Handbook of Multimedia Information Security:
Techniques and Applications

Amit Kumar Singh • Anand Mohan
Editors

Handbook of Multimedia Information Security: Techniques and Applications

 Springer

Editors
Amit Kumar Singh
Department of Computer
Science and Engineering
NIT Patna, Patna, India

Anand Mohan
Department of Electronics Engineering
Indian Institute of Technology, BHU
Varanasi, Uttar Pradesh, India

ISBN 978-3-030-15889-7   ISBN 978-3-030-15887-3   (eBook)
https://doi.org/10.1007/978-3-030-15887-3

This Springer imprint is published by the registered company Springer Nature Switzerland AG.
The registered company address is: Gewerbestrasse 11, 6330 Cham, Switzerland

Foreword

The book entitled *Handbook of Multimedia Information Security: Techniques and Applications* is a significant effort on the multimedia, which focuses on the emerging applications. The handbook intends to enhance the understanding of opportunities and challenges in multimedia security and processing for real-world applications at the global level.

It is a challenge for any researchers and scholars to identify the most popular topics on multimedia in any instant of time due to rapid progress on research and development. This book summarizes the recent trends in multimedia in terms of security, processing, and applications and focuses on identifying new directions for academic professionals, practicing engineers, and scientists. Given this, summarizing the vast literature in multimedia and identifying the most cutting-edge phenomena is a huge task. I hope the readers will find the book of great value in its visionary words.

I congratulate the editors for this book and look forward to seeing it in print soon.

Department of Computer Science and Engineering   Saraju P. Mohanty
University of North Texas, Denton, TX, USA

Preface

Recently, multimedia stands as one of the most demanding and exciting aspects of the information era, and every second, a lot of multimedia information are created and transmitted all around the world through different unsecured networks. The multimedia information distribution through open channel using information and communication technology (ICT) is an indispensable and cost-effective technique for dissemination and distribution of digital data/media files. However, the prevention of copyright violation, authenticity, confidentiality, ownership identification, and identity theft have been challenging issues due to attempts of malicious attacks or hacking of the open-channel information. Criminal offence ranging from identity theft to copyright violation and from personal information exposure to medical history disclosure is being made every day. However, research established that the authenticity of multimedia information/documents is strongly required in various emerging applications such as e-health, secure multimedia contents on social network, secured e-voting systems, automotive industries, military, digital forensic, digital cinema, education and insurance companies, driving license/passport, as well as many real-time applications. Furthermore, multimedia processing is a multi-rate computing problem and requires low-cost implementation of high-volume markets, high computation rates, and large memory bandwidth, which makes it a challenging domain for potential researchers.

Outline of the Book and Chapter Synopsis

In view of addressing the above challenges, this handbook presents the recent trends in multimedia in terms of security, processing, and applications at the global level. We have provided potential thoughts and methodology that help senior undergraduate and graduate students, researchers, programmers, and industry professionals in creating new knowledge for the future to develop efficient techniques/framework for multimedia applications.

A brief and orderly introduction to the book chapters in this handbook, organized under three major parts, is provided in the following:

Part I includes 15 interesting chapters dealing with multimedia security for emerging applications. The chapters include basic concepts of multimedia tools and applications, biological and behavioral biometrics, effective multimedia encryption and secure watermarking techniques for emerging applications, an adaptive face identification approach for android mobile devices, and multimedia using chaotic and perceptual hashing function.

Part II of the book includes 11 chapters dealing with multimedia processing for various potential applications. The chapters include a detailed survey of image processing-based automated glaucoma detection techniques and role of de-noising, recent study of dictionary learning-based image reconstruction techniques for analyzing the big medical data, brief introduction of quantum image processing and its applications, a segmentation-less efficient Alzheimer detection approach, object recognition, image enhancements and de-noising techniques for emerging applications, improved performance of image compression approach, and automated detection of eye-related diseases using digital image processing.

Part III of the book includes 11 interesting chapters dealing with multimedia applications. The chapters include the extensive survey on the role of multimedia in medicine and multimedia forensic classification, a fingerprint-based authentication system for e-health security, and analysis of recently developed deep learning techniques for emotion and activity recognition. Further, the book introduces a case study on the change of ECG according to time for user identification, role of multimedia in big data, cloud computing, the Internet of things (IoT), and blockchain environment in detail for real-life applications.

To conclude, we would like to sincerely thank all the authors for submitting their high-quality chapters to this book and the large number of potential reviewers who have participated in the review process and provided helpful comments and suggestions to the authors to improve their chapters.

We especially thank the Multimedia Systems and Applications Series Editor, *Prof. Borko Furht*, for his continuous support and great guidance.

We are also grateful to *Prof. Saraju P. Mohanty*, Department of Computer Science and Engineering University of North Texas, Denton, TX, for his inspirational foreword for the book.

We would also like to thank the publishers at Springer, in particular *Susan Lagerstrom-Fife*, Senior Publishing Editor/CS Springer, for their helpful guidance and encouragement during the creation of this book.

We are sincerely thankful to all authors, editors, and publishers whose works have been cited directly/indirectly in this book.

We believe that our book will be helpful to the senior undergraduate and graduate students, researchers, industry professionals, healthcare professionals, and providers working in the area demanding state-of-the-art solutions for multimedia applications.

Patna, India   Amit Kumar Singh
Varanasi, India   Anand Mohan

Special Acknowledgments

The first author gratefully acknowledges the authorities of *National Institute of Technology Patna, India*, for their kind support to come up with this book.

The second author gratefully acknowledges the authorities of *Indian Institute of Technology (BHU), Varanasi, India,* for their kind support to come up with this book.

Contents

About the Editors

Amit Kumar Singh received his bachelor's degree in computer science and engineering from the Institute of Engineering and Technology, VBS Purvanchal University, Jaunpur, India, in 2005; M.Tech. degree in computer science and engineering from Jaypee University of Information Technology, Waknaghat, India, in 2010; and Ph.D. degree in computer engineering from the National Institute of Technology, Kurukshetra, India, in 2015. He was with the Computer Science and Engineering Department, Jaypee University of Information Technology, from 2008 to 2018. He is currently an Assistant Professor with the Computer Science and Engineering Department, National Institute of Technology (an Institute of National Importance), Patna, India. He has authored over 70 peer-reviewed journals, conference publications, and book chapters and 2 books entitled *Medical Image Watermarking: Techniques and Applications*, in 2017, and *Animal Biometrics: Techniques and Applications*, in 2018 (Springer International Publishing). He has also edited the book *Security in Smart Cities: Models, Applications, and Challenges* (Springer International Publishing, 2019), the Proceedings of 4th IEEE International Conference on Parallel, Distributed and Grid Computing in 2016, and the Proceedings of 4th International Conference on Image Information Processing in 2017. He currently serves on the Editorial Board of two peer-reviewed international journals, namely, the *IEEE Access* and *Multimedia Tools and Applications* (Springer). He has edited various international journal special issues as a Guest Editor, such as *IEEE Consumer Electronics Magazine, IEEE Access, Multimedia Tools and Applications* (Springer), *International Journal of Information Management* (Elsevier), *Journal of Ambient Intelligence and Humanized Computing* (Springer), *Multimedia Systems* (Springer), *International Journal of Information and Computer Security* (Inderscience), *International Journal of Grid and Utility Computing* (Inderscience), and *Journal of Intelligent Systems* (Walter de Gruyter GmbH & Co. KG, Germany). His research interests include data hiding, biometrics, and cryptography.

Anand Mohan has nearly 42 years rich experience of teaching, research, administration, and managing higher educational institutions. He began his career in December 1975 as R&D Engineer of Murphy India Ltd., Thane, Maharashtra, and subsequently joined as Faculty in April 1979 at Electronics Engineering, Institute of Technology, now IIT (BHU), where he is currently working as Institute Professor. He has provided national-level leadership to the defense-related R&D activities as Chairman, Armament Sensors & Electronics (ASE) Panel under ARMREB, DRDO, Ministry of Defence, Government of India. As part of a doctoral research, he has developed a potential technology for application in "Neutron Detection Reader" system for defense applications. Prof. Mohan has active research collaboration with Louisiana State University, USA; Curtin University, Malaysia; Kathmandu University, Nepal; and Central Electronics Engineering Research Institute (CEERI), Pilani, Rajasthan. He has made notable academic and research contributions in the field of Electronics Engineering at IIT (BHU) by creating a dedicated research group of eminent academicians and researchers from the country and abroad. He has established state-of-the-art research facilities and conducted high-quality research in the areas of fault-tolerant/survivable system design, steganography, and embedded system design. His current areas of research interest are intelligent instrumentation, fault-tolerant design, robust watermarking algorithms, and information security. He has authored 145 research papers published in reputed international/national journals and conference proceedings. He has supervised 11 Ph.D. theses and made 4 chapter contributions in books. His coauthored book, *Medical Image Watermarking: Techniques and Applications*, has been published by Springer. Academic and research contributions of Prof. Mohan are internationally/nationally acknowledged.

Part I
Multimedia Security

Chapter 1
Introduction to Multimedia Tools and Applications

Abdul Rahaman Wahab Sait, J. Uthayakumar, K. Shankar, and K. Sathesh Kumar

1.1 Introduction

Multimedia is an innovation that enables us to introduce text, audio, images, animations, and video in an intelligent way, and has made an enormous effect on all parts of our everyday life. It likewise can possibly keep on making always captivating applications, some of which are portrayed in articles recorded in the references. Notwithstanding, the innovation without anyone else's input cannot modify the world. The general population receives and utilizes the innovation that rolls out the improvements. In this manner, the inborn property of multimedia is to help human-centered computing (HCC) might be credited for its touchy development in every aspect of use as is obvious from a few research works incorporated into the references. Becvar has examined how video blogging ("vlogging") frameworks influence the learning rehearses engaged with preparing learner experts, and how coordinating new innovation changes the perplexing social elements of expert preparing [1]. Present-day data access, which is a piece of our regular day to day existence, constantly includes multimedia information in some shape or another. The utilization of multimedia upgrades a client's capacity to impart and team up. A noteworthy part required in multimedia applications is a computer with high processing rate and extensive stockpiling limit. The equipment cost is diminishing at

A. R. W. Sait
Center of Documents, Archives and Communication, King Faisal University, Hofuf, Kingdom of Saudi Arabia
e-mail: asait@kfu.edu.sa

J. Uthayakumar
Department of Computer Science, Pondicherry University, Puducherry, India

K. Shankar (✉) · K. S. Kumar
School of Computing, Kalasalingam Academy of Research and Education, Krishnankoil, Tamil Nadu, India

© Springer Nature Switzerland AG 2019
A. K. Singh, A. Mohan (eds.), *Handbook of Multimedia Information Security: Techniques and Applications*, https://doi.org/10.1007/978-3-030-15887-3_1

3

a rate never observed, alongside a quick increment in the capacity limit, computing force, and system transmission capacity. Multimedia innovation has shown the possibility to develop the worldview of end-client computing, from intuitive text and illustrations display, into one increasingly perfect with the advanced electronic universe of the twenty-first century. It is relatively difficult to follow the size and broadness of the progressions that multimedia and correspondence innovation is experiencing. This is an introductory chapter which focuses to demonstrate common terminology, tools, formats employed in multimedia applications and their development. It also involves a broad list of references on newest research problems and future trends over multimedia application areas and development.

1.2 What Makes an Application Multimedia?

A common meaning of a multimedia applications is one that includes the intuitive demonstration of a few media types. Through this, we signify presentation as well as analysis, computing of multimedia information, synchronization in the display of various media things as well as the capacity to help connection with the information. This intelligent introduction does not need to be completely overseen inside one program. A program can simply be a controlling substance for a variety of scattered parts, every one of that is in charge of overseeing one part of the multimedia control. These parts together speak to the application. Figure 1.1 demonstrates a monolithic application in that the entire usefulness is performed inside one program. Over a solitary client remain solitary workstation the information streams from nearby gadgets and is shown locally. On a few frameworks hard-wired arrangements are utilized for nonstop media that don't permit media processing previously shown. Figure 1.2 represents creating and interconnecting individual parts, every one conceivably executes on discrete machines. Even though, every segment can be seen as a program in its very own right, they present mutually to a multimedia applications. Building up an application and is more adaptable and fast than building up a massive arrangement.

Multimedia applications are not really exclusively worried about intuitive introduction. People who remark on the constrained helpfulness of multimedia frequently mistakenly imagine that a multimedia applications is a dark planet, the usefulness of that is restricted to the showcase of media segments and association with it. In established truth, this is regularly a subset of the application's usefulness. An ongoing study [WB92] outlined that multimedia has suggestions for a extensive scope of standard zones, involving office mechanization, benefit industry applications, (for example, in training, money related administrations and wellbeing), retail applications, (for example, in distributing, travel and property), local applications, science, designing and social exercises. Because of the ongoing enthusiasm for the joining of audio and video into the workstation condition, a misinterpretation has risen which multimedia implies video and audio that is inaccurate. Multimedia speaks to the accessibility and compatibility of media kinds in an incorporated

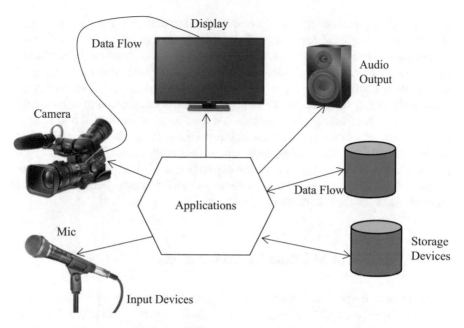

Fig. 1.1 A monolithic multimedia application

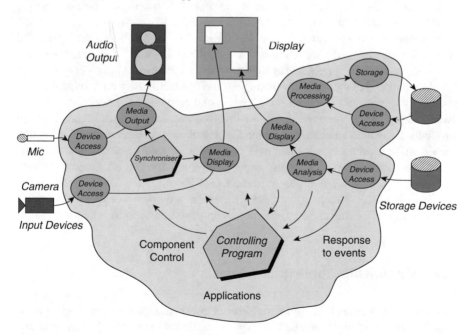

Fig. 1.2 A distributed multimedia application [2]

domain. An application designer comprise the decision of utilizing media types suitable for a individual application. Likewise, as asset accessibility can fluctuate at executing-time and among various situations, one media blend can be supplanted by another, e.g. substituting video and audio for audio with text captions. When to see the upcoming things, new media types with capable for cooperation and introduction are developing. Virtual Reality (VR) movement speaks to an energizing new showcase medium. Collaboration would develop by utilization of new kinds of info gadget both related with VR and mobility. Dynamic identifications [HH94] are the instances of versatile info gadgets, which frequently transmits a flag to enable people's areas. It is alluring to have the capacity to utilize these innovative media reciprocally in applications. Some conditions like incorporating pictures, audio, text and video, are not the constraint of multimedia, but rather the start.

1.3 Evolution of Multimedia Applications

In the present times, multimedia is a emerging study domain and a novel field. With a estimation of $50 billion in entire market, multimedia field has developed significantly. Over the past years, the revolution of digital media was initiated. But, long before, the seeds were sown. In Fig. 1.3, the digital media timeline were demonstrated that shows the basic technologies like video games, electronic encyclopedias and interactive Laser disks were explored. The technologies like interactive television, digital libraries, videoconferencing and interacting television are the present "bot" applications that the seed were sown. Other perspective of revolution in digital media is the making a novel media industry containing of communication, consumer electronics companies and computer. For adopting itself for twenty-first century, Various industry are involved now in making novel services and products. It involves satellite TV companies, telephone, communication equipment, movie studios, produce software tools companies, consumer electronics vendors, record companies, cable channels, vendors in computer add-on, Internet service providers, consumer electronics vendors, CD-ROM title creators, computer companies and semiconductor vendors, Internet service providers, consumer electronics vendors, CD-ROM title creators, computer companies and semiconductor vendors.

1.4 Multimedia Application Types

In the digital era protecting digital multimedia information is becoming more necessary. The source of digital media's growth can be linked to the wealth of information provided by the internet [22–27]. Instead of providing a detailed explanation of each of the available multimedia application, this subsection summarizes some of the important fields in multimedia has become part of applications. The platform intends to support the important needs of these kinds of applications.

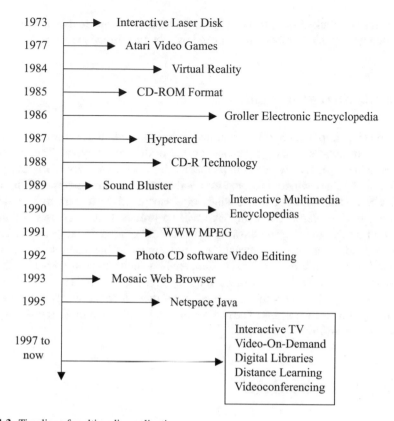

1973	Interactive Laser Disk
1977	Atari Video Games
1984	Virtual Reality
1985	CD-ROM Format
1986	Groller Electronic Encyclopedia
1987	Hypercard
1988	CD-R Technology
1989	Sound Bluster
1990	Interactive Multimedia Encyclopedias
1991	WWW MPEG
1992	Photo CD software Video Editing
1993	Mosaic Web Browser
1995	Netspace Java
1997 to now	Interactive TV Video-On-Demand Digital Libraries Distance Learning Videoconferencing

Fig. 1.3 Timeline of multimedia applications

1.4.1 Time-Driven Presentation

An application involves time-driven presentation that displays multimedia data by the use of time dimension as the driving force. The definition of presentation time begins at application start-up. The arrangement of media items could be initiated through a particular position in the time being reached. Few of the applications enable to interact with the functionalities at temporal coordinates.

1.4.2 Hypermedia Document

In hypermedia applications, the media elements indicate the data nodes. The virtual links among the nodes can be moved to interact with every portion of an data node. The instances of the related video clips portray when the vocabulary in a text document are clicked on, otherwise portray the picture and text biography about someone when which individual is clicked over in an audio visual story.

1.4.3 Conferencing System

Conferencing application offer multimedia based method for formal otherwise informal presentations among persons located in different regions. The text-based conferencing systems have been implemented between two users where every one of them has a text window to type into and other sees the outcome of the other user. The mutual drawing tool enables the distributed customers to integrate in the visualization ideas. A drawing area will be provided to every user and also a choice of drawing tools. The drawing strokes will be transmitted to the display of the every individual user. In recent days, more interest has been shifted towards the audiovisual conferencing. This system enables multiple customers to take over a discussion by watching and hearing the other conferences. The influence of a collaborated multimedia platform is that any of these techniques of discussing can be employed interchangeably. The choices are prepared based on the suitability and resource accessibility.

1.4.4 Multimedia Agents

Multimedia agent makes use of intelligence heuristics to multimedia filtering. Some of the instances are automation of filtering text files like mail or news, or searching for a in a video stream to help the security guards. A number of simple agents can be integrated to generate a complex applications.

1.4.5 Multimedia Tools

Multimedia tools involve a set of hardware and software employed in the task of developing multimedia applications, to multimedia products and for future use and also for modifying the products. The widely employed multimedia hardware comprises of video, sound cards, player, and recording devices. Recently, the hardware components are facing exponential enhancements even on a daily basis in their characteristics and usability. The software development tools can be classified into various ways based on the usage and are listed below:

1. Classifying multimedia tools depending upon its usage in various stages of application development.

- *Analysis Tools*: It helps the designers to investigate the available models to detect the advantages, drawbacks, and chances of enhancements and also investigates the requirement and aim of the project scope.
- *Design Tools*: It finds helpful to plan the project development, comprising the user features and particular contributions.
- *Management Tools*: It is usually employed to manage the entire multimedia development process.
- *Production Tools*: It is used in the real productivity of the multimedia product.
- *Evaluation Tools*: It supports the process of creating evaluations using diverse ways.

2. Classifying multimedia tools depending upon media type for which a software tool is useful.

- Audio software
- Graphic software
- Video software

3. *Classifying multimedia tools depending upon its function.* Multimedia software tools include a broad range of software in which the developer is required to employ to assist various functionalities, for instance, capture, play, combine images, text, music and sound, animation, video, and other particular effects. Few of the software tools depend upon their characteristics belong to every individual media categories (i.e., audio, video, text and graphics)

- Media editors
- Media viewers
- Media recorders
- Media format converters (e.g. bmp to jpeg)
- Media converters (e.g. text to speech or speech to text converter etc.)
- Media capture
- Animators
- Movie joiner and splitter
- Watermarking tool
- Multimedia for the Web
- Business presentation tool
- Creating Screen saver
- Slide show software
- Multimedia photo albums
- Multimedia authoring

Various software tools exist which has the capability to provide the above processes in a separate manner and for every diverse media. In addition, the widely employed tools have many in built functions for supporting different formats and media. For instance, Windows media player plays both audio and video in different formats, like Real Video/Real Audio 4.0, MPEG 1, WAV, VOD, QuickTime files, AU, ASF, Real Video/Real Audio 4.0, MPEG 2, AVI, MIDI, MOV, MP3, and QuickTime files etc.

1.5   Issues, Trends, and Effects of Multimedia

With the rapid development of multimedia data, it is important to maintain the confidentiality of such data. Over the entire domain like transportation of huge volumes of media produced data, data management, synchronization, retrieval are the novel issues that are rising nowadays with the enhanced ease of access and availability to electronic multimedia data. And, it should be noted that the number of designing problems, technology and management [27–30].

1.5.1   Managing Multimedia Projects

Sorting out and overseeing multimedia IT anticipates remains a test. Imagination is a critical main term in creating multimedia IT. It is exceptionally hard to gauge the dimension of innovativeness in every one of the players of a venture, specifically the representatives who are associated with making and conveying the task inside the given dead line and the customers with shifting desire for the inventiveness. For an ideal decent yield the businesses need to guarantee an inventive domain with the goal that the representatives can think imaginative and work at their own pace. The reality remains that "a few representatives can turn on innovativeness like a light switch and others require imagination to come to them". Interoperability is additionally an imperative issue. The applications should be coded in one institutionalized coding design, making them open to an entire scope of end-frameworks supporting constant audio/video stream and synchronization. There likewise should be a lot of conventions characterized to execute exchange everything being equal and dataflow in the framework. Portals should be indicated to coordinate different advanced administrations and bolster the relating designs. In multimedia applications, computerized symbolism and video has extended its mindset in numerous ways, bringing about a blast in the volume of picture, audio, and video information required to be sorted out and recovered. Likewise, an extraordinary increment is seen in the research of multimedia retrieval; which has prepared for new methods and captivating applications [3–7].

1.5.2   Managing Multimedia Resources

Because of large file sizes of audio and video contents, communication over the Internet involving multimedia data consumes lots of network bandwidth, occupies large storage space, and requires high processing time both on the client and on the server side. With huge multimedia files the utmost serving capacity of a server decreases exponentially, which is true even in case of an infinitely fast server. It is said, "The backbone of the Internet may have been modeled to endure nuclear attack, however it will never survive the onslaught of multimedia on the Web". The large multimedia file sizes not only consume more bandwidth during transmission, they occupy connections for long time, which causes delay to other real-time data transfers and also decrease the total number of connections available at any present time. In the long run, these connections create it simpler for a server to execute out of TCP/IP kernel resources.

1.5.3   Trends in Mobile Multimedia

Amid the most recent decade the systems administration speed has developed from 10 megabit to gigabit run, yet the hazardous development in the quantity of the Web clients has made the measure of traffic grow a few times more. In the meantime because of the critical advances in the VLSI innovation, there is an expanding interest for compact multimedia machines equipped for taking care of cutting edge calculations required in all types of correspondence. Throughout the years, we have seen a relentless move from remain solitary (or work area) multimedia to profoundly appropriated multimedia frameworks. Remote computing is surprising the world to serve our information require. Along these lines, there is a requirement for proficient mapping of the necessities of multimedia frameworks onto versatile systems administration conditions. The achievement criteria for a portable application configuration is to locate the best mapping onto the structural assets, while fulfilling a forced arrangement of plan limitations (e.g., least power dissemination, greatest execution) and indicated QoS measurements (e.g., end-to-end inactivity, jitter, misfortune rate) which straightforwardly affect the media quality. Applications are developing so as to help the present assembled working environment and way of life. Be that as it may, multimedia frameworks yet need to wind up progressively versatile or adaptable concerning the fluctuating system condition [8–14].

1.5.4   Trend in Multimedia Research

Multimedia research will keep on tending to the urgent issues that are advancing each day as endeavors are being accomplished to bring the fantasy applications. On account of the predominant computing remaining task at hand of multimedia applications in computer frameworks and in remote based gadgets, and because of their dreary computing and memory concentrated nature [16], recommended to take compelling favorable position from processor-in-memory (PIM) innovation and proposed an amazing failure control PIM-based 32-bit reconfigurable data path improved for multimedia applications.

1.5.5   Social Impact

One other essential angle is the social ramifications that multimedia-based applications may have [15]. The positive perspectives are clearer than the negative ones. With such a large number of offices promptly accessible at homes, workplaces, and shops, there are a few inquiries remain yet to be addressed, for example, how the decrease in human contact will influence the social conduct—will the workplaces, the play areas, or the shopping centers have a left look? Since, the general population like to telecommute or they would invest more energy in diversions and virtual reality maintaining a strategic distance from open air works out, breathing natural air or they incline toward requesting through intelligent TV while viewing a film. There is dependably an equalization which can be found to profit by a creating innovation like multimedia and it beyond any doubt will make information and correspondence simple to access and utilize.

1.5.6   Human-Centered Multimedia: Cultural Impact

The wide acknowledgment of multimedia might be credited to the human-centered characters innate in media blends. In any case, the social piece of the human-centered methodology did not get much thought in plan of multimedia advancement devices and applications. We frequently overlook that the improvement of multimedia interfaces and correspondence are dialect and culture-explicit. The clients feel much great when they can act to the social context to which they have a place [17, 18]. Instances of how culture influences content generation and programmed analysis methods might be found at http://www-nlpir.nist.gov/ventures/trecvid/ (The TREC video retrieval assessment, 2005). Ongoing patterns are to adjust specialized advancement to social and social improvement including new models that grasps multiculturalism and perceives the human effect. Some ongoing examination is incorporated into the reference list. Research works in multimedia has been reached out from programming advancement to idea of probabilistic structure for multimedia installed frameworks, which efficiently would consolidate execution prerequisites of multimedia application, vulnerabilities in run time, and resistance for sensible execution disappointments [19–21].

1.6   Summary

In this chapter, the overview of multimedia data, the timeline of multimedia applications are explained. In addition, the different real time applications of multimedia and its tools are also discussed briefly. At the end, the various issues and challenges exist in the multimedia data are also discussed. Furthermore, due to the presence of large file sizes of multimedia data, the communication process requires high network bandwidth, large storage space, and requires high processing time both on the client and on the server side. Keeping this in mind, in future, we try to develop a universal data aggregation technique commonly for all kinds of multimedia data for effective utilization of available resources.

References

1. Becvar, L. A. (2007). Social impacts of a video blogging system for clinical instruction. CHI 2007, ACM Student Research Competition, San Jose, CA, USA.
2. Furht, B. ed., 2012. *Multimedia tools and applications* (Vol. 359). Springer Science & Business Media.
3. Datta, R., Li, J., & Wang, J. Z. (2005). Multimedia information retrieval: Challenges and real-world applications: Content-based image retrieval: approaches and trends of the new age. Proceedings of the 7th ACM SIGMM International Workshop on Multimedia Information Retrieval MIR'05.
4. Nang, J., & Park, J. (2007). Database theory, technology, and applications. An efficient indexing structure for content based multimedia retrieval with relevance feedback. Proceedings of the 2007 ACM Symposium on Applied Computing SAC'07.
5. Rowe, L. A., & Jain, R. (2005). ACM SIGMM retreat report on future directions in multimedia research. ACM Transactions on Multimedia Computing, Communications, and Applications (TOMCCAP), 1(1).
6. Sebe, N., & Tian, Q. (2007). Personalized multimedia information retrieval: Personalized multimedia retrieval: the new trend? Proceedings of the International Workshop on Workshop on Multimedia Information Retrieval MIR '07.
7. Yang, J., Li, Q., & Zhuang, Y. (2002). Multimedia: OCTOPUS: Aggressive search of multi-modality data using multifaceted knowledge base. Proceedings of the 11th International Conference on World Wide Web WWW '02.
8. Cai, L. X., Cai, L., Shen, X., & Mark, J. W. (2006). Multimedia capacity of UWB networks supporting multimedia services. Proceedings of the 3rd International Conference on Quality of Service in Heterogeneous Wired/Wireless Networks QShine '06.
9. Farnham, T., Sooriyabandara, M., & Efthymiou, C. (2007). Enhancing multimedia streaming over existing wireless LAN technology using the unified link layer API. International Journal of Network Management, 17(5).
10. Fernando, X. (2006). Radio over fiber in multimedia access networks. Proceedings of the 1st International Conference on Access Networks AccessNets '06.
11. Koutsakis, P. (2007). Mobile computing symposium: Movement prediction and planning: Integrating latest technology multimedia traffic over high-speed cellular networks. Proceedings of the 2007 International Conference on Wireless Communications and Mobile Computing IWCMC '07.
12. Pham, B., & Wong, O. (2004). Computer human interface: Handheld devices for applications using dynamic multimedia data. Proceedings of the 2nd International Conference on Computer Graphics and Interactive Techniques in Australasia and South East Asia GRAPHITE.
13. Thwaites, H. (2006). Human computer interaction: Cyberanthropology of mobility. Proceedings of the 3rd International Conference on Mobile Technology, Applications & Systems Mobility '06.
14. Verkasalo, H. (2006). Empirical observations on the emergence of mobile multimedia services and applications in the U.S. and Europe. Proceedings of the 5th International Conference on Mobile and Ubiquitous Multimedia MUM '06.

15. Hua, S., Qu, G., & Bhattacharyya, S. S. (2007). Probabilistic design of multimedia embedded systems. ACM Transactions on Embedded Computing Systems (TECS), 6(3).
16. Lanuzza, M., Margala, M., & Corsonello, P. (2005). Special purpose processing: Cost-effective lowpower processor-in-memory-based reconfigurable datapath for multimedia applications. Proceedings of the 2005 International Symposium on Low Power Electronics and Design ISLPED '05.
17. Dimitrova, N. (2004). Context and memory in multimedia context analysis. IEEE Multimedia, 11(3), 7-11.
18. Rowe, L., & Jain, R. (2005). ACM SIGMM Retreat Report. ACM Trans. Multimedia Computing, Communications, and Applications, 1(1), 3-13.
19. El-Bendary, M. A., & El-Azm, A. A. (2018). Complexity considerations: efficient image transmission over mobile communications channels. *Multimedia Tools and Applications*, 1-32.
20. Shi, J., Yang, Z., & Zhu, J. (2018). An auction-based rescue task allocation approach for heterogeneous multi-robot system. *Multimedia Tools and Applications*, 1-10.
21. Fernández, D. G., Botella, G., Del Barrio, A. A., García, C., Prieto-Matías, M., & Grecos, C. (2018). HEVC optimization based on human perception for real-time environments. *Multimedia Tools and Applications*, 1-33.
22. K. Shankar, SK. Lakshmanaprabu, Deepak Gupta, Ashish Khanna, Victor Hugo C. de Albuquerque, "Adaptive Optimal Multi Key Based Encryption for Digital Image Security", Concurrency and Computation: Practice and Experience, December 2018. https://doi.org/10.1002/cpe.5122
23. K. Shankar, Mohamed Elhoseny, R. Satheesh Kumar, S. K. Lakshmanaprabu, Xiaohui Yuan, Secret image sharing scheme with encrypted shadow images using optimal homomorphic encryption technique, Journal of Ambient Intelligence and Humanized Computing, December 2018. https://doi.org/10.1007/s12652-018-1161-0
24. Deepak Gupta, Ashish Khanna, Lakshmanaprabu SK, Shankar K, Vasco Furtado, Joel J. P. C. Rodrigues, Efficient Artificial Fish Swarm Based Clustering Approach on Mobility Aware Energy-Efficient for MANET, Transactions on Emerging Telecommunications Technologies, November 2018. https://doi.org/10.1002/ett.3524
25. K. Shankar, Mohamed Elhoseny, E. Dhiravida chelvi, SK. Lakshmanaprabu, Wanqing Wu, An Efficient Optimal Key Based Chaos Function for Medical Image Security, IEEE Access, Vol.6, Issue.1, page(s): 77145-77154, December 2018. https://doi.org/10.1109/ACCESS.2018.2874026
26. Mohamed Elhoseny, K. Shankar, S. K. Lakshmanaprabu, Andino Maseleno, N. Arunkumar, Hybrid optimization with cryptography encryption for medical image security in Internet of Things, Neural Computing and Applications, October 2018. https://doi.org/10.1007/s00521-018-3801-x
27. T. Avudaiappan, R. Balasubramanian, S. Sundara Pandiyan, M. Saravanan, S. K. Lakshmanaprabu, K. Shankar, Medical Image Security Using Dual Encryption with Oppositional Based Optimization Algorithm, Journal of Medical Systems, Volume 42, Issue 11, pp.1-11, November 2018.
28. K.Shankar and P.Eswaran. "RGB Based Multiple Share Creation in Visual Cryptography with Aid of Elliptic Curve Cryptography", China Communications, Volume. 14, Issue. 2, page(s): 118-130, February 2017.
29. Lakshmanaprabu SK, K. Shankar, Ashish Khanna, Deepak Gupta, Joel J. P. C. Rodrigues, Plácido R. Pinheiro, Victor Hugo C. de Albuquerque, "Effective Features to Classify Big Data using Social Internet of Things", IEEE Access, Volume.6, page(s):24196-24204, April 2018.
30. K.Shankar and P.Eswaran. "RGB Based Secure Share Creation in Visual Cryptography Using Optimal Elliptic Curve Cryptography Technique", Journal of Circuits, Systems, and Computers, Volume. 25, No. 11, page(s): 1650138-1 to 23, November 2016.

Chapter 2
An Overview of Biometrics Methods

Muhammad Sharif, Mudassar Raza, Jamal Hussain Shah, Mussarat Yasmin, and Steven Lawrence Fernandes

2.1 Introduction

Biometric is a dual combination of technological and scientific authentication methods majorly based on human biology and extensively used in information assurance (IA) [1]. Biometric is a measurement and statistical test for the representation of unique intellectual and behavioral individuals. This technique is mainly used for identification and access control or to identify persons who are being monitored. The fundamental principle of biometric verification is that every person can be determined correctly via his/her inner physical or behavioral characteristics.

The term "biometrics" is derived from the Greek word "metric" which means to measure and "Bio" means life. Hence, Biometric means identification via body parts. Through biometrics, authentication of identification can be made secure by accessing human biological information [2] such as retina [3], DNA, fingerprint, voice etc. which are the common biometrics. Biometrics is unique and as every human acquires these characteristics uniquely, so these are the most reliable methods to authenticate any identification securely. Figure 2.1 depicts various types of biometrics.

M. Sharif · M. Raza · J. H. Shah · M. Yasmin (✉)
COMSATS University Islamabad, Wah Campus, Pakistan

S. L. Fernandes
Department of Electronics and Communication Engineering, Sahyadri College of Engineering and Management, Mangaluru, India

© Springer Nature Switzerland AG 2019
A. K. Singh, A. Mohan (eds.), *Handbook of Multimedia Information Security: Techniques and Applications*, https://doi.org/10.1007/978-3-030-15887-3_2

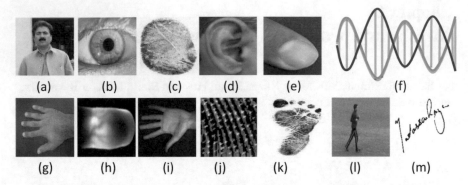

Fig. 2.1 Biometric Types (**a**) face (**b**) iris (**c**) finger print (**d**) ear (**e**) nail bit (**f**) DNA (**g**) hand (**h**) finger vein (**i**) Palm vein (**j**) sweat pores (**k**) foot print (**l**) gait (**m**) signature

2.2 Applications of Biometrics

Biometric Identification Management Systems (BIMS) deal with the highest levels of security. Trust, convenience, responsibility, and meticulous audits are all functions that motivate companies to search for technology and apply it to their own goals. Common applications are in the fields of:

- Banking Authentication
- Airport Security
- National level Identification
- Law Enforcement
- Access Control and Single Sign On (SSO)
- Time and Attendance

Creating a safe biological system is not easy. The term biometric technology is used as an ideal security alternative. A lot of research has been led for people's recognizable proof utilizing biometrics; be that as it may, there is a space for promoting change. A short survey of some biometrics is talked about in the next section.

2.3 Biometrics Categories

Automatic human recognition by utilizing biometrics tools takes after a general strategy in which an image taken through a few sensors is supplied to the biometric system. The system then checks input image from the database via some specific algorithm and displays the recognition results. Biometrics types are generally classified under two main categories (see Fig. 2.2) such as:

(1) Biological Biometrics

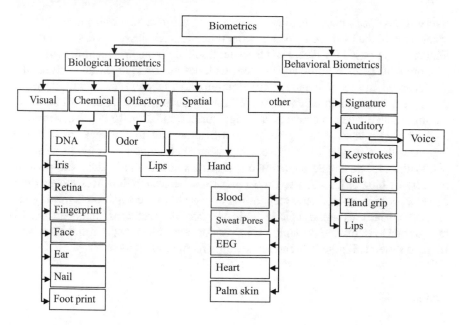

Fig. 2.2 Biometrics categories

(2) Behavioral Biometrics

These categories are further briefed in the accompanying section.

2.3.1 Biological Biometrics

Biological biometrics deals with size, shape and biological characteristics of human body. This category can further be divided into visual, chemical, olfactory, spatial and other categories. This section discusses biometrics types under these categories.

2.3.1.1 Visual Biometrics

The types of biometrics under visual biometrics depend on human organs that can be seen through human eyes.

Iris

Iris plays a vital role in the biometric recognition system as its complex texture conveys extremely distinguishing information valuable for person identification.

Every iris is specific and just like fingerprints; even identical twins have different irises. One of the iris based biometric identification includes a process for finding a feature vector based iris digest and then developing a biometric identifier [4].

Common iris based biometric system includes an iris scanner, an analyzer that produces an image of a human iris minimizing the presence of eye lashes in the image. The distinct characteristic of iris originates from randomly distributed features unlike other biometrics as finger prints and face [6, 7]. This prompts its high dependability for personal identification and in the meantime, it also increases the difficulty to effectively represent such complex details in an image [8]. With an increasing accentuation on security, automatic individual identification in view of biometrics has been receiving broad consideration over the previous decade. As a rising biometric recognition approach, iris recognition is turning into an exceptionally dynamic topic in both research and real world applications. Iris recognition systems can be deployed in various areas like passports and in national ID card systems. Figure 2.3 represents an iris recognition system.

Retina

The retina of eye is an important part for human vision. It can also be used for person identification due to its unique structure of blood vessels in every human being unless affected by the disease. The digital retinal image [9] can also be used for automated person identification through mapping of segmented retinal blood vessels image with the recorded sample. The biometric through retina is most suitable authentication system after DNA due to negligible error rate [10] and low cost of digital retinal camera. Figure 2.4 shows a retinal image and the segmented blood vessels.

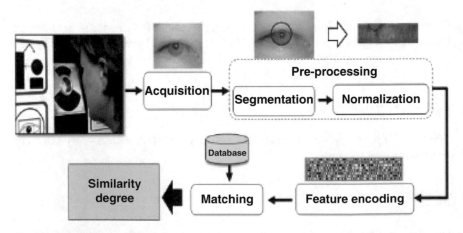

Fig. 2.3 Iris recognition system [5]

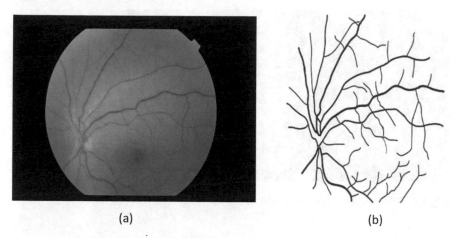

(a)   (b)

Fig. 2.4 (**a**) Retinal image (**b**) Retinal vessels [11]

Fingerprint Biometric Security System

Finger print biometric security systems (FPBSS) are the personal identification systems. FPBS system is an automatic identification and authentication system that involves the physiological features of a person. This system known as a bio-crypto system [12] has a basic goal to save and match the template to ensure security of the system. FPBS system uses uni biometrics and multi biometrics for security and recognition accuracy in person identification and recognition environments. For the FPBS system, uni biometrics appeared with many limitations in accuracy and security. Nowadays multi biometrics system known as fused system is intensively used in person recognition for security purposes. In fused finger print biometric security system, fingerprints and finger veins are used at feature level to generate a unique template (feature set) which are further evaluated and protected for revocability in later systems. Recently FPBS systems face problems in template matching [13] for person identification when sides and toe of finger template are not fully scanned. Spoofing templates and vulnerable fused patterns for generalized matching are also big issues in finger print matching and biometric security systems. To overcome these problems, researchers are working and developing their practically implementable models for improved system accuracy and security in the biometrically secured environment.

Face Recognition

Face recognition (see Fig. 2.5 for a facial recognition system) is one of the famous biometrics [14–20]. It deals with the clearest human identifier i.e., the facial region. Rather than expecting individuals to put their hand on a scanner or exactly place eye

Fig. 2.5 A face recognition system [21]

before an eye reader, face biometric system subtly take photos of individuals. There is no interruption and as a rule, people are completely ignorant of the procedure and they don't feel themselves under observation.

Face recognition is a renowned biometric technique utilized for investigation reason [22–25]. Face recognition is utilized as a part of much security and observation related areas like international ID, identity cards, live reconnaissance and so forth. The recognition process includes preprocessing of face picture which can be standardization, resizing and identification. Subsequent to preprocessing, the face image is looked from the database to be perceived [26]. The elements influencing recognition process are posture varieties, illumination, occlusions and so forth [27–31].

Ear Biometrics

The word "Ear Biometrics" denotes to auto person recognition based on characteristics of ear (physiological). The selection is made from the functions that are usually calculated on the basis of two-dimensional or three-dimensional recorded images.

Ear parameters employed in the identification procedure are geometric ear shape (Fig. 2.6), distinctive ear tips, universal ear imaging functions, local ear imaging functions and three-dimensional models [32]. Ears are not completely random structures. The ear differs from the human face because it has completely no change in color and expression and has no effect of make-up. While studying the use of ear identification information, the question remains open to determine whether the ear can be considered unique or unique to use in biometrics, hence because of any physical or behavioral characteristics of common identity verification mechanisms, each with a unique identifier remains unique to everyone. New researches [33] are working on the detailed structure of ear that it is not only unique in form but also permanent and does not change in entire human life. Because these qualities are of a system of interest determination, a significant increase in recent years using the ear as biometric automatically leads to an increase the person needs to authenticate.

Fig. 2.6 (a) Original ear (b) Geometric feature points extracted for identification

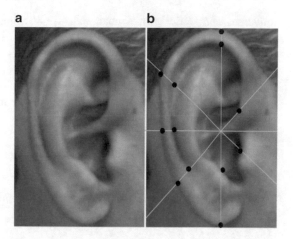

In contrast to facial scans or finger prints, ear identification system looks more natural. As one does not have to do body movements any more like moving fingers or face, therefore, it is very easy to perform persistent verification. Even in case of any movement, the system can be used effectively. The ear, therefore, contains all biometric characteristics i.e., uniqueness, durability, diversity, and collection [34].

Finger Nail

A finger nail bit generally stores unique data about individuals [35]. It is one of the safest biometric verification methods. As the data of nail bit cannot be copied easily, so it can be safely used for individual identification, individual authentication for security purposes, accessing bank accounts or entry point of any important occasion etc. Data written on finger nail can be read using Femto second laser pulse. All the data taken is firstly stored on some database. That data is then compared with data taken on the time of testing to check for the authorized user. In comparison with other biometrics, it is safer because finger prints can be copied easily by taking prints from any object touched by the person or faces can be copied as well through a number of picture editing software. Although iris cannot be copied but it is difficult to get the correct information using damaged iris, so it is also not considered safe. DNA is safest among all kinds of physiological biometric verification systems but it is time consuming. Although nail bit is same as finger print but little bit complex hence making it most safe to use for correct identification.

Foot Print and Foot Dynamics

Person identification through foot print is another biometric parameter [36]. Foot-print shape and patterns are used to recognize an individual. It is easy to capture, universal and static with a change in time. Sometimes it is not convenient to use as it needs bare footed images [37]. First, the raw input images of both feet are normalized in the form of direction as well as for position and then processed input image and registered foot image are compared. Sometimes useful information might be occluded as a result of normalization, so to avoid this problem, geometric information of input pair images before normalization is considered into an evaluation function.

2.3.1.2 Chemical Biometrics

The biometrics under this category deals with chemical composition pattern available in human DNA.

DNA

DNA is an abbreviation of deoxyribonucleic acid present in every cell of human body. The DNA is made of four bases in which the information is stored. These are Adenine (A), Guanine (G), cytosine (C) and thymine (T). These bases are attached to each other to make a pair. DNA is an important part player in solving security issues nowadays. As the DNA of every person is different, it helps in identifying personal information [38]. The DNA can be used for privacy concerns as for finding a serial killer, house breakers or solving rape cases. The forensic experts find samples from the crime place from which they can obtain cells of human body like blood, hair, and nails. Because the DNA of each person is different, so these are the powerful tools for identification [39].

2.3.1.3 Olfactory Biometrics

The biometrics under this category deals with human body odor.

Body Odor

One of the most revolutionary biometrics nowadays grabbing lots of attention from researchers is the body odor biometric. Body odor basically occurs due to the bacterial activity influenced by some specific skin gland. A person body condition can easily be determined by the composition (quantitative and qualitative information constituted by VOCs (Volatile compound (VOCs) [40]). Many stable recognizable patterns are present in human body. Body order being unique for ever person makes it possible to recognize an individual within a crowd. Few biometric approaches like iris and fingerprint although have little chances of error but as these are generally linked to illegal activities, so a person usually reserves to cooperate to get him recognized by a security system. Recognition of body odor is not a fresh idea as it is being used over decades by the forces and people with the help of hunting dogs educated at their early phases of life for such tasks [41]. The capability of these dogs to go after the culprit track from an illustration of individual odor is a famous proof that its usage is useful in biometric recognition. Past work on body odor has not achieved much higher accuracy with an error rate of 15% in the examination of 13 people out of 28 during a session [42]. The reality states that body odor has a giant potential in using it as a biometric detection.

2.3.1.4   Spatial Biometrics

Biometrics under this category depends upon the geometric shapes of body organs.

Hand Geometry

Hand geometry is basically an effective biometric used to identify the user by measuring the shape of hands. It is the most reliable kind of personal identification. For the identification of an individual, hand geometry plays a vital role as the shape of hands and palms holds a lot of useful information. Every person has different hand shape and different palm lines pattern and this information never changes throughout life, so everyone has distinct measurements (mentioned above) in this world.

Hand geometry scanner first extends the size of palm and palm lines pattern etc. and then compares obtained measurements with the measurements already stored in the system (see Fig. 2.7).

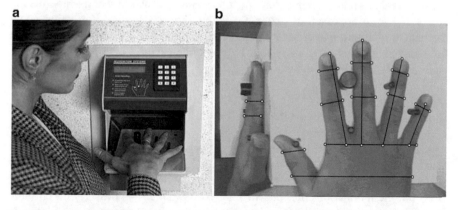

Fig. 2.7   (a) Hand geometry scanner (b) Scanned hand geometry [43]

Lips Geometry

Human lip features are basically a geometric feature that has specific height, width, contouring, and centroid [44]. Both face and lips features are sometimes fused together to enhance the identification performance and get low error rate.

2.3.1.5 Other Biological Biometrics

Some more biometrics under this category is discussed as under:

Biometrics Security Based on Blood Vein Patterns

Biometrics security with the help of vein patterns is very popular nowadays. In human beings, interconnected blood arteries are present which are enormous in number and are called vein patterns used for security identification in biometrics. Vein patterns of every human being are different and distinctive from others. Vein pattern is very unique and powerful identification method because it cannot be observed by naked eyes. Other attributes used for biometrics can easily be attacked by criminals, so nowadays new identification approaches like vein patterns of fingers and palm dorsa are more secure and less prone to error rate. Mostly finger veins pattern is used for biometrics security. To detect veins pattern of a finger, first of all the image of a finger is taken with the help of infrared rays which shows minute and accurate details of veins [45]. In a biometrics security system, palm dorsa are equally important as finger veins pattern. Palm dorsa technique also makes use of devices which capture images by using infrared light. After getting images, the main target is to extract useful information or features for further processing. Feature extraction helps to analyze images more clearly [46]. Feature extraction using shape feature is a very useful approach as geometric features give a lot of information about the pattern of input image. Most of the recent researches used a hybrid approach for biometrics authentication system by combining palm dorsa and finger veins patterns [47].

Biometrics Analysis of Sweat Pores

A research on sweat pores was done by Locardin 1912 and according to this research; the amount of pores recurrence and shape can possibly become the root of recognition. Moreover, 25–45 pores are enough to recognize an individual. However, the number of pores per inch are 10–19 and 23–46 [48]. Hydro chromic materials were designed for mapping sweat pores. These materials are also able to identify the difference between active and active pores [49]. The hydrophilic polymer film is also used for mapping sweat pores. Distinct micro dimples are produced by sweat pores on the hydrophilic polymer film. This technique is used in many detection applications. An image processing based algorithm for the extraction of sweat pores was proposed by [50]. The algorithm employed neural network based computational intelligent technique that was enabled to select true sweat pores from a group of contestant points. An excellent sweat pore matching algorithm based on geometric conversions and bipartite graph techniques was proposed by [51]. This algorithm magnificently eliminated the need for finger print devices and improved the performance of finger print identification systems. For the authentication of a person, a biometric system consists of a sensor that generates the image containing information about sweat glands.

EEG Signal

Recently, the scientific community has shown their interest in the usage of brain signals to recognize people automatically. Traditional biometrics methods like face, fingerprint or iris are slowly being replaced by the methods like ECG, EDR and BVP as these approaches had shown the notable advantage of being secured and hard to forge. Analysis of brain signals acquired through EEG (Electroencephalogram) (Fig. 2.8) generates high temporal resolution activities with inexpensive devices [52].

Different EEG behaviors can be observed using acquisition protocols. A major challenge faced by EEG biometric is the presence of noise in acquired data because of EMG activities and electrode impedance [54].

Heart Sound

One of the most important physiological signals in human body is heart sounds which contain significant information regarding the physiological state of a person.

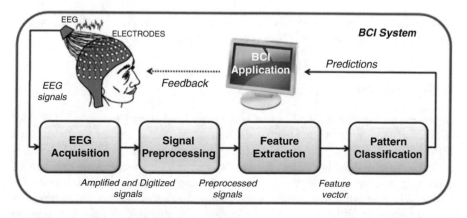

Fig. 2.8 An EEG model for pattern classification [53]

This information is captured using ventricles, atria, great vessels and functional status of each valve. When a human heart pumps blood, it generates a sound or vibration called phonocardiography [55]. High universality is undeniably true as if the body does not generate heart beats which makes the authentication of living or non-living human. This property can be helpful for the identification of organs like brain whose functionalities are critical. The major con of heartbeat biometric is the low presentation as biometric traits.

Biometric of Palmer Skin

Palm vein recognition is the most leading approach used for human identification, offers a high degree of security because veins pattern lies under the skin and cannot be seen through eyes. It cannot duplicate the vein structure of people and can be seen only through a sensor device emitted infrared radiation [56]. The foremost advantage of human palm vein is that it remains constant i.e., not changeable throughout one's life which is incredibly hard to modify. The three layers observed from the cross section of human skins are epidermis, inner dermis and hypodermic. All three layers consist of arteries, fat, and blood with diverse proportions. The wavelength produced by the incident of illumination has different responses to an individual's skin. Veins pattern regions are obtained with the assistance of NIR sensors that solely add the presence of real blood, creating it laborious to trick. Infrared radiation passes through the tissues of skin layer which block the pigments i.e., hemoglobin. As hemoglobin consists of densely blood vessels, therefore incursion of infrared radiation over the palm skin causes shine in veins to look as dark shadow outlines within the output image.

2.3.2   Behavioral Biometrics

The biometrics types under this category include signature, voice, key stroke dynamics, gait and hand grip. These types are discussed as under.

2.3.2.1   Signature

Signature recognition or verification is a type of behavioral biometrics [57–59]. It is a physical activity to identify an individual. Static and dynamic are two different ways to exam the individual. In the static method, individual provides its hand-written signature which is transformed into an image with the help of a scanner or a camera. After that, data turns into text data or other images for verification using different image processing and machine learning algorithms. It is also known as offline signature verification. The dynamic method is related to advanced technology in which individuals use smart phones, tablets or PDAs to sign with a finger or an appropriate pen. Individual signatures are verified with the properties of captured direction, stroke, pressure, and shape. The advantage of dynamic signature verification over static is that dynamic signature recognition is almost impossible to replicate and easy to find the human forger.

2.3.2.2   Auditory

Some auditory biometrics includes voice, breath and lips movements. These are discussed as follows:

Voice

According to Unisys survey, most biometric consumers think voice biometric as a top biometric tool [60]. Speaker recognition as biometric can be used in highly sensitive secure areas. In most of the investigation cases where the investigator has just a clue of voice, speaker recognition tool can be the only tool to identify the criminal. Speaker recognition is also used for remote verification on VOIP at some most sensitive telephone networks. Automatic speaker recognition can be helpful in the field of defense, law enforcement, business interactions, call centers, forensics, and security. One of the states of art techniques is Mel-frequency cepstral coefficients (MFCCs) [61] to recognize speaker through voice. Mel-frequency scale is 1000 Hz to 1 kHz [62]. Speaker recognition based on wavelet analysis and deep learning model is found more accurate [63].

Breath

Breath is an offensive technique available to uniquely identify an individual. It can be taken as an anatomic biometric of respiratory system because of its intrapulmonary stress managed by trachea, vocal tract, respiratory muscles, lungs and diaphragm [64]. Breath can also be used as a distinctive identification element because of its changing structure of inner microbes that reside in human body. In near future, it may be used in medical diagnostics figuring out the drugs taken by an individual and it is also able to identify whether an athlete is doping or not. The exhaled air contains such type of compounds that contain discriminating features and steady molecular breath print that can be used to check medication reaction and disease monitoring. Human breath as biometric is also named as breath print; it takes the sounds created by an individual's breathing recorded by taking microphone sensor closer to the human nose. If the biometric of breathing sound remains distinct and unchanged, then breath print gives a convincing way of verification. It is a universal feature than other biometrics. Breathing is a natural phenomenon and it does not require supplementary corporeal and cognitive efforts [65].

Fig. 2.9 Lips dynamics [67]

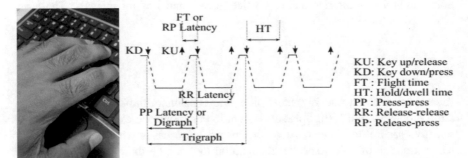

Fig. 2.10 Keystrokes timing information [70]

Lips Movements

Lips centroid and rotation movement play a vital role in human identification. Dynamic deformation lips shaped features and static [66] lips (see Fig. 2.9) features obtained significant high identification performance rate.

2.3.2.3 Keystroke Dynamics

Keystroke dynamics is a biometric approach used for person verification. It is a non-static biometric method that expects to distinguish persons in view of unique typing style [68, 69].

Keystroke progression is the point by point timing data that depicts precisely when each key was squeezed and when it was discharged as a man is writing at a PC console (see Fig. 2.10). The recorded keystroke timing information is then handled through an algorithm which decides an essential example for future correlation. A biometric framework comprises of three noteworthy parts: Data acquisition, Feature Extraction and Mapping [3]. It has numerous focal points, for example, it is (1) a product just strategy and does not require any equipment with the exception of a console, (2) generally acknowledged and simple to convey, (3) practical, and (4) does not require any end client training. It additionally has a few down sides, for example, (1) user's helplessness to fatigue, (2) dynamic change in writing designs, (3) injury, the expertise of client and (4) change of console equipment.

2.3.2.4   Gait

Gait is a human walking style that can be used to identify an individual [71]. Many physiological studies have proved that each individual has its unique walking style which is difficult to copy. Gait as a biometric plays a vital role in video surveillance for security purpose and to find lost people as video sequences for human identification can be taken from distance using multiple cameras and from various angles even in dense environment. Unlike other biometric technologies that use contact based estimation, gait employs non-contact acquisition of data [72]. The factors that affect the gait recognition process include various carrying conditions, clothing, illumination effects, shadow under feet, and walking speed [73].

To overcome these challenges, many state-of-art methods have been proposed that divide the gait recognition process in two different approaches i.e., model-free and model-based approaches. Figure 2.11 represents a sample gait recognition system. In model-based approach, structure of a human body with joint angles is used to track the body movement. It is view and scale invariant method that gives more information. It is computationally expensive and requires high quality video for feature extraction. Model-free approach is also named as appearance-based approach. This approach directly takes human silhouette as input for useful feature extraction [75]. Moreover, it is used to analyze spatiotemporal structure of subject in each gait cycle and then converting each gait cycle in to a single template named as gait energy image GEI [76]. For biometric gait identification, different floor sensors and sensors placed in body are also used such as micro-electro-mechanical system (MEMS). It is a small inertial sensor device fixed in to smart shoes. It is able to collect motion signals and then transmit them in to the server [77].

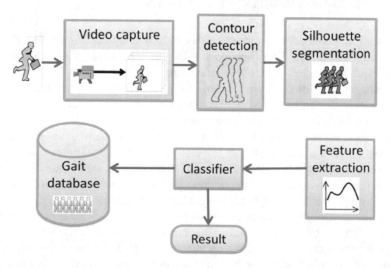

Fig. 2.11 A gait recognition system [74]

2.3.2.5 Hand Grip

Hand grip is holding capacity of a hand. The ability of grasping can act as a parameter to check the physical status of a human being. Hand grip strength directly depends on some physical properties as age, nutritional status, health etc. So hand grip strength varies between old age and young person just as between sick and healthy person. Hand grip strength is also affected by the weight of the thing going to be grasped. Nutritionists and dietitians use the hand grip strength as a measure of screening to know how many of the patients are suffering from malnutrition [78]. Hand grip as a biometric includes the pattern and behavior of grasped hand. The pressure rate of hand may vary because of the sickness and healthiness of the person. A monography system for hand grip measurement using Jamar electronic dynamometer measures the hand grip strength of healthy adults by considering some parameters including training, hand length, strength etc. Jamar dynamometers are good for clinical practices but at the same time having a drawback of being unidirectional [79]. Low power and inexpensive sensors called COTS are used to detect the fire arm. The hand pressure biometric is detected through some small sensors. Still the challenge is to implement an entire detection system for fire arm [80]. In winters, clipping the vineyard is far difficult and directly depends on the pruner's capability of handling the shears. The pruner may face musculoskeletal or wrist disorder when working with the shears. The muscle strength of the pruner is determined through a measure GS (Grip Strength) while holding distinct shears under different working conditions [81].

2.4 Important Findings and Discussion

The biometrics market is progressing day by day and according to an estimate, the market will worth 30 billion dollars by the year 2022 [82]. The traditional recognition approaches utilize magnetic cards, passwords and PINs for person identification. Most of the users demand easier ways for authentications. Biometrics is the answer to handle this issue. Biometrics is suitable by providing speedy and strong authentication. In addition, the biometrics are time saving, convenient to use and versatile. However, apart from the benefits, there are many issues that can raise questions on the usage of these systems. One problem is that all biometrics types are not applicable in all authentication domains. For example, DNA biometrics cannot be beneficial in attendance management systems. Moreover, biometrics security can be compromised through hacking. Most of biometrics is open to show to others such as face, ears, voice etc. Also, we can leave our finger prints on many things which can be useful to hackers to compromise the security. To answer such issues, the researchers are working on multi and hybrid biometrics techniques. An example of multi biometrics approach is the use of multiple prints of fingers at a time to authenticate. In hybrid biometrics, more than one biometrics is used at a time, for example, iris and finger print based authentication approach can be used simultaneously to increase authentication process security.

2.5 Summary

Biometrics is a practical swap or improvement to the utilization of passwords or PINs to recognize a person. Every individual's qualities are unique. Indeed, even identical twins do not have precisely the same qualities. Biometrics is an alternate of passwords or pins to recognize people. Biometrics innovation is persistently creating to enhance exactness and security which has seen the development of second era biometrics that use multi types of biometrics including biological and physiological biometrics. Any natural conduct or attribute can be utilized to recognize people if it meets the accompanying prerequisites: (a) Collectability (the components can be estimated), (b) All-inclusiveness (the component available in all individuals), (c) Uniqueness (the component must be unique to every individual) and (d) Lastingness (component must retain its properties long lasting). This chapter provides a brief introduction to many types of biometrics under the categories of biological and physiological biometrics. The importance and applicability of all types are discussed briefly.

New biometrics types can be generated by combining two or more biometrics (multi modal biometrics) to acquire more system robustness. Also, there are still some constraints and accuracy issues in existing biometrics systems which show that there are requirements of further research in the area of biometrics to achieve better performance.

References

1. R. Alexander, Using the Analytical Hierarchy Process Model in the Prioritization of Information Assurance Defense In-Depth Measures?—A Quantitative Study, Journal of Information Security, 8 (2017) 166.
2. D.W. Sanders, S.K. Kaufman, B.B. Holmes, M.I. Diamond, Prions and protein assemblies that convey biological information in health and disease, Neuron, 89 (2016) 433-448.
3. M.W. Khan, M. Sharif, M. Yasmin, S.L. Fernandes, A new approach of cup to disk ratio based glaucoma detection using fundus images, Journal of Integrated Design and Process Science, 20 (2016) 77-94.
4. R.P. Wildes, Iris recognition: an emerging biometric technology, Proceedings of the IEEE, 85 (1997) 1348-1363.
5. J.M. Colores-Vargas, M. García-Vázquez, A. Ramírez-Acosta, H. Pérez-Meana, M. Nakano-Miyatake, Video images fusion to improve iris recognition accuracy in unconstrained environments, Mexican Conference on Pattern Recognition, (Springer2013), pp. 114-125.
6. M. Sharif, M.A. Ali, M. Raza, S. Mohsin, Face recognition using edge information and DCT, Sindh University Research Journal-SURJ (Science Series), 43 (2015).
7. J.H. Shah, M. Sharif, M. Raza, A. Azeem, A Survey: Linear and Nonlinear PCA Based Face Recognition Techniques, Int. Arab J. Inf. Technol., 10 (2013) 536-545.

8. L. Ma, T. Tan, Y. Wang, D. Zhang, Efficient iris recognition by characterizing key local variations, IEEE Transactions on Image processing, 13 (2004) 739-750.
9. F. Bokhari, T. Syedia, M. Sharif, M. Yasmin, S.L. Fernandes, Fundus image segmentation and feature extraction for the detection of glaucoma: a new approach, Current Medical Imaging Reviews, 14 (2018) 77-87.
10. P. Cofta, H. Lacohée, Understanding public perceptions: trust and engagement in ICT-mediated services (Intl. Engineering Consortiu, 2008).
11. S. Akbar, M.U. Akram, M. Sharif, A. Tariq, U. ullah Yasin, Decision support system for detection of papilledema through fundus retinal images, Journal of medical systems, 41 (2017) 66.
12. A. Panwar, P. Singla, M. Kaur, Techniques for Enhancing the Security of Fuzzy Vault: A Review, Progress in Intelligent Computing Techniques: Theory, Practice, and Applications, (Springer, 2018), pp. 205-213.
13. A. Manickam, E. Devarasan, G. Manogaran, M.K. Priyan, R. Varatharajan, C.-H. Hsu, R. Krishnamoorthi, Score level based latent fingerprint enhancement and matching using SIFT feature, Multimedia Tools and Applications, (2018) 1-21.
14. M. Sharif, F. Naz, M. Yasmin, M.A. Shahid, A. Rehman, Face Recognition: A Survey, Journal of Engineering Science & Technology Review, 10 (2017).
15. J. Hussain Shah, M. Sharif, M. Raza, M. Murtaza, S. Ur-Rehman, Robust Face Recognition Technique under Varying Illumination, Journal of applied research and technology, 13 (2015) 97-105.
16. J.H. Shah, M. Sharif, M. Raza, A. Azeem, Face recognition across pose variation and the 3S problem, turkish journal of electrical engineering & computer sciences, 22 (2014) 1423-1436.
17. A. Aisha, S. Muhammad, S.J. Hussain, R. Mudassar, Face recognition invariant to partial occlusions, KSII Trans. Internet Inf. Syst.((TIIS)), 8 (2014) 2496-2511.
18. M. Murtaza, M. Sharif, M. Raza, J. Shah, Face recognition using adaptive margin fisher's criterion and linear discriminant analysis, International Arab Journal of Information Technology, 11 (2014) 1-11.
19. M. Sharif, J.H. Shah, S. Mohsin, M. Raza, Facial Feature Detection and Recognition for Varying Poses, World Congress on Engineering and Computer Science2014), pp. 22-24.
20. A. Azeem, M. Sharif, M. Raza, M. Murtaza, A survey: Face recognition techniques under partial occlusion, Int. Arab J. Inf. Technol., 11 (2014) 1-10.
21. Large-scale dynamic face recognition system, 2014).
22. M. Sharif, A. Khalid, M. Raza, S. Mohsin, Face detection and recognition through hexagonal image processing, Sindh University Research Journal-SURJ (Science Series), 44 (2012).
23. M. Sharif, S. Mohsin, M.Y. Javed, A survey: face recognition techniques, Research Journal of Applied Sciences, Engineering and Technology, 4 (2012) 4979-4990.
24. M. Sharif, S. Mohsin, M.Y. Javed, M.A. Ali, Single Image Face Recognition Using Laplacian of Gaussian and Discrete Cosine Transforms, Int. Arab J. Inf. Technol., 9 (2012) 562-570.
25. M. Sharif, M.Y. Javed, S. Mohsin, Face recognition based on facial features, Research Journal of Applied Sciences, Engineering and Technology, 4 (2012) 2879-2886.
26. M. Sharif, K. Ayub, D. Sattar, M. Raza, S. Mohsin, Enhanced and fast face recognition by hashing algorithm, Journal of applied research and technology, 10 (2012) 607-617.
27. M. Sharif, S. Anis, M. Raza, S. Mohsin, Enhanced SVD Based Face Recognition, Journal of Applied Computer Science & Mathematics, (2012).
28. M. Sharif, A. Khalid, M. Raza, S. Mohsin, Face Recognition using Gabor Filters, Journal of Applied Computer Science & Mathematics, (2011).
29. M. Sharif, S. Mohsin, R.A. Hanan, M.Y. Javed, M. Raza, Using nose heuristics for efficient face recognition, Sindh University Research Journal-SURJ (Science Series), 43 (2011).
30. M. Sharif, S. Mohsin, M.J. Jamal, M.Y. Javed, M. Raza, Face recognition for disguised variations using gabor feature extraction, Australian Journal of Basic and Applied Sciences, 5 (2011) 1648-1656.

31. M. Sharif, S. Mohsin, M.J. Jamal, M. Raza, Illumination Normalization Preprocessing for face recognition, Environmental Science and Information Application Technology (ESIAT), 2010 International Conference on, (IEEE2010), pp. 44-47.
32. D.P. Chowdhury, S. Bakshi, G. Guo, P.K. Sa, On applicability of tunable filter bank based feature for ear biometrics: a study from constrained to unconstrained, Journal of medical systems, 42 (2018) 11.
33. D. Zhang, G. Lu, L. Zhang, Online 3D Ear Recognition, Advanced Biometrics, (Springer, 2018), pp. 309-328.
34. M. Boczek, Ear biometric capture, authentication, and identification method and system, (Google Patents2017).
35. I.B. Barbosa, T. Theoharis, A.E. Abdallah, On the use of fingernail images as transient biometric identifiers, Machine Vision and Applications, 27 (2016) 65-76.
36. A. Uhl, P. Wild, Footprint-based biometric verification, Journal of Electronic Imaging, 17 (2008) 011016.
37. X. Wang, H. Wang, Q. Cheng, N.L. Nankabirwa, T. Zhang, Single 2D pressure footprint based person identification, Biometrics (IJCB), 2017 IEEE International Joint Conference on, (IEEE2017), pp. 413-419.
38. A. Brown, DNA as an investigative technique, Science and Justice, 38 (1998) 263-265.
39. C. Forr, B. Schei, L.E. Stene, K. Ormstad, C.T. Hagemann, Factors associated with trace evidence analyses and DNA findings among police reported cases of rape, Forensic science international, 283 (2018) 136-143.
40. M. Shirasu, K. Touhara, The scent of disease: volatile organic compounds of the human body related to disease and disorder, The Journal of Biochemistry, 150 (2011) 257-266.
41. S. Haze, Y. Gozu, S. Nakamura, Y. Kohno, K. Sawano, H. Ohta, K. Yamazaki, 2-Nonenal newly found in human body odor tends to increase with aging, Journal of investigative dermatology, 116 (2001) 520-524.
42. I. Rodriguez-Lujan, G. Bailador, C. Sanchez-Avila, A. Herrero, G. Vidal-De-Miguel, Analysis of pattern recognition and dimensionality reduction techniques for odor biometrics, Knowledge-Based Systems, 52 (2013) 279-289.
43. Hand, finger geometry, 2018).
44. C.M. Travieso, J. Zhang, P. Miller, J.B. Alonso, M.A. Ferrer, Bimodal biometric verification based on face and lips, Neurocomputing, 74 (2011) 2407-2410.
45. Y. Vasquez, C. Beltrán, M. Gómez, M. Flórez, J.L. Vázquez-González, Features extraction in images on finger veins with hybrid curves, Humanitarian Technology Conference (MHTC), IEEE Mexican, (IEEE2017), pp. 34-38.
46. W. Yang, S. Wang, J. Hu, G. Zheng, C. Valli, A fingerprint and finger-vein based cancelable multi-biometric system, Pattern Recognition, 78 (2018) 242-251.
47. P. Gupta, S. Srivastava, P. Gupta, An accurate infrared hand geometry and vein pattern based authentication system, Knowledge-Based Systems, 103 (2016) 143-155.
48. E.J. Esekhaigbe, Contributions to Biometric Recognition: Fingerprint For Identity Verification, Cardiff Metropolitan University, 2016.
49. D.-H. Park, B.J. Park, J.-M. Kim, Hydrochromic approaches to mapping human sweat pores, Accounts of chemical research, 49 (2016) 1211-1222.
50. A. Genovese, E. Munoz, V. Piuri, F. Scotti, G. Sforza, Towards touchless pore fingerprint biometrics: a neural approach, Evolutionary Computation (CEC), 2016 IEEE Congress on, (IEEE2016), pp. 4265-4272.
51. M.-j. Kim, W.-Y. Kim, J. Paik, Optimum Geometric Transformation and Bipartite Graph-Based Approach to Sweat Pore Matching for Biometric Identification, Symmetry, 10 (2018) 175.
52. P. Campisi, D. La Rocca, Brain waves for automatic biometric-based user recognition, IEEE transactions on information forensics and security, 9 (2014) 782-800.
53. P.J. García-Laencina, G. Rodríguez-Bermudez, J. Roca-Dorda, Exploring dimensionality reduction of EEG features in motor imagery task classification, Expert Systems with Applications, 41 (2014) 5285-5295.

54. S. Romero, M. Mañanas, M. Barbanoj, Ocular reduction in EEG signals based on adaptive filtering, regression and blind source separation, Annals of biomedical engineering, 37 (2009) 176-191.
55. K. Phua, J. Chen, T.H. Dat, L. Shue, Heart sound as a biometric, Pattern Recognition, 41 (2008) 906-919.
56. M.S.N. Dere, A. Gurjar, Identification of Human using Palm-Vein Images: A new trend in biometrics, International Journal Of Engineering And Computer Science ISSN, 2319-7242.
57. V.S. Nalwa, Automatic on-line signature verification, Proceedings of the IEEE, 85 (1997) 215-239.
58. D.B.S. Netto, M. Fornazin, M.A. Cavenaghi, R. Spolon, R.S. Lobato, A practical approach for biometric authentication based on smartcards, Information Systems and Technologies (CISTI), 2010 5th Iberian Conference on2010), pp. 1-5.
59. M. Sharif, M.A. Khan, M. Faisal, M. Yasmin, S.L. Fernandes, A framework for offline signature verification system: Best features selection approach, Pattern Recognition Letters, (2018).
60. M. Khitrov, Talking passwords: voice biometrics for data access and security, Biometric Technology Today, 2013 (2013) 9-11.
61. K.S.R. Murty, B. Yegnanarayana, Combining evidence from residual phase and MFCC features for speaker recognition, IEEE signal processing letters, 13 (2006) 52-55.
62. M. Bezoui, A. Elmoutaouakkil, A. Beni-hssane, Feature extraction of some Quranic recitation using mel-frequency cepstral coeficients (MFCC), Multimedia Computing and Systems (ICMCS), 2016 5th International Conference on, (IEEE2016), pp. 127-131.
63. N. Almaadeed, A. Aggoun, A. Amira, Speaker identification using multimodal neural networks and wavelet analysis, IET Biometrics, 4 (2015) 18-28.
64. L. Lu, L. Liu, M.J. Hussain, Y. Liu, I sense you by Breath: Speaker Recognition via Breath Biometrics, IEEE Transactions on Dependable and Secure Computing, (2017) 1-1.
65. J. Chauhan, Y. Hu, S. Seneviratne, A. Misra, A. Seneviratne, Y. Lee, BreathPrint: Breathing acoustics-based user authentication, Proceedings of the 15th Annual International Conference on Mobile Systems, Applications, and Services, (ACM2017), pp. 278-291.
66. D. Stewart, A. Pass, J. Zhang, Gender classification via lips: static and dynamic features, IET biometrics, 2 (2013) 28-34.
67. S.-L. Wang, A.W.-C. Liew, Physiological and behavioral lip biometrics: A comprehensive study of their discriminative power, Pattern Recognition, 45 (2012) 3328-3335.
68. M. Raza, M. Iqbal, M. Sharif, W. Haider, A survey of password attacks and comparative analysis on methods for secure authentication, World Applied Sciences Journal, 19 (2012) 439-444.
69. M. Sharif, T. Faiz, M. Raza, Time signatures-an implementation of keystroke and click patterns for practical and secure authentication, Digital Information Management, 2008. ICDIM 2008. Third International Conference on, (IEEE2008), pp. 559-562.
70. S.P. Banerjee, D.L. Woodard, Biometric authentication and identification using keystroke dynamics: A survey, Journal of Pattern Recognition Research, 7 (2012) 116-139.
71. M.H. Khan, F. Li, M.S. Farid, M. Grzegorzek, Gait recognition using motion trajectory analysis, International Conference on Computer Recognition Systems, (Springer2017), pp. 73-82.
72. S. Yu, H. Chen, Q. Wang, L. Shen, Y. Huang, Invariant feature extraction for gait recognition using only one uniform model, Neurocomputing, 239 (2017) 81-93.
73. S.D. Choudhury, T. Tjahjadi, Clothing and carrying condition invariant gait recognition based on rotation forest, Pattern Recognition Letters, 80 (2016) 1-7.
74. R. Amin, T. Gaber, G. ElTaweel, A.E. Hassanien, Biometric and traditional mobile authentication techniques: Overviews and open issues, Bio-inspiring cyber security and cloud services: trends and innovations, (Springer, 2014), pp. 423-446.
75. J.N. Mogan, C.P. Lee, A.W. Tan, Gait recognition using temporal gradient patterns, Information and Communication Technology (ICoIC7), 2017 5th International Conference on, (IEEE2017), pp. 1-4.

76. C.-C. Huang, C.-C. Hsu, H.-Y. Liao, S.-H. Yang, L.-L. Wang, S.-Y. Chen, Frontal gait recognition based on spatio-temporal interest points, Journal of the Chinese Institute of Engineers, 39 (2016) 997-1002.
77. S. Tao, X. Zhang, H. Cai, Z. Lv, C. Hu, H. Xie, Gait based biometric personal authentication by using MEMS inertial sensors, Journal of Ambient Intelligence and Humanized Computing, (2018) 1-8.
78. A. Byrnes, A. Mudge, A. Young, M. Banks, J. Bauer, Use of hand grip strength in nutrition risk screening of older patients admitted to general surgical wards, Nutrition & Dietetics, (2018).
79. A. Wichelhaus, C. Harms, J. Neumann, S. Ziegler, G. Kundt, K.J. Prommersberger, T. Mittlmeier, M. Mühldorfer-Fodor, Parameters influencing hand grip strength measured with the manugraphy system, BMC musculoskeletal disorders, 19 (2018) 54.
80. M.S. Islam, M. Ali, K.H. Zubaer, S. Sarmin, M.T. Islam, B. Islam, A.A. Al Islam, A.M. Sadri, Trusted Worrier: A low-cost and high-accuracy user authentication system for firearm exploiting dynamic hand pressure biometrics, Networking, Systems and Security (NSysS), 2017 International Conference on, (IEEE2017), pp. 87-95.
81. B. Çakmak, E. Ergül, Interactions of personal and occupational risk factors on hand grip strength of winter pruners, International Journal of Industrial Ergonomics, 67 (2018) 192-200.
82. K. Howell, 3 Reasons Biometrics Are Not Secure, (ipswitch2017).

Chapter 3
SIE: An Application to Secure Stereo Images Using Encryption

Sanoj Kumar and Gaurav Bhatnagar

3.1 Introduction

In the era of substantial escalation in the discipline of communication and network technology, digital data sharing over insecure networks and their storage on advanced web servers becomes considerably easy. A conspicuous fact is that this ease is contingent on the cyber-attacks making the data less secure on a public platform. Cryptography/Encryption techniques has been materialized as an essential mechanism for ensuring the security of digital data during the communication [1]. Generally, the encryption procedure is composed of two stages: (1) scrambling of digital data, and (2) diffusion of scrambled information. The former cast the digital data elements into daze by changing their position such that the original data is not recognizable. However, inverse operations can be used to obtain original data. Therefore, the security is further enhanced by the latter stage wherein the scrambled data is altered to break the strong correlative relationship among the neighboring data elements. The second stage is essentially performed by several cryptographic methods such as SCAN based methods [2], chaos based methods [3–6] and other miscellaneous methods [7, 8].

On the other hand, the 3D realization of an object/scene is provided by stereo vision. The core idea is to record two images of the same scene from two slightly distinct perspectives. These two images are generally called stereo image pair and are discerned as left and right stereo images [9]. Stereo vision has a vast range of

S. Kumar
Department of Mathematics, University of Petroleum and Energy Studies, Dehradun, Uttarakhand, India
e-mail: sanoj.kumar@ddn.upes.ac.in

G. Bhatnagar (✉)
Department of Mathematics, Indian Institute of Technology, Jodhpur, India
e-mail: goravb@iitj.ac.in

© Springer Nature Switzerland AG 2019
A. K. Singh, A. Mohan (eds.), *Handbook of Multimedia Information Security: Techniques and Applications*, https://doi.org/10.1007/978-3-030-15887-3_3

applications in robot vision, medical surgery, aerial mapping, visual surveillance, 3D television, 3D video applications, autonomous navigation, virtual machines and so forth. Typically, the storage and communication requirement for stereo image pair is twice the requirement of monocular vision system. The current trend is to compress the stereo images using some stereo coding algorithm before transmission to reduce data volume [10–14]. The main drawback of existing stereo coding algorithms is the revelation of the content present in the stereo images [15]. Therefore, there is a need to develop some stereo image coding algorithm which not only reduce the data volume but also hide the content of the stereo images. In light of this, an encryption technique for stereo image pair can be useful for secure and durable stereo images communication, wherein the storage and communication rate requirement is as par with monocular image. Thus, usage of encryption technique leads to secure and durable stereo image coding system.

In this chapter, a novel stereo image coding algorithm via image encryption technique is presented. The proposed algorithm is based on the step space filling curve, non-linear chaotic map and singular value decomposition. The core idea is to scramble image pixels positions using step space filling curve followed by altering the pixel values based on singular value decomposition coupled with non-linear chaotic map. For this, a random matrix is generated from chaotic map and a hankel matrix is then obtained using singular values of random matrix. Now, a secret image is acquired using left and right singular vectors of hankel matrix. This secret image is used to encrypt both the stereo images. An images is finally derived by unifying left and right encrypted stereo images. This image is treated as the final encrypted image and may be used for communication and transmission purposes. At the receiver end, final encrypted images is first detached into left and right encrypted images, which will then undergo the decryption process. Extensive experimental results on different stereo images are presented to illustrate the performance of the proposed algorithm.

This chapter is organized as follows: Sect. 3.2 presents a brief literature review of relevant research in the area of encryption techniques followed by the underlying mathematical preliminaries are discussed in Sect. 3.3. The Step space filling curve is presented in Sect. 3.4. The proposed algorithm is explained in detail in Sect. 3.5. In Sect. 3.6, the efficacy of the proposed technique is demonstrated through extensive experiments. Finally, the concluding observations are discussed and presented in Sect. 3.7.

3.2 Review of Existing Encryption Techniques

The core idea behind the encryption techniques is to modify the data, which is usually text, image, audio or video, in an effort to make the data unintelligible and only legitimate recipient can reconstruct and access the data [16]. These techniques are used to achieve one (or all) of the following goals [17]:

- *Data integrity*: It essentially clinches that the data has not been altered by unauthorized personnel and all legitimate recipients must detect the alteration, if the data is altered.
- *Confidentiality*: It refers to the protection of data from unauthorized personals. This goal is considered as one of the basic requirement to be catered by the encryption technique.
- *Authentication*: It assess the data origin authentication in regard of data source and integrity, however, it does not guarantee the uniqueness and time alacrity.
- *Non-repudiation*: It essentially ensures that the sender cannot claim that he/she encrypt and communicate the data.

Owing these goals, several image encryption techniques have been proposed in the literature. These techniques can be classified in many ways as per underlying classification criteria (rules). A general classification of these techniques is illustrated in Fig. 3.1. The most common classification is according to the structure of encryption technique. According to structure, the techniques are classified into full, selective and compression-combined encryption techniques. The complete image is encrypted in the former techniques [18–23] whereas only some significant portions of the image are encrypted in the partial encryption techniques [24–30]. In the latter techniques, the encryption operations are coupled with the compression operations and are executed concurrently [31–36]. Instinctively, full encryption is highly secure as the full image is encrypted while selective and compressed-combined encryption techniques reduces the data volume to be encrypted and lead to the higher efficiency.

According to working domain, encryption techniques can be classified into two types: (1) spatial [37–44], and (2) frequency domain techniques [45–50]. Spatial domain techniques are simple but are having less security when compared to frequency domain techniques. Spatial domain techniques are simple but not robust when compared to frequency domain techniques. This stems from the fact that when inverse transformation is applied, the encrypted information is distributed irregularly over the image, making it difficult to read or modify [51]. According to encryption properties, techniques can be classified into perceptual or scalable encryption techniques. In the former, an image is encrypted where the image perceptibility is controlled by a parameter, usually, called encryption strength

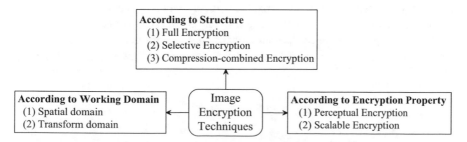

Fig. 3.1 A general classification of image encryption techniques

[52–54]. One of the typical scenario is when an image is encrypted and the preview is only available after payment. In the latter, image is encrypted with respect to layers in a gradual manner owing the importance of the layers [55–58].

3.3 Mathematical Preliminaries

This section narrates the description of mathematical notions that are forming a necessary base for the craved objective. These notions comprises of the following:

3.3.1 Singular Value Decomposition

The singular value decomposition (SVD) is an important factoring procedure for a real (complex) rectangular matrix with numerous applications in the broader area of signal and image processing. In mathematical terms, SVD of a matrix Σ can be expressed as

$$\Sigma = U_\Sigma S_\Sigma V_\Sigma^T \tag{3.1}$$

where U_Σ and V_Σ are *orthogonal(unitary)* and $S_\Sigma = diag(\sigma_1, \sigma_2, ..., \sigma_r)$, where σ_i are the singular values of the matrix Σ with $r = min(m, n)$ and satisfying $\sigma_1 \geq \sigma_2 \geq ... \geq \sigma_r$. The first r columns of U_Σ and V_Σ are called *left singular* and *right singular vectors* respectively.

3.3.2 Non-linear Chaotic Map

A complex system is termed chaotic if it is a deterministic system, mostly non-linear, with pseudo-stochastic features. These compelling features, comprises of aperiodicity, unpredictability, Gauss like statistical characteristics and exceptional sensitivity to internal parameters, make chaotic system a perfect choice for random sequence generator. In this work, a non-linear chaotic piece-wise system is used to design a digital sequence. Mathematically, this system is represented by a map $\mathscr{F} : I \rightarrow I$ with $I = [0, 1]$, which is called the length of the region, is described as [59]

$$\mathscr{F}(y_{k+1}) = \begin{cases} \left(\frac{1}{I_{i+1}-I_i} + b_i\right)(y_k - b_i) - \frac{b_i}{I_{i+1}-I_i}(y_k - b_i)^2, \\ \qquad\qquad\qquad \text{if } y_k \in [I_i, I_{i+1}) \\ 0, \qquad\qquad\quad \text{if } y_k = 1/2 \\ \mathscr{F}(y_k - 1/2), \quad \text{if } y_k \in (1/2, 1] \end{cases} \tag{3.2}$$

where $y_k \in [0, 1]$ and I_i is the sub-interval of $[0,1]$ such that $0 = I_0 < I_1 < \cdots < I_i < \cdots < I_{n+1} = 1/2$ and $b_i \in (-1, 0) \cup (0, 1)$ is the parameter to tune digital sequence in ith interval such that $\sum_{i=0}^{n-1} (I_{i+1} - I_i)b_i = 0$. The compelling properties of this map can be summarized as follows.

- The iterative system obtained by Eq. (3.2) is chaotic for all $y_k \in [0, 1]$.
- The generated sequence $\{y_k\}_{k=1}^{\infty}$ is ergodic in $[0,1]$.
- The underlying probability distribution function is uniform, which further shows the uniformity of the map.
- The sequence $\{y_k\}_{k=1}^{\infty}$ has the auto-correlation function of δ type and is given as

$$R_{\mathscr{F}}(r) = \lim_{j \to \infty} \frac{1}{j} \frac{\sum_{k=1}^{j} y_k y_{k+r}}{\sum_{k=1}^{j} y_k y_k}, r \geq 0$$

3.4   Step Space Filling Curve

A space-filling curve (SFC) [60] is a continuous scan that travel across every pixel of an image precisely once. Due to this, SFCs have gained the interest of image-space models that are founded on the spatial coherence of neighbouring pixels. SFCs essentially provide a sequence of pixels, which can be processed as per the requirement of intended application and finally the sequence, possibly altered, is mapped to its original position using the same SFC.

In this section, a new SFC namely Step SFC is illustrated which traverse every pixel of an image having size $m \times m$ in the shape of steps/stairs [15]. Therefore, we termed proposed SFC as Step SFC. The core idea behind the Step SFC is to divide the image into two matrices according to its leading diagonal. Among these matrices, one matrix is upper diagonal matrix including the leading diagonal of the original matrix. On the other hand, second matrix is the strictly lower diagonal matrix i.e. having zeros on its diagonal. The Step SFC utilizes the property of images (matrices) that the pixel in the superdiagonal or subdiagonal are perpendicular to the neighbor pixels of the diagonal. Therefore, the pixels of super diagonal or subdiagonal can be inserted between the neighbor pixels of the diagonal.

In order to elaborate the mechanism of Step SFC, a simple example is considered having size 4×4. The whole process is depicted in Fig. 3.2. In upper triangular matrix, the diagonal having the pixels with positions (1,1), (2,2), (3,3) and (4,4) whereas the first superdiagonal containing the pixels with positions (1,2), (2,3) and (3,4). The pixel at (1,2) is the perpendicular to the pixels at (1,1) and (2,2). Therefore, pixel at (1,2) can be inserted between the pixels at (1,1) and pixel (2,2). Similarly, pixel at (2,3) can be inserted between pixels (2,2) and (3,3); pixel at (3,4)

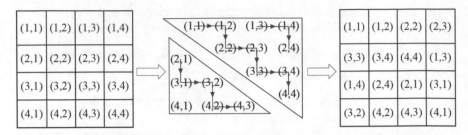

Fig. 3.2 Illustration of step SFC on an image patch

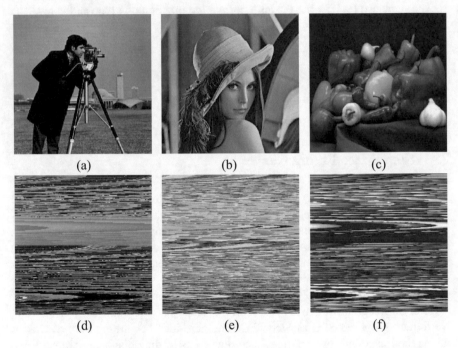

Fig. 3.3 Visual assessment of step SFC: original images (**a**) Cameraman, (**b**) Lena, (**c**) Peppers; Scrambled images (**d**) Cameraman, (**e**) Lena, (**f**) Peppers

can be inserted between pixels (3,3) and (4,4). Once the leading diagonal and first superdiagonal traverses, the same mechanism is applied to the third and fourth superdiagonal, fifth and sixth superdiagonal until all the elements are traversed. In the same manner, every pixel is traversed in strictly lower triangular matrix considering subdiagonals. The visual effect of Step SFC on different standard images, namely Cameraman, Lena and Peppers, are shown in Fig. 3.3.

3.5   Proposed Algorithm

In this section, some of the inspiring facets in the design of proposed encryption technique for stereo images are discussed. The proposed algorithm uses a pair of stereo images and gives an encrypted image in which both the encrypted stereo images are merged. At the receiver end, the encrypted left and right images are separated followed by the decryption of the images for varied objectives. Without loss of generality, let us assume that $F_\ell : \ell \in \{L, R\}$ represents the original left and right stereo images each of size $M \times N$. The proposed technique can be summarized as follows.

3.5.1   Pre-processing

The goal of pre-processing is to produce square reference left and right stereo image by adding redundancy in it. The pre-processing is done whenever the original stereo images are rectangular images. The complete process can be elaborated as follows.

1. Apply the discrete cosine transform (DCT) on the rectangular stereo images (F_ℓ).
2. Modify DCT transformed stereo images as follows

   (i) Add $(M - N)$ columns having zeros, if $M > N$.
   (ii) Add $(N - M)$ columns having zeros, if $M < N$.

3. Apply inverse DCT to construct reference stereo images, denoted by F_ℓ^{ref}.

3.5.2   Encryption Process

1. **First Phase:** Scramble reference left and right stereo image pixel positions using Step SFC which are denoted by F_ℓ^s.
2. Construct two sequences $K_i : i = 1, 2$ of length MN by adopting $\{key_i : i = 1, 2\}$ as keys to iterate non-linear chaotic map.
3. Convert sequences K_i into integer sequences Z_i as follows

$$\text{if } K_i(j) \in \left[\frac{k}{M \times N}, \ \frac{k+1}{M \times N} \right), \text{ then } Z_i(j) = k \qquad (3.3)$$

   where $j, k = 1, 2, 3, ..., M \times N$.
4. Arrange integer sequences Z_i into two random matrices (R_i^Z) of size $M \times N$ followed by SVD on it.

$$R_i^Z = U_{R_i^Z} \, S_{R_i^Z} \, V_{R_i^Z}^T \tag{3.4}$$

5. Obtain two Hankel Matrices using singular values (SVs) of R_i^Z denoted by $H_{R_i^Z}$ and is given by

$$H_{R_i^Z} = \begin{pmatrix} \sigma_i^1 & \sigma_i^2 & \sigma_i^3 & \cdots & \sigma_i^{r-1} & \sigma_i^r \\ \sigma_i^2 & \sigma_i^3 & \sigma_i^4 & \cdots & \sigma_i^r & 0 \\ \vdots & \vdots & \vdots & \ddots & \vdots & \vdots \\ \sigma_i^{r-1} & \sigma_i^r & 0 & \cdots & 0 & 0 \\ \sigma_i^r & 0 & 0 & \cdots & 0 & 0 \end{pmatrix} \tag{3.5}$$

where $S_{R_i^Z} = diag(\sigma_i^1, \ldots, \sigma_i^r)$.

6. Compute SVD of the obtained Hankel matrices.

$$H_{R_i^Z} = U_{H_{R_i^Z}} \, S_{H_{R_i^Z}} \, V_{H_{R_i^Z}}^T \tag{3.6}$$

7. Obtain the matrix keys ($\mathcal{K}_i$) by $U_{H_{R_i^Z}}$ and $V_{H_{R_i^Z}}$ as

$$\mathcal{K}_i = U_{H_{R_i^Z}} V_{H_{R_i^Z}}^T \tag{3.7}$$

where the matrix keys $\mathcal{K}_i$ are orthogonal matrices, i.e., $\mathcal{K}_i \mathcal{K}_i^T = I$.

8. **Second Phase**: The pixel values of scrambled left and right stereo images are changed using matrix keys $\mathcal{K}_i$ to get encrypted stereo images F_ℓ^e as

$$F_\ell^e = \mathcal{K}_i F_\ell^s \Rightarrow \begin{cases} F_L^e = \mathcal{K}_1 F_L^s \\ F_R^e = \mathcal{K}_2 F_R^s \end{cases} \tag{3.8}$$

9. **Third Phase**: In this phase, the encrypted left and right stereo images are merged into single image, which is further termed as the final encrypted image. The merging process is as follows.

   a. Adopting key_3 as key, iterate non-linear chaotic map to get a sequence K_3 of length $M \times N$ followed by generation of random matrix R_3^Z using **steps 2** and **3** of Sect. 3.5.2.

   b. Construct final encrypted image F_m^e as

$$F_m^e \text{s.t} \begin{cases} F_m^e(:,:,1) = F_L^e \\ F_m^e(:,:,2) = R_3^Z \\ F_m^e(:,:,3) = F_R^e \end{cases} \tag{3.9}$$

3.5.3   Decryption Process

The decryption process starts after receiving the final encrypted image and the keys. The complete decryption process can be summarize in the following steps.

1. *First Phase:* In this phase, the encrypted left and right stereo images are extracted from final encrypted image (F_m^e). The extraction process is given by following equation.

$$\begin{cases} F_L^e = F_m^e(:, :, 1) \\ F_R^e = F_m^e(:, :, 3) \end{cases} \tag{3.10}$$

2. By adopting keys $\{key_i \; : \; i = 1, 2\}$, **steps 2** to **7** of encryption process are performed to get matrix keys $\mathscr{K}_i$.
3. Decrypted scrambled images are obtained from F_L^e and F_R^e by utilizing matrix keys, i.e.,

$$F_\ell^{s,d} = inv(\mathscr{K}_i) F_\ell^e \Rightarrow \begin{cases} F_L^{s,d} = \mathscr{K}_1^T F_L^e \\ F_R^{s,d} = \mathscr{K}_2^T F_R^e \end{cases} \tag{3.11}$$

Since, matrix keys ($\mathscr{K}_i$) are orthogonal matrices, therefore, $inv(\mathscr{K}_i) = \mathscr{K}_i^T$.

4. *Second Phase:* Undo scramble pixels of $F_\ell^{s,d}$ to get decrypted reference stereo images $F_\ell^{ref,d}$.

3.5.4   Inverse Pre-processing

The central idea of inverse pre-processing is to obtain decrypted rectangular stereo images (F_ℓ^d) from $F_\ell^{ref,d}$ by removing redundancy from it. The process is as follows.

1. Apply DCT on the decrypted reference stereo images ($F_\ell^{ref,d}$).
2. Modify DCT transformed stereo images as follows

    (i) Remove ($M - N$) columns having zeros, if $M > N$.
    (ii) Remove ($N - M$) columns having zeros, if $M < N$.

3. Perform inverse DCT to obtain the decrypted stereo images, denoted by F_ℓ^d.

3.6 Results and Discussions

The capability and potential of the proposed stereo image coding algorithm via encryption is revealed using several experiments on MATLAB platform. Different stereo images namely Cones, Teddy, Art and Books are used as original stereo images and all are having the size of 450×375. The experimental stereo images are shown in Fig. 3.4. Here, the visual results, statistical and information entropy analysis are given for all stereo images. In the proposed algorithm, three parameters are used as the keys, these parameters are $key_i : i = 1, 2, 3$. All these keys are used as the initial seed for the non-linear chaotic map. The first two keys are used to produce matrix keys for the encryption of left and right stereo images and are taken as $key_1 = 0.4568$ and $key_2 = 0.8597$. The third key, $key_3 = 0.0154$, is used to merge left and right stereo image but has no impact on the security of the proposed algorithm. Therefore, only two keys i.e. key_1 and key_2 plays an vital role in the security of proposed algorithm. The encrypted and decrypted stereo images, using above mentioned keys, are shown in Figs. 3.5, 3.6, 3.7, and 3.8.

One of the main concern for encryption techniques is its security. Chiefly, a good encryption technique must resist against all sort of cryptanalytic, brute-force and statistical attacks. A comprehensive inquisition has been actualized to confirm the security of proposed technique. This essentially include key-sensitivity, information entropy, histogram and correlation analysis. These analysis evinced the high level of security against most common distortions. For brevity, these analysis can be summarized as follows:

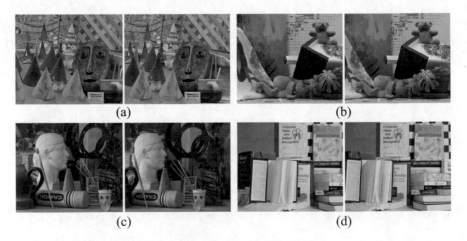

(a)   (b)

(c)   (d)

Fig. 3.4 Experimental left and right stereo images (**a**) Cones (**b**) Teddy (**c**) Art (**d**) Books

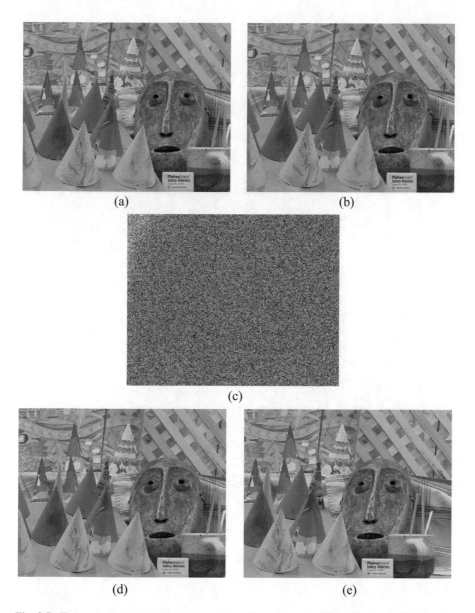

Fig. 3.5 Encryption and decryption process of cone stereo images (**a**) left image, (**b**) right image, (**c**) encrypted image, (**d**) decrypted left image and (**e**) decrypted right image

3.6.1 Key Sensitivity Analysis

For an ideal encryption technique, a subtle amendment in the underlying keys never produces the perfect decryption results. In this context, the sensitivity of the

Fig. 3.6 Encryption and decryption process of teddy stereo images (**a**) left image, (**b**) right image, (**c**) encrypted image, (**d**) decrypted left image and (**e**) decrypted right image

proposed technique on the keys is validated in this section. The proposed technique realizes on two keys ($key_i : i = 1, 2$) and have repercussions on the security. Figure 3.9d–i shows the decrypted images when key_1, key_2 and both $key_i : i = 1, 2$ are wrong respectively. The modification in keys are done such that older

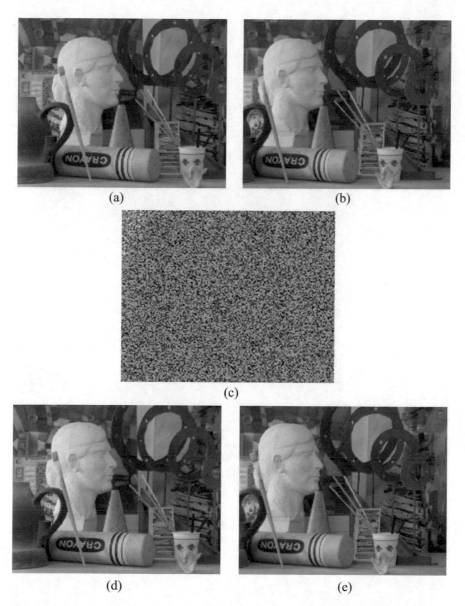

Fig. 3.7 Encryption and decryption process of art stereo images (**a**) left image, (**b**) right image, (**c**) encrypted image, (**d**) decrypted left image and (**e**) decrypted right image

($key_1 = 0.4568$, $key_2 = 0.8597$) and newer values ($key_1 = 0.456811111$, $key_2 = 0.859699999$) are roughly similar. If the left and right decrypted stereo images with changed keys are considered then one can observe that there is no similarity between the original and decrypted left and right stereo images according to human visual

Fig. 3.8 Encryption and decryption process of book stereo images (**a**) left image, (**b**) right image, (**c**) encrypted image, (**d**) decrypted left image and (**e**) decrypted right image

system. Therefore, a slight modification in the involved keys lead to incomplete decryption. This fact further validates the exorbitant key sensitivity of the proposed technique.

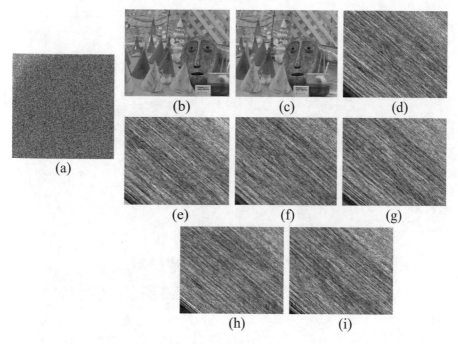

Fig. 3.9 (a) Final encrypted image; decrypted left and right stereo images with (**b, c**) all correct keys (**d, e**) wrong key_1 (**f, g**) wrong key_2 (**h, i**) all wrong keys

3.6.2 Statistical Analysis: Histogram and Correlation Analysis

An alternate way to assess the performance of proposed technique is statistical analysis, which comprises of two procedures: (1) Histogram, and (2) Correlation analysis. The former procedure communicate that the histogram of image after encryption becomes uniform. The histogram analysis ensures that the information is not leaked to the attackers as by uniform histogram none can judge the distribution of the original image pixels. Figure 3.10a, b, e, f illustrates the histograms of original and encrypted stereo images wherein it is confirmed that the histogram after encryption becomes uniform. Therefore, the proposed algorithm is statistically secure and does not reveal any evidences of original stereo images to the attackers.

On the other hand, the second procedure communicates that there is no correlation among the neighboring pixels. Given that, the correlation between two adjacent pixels are calculated. In general, lower values of correlation ensures efficient encryption. In this regard, $\mathscr{P}$ pairs of adjacent pixels in any direction are randomly selected followed by the correlation estimation. Figure 3.10c, d, g, h shows the correlation distribution of two horizontally adjacent pixels in the original and encrypted left and right stereo images. The correlation coefficients in all directions are shown in Table 3.1, which are far apart. It is very prominent from Fig. 3.10 and Table 3.1 that there is no correlation among the pixels of encrypted

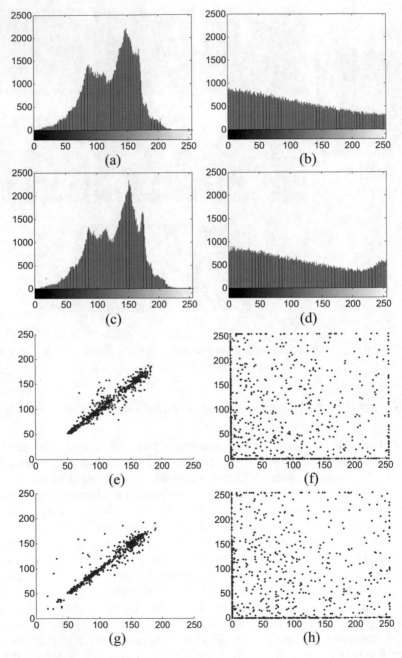

Fig. 3.10 Histogram of (**a**, **c**) original left and right stereo (**b**, **d**) encrypted left and right stereo images; Correlation plot of two horizontal adjacent pixels in (**e**, **g**) original left and right stereo (**f**, **h**) encrypted left and right stereo images

Table 3.1 Correlation coefficients analysis of two adjacent pixels in original and encrypted images

Correlation coefficient in	Image		Direction		
			Horizontal	Vertical	Diagonal
Original stereo images	Cones	Left	0.9981	0.9928	0.9995
		Right	0.9990	0.9954	0.9948
	Teddy	Left	0.9913	0.9995	0.9979
		Right	0.9990	0.9996	0.9914
	Art	Left	0.9963	0.9916	0.9942
		Right	0.9910	0.9996	0.9991
	Books	Left	0.9973	0.9957	0.9986
		Right	0.9971	0.9976	0.9967
Encrypted stereo images	Cones	Left	0.0713	0.0611	−0.0635
		Right	−0.0864	0.0682	0.0029
	Teddy	Left	0.0590	0.0669	0.0249
		Right	0.0032	−0.0353	−0.0042
	Art	Left	−0.0764	0.0590	0.0087
		Right	−0.0841	−0.0154	0.0741
	Books	Left	0.0046	0.0317	−0.0382
		Right	−0.0823	0.0034	−0.0795

left and right encrypted images. Hence, proposed technique is able to break the high correlation among the pixels.

3.6.3 Information Entropy Analysis

Information entropy (IE) quantify the precariousness linked with a aleatory variable by providing the information in terms of bits. Mathematically, IE of source m can be written as

$$IE(m) = \sum_{\forall i} Pb(m_i) log_2 \frac{1}{Pb(m_i)} \qquad (3.12)$$

where $Pb(m_i)$ is the probability of the symbol m_i. Assume that m effuse 2^8 equal probable symbols. A prompt analysis of Eq. (3.12) reveals that a truly random source is having IF close to eight. The IF for encrypted left and right stereo images are listed in Table 3.2 wherein it is visible that IF is in the vicinity of the theoretical value of eight. Therefore, it is apposite to mention that the proposed technique ensures no information leakage by the encrypted images.

Table 3.2 Information
entropy analysis for the
proposed algorithm

Stereo images		Entropy
Cones	Left	7.9427
	Right	7.9489
Teddy	Left	7.9328
	Right	7.9284
Art	Left	7.8974
	Right	7.9023
Book	Left	7.9491
	Right	7.9317

3.6.4 Effect of Proposed Algorithm on Disparity Estimation

Disparity estimation refers to the determination of local displacement, which can align two different images of a scene. Let $I_i(\mathbf{x}) : i = 1, 2$ and $\mathbf{x} = (x, y)^T \in \mathbb{R}^2$ are the two images of the same scene differing by a local displacement. In mathematical terms,

$$I_1(\mathbf{x}) = I_2(\mathbf{x} + \mathbf{d}(\mathbf{x})) \tag{3.13}$$

where $\mathbf{d}$ is the disparity field, which can be expressed by combining horizontal (d_x) and vertical (d_y) disparities as $\mathbf{d} = (d_x, d_y)^T$. The foremost requirement is that $\mathbf{d}(\mathbf{x})$ must possess small range when compared to the domain of $I_i(\mathbf{x})$ else the objects/structures available in $I_1(\mathbf{x})$ would not be present in the domain of $I_2(\mathbf{x})$. In the case of stereo images, the disparity is estimated only along the horizontal direction because both the images are rectified. With the aim of evaluating the effect of proposed algorithm on disparity estimation, three famous block matching methods have been considered. These methods include matching algorithms based on Sum of Absolute Difference (SAD), Sum of Square Differences (SSD) and Normalized Cross-Correlation (NCC) [61].

3.6.4.1 Sum of Absolute Differences (SAD)

It is a most common matching algorithm. SAD is more important when we need the speed of computation because it requires least computations. In SAD, each block from the right stereo image is equated with the block in the left stereo image sequentially by shifting the right block across the searching area of pixels in the left image. For the matching ease, the blocks should be on epipolar lines. Comparing parameters in the matching algorithm is intensity or color of the two blocks, one in the left image and another one is in the right image. At each shift, the sum of the comparing parameters of the two blocks is computed and saved. The stereo similarities between the pixels is computed with absolute differences of pixel intensities. The SAD of pixels in a block (or window) surrounding is calculated. The best match is the disparity corresponding to the smallest SAD value. The SAD between a block in a left image and the block after it displaced horizontally by d in the reference image, is formulated as

$$SAD = \sum_{\forall \mathbf{x}} |I_1(\mathbf{x}) - I_2(\mathbf{x} + \mathbf{d})| \qquad (3.14)$$

where $\mathbf{d} = [d_x, 0]^T$ and SAD function measures the disparity at every pixel. It aggregates the intensities of all neighboring pixels of $\mathbf{x}$ in the left I_1 and right image I_2. Then, the absolute difference between these two sums is computed. In right image, the best matching pixel at the same scan line is chosen for which the absolute difference is minimum. Then, the disparity is calculated which is equal to the actual horizontal pixel difference. The disparity is calculated for all pixels of the image which gives the disparity image. The depth information can finally be calculated imposing inverse on the obtained disparities.

3.6.4.2 Sum of Square Differences (SSD)

SSD is another commonly used matching algorithm. The SSD function essentially determines a quality value using least square comparison of corresponding pixel intensities in left and right stereo images. SSD produces excellent results in feature-rich regions whereas comparatively noisy results in homogeneous area. Overall, SSD is preferred over SAD as it provides results of higher quality than that of SAD method. Owing the disparity field $\mathbf{d} = [d_x, 0]^T$, SSD can be written as

$$SSD = \sum_{\forall \mathbf{x}} [I_1(\mathbf{x}) - I_2(\mathbf{x} + \mathbf{d})]^2 \qquad (3.15)$$

3.6.4.3 Normalized Cross-Correlation (NCC)

Unlike SAD and SSD, NCC is an exemplar statistical model to determine similarities for disparity estimation. The correlation between two signals is selected for feature detection. It is the normalization of cross-correlation (CC) in terms of mean and variance which makes it relatively insensitive to radiometric gain and bias to luminance scale and level. The foremost advantage of the NCC over CC is its non-sensitivity to the linear changes in the amplitude of signals. It is worth mentioning that NCC is impounded in the interval $[-1, 1]$. NCC is computationally expensive due to the normalization and increases exponentially with the size of underlying template, however, it provides lowest error rates and thus producing better results compare to SAD and SSD. NCC may be expressed mathematically as

$$NCC = \sum_{\forall \mathbf{x}} \left(\frac{(I_1(\mathbf{x}) - \bar{I}_1)}{\sqrt{\sum_{\forall \mathbf{x}}(I_1(\mathbf{x}) - \bar{I}_1)^2}} - \frac{(I_2(\mathbf{x} + \mathbf{d}) - \bar{I}_2)}{\sqrt{\sum_{\forall \mathbf{x}}(I_2(\mathbf{x} + \mathbf{d}) - \bar{I}_2)^2}} \right)^2 \quad (3.16)$$

where $\mathbf{d} = [d_x, 0]^T$ is the disparity field, $\bar{I}_1$ is the mean value of left image and $\bar{I}_2$ is the mean value of right image.

The disparity is estimated from both original and decrypted stereo image pairs followed by their quantitatively comparison. The quantitative comparison is done using two different quality metrics: (1) root mean square error (RMSE), and (2) percentage of bad matching pixels. The estimated disparities for Cone, art, teddy and book stereo images, in both the cases, are depicted in Figs. 3.11–3.14, respectively whereas the quantitative results, for all the experimental images, are given in Table 3.3. For qualitative results, the root mean square error (RMSE) and bad matching pixels (BMP) are considered. The similarity between disparities in Figs. 3.11–3.14 indicates that the proposed algorithm has not introduced any significant degradation in stereo images and hence in disparity estimation. This fact is also justified by Table 3.3 where all quantitative values are close to each other. Therefore, the proposed algorithm is highly suitable for the stereo images with trifling effect on the disparity estimation.

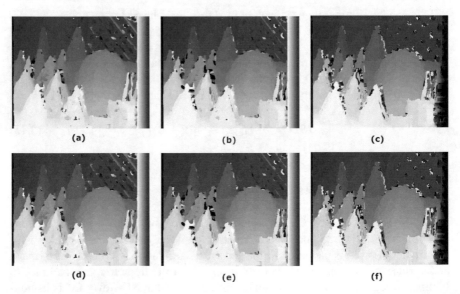

Fig. 3.11 Disparity estimated using the (**a–c**) original (**d–f**) decrypted cones stereo images by (**a, d**) SAD (**b, e**) SSD (**c, f**) NCC algorithms

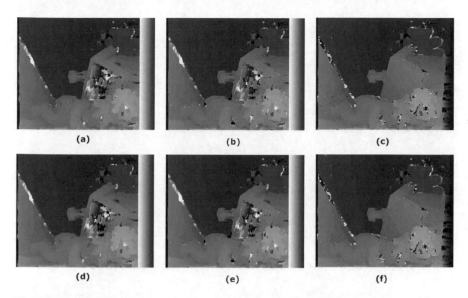

Fig. 3.12 Disparity estimated using the (**a–c**) original (**d–f**) decrypted teddy stereo images by (**a, d**) SAD (**b, e**) SSD (**c, f**) NCC algorithms

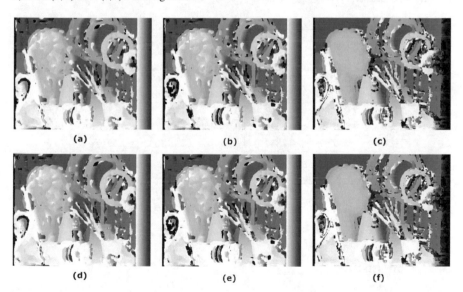

Fig. 3.13 Disparity estimated using the (**a–c**) original (**d–f**) decrypted art stereo images by (**a, d**) SAD (**b, e**) SSD (**c, f**) NCC algorithms

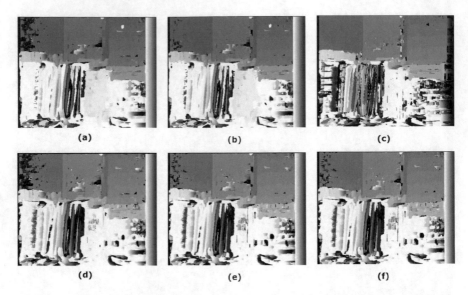

(a)   (b)   (c)

(d)   (e)   (f)

Fig. 3.14 Disparity estimated using the (**a–c**) original (**d–f**) decrypted book stereo images by (**a, d**) SAD (**b, e**) SSD (**c, f**) NCC algorithms

Table 3.3 Quantitative evaluation for the effect on disparity estimation of proposed algorithm

Images		RMSE			BMP (%)		
		SAD	SSD	NCC	SAD	SSD	NCC
Cones	O	0.1752	0.1911	0.1942	8.7369	9.5876	9.7850
	D	0.1763	0.1919	0.1947	8.7265	9.5896	9.7903
Teddy	O	0.2009	0.2043	0.2100	14.5650	14.6601	14.5516
	D	0.2015	0.2025	0.2144	14.4223	14.6675	14.5560
Art	O	0.2687	0.2844	0.2997	21.1864	22.1658	23.6431
	D	0.2705	0.2851	0.2984	21.1929	22.1669	23.6395
Books	O	0.2471	0.2530	0.2482	21.1431	21.3964	21.2102
	D	0.2492	0.2551	0.2528	21.1542	21.4036	21.2083

O Disparity estimation with original stereo pairs
D Disparity estimation with decrypted stereo pairs

3.7 Conclusions

In this chapter, a novel application of encryption is proposed to secure Stereo Images. The proposed technique is realized on non-linear chaotic map, step-space filling curve and singular value decomposition. The core idea is to first scramble the pixels using step-space filling curve and the diffusion is then done by chaotic map and singular value decomposition. It is confirmed from the extensive experiments on different stereo images that the proposed technique is inordinately efficient and only the right combination of underlying keys reveal the stereo images. The exhaustive security analysis finally demonstrate that the proposed scheme is highly suitable for stereo images and not only attaining high quality encryption results, but also secure enough to resist against common attacks.

References

1. S. Lian, MultiMedia Content Encryption: Techniques and Applications, CRC Press, Boca Raton, FL, 2008.
2. S.S. Maniccam and N.G. Bourbakis, Image and video encryption using SCAN patterns, Pattern Recognition, 37(4), 2004, 725–737.
3. H. Gao, Y. Zhang, S. Liang and D. Li, A new chaotic algorithm for image encryption, Chaos, Solitons & Fractals, 29(2), 2006, 393–399.
4. T.G. Gao and Z.Q. Chen, Image encryption based on a new total shuffling algorithm, Chaos, Solitons & Fractals, 38(1), 2008, 213–220.
5. X. Tong and M. Cui, Image encryption scheme based on 3D baker with dynamical compound chaotic sequence cipher generator, Signal Processing, 89(4), 2009, 480–491.
6. Y. Wang, K.W. Wong, X.F. Liao and G.R. Chen, A new chaos-based fast image encryption algorithm, Applied Soft Computing, 11(1), 2011, 514–522.
7. X. Li, J. Knipe and H. Cheng, Image compression and encryption using tree structures, Pattern Recognition Letters, 18(11–13), 1997, 1253–1259.
8. Y. Mao, G. Chen and S. Lian, A novel fast image encryption scheme based on 3D chaotic baker maps, International Journal of Bifurcation and chaos, 14(10), 2004, 3613–3624.
9. M.G. Perkins, Data compression of stereopairs, IEEE Transactions on Communications, 40, 1992, pp. 684–696.
10. H. Aydinoglu and M. H. Hayes, Stereo image coding: A projection approach, IEEE Transactions on Image Processing, 7(4), 1998, 507–516
11. T. Frajka, and K. Zeger, Residual Image Coding for Stereo Image Compression, Optical Engineering, 42(1), 2003, 182–189.
12. M. Kaaniche, A. Benazza-Benyahia, B. Pesquet-Popescu and J.C. Pesquet, Vector Lifting Schemes for Stereo Image Coding, IEEE Transactions on Image Processing, 18(11), 2009, 2463–2475.
13. Gaurav Bhatnagar, Sanjeev Kumar, R. Balasubramanian and N. Sukavanam, Stereo image coding via digital watermarking, Journal of Electronic Imaging, 18(3), 2009, 0330121–9.
14. L.F.R. Lucas, N.M.M. Rodrigues, E.A.B. da Silva and S.M.M. de Faria, Stereo image coding using dynamic template-matching prediction, In proceeding of International Conference on Computer as a Tool (EUROCON), Lisbon, 2011, 1–4.
15. S. Kumar, G. Bhatnagar, B. raman and N. Sukavanam, Security of Stereo Images During Communication and Transmission, Advanced Science Letters, 6, 2012, 173–179.
16. F. A El-Samie, H.H. Ahmed, I.F. Elashry, M.H. Shahieen, O.S. Faragallah, E.M. El-Rabaie, S.A. Alshebeili, Image Encryption: A Communication Perspective, CRC Press, 2014.
17. D. Stinson, Cryptography: Theory and Practice, 2nd edition, Chapman & Hall/CRC Press, Boca Raton, FL, 2002.
18. Y. Kim, J. Song, I. Moon and Y. Lee, Interference-based multiple-image encryption using binary phase masks, Optics and Lasers in Engineering, 7, 2018, 81–287.
19. Yong Wang, Yi Zhao, Qing Zhou and Zehui Lin, Image encryption using partitioned cellular automata, Neurocomputing, 275, 2018, 1318–1332.
20. Y. Xiong, C. Quan and C.J. Tay, Multiple image encryption scheme based on pixel exchange operation and vector decomposition, Optics and Lasers in Engineering, 101, 2018, 113–121.
21. X. Li, C. Li and I. Lee, Chaotic image encryption using pseudo-random masks and pixel mapping, Signal Processing, 125, 2016, 48–63.

22. W. Yap, R.C.-W. Phan, B. Goi, W. Yau and S. Heng, On the effective subkey space of some image encryption algorithms using external key, Journal of Visual Communication and Image Representation, 40, 2016, 51–57.
23. M. García-Martínez, L.J. Ontañón-García, E. Campos-Cantón and S. Čelikovský, Hyper-chaotic encryption based on multi-scroll piecewise linear systems, Applied Mathematics and Computation, 270, 2015, 413–424.
24. D. Liu, W. Zhang, H. Yu and Z. Zhu, An image encryption scheme using self-adaptive selective permutation and inter-intra-block feedback diffusion, Signal Processing, 151, 2018, 130–143.
25. M.K. Abdmouleh, A. Khalfallah and M.S. Bouhlel, A Novel Selective Encryption Scheme for Medical Images Transmission based-on JPEG Compression Algorithm, Procedia Computer Science, 112, 2017, 369–376.
26. M. Hamdi, R. Rhouma and S. Belghith, A selective compression-encryption of images based on SPIHT coding and Chirikov Standard Map, Signal Processing, 131, 2017, 514–526.
27. T. Xiang, J. Hu and J. Sun, Outsourcing chaotic selective image encryption to the cloud with steganography, Digital Signal Processing, 43, 2015, 28–37.
28. T.Xiang, J. Qu and D. Xiao, Joint SPIHT compression and selective encryption, Applied Soft Computing, 21, 2014, 159–170.
29. G. Bhatnagar and Q.M. Jonathan Wu, Selective image encryption based on pixels of interest and singular value decomposition, Digital Signal Processing, 22(4), 2012, 648–663.
30. W. Zeng and S. Lei, Efficient frequency domain selective scrambling of digital video, IEEE Transactions on Multimedia 5(1), 2003, 118–129.
31. C. Wu, and C.C. Jay Kuo, Efficient multimedia encryption via entropy codec design, In Proceeding of SPIE International Symposium on Electronic Imaging, San Jose, CA, 4314, 2001, 128–138.
32. Y. Zhang, B. Xu and N. Zhou, A novel image compression–encryption hybrid algorithm based on the analysis sparse representation, Optics Communications, 392, 2017, 223–233.
33. G. Hu, D. Xiao, Y. Wang and T. Xiang, An image coding scheme using parallel compressive sensing for simultaneous compression-encryption applications, Journal of Visual Communication and Image Representation, 44, 2017, 116–127.
34. X. Chai, Z. Gan, Y. Chen and Y. Zhang, A visually secure image encryption scheme based on compressive sensing, Signal Processing, 134, 2017, 35–51.
35. R. Fay, Introducing the counter mode of operation to Compressed Sensing based encryption, Information Processing Letters, 116(4), 2016, 279–283.
36. C. Wang, J. Ni and Q. Huang, A new encryption-then-compression algorithm using the rate–distortion optimization, Signal Processing: Image Communication, 39, 2015, 141–150.
37. Z. Hua, F. Jin, B. Xu and H. Huang, 2D Logistic-Sine-coupling map for image encryption, Signal Processing, 149, 2018, 48–161.
38. W. Cao, Y. Zhou, C.L.P. Chen and L. Xia, Medical image encryption using edge maps, Signal Processing, 132, 2017, 96–109.
39. C. Li, Cracking a hierarchical chaotic image encryption algorithm based on permutation, Signal Processing, 118, 2016, 203–210.
40. X. Wang, Q. Wang and Y. Zhang, A fast image algorithm based on rows and columns switch, Nonlinear Dynamics, 79(2), 2015, 1141–1149.
41. M. Murillo-Escobar, C. Cruz-Hernndez, F. Abundiz-Prez, R. Lpez-Gutirrez and O.A.D. Campo, A RGB image encryption algorithm based on total plain image characteristics and chaos, Signal Processing, 109, 2015, 119–131.
42. G. Ye and J. Zhou, A block chaotic image encryption scheme based on self-adaptive modelling, Applied Soft Computing, 22, 2014, 351–357.
43. Y. Zhou, K. Panetta, S. Agaian and C.L.P. Chen, Image encryption using P-Fibonacci transform and decomposition, Optics Communication, 285(5), 2012, 594–608.
44. J. Hu and F. Han, A pixel-based scrambling scheme for digital medical images protection, Journal of Network and Computer Applications, 32(4), 2009, 788–794.
45. C. Li, H. Li, F. Li, D. Wei, X. Yang and J. Zhang, Multiple-image encryption by using robust chaotic map in wavelet transform domain, Optik, 71, 2018, 277–286.

46. X. Li, X. Meng, Y. Wang, X. Yang, Y. Yin, X. Peng, W. He, G. Dong and H. Chen, Secret shared multiple-image encryption based on row scanning compressive ghost imaging and phase retrieval in the Fresnel domain, Optics and Lasers in Engineering, 96, 2017, 7–16.
47. L. Yuan, Q. Ran and T. Zhao, Image authentication based on double-image encryption and partial phase decryption in nonseparable fractional Fourier domain, Optics & Laser Technology, 88, 2017, 111–120.
48. J.B. Lima, E.S. da Silva and R.M. Campello de Souza, Cosine transforms over fields of characteristic: Fast computation and application to image encryption, Signal Processing: Image Communication, 54, 2017, 130–139.
49. J.B. Lima, F. Madeiro and F.J.R. Sales, Encryption of medical images based on the cosine number transform, Signal Processing: Image Communication, 35, 2015, 1–8.
50. H. Li and Y. Wang, Double-image encryption based on discrete fractional random transform and chaotic maps, Optics and Lasers in Engineering, 49(7), 2011, 753–757.
51. B. Furht and D. Socek, Multimedia Security: Encryption Techniques, IEC Comprehensive Report on Information Security, International Engineering Consortium, Chicago, IL, 2003.
52. J. Kumar and S. Nirmala, A Novel and Efficient Perceptual Image Encryption Based on Knight Moves and Genetic Operations. In: Saeed K., Chaki N., Pati B., Bakshi S., Mohapatra D. (eds) Progress in Advanced Computing and Intelligent Engineering. Advances in Intelligent Systems and Computing, vol 563. Springer, Singapore.
53. P. Jagadeesh, P. Nagabhushan and R.P. Kumar, A Novel Perceptual Image Encryption Scheme Using Geometric Objects Based Kernel, International Journal of Computer Science and Information Technology, 5, 2013, 165–173.
54. B. Yang, C. Busch and X. Niu, Perceptual image encryption via reversible histogram spreading, In Proceedings of International Symposium on Image and Signal Processing and Analysis, Salzburg, 2009, 471–476.
55. M.T.I. Ziad, A. Alanwar, M. Alzantot and M. Srivastava, CryptoImg: Privacy preserving processing over encrypted images, In Proceedings of IEEE Conference on Communications and Network Security (CNS), Philadelphia, PA, 2016, 70–575.
56. M. Li, X. Yi and H. Ma, A scalable encryption scheme for CCSDS image data compression standard, In Proceedings of IEEE International Conference on Information Theory and Information Security, Beijing, 2010, 646–649.
57. O. Watanabe, A. Nakazaki and H. Kiya, A scalable encryption method allowing backward compatibility with JPEG2000 images, In Proceedings of IEEE International Symposium on Circuits and Systems, Kobe, 2005, 6324–6327.
58. S.J. Wee and J.G. Apostolopoulos, Secure scalable video streaming for wireless networks, In Proceedings of the IEEE International Conference on Acoustics, Speech, and Signal Processing, Salt Lake City, UT, 4, 2001, 2049–2052.
59. T. Sang, R. Wang and Y. Yan, Generating binary Bernoulli sequences based on a class of even-symmetric chaotic maps, IEEE Transactions on Communications, 49(4), 2001, 620–623.
60. H. Sagan, Space-filling curves, Springer, New York, 1994.
61. D.N. Bhat and S.K. Nayar, Ordinal Measures for Image Correspondence, IEEE Transactions on Pattern Analysis and Machine Intelligence, 20, 1998, 415–423.

Chapter 4
Example Based Privacy-Preserving Video Color Grading

Amitesh Singh Rajput and Balasubramanian Raman

4.1 Introduction

The swift technological growth of advanced camera sensors has made high availability of digital multimedia nowadays. In addition, due to growing Internet facilities, it has become very easy to copy and distribute them. However, there is always a threat of security when moving to third party driven infrastructures like cloud [29]. To avoid this vulnerability, one can encrypt his/her multimedia data before transmission. During the past two decades, various schemes have been proposed in the literature for image/video encryption. The multimedia data is of very large size as compared to simple text data, and forms a special case of encryption. Existing schemes supporting multimedia encryption use diverse techniques such as permutation, substitution and diffusion for obfuscation of the multimedia content (e.g. structure, histogram etc.). An example is shown in Fig. 4.1 where a plain secret image is encrypted using image encryption algorithm and a secret key k, resulting an encrypted image. On the other hand, the secret image is recovered back using the same secret key k while decryption. The scenario can be extended to multiple keys using a public key cryptosystem.

Moreover, other techniques like steganography, watermarking, fingerprinting etc. have been developed to protect valuable multimedia information from unauthorized access and tampering. The existing multimedia encryption schemes support secure storage. However, think of a scenario where multimedia data needs to be processed while remaining in encrypted form. This can be considered as a step ahead of traditional multimedia encryption and is actively evolving today, discussed in the next subsection.

A. S. Rajput (✉) · B. Raman
Department of Computer Science and Engineering, Indian Institute of Technology Roorkee, Roorkee, India
e-mail: arajput@cs.iitr.ac.in; balarfma@iitr.ac.in

© Springer Nature Switzerland AG 2019
A. K. Singh, A. Mohan (eds.), *Handbook of Multimedia Information Security: Techniques and Applications*, https://doi.org/10.1007/978-3-030-15887-3_4

Plain secret image   **Secret key (k)**   **Encrypted image**   **Secret key (k)**   **Decrypted image**

Fig. 4.1 Generic multimedia encryption and decryption system

4.1.1   Importance of Privacy-Preserving Multimedia Processing

The high availability of smart digital cameras, coupled with cloud computing has changed the way multimedia was actually captured and processed. Previously, multimedia was captured through a large, heavy weight camera consisting of additional flash and lenses, adjusted by the user for capturing a particular scene. Once captured, the multimedia content was then developed which is a time consuming task. Nowadays, this scenario is completely changed as camera hardware has become very small and advanced facilities such as face detection, auto-focus, depth effects etc. are introduced. The scenario has been further upgraded to another step with the involvement of cloud computing, using which the user can process his/her captured multimedia files remotely. This saves the storage as well as hardware/software overheads required to process multimedia locally. In addition, various facilities, which are not available with user device can be accessed over the cloud in a cost effective manner. Examples of such services include Google Photos, Cloudinary, Uploadcare etc. These services have been deployed pleasantly enabling remote users to process their large multimedia files without requiring any software locally. However, cloud servers are assumed untrusting and users are always concerned regarding privacy of their personal data when moving to these third party driven infrastructures. To avoid this, one can encrypt his/her multimedia files before transmission to the cloud, although intermediate decryption is required for processing over the cloud server. This is due to the fact that the existing multimedia encryption schemes use integration of different techniques including permutation, substitution etc. leveraging distortion of multimedia content while processing. As a result, the decryption completely fails.

Hence, state-of-the-art requirements leverage the need of homomorphic encryption in such a way that the intended task of processing user files can be performed without requiring any intermediate decryption. Homomorphic encryption allows one to perform specific computations over encrypted data in a manner such that equivalent effects, as of processing in the plain domain can be achieved when the processed data is decrypted. Using homomorphic encryption, one can encrypt his/her multimedia files and transmit them to the cloud server for further processing. An illustration is depicted in Fig. 4.2 where original secret image is encrypted before transmission to the cloud server. The encrypted image is then processed (e.g. color enhancement) at cloud server and returned back. Once received, the user can decrypt the image where processing effects can clearly observed.

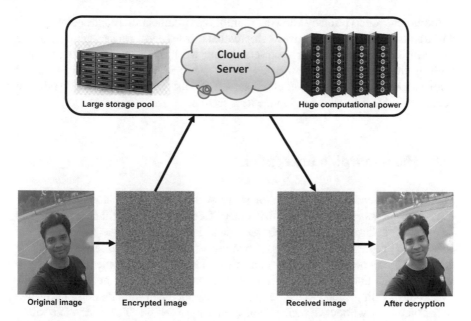

Fig. 4.2 Privacy-preserving cloud based image processing

4.1.2 Secure Multi-Party Computation

As our work is based on secure multi-party computation, we describe it solely here. Introduced in the early eighties by Yao [51], Secure Multi-Party Computation (SMC) involves distributing the computation ζ among η number of participants in a manner such that none of the participant can get any information about the data. Let us consider the simplest form of secure two-party computation, where two parties Alice ($\mathbb{A}$) and Bob ($\mathbb{B}$), wish to jointly process a function $f(\lambda_\mathbb{A}, \lambda_\mathbb{B})$ on their corresponding data $\lambda_\mathbb{A}$ and $\lambda_\mathbb{B}$. The function f can be made public however, the data needs to be protected. Hence, f needs to process the intended task in a manner such that, apart from output, either party cannot learn any useful information about other's data i.e. $\mathbb{A}$ should not learn about $\lambda_\mathbb{B}$ and similarly $\mathbb{B}$ with $\lambda_\mathbb{A}$. The scenario can naturally be extended to multi-parties. Various schemes have been proposed to support SMC including garbled circuits and oblivious transfer. Their main objective is to provide robust privacy protection by allowing secret data to be shared among the parties involved.

While existing protocols enable processing to be carried out without revealing any information among the participants, expensive computational overheads are involved due to the use of strong cryptographic algorithms. In addition, implementation challenges may occur due to protocol-specific overhead costs. Due to this, research communities are using SMC with homomorphic encryption jointly. The usual scenario consists of outsourcing computations to a third party server using homomorphic encryption by allowing multiple communication rounds between user and untrusted servers. This saves computational overheads at user end by shifting the computations to third party servers. In our work, we propose to encrypt user multimedia files before transmission to the cloud server such that no personal information can be obtained at cloud server. We use homomorphic encryption to accomplish this task, discussed in the next section.

4.2 Homomorphic Encryption

Homomorphic encryption exhibits majority of the features of classical cryptography, however can be considered as a step ahead by allowing the processing to be performed directly on the encrypted data. For instance, let $\hat{a} \leftarrow E_k[a]$ and $\hat{b} \leftarrow E_k[b]$ represent encryptions of two secret values a and b, respectively. The additive homomorphism property consists of adding two encrypted values $\hat{a} \oplus \hat{b}$ with assurance that the decrypted result $D_k(\hat{a} \oplus \hat{b})$ will match the addition of the two corresponding secret values $a + b$. Hence, one can compute addition of two secret numbers without knowing their actual information. The encrypted values $\hat{a}$ and $\hat{b}$ cannot reveal any information about the secret values (a, b) and so the processing $\oplus$ is. Unlike processing for basic addition, the homomorphic operation $\oplus$ consists of certain complex computations and depends on the type of cryptosystem used. Similar to addition, multiplicative operations can also be performed over $\hat{a}$ and $\hat{b}$ and the schemes supporting both addition as well as multiplication falls in the category of *Fully Homomorphic Encryption* (FHE). On the contrary, the schemes comprising between FHE and no homomorphism are known as *Partially Homomorphic Encryption* (PHE).

4.2.1 Classification of Homomorphic Cryptosystems

Rivest et al. [40] first proposed the concept of FHE supporting unlimited number of additions and multiplications over the encrypted data and remained elusive for the next three decades. During 1999, Boneh et al. [3] proposed another FHE scheme by allowing unlimited homomorphic additions. However, the number of multiplications is restricted to only one. Hence, after another decade, Gentry [12] proposed a strongly secure FHE supporting unlimited addition and multiplication operations. Their scheme was very complex to be deployed for practical applications and still required efficient enhancements, although considered as one of the pioneering work in this field. After Gentry's scheme, a number of FHE schemes have been proposed including [4, 8, 13–15, 18, 19, 44, 48]. The research groups tried their best to reduce computational complexity of FHE, however efficient implementation for multimedia data is still missing and remains an open problem.

Instead of FHE, various schemes supporting PHE have also been emerged in the literature. PHE can be considered as an intermediary solution between FHE and non-homomorphic encryption. A variety of schemes have been proposed including the pioneering schemes of RSA proposed by Rivest et al. [40] and Elgamal [9] supporting multiplicative homomorphism; Goldwasser et al. [16] for homomorphic addition modulo 2; Shamir's secret sharing [41] for additive and multiplicative homomorphism; Paillier cryptosystem [32] for homomorphic addition and multiplication, and Boneh et al. [2] for homomorphic addition/subtraction. In addition to FHE and PHE, another interesting part lies in *Somewhat Homomorphic Encryption* (SHE). This part supports additive and multiplicative homomorphism, however is restricted to the number of operations depending on the noise-level of the ciphertext. After performing a few operations, if the ciphertext noise-level grows sufficiently high such that the resulting ciphertext can cause infeasible decryption, the computations are stopped. Hence, the cryptographic parameters need to be selected very precisely such that the desired operations can be performed with respect to the threshold noise-level.

In comparison to text data, multimedia data is of very large size and implementation of FHE becomes infeasible. Hence, the existing multimedia applications use PHE leveraging a significant portion of processing to be performed over the encrypted data. This reduces computational complexity while still achieving the security. After the significant advancement of cloud computing, research work in this area is gradually increasing and some preliminary schemes have been proposed to process multimedia data while remaining in encrypted form. This emerging field of processing the secret while remaining in encrypted form is known as *Encrypted Domain* (ED) processing or *Privacy-Preserving* processing.

4.3 Review of Recent Advancements in the ED

We review the recent advancements supporting privacy-preserving processing in this section. For convenience in understanding, the description is categorized into two subsections; (1) privacy-preserving data processing and, (2) privacy-preserving multimedia processing, and a brief summary is depicted in Table 4.1.

4.3.1 Privacy-Preserving Data Processing

Privacy-preserving data processing consists of performing computations on the encrypted data using SMC and FHE jointly. Nowadays, privacy-preserving cloud based data processing is emerging as a new area, and techniques to securely store and process user data are evolving gradually. Based on the nature of the job, each scheme is different and requires corresponding pre-processing and post-processing mechanisms.

Table 4.1 Summary of existing privacy-preserving schemes with respective cryptosystems

Work	Area of specialization	Cryptosystem used
[7]	Large scale of linear equation	Sparse matrix has been used to outsource large scale of linear equations securely
[34]	Clinical decision support system	Paillier cryptosystem
[42]	Data deduplication over the cloud	POB based number system and CRT
[22]	k-means clustering	Yao' circuit evaluation protocol with random shares
[26, 27]	Image enhancement	Shamir's secret sharing scheme in both the works
[20]	Privacy-preserving SIFT	Paillier cryptosystem
[17]	Moving object detection	Color flipping and matrix permutation
[33]	Facial expression recognition	Paillier cryptosystem
[29, 30]	Image scaling and cropping	Shamir's secret sharing scheme, proxy encryption based Paillier cryptosystem
[52]	E-healthcare system using data aggregation	The authors proposed a fully-homomorphic scheme to support data aggregation in the ED
[49, 50]	Speech noise reduction using comb filter	Shamir's secret sharing scheme
[28]	SVM and Fuzzy C-means clustering for classification of user data	Pixel-level extraction followed by SVM classifier has been used to segment the image and hide identity
[31]	Pre-classification volume ray casting	Shamir's secret sharing scheme
[10]	Face recognition	Paillier cryptosystem along with Damgard, Geiser and Kroigoard cryptosystem (DGK)
[45]	Multimedia Similarity Search	Paillier cryptosystem
[6]	Crowd monitoring	The authors used special purpose cameras that output low-level features. Thus avoiding visual record of the people
[1]	Fingerprint recognition	Paillier cryptosystem, ElGamal cryptosystem
[23]	Smart room tracking	Image down sampling has been used to preserve the privacy
[21]	Non-local denoising	Paillier cryptosystem, privacy-preserving transform
[47]	Content Based Image Retrieval	Distance recoverable encryption supporting secure k-NN, Tunable privacy has been implemented using hash-based piece-wise inverted indexing
[43]	Tamper detection and localization	POB based number system

Rahulamathavan et al. [34] proposed a clinical decision support system using Gaussian kernel-based classification in the ED. The authors used Paillier cryptosystem [32] enabling the clinical to generate and distribute public key to the cloud server while keeping the secret key safe. A privacy-preserving data deduplication scheme was presented by Singh et al. [42]. Due to huge data overheads at cloud servers, the authors proposed a novel approach for eliminating duplicate files without knowing its contents. Permutation Ordered Binary (POB) number system along with Chinese Remainder Theorem (CRT) were used as the cryptographic primitive for data security. Chan et al. [6] proposed a crowd monitoring scheme by implementing special-purpose cameras that do not produce visual record of the people. The authors addressed pedestrian counting problem and accounted for multiple pedestrian flows. A privacy-preserving approach for k-means clustering using a secure scalar product protocol was proposed by Jagannathan et al. [22]. Addressing higher computational and storage overheads of large data repositories, the authors efficiently utilized Yao's circuit evaluation protocol [51] in combination with random shares. Furthermore, other generic data mining algorithms in the ED were addressed in [25] and [38]. Yakubu et al. [50] proposed a speech noise reduction scheme by utilizing comb filter in the ED. The authors used Shamir's secret sharing to process encrypted data which they further explored in [49].

A cloud assisted e-healthcare system was proposed by Zhou et al. [52]. Specific to the problem addressed, the authors devised a privacy-preserving fully homomorphic data aggregation scheme to support simultaneous addition and multiplication operations. Moving ahead, Barni et al. [1] proposed a novel approach for privacy-preserving fingerprint recognition by utilizing the notion of additive homomorphic encryption. The authors utilized Paillier cryptosystem with a known variant of ElGamal encryption scheme [9] to support processing in the ED. Recently, Marwan et al. [28] attempted to process user data while maintaining privacy using machine learning techniques in the ED. The authors utilized Support Vector Machine (SVM) and Fuzzy C-means Clustering (FCM) to classify user data more efficiently. Chen et al. [7] proposed a privacy-preserving scheme to process large-scale system of linear equations over the cloud. The authors utilized sparse matrix with only one round of communication with the third party server. A privacy-preserving smart room tracking approach was proposed by Jia el at. [23]. The ceiling-mounted, downward-pointed time-of-flight sensors were used to estimate human occupancy and pose in real time.

4.3.2   Privacy-Preserving Multimedia Processing

Digital image forms the basic element of multimedia. It is a two-dimensional array with pixel intensity values in the range [0,255], and requires high computational as well as storage cost (as compared to the text data) for processing. In addition, correlation between adjacent pixels in a digital image is usually high, and if not considered properly during encryption, the image structure may be revealed. Similarly, a video sequence consists of a set of image frames and suffers from the same problem. Hence, special attention needs to be delineated when dealing with digital multimedia.

The emerging trend towards cloud computing coupled with smart devices has attracted the research communities to develop interesting privacy-preserving multimedia processing solutions. As a result, new techniques are emerging gradually. Wang et al. [45] proposed a novel approach for large scale similarity search over encrypted feature rich multimedia data. The authors considered search criteria as high dimensional feature vector and proposed a similarity search index supporting efficient file and index updates. Erkin et al. [10] proposed a privacy-preserving face recognition scheme based on SMC over the untrusted cloud server. Specifically designed for biometric data, the authors proposed a technique to hide biometric data along with authentication results from cloud server. A privacy-preserving spatial domain image enhancement scheme was proposed by Lathey et al. [26]. Shamir's secret sharing scheme was used to generate multiple shares. Different operations including low-pass filtering, anti-aliasing and haze removal have been performed and equivalent effects were observed in the ED as of processing in the Plain Domain (PD).

Mohanty et al. [29] proposed an ED image scaling and cropping scheme, where a space efficient block-level scheme was proposed to support multi-user image scaling and cropping operations over the cloud. Essence of their scheme lies in encrypting a block of pixels instead of per pixel encryption, which saves the space overheads caused by the basic Paillier cryptosystem. Addressing the importance of SIFT algorithm, Hsu et al. [20] proposed a homomorphic encryption based secure SIFT scheme. Their scheme consisted of performing homomorphic comparisons such that local extrema can be securely detected for SIFT feature point extraction. The authors used Paillier cryptosystem as the platform for designing their method. A novel scheme for facial expression recognition in the ED was proposed by Rahulamathavan et al. [33]. The authors utilized a PCA based method to recognize the identity of human subjects in the ED. Content Based Image Retrieval (CBIR) has been one of the important tasks used to extract images from a large database. Different aspects of CBIR with copy-deterrence and watermarking have been addressed effectively by Xia et al. [47], whereas Weng et al. [46] introduced the concept of tunable privacy. Ferreira et al. [11] proposed to separate color information from texture information enabling the utilization of different encryption techniques individually. A novel approach for image tampering detection and localization in the ED was proposed by Singh et al. [43]. The authors performed image encryption using POB number system, and further authenticated at pixel level.

4.3.2.1 Privacy-Preserving Color Transfer Between Images

Color transfer consists of modifying colors of a test image by considering colors of another image as the reference. The image whose colors need to be transformed is known as target image, whereas the image whose colors are considered as ideal falls in the category of reference image. Initial efforts for color transfer include linear color transformation mappings proposed by Reinhard et al. [39] in the PD.

Their method consisted of transforming image colors using mean and standard deviation based statistical transformations. Based on this, three main research works have been proposed for processing image colors in a privacy-preserving manner in [35–37]. The schemes effectively accomplished the task of color transfer in the ED. However, they suffered from the drawback of computational and storage overhead, and becomes non-trivial in case of videos. The initial two schemes used Shamir's secret sharing and its variant (Ramp secret sharing) for generation of obfuscated image shares. The shares do not reveal any information about the secret image. However, there is always a requirement of additional n cloud servers, which increases the storage and computational cost. In addition, there is a risk of collusion attack when using Shamir's secret sharing.

Moving ahead, the last attempt consisted of securing color transfer operations over a single cloud server. Image encryption is accomplished by using Paillier cryptosystem, due to which only one encrypted image is obtained. Hence, the requirement of multiple cloud datacenters (n) is removed and so the collusion attack. Furthermore, quality of the color transfer is improved as compared to the previous schemes. However, high computations are required for image encryption and decryption operations. The number of encryptions per second for the basic Paillier cryptosystem with minimal secret key k of size 1024 bits is 1898 [24]. According to [29], the 24 bit color is represented by $4k$ bits when using the naive approach. Hence, the total time increases to $(m \times n \times 4096)/1898$ which is very high for video based applications. For example, let the size of a color image with 24 bits per pixel (8 bit per RGB—Red, Green and Blue) is 128×128, hence the total time requirement to encrypt the entire image using the naive approach would result to 589 min (approximately 10 h). In addition, the storage cost is increased to 170 times during encryption. For video sequences, the same terminology can be applied on a per frame basis, however it may cause high computational as well as storage overheads, as video sequences consists of a large number of image frames. Addressing this problem, we propose an efficient video color grading approach in this chapter by reducing the storage and computational overheads, discussed in detail in the next section.

4.4   Proposed Approach

Video color grading is the process of adjusting color palette of the video sequence for achieving a certain visual look. We automate this process by transforming colors of the video frames as per the colors of a particular scene/mood (reference). For example, suppose a user captures a video sequence using his/her mobile phone during a cloudy weather. The lightning exposure during cloudy weather is dull as compared to the sunny day, and may affect the captured video sequence. Figure 4.3a shows the original video frames captured during a cloudy weather. Now, if we consider an image captured during a sunny day as the reference (depicted in Fig. 4.3b) and transfer its colors to the video sequence, the results are adorably improved. The

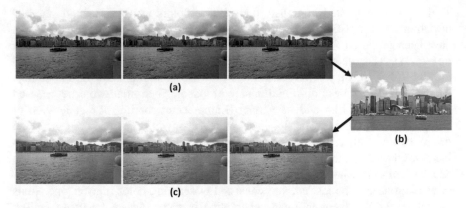

Fig. 4.3 An illustration of example based video color grading. (**a**) Original video frames. (**b**) Reference image. (**c**) Resulting video frames

resulting video frames are shown in Fig. 4.3c and effective colors can be clearly observed. Hence, a user can transform visual appearance of the captured video sequence using video color grading. However, a video sequence consists of a large number of frames and adjusting colors of each frame manually is a painstakingly task. In addition, the hand-held devices consist of low computational and storage capabilities as compared to a desktop PC, workstation etc. and processing video sequences locally further complicates the problem. Hence, we propose to process them over cloud servers in a secure manner. The user can capture video sequences from his device, encrypt them and send to the cloud server for processing/storage. This removes the burden of computational and storage overheads locally, while still assuring privacy.

4.4.1 Overview of the Proposed Approach

A block-wise representation of the proposed approach is shown in Fig. 4.4. The trust server is a user accessible physical device such as mobile phone, laptop, tablet etc. using which the user can encrypt the captured video sequence and send to the cloud server for secure storage/processing. We assume the cloud server to be based on "honest-but-curious" adversary model, wherein the cloud server will perform all the assigned tasks, however is curiously inquisitive regarding user data. Initially, the user needs to provide captured video sequence followed by a reference image. The video sequence is then pre-processed to identify color transformation parameters, followed by encryption and transmission to the cloud server. The cloud server then performs the task of video color grading over the encrypted video sequence during storage.

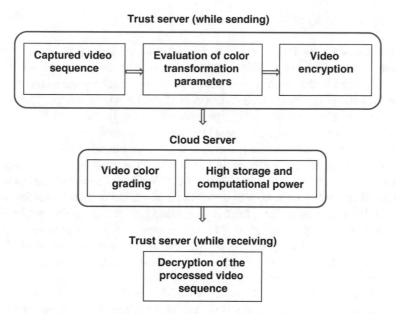

Fig. 4.4 Block-wise representation of the proposed approach

The cloud server needs to be prepared for a multi-user environment by possessing services like load balancing, scalability and service latency, enabling user requests to be fulfilled in a timely manner. Once processed, the encrypted video sequence is transmitted back to the trust server for decryption.

4.4.2 Methodology

The recent scheme proposed in [37] consisted of superior color transfer effects. However one cannot implement the method directly over video sequences due to high computational and storage overheads. Let $V=\{f_1, f_2, \ldots f_n\}$ represents the video sequence with n number of image frames (f). The scheme proposed in [37] used Paillier cryptosystem for image encryption. Due to this, more than 170 times storage is required for encrypted image. Considering this fact, if we apply the previous scheme over V with n image frames, the storage overhead drastically increases to $170 \times n$. In addition, the computational complexity also increases as the number of encryptions bits per second for the Paillier cryptosystem is 1898 [24], which will be very costly for encrypting a complete video sequence. Hence, we further enhance the previous framework for efficient compatibility with video sequences in this section. The proposed methodology consists of three phases, described in detail in the next subsections.

4.4.2.1 Reckoning at Trust Server

Evaluation of Color Transformation Parameters Initially, evaluate color transformation parameters of individual RGB channels of the video frames at trust server and send to the cloud server. The color transformation parameters consist of computing mean (μ) and standard deviation (δ) of the video frames. The original video sequence V consists of a large number of image frames $\{f_1, f_2, \ldots f_n\}$ and computing individual color transformation parameters $\mu_i = \{\mu_r, \mu_g, \mu_b\}$ and $\delta_i = \{\delta_r, \delta_g, \delta_b\}$, for each image frame f_i is a resource intensive task. For example, let n depicts the total number of image frames contained in a video sequence V, the time complexity for evaluation of color transformation parameters is dominated by O(nf). Hence, we propose to evaluate color transformation values for each alternate frame. Since neighboring video frames are highly correlated, the difference of corresponding pixel intensity values used for evaluation of μ and δ is very less. Based on this, two consecutive frames can be processed using a single set of $\mu = \{\mu_r, \mu_g, \mu_b\}$ and $\delta = \{\delta_r, \delta_g, \delta_b\}$. This reduces the computational complexity to half as compared to evaluating the color transformation parameters μ and δ for each frame i.e. O($nf/2$) <O(nf). Let $\mu = \{\mu_1, \mu_3, \mu_5, \ldots, \mu_n\}$ and $\delta = \{\delta_1, \delta_3, \delta_5, \ldots, \delta_n\}$ represent the final set consisting of alternate color transformation parameters, transmit them to the cloud server along with reference image R.

Video Encryption We use proxy encryption based Paillier cryptosystem proposed by Bresson et al. [5] for video encryption. As discussed in Sect. 4.3.2.1, the basic Paillier cryptosystem [32] is computationally expensive and increases size of the encrypted multimedia to a higher extent making a non-trivial situation for video encryption. Though, proxy encryption has proved to be less complex and saves the computational and storage cost. Proposed by Bresson et al. in the year 2003, this cryptosystem decomposed the original Paillier's encryption mechanism into two parts. As a result, the complexity and data expansion is reduced while still preserving homomorphic properties of the original cryptosystem. Let the public key of user U is represented as $(n, g, h = g^\nu)$, where $n = pq$ (p and q are two primes), $\nu \in [1, n^2/2]$ is a random integer and forms the secret key, and g is a generator of order $(p - 1)(q - 1)/2$. Hence, to encrypt a message m, one needs to select a random integer $\sigma_1 \in [1, n/4]$ and generate the ciphertext pair (e_1, e_2), as follows:

$$e_1 = g^{\sigma_1} \bmod n^2 \text{ and } e_2 = h^{\sigma_1}(1 + mn) \bmod n^2 \tag{4.1}$$

The ciphertexts are further re-encrypted using the same public key (n, g, h) but with a different random integer $\sigma_2 \in [1, n/4]$:

$$\hat{e}_1 = g^{\sigma_2} e_1 \bmod n^2 \text{ and } \hat{e}_2 = h^{\sigma_2} e_2 \bmod n^2 \tag{4.2}$$

The set $(\hat{e}_1, \hat{e}_2)$ forms the final ciphertext. On the contrary, decryption is accomplished by using private key ν:

$$m = \wedge(\hat{e}_2 / \hat{e}_1^{\nu}) \tag{4.3}$$

where $\wedge(a) = \frac{(a-1) \ mod \ n^2}{n}$, for all $a \ \epsilon \ a \leq n^2 \ |a = 1 \ mod \ n$. We implement the proxy encryption method to all video frames using the same public key $(n, g, h = g^v)$. It is worth to note that only $\hat{e}_2$ considers secret data m during encryption in Eq. (4.2) whereas $\hat{e}_1$ is independent of the m. Hence, we represent encrypted video frames $[\![V]\!] = \{[\![f_1]\!], [\![f_2]\!], \ldots, [\![f_n]\!]\}$ with respect to $\hat{e}_2$ throughout the proposed methodology. Upon encryption, transmit the video frames $[\![V]\!] = \{[\![f_1]\!], [\![f_2]\!], \ldots, [\![f_n]\!]\}$ along with public key (n, g, h) to the trust server.

4.4.2.2 Processing for Video Color Grading over the Cloud Server

After receiving the encrypted video sequence $[\![V]\!] = \{[\![f_1]\!], [\![f_2]\!], \ldots, [\![f_n]\!]\}$, reference image R along with $\mu = \{\mu_1, \mu_3, \mu_5, \ldots, \mu_n\}$ and $\delta = \{\delta_1, \delta_3, \delta_5, \ldots, \delta_n\}$, the cloud server performs the task of video color grading in the ED. The video sequence is processed over cloud server on a per frame basis. Here, we describe the methodology for a single image frame $[\![f_i]\!]$, however the same methodology needs to be performed over all the fames for effective result. The step-by-step flow of the methodology is described as follows:

1. Similar to computing color transformation parameters at trust server for test video frames, evaluate the mean μ_{ref} and standard deviation δ_{ref} of the reference image R here.
2. Now, evaluate the division of standard deviation scores of the reference image δ_{ref} and received $\delta = \{\delta_1, \delta_3, \delta_5, \ldots, \delta_n\}$ for each δ_i as follows:

$$\delta_i' = \lfloor \delta_{ref}/\delta_i \rceil \qquad (4.4)$$

   where $\lceil . \rfloor$ is a rounding function used to convert the resulting set into integer values $\delta' = \{\delta_1', \delta_3', \delta_5', \ldots, \delta_n'\}$. This is due to the fact that the selected cryptosystem works only in the integer domain.
3. Like previous step, round the received $\mu = \{\mu_1, \mu_3, \mu_5, \ldots, \mu_n\}$ along with μ_{ref} using rounding function $\lceil . \rfloor$, and encrypt using public key $(n, g, h = g^v)$, such that processing with respect to encrypted video frames $\{[\![f_1]\!], [\![f_2]\!], \ldots, [\![f_n]\!]\}$ can be successfully accomplished in the next steps. In addition, initialize $i{=}1$ and repeat the following steps until all encrypted video frames $\{[\![f_1]\!], [\![f_2]\!], \ldots, [\![f_n]\!]\}$ are processed.
4. Select two consecutive video frames $[\![f_i]\!]$ and $[\![f_{i+1}]\!]$ along with corresponding standard deviation δ_i and encrypted mean value $[\![\mu_i]\!]$ respectively.
5. Extract individual RGB color channels of encrypted video frames $[\![f_i]\!]$ and $[\![f_{i+1}]\!]$, and process for color transformation using $[\![\mu_i]\!]$ obtained from step 3. Let $\{[\![R_i]\!], [\![G_i]\!], [\![B_i]\!]\}$ and $\{[\![R_{i+1}]\!], [\![G_{i+1}]\!], [\![B_{i+1}]\!]\}$ represent the extracted RGB channels of $[\![f_i]\!]$ and $[\![f_{i+1}]\!]$ respectively, process them using $[\![\mu_i]\!]$ as follows:

$$[\![f_i']\!] = \left(\frac{[\![f_i]\!]}{[\![\mu_i]\!]} \right)^{\delta_i'} \quad \text{and} \quad [\![f_{i+1}']\!] = \left(\frac{[\![f_{i+1}]\!]}{[\![\mu_i]\!]} \right)^{\delta_i'}$$

where $[\![f_i']\!]$ and $[\![f_{i+1}']\!]$ represent the partially processed video frames.

Note: It is worth to note that $[\![\mu_i]\!]$ and δ_i remained same while processing both the video frames $[\![f_i]\!]$ and $[\![f_{i+1}]\!]$.

6. The partially processed video frames $[\![f_i']\!]$ and $[\![f_{i+1}']\!]$ are further transformed using $[\![\mu_{ref}]\!]$:

$$[\![\hat{f}_i]\!] = [\![f_i']\!] \times [\![\mu_{ref}]\!] \text{ and } [\![\hat{f}_{i+1}]\!] = [\![f_{i+1}']\!] \times [\![\mu_{ref}]\!]$$

the $[\![\hat{f}_i]\!]$ and $[\![\hat{f}_{i+1}]\!]$ represent the completely processed video frames in the ED.

7. Increment $i=i+2$ and goto step 4.
8. Once processed, transmit the video sequence $[\![\hat{V}]\!] = \{[\![\hat{f}_1]\!], [\![\hat{f}_2]\!], \ldots, [\![\hat{f}_n]\!]\}$ to the trust server for decryption. Rest of the remaining data including $[\![\mu]\!]$ and $\delta' = \{\delta_1', \delta_3', \delta_5', \ldots, \delta_n'\}$ can be deleted or retained, based on regulations of the cloud service provider.

4.4.2.3   Decryption at Trust Server

The processed video frames $[\![\hat{V}]\!] = \{[\![\hat{f}_1]\!], [\![\hat{f}_2]\!], \ldots, [\![\hat{f}_n]\!]\}$ are received at trust server for decryption. The decryption is performed by using private key v of the selected cryptosystem. Unlike the privacy-preserving color transfer method proposed in [37], the overheads of post-processing are removed here. Hence, the trust server only needs to decrypt the received video frames to obtain the processed video sequence $\hat{V} = \{\hat{f}_1, \hat{f}_2, \ldots, \hat{f}_n\}$.

4.4.3   Results and Performance Analysis

The video color grading effects achieved by the proposed approach are analyzed in this section. Since video color grading is the process of adjusting colors of a video sequence as per the reference scene/mood image, we analyze the color transformation of test video sequences before and after application of the proposed approach. Figures 4.5, 4.6 and 4.7 shows the color transfer effects for *Building* video sequence with three different reference images. The top row with a single image shows the reference image, followed by second row and third rows for original and processed video frames respectively. For effective analysis, three different images with "morning", "day" and "evening" time are selected as reference in Figs. 4.5, 4.6 and 4.7 respectively. Upon analysis from Figs. 4.5, 4.6 and 4.7, it can be clearly observed from the last row that color palette of the original video frames (depicted in the second row) has been successfully processed with respect to colors of the corresponding reference images. The same analysis can be observed from Figs. 4.8, 4.9 and 4.10 for *Bay* video sequence.

Fig. 4.5 Sample video frames of *Building* video sequence using a "morning" time image as the reference

Fig. 4.6 Sample video frames of *Building* video sequence using a "day" time image as the reference

Fig. 4.7 Sample video frames of *Building* video sequence using an "evening" time image as the reference

Fig. 4.8 Sample video frames of *Bay* video sequence using a "morning" time image as the reference

Fig. 4.9 Sample video frames of *Bay* video sequence using a "day" time image as the reference

Fig. 4.10 Sample video frames of *Bay* video sequence using an "evening" time image as the reference

4.4.3.1 Comparison of Mean Color Intensity Scores

Instead of visual comparison, rigorous numerical analysis has been performed to validate the color grading effects achieved by the proposed approach. The *Building* and *Bay* video sequences along with their corresponding reference images, depicted in Figs. 4.5, 4.6 and 4.7 and Figs. 4.8, 4.9 and 4.10 are considered for this purpose. Since color transfer involves transforming color intensity values of the target image t with respect to color palette of the reference image r, colors of the reconstructed target image t_r should match as of the reference image r. On the other hand, a considerable difference should be observed when comparing colors of the target image t with reference r and reconstructed images t_r respectively. To accomplish this purpose, we compute Mean Color Intensity (MCI) scores by working on average of individual RGB color channels and mapping them into a single value. The mapping is performed with the help of a transformation $f : S \subseteq \mathbb{R}^3 \to \mathbb{R}$ as follows:

$$f(\mu_1, \mu_2, \mu_3) = \frac{\sum_{i=1}^{3}(\mu_i)}{3} \tag{4.5}$$

where mean scores of RGB color channels of the test image is represented by μ_1, μ_2 and μ_3. Since the proposed approach addresses the task of video color grading where multiple image frames are processed, we evaluate the average of MCI scores of the processed video frames and compared with original video frames (target frames) and reference image. The comparison is depicted in Table 4.2 for various scenarios depicted in Figs. 4.5, 4.6, 4.7, 4.8, 4.9, and 4.10. Upon analysis, it can be observed that the resulting average of MCI scores achieved by the proposed approach is very close to the reference image, meaning that average colors of the processed video frames are highly similar to the colors of the reference image. On the contrary, a huge difference can be observed between average MCI scores of the

Table 4.2 Comparison of MCI scores of the video sequences depicted in Figs. 4.5, 4.6, 4.7, 4.8, 4.9, and 4.10

	Building "morning"	Building "day"	Building "evening"	Bay "morning"	Bay "day"	Bay "evening"
Original frames	91.15	91.15	91.15	121.54	121.54	121.54
Reference image	125.42	148.81	68.14	144.52	169.93	127.98
Proposed approach	121.98	142.36	69.79	143.59	165.23	127.70
Difference (original)	34.26	57.65	23.01	22.97	48.38	6.44
Difference (proposed)	3.44	6.45	1.64	0.92	4.70	0.28
Reduction (%) achieved by the proposed approach	**89.94%**	**88.80%**	**92.84%**	**95.96%**	**90.28%**	**95.54%**

The bold values depict superior results achieved by the proposed method. The results are evaluated with respect to the difference of MCI (Mean Color Intensity) scores evaluated between original-reference and proposed-reference image pairs respectively

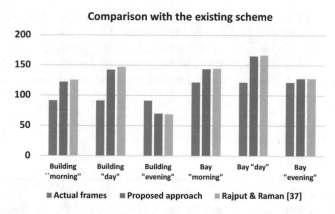

Fig. 4.11 Comparison of MCI scores with the existing scheme

original and reference image. Hence, the proposed approach successfully achieved colors of the reference image with high-level of similarity. The last row shows the percentage of difference reduced by the proposed approach before and after processing video sequences with respect to the reference image, and sufficiently higher scores are achieved. Furthermore, a graphical comparison with the existing scheme proposed in [37] is shown in Fig. 4.11 and it can be observed that the MCI scores achieved by the proposed approach are almost equivalent to the previous scheme. Hence superiority of the color transfer is maintained with drastic reduction in computational and storage overheads, discussed in the next subsection.

4.4.4   Performance Analysis

We implemented the proposed block based image encryption method over a desktop PC with Intel core i7 processor and 4 GB RAM. Matlab R2015b is used as the programming platform and the operating system is Windows 10. In this section, we assess the proposed approach and compare with the naive Paillier cryptosystem. Consider λ as the key size of the naive Paillier cryptosystem with 1024 bits [29]. Therefore, upon implementing the naive Paillier cryptosystem for an RGB image of size 256×256, each pixel value of 24-bit will be represented by 4λ. Thus, size of the resulting image becomes 32 MB which is approximately 177 times higher than the original image (0.18 MB).

Since the proposed approach is designed to support video color grading in the ED, implementing naive Paillier cryptosystem for a video sequence of 50 frames (each of size 256×256) would require 1.56 GB space for encrypted video sequence. Thus, making a non-trivial case for video processing. In addition, the evaluation of color transfer values for a large video sequence further increases the computational complexity at user end (trust server). Addressing these problems, we propose to evaluate color transformation values for each alternate video frame, followed by using Paillier cryptosystem based proxy encryption method for encryption. As a result, the computational complexity is reduced from $O(nf)$ to $O(nf/2)$ (where n and f depicts the total number of video frames and size of each frame respectively), along with drastic reduction in storage overhead as the proposed approach reduces storage overhead from **1.56 GB** to **800 MB**. Thus, achieving secure and effective video color grading effects with less computational and storage overheads.

4.5   Security Analysis

After successful assessment of video color grading effects in the previous subsection, robustness of the proposed approach is analyzed here. We use proxy encryption based Paillier cryptosystem to encrypt the video sequence. The encryption process consists of considering each video frame individually and applying proxy based Paillier cryptosystem. In a generic sense, a cryptosystem is considered robust if its probability of guessing is highly unbreakable. Hence, security of the selected cryptosystem is described with the help of two features, described as follows.

4.5.1   One-Wayness

Let us assume a third party T with access to the ciphertext $\hat{e}$ and public key ρ, the one-wayness assures that it is hard to retrieve plain text information from $\hat{e}$. While referring to the original article in [5], we came to know that authors analyzed security strengths of proxy based modified Paillier cryptosystem in association with *Lift Diffie-Hellman* problem. The *Lift Diffie-Hellman* problem has been proved to be hard by considering a negligible function for each Probabilistic Polynomial time algorithm, and authors used it to prove that the proxy encryption based Paillier cryptosystem is one-way.

Theorem 4.1 *The proxy encryption based Paillier cryptosystem is one-way if and only if the Lift Diffie-Hellman problem is hard.*

Proof Consider ω as a plain text message encrypted using public key ρ of the cryptosystem with $(\hat{e}_1, \hat{e}_2) = (g^\sigma, h^\sigma(1 + \omega n))$ as ciphertexts. An adversary requiring plain text message ω needs to evaluate $\kappa = h^\sigma \bmod n^2$ on input $\vartheta = g^\sigma, \varphi = h$ and $\kappa = h^\sigma(1 + \omega n)$ to solve the *Lift Diffie-Hellman* problem. Contradictory, one can generate the ciphertext $(\hat{e}_1, \hat{e}_2)$ for an arbitrary message ω by modifying the public key $(g, h = \varphi, n), \hat{e}_1 = \vartheta$ and $\varphi = \kappa(1 + \omega n) \bmod n^2$. Therefore, if one can extract plain text message ω from $(\hat{e}_1, \hat{e}_2)$, such intelligence can be utilized to solve *Lift Diffie-Hellman* problem. While our objective is to extract $\beta = g^{\kappa\rho} \bmod n^2$, let ζ be the extracted plaintext from $(\hat{e}_1, \hat{e}_2)$, by definition [5]:

$$\hat{e}_2 = \beta(1 + \zeta n) = \beta + \beta\zeta n = \beta + (\beta \bmod n)\zeta n = \beta + \kappa\zeta n \bmod n^2$$

Hence, it has become possible to efficiently compute $\beta = \kappa(1 + (\omega - \zeta)n) \bmod n^2$ leveraging establishment of an explicit relation between the *Lift Diffie-Hellman problem* and the Partial Discrete Logarithm problem. Thus, the selected cryptosystem is highly secure with the fact that the *Lift Diffie-Hellman problem* is as hard as Partial Discrete Logarithm problem. For detailed description, the reader is advised to [5].

4.5.2   Semantic Security

In order to resist differential attacks, the adversary should not be able to differentiate between two ciphertexts $(\hat{e}_1, \hat{e}_2)$ generated from the same plain text ω. This property falls under semantic security and is associated to Decisional Diffie-Hellman Assumption in $\mathbb{Z}_{n^2}$.

Theorem 4.2 *The proxy encryption based Paillier cryptosystem is semantically secure if Decisional Diffie-Hellman Assumption holds in $\mathbb{Z}_{n^2}$.*

Proof Let us consider a polynomial time distinguisher D_p that can break the semantic security of the cryptosystem. Provided a quadruple $\mathbb{G} = (g, g^\vartheta, g^\varphi, g^\kappa)$, our aim is to classify whether it is a Diffie-Hellman or random one using D_p. To perform this, one can proceed by first declaring the public key ρ and waiting for adversary to chose the messages ω_0 and ω_1. Then, a bit d can be flipped and encrypted (ω_d) to get $(\hat{e}_1, \hat{e}_2)$, where $\hat{e}_1 = g^\varphi$ and $\hat{e}_2 = g^\kappa(1 + \omega n) \bmod n^2$. In this situation, a right response will be received by the polynomial time distinguisher D_p for a Diffie-Hellman quadruple. On the other hand, no information can be extracted even by implementing a polynomially unbounded approach. The obtained information will be of the following form:

$$g^\varphi \bmod n \text{ and } g^{\vartheta\varphi+\sigma}(1 + \omega_d n) \bmod n^2$$

Focusing on the second value, assume $c = \vartheta\varphi + \sigma \bmod ord(\mathbb{G})$. The σ is a random integer steadily distributed in $[1, ord(\mathbb{G})]$, and can be inscribed as $\sigma_1 + \sigma_2\lambda(n)/2$, with $\sigma_1, \sigma_2 \in \mathbb{Z}_n$. Therefore,

$$g^{\vartheta\varphi+\sigma}(1 + \omega_b n) = g^{\vartheta\varphi}g^{\sigma_1}g^{\sigma_2\lambda(n)/2}(1 + \omega_d n) \bmod n^2$$
$$= g^{\vartheta\varphi+\sigma_1}(1 + n)^{\sigma_2}(1 + \omega_d n) \bmod n^2$$
$$= g^{\vartheta\varphi+\sigma_1}(1 + (\sigma_2 + \omega_d)n) \bmod n^2$$

Therefore, it is important to observe that σ_2 hides ω_d admirably and D_p cannot guess the inserted bit d. In addition, the modified Paillier cryptosystem been proved to be INDistinguishable under Chosen Plaintext Attack (IND-CPA) in [29] and the reader is advised to refer to [29] for more description.

4.6   Conclusion

In this chapter, we have presented a video color grading approach using an example image as the reference in the ED. A descriptive review of multimedia encryption along with emergence of homomorphic encryption schemes has been presented. Furthermore, we emphasized the feasibility of performing effective color transfer operations with least storage and computational overheads by using alternate frame based video color transfer. Initially, color transformation parameters are evaluated at trust server for every alternate video frame, followed by using proxy encryption based Paillier cryptosystem for video encryption. Due to this, the storage overhead is drastically reduced. For example, when encrypting a video sequence of 50 frames, each of size 256×256, the storage overhead is reduced from $1.56\,\text{GB}$ to $800\,\text{MB}$ (as compared to the naive approach). In addition, effective quality of video color grading achieved by the proposed approach has been successfully assessed. Security analysis has been performed thoroughly, and the proposed approach has proved to be semantically secure along with complete assurance of one-wayness.

Acknowledgement This work was supported by Information Security Education and Awareness (ISEA) Project (phase II), Deity, Government of India.

References

1. Barni, M., Bianchi, T., Catalano, D., Di Raimondo, M., Donida Labati, R., Failla, P., Fiore, D., Lazzeretti, R., Piuri, V., Scotti, F. et al. [2010], Privacy-preserving fingercode authentication, *in* 'Proceedings of the 12th ACM workshop on Multimedia and security', ACM, pp. 231–240.
2. Boneh, D., Goh, E.-J. and Nissim, K. [2005], Evaluating 2-dnf formulas on ciphertexts, *in* 'Theory of Cryptography Conference', Springer, pp. 325–341.
3. Boneh, D. et al. [1999], 'Twenty years of attacks on the rsa cryptosystem', *Notices of the AMS* **46**(2), 203–213.
4. Brakerski, Z. [2012], Fully homomorphic encryption without modulus switching from classical gapsvp, *in* 'Advances in cryptology–crypto 2012', Springer, pp. 868–886.
5. Bresson, E., Catalano, D. and Pointcheval, D. [2003], A simple public-key cryptosystem with a double trapdoor decryption mechanism and its applications, *in* 'International Conference on the Theory and Application of Cryptology and Information Security', Springer, pp. 37–54.
6. Chan, A. B., Liang, Z.-S. J. and Vasconcelos, N. [2008], Privacy preserving crowd monitoring: Counting people without people models or tracking, *in* 'Computer Vision and Pattern Recognition, 2008. CVPR 2008. IEEE Conference on', IEEE, pp. 1–7.
7. Chen, X., Huang, X., Li, J., Ma, J., Lou, W. and Wong, D. S. [2015], 'New algorithms for secure outsourcing of large-scale systems of linear equations', *IEEE transactions on information forensics and security* **10**(1), 69–78.
8. Coron, J.-S., Mandal, A., Naccache, D. and Tibouchi, M. [2011], Fully homomorphic encryption over the integers with shorter public keys, *in* 'Annual Cryptology Conference', Springer, pp. 487–504.
9. ElGamal, T. [1985], 'A public key cryptosystem and a signature scheme based on discrete logarithms', *IEEE transactions on information theory* **31**(4), 469–472.

10. Erkin, Z., Franz, M., Guajardo, J., Katzenbeisser, S., Lagendijk, I. and Toft, T. [2009], Privacy-preserving face recognition, *in* 'International Symposium on Privacy Enhancing Technologies', Springer, pp. 235–253.
11. Ferreira, B., Rodrigues, J., Leitao, J. and Domingos, H. [2015], Privacy-preserving content-based image retrieval in the cloud, *in* 'Reliable Distributed Systems (SRDS), 2015 IEEE 34th Symposium on', IEEE, pp. 11–20.
12. Gentry, C. [2010], 'Computing arbitrary functions of encrypted data', *Communications of the ACM* **53**(3), 97–105.
13. Gentry, C., Halevi, S. and Smart, N. P. [2012 *a*], Better bootstrapping in fully homomorphic encryption, *in* 'International Workshop on Public Key Cryptography', Springer, pp. 1–16.
14. Gentry, C., Halevi, S. and Smart, N. P. [2012 *b*], Fully homomorphic encryption with polylog overhead, *in* 'Annual International Conference on the Theory and Applications of Cryptographic Techniques', Springer, pp. 465–482.
15. Gentry, C., Sahai, A. and Waters, B. [2013], Homomorphic encryption from learning with errors: Conceptually-simpler, asymptotically-faster, attribute-based, *in* 'Advances in Cryptology–CRYPTO 2013', Springer, pp. 75–92.
16. Goldwasser, S. and Micali, S. [1982], Probabilistic encryption & how to play mental poker keeping secret all partial information, *in* 'Proceedings of the fourteenth annual ACM symposium on Theory of computing', ACM, pp. 365–377.
17. Guo, J., Zheng, P. and Huang, J. [2017], 'An efficient motion detection and tracking scheme for encrypted surveillance videos', *ACM Transactions on Multimedia Computing, Communications, and Applications (TOMM)* **13**(4), 61.
18. Halevi, S. and Shoup, V. [2014], Algorithms in helib, *in* 'International Cryptology Conference', Springer, pp. 554–571.
19. Halevi, S. and Shoup, V. [2015], Bootstrapping for helib, *in* 'Annual International conference on the theory and applications of cryptographic techniques', Springer, pp. 641–670.
20. Hsu, C.-Y., Lu, C.-S. and Pei, S.-C. [2012], 'Image feature extraction in encrypted domain with privacy-preserving sift', *IEEE Transactions on Image Processing* **21**(11), 4593–4607.
21. Hu, X., Zhang, W., Li, K., Hu, H. and Yu, N. [2016], 'Secure nonlocal denoising in outsourced images', *ACM Transactions on Multimedia Computing, Communications, and Applications (TOMM)* **12**(3), 40.
22. Jagannathan, G. and Wright, R. N. [2005], Privacy-preserving distributed k-means clustering over arbitrarily partitioned data, *in* 'Proceedings of the eleventh ACM SIGKDD international conference on Knowledge discovery in data mining', ACM, pp. 593–599.
23. Jia, L. and Radke, R. J. [2014], 'Using time-of-flight measurements for privacy-preserving tracking in a smart room', *IEEE Transactions on Industrial Informatics* **10**(1), 689–696.
24. Jost, C., Lam, H., Maximov, A. and Smeets, B. J. [2015], 'Encryption performance improvements of the paillier cryptosystem.', *IACR Cryptology ePrint Archive* **2015**, 864.
25. Kargupta, H., Datta, S., Wang, Q. and Sivakumar, K. [2005], 'Random-data perturbation techniques and privacy-preserving data mining', *Knowledge and Information Systems* **7**(4), 387–414.
26. Lathey, A. and Atrey, P. K. [2015], 'Image enhancement in encrypted domain over cloud', *ACM Transactions on Multimedia Computing, Communications, and Applications (TOMM)* **11**(3), 38.
27. Lathey, A., Atrey, P. K. and Joshi, N. [2013], Homomorphic low pass filtering on encrypted multimedia over cloud, *in* 'IEEE Seventh International Conference on Semantic Computing (ICSC)', IEEE, pp. 310–313.
28. Marwan, M., Kartit, A. and Ouahmane, H. [2018], 'Security enhancement in healthcare cloud using machine learning', *Procedia Computer Science* **127**, 388–397.
29. Mohanty, M., Asghar, M. R. and Russello, G. [2016], '2dcrypt: Image scaling and cropping in encrypted domains', *IEEE Transactions on Information Forensics and Security* **11**(11), 2542–2555.

30. Mohanty, M., Ooi, W. T. and Atrey, P. K. [2013 *a*], Scale me, crop me, knowme not: Supporting scaling and cropping in secret image sharing, *in* 'IEEE International Conference on Multimedia and Expo (ICME)', IEEE, pp. 1–6.

31. Mohanty, M., Ooi, W. T. and Atrey, P. K. [2013 *b*], Secure cloud-based volume ray-casting, *in* 'International Conference on Cloud Computing Technology and Science (CloudCom)', Vol. 1, IEEE, pp. 531–538.

32. Paillier, P. [1999], Public-key cryptosystems based on composite degree residuosity classes, *in* 'International Conference on the Theory and Applications of Cryptographic Techniques', Springer, pp. 223–238.

33. Rahulamathavan, Y., Phan, R. C.-W., Chambers, J. A. and Parish, D. J. [2013], 'Facial expression recognition in the encrypted domain based on local fisher discriminant analysis', *IEEE Transactions on Affective Computing* **4**(1), 83–92.

34. Rahulamathavan, Y., Veluru, S., Phan, R. C.-W., Chambers, J. A. and Rajarajan, M. [2014], 'Privacy-preserving clinical decision support system using gaussian kernel-based classification', *IEEE journal of biomedical and health informatics* **18**(1), 56–66.

35. Rajput, A. S. and Raman, B. [2017], Color me, store me, know me not: Supporting image color transfer and storage in encrypted domain over cloud, *in* 'International Conference on Multimedia & Expo Workshops (ICMEW)', IEEE, pp. 291–296.

36. Rajput, A. S. and Raman, B. [2018 *a*], 'Cloud based image color transfer and storage in encrypted domain', *Multimedia Tools and Applications*. https://doi.org/10.1007/s11042-017-5580-2 pp. 1–29.

37. Rajput, A. S. and Raman, B. [2018 *b*], 'Cryptoct: towards privacy preserving color transfer and storage over cloud', *Multimedia Tools and Applications*. https://doi.org/10.1007/s11042-018-5729-7 pp. 1–23.

38. Rane, S. and Boufounos, P. T. [2013], 'Privacy-preserving nearest neighbor methods: Comparing signals without revealing them', *IEEE Signal Processing Magazine* **30**(2), 18–28.

39. Reinhard, E., Adhikhmin, M., Gooch, B. and Shirley, P. [2001], 'Color transfer between images', *IEEE Computer graphics and applications* **21**(5), 34–41.

40. Rivest, R. L., Shamir, A. and Adleman, L. [1978], 'A method for obtaining digital signatures and public-key cryptosystems', *Communications of the ACM* **21**(2), 120–126.

41. Shamir, A. [1979], 'How to share a secret', *Communications of the ACM* **22**(11), 612–613.

42. Singh, P., Agarwal, N. and Raman, B. [2018], 'Secure data deduplication using secret sharing schemes over cloud', *Future Generation Computer Systems*.

43. Singh, P., Raman, B., Agarwal, N. and Atrey, P. K. [2017], 'Secure cloud-based image tampering detection and localization using pob number system', *ACM Transactions on Multimedia Computing, Communications, and Applications (TOMM)* **13**(3), 23.

44. Van Dijk, M., Gentry, C., Halevi, S. and Vaikuntanathan, V. [2010], Fully homomorphic encryption over the integers, *in* 'Annual International Conference on the Theory and Applications of Cryptographic Techniques', Springer, pp. 24–43.

45. Wang, Q., He, M., Du, M., Chow, S. S., Lai, R. W. and Zou, Q. [2016], 'Searchable encryption over feature-rich data', *IEEE Transactions on Dependable and Secure Computing*.

46. Weng, L., Amsaleg, L., Morton, A. and Marchand-Maillet, S. [2015], 'A privacy-preserving framework for large-scale content-based information retrieval', *IEEE Transactions on Information Forensics and Security* **10**(1), 152–167.

47. Xia, Z., Wang, X., Zhang, L., Qin, Z., Sun, X. and Ren, K. [2016], 'A privacy-preserving and copy-deterrence content-based image retrieval scheme in cloud computing', *IEEE Transactions on Information Forensics and Security* **11**(11), 2594–2608.

48. Yagisawa, M. [2015], 'Fully homomorphic encryption without bootstrapping.', *IACR Cryptology ePrint Archive* **2015**, 474.

49. Yakubu, A. M., Maddage, N. C. and Atrey, P. K. [2017], 'Securing speech noise reduction in outsourced environment', *ACM Transactions on Multimedia Computing, Communications, and Applications (TOMM)* **13**(4), 51.

50. Yakubu, M. A., Maddage, N. C. and Atrey, P. K. [2016], Encrypted domain cloud-based speech noise reduction with comb filter, *in* 'Multimedia & Expo Workshops (ICMEW), 2016 IEEE International Conference on', IEEE, pp. 1–6.
51. Yao, A. C. [1982], Protocols for secure computations, *in* '23rd Annual Symposium on Foundations of Computer Science', IEEE, pp. 160–164.
52. Zhou, J., Cao, Z., Dong, X. and Lin, X. [2015], 'Ppdm: A privacy-preserving protocol for cloud-assisted e-healthcare systems', *IEEE Journal of Selected Topics in Signal Processing* **9**(7), 1332–1344.

Chapter 5
A Novel Watermarking Technique for Multimedia Security

Satendra Pal Singh and Gaurav Bhatnagar

5.1 Introduction

In the digital era, advance development in network technologies and wide availability of internet increases the access to digital media through online services. As a result, sharing of multimedia data such as images, audio and videos are significantly increased and become widespread practice between the end users. At the same time, illegal copying, distribution, unlawful editing of multimedia data become an easy task due to the wide availability of sophisticated softwares. This has led to a serious concern of the privacy and ownership issues. Moreover, this can be the reason for considerable financial loss for media producers. Therefore, the protection of intellectual property right (IPR) emerged as the one of the major challenges in information security [1]. This fact motivates the researcher to develop some solution to address these issues. As a solution, multimedia encryption [2] is a simple way to secure the multimedia data. Encryption is used to transform the original data into cipher data which can be decrypted at the later stage to reproduce the multimedia data. This technique is effectively used to secure the multimedia data during the transmission and to protect the content during the storage of the multimedia data. However, this process has some limitation that data is no longer secured after the decryption of the multimedia data. It mainly used for secure communication and protect the content of the multimedia data but not the ownership and copyright protection.

Hash functions [3] are another common approach to secure the multimedia data. Generally, hash functions are categorized into two groups: (1) Cryptographic, and (2) Content based hash functions. Cryptographic hash functions are bit sensitive

S. P. Singh · G. Bhatnagar (✉)
Department of Mathematics, Indian Institute of Technology, Jodhpur, India
e-mail: pg201383504@iitj.ac.in; goravb@iitj.ac.in

© Springer Nature Switzerland AG 2019
A. K. Singh, A. Mohan (eds.), *Handbook of Multimedia Information Security: Techniques and Applications*, https://doi.org/10.1007/978-3-030-15887-3_5

89

and key dependent. These hash functions are designed mainly for data integrity [4]. These types of functions are not appropriate to secure the multimedia data. In contrast, content based hash function can secure the data but provide limited robustness. These techniques have various advantages in classification and identification. Therefore, these techniques are widely used in multimedia authentication.

Recently, digital watermarking emerges as a prominent solution for aforementioned issues [5]. Basically, watermarking used to describe the convey information in a hiding manner by embedding the information into host data. The concept of watermarking have been used in various forms and can be traced back to the thirteenth century. Watermarks were made on the paper using the thin translucent layer and wire to specify the brand and producer name as the registered trademark for the product in Italy. The watermarks began to be used for different prospective during sixteenth century and by eighteenth century, it has been used as anti-counterfeiting measures on currencies and other documents. Thereafter, digital watermarking gained the considerable attention and researcher actively contribute intense research work in this area in past few years.

Digital watermarking is a process in which an ownership sign or information is imperceptibly embedded into multimedia signal and can be extracted at later stage for verification or authentication purposes. The embedded information into the signal is called a digital watermark and the signal in which the watermark is embedded is know as the host signal whereas the embedded signal termed as the watermarked signal. The watermarked signal is usually stored or transmitted between the different channel for communication purpose. During the transmission, if the watermarked signal is unmodified then watermark information is still present in the signal and can be extracted. For a robust watermarking algorithm, the watermark information can also be recovered even the watermarked signal is modified strongly. The quality of original and extracted watermark signal should be perceptually similar. The perceptual transparency can be ensure using some perceptibility criterion. This can be adaptive or fixed. The watermark information remain confined with the watermarked signal to protect the ownership. If watermarked signal is copied then copied version also contains the embedded information present in the signal. Generally, an ideal watermarking algorithm have good perceptual quality as well as robustness.

5.2   General Framework of Watermarking System

Generally, a watermarking system [6–8] comprise of two components: (1) Watermark embedder, and (2) Watermark extractor/detector. The watermark embedder requires three inputs that includes original host media, watermark and a secret key to produce the watermarked media. The embedder inserts a machine-readable watermark into the host media by modifying the media object which is generally controlled by a private key. The private key is assigned to ensure the security during the complete procedure. In contrast, secret key and watermarked media are produced

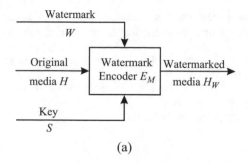

(a)

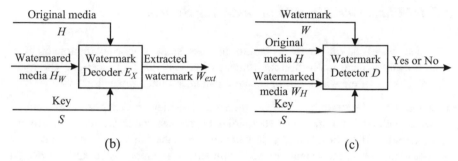

(b)   (c)

Fig. 5.1 A general framework for watermarking system. (**a**) Watermark encoder/embedder. (**b**) Watermark decoder/extractor. (**c**) Watermark detector

as the output, which can be utilized for extraction purposes. From the watermarked media, the embedding of watermark can be confirmed by the watermark detector or extractor. However, the terms 'extractor' and 'detector' do not have same meaning. The former is employed to extract the embedding information from the watermarked media, whereas the later defines the existence of the watermark in the media. A typical watermarking system can be observed from Fig. 5.1.

In embedding process, encoder combines the host media (H), watermark code (W), a secret key (S) and an embedding algorithm to create the watermarked media (H_W). Mathematically, the embedding process can be express as follows:

$$H_W = E_M\left(H, W, [S]\right) \tag{5.1}$$

where $E_M(\cdot)$ is the embedding function and $[\cdot]$ indicate the optional nature of the parameters and can be used to extend the watermark embedder. The considering key (S) may be disclosed privately or publically. In extraction process, the watermarked media, secret key, original media and extraction algorithm is required to extract the watermark (W_{ext}). Mathematically, the extraction process can be illustrated as given below:

$$W_{ext} = E_X\left(H_W, [H], [S]\right) \tag{5.2}$$

where $E_X(\cdot)$ represent the extraction function. In detection process, detector is used to confirm the existence of watermark and can be summarized as:

$$D\left(H_W, [H], W, [S]\right) = \begin{cases} 0 & \text{There is no watermark} \\ 1 & \text{There is a watermark} \end{cases} \tag{5.3}$$

where $D(\cdot)$ denote the detection function.

5.2.1 Characteristic of Watermarking System

An ideal watermarking system should possess some important characteristics. They mainly depend upon the requirement of the intended application. The main characteristics of the watermarking system can be summarized as follows:

1. *Robustness:* The term 'robustness' referred to resilience ability of the embedded watermark against removal by standard data processing operations. A watermark is considered to be robust if it can survive under distortion introduced by intentional or unintentional attacks. Typically, it is almost impossible to design a perfect watermarking system which is robust against all potential attacks. This property mainly depends on the working medium (image, audio, video) and the type of application. Therefore, it may possible that a watermarking system may be required resistance for only some of the attacks.
2. *Imperceptibility:* Imperceptibility of the watermark can be described in terms of perceptual transparency. The perceptual transparency is the degree of invisibility of the watermark in the watermarked signal, i.e., a watermark is said to be truly imperceptible to human eye if no perceptual difference can be detected between watermarked and the original media.
3. *Capacity:* Capacity is referred as maximum amount of information that can be hide in the host media without noticeably reducing perceptual quality. Generally, a technique with higher capacity is more desirable because, more data information can be embedded in the host multimedia.
4. *Security:* Watermark security refers to the ability to resist against the hostile attacks. The hostile attacks indicates the process that can destroy the requirement of the watermark. There are different kind of hostile attacks and hence each watermark application required its own type of security. The security of a watermarking system can be compromised, if an intruder have raw information about the secret key and corresponding system. In this scenario, the attacker will have the details about the specified watermark embedding locations or watermark bits with respective frequencies. The prediction of the secret key becomes possible by analyzing the similarity between the characteristics of a set of watermarked media.

Fig. 5.2 Trade-off between
the different characteristics of
watermarking system

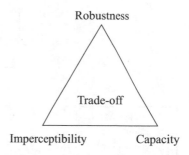

The above characteristics generally oppose each other and hence a trade-off is essential between them. A possible trade-off is illustrated in Fig. 5.2. Usually, imperceptibility is the basic and most important requirement for a watermarking system. This is directly connected to robustness and capacity. The amount of embedding information may lead to some artifact or less imperceptibility between watermarked and original multimedia. However, improvement in imperceptibility may lead to less robustness and conversely. Both of the factor depends on the capacity, i.e., if the capacity is increased then robustness may increases but imperceptibility will be compromised. Therefore, these constraints can optimized significantly for the watermarking system.

5.2.2 Classification of Watermarking Techniques

Watermarking techniques can be categorised in different ways as per underlying classification criteria (rules). The most common classification of watermarking techniques have been illustrated in Fig. 5.3 which shows that classification arc based on numerous factor that includes working domain, type of data, human perception, robustness and extraction strategies. Among these, watermarking techniques based on human perception and working domain have received considerable attention by the researchers in past few decades. Considering to working domain, spatial domain techniques are simple but not robust when compared to frequency domain techniques. The main reason behind this fact is that, when inverse process is performed on the image, the embedding information is scattered irregularly over the entire image, which making the attacker difficult to read or modify. Based on human perception, watermark is either visible or invisible to viewers. In visible watermarking, the embedded watermark is perceptually visible to the viewer whereas in invisible watermarking, watermark is embedded in a manner, such that it cannot be perceptually noticed.

In addition, watermarking techniques can be divide based on robustness of feature into three groups namely robust, fragile and semi-fragile. Firstly, the robust watermarking techniques are mainly designed for copyright protection and identi-fication of ownership [9]. In these type of techniques, user embed the watermark

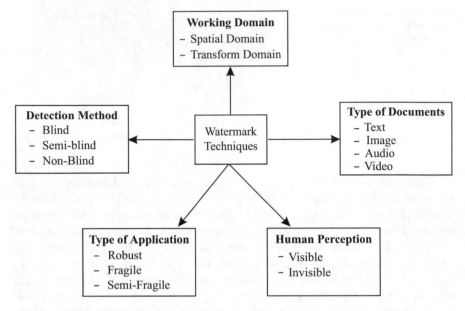

Fig. 5.3 Classification of watermarking techniques

or proof of ownership into the host media with some perceptible distortion. This watermarked media can be transmitted over the secure or insure network for the communication purpose. At the other end, receiver can extract the embedding information through the extraction process. During the transmission, watermark may undergo some attacks like white Gaussian noise, filtering operation, geometric attacks or data compression. The robust watermarking has ability to tolerant certain signal processing operation or attacks upto some extent which can occurs during the life of watermarked media. Secondly, fragile watermarking is employed to verify the integrity of the multimedia object [10]. This watermarking has the ability to detect the small changes in the original multimedia object and locate the corresponding regions i.e., any alteration in the pixel values by the attacks or modification can be detected. Fragile watermarking is commonly used for the temper detection and to authenticate the multimedia object. Lastly, semi-fragile schemes are designed for the localisation of tempered media [11]. The schemes is employed for content authentication of media object. The scheme has the ability to resist unintentional changes or modification caused by common signal processing operations. Due to this fact, it is possible to verify the content of the object with some perceptible distortion which may be arises due to transmission or non-malicious operation. However, semi-fragile scheme detect the malicious or intentional attacks rather than validating the original media.

The extraction of watermark is carried out to obtain an estimate of embedded watermark using a private or public keys. Therefore, watermarking techniques can be divide into three groups based on information required in the extraction process.

1. *Non-blind Extraction:* This scheme also referred as the private watermarking scheme. The schemes requires the original media and extraction key to extract the watermark.
2. *Semi-blind Extraction:* This type of scheme is usually called as the semi-private watermarking scheme. The extraction process requires the information about the watermark and the related keys to extract the watermark.
3. *Blind Extraction:* The scheme is considered as the public watermarking scheme. In extraction process, the information about the original media and watermark is not required. The knowledge of extraction key is sufficient to extract the watermark.

5.3 Literature Survey of Digital Watermarking

There are several watermarking taxonomies have been reported in the existing literature. Among them, watermarking taxonomies based on working domain are most popular and represented by spatial and transform domain. In spatial domain approaches [12–20], embedding of watermark directly change the gray values of the image. These techniques are easy to implement and requires low computational cost, but less robust against several type of distortions. In contrast, the transform domain approach [21–25, 27–35] are more robust. This is due to the fact that watermarking information is embedded into the transformed coefficients and the inverse process distribute it irregularly over the entire image. This make difficult to modify or remove the watermark. A range of transform domain techniques have been proposed in the literature based on discrete fourier transform (DFT) [21], discrete cosine transform [23–25], discrete wavelet transform (DWT) [22, 27] and others [37–42].

In spatial domain, the most common watermarking approach are based on least significant bit (LSB) using PN sequence. In LSB techniques, the watermark is embedded by changing the least significant bit of the host data. The change introduced in the pixel values due to LSB modification are visually less significant which ensure the invisibility of the watermark. Schyndel et al. [12] proposed two LBS based techniques. Firstly, they replace the least significant bit by PN sequence to modify the pixel values whereas a PN sequence is added in LSB of the pixel values in the second technique. Bender et al. [13] developed a statistical scheme based on spread spectrum principle. They select m pairs (u, v) randomly in an image, then increase the value u by one unit and decrease v in the same amount simultaneously. Nikolaidis et al. [14] present a binary watermarking scheme in which they modifies the intensity levels at randomly selected location by adding a small positive quantity. In detection process, the mean value of marked pixel is compared with unmarked pixels to verify the presence of the watermark. Voyatzis et al. [15] utilized the toral automorphism to generate a chaotic sequence and hide the watermark at different locations given by chaotic sequence which are dense in spatial domain. Pita et al. [16] proposed a watermarking scheme in which the host image is randomly split into two parts of equal size. For watermark embedding, the mean value of one of the selected part is increased by a factor and authors investigate security of spread spectrum communication based watermarking theoretically and practically. Bas et al. [18] developed a new security measure based on the effective key length. The author estimate the effective key length for spread spectrum communication (SSC) and improved SSC. Chen et al. [19] reported a optimal watermarking scheme based on integrated quantization embedding. The watermark is embedded into low frequency component of the discrete wavelet transform (DWT) using amplitude quantization to ensure the robustness. Singh et al. [20] present efficient watermarking scheme using the spread spectrum principle. They embedded a binary watermark using the PN sequence generated from linear feedback shift register (LFSR). In general, the LSB based approach that modifies the image data using a PN sequence of fixed magnitude are highly vulnerable to signal processing attacks. The main reason behind this weakness is due to limited magnitude of the embedded noise which ensure the invisibility of the watermark.

Generally, transform domain approaches are more resilient to signal processing operations in compare to spatial domain. Cox et al. [21] proposed a watermarking scheme using the spread spectrum principle. The watermark embedding is carried out using first ℓ highest magnitude coefficients of DFT/DCT, whereas comparison the DFT/DCT coefficients of the watermarked and original image to extract the watermark. Barni et al. [22] reported a watermarking scheme in DCT domain wherein watermark is embedded in DCT coefficients considering a sequence of real numbers. Huang et al. [23] presented an adaptive watermarking scheme utilizing luminance and texture in DCT domain. The watermark is embedded in DC coefficients, due to larger perceptually capacity than AC coefficients which ultimately improves the robustness. Several other watermarking scheme based on block-based DCT can be found in [24].

In past few years, a new mathematical transform namely discrete wavelet transform is frequently used in watermarking [25–31]. DWT has several advantage over other frequency domain approaches such as multiresolution property, better energy compaction and effective scale space approximation. Zhu et al. [27] have presented a unified approach for digital watermarking using multi-level discrete wavelet transform. This method adds the watermark using a Gaussian distributed random vector in high frequency band. Liu et al. [28] present robust watermarking scheme based on singular value decomposition (SVD). In this method, singular values (SVs) of cover and watermark images are estimated and modified in order to embed the watermark. The modified singular values and know components are combined to produced the watermarked image. Ganic et al. [29] reported a watermarking scheme in which the payload factor is determined by considering the SVs of the cover and watermark image. Ganic et al. [30] proposed an optimal watermarking scheme utilizing DWT and SVD. The SVD is performed to the each wavelet sub-bands of the images and modifies the singular values to produced the watermarked image. Lin et al. [31] design a blind watermarking scheme based on the significant difference of wavelet coefficients. In extraction process, maximum wavelet coefficients are quantized and the energy difference between the significant difference are used to estimate the extracted watermark. The embedding in frequency domain can be further extended to the multiple frequency domain. The use of multiple frequency domain for embedding purpose can have the combined advantages derived from each domain. Zhao et al. [32] has proposed a watermarking scheme in dual domain comprise of DCT and DWT, where DCT transform is utilize for watermark generation and embedded in the DWT domain. A detailed review on recent watermarking techniques can be seen in [36].

Recently, a new approach based on stochastic resonance (SR) have been used to determine the existence of the watermark [37]. The core idea involves the detection of the watermark signal from the possible attacked watermarked image and therefore SR phenomena is employed to optimize the authenticity of the watermark in extraction process. Thereafter, numerous watermarking scheme have been proposed by the incorporation of stochastic resonance with different philosophies [38–43]. Sun et al. [38], design a new watermarking system based on aperiodic signal processor and DCT, where embedding is done in DCT coefficients and aperiodic signal processor employed to detect the binary pulse amplitude modulation (PAM) signals. A more efficient watermarking technique have been developed based on dynamic stochastic resonance (DSR) [40, 41]. In former technique, a binary watermark is embedded in DCT domain using pseudo random sequence whereas multilevel DWT and DCT is considered in later one. In both the case, dynamic stochastic resonance (DSR) based detector is employed to improve the authenticity of the watermark. Jha et al. [42] embedded a gray scale logo by modifying the singular values whereas the incorporation of DSR and singular values extract the watermark. The major drawback of the algorithm is that it has limited robustness and suffer from false positive problem. Singh et al. [43] embedded the watermark in integer DCT domain and remove the falsification problem which essentially resolve the existing problem.

5.4   Mathematical Preliminaries

5.4.1   Singular Value Decomposition

In linear algebra, singular value decomposition (SVD) is an efficient numerical technique for the matrix decomposition. Due to usefulness, it is widely used in many application like statistical data analysis, image processing, data compression, dimension reduction [44]. This transform was discovered independently by Beltrami [45] in 1873 and Jordan [46] in 1874 for square matrices. Later on, Eckart and Young [47] extended the concept for the rectangular matrices. The main motivation behind SVD is that it transforms a high dimensional data into lower dimensional subspace, in which substructure of original data is arranged in lower dimension. In other words, the original correlated variables can be express in the form of uncorrelated variables that exhibits the crucial information regarding the original data points.

The singular value decomposition factorize a linear operator $X : R^n \rightarrow R^m$ into three distinct linear operator U, Σ and V such that $U : R^k \rightarrow R^m$, $\Sigma : R^k \rightarrow R^k$ and $V : R^n \rightarrow R^k$, where R^n denote a n-dimensional vector space. Let A be the matrix of size $m \times n$ corresponding to operator X defined over the field $\mathbb{F}$. Then, singular value decomposition [48] of matrix A can be defined as:

$$A = U_A \Sigma_A V_A^T \tag{5.4}$$

$$A = \begin{bmatrix} u_{1,1} & \cdots & u_{1,k} \\ \vdots & \ddots & \vdots \\ u_{m,1} & \cdots & u_{m,k} \end{bmatrix} \begin{bmatrix} \sigma_{1,1} & \cdots & 0 \\ \vdots & \ddots & \vdots \\ 0 & \cdots & \sigma_{k,k} \end{bmatrix} \begin{bmatrix} v_{1,1} & \cdots & v_{1,k} \\ \vdots & \ddots & \vdots \\ v_{n,1} & \cdots & v_{n,k} \end{bmatrix}^T$$

where U_A and V_A are orthogonal (unitary) matrices of size $m \times k$ and $k \times n$ respectively. Σ_A is a diagonal matrix $\Sigma = diag(\sigma^{(i)})$, $i = 1 \ldots k$, where $\sigma^{(i)}$ denote the singular values and k is the rank of matrix A with $k = \min(m, n)$. All the singular values are non-negative and are arranged in the following order:

$$\sigma_1 \geq \sigma_2 \geq \cdots \geq \sigma_{k-1} \geq \sigma_k \geq 0 \tag{5.5}$$

From Eq. (5.4), A can be written as

$$A = \sum_{i=1}^{k} u^{(i)} \sigma_i v^{(i)T} \tag{5.6}$$

where matrix $u^{(i)} v^{(i)T}$ is referred as the outer product between ith row of U_A and corresponding column of V_A. The columns of matrix U_A and V_A are called singular vectors, in which first k columns of V_A spanned the row space of A. However, first k columns of U_A and last $(n - k)$ columns of V_A spanned the column and null space of A respectively. The relation between the singular values can be express as follows:

$$Av^{(i)} = \sigma_i u^{(i)}, \qquad i = 1 \ldots r \tag{5.7}$$

$$A^T u^{(i)} = \sigma_i v^{(i)}, \qquad i = 1 \ldots r \tag{5.8}$$

The SVD transformation can be illustrated using geometry of linear transformation as shown in Fig. 5.4. Let U, V and Σ represent a rotation, reflection and stretching matrix corresponding to the transformations. For this purpose, consider a matrix $V = (y^{(1)}, y^{(2)})$ of size 2×2, where $y^{(1)}$ and $y^{(2)}$ are unit vectors. In first step, V^T is applied on the vectors, which resulted in rotation by unit vectors $i = (0, 1)^T$ and $j = (1, 0)^T$. In next step, Σ stretches the resulting vectors i and j to $\sigma_1 i$ and

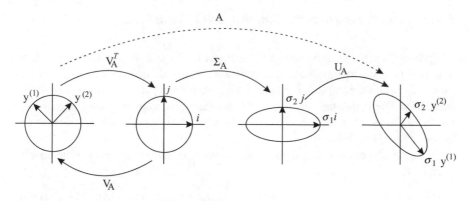

Fig. 5.4 Illustration of SVD transformation

$\sigma_2 j$ with scaling factor σ_1 and σ_2 respectively. Finally, these vectors undergo in a rotation due to matrix U and become $\sigma_1 y^{(1)}$ and $\sigma_2 y^{(2)}$. For digital image, singular values and singular vector specify the luminance (energy) and intrinsic properties of the image. The characteristic of singular values can be summarized as follows:

1. Let F is original image and F^T denote the corresponding transposed image. Then F and F^T have the same singular values.
2. A slight variation in an image does not lead to larger disturbance in the singular values.
3. A slight variation in the singular values of an image does not lead to larger impact on the visual quality of the image. This shows the stable behaviour of singular values.
4. SVD has ability to extract the invariance features up to some extent from the image.
5. SVD localize most of the energy of the image into few singular values.
6. An image and corresponding flipped version about the horizontal or vertical axis have the same singular values.
7. If λ and μ^s represent the non-zero singular value of A and corresponding scaled (either row or column) version A^S then they satisfied the following condition:

$$\mu^S = \sqrt{S^f} * \lambda \tag{5.9}$$

where S^f is the factor in which every row (or column, but not both) is increased in respective scaled version. If A is row scaled S^R times and column scaled S^C then each non-zero singular values μ^{RS} of row-column scaled version A^{RS} satisfied the following condition

$$\mu^{RS} = \sqrt{S^R * S^C} * \lambda \tag{5.10}$$

5.4.2 All Phase Discrete Biorthogonal Transform

All phase discrete biorthogonal transform (APDBT) is a mathematical transform and widely used in the image compression, image de-noising and other image processing application [49]. The basic idea is inspired by the superimposing digital filter [50]. The main steps involve in the designing the superimposing digital filter has been discussed in [51]. A general approach for all phase sequence filtering can be summarized as follows:

A digital sequence $\{U(r)\}$ required R, R-dimensional vectors which contain $u(r)$ such that:

$$
\begin{cases}
U_0 = [u(r), u(r+1), \ldots, u(r+R-1)]^T \\
u_1 = X^{-1}u_0 = [u(r-1), u(r), u(r+1), \ldots, u(r+R-3), u(r+R-2)]^T \\
\qquad\qquad \cdots\cdots\cdots\cdots\cdots\cdots\cdots\cdots\cdots\cdots\cdots \\
u_{R-1} = X^{-R+1}u_0 = [u(r-R+1), u(r-R+2), \ldots, u(r-1), u(r)]^T
\end{cases}
$$
$$(5.11)$$

where $X^{-\ell}, \ell = 1, 2 \ldots R - 1$ represent the delay operator. Each member of sequence yields R different values. The average of these values can be assigned as the all phase filtering. The outcome can be expresses as:

$$
w(r) = \frac{1}{R} \sum_{p=0}^{R-1} Z_p(p) \tag{5.12}
$$

$$
w(r) = \frac{1}{R} \sum_{p=0}^{R-1} \sum_{q=0}^{R-1} [H(p,q)u(r-p+q)] \tag{5.13}
$$

where

$$
H(p,q) = \sum_{p=0}^{R-1} F(k)[T^{-1}(i,k) * T(k,j)] \tag{5.14}
$$

where T and T^{-1} represent the $R \times R$ matrices corresponding to discrete orthogonal transform. From Eqs. (5.13) and (5.14), we get

$$
w(r) = \sum_{q=-(R-1)}^{R-1} h(q)u(r-q) \tag{5.15}
$$

where $h(q)$ represent the unit impulse response and can be express as given below:

$$h(q) = \begin{cases} \sum_{p=q}^{R-1} H(p, p-q) & q = 0, 1....., R-1 \\ \sum_{p=0}^{q+R-1} H(p, p-q) & q = -1, -2...., -R+1 \end{cases} \qquad (5.16)$$

5.4.2.1 All Phase Discrete Biorthogonal Cosine Transform

All phase discrete biorthogonal cosine transform (APDCT) [52] can be derived from the discrete cosine transform using all phase sequence filtering. It has more advantage than the conventional transform due to better energy compaction in the low-frequency component. Discrete cosine transform (DCT) can be described as in [53] as follows:

$$C_{DCT}(\bar{u}, \bar{v}) = \mathscr{C}(\bar{u})\mathscr{C}(\bar{v}) \sum_{p=1}^{R} \sum_{q=1}^{S} f(p, q) \cos\left[\frac{\bar{u}(2r+1)\pi}{2R}\right] \cos\left[\frac{\bar{v}(2s+1)\pi}{2S}\right]$$

$$(5.17)$$

where $\bar{u}, \bar{v} = 1, 2, \cdots R$. The factors $\mathscr{C}(\bar{u})$ and $\mathscr{C}(\bar{v})$ are given as:

$$\mathscr{C}(\bar{u}) = \begin{cases} \frac{1}{\sqrt{R}}, & \bar{u} = 0 \\ \sqrt{\frac{1}{R}}, & 1 \le \bar{u} \le M-1 \end{cases}, \qquad \mathscr{C}(\bar{v}) = \begin{cases} \frac{1}{\sqrt{S}}, & \bar{v} = 0 \\ \sqrt{\frac{1}{S}}, & 1 \le \bar{v} \le N-1 \end{cases}$$

$$(5.18)$$

Also

$$T(p, q) = C_{DCT}(p, q), \qquad T^{-1}(p, q) = C_{DCT}^{-1}(p, q) \qquad (5.19)$$

where C_{DCT} denote the square DCT matrix of size $N \times N$. From Eqs. (5.14) and (5.17)

$$H(p, q) = \frac{1}{R}\left[F(0) + \sum_{k=1}^{R} 2\cos\left[\frac{k(2p+1)\pi}{2R}\right]\cos\left[\frac{k(2q+1)\pi}{2R}\right]F(k)\right]$$

$$(5.20)$$

From Eqs. (5.16) and (5.20),

$$h(q) = \sum_{m=0}^{R-1} V(q, k)F_R(k) \qquad q = 0, 1....., R-1 \qquad (5.21)$$

Matrix representation of Eq. (5.21) can be express as $h = VF$, where the transformation corresponding to matrix V is used to describe the relationship between unit-pulse time response in time domain and sequence response in transform domain. This matrix V is know as APDCT matrix and element of V can be represented as:

$$V(q, k) = \frac{1}{R} \sum_{p=0}^{R-1-p} C(q, k) C^T(q, q+p) \tag{5.22}$$

From Eqs. (5.17) and (5.22), All phase discrete biorthogonal cosine transform is given as:

$$V(p, q) = \begin{cases} \frac{R-i}{R^2} & p = 0, 1, \ldots, R-1 \\ \frac{1}{R^2} * \left[(R-p) \cos \frac{pq\pi}{R} - \csc \frac{q\pi}{R} \sin \frac{pq\pi}{R} \right] & p = 0, \ldots, R-1, \\ & q = 1 \ldots, R-1 \end{cases} \tag{5.23}$$

5.4.2.2 All Phase Discrete Biorthogonal Sine Transform

All phase discrete biorthogonal sine transform (APDBST) [54] is similar transform to (APDBCT) based on all phase sequence filtering. It has been derived from the discrete sine transform. Mathematically, APDBST can be expressed as:

$$V(p, q) = \begin{cases} \frac{1}{R} & p = 0, q = 0, 1, \ldots, R-1 \\ \frac{4}{R(2R+1)} * \beta & p = 1, \ldots, R-1 \\ & q = 0, 1, \ldots, R-1 \end{cases} \tag{5.24}$$

where

$$\beta = \sum_{p=0}^{R-1-p} \sin \frac{(2q+1)(l+1)\pi}{(2R+1)} \sin \frac{(2q+1)(l+p+1)\pi}{(2R+1)} \tag{5.25}$$

5.5 Stochastic Resonance

The phenomena 'stochastic resonance' describe the behaviour of a non-linear system where the performance is optimized in the presence of particular level of noise. Benzi et al. [55] introduced the stochastic resonance (SR) by addressing the issue of periodic occurrences of the earth's ice ages in climatic change model. Since then, stochastic resonance got considerable attention and the applications are significantly increasing in various fields like optical system [56], mechanical system [57] and biological system [58], engineering systems [59], and signal processing

Fig. 5.5 A general structure of stochastic resonance

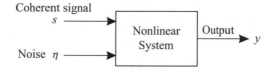

applications [60]. Generally, noise can degrade the quality of the signal and considered as a hindrance for the system. Therefore, it is believed that performance of the system may be worse in the presence of the noise. However, an extra amount of noise may enhanced the performance rather than worse [61]. When a non-linear interaction take place between the signal and noise then there is a possibility of cooperation between them. This cooperation turns out beneficial with some extra amount of noise and it leads to the improvement in the performance of the system. This type of non-linear effect strengthens the concept of stochastic resonance (SR). The various form of SR can be synthesized as shown in Fig. 5.5. The stochastic resonance comprise of four basic components:

1. *An input signal* (s): It may be periodic or non-periodic.
2. *A source of noise* (η): May be of different kind based on the statistical property like Gaussian noise etc.
3. *A transmission system:* A non-linear system receive input in the form of information carrying signal (s) and noise (η) which produced an enhanced output signal y under the influence of (η).
4. *An objective metric:* The metric like PSNR, entropy, correlation coefficient used for performance evaluation, that quantifies the similarity between input signal (s) and output signal (y).

The SR phenomena can be observed based on above elements due to resonance-like behaviour in the response of a system. The Basic mechanism of SR is simple and robust. The SR effect can be analyzed on the basis of the dynamics of the system and can be divide into two parts as: (1) Dynamic Stochastic Resonance (DSR), and (2) Non-dynamic Stochastic Resonance (NDSR).

5.5.1 Dynamic Stochastic Resonance

Dynamic stochastic resonance refers to the generic phenomena for physical system and can be illustrate using a dynamic and bistable double well potential system. For this purpose, consider the Brownian motion of an overdamped particle in double well bistable system in the presence of weak periodic force as described in Fig. 5.6. Mathematically, this can express as follows:

$$\dot{x}(t) = -U'(x) + C_0 \sin(wt) + \sqrt{D}\eta(t) \tag{5.26}$$

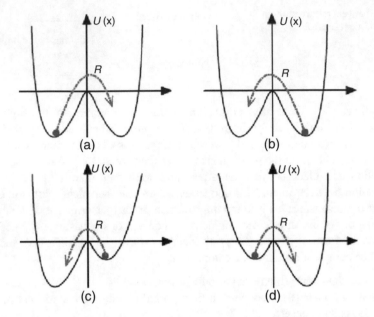

Fig. 5.6 Illustration of motion of a particle from one state to another state in bistable double potential system. (**a–b**) particle not able to cross the barrier, (**c–d**) particle crossing the barrier when signal reaches peak

such that

$$U'(x) = -cx(t) + dx^3(t) \tag{5.27}$$

From Eqs. (5.26) and (5.27)

$$\dot{x}(t) = [cx(t) - dx^3(t)] + C_0 \sin(wt) + \sqrt{D}\eta(t) \tag{5.28}$$

where C_0, w represent signal amplitude and frequency respectively. The particle's normalized position $x(t)$ can be obtained using the Langevin equation [62] as shown in Fig. 5.6a Also, $U(x)$ denotes the bistable potential can be described as follows:

$$U(x) = -(c/2)x^2 + (d/4)x^4 \tag{5.29}$$

where $c > 0$ and $d > 0$ are the bistable system parameters. The potential function correspond to two different stable states separated by a barrier with height $\Delta h = c^2/4d$ at $x_{st} = \pm\sqrt{c/d}$. The potential well is modulated in the presence of periodic fluctuation and as a results potential well is raising and lowering successively in asymmetric fashion around left and right of the barrier. If the amplitude of the weak periodic signal is small, then particle is unable to cross over the barrier between the potential well. In absence of the external noise, there is no transition of the particle from one well to the other and it remains in its local state. However, if a small amount of stochastic noise is applied to the particle, then there exists a cooperative effect between particle and noise which cause the transition of the particle from one state to another. The associated autocorrelation can be determined defined as:

$$< \eta(t), \eta(0) >= 2D * w(t) \tag{5.30}$$

where D represent the noise intensity. The noise induced transition of the particle r_k between equilibrium state is estimated by Kramer's rate [62] as:

$$r_k = \frac{c}{\sqrt{2\pi}} \exp\left(-\frac{\Delta U}{D}\right) \tag{5.31}$$

The noise driven transition is synchronized with a weak periodic force between the double well potential. The average waiting time in the synchronization is determined as given below:

$$T_w = 2T_k(D) \tag{5.32}$$

where T_k denote the period of the input periodic force. The stochastic resonance phenomena occur at moderate noise level which allows the signal to reach the threshold barrier and increase signal to noise ratio (SNR). The SNR is considered as the optimal objective metric which quantifies the SR effect for bistable system and can be described as:

$$SNR = \pi \left(\frac{C_0 X_m}{D}\right)^2 r_k \tag{5.33}$$

From Eqs. (5.31) to (5.33), we get

$$SNR = \left[\frac{c}{\sqrt{2\pi}} \pi \left(\frac{C_0 X_m}{D}\right)^2\right] \exp\left(-\frac{c}{2\sigma_0^2}\right) \tag{5.34}$$

A typical SNR [62] is depend upon σ_0 and determined by following expression:

$$SNR = \left[\frac{4c}{\sqrt{2}(\sigma_0\sigma_1)^2}\right] \exp\left(-\frac{c}{2\sigma_0^2}\right) \tag{5.35}$$

Here (σ_0, σ_1) denote the standard deviation of internal and additional external noise, which are obtained from the original bistable system and SR enhanced bistable system. From Eq. (5.28) and using the Eluer-Maryama's iterative method [63], the system can be modelled as:

$$x(t+1) = x(t) + \Delta t[c * x(t) - d * x^3(t) + input] \tag{5.36}$$

where Δt is a bistable parameter represent the sampling time. The term 'input' is used for sequence of input signal.

5.5.2 Parameter Selection

5.5.2.1 Selection of c

SR can be seen by appropriate selection of the bistable parameters c and d. These parameters can be produced by the maximization of SNR. In order to maximize SNR, differentiate Eq. (5.35) with respect to parameter c and estimate the corresponding value as follows:

$$\frac{d(SNR)}{d(c)} = \frac{1}{\sqrt{2}} \left[\frac{1}{(\sigma_0, \sigma_1)^2} \right] \exp\left(-\frac{c}{2\sigma_0^2}\right)$$

$$- \frac{c}{\sqrt{2}} \left[\frac{1}{(\sigma_0, \sigma_1)^2} \right] \left(\frac{1}{2\sigma_0^2}\right) \exp\left(-\frac{c}{2\sigma_0^2}\right) = 0 \qquad (5.37)$$

Solving above equation gives the optimal value of $c = \sigma_0^2$ that results the maximum SNR.

5.5.2.2 Selection of d

The considering input signal can be defined as the subthreshold signal. This can be ensured by deriving a condition on the value of the parameter d. The derivative of bistable potential function $U(x)$ express the periodic fluctuation in Eq. (5.26). The maximum possible value of the periodic signal at which the bistable potential still remains in the stable state, can approximate the final value. Let $Q = C_0 \sin(wt)$ represent the input signal. Then,

$$Q = \frac{dU(x)}{dx} = -cx + dx^3, \frac{dQ}{dx} = -c + 3dx^2 = 0 \qquad (5.38)$$

This gives $x = \sqrt{\frac{c}{3d}}$ and the corresponding maximum force can be observe as $\sqrt{\frac{4c^3}{27d}}$. Therefore,

$$C_0 \sin(wt) < \sqrt{\frac{4c^3}{27d}} \qquad (5.39)$$

In order to obtain a maximal signal, it is assumed that sine term attains its maximum value. Thus, Eq. (5.39) reduces to the following.

$$1 < \sqrt{\frac{4c^3}{27d}} \qquad (5.40)$$

This essentially implies that $d < \frac{4c^3}{27}$ for a weak input signal. Finally, the values of parameters are taken in a manner so that maximum correlation coefficients can be achieved. The desired maximum correlation coefficients can be obtained by taking the values of parameters as $c = \sigma_0^2$ and $d < 4c^3/27$.

5.6   Proposed Watermarking Technique

The basic steps involved in the designing of the proposed watermarking scheme have been explained in this section. The procedure initiates with the transformation of the cover image into frequency domain and then watermark embedding is carried out using the singular values. At the receiver end, a DSR based approach is employed for watermark extraction. The DSR based approaches mainly depend on the selection bistable parameters and therefore, parameters are optimized to improve the performance of the scheme.

5.6.1   Embedding Process

Let H and W represent the gray-scale host and watermark image of size $M \times N$ and $m \times n$ respectively. The embedding procedure is briefly described as follows:

1. The host image (H) is partitioned into different blocks of size $k \times k$ and then apply the APDBT on each block. Let H_f denote transformed image.

$$H_f = APDBT\{H\} \tag{5.41}$$

2. Extract singular values of the watermark W and transformed image H_f.

$$W = U_w S_w V_w^T \tag{5.42}$$

$$H_f = U_f S_f V_f^T \tag{5.43}$$

3. Embed the singular values of the transformed image H_f as follows.

$$H_f^{\ w} = S_f + \alpha * S_w \tag{5.44}$$

where α represent the payload factors.

4. Apply the inverse SVD process to construct the $H_f^{\ new}$ as follows.

$$H_f^{\ new} = U_f H_f^{\ w} V_f^T \tag{5.45}$$

5. Modified coefficients $\left(H_f^{new}\right)$ are partitioned into the different blocks and each block is transformed using inverse IAPDBT to produce the watermarked image H_W as:

$$H_W = IAPDBT\{H_f^{new}\} \tag{5.46}$$

5.6.2 Extraction Process

The extraction process is deployed to obtain an estimate of the watermark from the watermarked image. The steps involved in the extraction process are described as follows:

1. Watermarked image H_W is divided into non-overlapping blocks of size $k \times k$ and then apply the APDBT on each block. Let H_W^f denote transformed watermarked image and is given by following equation:

$$H_f^{W} = APDBT\{H_W\} \tag{5.47}$$

2. Extract singular values of the transformed watermarked image H_f^W.

$$H_f^{W} = U_f^W S_f^W V_f^{W^T} \tag{5.48}$$

3. Dynamic stochastic resonance (DSR) process is initialized using the singular values and the corresponding bistable system parameters as given below:

$$x(0) = 0; c = 2 * \sigma_k^2; d = k * \frac{4c^3}{27} \tag{5.49}$$

where σ_k is the standard deviation of singular values of the watermarked image in APDBT domain, k is an empirical factor and is set to less than one ($k < 1$) to ensure the sub threshold condition in DSR.

4. Obtained the tuned coefficients of input vector in the iterative process as discussed in Eq. (5.36).

5. Estimate singular values of the extracted watermark from the DSR enhanced singular values as given below:

$$\mu_{ext} = \frac{x_i - \mu_{S_f}}{\alpha} \tag{5.50}$$

where μ_{ext} are extracted bits of watermark, μ_{S_f} are singular values of transformed image and $x = \{x_i | i = 1 \cdots n\}$ is the set of DSR tuned singular values.

6. Obtained an estimate of watermark image (W_{ext}) using inverse SVD transform and singular vector as follows:

$$W_{ext} = U_w * \mu_{ext} * V_w^T \tag{5.51}$$

7. The estimated watermark is compared with original one by computing the correlation coefficients (ρ). To make the proposed algorithm adaptive, the iterative process continue until the jth iteration, in which ρ start decreasing after attaining its maximum value. The watermark corresponding to maximum ρ is the optimal and final watermark image.

5.7 Experimental Results and Discussions

The performance of the proposed scheme is examined through a series of experiments using MATLAB platform on a PC with core i5 processor and 4 GB RAM. In these experiments, four gray-scale images namely Barbara, Lake, Pirate and House of size 256×256, are considered as the host images whereas four gray-scale logos image namely copyright sign, cross sign, circle and tree are taken as the watermark. The host image and corresponding watermarks are of same the size as shown in Fig. 5.7. The quality of watermarked image is evaluated quantitatively using peak signal-to-noise ratio (PSNR). The PSNR value is controlled by a parameter α. In general, if the value of α is decreased then the perceptual fidelity of watermarked image will increase and vice versa. However, this change will affect the robustness of the scheme and Hence, a trade-off can be observe between the perceptual fidelity and robustness of the scheme. The empirical optimal value of α is set to 0.03 to achieve the optimal results. Mathematically, PSNR between two images f and g can be computed as follows:

$$PSNR(f, g) = 10 \log_{10} \frac{255^2}{\frac{1}{M \times N} \sum_{a,b} [f(a, b) - g(a, b)]^2} \tag{5.52}$$

where $M \times N$ denote the size of the image. The PSNR value of watermarked image Lena, Barbra, Boat and House are 30.56, 29.54, 28.78, and 29.11 respectively.

In extraction process, the embedded watermark is extracted from the watermarked image and then compared with the original one to verify the presence of the watermark. For this purpose, the normalized correlation is estimated between the embedded and extracted watermark. Mathematically, normalized correlation (ρ) is computed as follows:

$$\rho(H, W) = \frac{\sum_{\mathscr{C}_1, \mathscr{C}_2} (H(\mathscr{C}_1, \mathscr{C}_2) - \mu_H)(W(\mathscr{C}_1, \mathscr{C}_2) - \mu_W)}{\sqrt{\sum_{\mathscr{C}_1, \mathscr{C}_2} (H(\mathscr{C}_1, \mathscr{C}_2) - \mu_H)^2} \sqrt{\sum_{\mathscr{C}_1 \mathscr{C}_2} (W(\mathscr{C}_1, \mathscr{C}_2) - \mu_W)^2}} \tag{5.53}$$

Table 5.1 Estimated correlation coefficients for experimental images

Image	APDBST		APDBCT	
	ρ	Iterations	ρ	Iterations
Barbara	1.00	46	1.00	44
Lake	0.9999	49	1.00	41
Pirate	0.9999	58	0.9999	56
House	0.9999	53	1.00	53

where H and W represent the original and extracted watermark images with their respective mean as μ_H and μ_W. The principle range of ρ lie between 0 and 1. If ρ attains the value one then, it indicates the maximum correlation. However, if ρ attains the value zero then it imply that there is no correlation between the images. The normalization coefficients between the embedded and extracted watermarks are computed for the experimental images considering the all phase discrete sine and cosine orthogonal transforms. The estimated values are depicted in Table 5.1. The watermarked image and corresponding extracted watermarks are shown in Fig. 5.7.

5.7.1 Parameter Optimization

Dynamic stochastic resonance (DSR) is optimized by the bistable potential parameters c, d, m, and δt. The optimal values of these parameters reduce the computational load and maximize the correlation. Generally, the value of bistable parameter m is set to less than one for the requirement of the subthreshold condition of the DSR. The optimal value of m is found to be 0.0001 and with this optimized value, the value of c which corresponds the maximum value of ρ is considered as the optimum value of c. The optimal values of c and δt are 0.05 and 0.055 respectively.

The number of iteration required for maximum value of ρ in the adaptive process is considered as optimal iteration index. The optimal iteration count is 49 for the watermark extraction. The graph of correlation coefficients (ρ) and number of iterations have been shown in Fig. 5.8a. In addition, the variation in correlation coefficients is also evaluated with DSR parameter c as shown in Fig. 5.8b and it can be observe that correlation is increased and attains the highest value at particular level and then start decreasing. This level gives the optimal value of a. It shows the converging nature of DSR and achieve the stability at the converging point. This verify the resonant nature of DSR system with optimal bistable parameters.

5.7.2 Robustness Analysis

Robustness is one of the important characteristic of a watermarking system. Generally, a good watermarking scheme should be robust enough against different

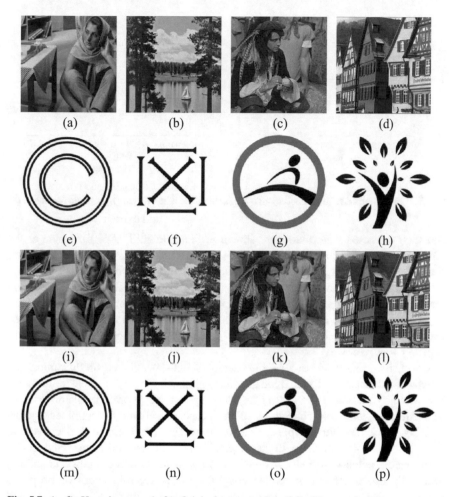

Fig. 5.7 (**a–d**) Host images; (**e–h**) Original watermarks; (**i–l**) Watermarked images; (**m–p**) Extracted watermarks

kind of attacks. Therefore, the robustness of proposed scheme is examined using a series of attacks namely Gaussian noise addition, salt and pepper noise, speckle noise, average and median filtering, Gaussian blur, JPEG compression, resizing, cropping, rotation, histogram equalization, sharpening, contrast adjustment, gamma correction, row-column deletion and wrapping. Noise addition is one of the main reason which can degrade the quality of watermarked as well as hidden information. Therefore, Gaussian noise addition (40%), salt and pepper noise (40%) and speckle noise (40%) are applied on the watermarked image to measure the effectiveness of proposed scheme against noisy attacks. After these attacks, the watermarks are extracted from the noisy watermarked images and compared with the original one in terms of normalization coefficients. The noisy images are shown in Fig. 5.9a–c

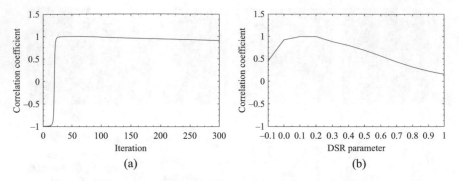

Fig. 5.8 Estimated correlation coefficient with: (**a**) numbers of iterations, (**b**) bistable parameter (*c*)

and their extracted watermarks are shown in Fig. 5.9e–g. The performance of the proposed scheme is measured against the average and median filtering with filter size (7 × 7). The watermark logos are extracted form the filtered image and normalized correlation is computed with the original watermarks. The average and median filtered image is depicted in Fig. 5.9d, i and corresponding watermarks are depicted in Fig. 5.9h, m. The watermarked is extracted from the Gaussian blurred watermarked image. The blurred image and extracted watermark are shown in Fig. 5.9j, n respectively.

Geometric distortions are another set of attacks which majorly affects the watermarked image and their hidden information. Therefore, an ideal watermarking scheme must have the ability to resist against the geometric distortion. For performance evaluation, robustness of the proposed scheme is examined against resizing attack. For this purpose, size of the watermarked image is decreased to 64 × 64 and then scale up to its original size. The resized image and corresponding extracted watermark is depicted in Fig. 5.9l, p. Image rotation is another frequently use operation in day to day life. Therefore, robustness of proposed scheme is also tested against image rotation. The watermarked image is rotated by 30° in counter-clockwise direction and then watermark is extracted from the rotated image. Both, rotated image and extracted watermark are shown in Fig. 5.9r, v respectively. In addition, efficiency of the proposed scheme is also tested against image cropping by erasing 50% area of the watermarked image, i.e., gray values of that area of the watermarked image is mapped to zero. The cropped watermarked image and the extracted watermark are shown in Fig. 5.9q, u. The visual quality of the extracted watermarks from the geometrically modified watermarked images indicate the higher degree of robustness of the proposed scheme.

Data compression is an important tool for efficient transmission and widely used to reduce the storage requirement of multimedia data. Therefore, performance of the proposed scheme is also analyzed through lossy compression. For this purpose,

Fig. 5.9 Attacked watermarked images: (**a**) Gaussian noise (40%), (**b**) salt and pepper noise (40%), (**c**) speckle noise (40%), (**d**) average filter (7 × 7), (**i**) median filter (7 × 7), (**j**) Gaussian blur (7 × 7), (**k**) JPEG compression (95%), (**l**) resizing (256 → 64 → 256), (**q**) cropping (50%), (**r**) rotation (30°), (**s**) histogram equalization, (**t**) sharpen (100%); second, fourth and sixth rows shows the corresponding extracted watermark

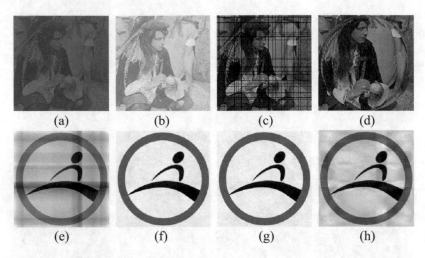

Fig. 5.10 (**a**) Contrast adjustment (-100%), (**b**) gamma correction ($\gamma = 3.5$), (**c**) row-column deletion, (**d**) wrapping (100%); second rows shows the corresponding extracted watermarks

watermark is extracted after applying JPEG compression (95%) on the watermarked image. The compressed image and corresponding extracted watermark are shown in Fig. 5.9k, o. Experimental analysis is extended to histogram equalization and image sharpen operation. The sharpening of the watermarked image is increased by 100%. The visual quality of affected images are depicted in Fig. 5.9s, t and the corresponding extracted watermarks are shown in Fig. 5.9w, x respectively. Moreover, efficiency of the proposed scheme is also tested against contrast adjustment and gamma correction operations. The contrast of the watermarked image is decreased by 100 % and watermarked image is corrected with $\gamma = 3.5$. The attacked image and corresponding watermarks are shown in Fig. 5.10a, b, e, f, respectively.

The robustness of the proposed framework is also tested against row-column deletion and image wrapping which is shown in Fig. 5.10c, d. In row-column deletion, twenty rows and columns are randomly deleted from the watermarked image. The extracted watermark form the row-column deleted and wrapped image is depicted in Fig. 5.10g, h respectively. From the Figs. 5.9 and 5.10, it can be observed that visual quality of extracted watermark form the attacked images is recognizable and perceptually similar to the original watermark. The same observation may be confirmed by the Table 5.2, where the correlation coefficients are listed for the extracted watermarks after attacks. Therefore, results indicate that higher level robustness is achieved against most of the attacks.

Table 5.2   Estimated correlation coefficients in watermark extraction after attacks

	APDBST		APDBCT	
Image	ρ	Iterations	ρ	Iterations
Gaussian noise addition (40%)	0.9590	68	0.9519	63
Salt and pepper noise (40%)	0.9826	66	0.9819	66
Speckle noise (40% area)	0.9901	56	0.9889	56
Gaussian blur (7×7)	0.9769	69	0.9768	69
Average filter (7×7)	0.9793	47	0.9508	59
Median filter (7×7)	0.9823	63	0.9822	62
Resizing ($256 \rightarrow 64 \rightarrow 256$)	0.9901	55	0.9899	55
Cropping (50%)	0.9790	83	0.9442	126
Rotation ($30°$)	−0.9952	11	−0.9951	37
Histogram equalization	0.9877	43	0.9873	36
Sharpen (100%)	0.7005	126	0.7638	104
Contrast adjustment (-100%))	0.9290	300	0.9309	300
Gamma correction ($\gamma = 3.5$)	0.9996	144	0.9996	142
Wrapping (100%)	0.9862	62	0.9860	61
JPEG compression (95%)	0.9955	88	0.9954	89
Row-column deletion (20R–20C)	0.9903	51	0.9793	49

5.8   Conclusions and Future Directions

In this chapter, a robust watermarking scheme has been presented using singular value decomposition (SVD), all phase discrete biorthogonal transformation (APDBT) and dynamic stochastic resonance (DSR). A remarkable improvement have been achieved in robustness against geometric and image processing attacks. A DSR based approach is employed in the extraction process which essentially improves the extraction of watermark. The noise introduced during the attack utilized to suppress the effect of noise which improves the overall performance of the scheme. An adaptive process is applied to optimized the bi-stable parameter to ensure the less computational complexity. The simulation results and analysis validate the feasibility of the proposed watermarking technique.

Based on our research experiences, the further research work can be summarized as follows:

- The proposed techniques are non-blind techniques and can be extended to make it blind.
- A further intensification in the proposed techniques could be possible, wherein the proposed techniques could be employed to protect different types of audio and video files.
- The current trend is to use multicore computing for an ease and the legitimate owner information also needs to be preserved. It could be a good future direction of research to deploy the proposed technique under multi-core platforms like NVIDIA-CUDA, ATI Radeon, etc.

References

1. Menezes, A.J., Van Oorschot, P.C. and Vanstone, S.A., Handbook of applied cryptography, CRC press, Boca Raton, (1996).
2. Singh S.P., Bhatnagar G., Gurjar D.K., A secure image encryption algorithm based on polar decomposition, International Colloquium on Signal Processing & Its Applications, pp 135–139, (2018).
3. Singh, S.P. and Bhatnagar, G., A robust image hashing based on discrete wavelet transform, International Conference on Signal and Image Processing Applications (ICSIPA), pp. 440–444, (2017).
4. Stallings, W., Cryptography and Network Security: Principles and Practice, Prentice-Hall, Upper Saddle River, (1999).
5. Katzenbeisser, S. and Petitcolas, F. A. P., Information hiding techniques for steganography and digital watermarking, Artech House, Boston, (2002).
6. Cox, I.J., Miller, M.L. and Bloom, J.A., Digital watermarking, Morgan Kaufmann, San Francisco, (2001).
7. Arnold, M., Schmucker, M. and Wolthusen, S.D., Techniques and applications of digital watermarking and content protection, Artech House, (2003).
8. Muharemagic, E. and Furht, B., Multimedia Security: Watermarking Techniques, Comprehensive Report on Information Security, International Engineering Consortium, Chicago, (2004).
9. Bhatnagar, G. and Raman, B., A new robust reference watermarking scheme based on DWT-SVD, Computer Standards & Interfaces, 31(5), pp. 1002–1013, (2009).
10. Izquierdo, E., Fragile watermarking for image authentication, Multimedia Security Handbook, CRC Press, Boca Raton, (2005).
11. Zhu, X., Ho, A.T.S. and Marziliano, P., A new semi-fragile image watermarking with robust tampering restoration using irregular sampling, Signal Processing, Image Communication, 22(5), pp. 515–528, (2007).
12. Schyndle, R.G.V., Tirkel, A.Z. and Osbrone, C.F., A Digital Watermark, International Conference on Image Processing, 2, pp. 86–90, (1994).
13. Bender, W., Gruhl, D., Morimoto, N. and Lu, A., Techniques for data hiding, IBM Systems Journal, 35(3-4), pp. 313–336, (1996).
14. Nikolaidis N. and Pitas I., Copyright protection of images using robust digital signatures, International Conference on Acoustics, Speech, Signal Processing, 4, pp. 2168–2171, (1996).
15. Voyatzis G. and Pitas I., Applications of toral automorphisms in image watermarking, International Conference on Image Processing, 2, pp. 237–240, (1996).
16. Pitas I. and Kaskalis, T.H., Applying signatures on digital images, Workshop on Non-linear Signal and Image Processing, pp. 460–463, (1995).
17. Perez-Freire L. and Perez-Gonzalez F., Spread-spectrum watermarking security, IEEE Transactions on Information Forensics and Security, 4(1), pp. 2–24, (2009).
18. Bas, P. and Furon, T., A new measure of watermarking security: The effective key length, IEEE Transactions on Information Forensics and Security, 8(8), pp. 1306–1317, pp. (2013).
19. Chen S. T., Huang H. N., Kung, W. M. and Hsu, C. Y., Optimization-based image watermarking with integrated quantization embedding in the wavelet-domain, Multimedia Tools and Applications, 75(10), pp. 5493–5511, (2016).
20. Singh S. P. and Bhatnagar G., A novel chaos based robust watermarking framework, International Conference on Computer Vision and Image Processing, 2, pp. 439–447, (2017).
21. Cox, I.J., Killian, J., Leighton, F.T. and Shamoon, T., Secure spread spectrum watermarking for multimedia, IEEE Transaction on Image Processing, 6(12), pp. 1673–1687, (1997).
22. Barni, M., Bartiloni, F. and Piva, A., Improved wavelet based watermarking through pixel wise masking, IEEE Transactions on Image Processing, 10, pp. 783–791, (2001).
23. Huang, J., Shi, Y.Q. and Shi, Y., Embedding image watermarks in dc components, IEEE Transactions on Circuits and Systems for Video Technology, 10(6), pp. 974–979, (2000).

24. Tao, H., Chongmin, L., Zain, J.M. and Abdalla, A.N., Robust image watermarking theories and techniques: A review, Journal of applied research and technology, 12(1), pp. 122–138, (2014).
25. Daren, H., Jiufen, L., Jiwu, H. and Hongmei, L., A DWT-based image watermarking algorithm, International Conference on Multimedia and Expo, pp. 313–316, (2001).
26. Serdean, C.V., Ambroze, M.A., Tomlinson, M. and Wade, J.G., DWT-based high-capacity blind video watermarking, invariant to geometrical attacks, Image and Signal Processing, 150(1), pp. 51–58, (2003).
27. Wenwu Zhu, Zixiang Xiong, and Ya-Qin Zhang, Multiresolution watermarking for images and video, IEEE Transactions on Circuits and Systems for Video Technology, 9(4), pp. 545–550, (1999).
28. Liu, R. and Tan, T., An SVD-Based Watermarking Scheme for Protecting Rightful Ownership, IEEE Transactions on Multimedia 4(1), pp. 121–128, (2002).
29. Ganic, E., Zubair, N. and Eskicioglu, A.M., An Optimal watermarking scheme based on singular value decomposition, International Conference on Communication, Network, and Information Security, pp. 85–90, (2003).
30. Ganic, E. and Eskicioglu, A.M., Robust embedding of visual watermarks using DWT-SVD, Journal of Electronic Imaging, (2005).
31. Lin, W. H., Horng, S. J., Kao, T. W., Fan, P., Lee, C. L. and Pan, Y., An efficient watermarking method based on significant difference of wavelet coefficient quantization, IEEE Transactions on Multimedia, 10(5), pp. 746–757, (2008).
32. Zhao, Y., Campisi, P. and Kundur, D., Dual domain watermarking for authentication and compression of cultural heritage images, IEEE Transactions on Image Processing, 13(3), pp. 430–448, (2004).
33. Singh S.P., Bhatnagar G., A robust watermarking scheme based on image normalization, International Colloquium on Signal Processing & Its Applications, pp 140–144, (2018).
34. Singh A.K., Kumar B, Singh S.K., Ghrera SP, Mohan A, Multiple watermarking technique for securing online social network contents using back propagation neural network, Future Generation Computer Systems, (2016).
35. Kumar C, Singh AK, Kumar P, Singh R, Singh S., SPIHT-based multiple image watermarking in NSCT domain, Concurrency and Computation: Practice and Experience, e4912, (2018).
36. Singh L, Singh AK, Singh PK, Secure data hiding techniques: a survey, Multimedia Tools and Applications, pp. 1–21, (2018).
37. Wu, G. and Qiu, Z., A novel watermarking scheme based on stochastic resonance, In: Proceedings of 8th International Conference on Signal Processing, 2, pp. 1–4, (2006).
38. Sun, S. and Lei, B., On an aperiodic stochastic resonance signal processor and its application in digital watermarking, Signal Processing, 88(8), pp. 2085–2094, (2008).
39. Chouhan R., Jha R.K., Chaturvedi A., Yamasaki T. and Aizawa K., Robust watermark extraction using SVD-based dynamic stochastic resonance, International Conference on Image Processing, 11, pp. 2745–2748, (2011).
40. Jha, R. K., Chouhan, R. and Aizawa, K., Dynamic stochastic resonance-based improved logo extraction in discrete cosine transform domain, Computers and Electrical Engineering, 40(6), pp. 1917–1929, (2014).
41. Jha, R. K., Biswas, P. K. and Shrivastava, S., Logo extraction using dynamic stochastic resonance, Signal, Image and Video Processing, 7(1), pp. 119–128, (2013).
42. Chouhan, R., Jha, R. K., Chaturvedi, A., Yamasaki, T. and Aizawa, K., Robust watermark extraction using SVD-based dynamic stochastic resonance, International Conference on Image Processing, pp. 2745–2748, (2011).
43. Singh, S.P., and Bhatnagar, G., A new robust watermarking system in integer DCT domain, Journal of Visual Communication and Image Representation, 53, pp. 86–101, (2018).
44. Wei, J.J., Chang, C.J., Chou, N.K. and Jan, G.J., ECG data compression using truncated singular value decomposition, IEEE Transactions on Information Technology in Biomedicine, 5(4), pp. 290–299, (2001).

45. Beltrami, E.: Sulle funzioni bilineari (On Bilinear Functions), Giornale di Matematiche ad Uso degli Studenti Delle Universita 11, pp. 98–106, (1873); An English translation by Boley, D. Tech. Report, Dept. of Computer Science, Univ. of Minnesota, Minneapolis, pp. 90–37, (1990).

46. Jordan, C., Memoire sur les formes bilineaires (Memoir on Bilinear Forms), Journal de Mathematiques Pures et Appliquees, Deuxieme Serie 19, pp. 35–54, (1874).

47. Eckart, C. and Young, G., The approximation of one matrix by another of lower rank, Psychometrika 1, pp. 211–218, (1936).

48. Andrews, H. and Patterson, C., Singular value decompositions and digital image processing, IEEE Transactions on Acoustics, Speech, and Signal Processing, 24(1), pp. 26–53, (1976).

49. Hou, Z. X., Wang, C. Y. and Yang, A. P., All phase biorthogonal transform and its application in JPEG-like image compression, Signal Processing: Image Communication, 24(10), pp. 791–802, (2009).

50. Hou, Z. and Yang, X., The all phase DFT filter, In Proc. of the 10th Digital Signal Processing (DSP) Workshop and Signal Processing Education (SPE) Workshop, pp. 221–226, (2002).

51. Hou, Z. X., Wang, Z. H., and Yang, X., Design and implementation of all phase DFT digital filter, Acta Electronica Sinica, 31(4), pp. 539–543, (2003).

52. Budagavi, M., Fuldseth, A. and Bjontegaard, G., HEVC transform and quantization, In High Efficiency Video Coding (HEVC), pp. 141–169, (2014).

53. Ahmed, N., Natarajan, T. and Rao, K.R., Discrete cosine transform, IEEE transactions on Computers, 100(1), pp. 90–93, (1974).

54. Zhou, X., Wang, C. and Jiang, B., All phase inverse discrete sine biorthogonal transform and its application in image coding, Journal of Communications, 12(1), (2017).

55. Benzi, R., Sutera, A. and Vulpiani, A., The mechanism of stochastic resonance, Journal of Physics A: mathematical and general, 14(11), (1981).

56. Gammaitoni, L., Hanggi, P., Jung, P. and Marchesoni, F., Stochastic resonance, Reviews of Modern Physics, 70(1), pp. 223–287, (1998).

57. Leng, Y. G., Wang, T. Y., Guo, Y., Xu, Y. G., and Fan, S. B., Engineering signal processing based on bistable stochastic resonance, Mechanical Systems and Signal Processing, 21(1), pp. 138–150, (2007).

58. Horsthemke, W., and Lefever, R., Noise-induced transitions in physics, chemistry, and biology, Noise-induced transitions: theory and applications in physics, chemistry, and biology, pp. 164–200, (1984).

59. Hongler, M. O., de Meneses, Y. L., Beyeler, A., and Jacot, J., The resonant retina: exploiting vibration noise to optimally detect edges in an image, IEEE Transactions on Pattern Analysis and Machine Intelligence, 25(9), pp. 1051–1062, (2003).

60. Badzey, R. L., and Mohanty, P., Coherent signal amplification in bistable nanomechanical oscillators by stochastic resonance, Nature, pp. 995–998, (2005).

61. Anishchenko, V.S., Neiman, A.B., Moss, F. and Schimansky-Geier, L., Stochastic Resonance: noise-enhanced order, Physics-Uspekhi, 42(1), pp. 7–36, (1999).

62. Hannes R., The Fokker-Planck Equation, Berlin, Heidelberg, (1996).

63. Gard, T.C., Introduction to Stochastic Differential Equation, Marcel-Dekker, New York, 1998.

Chapter 6
A Secure Medical Image Watermarking Technique for E-Healthcare Applications

Nasir N. Hurrah, Shabir A. Parah, and Javaid A. Sheikh

6.1 Introduction

The rapid advancements in technology has equipped designers with easy to use and low-cost methods to analyze and treat diseases. If the patient medical records collected across providers in the form of electronic medical record (EMR) by different systems and wearables is merged, the organization and processing of data is possible beyond current clinical scenarios. Thankfully advances in system automation and cloud architectures can significantly reduce or eliminate many of the risks in diagnosis/treatment associated with healthcare setup. When worked in combination, the care-takers and patients can lead to efficient ways of patient health monitoring and diagnosis, enabling accurate adjustment treatments. While there are opportunities there are also many challenges which can be dealt with by intelligently combining and using clinical and consumer source data. Also passive technologies can be used to better track patient data in order to reduce risks by automatic system recovery. So it is now possible to provide better healthcare through better technology. For example, IOT has proven to be an efficient technology which has equipped different systems in the E-healthcare sector to collect medical information from easy to use devices, view patient information and diagnose in real-time [1, 2]. Effective healthcare depends on accuracy and speed of its services, for that a huge range of devices connected as IOT takes hold. It has been estimated that about 50% of devices using healthcare networking platforms will be based on IoT systems in the next few years. The devices ranging from handheld modules to recording systems to other healthcare equipment's, the industries are progressing towards a central system of connected things. Using the latest state of devices, the

N. N. Hurrah · S. A. Parah (✉) · J. A. Sheikh
Department of Electronics and Instrumentation Technology, University of Kashmir, Srinagar, Jammu and Kashmir, India

© Springer Nature Switzerland AG 2019
A. K. Singh, A. Mohan (eds.), *Handbook of Multimedia Information Security: Techniques and Applications*, https://doi.org/10.1007/978-3-030-15887-3_6

monitoring and managing of patients has become easy and saves lot of valuable time. The doctors can diagnose/track numerous patients remotely and prescribe effective treatments. This is achieved by utilizing sensors employed in medical devices which are connected through internet.

The rise in exchange of information through various networks using internet has posed numerous security issues to both the users and service providers. In addition, the availability of different data editing tools and hacking software's, the risk to the information exchanged through different networks is also rising. In this scenario most of the agencies and organizations spend a lot of money to secure the information exchanged/stored while dealing with sharing of data. With the increase of data exchange over various networks, the requirement of designs which are theft-proof, hack-proof and piracy-proof has increased proportionally. In past few years, various state of art solutions have been proposed by researchers and other concerned institutions to curb the menace of data breaches [3–6]. The main focus of the people has been mainly in the health sector, film industry, defense, space communication and social media. But until now no method has been devised which can provide complete security to the data exchange. In contrast, the new challenges are rising rapidly due to the vulnerability of the insecure networks to adversaries. In this scenario, it is highly needed to devise a framework which can ensure the best possible security and privacy to the users exchanging sensitive information.

The medical images shared in an e-healthcare system are very sensitive to any data breach as they carry patient's private information necessary for treatment of various diseases. Any change in this medical data can lead to the diagnosis which may result to wrong treatments and even death [7–12]. In case of e-healthcare applications it is necessary to ensure integrity and better security while sharing of medical images. Privacy and copyright protection are the key requirements to ensure trustworthy exchange of information over different platforms which are usually insecure. In order to achieve the above discussed requirements the information is usually pre-processed before transmission/storage. These pre-processing operations include filtering, compression, equalization and various geometrical operations. Conventional data security procedures are able to ensure data security to some extent but the level of resistance against most of the commonly occurring attacks is not met up to an efficient level. Digital watermarking (WM) technique, which involves hiding of some secret data in some cover media has proven to be one of the best technique for securing information exchange. The data hiding in watermarking involves the state of art mechanisms which ensure that visual quality is kept intact even after embedding additional data. The cover media in which secret data, known as watermark, is stored may be an image, audio or video file [13–15].

Digital watermarking algorithms are usually implemented according to the requirement of application in one of the two domains: spatial domain or transform domain. Spatial domain based schemes offer simple design, low computational complexity and good perceptual quality of watermarked images but the robustness is weak against signal processing attacks. In contrast, the schemes implemented in transform domain high robustness to the watermark at the cost of some design complexity. The commonly used transform domains include DCT, DWT, SVD and IWT. The watermarking techniques can also be categorized on the basis of need of original image at the time of extraction of watermark. Whereas blind WM techniques doesn't require original image for extraction of watermark, non-blind technique requires original image. The blind techniques are popular ones due to the fact that the load on the bandwidth and storage is less as watermark can be extracted remotely without need of cover image [3, 8]. On the basis of requirement of an application the WM techniques can be further categorized in robust and fragile techniques. Whereas robust WM techniques are devised for application where copyright protection is main requirement, the fragile techniques are devised for application with authentication and tamper detection as main requirement [16, 17]. The robust watermark remains intact if the image is attacked by the unauthorized user while as fragile watermark gets destroyed with any kind of manipulation to indicate tampering [18]. The robust WM schemes show better performance if embedding is done in transform domain while as fragile WM schemes are generally implemented in spatial domain [18–22].

It is generally required for watermarking schemes to be multipurpose such that a single scheme can work for different applications. But majority of WM schemes proposed until now generally target a particular requirement such that a separate algorithm is needed for every application. In this chapter a robust watermarking scheme has been proposed with high level security in order to ensure the originality and authenticity of the embedded data while being received. This is done by scrambling the secret data to be embedded via a unique key followed by embedding of this encrypted data by modifying the transform domain coefficients of the cover image. The cover image is divided into blocks of fixed size followed by application of transform domain technique (DCT) on the blocks. Watermark is then embedded in SVD coefficients by application of proposed watermarking algorithm. The experimental results show that the scheme offers a great imperceptivity and robustness against all intentional/unintentional signal processing and geometrical attacks.

6.2   Literature Review

The recent trend in data exchange through various networking channels has put the privacy of the data at high risk. The research on data hiding increased many folds to counter the issues. Data hiding techniques have proven to be highly effective ensuring integrity, privacy and authenticity of the images along with most desirable demand of copyright protection. Since the demand for exchange of medical images and their storage between patients, doctors and institutes over the internet and other networks has increased in recent years. The need for securing this data exchange has also increased rapidly and millions of dollars are being spent throughout the globe to achieve this aim. Digital image watermarking techniques is one of the effective data hiding techniques used for hiding the medical information in some other media to ensure this security. The WM schemes are either implemented in pixel (spatial) domain or coefficient (frequency) domain [23–25]. The spatial domain data hiding techniques involve embedding of the secret data directly in the original pixel intensities of the cover image. The transform domain techniques first transform the pixels in frequency domain coefficients and then carry out the process of data embedding. The coefficients needed for embedding are obtained after application of transforms like DWT, DCT, IWT etc. is achieved by using transforms live Although the spatial domain techniques are easy to implement the robustness of the embedded watermark is weak against most of the signal processing attacks [26]. However, they are suitable for the applications where authentication of the information is key requirement along the design simplicity. In order to achieve high level of robustness the transform domain techniques have proven to be highly effective [27–29].

A Digital Watermarking has been implemented by using combination of a spatial domain technique (SVD) and a transform domain technique (DWT). After applying fourth level DWT to the medical image the singular value of HH band is exchanged with singular value of watermark image to complete the embedding process. The watermark authenticity is checked at the receiver by comparing the watermark signature in the received image with the already available watermark. For extraction of the watermark signature the authorized users need the original watermark and technique as such is non blind as we always require the original watermark. Also since high frequency coefficients have been used for embedding watermark the robustness of the scheme should be quite low and as such has not been evaluated [30]. In [31] a blind and robust watermarking technique has been proposed in the DCT domain using inter-block coefficient differencing method. The cover image is divided in blocks each of size 8 × 8 and DCT is applied on each block. From the two neighbouring blocks the difference between to coefficients at predefined locations is calculated and the coefficients are modified according to the watermark bit to be embedded. The proposed scheme performs well in terms of robustness when subjected to various image processing attacks. A robust watermarking technique based on both DCT and DWT domains applicable to medical images has been proposed in [32]. The cover image is divided in the two regions: region of interest (ROI) and region of non interest (RONI). In the two regions an image watermark and a text watermark is embedded. The security of the watermarks has been achieved by using Rivest-Shamir-Adleman (RSA) encryption technique. In [33] a blind and robust watermark method based on Lift Wavelet Transform (LWT) has been proposed. The LWT offers the energy compaction property which is used along with a block based concept to achieve a good resistance against image distortion and a better security as compared to previous traditional techniques. The limitation of the technique is its poor robustness performance in presence of salt & pepper noise and some of the geometrical and filtering attacks.

For achieving high level of security multiple transform domain techniques have been used in many techniques which ensure employment of their combined advantages in one scheme. Such schemes offer high level of robustness and security to the embedded watermark. Kang et al. [34] has proposed an image watermarking scheme using combination of DWT and DFT. In order to embed watermark the proposed algorithm takes advantage of their decomposition property and mid frequency coefficients are used for embedding. Feng et al. [35] proposed a DCT-DWT based blind watermarking scheme in which two PN-sequences of an encrypted watermark is embedded in an image. For embedding this watermark DWT is applied on the cover image and LL sub-band is used for carrying out block based DCT transform. From these DCT blocks watermark is embedded in the mid-frequency coefficients. Laskar et al. [36] has proposed a similar technique wherein cover image is subjected to many stages of DWT transform and resulting sub-bands are used to carry out embedding of the watermark. Similarly, Benoraira et al. [37] proposed a watermarking scheme based on DCT-DWT domains but the watermark embedding capacity is very low, only 256 bits.

Previously mentioned schemes lack the important factor that is essential for robustness of the watermark embedded in a cover image i.e. security. The security is important parameter considering the case when an unauthorized person succeeds in cracking extraction algorithm to access the watermark information. If there is no watermark security procedure the information may be lost to this attacker easily. However, if the watermark security mechanism has been devised the attacker will get no information without the secret keys only know to authorized users. In order to secure the watermark various encryption/encoding techniques available can be employed [38–40]. For copyright protection of the information a robust WM technique using chaotic encryption has been presented in [41]. A similar watermark approach for both medical and general images using swap permutation approach along with nonlinear inter-pixel computation has been proposed in [42]. Chaotic encryption has been used to secure watermark information. In [43] a robust image encryption technique has been proposed by employing chaotic maps. The robustness against differential and statistical attacks has been achieved by using block mixing procedure.

As discussed, the most of the techniques proposed till now only offer better imperceptivity or security or robustness and as such no technique offers the discussed factors simultaneously. To meet all the above discussed requirement a secure digital image watermarking technique has been proposed which offers high imperceptivity along with efficient robustness performance to both singular and combined attacks. A combination of spatial/transform domain techniques is used to achieve high level robustness and better security of the electronic health record. Digital Watermarking algorithm is implemented using combination DCT and SVD. As such proposed watermarking technique utilizes the strengths of both the spatial and transform domain. The efficiency of the proposed system is checked for various attacks. The technique offers better data hiding solution for copyright protection evident from both objective and subjective results obtained. The balance between imperceptivity and robustness has been achieved by embedding the watermark after optimal modification of the singular values of the DCT coefficients. The security of the watermark has been ensured by two level encryption using Arnold transform along with chaos encryption.

6.3 Preliminaries

In the proposed scheme several state of art procedures are employed at different stages to achieve the robust and secure watermarking system. Two main techniques used for achieving the goal of high robustness are DCT and SVD. DCT is a transform domain technique and SVD is a spatial domain technique. DCT has been discussed thoroughly in various papers [44]. Since embedding is done by using the matrices obtained after applying SVD, a brief discussion on SVD with be carried out in this section.

6.3.1 Singular Value Decomposition (SVD)

SVD is a matrix decomposition technique which applied on a rectangular matrix (R) results in a column matrix of non-negative real values in decreasing order. These values are called singular values and the first value is the largest value of this column vector, 'S'. The SVD operation is usually represented as a group of vectors with different properties as below:

$$R = U^*S^*V \tag{6.1}$$

where 'U' is the left singular vector matrix, 'V' is the right singular vector matrix and 'S' is a diagonal matrix of singular values. As already mentioned the values of the singular matrix are zero except diagonal ones which are positive real values. The values of matrices 'U' and 'V' are integer values less than unity such that both matrices are orthonormal with $UU^T = I$ and $VV^T = I$, where I is the identity matrix. For a square matrix of size n × n all the three matrices U, S and V are of the same size. If the size of matrix 'R' is with m > n then size of 'U' is m x m, size of 'S' is m x n and size of 'V' is n x n. If size of matrix 'R' is with m < n then size of U is n × n, size of 'S' is m x n and size of V is n x n. The inverse equation of SVD transform gives back the original matrix as described by the following equation:

$$U^*S^*V^T = R \tag{6.2}$$

where 'V^T' is the transposed version of orthonormal matrix 'V'. In the SVD form if the values of singular values are varied the effect on the visual quality of the image is not that munch ensuring better imperceptivity along with high robustness.

6.3.2   Chaos Encryption

The security of the watermark is extremely essential in case the watermark has to survive against the unauthorized access. Usually robust watermarking is not sufficient to secure the sensitive information against several signal processing attacks and if the embedding algorithm is somehow broken down by the unauthorized person the information will be lost. In such a scenario it is highly encouraged to increase the security and set multiple security procedure that if one is cracked in some extreme scenario other comes at rescue. Keeping these factors in mind an encryption technique is the best procedure to save the watermark from any remote unauthorized access. The encryption technique ensures that nobody can access our private data without being provided with secret keys used in the encryption technique. Chaos encryption has proved to be the best encryption technique which manipulates the private information and sets high security to the data. Chaotic maps offer properties like irreversibility, pseudo-randomness, dynamic behaviour and highly sensitive initial parameters. The result of application chaotic maps is a sequence having similar properties as that of white noise with random behaviour, less complexity and improved correlation [44].

$$a\,(x+1) = \beta \times a(x) \times [1 - a(x)] \tag{6.3}$$

where the parameter 'β' defines the randomness and $0 < \beta < 4$. If the value of β is set to 3.99 the randomness is highest. From Eq. (6.3), the x + *l*th value generated is given as $a(x+1)$ and $0 < a(x) < 1$. By varying value of x from 0 to *P-1* different values of a*(x)* are obtained. '*P*' gives the upper limit of the chaotic values to be obtained from the equation. The initial values of 'β' and a*(0)* set at start of the encryption process in order to obtain chaotic signal. The detailed process for encryption is described in [44]. The result of encryption on the watermark is described in Fig. 6.1.

| 64 x 64 Original Watermark | Encrypted Watermark | 128 x 128 watermark logo | Encrypted watermark |

Fig. 6.1 Original and corresponding encrypted watermarks

6.4   Proposed Scheme

The proposed robust watermarking technique for secure medical data exchange is described in detail in this section. DCT and SVD transforms are employed to formulate a new robust and blind WM scheme to achieve copyright protection. The proposed scheme performs efficiently and meets the demands of imperceptivity, security and robustness under various attacks and is hence suitable for copyright and privacy protection of medical images shared in e healthcare applications. The embedding is done using the advantages of multiple transform domains in order to achieve high levels of robustness. Sections 6.4.1 and 6.4.2 discusses in detail the steps of embedding and extraction. The concept of image blocking along with cryptographic method in order to avoid blocking artefacts and search out best possible coefficients for embedding watermark. The watermark is first secured using an encryption algorithm before embedding in the cover image. The use of DCT transformed blocks for embedding watermark ensure that blocking artefacts are avoided.

6.4.1   Embedding Algorithm

Before starting the embedding process, the watermark is encrypted using the chaotic encryption. The block diagram of the proposed watermarking scheme is shown in Fig. 6.2. The cover image is first divided into 8×8 blocks and Arnold transform is applied on each block followed by application of DCT on each block. The number of iterations (n) for carrying out Arnold transform is different for each block and function of block number. From each of the DCT block middle frequency coefficients are randomly selected through zigzag scanning of the 8×8 DCT block. It has been found that middle frequency coefficients show better results in terms of robustness and imperceptivity [45]. Hence eight middle frequency coefficients are chosen at random and two matrices 'C_{i1}' and 'C_{i2}' are formed. The coordinates of these eight coefficients is different for each block and is again function of block number. Embedding is done using the singular values after applying SVD transform on each of the 'C_{i1}' and 'C_{i2}' using algorithm.

The embedding of the watermark begins after the watermark is encrypted. The watermark used in this scheme is a 64 x 64 binary logo which is to be embedded in a 512×512 cover image. This encrypted watermark is embedded by employing the following steps:

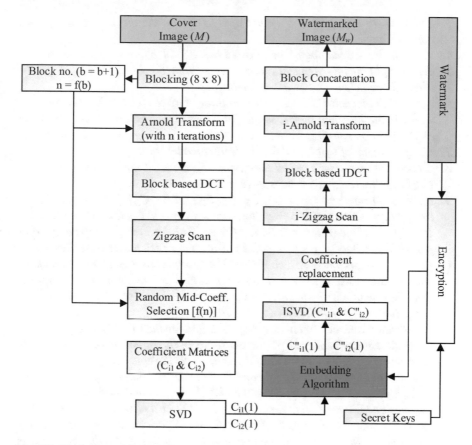

Fig. 6.2 Block diagram for embedding watermark

1. *Perform encryption of the watermark 'w' which is to be embedded in the cover image using encryption technique discussed in Sect. 6.3.2. The result is the encrypted watermark, 'w_e'.*
2. *Arrange the cover image into an array of 8 × 8 blocks. The total number of blocks is*

$$T = \frac{m/2 \times n/2}{8 \times 8}$$

Let B_i is the ith block put forward for embedding a watermark bit.

3. *Select an ith 8×8 block (B_i) and apply DCT on the block to get frequency domain coefficients.*
4. *Perform zigzag scanning of the selected 8×8 DCT block.*
5. *Select eight middle frequency coefficients from the block and arrange the selected coefficients into two 2×2 matrices.*
6. *Apply SVD on each 2×2 matrix to get three matrices (U, S & V). The S matrix which is the diagonal matrix is put forward for embedding watermark. After SVD operation two singular matrices obtained are designated as C_{i1} and C_{i2}.*
7. *Compute mean of $C_{i1}(1)$ and $C_{i2}(1)$ designated by 'M_i'.*
8. *Embed the watermark bit by modifying the selected coefficients $C_{i1}(1)$ and $C_{i2}(1)$ as described in the steps 9–12 and Fig. 6.3.*
9. *Initialize parameters like δ, α_1, α_2, β_1, β_2 and β_3. $C_{i1}(1)$ and $C_{i2}(1)$ be the original coefficients of two singular matrices C_{i1} and C_{i2} for a selected 8×8 DCT block. If the watermark bit is '1' then $C_{i1}(1)$ and $C_{i2}(1)$ are modified as per the Fig. 6.3 using the predefined parameters which act as secret keys.*
10. *For a watermark bit '1' check if $C_{i1}(1)$ is greater than $C_{i2}(1)$ by a predefined value. Otherwise, perform a series of modifications as described in Fig. 6.3 meet the condition. The result of embedding watermark bit '1' are the modified coefficients are designated as $C_{i1}*(1)$ and $C_{i2}*(1)$.*
11. *For a watermark bit '0' check if $C_{i2}(1)$ is greater than $C_{i1}(1)$ by a predefined value. As defined in step 11 perform a series of operations to meet the desired condition the result of which are the modified coefficients $C_{i1}°(1)$ and $C_{i2}°(1)$.*
12. *The modified coefficients $C_{i1}*(1)$ and $C_{i1}°(1)$ are designated by $C''_{i1}(1)$ while as $C_{i2}*(2)$ and $C_{i2}°(2)$ are designated by $C''_{i2}(1)$ in combination. Replace the original coefficients $C_{i1}(1)$ and $C_{i2}(1)$ with the corresponding modified ones to get the matrices C''_{i1} and C''_{i2}. Perform ISVD operation on the resulting matrices and place the resulting coefficients at the corresponding positions in the selected DCT block. Apply IDCT operation on the resulting block.*
13. *Perform steps 9–12 for embedding a watermark bit. After embedding the whole watermark reshape and rearrange the array of 8×8 blocks to get the watermarked image.*

Figure 6.3 shows the flow diagram for embedding watermark which involves the steps from 9 to 11 of the embedding algorithm. Note that algorithm requires first coefficients of matrices C_{i1} and C_{i2}, the input parameters δ, α_1, α_2, β_1, β_2 and β_3 that act as secret keys only known to the authorized users. Any variation in these parameters will result in a logo which is totally meaningless. The result of the embedding algorithm is set of modified coefficients $C_{i1}*(1)$ and $C_{i2}*(1)$ if watermark bit '1' is embedded or $C_{i1}°(1)$ and $C_{i2}°(1)$ if watermark bit '0' is embedded.

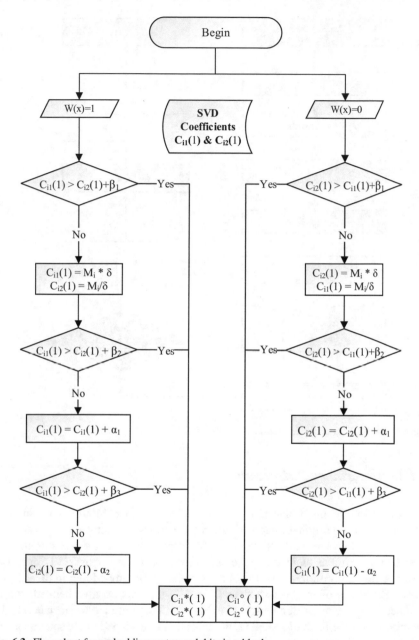

Fig. 6.3 Flow chart for embedding watermark bits in a block

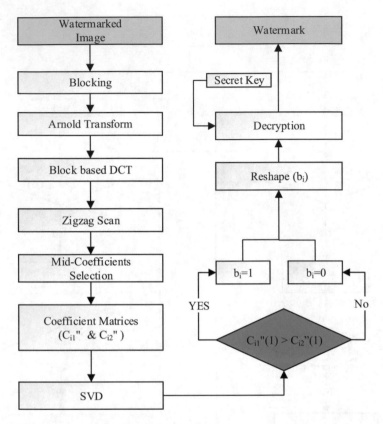

Fig. 6.4 Block Diagram for extraction of watermark

6.4.2 Watermark Extraction

The extraction of the watermark at the receiver is done blindly without prior information of the original image. Figure 6.4 describes the steps to be followed for extraction of the watermark. It is evident from the figure that the steps up to SVD operation are similar as in case of embedding process. After the SVD operation the extraction algorithm is used to get the watermark bit embedding in the selected block. The status of the bit (whether '0' or '1') that has been embedded, can be obtained using the algorithm presented in Fig. 6.4. The extracted watermark bits (b_i) are arranged in the form of a single row array and the reshaped into a square matrix. This watermark matrix doesn't provide any information and is hence decrypted using the predefined secret keys only known by the authorized user. The result of decryption is the actual watermark which was embedded in the medical image.

6.5 Experimental Analysis

In this section, the proposed scheme is analysed for its performance by measuring watermark robustness and invisibility under various attacks. Various medical images used for the analysis are taken MedPix® and Open-i which are free open-access online databases of medical images [46, 47]. Some of the images have been taken from USC-SIPI Image Database only meant for the research purposes [48]. These images are shown in the Fig. 6.5. The proposed technique has been implemented in Matlab 2015b with the system having 8GB RAM and 2.30 GHz Intel Core processor. For embedding the 64 x 64 binary watermark various images of size 512×512 have been used in the proposed scheme. The performance of the proposed scheme has been efficiently described using both subjective and objective analysis.

Robustness is an important parameter to estimate the effect of different attacks on a watermarked image. Robustness is defined as the level of resistance offered by a watermarking scheme under different unauthorized manipulations and is should be as high as possible. Bit error rate (BER) and Normalized Cross correlation (NCC) are the two mainly used values for the calculation of robustness and are usually calculated with respect to secret logos embedded and extracted in case of a data hiding scheme. Imperceptibility is another important parameter which gives the variation in quality of a cover image before and after embedding watermark. For calculation of the imperceptibility, the values of factors like Peak Signal to Noise Ratio (PSNR) and Structural Similarity (SSIM) are generally used. PSNR & SSIM

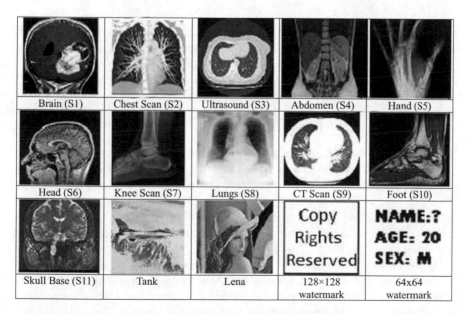

Fig. 6.5 Medical and other gray scale images used in the proposed scheme

are evaluated with respect to the original and watermarked. The peak PSNR is mathematically given by the formula:

$$PSNR\ (dB) = 10\log\frac{(2^n - 1)^2}{MSE} \tag{6.4}$$

The variable 'n' represents the number of bits used to represent a pixel in terms of its intensity level in an image. The parameter MSE gives the mean square error representing the similarity difference between the two images of same size. It is evident that for a low value of MSE the value of PSNR will be higher depicting that the error pixels in the two images is less.

$$MSE = \frac{1}{MN}\sum_a^M \sum_b^N \left(G\,(a,b) - \hat{G}\,(a,b)\right) \tag{6.5}$$

The mathematical formula for calculation of BER is given as follows:

$$BER\ (\%) = 1/MN\left[\sum_{a=0}^{M-1}\sum_{b=0}^{N-1} W\,(a,b) \oplus \hat{W}\,(a,b)\right] \times 100 \tag{6.6}$$

where $(a,\,b)$ represents the coordinates of the images W and $\hat{W}$ with identical size. The value of BER should be as small as possible in order to designate that the error bits of the extracted watermark are less. Mathematically NCC is given by the expression:

$$NCC = \frac{\sum_{a=1}^M \sum_{b=1}^N W\,(a,b)\,\hat{W}\,(a,b)}{\sqrt{\sum_{a=1}^M \sum_{b=1}^N [W\,(a,b)]^{2*}\sum_{a=1}^M \sum_{b=1}^N \left[\hat{W}\,(a,b)\right]^2}} \tag{6.7}$$

6.5.1 Imperceptivity Analysis

As discussed earlier the imperceptivity gives the visual quality of the images in which watermark is embedded. In this section, the imperceptivity analysis has been presented through both subjective and objective metrics. SSIM and PSNR metrics have been for evaluating the imperceptivity of the watermarked image obtained by proposed technique. The objective metrics of watermarked images with size 512×512 and extracted watermark with size 64×64 obtained using proposed algorithm have been shown in Table 6.1.

The average PSNR value of watermarked image is above 40 dB while as BER of value zero and NCC with value unity has been obtained. From the above results obtained with the proposed algorithm it is clear that high imperceptivity is maintained for watermarked image and thus scheme could be used in many applications.

Table 6.1 Perceptual quality parameters of watermarked images

Images	PSNR	NCC	SSIM
Scan 1	42.8838	1.0000	0.97572
Scan 2	41.9171	1.0000	0.96761
Scan 3	42.8796	1.0000	0.97559
Scan 4	41.9012	1.0000	0.97532
Scan 5	40.8921	1.0000	0.95123
Scan 6	42.8909	1.0000	0.98547
Scan 7	41.9133	1.0000	0.96304
Scan 8	42.6007	1.0000	0.97456
Scan 9	41.9041	1.0000	0.97751
Scan 10	40.7189	1.0000	0.96427
Scan 11	42.601	1.000	0.9821
Lena	43.9677	1.0000	0.98594
Plane	43.2083	1.0000	0.9816

6.5.2   Robustness Analysis

In the proposed watermarking scheme, data embedding is accomplished by modifying the diagonal coefficients of singular matrices according to the watermark bits as defined in Sect. 6.4. For attaining the strong robustness maximum possible difference is set between two values optimized according to the perceptual quality of the cover image. For analysing the robustness of the scheme, watermarked images are subjected to different attacks and the results in the form of extracted watermark are recorded. The attacks include salt & pepper (SP) noise, Gaussian noise (GN), histogram equalization (HE) etc. If the extracted watermark is fairly recognizable the robustness of the scheme is considered to be high for that attack. In Fig. 6.6, the results obtained after several attacks on the watermarked image in terms of NCC and BER have been recorded. The robustness analysis has been done on the watermarked images subject to various attacks like noise addition, Filtering [3 3], compression (at quality 50) and other geometrical operations. It is clear from the resulted recoded in the table that the proposed scheme is highly resilient to all of the image processing operations as such highly robust watermark is obtained. The objective and subjective results under different attacks are presented in Fig. 6.6.

From the results described in the table it is clear that the proposed scheme offers strong robustness and could performs efficiently against all of the mentioned attacks.

6.5.2.1   Rotation

One of the most difficult geometrical attack to survive for a robust watermark is the rotation attack on the watermarked image. This is because the rotation attack modifies the corners on the all four dimensions and amount of severity depends

Attack Type	No Attack	S & P Noise	Histogram Equal. (HE)	JPEG 2000 (CR = 4)	Smoothing Filter
Extracted Watermark	NAME:? AGE: 20 SEX: M	NAME:? AGE: 20 SEX: M	NAME:? AGE: 20 SEX: M	NAME:? AGE: 20 SEX: M	NAME:? AGE: 20 SEX: M
NCC	1	0.9901	0.9994	1	1
BER(%)	0	1.39	0.0977	0	0
Attack Type	Rotation (40°)	Speckle Noise	Scaling (Down 25%)	JPEG (QF=50)	JPEG 2000 (CR = 8)
Extracted Watermark	NAME:? AGE: 20 SEX: M	NAME:? AGE: 20 SEX: M	NAME:? AGE: 20 SEX: M	NAME:? AGE: 20 SEX: M	NAME:? AGE: 20 SEX: M
NCC	0.9812	0.99	0.9987	0.9915	0.9998
BER(%)	2.0723	0.26	0.8789	1.46	0.0244
Attack Type	Low Pass Filter (LPF)	Sharpening	Wiener Filter	Gaussian LPF	Poisson Noise
Extracted Watermark	NAME:? AGE: 20 SEX: M	NAME:? AGE: 20 SEX: M	NAME:? AGE: 20 SEX: M	NAME:? AGE: 20 SEX: M	NAME:? AGE: 20 SEX: M
NCC	0.9620	0.9998	0.9806	1	0.9542
BER(%)	5.9326	0.0244	3.0029	0	7.4720
Attack Type	LSB Reset (1-4)	Gamma Correction	Median Filter	Crop (10%)	Average Filtering
Extracted Watermark	NAME:? AGE: 20 SEX: M	NAME:? AGE: 20 SEX: M	NAME:? AGE: 20 SEX: M	NAME:? AG 20 SEX: M	NAME:? AGE: 20 SEX: M
NCC	0.9946	1	0.98	0.9842	0.9557
BER(%)	0.8301	0	2.56	2.4431	6.7325

Fig. 6.6 Extracted watermarks after attacks with corresponding NCC and BER

on the rotation angle. The proposed robust watermarking scheme efficiently resists the rotation attacks and a well recognizable watermark is obtained even after the attack. The results obtained for rotational attacks of various degrees are shown in the Fig. 6.7.

It is evident from the above figure that watermark shows high level of robustness as depicted by NCC and BER values.

Rotation Attack	Scan 1		Scan 2		Scan 3		Lena	
	NCC	*BER*	*NCC*	*BER*	*NCC*	*BER*	*NCC*	*BER*
Rotate(10°)	0.9991 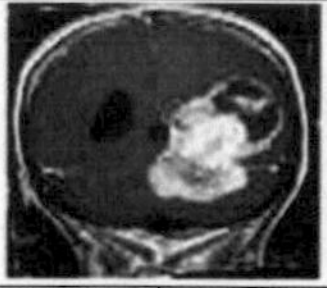	0.9312	0.9914 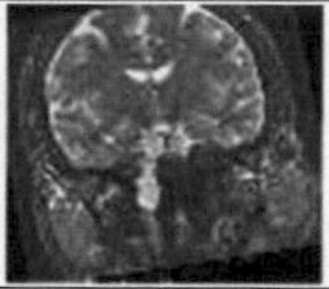	1.2451	0.991 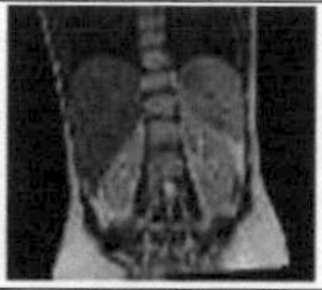	1.65	0.993 	1.76
Rotate(20°)	0.9899 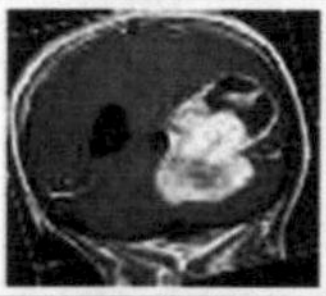	1.3741	0.9851 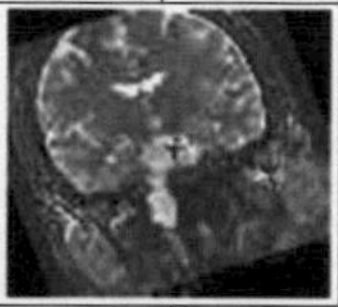	2.1243	0.989 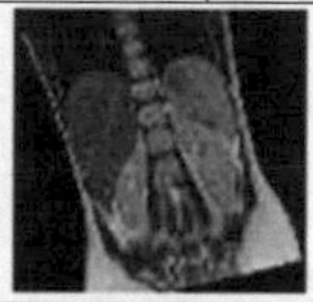	2.66	0.985 	1.98
Rotate(30°)	0.9801 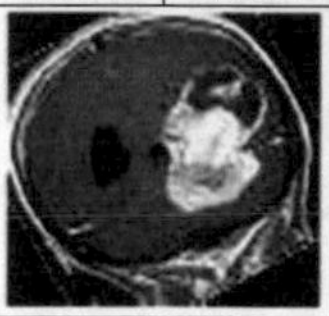	1.9231	0.9807 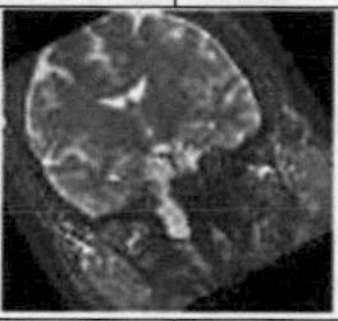	2.9531	0.971 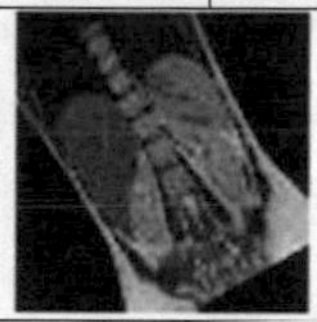	3.01	0.978 	2.09
Rotate(40°)	0.9721 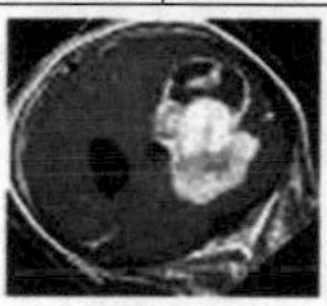	2.3422	0.9635 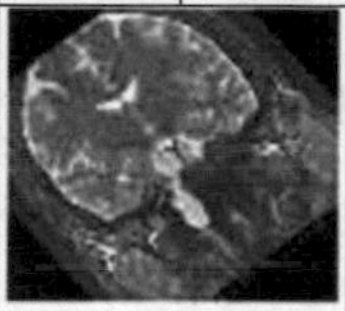	3.2251	0.950 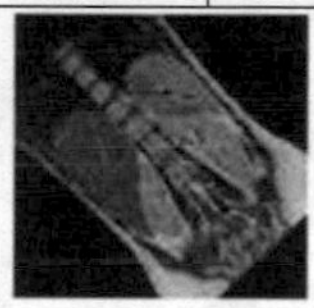	3.94	0.967 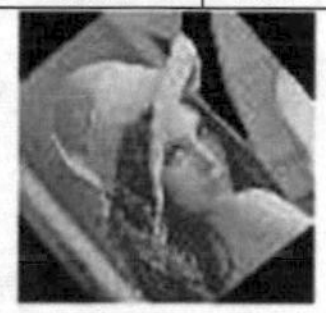	3.71

Fig. 6.7 Watermarked images after rotation attack with corresponding NCC and BER

6.5.2.2   Robustness Against Combined Attacks

In practical scenario the attacks may happen on a watermarked image one after other. Hence the performance of the proposed scheme has also been tested under worst case scenarios of multiple attacks on the watermarked image one after other. For evaluating the results some cases of dual and triple simultaneous attacks are taken and the results are shown in the Fig. 6.8.

6.6   Comparison Results

The proposed scheme is compared with [49, 50] and the results for the Lena image of size 512×512 and watermark of size 64 x 64 are recorded in the Table 6.2 below. The results are obtained for the Lena gray scale image and various parameters related to the attack are specified along with the attack in the table. It is evident from

Dual Attacks	SP (0.001) and GN (0.001)	SP Noise (0.001) and Hist. Equal.	SP Noise(0.001) and JPG (Q=80)	GN (0.001) and JPEG (Q=80)
Extracted Watermark	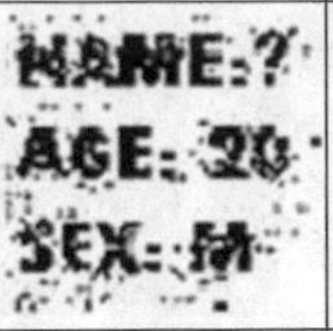 NAME:? AGE: 20 SEX: M	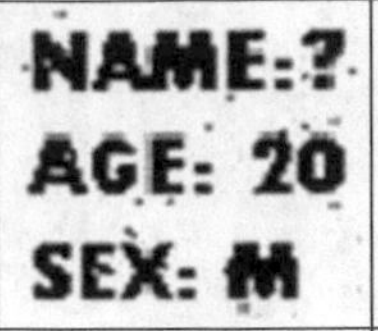 NAME:? AGE: 20 SEX: M	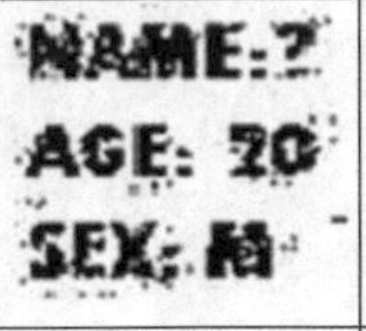 NAME:? AGE: 20 SEX: M	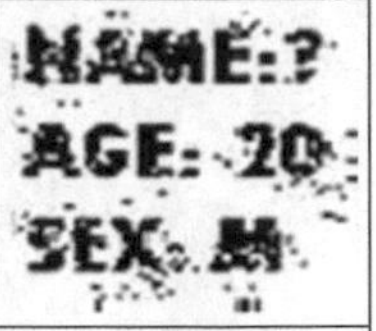 NAME:? AGE: 20 SEX: M
BER *NCC*	5.8801 0.9652	0.7568 0.9956	3.6865 0.9758	4.8828 0.9680
Dual Attacks	Gaussian Noise (0.001) and Sharpening	JPEG (Q=80) and Rotate (10°)	JPEG (Q=80) and Crop (10%)	Rotate (10°) and Upscaling (400%)
Extracted Watermark	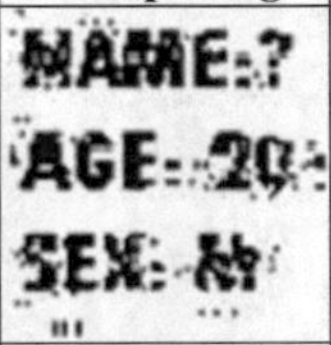 NAME:? AGE: 20 SEX: M	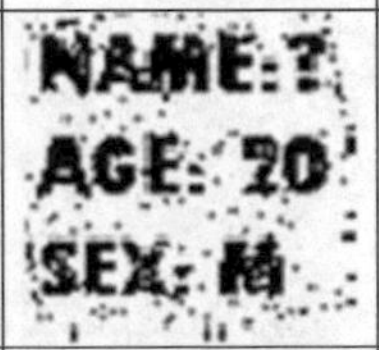 NAME:? AGE: 20 SEX: M	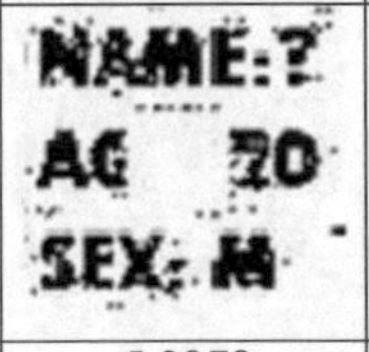 NAME:? AG 20 SEX: M	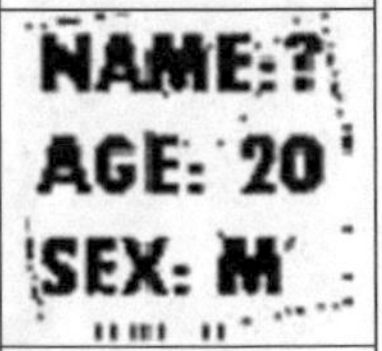 NAME:? AGE: 20 SEX: M
BER *NCC*	4.8584 0.9683	5.4932 0.9636	5.2979 0.9655	2.002 0.9868
Triple Attacks	GN (0.001), Sharp.& Rot. (10°)	Sharpening, HE and Upscaling (400%)	Sharpening, HE and Rot. (10°)	SP Noise (0.001), HE and Sharpening
Extracted Watermark	 NAME:? AGE: 20 SEX: M	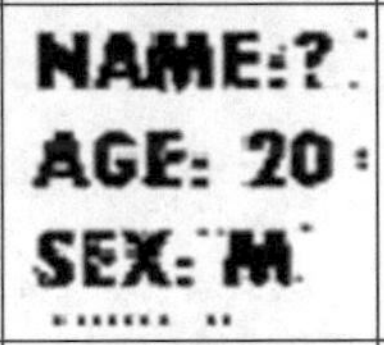 NAME:? AGE: 20 SEX: M	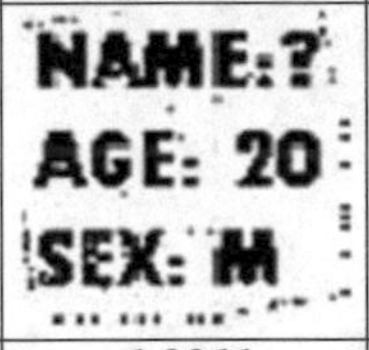 NAME:? AGE: 20 SEX: M	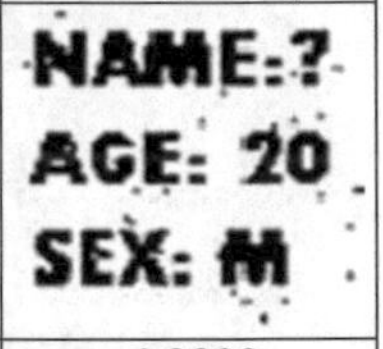 NAME:? AGE: 20 SEX: M
BER *NCC*	4.6874 0.9691	1.2451 0.9918	1.8311 0.98801	1.2828 0.9880

Fig. 6.8 Extracted watermarks after dual/triple attacks with NCC and BER values

the table that the proposed scheme performs better as compared to the scheme under comparison. Also it is to be noted that the expression for calculation of NCC in the paper [49] is different and for such expression our results are far better. The accurate expression for calculation of NCC is described in the Eq. (6.7).

Four medical images of size 1024×1024 and watermark of size 128×128 are taken for comparing robustness of the proposed scheme. The results hence obtained for an X-ray medical image have been compared with [51] and are recorded in Table 6.3.

Table 6.2 Robustness performance in case of Lena image

Attacks	Zhang [49]	Zhu [50]	Proposed
No attack	1	1	1
Salt & pepper noise (0.001)	0.9923	NA	0.9891
Salt & pepper noise (0.005)	0.9566	NA	0.9639
Salt & pepper noise (0.02)	NA	0.81	0.8911
Gaussian noise (0,0.0001)	0.9693	NA	0.9973
Gaussian noise (0,0.0005)	0.7099	NA	0.9799
Speckle noise (0.0001)	0.9944	NA	1
Speckle noise (0.0005)	0.8379	NA	0.9989
Median filter (3 × 3)	0.9386	0.79	0.9725
Average filter (3 × 3)	0.8641	NA	0.9531
Image sharpening	0.9741	NA	0.9998
JPEG (Q = 90)	1	NA	1
JPEG (Q = 80)	0.9986	NA	1
JPEG (Q = 70)	0.9793	NA	1
JPEG (Q = 60)	NA	0.98	0.9915
Rescaling (2, 0.5)	1	NA	1
Rescaling (0.5, 2)	0.9538	NA	0.9871
Cropping (top 25%)	0.7828	NA	0.9651
Cropping (middle 25%)	0.7083	NA	0.9324
Cropping (right 25%)	0.7297	NA	0.9595
Rotation (5°)	NA	0.99	0.9963
Shear (1/4)	NA	0.90	0.9551

Table 6.3 Robustness performance under different attacks in case of X-ray image

Attacks	Thanki [51]	Proposed
JPEG (Q = 90)	0.9806	1
Sharpening	0.9674	0.9998
Median (2 × 2)	0.9607	0.9768
Gaussian LPF	0.9668	0.9925
Gaussian noise ($\mu = 0$, $\sigma = 0.01$)	0.6377	0.8265
Salt & pepper noise ($\sigma = 0.1$)	0.7532	0.6791
Histogram equalization	0.9708	0.9994

It is clear from the Table that the proposed scheme outperforms the scheme under comparison in all of the attacks under consideration. Similarly, very high robustness is achieved for other attacks not mentioned in the table. Only in case of salt & Pepper noise with high variance the proposed scheme shows weaker robustness due to the fact that most of the pixels attain the value of either '0' or '255' resulting in wrong decisions during extraction. Similar results can be seen for other medical images like MRI, US and CT using proposed scheme.

6.7   Conclusion

In this chapter, a digital image watermarking technique has been proposed with high robustness applicable for copyright protection of medical images. The security of the watermark is enhanced before embedding in a medical image by encryption techniques. The embedding is done by modifying the values of the diagonal coefficients of singular matrices in the SVD domain. The modification factor is decided by a watermark bit of a binary logo and coefficients are set accordingly. The singular matrices are obtained by selecting middle frequency coefficients from a DCT block and arranging them in two matrices. The performance of the proposed scheme has been analysed under various image processing operations including noise addition, filtering and geometrical manipulations. The results hence obtained prove that the scheme is highly robust to both singular and simultaneous attacks. The comparison with state of art technique prove the superiority of the proposed scheme in terms of both robustness, security, payload and imperceptivity. Given the strengths of the proposed technique it can be used for the applications where copyright protection and user privacy is of greater concern. E-healthcare is one of the prospective areas where it can be used to counter various challenges and ensure integrity of medical images, protect EPR and secure file sharing. In future, tamper localization module will be added to the system to trace and localize forgery attacks.

Acknowledgments This publication is an outcome of the R&D work undertaken project under the Visvesvaraya PhD Scheme of Ministry of Electronics & Information Technology, Government of India, being implemented by Digital India Corporation and in part is supported by Department of Science and Technology (DST) New Delhi under DST inspire scheme.

References

1. Loan NA, Parah SA, Sheikh JA, Akhoon JA, Bhat GM (2017). Hiding Electronic Patient Record (EPR) in medical images: A high capacity and computationally efficient technique for e-healthcare applications. *Journal of biomedical informatics*, *73*, 125-136.
2. Parah SA, Sheikh JA, Ahad F, Bhat GM (2018). High Capacity and Secure Electronic Patient Record (EPR) Embedding in Color Images for IoT Driven Healthcare Systems. In *Internet of Things and Big Data Analytics Toward Next-Generation Intelligence* (pp. 409-437). Springer, Cham.
3. Cox I, Miller M, Bloom J, Fridrich J, Kalker T (2008) *Digital Watermarking and Steganography*, 2nd edn. (Morgan Kaufmann Publishers Inc., San Francisco, CA, USA, 2008).
4. Kumar C, Singh AK, Kumar P, Singh R, Singh S. SPIHT-based multiple image watermarking in NSCT domain. *Concurrency and Computation: Practice and Experience*, Wiley, DOI:10.1002/cpe.4912.
5. Singh, AK, Kumar B, Singh SK, Ghrera SP, Mohan A (2016) Multiple watermarking technique for securing online social network contents using back propagation neural network. *Future Generation Computer Systems*. Elsevier, pp.1-16, DOI: 10.1016/j.future.2016.11.023.
6. https://online.norwich.edu/academic-programs/masters/nursing/resources/infographics/healthcare-data-breaches-the-costs-and-solutions.

7. Parah SA, Ahad F, Sheikh JA, Loan NA, Bhat GM (2016c) A New Reversible and high capacity data hiding technique for e-healthcare applications, *Multimedia Tools and Applications*, Springer, DOI: 10.1007/s11042-016-4196-2.

8. Kumar C, Singh AK, Kumar P (2018) A recent survey on image watermarking techniques and its application in e-governance. *Multimedia Tools and Applications*, Springer, 77(3), pp. 3597–3622, DOI: 10.1007/s11042-017-5222-8.

9. Ahad F, Loan NA, Parah SA, Sheikh JA, Bhat GM, (2016a) Pixel repetition technique: a high capacity and reversible data hiding method for e-healthcare applications, *Intelligent Techniques in Signal Processing for Multimedia Security*, Vol. 660, Springer, DOI: 10.1007/978-3-319-44790-2_17.

10. Parah SA, Sheikh JA, Akhoon JA, Loan NA (2018) Electronic Health Record hiding in Images for smart city applications: A computationally efficient and reversible information hiding technique for secure communication. *Future Generation Computer Systems*.

11. Parah SA, Ahmad I, Loan NA, Muhammad K, Sheikh JA, Bhat GM. (2019). Realization of an adaptive data hiding system for electronic patient record, embedding in medical images. In Security in smart cities: models, applications, and challenges (pp. 47–70). Springer, Cham.

12. Parah SA, Sheikh JA, Ahad F, Loan NA, Bhat GM (2017). Information hiding in medical images: a robust medical image watermarking system for E-healthcare. *Multimedia Tools and Applications*, 76(8), 10599-10633.

13. Singh L, Singh AK, Singh PK (2018) Secure data hiding techniques: A survey, Multimedia Tools and Applications, Multimed. Tools Appl., Springer DOI: 10.1007/s11042-018-6407-5.

14. Natasa Zivic: Robust Image Authentication in the Presence of Noise. springer (2015).

15. Parah SA, Sheikh JA, Ahad F, Loan NA, Bhat GM (2015d) Information hiding in medical images: a robust medical image watermarking system for E-healthcare. *Multimedia Tools and Applications. 2017 Apr 1;76(8):10599-633.* Springer.

16. Chang CC, Chen KN, Lee CF, Liu LJ. A secure fragile watermarking scheme based on chaos-and-hamming code. J Syst Softw 2011;84(9):1462–70.

17. Loan NA, Hurrah NN, Parah SA, Sheikh JA (2017) High capacity reversible stenographic technique based on image resizing and pixel permutation. In *Image Information Processing (ICIIP), 2017 Fourth International Conference on* (pp. 1-6). IEEE.

18. Kumar, C., Singh, A. K., & Kumar, P. (2018). Improved wavelet-based image watermarking through SPIHT. *Multimedia Tools and Applications*, Springer, pp. 1-14, DOI: 10.1007/s11042-018-6177-0.

19. Lin S, Chen CF (2000) A robust dct-based watermarking for copyright protection. *IEEE Transactions on Consumer Electronics, 46* (3), 415–421.

20. Srivastava R, Kumar B, Singh AK, Mohan A (2018) Computationally efficient joint imperceptible image watermarking and JPEG compression: a green computing approach. Multimedia Tools and Applications, 77(13), 16447-16459, Springer US DOI: 10.1007/s11042-017-5214-8.

21. Parah SA, Sheikh JA, Loan NA and Bhat GM (2016b) Robust and blind watermarking technique in DCT domain using inter-block coefficient, *Digital Signal Processing*, Elsevier, DOI: 10.1016/j.dsp.2016.02.005.

22. Sheikh JA, Parah SA, Assad UI, Bhat GM (2016b) Realization and robustness evaluation of a blind spatial domain watermarking technique', *International Journal of Electronics*, DOI: 10.1080/00207217.2016.1242162.

23. Singh AK, Kumar B, Singh G, Mohan A (Eds.) (2017). Medical image watermarking: techniques and applications. Springer, ISBN: 978-3319576985.

24. Parah S, Sheikh J, Bhat, GM (2012a) On the realization of secure and efficient data hiding system using ISB and LSB technique, *Engineering E-Transaction, Malaysia, Vol. 7, No. 2,* pp.48–53, ISSN: 1823-6379.

25. Parah S, Sheikh J, Bhat GM (2013a) High capacity data embedding using joint intermediate significant bit and least significant technique', *International Journal of Information Engineering and Applications, Vol. 2, No. 11,* pp.1–11.

26. Hurrah NN, Loan NA, Parah SA, Sheikh JA (2017, December). A transform domain based robust color image watermarking scheme for single and dual attacks. In *Image Information Processing (ICIIP), 2017 Fourth International Conference on* (pp. 1-5). IEEE.

27. Hurrah NN, Parah SA, Loan NA, Sheikh JA, Elhoseny M, Muhammad K, (2019). Dual watermarking framework for privacy protection and content authentication of multimedia. *Future Generation Computer Systems, 94*, 654–673. DOI: 10.1016/j.future.2018.02.023.

28. Loan NA, Parah SA, Sheikh JA, Bhat GM (2017) Utilizing neighbourhood coefficient correlation: a new image watermarking technique robust to singular and hybrid attacks, Multidimentional Systems and Signal Processing, DOI: 10.1007/s11045-017-0490-z.

29. Ahad F, Parah SA, Sheikh JA, Bhat GM (2017) Hiding clinical information in medical images: a new high capacity and reversible data hiding technique, Journal of Biomedical Informatics, February, Vol. 66, pp.214–230 [online] DOI: https://doi.org/10.1016/j.jbi.2017.01.006 (accessed 21 September 2017).

30. Kavitha KJ, Shan PB (2018) Joint Digital Water Marking for Medical Images for Improving Security. *Biomedical and Pharmacology Journal, 11*(2).

31. Loan NA, Parah SA, Sheikh JA, Bhat GM (2016b) A robust and computationally efficient digital watermarking technique using inter block pixel differencing, *Multimedia Forensics and Security*, Vol. 115, Springer DOI: 10.1007/978-3-319-44270-9_10.

32. Abhilasha Sharma, Amit Kumar Singh and S P Ghrera, Sharma, Secure Hybrid Robust Watermarking Technique for Medical Images. *Procedia Computer Science 70 (2015)*, 778 – 784.

33. Verma VS, Jha RK, Ojha A (2015) Significant region based robust watermarking scheme in lifting wavelet transform domain. *Expert Systems with Applications, 42*(21), pp.8184-8197.

34. Kang X, Huang J, Shi YQ, Lin Y (2003) A DWT-DFT composite watermarking scheme robust to both affine transform and jpeg compression. IEEE T. Circ. Syst. Vid. 13, 776–786 (2003). doi:10.1109/TCSVT.2003.815957.

35. LP Feng, LB Zheng, P Cao, in 3rd IEEE International Conference on Computer Science and Information Technology (ICCSIT). A DWT-DCT Based Blind Watermarking Algorithm for Copyright Protection, vol. 7, (2010), pp. 455–458. doi:10.1109/ICCSIT.2010.5565101.

36. RH Laskar, M Choudhury, K Chakraborty, S Chakraborty, in *Computer Networks and Intelligent Computing. Communications in Computer and Information Science*. A Joint DWT-DCT Based Robust Digital Watermarking Algorithm for Ownership Verification of Digital Images, vol. 157 (Springer Berlin, Germany, 2011), pp. 482–491. doi:10.1007/978-3-642-22786-8_61.

37. Benoraira A, Benmahammed K, Boucenna N (2015) Blind image watermarking technique based on differential embedding in DWT and DCT domains. EURASIP Journal on Advances in Signal Processing, 2015(1), p.55.

38. Thakur S, Singh AK, Ghrera SP, Mohamed Elhoseny (2018) Multi-layer security of medical data through watermarking and chaotic encryption for tele-health applications, Multimedia Tools and Applications, Springer, pp. 1-14, DOI: 10.1007/s11042-018-6263-3

39. Parah SA, Sheikh JA, Bhat GM (2015e) Hiding in encrypted images: a three tier security data hiding system, Multidimensional Systems and Signal Processing, September, Springer, DOI: 10.1007/s11045-015-0358-z.

40. Thakur, S., Singh, A. K., Ghrera, S. P., & Mohan, A. (2018). Chaotic based secure watermarking approach for medical images. Multimedia Tools and Applications, 1-14. Springer, DOI: 10.1007/s11042-018-6691-0.

41. Shao Z, Shang Y, Zhang Y, Liu X, Guo G (2016) Robust watermarking using orthogonal Fourier–Mellin moments and chaotic map for double images. Signal Processing, 120, pp.522-531.

42. Chen JX, Zhu ZL, Fu C, Zhang LB, Zhang Y (2015) An image encryption scheme using nonlinear inter-pixel computing and swapping based permutation approach. *Communications in Nonlinear Science and Numerical Simulation, 23(1), 2015,* 294-310.

43. Kanso A, Ghebleh M (2015) An efficient and robust image encryption scheme for medical applications. *Communications in Nonlinear Science and Numerical Simulation, vol. 24, no. 1, 2015*, pp. 98-116.
44. Loan NA, Hurrah NN, Parah SA, Lee JW, Sheikh JA, Bhat GM (2018) Secure and Robust Digital Image Watermarking Using Coefficient Differencing and Chaotic Encryption. *IEEE Access, 6*, 19876-19897.
45. Lin YK, A data hiding scheme based upon DCT coefficient modification *Comput. Standards Int.*, vol. 36, no. 56, pp. 855-862, 2014.
46. MedPix™ Medical Image Database, available at: http://rad.usuhs.mil/medpix/medpix.html, https://medpix.nlm.nih.gov/home.
47. Openi™ Medical Image Database, available at: https://openi.nlm.nih.gov/index.php.
48. The USC-SIPI Image Database, available at: http://sipi.usc.edu/database/.
49. Zhang H, Wang C, Zhou X (2017) A robust image watermarking scheme based on SVD in the spatial domain. *Future Internet, 9*(3), 45.
50. Yuefeng Z, & Li, L. (2015). Digital image watermarking algorithms based on dual transform domain and self-recovery. *International Journal on Smart Sensing & Intelligent Systems, 8*(1).
51. Thanki R, Borra S, Dwivedi V, Borisagar K (2017) An efficient medical image watermarking scheme based on FDCuT–DCT. *Engineering Science and Technology, an International Journal, 20*(4), 1366-1379.

Chapter 7
Hybrid Transforms Based Oblivious Fragile Watermarking Techniques

Geeta Kasana

7.1 Introduction

With the advancement in information technology, the illegal use, manipulation and tampering of the digital data has become very easy. Due to these threats, security of the digital data has become very important. Digital watermarking is one of the approach which is used to handle the threats to the digital data [9, 10, 19–21, 23, 24]. The watermark is a secret data to be embedded into any digital media like image, video, audio or text file which is further used for copyright protection and authentication of the data. The image in which the watermark is embedded, is termed as cover image and after embeddeding a cover image is termed as watermarked image. A general digital watermarking technique consists of a embedding and extraction algorithms, as shown in Fig. 7.1. The embedding algorithm embeds a watermark into the cover image and the watermarked image is generated. The watermarked image is further processed by an extraction algorithm to extract the watermark when required. To check the features such as robustness, fragility etc. attacks are executed on the watermarked image and then the watermark is extracted from it.

G. Kasana (✉)
Computer Science and Engineering Department, Thapar Institute of Engineering and Technology, Patiala, Punjab, India
e-mail: gkasana@thapar.edu

© Springer Nature Switzerland AG 2019
A. K. Singh, A. Mohan (eds.), *Handbook of Multimedia Information Security: Techniques and Applications*, https://doi.org/10.1007/978-3-030-15887-3_7

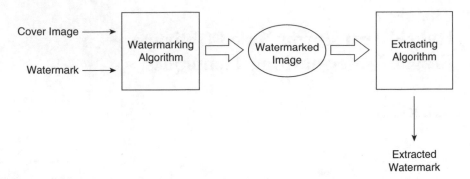

Fig. 7.1 General image watermarking framework

7.1.1   Types of Watermarking

Watermarking techniques are classified into following types:

1. Robust Watermarking: In this technique, watermarks can survive various attacks on them. Watermarks are embedded with such algorithms that they could resist attacks and have minimal damage.
2. Fragile and Semi-Fragile Watermarking: In Fragile watermarking, watermarks are very sensitive and get easily distorted upon modification. These are mostly used to find whether data had been tampered or not where as in semi-fragile watermarking the watermarks can handle unintentional attacks such as JPEG compression but can survive the intentional attacks like cropping, rotation etc.
3. Blind and Semi-Blind Watermarking: In blind watermarking also known as public watermarking, during detection or extracting process, host image is not needed where as in semi blind watermarking some part of host image is required.
4. Non-Blind Watermarking: In non-blind watermarking, the host image is needed during the detection and extraction process. This watermarking is also known as private watermarking.
5. Visible Watermarking: In visible watermarking, watermarks are easily visible or noticeable to human eyes. For example like stamp papers and television channel logo.
6. Invisible Watermarking: Invisible watermarking is the one's which holds the imperceptibility property. Embedded watermark is not visible to viewers and can be seen only after extraction process.

7.1.2   Features of Digital Watermarking

The features of the watermarking are the properties which are meant to be present in the watermarking algorithm. Some of the features of Digital Watermarking are described as.

1. **Robustness**: It is defined as a property of the watermarking technique if a watermark is not degraded, displaced or distorted on applying attacks like cropping, noise, rotation, quantization, scaling and JPEG compression. This property is important in the copyright material which is used for authentication.
2. **Imperceptibility**: In digital watermarking the watermark shouldn't be noticeable or visible to the viewer and the quality of the digital data should not be degraded. The only way to view watermark should be applying some kind of extraction algorithm in order to view it.
3. **Security**: When a digital watermarking technique is able to prevent any detection and modification of the watermark embedded in the cover image from any unauthorized users then it is said to be secure. Watermark keys are used to ensure that only authorised users are able to extract or transform the watermark. User having all information of embedding and extracting algorithm and nature of watermark should be able to get access. Watermark information has the unique sign for identification that only the users who are authorised can detect, extract or modify the watermark legally, and be able to provide the copyright protection.
4. **Capacity**: This property describes what amount of data or information bits can be inserted in the host image successfully. It describes the potential of embedding more than one watermarks in single digital file. This feature always contest with two other important features, which are, robustness and imperceptibility. A large capacity could be obtained but at the cost of either robustness, imperceptibility or sometimes both.

7.2   Review of Existing Watermarking Techniques

This section includes a review of existing watermarking techniques. The most of the work discussed here includes watermarking techniques based on Singular Value Decomposition (*SVD*).

A hybrid non-blind watermarking algorithm using *DWT* and *SVD* has been proposed by Ganic et al. [5]. The host image is transformed into subbands by using *DWT*. *SVD* is applied further to each of the subband, and then the singular values of these subbands are modified with the watermark's singular values. Modification in the frequencies made a watermarking algorithm robust to a many type of attacks. The authors compared their algorithm with *SVD*-based algorithms, and showed that their algorithm is robust to attacks and more reliable. Shieh et al. [18] proposed a robust watermarking system for embedding grayscale watermarks into cover images. The image quality parameters prove that the their technique ensures the extracted watermark has the mean *PSNR* value of 24.91 dB and the worst *PSNR* values of 19.96 dB, respectively. A digital watermarking technique based on *SVD* and *GA* was proposed by Aslantas [1]. In the embedding process of the technique, the singular values of the cover image are remodeled by multiple scaling factors. Further, modifications are optimized using genetic algorithm and the highest of the possible robustness are obtained without losing the transparency.

Dogan et al. [3] proposed a scheme for watermarking using *SVD* applicable to the color images. In *SVD* centered watermarking techniques, the watermark is inserted by changing the *LSB* of the singular value matrix. A digital image watermarking technique by using a tiny genetic algorithm and *SVD* is proposed by Lai [11]. Tiny-GA is used to find the correct values in order to enhance the robustness of the technique and the imperceptibility standard of the watermarked image as the values of scale factors were used to find the strength of watermark. Jose et al. [7] proposed a hybrid digital watermarking technique based on *DCT – DWT – SVD*. The cover image is re-arranged before applying the *DCT*. *DCT* coefficients of the re-arranged image are decomposed into subbands by applying *DWT*. The singular quantities of the central sub bands were determined and then watermark is embedded.

Su et al. [22] proposed an image watermarking technique in which blocks of watermark are embedded and then distortion in the watermarked image is compensated by using improved optimization operation to achieve higher *PSNR* values. Caragata et al. [2] has proposed a new technique that is based on the cryptanalysis of the *CWSA* technique. The technique is robust from cryptanalysis, less perceptible, faster and also preserves the advantages of *CWSA*. It uses two chaotic maps: a chaotic generator which comprises of two perturbed recursive filters with a nonlinear function, which is Skew Tent map and the piecewise linear chaotic map. Keshavarzian et al. [8] proposed a blind and robust watermarking technique based on concept of Region of Interest using the Arnold Transform. A technique for an invisible and secure watermarking is proposed by Saikrishna et al. [15]. The cover image is classified into white and black textured areas by the determined location of embedding through initially entered key. The watermark image is then transformed by applying Arnold scrambling. *DWT* is used for inserting the transformed watermark into the regions having white textures. Singh and Singh [4] proposed a watermarking technique for copyright protection based on *DCT*, *DWT* and *SVD* with Arnold Cat Map encryption. Their technique is able to solve problem of unauthorised reading and false-positive detection and is robust. Haddada et al. [6] proposed a watermarking technique that safeguards the security of the biometric data of the person and the computational complication of the proposed technique. The better visual standards of the watermarked image and reduced storage space had been maintained. By various tests performed, robustness to several signal processing attacks had been demonstrated by their technique. Loukhaoukha et al. [12] used the *SVD* and redundant discrete wavelet transform (*RDWT*) to propose a copyright protection technique.

Solorio et al. [16] proposed a technique in which two series of reference bits of the five most significant bit-planes of the image are generated. Some authentication bits and reference bits are then assigned to the three least significant bit-planes (*LSBPs*) of the image. The verified bits are used by the receiver to localize the changed pixel-blocks. An iterative restoration mechanism is executed to determine the genuine value of the watermarked pixels. Sangeetha et al. [17] proposed digital image watermarking technique by using the entropy of cover images and texture of the watermarks. The evaluation of the Entropy is done by the coefficients determined by applying *DWT* of the cover image were used. The experimental results are used to show the effectiveness of the technique.

7.2.1   Motivation

In the light of the literature review conducted on the existing watermarking techniques, following gaps have been identified:

1. Most of the *SVD* based watermarking techniques are non-blind in nature.
2. Mostly techniques are having the false positive problem.

7.2.2   Contribution

Contributions of the proposed chapter are summarized as:

1. Proposed watermarking techniques are free from false positive detection.
2. Both the techniques are blind in nature, so no overhead is required to extract the watermark on the receiver side.

7.3   Proposed Watermarking Techniques

In this section, two watermarking techniques for grayscale images have been proposed. The first technique is Entropy based blind watermarking technique which uses *DWT* and *SVD* transforms. After applying *DWT* to the host image, sub-band having maximum entropy is selected and is partitioned into 4×4 sized non overlapping blocks. *SVD* is then applied on each 4×4 block and then watermark bit is embedded into one of the singular value of each block. Singular values are selected in such a way that imperceptibility as well as visual quality of extracted watermark are maintained.

Whereas in second technique, *DWT*, *DCT* and *SVD* transforms have been used. *DWT* is applied on the host image and then it is decomposed into 4×4 sized non overlapping blocks. Then *DCT* and *SVD* are applied on the blocks and a watermark bits are embedded into the singular values of the non-overlapping blocks to get the watermarked image.

7.3.1   Entropy Based Watermarking Technique

The properties of the *SVD* of the host image are utilized to embed the watermark. For this, it has been observed that bigger the singular value utilized for watermark embedding, lesser will be the impact of watermark on host image. The number of designated singular values are similar as the amount of pixels in watermark image but good quality of extracted watermark. These factors support the idea behind developing the proposed *SVD* based watermarking technique.

7.3.1.1 Embedding Method

Embedding method of the proposed technique is shown in Fig. 7.2 and steps are explained below:

Step 1: Decompose the host image H into four sub-bands, HL, LH, HH and LL using DWT.

$$[LL, LH, HL, HH] = DWT(H,'haar')$$

Step 2: Find out the entropy of each sub-band. Choose the sub-band, X_{sub}, for embedding having maximum entropy.

Step 3: Divide the X_{sub} into non-overlapping blocks of dimension 4×4.

Step 4: Apply the SVD on each non-overlapping blocks of X_{sub} sub-band.

$$[u, s, v] = svd(B_i)$$

where B_i is the input block.

Step 5: Read the watermark W and reshuffle it using Arnold transform.

Step 6: Modify the singular values of eack block B_i to embedding the watermark bit W_i by performing following steps:

- If W_i is '1' and the largest singular value is odd then there will be no variation in the singular value otherwise increment the singular value by one.
- If W_i is '0' and largest singular value is even then there will be no variation in the singular value otherwise increment the singular value by one.

Step 7: Apply inverse SVD on every block and then join all blocks to restore the sub band.

Step 8: Apply inverse wavelet $IDWT$ on modified X_{sub} and other three sub-bands to obtain watermarked image W'.

To increase watermarking security, a pseudo random number generator ($PRNG$) is adopted to select the block from where watermark bit starts embedding.

7.3.1.2 Extraction Method

Extraction method of the proposed technique is shown in Fig. 7.3 and steps are discussed below:

Step 1: Apply DWT on the watermarked image W' to form sub bands.

Step 2: Find the entropy of each sub-band and select the sub-band having maximum entropy.

Step 3: Divide the selected sub-bands into non overlapping blocks of size 4×4.

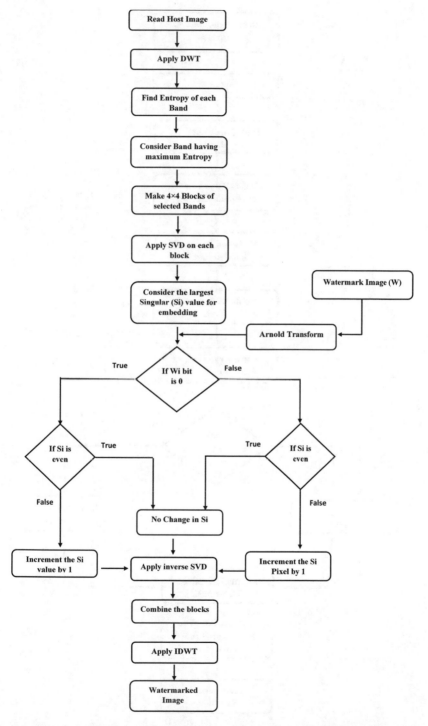

Fig. 7.2 Flowchart depicting embedding method of entropy based technique using *DWT* and *SVD*

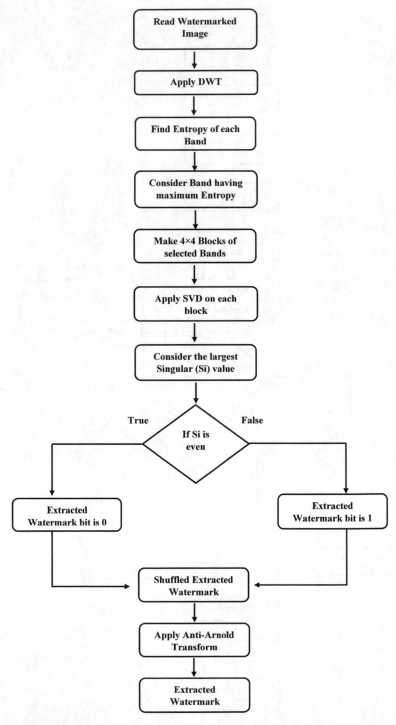

Fig. 7.3 Flowchart depicting extraction method of entropy based technique using *DWT* and *SVD*

Step 4: Apply *SVD* to every block of selected sub-band by

$$[u, s, v] = svd(B_i)$$

Step 5: Largest singular value of every block is obtained.

- If singular value is even then watermark bit $= 0$.
- If singular value is odd then watermark bit $= 1$

Step 6: Apply Inverse Arnold on the extracted watermark.

7.3.2 Watermarking Technique Based on DWT, DCT and SVD

In this section, technique based on the concepts of the *DWT, DCT* and *SVD* is proposed. This technique also has Embedding and the Extraction method which are explained with steps and detailed flowchart in Fig. 7.4.

7.3.2.1 Embedding Method

Embedding method of the proposed technique is shown in Fig. 7.4 and steps are explained below:

Step 1: Apply single level *DWT* on the host image to divide it into four sub-bands *LL, LH, HL* and *HH*.

$$[LL, LH, HL, HH] = DWT(H, 'haar')$$

Step 2: Divide the sub-band *LL* into non-overlapping blocks of size 4×4.

Step 3: Apply *DCT* on each block of sub-band $DCT(B_i)$.

Step 4: Execute *SVD* operation on each and every blocks of the *LL* sub-band.

$$[u_i, s_i, v_i] = svd(B_i)$$

Step 5: Read the watermark and apply Arnold Transform on it.

Step 6: Modify the singular value S_i of the block b_i with the watermark bit W_i by the following steps.

- If W_i is '1' and the largest singular value is odd then there will be no variation in the singular value otherwise increment the singular value by one.
- If W_i is '0' and integer part of the singular value is even then there will be no variation in the singular value otherwise increment the singular value by one.

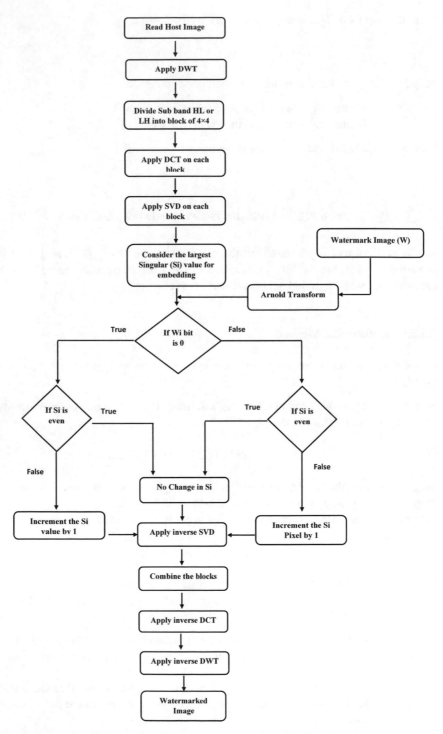

Fig. 7.4 Flowchart depicting embedding method of technique based on *DWT*, *DCT* and *SVD*

Step 7: Perform inverse *SVD* on each and every blocks, and merge the modified *LL* sub band.

Step 8: Implement inverse of *DCT* to each block.

Step 9: Apply inverse *IDWT* to obtain the watermarked image.

7.3.2.2 Extraction Method

Extraction method of the proposed technique is shown in Fig. 7.5 and steps are discussed below:

Step 1: Consider the host image and apply single level *DWT* on the host image to decompose it into four sub-bands *LL*, *LH*, *HL* and *HH*.

Step 2: Divide the sub-band *HL* or *LH* into non-overlapping block of 4×4 elements.

Step 3: Apply *DCT* on each block of sub-band $DCT(B_i)$.

Step 4: Implement *SVD* on all blocks of the sub-band.

$$[u_i, s_i, v_i] = svd(B_i)$$

Step 5: Largest singular value of each block is processed using the following rules.

- If singular value is even then $W_i = 0$.
- If singular value is odd then $W_i = 1$.

Using these steps, shuffled watermark is obtained.

Step 6: Apply the Inverse Arnold Transform on shuffled watermark to get original watermark.

7.4 Experimental Results and Discussions

Proposed watermarking techniques are implemented in MATLAB. To analyse the performance of the proposed techniques, few images like Baboon, Boat, Lena, Girlface, Crowd and Zelda are considered as host image for experiment. All these images are of size 512×512 and some of these are shown in Fig. 7.6a and b. The considered watermarks are logo and copyright of size 32×32, as shown in Fig. 7.7.

7.4.1 Image Quality Metrics

Image quality metrics are used to analyze the changes in visual quality of image after embedding, extracting and attacking process.

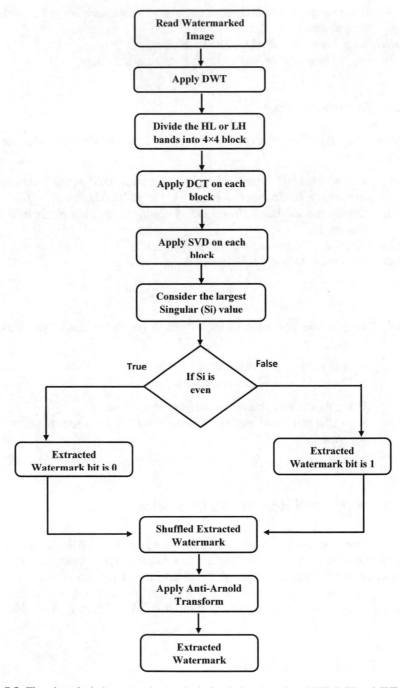

Fig. 7.5 Flowchart depicting extracting method of technique based on *DWT*, *DCT* and *SVD*

Fig. 7.6 Watermarks. (**a**) Logo image. (**b**) Copyright image

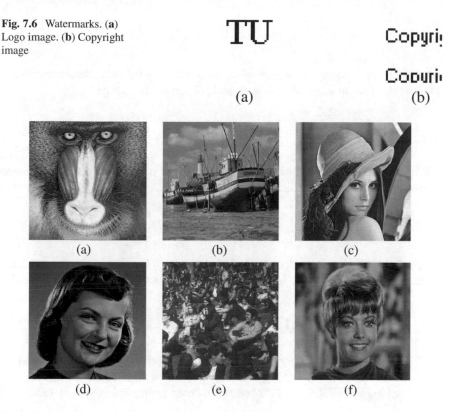

TU

Copyri<

Copuri<

(a)

(b)

(a)   (b)   (c)

(d)   (e)   (f)

Fig. 7.7 Host images. (**a**) Baboon. (**b**) Boat. (**c**) Lena. (**d**) Girlface. (**e**) Crowd. (**f**) Zelda

7.4.1.1 Peak Signal-to-Noise Ratio

PSNR determines the peak signal-to-noise ratio, in decibels, among the two images. This ratio is frequently used as an image quality metric among the host and the watermarked image. Higher the value of *PSNR* shows that imperceptibility of the watermarked image is better. It is defined by using the following equation

$$PSNR = 10 \, log_{10} \frac{(2^b - 1)^2}{MSE} \tag{7.1}$$

where b is bit depth of an image. Mean Square Error *(MSE)* is also an image quality metric used for comparison between the image quality and it shows the cumulative squared error between the watermarked and the host image, and quantity of the peak error is *PSNR*. *MSE* is evaluated as the root mean square of difference of the corresponding pixel values of the host image and watermarked image. Minimum the Mean Square error is, better the watermarking is. The Mean Square error can expressed as:

$$MSE = \frac{\sum [I_1(i, j) - I_2(i, j)]}{M \times N} \tag{7.2}$$

where $I_1(i, j)$ is cover image pixel at (i, j) location, $I_2(i, j)$ is watermarked image pixel at (i, j) location. $M \times N$ is rows and columns of the image.

7.4.1.2 Bit Error Rate

Bit Error Rate *(BER)* is defined as the number of the bit changed during extraction to the bits that were embedded in cover image.

$$BER = \frac{\sum [I_1(i, j) \oplus I_2(i, j)]}{M \times N} \tag{7.3}$$

where $I_1(i, j)$ is original watermark image pixel at (i, j) location, $I_2(i, j)$ is extracted watermark image pixel at (i, j) location. $M \times N$ is rows and columns of the image.

7.4.1.3 Bit Correction Rate

Bit Correction Rate (*BCR*) implies resemblance between the host watermark and the extracted watermark. It is defined as the ratio of the bit remained unchanged during extraction to the bits that were embedded in cover image and is usually calculated as:

$$BCR = 100 - BER \tag{7.4}$$

7.4.1.4 Normalized Correlation

Normalized Correlation (*NC*) is used to evaluate the quality among the original and the extracted watermark. This parameter is defined by using the following expression:

$$NC = \frac{\sum (x - x') \times (y - y')}{\sqrt{\sum (x - x')^2 \times (y - y')^2}} \tag{7.5}$$

where x is the pixel of watermark, x' is the mean of the watermark, y is the pixel of extracted watermark, y' is the mean of the extracted watermark.

7.4.1.5   Similarity Index Modulation

Similarity Index Modulation (*SIM*) is used to measure the similarity between the original and extracted watermarks and it is expressed by:

$$SIM = \frac{\sum_i \sum_j I_1(i, j) \times I_2(i, j)}{\sum_i \sum_j [I_1(i, j)]^2} \tag{7.6}$$

where $I_1(i, j)$ is the original watermark pixel while $I_2(i, j)$ is the extracted watermark.

7.4.2   Entropy Based Algorithm Using DWT and SVD

Using this technique, watermarked images are formed, which are shown in Fig. 7.8. If we compare the watermarked image with their host image, the visual quality of both are similar i.e., they maintains the imperceptibility. The entropy of each sub band of host images and *PSNR* between host and watermarked images after embedding 32×32 copyright watermark is shown in Table 7.1.

From Tables 7.1 and 7.2 we can conclude that, diagonal sub bands of *DWT* have maximum entropy and *PSNR* is also indication to high imperceptibility. In order to show the effectiveness of technique, Tables 7.3 and 7.4 contain the *PSNR* between

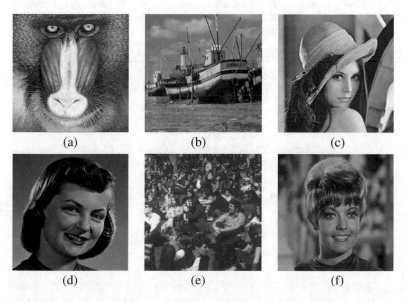

(a)   (b)   (c)

(d)   (e)   (f)

Fig. 7.8 Watermarked images by entropy based technique using *DWT* and *SVD*. (**a**) Baboon. (**b**) Boat. (**c**) Lena. (**d**) Girlface. (**e**) Crowd. (**f**) Zelda

host and watermarked images, *NC*, *BCR*, *BER*, *SIM* between original watermarks and extracted watermarks, and the watermark extracted from different watermarked images obtained is shown.

Tables 7.3 and 7.4 summarize the performance of the entropy based technique after embedding watermark of size 32 × 32. The *PSNR* between host image and watermarked image is approximately 70 dB. It shows that this technique maintains the imperceptibility and visual quality of watermarked image is better whereas *NC* and *SIM* between original and extracted watermark is '1', *BCR* is 100 and BER is 0% which depicts the extracted watermark image quality is exactly similar to the original watermark.

In order to use characteristics of *SVD* domain to embed a watermark in host image, different singular values are used for determining image quality metrics. As we apply the *SVD* on 4 × 4 block, four non-zero singular values obtained.

Table 7.1 Entropy of the sub-bands of the host images and *PSNR* (dB) between host and watermarked images after embedding 32 × 32 copyright watermark

Images	Baboon		Boat		Lena	
Subband	Entropy	*PSNR*	Entropy	*PSNR*	Entropy	*PSNR*
LL	0	4.737	0	5.361	0	4.829
HL	1.1516	25.163	1.253	33.638	1.255	33.449
LH	1.1569	75.147	1.217	30.328	1.232	33.285
HH	1.336	29.743	1.275	75.189	1.421	75.156

Table 7.2 Entropy of the sub-bands of the host images and *PSNR* (dB) between host and watermarked images after embedding 32 × 32 copyright watermark

Images	Girlface		Crowd		Zelda	
Subband	Entropy	*PSNR*	Entropy	*PSNR*	Entropy	*PSNR*
LL	0.138	6.478	0	8.247	0	5.464
HL	1.308	33.481	1.323	32.837	1.337	37.105
LH	1.385	73.386	1.316	33.634	1.260	33.880
HH	1.435	35.044	1.404	74.893	1.367	72.462

Table 7.3 *PSNR* (in dB) between host and watermarked image, *NC*, *BCR* (in %), *BER* (in %), *SIM* between original copyright watermark and extracted watermark, and watermark extracted from different watermarked images

	Baboon	Boat	Lena	Girlface	Crowd	Zelda
PSNR	75.147	75.189	75.156	73.386	74.893	72.462
NC	1	1	1	1	1	1
BCR	100	100	100	100	100	100
BER	0	0	0	0	0	0
SIM	1	1	1	1	1	1
Extracted watermark	Copyri Copyri	Copyri Copyri	Copyri Copyri	Copyri Copyri	Copyri Copyri	Copyri Copyri

Table 7.4 *PSNR* (in dB) between host and watermarked image, *NC*, *BCR* (in %), *BER* (in %), *SIM* between logo watermark and extracted watermark, and watermark extracted from different watermarked images

	Baboon	Boat	Lena	Girlface	Crowd	Zelda
PSNR	74.387	74.547	74.493	72.687	74.310	71.797
Correlation	1	1	1	1	1	1
BCR	100	100	100	100	100	100
BER	0	0	0	0	0	0
SIM	1	1	1	1	1	1
Extracted watermark	TU	TU	TU	TU	TU	TU

Table 7.5 *PSNR* (in dB) between watermarked and host image, *NC*, *BCR* (in %), *BER* (in %), *SIM* between original and extracted watermark without any attack embedded in *S(1,1)* and image of extracted watermark

	Baboon	Boat	Lena	Girlface	Crowd	Zelda
PSNR	75.147	75.189	75.156	73.386	74.893	72.462
NC	1	1	1	1	1	1
BCR	100	100	100	100	100	100
BER	0	0	0	0	0	0
SIM	1	1	1	1	1	1
Extracted watermark	Copyri Copuri	Copyri Copuri	Copyri Copuri	Copyri Copuri	Copyri Copuri	Copyri Copuri

Table 7.6 *PSNR* (in dB) between watermarked and host image, *NC*, *BCR* (in %), *BER* (in %), *SIM* between original and extracted watermark without any attack embedded in *S(2,2)* and image of extracted watermark

	Baboon	Boat	Lena	Girlface	Crowd	Zelda
PSNR	75.274	75.181	75.438	73.270	75.634	72.445
NC	1	0.983	0.916	0.909	0.901	0.934
BCR	100	99.609	97.949	97.753	97.656	98.437
BER	0	0.390	2.050	2.246	2.343	1.562
SIM	1	1	1	1	1	1
Extracted watermark	Copyri Copuri	Copyri Copuri	Copyri Copuri	Copyri Copuri	Copyri Copuri	Copyri Copuri

Tables 7.5, 7.6, 7.7, 7.8 show which nonzero singular values give better imperceptibility and extraction of watermark after embedding.

After observing the *PSNR* values for different images in the given tables we observed that data embedded into highest singular value gives better *PSNR* i.e., imperceptibility maintained and *BCR* having value above 90 and very low *BER*, it infer that quality of extracted watermark is comparable to original watermark. To show the fragility of the watermarking technique, different attacks on the watermarked image have been applied. After applying these attacks the values of *NC*, *BCR* and *BER* between original and extracted watermark are tabulated in Table 7.9.

Table 7.7 *PSNR* (in dB) between watermarked and host image, *NC*, *BCR* (in %), *BER* (in %), *SIM* between original and extracted watermark, without any attack embedded in *S(3,3)* and image of extracted watermark

	Baboon	Boat	Lena	Girlface	Crowd	Zelda
PSNR	75.040	75.215	74.958	73.905	74.949	72.487
NC	0.987	0.971	0.758	0.8302	0.834	0.897
BCR	99.707	99.316	92.773	95.605	95.507	97.363
BER	0.293	0.683	7.226	4.394	4.492	2.636
SIM	1	1	1	1	1	1
Extracted watermark	Copyri Coperi	Copyri Coperi	Copyri Cobuh	Copyri Copuri	Copyri Coburh	Copyri Copuri

Table 7.8 *PSNR* (in dB) between watermarked and host image, *NC*, *BCR* (in %), *BER* (in %), *SIM* between original and extracted watermark, without any attack embedded in *S(4,4)* and image of extracted watermark

	Baboon	Boat	Lena	Girlface	Crowd	Zelda
PSNR	74.765	74.592	73.315	71.871	73.568	71.246
NC	0.970	0.949	0.449	0.739	0.513	0.819
BCR	99.316	98.828	71.679	92.089	77.050	95.312
BER	0.683	1.171	28.320	7.910	22.949	4.687
SIM	1	1	1	1	1	1
Extracted watermark	Copyri Coperi	Copyri Coburi		Copyri Copuri		Copyri Copufi

Table 7.9 *NC*, *BCR* and *BER* between original and extracted watermark after attack on watermarked image

Image	Attacks	*NC*	*BCR*	*BER*
Baboon	Averaging filtering	0.057	51.85	48.14
	JPEG compression	0.017	13.28	86.71
	Salt & pepper	0.012	13.183	86.816
Boat	Averaging filtering	0.015	14.74	85.25
	JPEG compression	NaN	13.08	86.91
	Salt & pepper	0.0242	13.476	86.523
Lena	Averaging filtering	0	18.06	81.93
	JPEG compression	NaN	13.08	86.91
	Salt & pepper	0.012	13.183	86.816
Girlface	Averaging filtering	0.027	35.05	64.94
	JPEG compression	−0.050	16.21	83.78
	Salt & pepper	0.010	16.406	83.593
Crowd	Averaging filtering	−0.017	17.96	82.03
	JPEG compression	NaN	13.08	86.91
	Salt & pepper	0.012	13.183	86.816
Zelda	Averaging filtering	−0.004	14.06	85.91
	JPEG compression	NaN	13.08	86.91
	Salt & pepper	0.017	13.085	86.914

Table 7.10 *PSNR* (dB) after embedding 32 × 32, 56 × 56 and 64 × 64 copyright watermarks

Image\size	32 × 32	56 × 56	64 × 64
Baboon	75.147	70.239	69.150
Boat	75.189	70.398	69.244
Lena	75.156	70.272	69.135
Girlface	73.386	68.544	67.371
Crowd	74.893	70.331	69.319
Zelda	72.462	67.730	66.568

From Table 7.9, we can conclude that after attacking the watermarked image by average filtering and salt n pepper noise the *NC* values are very less and *BCR* value is also below 50%, which shows the watermarking scheme can be used for fragile watermarking. In Table 7.10 the *PSNR* between host and watermarked image after embedding copyright watermark of different sizes are tabulated. From Table 7.10 we can conclude that on embedding different sizes of watermark, the *PSNR* is more than or near to 70 dB.

7.4.3   Results Analysis of DWT, DCT and SVD Based Technique

By implementing this technique, watermarked images are formed, which are shown in Fig. 7.9. If we compare the visualization of the watermarked image with their host images, then we notice that they both look similar, i.e., the imperceptibility is maintained.

In order to show the effectiveness of the technique, Tables 7.11, 7.12, 7.13, 7.14 contains the *PSNR* between host and watermarked images, *NC*, *BCR*, *BER*, *SIM* between original and extracted watermark, and the extracted watermark image from different watermarked images obtained is shown.

Tables 7.11, 7.12, 7.13, 7.14 show that the *NC* and *BCR* values are 1 and 100 respectively and the *PSNR* is approximately 75 dB. After analyzing the result values we can observe that applying *DCT* on 4 × 4 block before *SVD*, gives better *PSNR* and other parameters. To show the fragility of the watermarking technique, different attacks on the watermarked image have been applied. After applying these attacks the values of *NC*, *BCR* and *BER* between original and extracted watermark are tabulated in Table 7.15.

From Table 7.15, we can conclude that after attacking the watermarked image by average filtering and salt and pepper noise, the *NC* values are very less, which shows the watermarking scheme can be used for fragile watermarking. In Table 7.16 the *PSNR* between host and watermarked image after embedding copyright watermark of different sizes are tabulated.

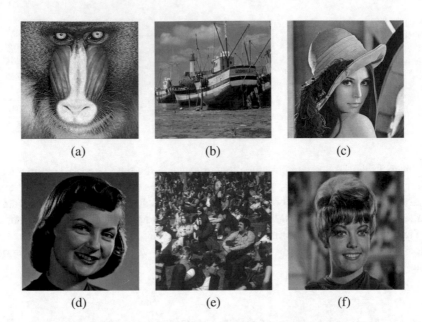

(a) (b) (c)

(d) (e) (f)

Fig. 7.9 Watermarked images from technique using *DWT*, *DCT* and *SVD*. (**a**) Baboon. (**b**) Boat. (**c**) Lena. (**d**) Girlface. (**e**) Crowd. (**f**) Zelda

Table 7.11 *PSNR* (in dB) between watermarked and host image, *NC*, *BCR* (in %), *BER* (in %), *SIM* between 32 × 32 original and extracted watermark and watermark extracted from different watermarked images

	Baboon	Boat	Lena	Girlface	Crowd	Zelda
PSNR	74.952	75.114	75.030	73.412	75.061	72.258
NC	1	1	1	1	1	1
BCR	100	100	100	100	100	100
BER	0	0	0	0	0	0
SIM	1	1	1	1	1	1
Extracted watermark	Copyri Copuri	Copyri Copuri	Copyri Copuri	Copyri Copuri	Copyri Copuri	Copyri Copuri

From Table 7.16 we conclude that after embedding large size of watermark, it maintains the imperceptibility. The comparison of proposed techniques with existing techniques with respect to *PSNR*, blindness and false positive are shown in Tables 7.17 and 7.18.

Table 7.12 *PSNR* (in dB) between watermarked and host image, *NC*, *BCR* (in %), *BER* (in %), *SIM* between 56 × 56 original and extracted watermark and watermark extracted from different watermarked images

	Baboon	Boat	Lena	Girlface	Crowd	Zelda
PSNR	70.385	70.290	75.340	68.619	70.309	67.713
NC	1	1	1	1	1	1
BCR	100	100	100	100	100	100
BER	0	0	0	0	0	0
SIM	1	1	1	1	1	1
Extracted watermark	Copyright Cc Copyright Cc Copyright Cc	Copyright Cc Copyright Cc Copyright Cc	Copyright Cc Copyright Cc Copyright Cc	Copyright Cc Copyright Cc Copyright Cc	Copyright Cc Copyright Cc Copyright Cc	Copyright Cc Copyright Cc Copyright Cc

Table 7.13 *PSNR* (in dB) between watermarked and host image, *NC*, *BCR* (in %), *BER* (in %), *SIM* between 64 × 64 original and extracted copyright watermark and watermark extracted from different watermarked images

	Baboon	Boat	Lena	Girlface	Crowd	Zelda
PSNR	69.175	69.154	69.219	67.460	69.122	66.504
NC	1	1	1	1	1	1
BCR	100	100	100	100	100	100
BER	0	0	0	0	0	0
SIM	1	1	1	1	1	1
Extracted watermark	Copyright Cc Copyright Cc Copyright Cc	Copyright Cc Copyright Cc Copyright Cc	Copyright Cc Copyright Cc Copyright Cc	Copyright Cc Copyright Cc Copyright Cc	Copyright Cc Copyright Cc Copyright Cc	Copyright Cc Copyright Cc Copyright Cc

Table 7.14 *PSNR* (in dB) between watermarked and host image, *NC*, *BCR* (in %), *BER* (in %), *SIM* between original and extracted logo watermark and watermark extracted from different watermarked images

	Baboon	Boat	Lena	Girlface	Crowd	Zelda
PSNR	74.496	74.205	74.448	72.737	74.415	71.712
NC	1	1	1	1	1	1
BCR	100	100	100	100	100	100
BER	0	0	0	0	0	0
SIM	1	1	1	1	1	1
Extracted watermark	TU	TU	TU	TU	TU	TU

7.5   Conclusion

In this work, transform based blind watermarking techniques for digital images have been proposed. In first technique, after its implementation the average *PSNR* was up to 74.372 dB with *NC* and *BCR* with values 1 and 100 and of the various watermarks of sizes 32 × 32 and 64 × 64. Even in the second proposed technique based on *DWT*, *DCT*, image quality metrics evaluated were showing the average *PSNR* up to

Table 7.15 *NC, BCR* and *BER* between original and extracted watermark after attack on watermarked image

Image	Attacks	*NC*	*BCR*	*BER*
Baboon	Average filtering	−0.034	49.902	50.097
	JPEG compression	−0.017	86.718	13.281
	Salt & pepper	NaN	86.914	13.085
Boat	Average filtering	0.003	48.828	51.171
	JPEG compression	NaN	86.914	13.085
	Salt & pepper	NaN	86.914	13.085
Lena	Averaging filtering	−0.011	47.363	52.636
	JPEG compression	NaN	86.914	13.085
	Salt & pepper	NaN	86.914	13.085
Girlface	Averaging filtering	0.017	50.585	49.414
	JPEG compression	0.026	82.519	17.480
	Salt & pepper	0.005	84.960	15.039
Crowd	Averaging filtering	−0.007	49.609	50.390
	JPEG compression	NaN	86.914	13.085
	Salt & pepper	NaN	86.914	13.085
Zelda	Averaging filtering	−0.067	47.363	52.636
	JPEG compression	NaN	86.914	13.085
	Salt & pepper	NaN	86.914	13.085

Table 7.16 *PSNR* (in dB) after embedding 32×32 and 64×64 copyright and logo watermarks

Size of watermark	32×32	64×64	Logo (32×32)
Baboon	74.952	69.175	74.496
Boat	75.114	69.154	74.205
Lena	75.030	69.219	74.448
Girlface	73.412	67.460	72.737
Crowd	75.061	69.122	74.415
Zelda	72.258	66.504	71.712

74.827 dB with *NC* and *BCR* with values 1 and 100%. Here also, various watermark were used and of different sizes of 32×32 and 64×64. After analyzing the all image quality metrics, it have been concluded the both proposed techniques are providing the better imperceptibility and free from false-positive problem. Further, both of techniques also include blindness feature as the host image is not required to extract the embedded watermark.

7.6 Future Scope

The proposed techniques are very much fragile but are not able to provide the robustness. So the work on the robustness of the techniques can be done in the near future.

Table 7.17 Comparison of the *PSNR* (in dB) between existing techniques with proposed techniques

	Jose et al. [7]	Sangeetha et al. [17]	Mishra et al. [13]	Proposed entropy based technique	Proposed *DWT*, *DCT* and *SVD* based technique
Airplane	–	28.66762	–	–	–
Baboon	–	28.58936	53.0487	75.147	74.952
Boat	–	28.65913	54.0508	75.189	75.114
Barbara	51.7341	28.61679	–	–	–
Crowd	–	–	–	74.893	75.061
Cameraman	–	–	53.5651	–	–
Girlface	–	–	–	73.386	73.412
Goldhill	–	28.66259	–	–	–
Lena	51.5564	–	53.3062	75.156	75.030
Man	–	–	53.7479	–	–
Pepper	51.7925	–	52.09	–	–
Zelda	–	28.66974	–	72.462	72.258

Table 7.18 Comparison of the false-positive problem and blindness with existing techniques

	Watermark type	Type of transform	Embedding sub band	Encryption	False-positive problem	Blindness
Mishra et al. [13]	Binary	*DWT* + *SVD*	LL3	No	Yes	No
Rastegar et al. [14]	Binary	*FRAT* + *SVD* + *DWT*	LL3, LH3	No	Yes	No
Proposed entropy based technique	Binary	*DWT* + *SVD*	Based on entropy	Yes	No	Yes
Proposed *DCT* based technique	Binary	*DWT* + *DCT* + *SVD*	HH	Yes	No	Yes

References

1. Aslantas V., "A singular-value decomposition-based image watermarking using genetic algorithm", International Journal of Electronics and Communications Vol. 62, pp. 386–394, 2008.
2. Caragata D., Assad S. E., Luduena M., "An improved fragile watermarking algorithm for JPEG images", International Journal of Electronics and Communications, pp. 1783–1794, 2015.
3. Dogan S., Tuncer T., Avci E., Gulten A., "A robust color image watermarking with Singular Value Decomposition method", Advances in Engineering Software, Vol. 42, pp. 336–346, April 2011.
4. Durgesh Singh, S. K. Singh, "DWT-SVD and DCT based robust and blind watermarking scheme for copyright protection", Multimed Tools Appl, Vol. 76, pp. 13001–13024, July 2016.
5. Ganic E., Eskicioglu A. M., "Robust Embedding of visual Watermarks using DWT-SVD", Department of Computer and Information Science, CUNY Brooklyn College, pp. 1–13, 2004.
6. Haddada L.R., Dorizzic B., Amara N. E. B., "A combined watermarking approach for securing biometric data", Signal Processing: Image Communication, Vol. 55, pp. 23–31, 2017.

7. Jose S., Roy R. C., Shashidharan S., "Robust Image Watermarking based on DCT-DWT-SVD Method", International Journal of Computer Applications, Vol. 58, Issue 21, pp. 12–16, 2012.
8. Keshavarziana R., Aghagolzadeh A., "ROI based robust and secure image watermarking using DWT and Arnold map", International Journal of Electronics and Communications, pp. 278–288, 2016.
9. Kumar C., Singh A. K., and Kumar P., "Improved Wavelet-Based Image Watermarking Through SPIHT, Multimedia Tools and Applications, Springer, pp. 1–14. https://doi.org/10.1007/s11042-018-6177-0
10. Kumar C., Singh A. K., and Kumar P., "A recent survey on image watermarking techniques and its application in e-governance, Multimedia Tools and Applications, Springer, Vol. 77, Issue 3, pp. 3597–3622. https://doi.org/10.1007/s11042-017-5222-8.
11. Lai C. C., "A digital watermarking scheme based on singular value decomposition and tiny genetic algorithm", Digital Signal Processing, Vol. 21, pp. 522–527, 2011.
12. Loukhaoukha K., Refaey A., Zebbiche K., "Ambiguity attacks on robust blind image watermarking scheme based on redundant discrete wavelet transform and singular value decomposition", Journal of Electrical Systems and Information Technology, pp. 359–368, 2017.
13. Mishra A., Agarwal C., Sharma A., Bedi P., "Optimized gray-scale image watermarking using DWT–SVD and Firefly Algorithm", Expert Systems with Applications, Issue 41, pp. 7858–7867, 2014.
14. Rastegar S., Namazi F, Yaghmaie K, Aliabadian A., "Hybrid watermarking algorithm based on singular value decomposition and radon transform", International Journal on Electronics Communication, Vol. 7, Issue 65, pp. 658–663, 2011.
15. Saikrishna N., Resmipriya M. G., "An Invisible Logo Watermarking using Arnold Transform", 6th International Conference on Advances in Computing and Communications, pp. 808–815, 2016.
16. Solorio S. Y., Calderon F., Lic C.T., Nandi A. K., "Fast fragile watermark embedding and iterative mechanism with high self-restoration performance", Digital Signal Processing, Issue 73, pp. 83–92, 2018.
17. Sangeetha N., Anita X., "Entropy based texture watermarking using discrete wavelet transform", Optik, Issue 160, pp. 380–388, 2018.
18. Shieh J.M., Lou D.C., Chang M.C., "A semi-blind digital watermarking scheme based on singular value decomposition", Computer Standards and Interfaces, Issue 28, pp. 428–440, 2005.
19. Sharma S., Singh A. K., Kumar P., "Computationally efficient joint imperceptible image watermarking and JPEG compression: A green computing approach, Multimedia Tools and Applications, Vol. 77, pp. 16447–16459, 2017. https://doi.org/10.1007/s11042-017-5214-8.
20. Singh A.K., Kumar B., Singh G. and Mohan A., "Medical Image Watermarking: Techniques and Applications, book series on Multimedia Systems and Applications, Springer, USA, ISBN: 978-3319576985, 2017.
21. Singh L., Singh A.K., and Singh P.K., "Secure data hiding techniques: A survey, Multimedia Tools and Applications, Springer. https://doi.org/10.1007/s11042-018-6407-5, 2018.
22. Su Q., Niu Y., Zhao Y., Pang S., Liu X., "A dual color images watermarking scheme based on the optimized compensation of singular value decomposition", International Journal of Electronics and Communications, Issue 67, pp. 652–664, 2013.
23. Thakur S., Singh A. K., Ghrera S. P. and Mohamed E. Multi-layer security of medical data through watermarking and chaotic encryption for tele-health applications, Multimedia Tools and Applications, Springer, pp. 1–14, 2018. https://doi.org/10.1007/s11042-018-6263-3.
24. Thakur S., Singh A. K., Ghrera S. P. and Mohan A. Chaotic based secure watermarking approach for medical images, Multimedia Tools and Applications, 2018. https://doi.org/10.1007/s11042-018-6691-0.

Chapter 8
Performance Analysis of Invariant Quaternion Moments in Color Image Watermarking

Khalid M. Hosny and Mohamed M. Darwish

8.1 Introduction

With the widespread of multimedia technology [1], protecting the copyright content and integrity of digital products becomes a great challenge. In the social networks such as Facebook, Twitter and Instagram, digital images are captured, stored and shared without any kind of protection [2]. The shared images can be accessed, downloaded, modified, and illegally reused by the others for different purposes [3]. Methods of information security could prevent these risks [4]. Watermarking the digital images is one of the most successful solutions for protecting digital contents such as audio, image, video and text [5]. Watermark methods are proposed to protect copyrights, detecting illegal distribution of digital contents and authentication [6]. According to their specific security purposes, three groups of watermarking methods are available: (1) robust. (2) semi-fragile. (3) fragile [7–9]. The digital watermarking plays an important role in Telemedicine [10], e-health [11], medical images [12–15], online social network [16], e-governance [17] and video streaming services [18]. Different applications of watermarking are displayed in Fig. 8.1.

Watermarking methods consists of two main stages. In the first stage, a digital watermark is embedded in the original/host digital content where this embedded watermark is a piece of digital data. In the second stage, the watermark information is detected or extracted where the watermark should be invisible and robust enough to resist different types of attacks. Robust image watermarking methods were developed for many applications [19–23]. Image watermarking methods suffered

K. M. Hosny (✉)
Department of Information Technology, Faculty of Computers and Informatics,
Zagazig University, Zagazig, Egypt

M. M. Darwish
Department of Mathematics, Faculty of Science, Assiut University, Assiut, Egypt

© Springer Nature Switzerland AG 2019
A. K. Singh, A. Mohan (eds.), *Handbook of Multimedia Information Security: Techniques and Applications*, https://doi.org/10.1007/978-3-030-15887-3_8

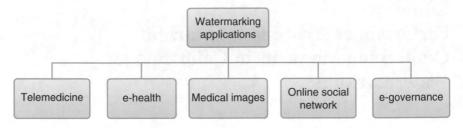

Fig. 8.1 Watermarking applications

from two challenging problems. First, the perceptibility in the embedding process where embedding the watermark results in a modification in the host image. The quality of the host image is degraded and the hidden information could be exposed. Different attacks represent the second challenge. Detection of digital watermark encounters attacks. The presence of one or more attacks negatively affect the detection of the embedded watermark due to its small size. Geometric attacks are more difficult than the common signal processing attacks due to their ability to modify the embedded content [24–27].

Alghoniemy and Tewfik [28] utilized the well-known Hu moment invariants in invariant digital watermarking. Despite their success in robustness against attacks, their watermarking method suffers from numerical instability and poor visual imperceptibility. Xin et al. [29] employed both orthogonal Zernike moments (ZMs) and pseudo-Zernike moments (PZMs) in invariant image watermarking. They computed both ZMs/PZMs in cartesian coordinates and selected ZMs/PZMs which show a great robustness against the geometric distortions. Ismail et al. [30] computed ZMs in polar coordinates and achieved better robustness against the geometric distortions. Zhu et al. [31] utilized the invariant complex moments and the Radon transform for invariant image watermarking. Zhang et al. [32] used affine Legendre moment invariants in invariant image watermarking where these moments successfully detect and extract watermark under affine transformation attacks. Li et al. [33] applied the invariant polar harmonic transforms (PHTs) in image watermarking.

In their remarked work [34], Papakostas and his co-authors evaluated the moment-based watermarking methods for grey-scale images using three criteria: Invisibility, Robustness, and Capacity of watermark information. They concluded that, orthogonal moments of the grey-scale images and their invariants to geometric transformations are successfully used in digital image watermarking. There are two reasons behind this success. First, orthogonal moments are able to reconstruct the initial host image before and after watermark embedding with high quality. Second, the orthogonal moments achieved the invariance to rotation, scaling and translation transformations which increased the watermark's robustness against attacks. Tsougenis et al. [35] applied invariant PHTs. The invariant radial harmonic Fourier moments (RHFMs) were used in [36, 37]. Qi et al. [38] used another polar harmonic transforms-based image watermarking method was proposed by.

A highly accurate polar harmonic transforms were used by Hosny and Darwish [39] in invariant image watermarking method. These remarkable works show that the invariant image watermarking methods are successful methods. However, most existing invariant watermarking methods are designed for monocoloured and grey-scale images.

Color information are useful in recognition and description of color images. Therefore, watermarking of color images becomes more important than the water-marking of the grey-scale images. Tsui et al. [40] proposed a watermarking method for color images in which the digital watermark was embedded in the Y component of the YCbCr color model. Hussein et al. [41] proposed non-blind luminance-based color image watermarking scheme. Peng et al. [42] used the support vector machines (SVM) in the multi-wavelet domain for color image watermarking. Niu et al. [43] used the three channels of the color images to embed the watermark. Liu [44] used the visual mask of wavelet transform in color image watermarking. Another method was proposed in [45] where the wavelet coefficients are used to embed a high-strength watermark. Basso et al. [46] decorrelated the RGB channels of the input color image using a Karhunen–Loève transform (KLT) and presented a blind watermarking method. A similar blind watermarking method was proposed by Su et al. [47]. A multiple watermarking method was proposed by Roy and Pal [48] where the discrete cosine transform (DCT) and the repetition code are used in blind color image watermarking. Su and Chen [49] utilized the upper Hessenberg matrix in blind watermarking of color images. More blind color image watermarking methods were proposed in [50–55].

Extensive analysis of above-mentioned watermarking methods shows that the correlation between channels of the color images are ignored which decreased the performance of the watermarking methods in terms of imperceptibility and robustness against the attacks. To avoid this problem, quaternion moments were applied in color image watermarking [56, 57] where quaternion moment-based color image watermarking handled the color image holistically. The quaternion moments are derived by integrating the quaternion algebra with the theory of orthogonal moments.

In this approach, the watermark is embedded in the color image, then the quaternion moments are computed for the watermarked image. Different quaternion moments are used by different researches for color image watermarking. Radial quaternion moments were used by Tsougenis et al. [58]. The orthogonal quaternion exponent moments (QEMs) were used in [59–61] to increase the robustness against different attacks. Quaternion radial harmonic Fourier moments (QRHFMs) [62] and quaternion polar harmonic transform (QPHTs) [63] were used in watermarking of color image.

Assessment the quaternion moment-based watermarking methods for color images [58–64] highlighted expensive computational demands and numerical insta-bility especially at high moment orders as challenging problems. In [58–64], the zero-order approximation (ZOA) computational method was employed to compute these quaternion moments. This method is very time-consuming and suffers from numerical and geometrical errors. The accumulation of these errors results in inaccurate quaternion moments which showed a non-acceptable performance in terms of imperceptibility and robustness against the attacks. These limitations and challenges motivated Hosny and Darwish [65] to introduce a robust watermarking method of color images.

An extensive comparative study is presented in this chapter where the different quaternion moment-based watermarking methods for color images are evaluated. In this comparative study, the radial kernels of quaternion moments are computed by using the accurate Gaussian integration method while an exact analytical integration method is used to compute the unified angular kernel over circular pixels. By this way, we remove the negative effect of the inaccurate and numerical instable quaternion moments. Therefore, the comparative study is fair and the performance of the quaternion moment-based watermarking methods of color image is dependent on the characteristics of the quaternion polynomials. Different experiments are conducted to evaluate the performance of quaternion moments. It is observed that QPHTs have the best performance followed by QLFMs, QRSCMs, QRHFMs and QEMs in terms of robustness against attacks.

The sections of this chapter are: The quaternion representation of color images, the quaternion moments and the unified accurate computational method are briefly described in Sect. 8.2. In Sect. 8.3, the robust quaternion moment-based watermarking approach for color images is presented. Experiments, results and discussions are presented in Sect. 8.4. The conclusion is presented in Sect. 8.5.

8.2 Some Preliminaries

8.2.1 Quaternion Representation of Color Images

Hamilton [66] defined quaternion numbers as generalized complex numbers where a quaternion number, qq, contain one real, a, and three imaginary components, b, c & d, as follows:

$$qq = a + bi + cj + dk \tag{8.1}$$

i, j, and k, are the imaginary units and defined as follows:

$$i^2 = j^2 = k^2 = ijk = -1,$$

$$ij = -ji = k, jk = -kj = i, ki = -ik = j \tag{8.2}$$

$$qq^* = a - bi - cj - dk, \tag{8.3}$$

$$|qq| = \sqrt{a^2 + b^2 + c^2 + d^2} \tag{8.4}$$

where qq^* and $|qq|$ are the conjugate and the modulus of the quaternion, qq. Ell and Sangwine [67] successfully used the pure quaternions, $a = 0$, to represent the RGB color images as follows:

$$f(r, \theta) = f_R(r, \theta) i + f_G(r, \theta) j + f_B(r, \theta) k \tag{8.5}$$

where $f_R(r, \theta)$, $f_G(r, \theta)$, and $f_B(r, \theta)$ represent the three channels of the image intensity function.

8.2.2   Quaternion Moments

The quaternion moments are defined over a unit circle in polar coordinates. These moments are orthogonal over the interval $[0, 1]$. For the image intensity function, $f(r, \theta)$, the different quaternion moments are defined through the following subsections.

8.2.2.1   Quaternion Zernike Moments (QZMs)

The right-side QZMs are defined as follows [68]:

$$QZ_{pq}^R = \frac{(p+1)}{\pi} \int_0^{2\pi} \int_0^1 R_{pq}^{ZM}(r) f(r, \theta) e^{-\mu q \theta} r \, dr \, d\theta \tag{8.6}$$

where the order p and repetition q are defined as: $p = 0, 1, 2, 3 \dots \quad \dots \quad \dots \quad \infty$, $|q| \le p$ & $p - |q|$ is even. The real-valued radial basis polynomials, $R_{pq}^{ZM}(r)$, are defined as follows:

$$R_{pq}^{ZM}(r) = \sum_{k=0}^{(p-|q|)/2} \frac{(-1)^k (p-k)!}{k! \left(\frac{p+|q|}{2} - k\right)! \left(\frac{p-|q|}{2} - k\right)!} r^{p-2k} \tag{8.7}$$

where $\mu = (i + j + k)/\sqrt{3}$ is the unit pure quaternion. Based on the orthogonality of $R_{pq}^{ZM}(r)$, the reconstructed color image is represented as:

$$f^{reco.}(r, \theta) = \sum_{p=0}^{\infty} \sum_{q=-p}^{p} Z_{pq}^R R_{pq}^{ZM}(r) e^{\mu q \theta} \tag{8.8}$$

The color image is approximately reconstructed using a finite number of moments, where Eq. (8.8) will be modified:

$$f^{reco.}(r, \theta) \approx \sum_{p=0}^{pmax} \sum_{q=-p}^{p} Z_{pq}^{R} R_{pq}^{ZM}(r) e^{\mu q \theta} \tag{8.9}$$

8.2.2.2 Quaternion Pseudo-Zernike Moments (QPZMs)

The right-side QPZMs are defined as follows [69]:

$$PZ_{pq}^{R} = \frac{(p+1)}{\pi} \int_{0}^{2\pi} \int_{0}^{1} R_{pq}^{PZM}(r) f(r, \theta) e^{-\mu q \theta} r dr d\theta, \tag{8.10}$$

where the order p and repetition q are defined as: $p = 0, 1, 2, 3 \ldots \ldots \ldots \infty$, $|q| \le p$. The real-valued radial basis polynomials, $R_{pq}^{PZM}(r)$, are defined as follow:

$$R_{pq}^{PZM}(r) = \sum_{k=0}^{p-|q|} \frac{(-1)^{k} (2p+1-k)!}{k! (p-|q|-k)! (p+|q|+1-k)!} r^{p-k} \tag{8.11}$$

The reconstructed color image using a finite number of QPZMs is defined as follows:

$$f^{reco.}(r, \theta) \approx \sum_{p=0}^{pmax} \sum_{q=-p}^{p} PZ_{pq}^{R} R_{pq}^{PZM}(r) e^{\mu q \theta} \tag{8.12}$$

8.2.2.3 Quaternion Orthogonal Fourier–Mellin Moments (QOFMMs)

The right-side QOFMMs are defined as follows [70]:

$$F_{pq}^{R} = \frac{(p+1)}{\pi} \int_{0}^{2\pi} \int_{0}^{1} R_{p}^{FM}(r) f(r, \theta) e^{-\mu q \theta} r dr d\theta, \tag{8.13}$$

where the order p and repetition q are defined as: $p = |q| = 0, 1, 2, 3 \ldots \ldots \ldots \infty$. The real-valued radial basis polynomials, $R_{pq}^{FM}(r)$, are defined as follow:

$$R_{p}^{FM}(r) = \sum_{k=0}^{p} \frac{(-1)^{p+k} (p+k+1)!}{k! (p-k)! (k+1)!} r^{k} \tag{8.14}$$

Similarly, the color image is reconstructed using a finite number of QOFMMs as follows:

$$f^{reco.}(r,\theta) \approx \sum_{p=0}^{pmax} \sum_{q=-p}^{p} F_{pq}^{R} R_{p}^{FM}(r) e^{\mu q \theta} \tag{8.15}$$

8.2.2.4   Quaternion Legendre-Fourier Moments (QLFMs)

The right-side QLFMs are defined as follows [65]:

$$L_{pq}^{R} = \frac{2p+1}{\pi} \int_{0}^{2\pi} \int_{0}^{1} R_{p}^{LFM}(r) f(r,\theta) e^{-\mu q \theta} r dr d\theta, \tag{8.16}$$

where the real-valued substituted shifted Legendre polynomials, $R_{p}^{LFM}(r)$, are defined as follow [71]:

$$R_{p}^{LFM}(r) = \sum_{k=0}^{p} (-1)^{p-k} \binom{p+k}{2k} \binom{2k}{k} r^{2k} = \sum_{k=0}^{p} (-1)^{p-k} \frac{(p+k)! r^{2k}}{(p-k)!(k!)^2} \tag{8.17}$$

These polynomials are computed recursively as follows:

$$R_{p+1}^{LFM}(r) = \frac{2p+1}{p+1} \left(2r^2 - 1\right) R_{p}^{LFM}(r) - \frac{p}{p+1} R_{p-1}^{LFM}(r), \tag{8.18}$$

where:

$$R_{0}^{LFM}(r) = 1, \; R_{1}^{LFM}(r) = 2r^2 - 1.$$

The image function $f(r,\theta)$ could be reconstructed using the QLFMs as follows:

$$f^{reco.}(r,\theta) = \sum_{p=0}^{\infty} \sum_{q=-\infty}^{\infty} L_{pq}^{R} R_{p}^{LFM}(r) e^{\mu q \theta} \approx \sum_{p=0}^{pmax} \sum_{q=-qmax}^{qmax} L_{pq}^{R} R_{p}^{LFM}(r) e^{\mu q \theta} \tag{8.19}$$

8.2.2.5   Quaternion Radial Substituted Chebyshev Moments (QRSCM)

Hosny and Darwish [72] presented new quaternion moments for color image description, which are called the quaternion radial substituted Chebyshev moments (QRSCMs). The right-side QRSCMs with order, p, and repetition, q, are:

$$SCM_{pq}^{R} = \frac{1}{2\pi a_p} \int_0^{2\pi} \int_0^1 R_p^{RSC}(r) f(r,\theta) e^{-\mu q\theta} W(r) r dr d\theta, \qquad (8.20)$$

where $p = 0, 1, 2, \ldots \ldots$, and $q = 0, \pm 1, \pm 2, \ldots \ldots$; The normalization constant is defined as follows:

$$a_p = \frac{C_p \pi}{2} \qquad (8.21)$$

where:

$$C_p = \begin{cases} 2, & for \ p = 0 \\ 1, & for \ p \geq 1 \end{cases} \qquad (8.22)$$

The real-valued radial substituted Chebyshev polynomials, $R_p^{RSC}(r)$, are:

$$R_p^{RSC}(r) = \sum_{k=0}^{p} \frac{(k!)^2}{(2k)!} \binom{p+k-1}{k} \binom{p}{k} (-4)^k (1-r)^k \qquad (8.23)$$

For $n \geq 1$. With the weight function:

$$W(r) = \frac{1}{\sqrt{(r-r^2)}} \qquad (8.24)$$

The real-valued radial substituted Chebyshev polynomials, $R_p^{RSC}(r)$, obey the following recurrence relation:

$$R_{p+1}^{RSC}(r) = 2(2r-1) R_p^{RSC}(r) - R_{p-1}^{RSC}(r) \qquad (8.25)$$

with:

$$R_0^{RSC}(r) = 1, R_1^{RSC}(r) = 2r - 1.$$

These polynomials, $R_p^{RSC}(r)$, are orthogonal with $0 < r < 1$ and satisfy the following orthogonally relation:

$$\int_0^1 R_p^{RSC}(r) R_q^{RSC}(r) W(r) \, dr = \frac{C_p \pi}{2} \delta_{p\,q} \qquad (8.26)$$

The original image function, $f(r,\theta)$, could be reconstructed as follows:

$$f^{reco.}(r, \theta) = \sum_{p=0}^{\infty} \sum_{q=-\infty}^{\infty} SCM_{pq}^{R} R_p^{RSC}(r)e^{\mu q\theta} \approx \sum_{p=0}^{pmax} \sum_{q=-qmax}^{qmax} SCM_{pq}^{R} R_p^{RSC}(r)e^{\mu q\theta}$$

(8.27)

8.2.2.6 Quaternion Polar Harmonic Transforms (QPHTs)

The polar harmonic transforms for grey-scale images were defined by Yap et al. in [73] while he quaternion polar harmonic transforms were defined by Wang et al. in [74] and accurately computed by Hosny and Darwish in [75, 76]. The right-side quaternion polar complex exponential transform (QPCET)are defined as follows:

$$P_{pq}^{R} = \frac{1}{\pi} \int_{0}^{2\pi} \int_{0}^{1} R_p^{PCET}(r) f(r, \theta) e^{-\mu q\theta} r dr d\theta,$$

(8.28)

where the order p and the repetition q are $|p| = |q| = 0, 1, 2, 3, \ldots \quad \ldots \quad \ldots \quad \infty$; and the polar harmonic polynomials, $R_p^{PCET}(r)$, are:

$$R_p^{PCET}(r) = e^{-\mu 2\pi p r^2}$$

(8.29)

The quaternion polar cosine transform (QPCT) and the quaternion polar sine transform (QPST) are:

$$PC_{pq}^{R} = \Omega_p \int_{0}^{2\pi} \int_{0}^{1} R_p^{C}(r) f(r, \theta) e^{-\mu q\theta} r dr d\theta$$

(8.30)

with $p = |q| = 0, 1, 2, 3, \ldots \quad \ldots \quad \ldots \quad \infty$.

$$PS_{pq}^{R} = \Omega_p \int_{0}^{2\pi} \int_{0}^{1} R_p^{S}(r) f(r, \theta) e^{-\mu q\theta} r dr d\theta,$$

(8.31)

With $p = 1, 2, 3, \ldots\ldots\ldots\infty$, $|q| = 0, 1, 2, 3, \ldots\ldots\ldots\infty$ where:

$$\Omega_p = \begin{cases} 1/\pi, & p = 0 \\ 2/\pi, & p \neq 0 \end{cases}$$

$$R_p^{C}(r) = \cos\left(\pi p r^2\right)$$

(8.32)

$$R_p^S(r) = \sin\left(\pi pr^2\right) \tag{8.33}$$

Digital image could be reconstructed using the quaternion polar harmonic transforms using the following equations:

$$f^{reco.}(r,\theta) = \sum_{p=-\infty}^{\infty} \sum_{q=-\infty}^{\infty} P_{pq}^R R_p^{PCET}(r)e^{\mu q\theta} \approx \sum_{p=-\infty}^{pmax} \sum_{q=-qmax}^{qmax} P_{pq}^R R_p^{PCET}(r)e^{\mu q\theta}, \tag{8.34}$$

Similarly,

$$f^{reco.}(r,\theta) = \sum_{p=0}^{\infty} \sum_{q=-\infty}^{\infty} PC_{pq}^R R_p^C(r)e^{\mu q\theta} \approx \sum_{p=0}^{pmax} \sum_{q=-qmax}^{qmax} PC_{pq}^R R_p^C(r)e^{\mu q\theta}, \tag{8.35}$$

$$f^{reco.}(r,\theta) = \sum_{p=1}^{\infty} \sum_{q=-\infty}^{\infty} PS_{pq}^R R_p^S(r)e^{\mu q\theta} \approx \sum_{p=1}^{pmax} \sum_{q=-qmax}^{qmax} PS_{pq}^R R_p^S(r)e^{\mu q\theta}. \tag{8.36}$$

8.2.2.7 Quaternion Radial Harmonic Fourier Moments (QRHFMs)

The right-side QRHFMs are [77]:

$$RH_{pq}^R = \frac{1}{2\pi} \int_0^{2\pi} \int_0^1 R_p^{RHFM}(r) f(r,\theta) e^{-\mu q\theta} r dr d\theta, \tag{8.37}$$

where $p = |q| = 0, 1, 2, 3 \ldots \ldots \ldots \infty$ and the radial basis polynomials, $R_p^{RHFM}(r)$, are:

$$R_p^{RHFM}(r) = \begin{cases} \sqrt{\frac{1}{r}}, \, p = 0 \\ \sqrt{\frac{2}{r}}\cos(p\pi r), \, p = even \\ \sqrt{\frac{2}{r}}\sin((p+1)\pi r), \, p = even \end{cases} \tag{8.38}$$

Reconstruction using the QRHFMs could be achieved using the following equation:

$$f^{reco.}(r, \theta) \approx \sum_{p=0}^{pmax} \sum_{-qmax}^{qmax} RH_{pq}^{R} R_{p}^{RHFM}(r)e^{\mu q\theta} \qquad (8.39)$$

8.2.2.8 Quaternion Exponent Moments (QEMs)

The right-side QEMs are defined [63]:

$$E_{pq}^{R} = \frac{1}{4\pi} \int_{0}^{2\pi} \int_{0}^{1} R_{p}^{EM}(r) f(r, \theta) e^{-\mu q\theta} r dr d\theta, \qquad (8.40)$$

where the order p and the repetition q are defined as $|p| = |q| = 0, 1, 2,$ $3, \ldots \ldots \ldots \infty$ and the real-valued radial polynomials, $R_{p}^{EM}(r)$, are:

$$R_{p}^{EM}(r) = \sqrt{\frac{2}{r}} e^{-\mu 2\pi pr} \qquad (8.41)$$

Using Eqs. (8.41) and (8.42), the digital images could be reconstructed using these moments as follows:

$$f^{reco.}(r, \theta) = \sum_{p=-\infty}^{\infty} \sum_{q=-\infty}^{\infty} E_{pq}^{R} R_{p}^{EM}(r)e^{\mu q\theta} \approx \sum_{-pmax}^{pmax} \sum_{q=-qmax}^{qmax} E_{pq}^{R} R_{p}^{EM}(r)e^{\mu q\theta}$$

$$(8.42)$$

The major characteristics of the quaternion-type moments including their normalization factor, and radial basis functions are shown in Table 8.1.

8.2.3 Accurate Computation of Quaternion Moments

In order to design accurate and robust watermarking algorithms, the computation process of the quaternion moments is performed in the polar domain using the polar raster [78, 79] where a hybrid accurate and stable method is utilized. In this method, the input color images are converted to the polar coordinates using accurate cubic interpolation [80]. For the interpolated image, $\hat{f}(r_i, \theta_{ij})$, the general formula of the right-side quaternion moments of order p with repetition q is defined as follows:

$$\Phi_{pq}^{R} = \Omega_{p} \sum_{i} \sum_{j} \hat{f}(\hat{r}_i, \theta_{i,j}) I_{p}(r_i) I_{q}(\theta_{ij}) \qquad (8.43)$$

The angular kernel is:

Table 8.1 Characteristics of quaternion moments

Orthogonal moments	Radial polynomial	Normalization factor
ZMs [68]	$R_{pq}^{ZM}(r) = \sum_{k=0}^{(p-|q|)/2} \dfrac{(-1)^k(p-k)!}{k!\left(\frac{p+|q|}{2}-k\right)!\left(\frac{p-|q|}{2}-k\right)!}\, r^{p-2k}$ p = 0, 1, 2, 3 … … … ∞, $|q| \leq p$, $p - |q|$ is even	$(p+1)/\pi$
PZMs [69]	$R_{pq}^{PZM}(r) = \sum_{k=0}^{p-|q|} \dfrac{(-1)^k(2p+1-k)!}{k!(p-|q|-k)!(p+|q|+1-k)!}\, r^{p-k}$ p = 0, 1, 2, 3 … … … ∞, $|q| \leq p$	$(p+1)/\pi$
OFMMs [70]	$R_p^{FM}(r) = \sum_{k=0}^{p} \dfrac{(-1)^{p+k}(p+k+1)!}{k!(p-k)!(k+1)!}\, r^k$ p = |q| = 0, 1, 2, 3 … … … ∞	$(p+1)/\pi$
RSCMs [72]	$R_p^{RSC}(r) = \sum_{k=0}^{n} \dfrac{(k!)^2}{(2k)!}\binom{n+k-1}{k}\binom{n}{k}(-4)^k(1-r)^k$	$\dfrac{1}{2\pi}a_p,\ a_p = \dfrac{C_p\pi}{2}\ C_p = \begin{cases} 2, & p=0 \\ 1, & p \geq 1 \end{cases}$
LFMs [65]	$R_p^{LFM}(r) = \sum_{k=0}^{p}(-1)^{p-k}\dfrac{(p+k)!\,r^{2k}}{(p-k)!(k!)^2}$	$\dfrac{(2p+1)}{\pi}$
PCET [73]	$R_p^{PCET}(r) = e^{-\mu 2\pi p r^2}$ |p| = 0, 1, 2, 3, … … … ∞	$1/\pi$
PCT [73]	$R_p^C(r) = \cos(\pi p r^2)$ p = |q| = 0, 1, 2, 3 … … … ∞	$\Omega_p = \begin{cases} \frac{1}{\pi}, & p=0 \\ \frac{2}{\pi}, & p \neq 0 \end{cases}$
PST [73]	$R_p^S(r) = \sin(\pi p r^2)$ p = 1, 2, 3, … … … ∞, |q| = 0, 1, 2 … … … … ∞	$2/\pi$
RHFMs [77]	$R_p^{RHFM}(r) = \begin{cases} \sqrt{\frac{1}{r}}, & p=0 \\ \sqrt{\frac{2}{r}}\cos(p\pi r), & p \text{ even} \\ \sqrt{\frac{2}{r}}\sin((p+1)\pi r), & p \text{ even} \end{cases}$ p = |q| = 0, 1, 2, 3, … … … ∞	$1/2\pi$
EMs [63]	$R_p^{EM}(r) = \sqrt{\frac{2}{r}}\,e^{-\mu 2\pi p r}$ |p| = 0, 1, 2, 3, … … … ∞	$1/4\pi$

$$I_q\left(\theta_{ij}\right) = \int\limits_{V_{ij}}^{V_{i,j+1}} e^{-\mu\, q\,\theta}\, d\theta \tag{8.44}$$

The radial kernel is:

$$I_p\left(\hat{r}_i\right) = \int\limits_{U_i}^{U_{i+1}} R(r) r\, dr \tag{8.45}$$

where $R(r)$ is given as:

$$R(r) = \begin{cases} R_{pq}^{ZM}(r)\, for\ QZM \\ R_{pq}^{PZM}(r)\, for\ QPZM \\ R_p^{FM}(r)\, for\ QOFMM \\ R_p^{LFM}(r)\, for\ QLFM \\ W(r) R_p^{RSC}(r)\, for\ QRSCM \\ R_p(r)\, for\, QPCET \\ R_p^{C}(r)\, for\, QPCT \\ R_p^{S}(r)\, for\ QPST \\ R_p^{RHFM}(r)\, for\ QRHFM \\ R_p^{EM}(r)\, for\ QEM \end{cases} \tag{8.46}$$

The angular kernel as defined by Eq. (8.44) could be exactly computed through the analytical integration of the exponential function over the polar pixels. Accurate Gaussian numerical integration method [81] is used to compute the radial kernels as defined by the Eqs. (8.45) and (8.46). This method was successfully used by Camacho-Bello et al. in [82, 83]. This method is defined as follows:

$$\int\limits_a^b g(z) dz \approx \frac{(b-a)}{2} \sum_{l=0}^{c-1} w_l g\left(\frac{a+b}{2} + \frac{b-a}{2} t_l\right) \tag{8.47}$$

where t_i and w_i refer to the locations of sampling points and weights; c is the order of the numerical integration with $i = 0, 1, 2, \ldots \ldots c - 1$. The values of w_i are fixed and $\sum_{i=0}^{c-1} w_i = 2$. The values of t_i can be expressed in terms of the integration limits, a & b. Using Eq. (8.47) in Eq. (8.45) yield:

$$I_p\left(\hat{r}_i\right) = \int\limits_{U_i}^{U_{i+1}} R(r) r\, dr \approx \frac{(U_{i+1} - U_i)}{2} \sum_{l=0}^{c-1} w_l R\left(\frac{U_{i+1} + U_i}{2} + \frac{U_{i+1} - U_i}{2} t_l\right) \tag{8.48}$$

where $R(r)$ is defined in Eq. (8.46). The angular kernel, $I_q(\theta_{ij})$, is exactly calculated using the principles of analytical integration as follows:

$$I_q\left(\theta_{ij}\right) = \begin{cases} \frac{\mu}{q}\left(e^{-\mu\,qV_{i,j+1}} - e^{-\mu\,qV_{i,j}}\right), q \neq 0 \\ V_{i,j+1} - V_{i,j}, q = 0 \end{cases} \qquad (8.49)$$

where:

$$U_{i+1} = R_i + \Delta R_i/2;\, U_i = R_i - \Delta R_i/2; \qquad (8.50)$$

$$V_{i,j+1} = \theta_{i,j} + \frac{\Delta\theta_{i,j}}{2};\, V_{i,j} = \theta_{i,j} - \Delta\theta_{i,j}/2 \qquad (8.51)$$

8.3 Robust Color Image Watermarking Using Quaternion Moments

In this section, the invariant quaternion moment-based color image watermarking approach is presented. In this approach, the quaternion moments (QMs) of the host color image are computed where accurate QMs are selected according to specific conditions. The binary watermark is embedded into the original color image by adaptively quantizing the modulus of the selected QMs. The watermark information is extracted from modulus QMs coefficients which improve the robustness against geometrical distortion. A flowchart diagram is displayed in Fig. 8.2.

8.3.1 Watermark Embedding

A host color image, $f(x, y)$, of size $N \times N$ and the binary watermark image of size $P \times Q$ are represented as follows:

$$F = \{f(x, y), 0 < x \leq N,\ 0 < y \leq N\}$$

$$B = \{b(i, j) \in \{0, 1\}, 0 \leq i < P, 0 \leq j < Q\}$$

8.3.1.1 Watermark Preprocessing

To increase the security level, the binary watermark image should be scrambled where the scrambling algorithm perturbed the content of the watermark image.

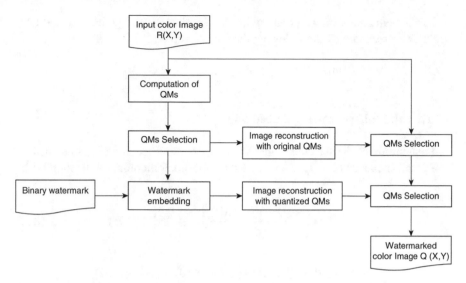

Fig. 8.2 The schematic diagram of color image watermarking

Arnold scrambling transform [29] is utilized in the pre-processing step where the Arnold transform is intuitionistic, simple, periodic, and easy to use. The binary watermark image, B, is scrambled by the Arnold transform where the scrambled binary image is B_1:

$$B_1 = \{b_1\,(i, j) \in \{0, 1\}\,, 0 \leq i < P, 0 \leq j < Q\}.$$

The scrambled binary image B_1 is transformed into a one-dimensional bit sequence as follows:

$$B_2 = \{b_2(l) = b_1\,(i, j) \in \{0, 1\}\,, 0 \leq i < P, 0 \leq j < Q, l = i \times Q + j\}.$$

8.3.1.2   Quaternion Moment Selection

Selection of the appropriate QMs increase the robustness of the watermarking methods based on quaternion moment. The QMs are selected according to the following conditions:

- QMs with $q = 4m$, $m \in Z$ are ignored [29].
- QMs with $q > 0$ are independent while the QMs with $q < 0$ are dependent which ignored.

The selected moments could be represented as follows:

$$S = \{\Phi_{pq}, q \neq 4m, m \in Z\}$$

For bit sequence of a watermark with the length, $l = P \times Q$, the selected QMs could be represented by the following the feature vector:

$$\Phi(l) = \left\{ \Phi_{p_1 q_1}, \Phi_{p_2 q_2}, \ldots \ldots \ldots, \Phi_{p_l q_l} \right\}$$

8.3.1.3 Digital Watermark Embedding

The magnitude of the selected moments, $\Phi(l)$, are modified and used to embed the scrambled sequence bits, B_2, using the following dither modulation function [29]:

$$\Phi'(l) = \left[\frac{\Phi(l) - d_k \, (b2(l))}{\Delta} \right] * \Delta + d_k \, (b2(l)) \tag{8.52}$$

$$0 \leq l < P \times Q, d_k(1) = \frac{\Delta}{2} + d_k(0), d_k(0) \in [0, 1]$$

where $\Phi'(l)$ and $\Phi(l)$ are the modified and unmodified QMs of host image respectively. The mathematical symbols, $d_k(\cdot)$, Δ, and $[\cdot]$ refer to the dither function, the quantization step and the rounding operator respectively. The subscript k of the dither function refers to the key.

8.3.1.4 Reconstruction of the Watermarked Color Image

The watermarked color image is composed of two parts, one part is represented by the image reconstructed from unmodified QMs moments, which is defined as follow [63]:

$$f_{rem} \, (r, \theta) = f \, (r, \theta) - f_M \, (r, \theta) \tag{8.53}$$

with:

$$f_M \, (r, \theta) = \sum_{i=0}^{P \times Q - 1} \Phi_{p_i q_i} L_{p_i q_i} \, (r, \theta) + \Phi_{p_i, -q_i} L_{p_i, -q_i} \, (r, \theta) \tag{8.54}$$

where the second part is contributed by the selected modified QMs' moments:

$$f_{M'} \, (r, \theta) = \sum_{i=0}^{P \times Q - 1} \Phi'_{p_i q_i} L_{p_i q_i} \, (r, \theta) + \Phi'_{p_i, -q_i} L_{p_i, -q_i} \, (r, \theta) \tag{8.55}$$

where $L_{pq}(r, \theta) = R_{pq}(r) e^{\mu q \theta}$.

As a result, the watermarked image, $f_w(r, \theta)$, is obtained by combining the two parts where $f_w(r, \theta)$ was formed as:

$$f_W(r, \theta) = f_{rem}(r, \theta) + f_{M'}(r, \theta) \tag{8.56}$$

8.3.2   Watermark Extraction

In the following subsections, the main steps of watermark extraction can be described.

8.3.2.1   Feature Selection

For watermarked color image, f_w, the processing of the QMs in both extraction and embedding processes is similar. Therefore, a similar feature vector, $\Phi^*(l) = \{\Phi^*_{p_1q_1}, \Phi^*_{p_2q_2}, \cdots\cdots\cdots, \Phi^*_{p_1q_1}\}$, is constructed using the same key.

8.3.2.2   Binary Watermark Extraction

With the same embedding process, the magnitude of each Φ'_i is quantized with the two dithers respectively:

$$\left|\Phi'(l)\right|_j = \left[\frac{|\Phi^*(l)| - d_k(j)}{\Delta}\right] * \Delta + d_k(j), \, j = 0, 1 \tag{8.57}$$

where:

$$\hat{b}_2(l) = \underset{j \in [0,1]}{argmin}\left(\left|\Phi'(l)\right|_j - \left|\Phi^*(l)\right|\right)^2 \tag{8.58}$$

The distance between the original and the quantized, $\Phi^*(l)$ & $\Phi'(l)$, values used to decide the value of $\hat{b}_2(l)$ to be 0 or 1.

8.4   Experiments

Experiments are conducted to evaluate the performance of the quaternion moment-based watermarking methods for color images. Different performance measures were used in quantative and qualitative evaluation of the performance. Peek signal-to-noise ratio (PSNR) and the structural similarity image index (SSIM) are used to

Fig. 8.3 Color images used to test the watermarking methods

Fig. 8.4 Binary watermark images

measure the watermark invisibility, while the bit error rate (BER) is used to measure the quality of the extracted watermark. The normalized correlation (NC) between the original and the extracted watermark is a measure of the robustness against the attacks.

Experiments were divided into three groups. In the first one, experiments were performed to evaluate the invisibility of the watermark using different host color images. In the second one, experiments were performed to evaluate the robustness of the different quaternion moment-based watermarking methods against various attacks. The CPU times required by the watermarking methods were evaluated in the third group of experiments.

Experiments were performed with 10 standard color images of size 256×256 as host images and different binary image with size 32×32 as watermarks. The color and the binary images are displayed in Figs. 8.3 and 8.4 respectively.

8.4.1 Watermark Invisibility

The PSNR and SSIM metrics are used to evaluate the invisibility of the embedded images by measuring the similarity between the host, f, and watermarked, f_w, color images. The PSNR is defined as follows:

$$PSNR(f, f_w) = 10\log_{10}\frac{255^2}{MSE} \tag{8.59}$$

where:

$$MSE = \frac{1}{N^2}\left(\sum_{i=1}^{N}\sum_{j=1}^{N}[f_w(i, j) - f(i, j)]^2\right) \tag{8.60}$$

The watermarked image quality is measured by the SSIM [84] The SSIM defined as follow:

$$SSIM(f, f_w) = \frac{\left(2\mu_f\mu_{f_w} + C_1\right)\left(2\sigma_{ff_w} + C_2\right)}{\left(\mu_f^2 + \mu_{f_w}^2 + C_1\right)\left(\sigma_f^2 + \sigma_{f_w}^2 + C_2\right)} \tag{8.61}$$

where μ_f & μ_{f_w} refer to average luminance values of the host, f, and watermarked, f_w, color images; σ_f and σ_{f_w} are the standard variance of host, f, and watermarked, f_w, color images; σ_{ff_w} is the covariance between f and f_w; C_1 and C_2 are small fixed positive constants.

The quaternion moment-based watermarking methods are used to embed a 512-bit watermark information in the host color image with, Δ, varying from 0.1 to 1.0. The corresponding PSNR value for each value of quantization step, Δ, is computed and depicted in Fig. 8.5. It is clear that, increasing the quantization step, Δ, results in decreasing the PSNR.

The color image of Lena with size 256×256 is watermarked with a binary image using the different quaternion moment-based watermarking methods. A 512-bit watermark information is embedded in the host color image with a quantization step $\Delta = 0.2$. The PSNR and SSIM values for each watermarking method are shown in Tables 8.2 and 8.3 respectively.

Tables 8.2 and 8.3 show that, in terms of visual imperceptibility, the QLFMs, QPCET, QPCTs, and QPSTs watermarking methods achieved better performance than the watermarking methods, QRSCMs, QRHFMs & QEMs. The performance of the watermarking methods, QZM, QPZM and QOFMM is very bad where their corresponding PSNR and SSIM values are very small.

The watermarked image is reconstructed using the different quaternion moments, which are displayed in Fig. 8.6.

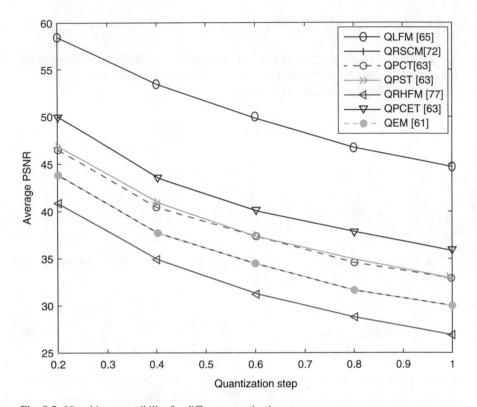

Fig. 8.5 Visual imperceptibility for different quantization steps

It is observed that, no distortion is noticed in the images reconstructed by using the QPHTs, QLFMs, QRSCMs, QRHFMs and QEMs which ensures their good imperceptibility. On the other side, poor imperceptibility is obtained when using QZMs, QPZMs, and QOFMMs watermarking methods.

8.4.2 Robustness of the Watermark

BER and NC are two quantitative measures used in evaluating the quality of the extracted watermark. The BER is defined as:

$$BER = \frac{B_{error}}{l} \tag{8.62}$$

where B_{error} represent the number of incorrectly extracted bits while $l = P \times Q$ is the total number of embedded bits. The NC is calculated as follows [38]:

Table 8.2 The average PSNR (dB) for quaternion watermarking methods with different values of (Δ)

Q.S.	QZMs [68]	QPZMs [69]	QOFMMs [70]	QLFMs [65]	QRSCMs [72]	QPHT [63] QPCET	QPCT	QPST	QRHFMs [77]	QEMs [61]
0.2	12.14	−190.50	−45.60	54.96	43.72	50.01	46.58	46.90	40.85	43.76
0.4	8.40	−191.81	−52.29	48.18	37.74	43.65	40.61	40.92	34.81	37.83
0.6	1.97	−197.25	−54.86	44.80	34.31	40.17	37.30	37.48	31.30	34.31
0.8	0.44	−199.83	−57.37	42.58	31.72	37.83	34.57	34.83	28.75	31.63
1.0	−2.71	−198.68	−58.55	40.53	29.72	35.86	32.77	32.88	26.86	29.90

Table 8.3 The average SSIM for various watermarking approaches with Different values of (Δ)

| Q.S. | QZMs [68] | QPZMs [69] | QOFMMs [70] | QLFMs [65] | QRSCMs [72] | QPHT [63] | | | QRHFMs [77] | QEMs [61] |
						QPCET	QPCT	QPST		
0.2	0.8354	0.2068	0.4524	0.9996	0.9937	0.9965	0.9948	0.9948	0.9859	0.9891
0.4	0.8168	0.2050	0.4254	0.9982	0.9765	0.9856	0.9794	0.9801	0.9517	0.9606
0.6	0.7856	0.1990	0.4153	0.9957	0.9527	0.9687	0.9596	0.9591	0.9084	0.9227
0.8	0.7794	0.1963	0.4025	0.9932	0.9257	0.9488	0.9312	0.9302	0.858	0.8745
1.0	0.7657	0.1962	0.3970	0.9892	0.8924	0.9247	0.8991	0.8987	0.8092	0.8381

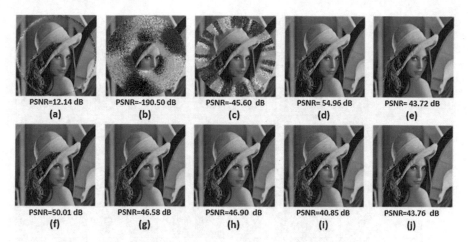

Fig. 8.6 The watermarked image of Lena ($\Delta = 0.2$, $L = 128$): (**a**) QZMs, (**b**) QPZMs, (**c**) QOFMMs, (**d**) QLFMs, (**e**) QRSCMs, (**f**) QPCETs, (**g**) QPCTs, (**h**) QPSTs, (**i**) QRHFMs and (**j**) QEMs

$$NC = \frac{\sum_{i=1}^{N}\sum_{j=1}^{N}\left[W\left(i,j\right)xw''\left(i,j\right)\right]}{\sum_{i=1}^{N}\sum_{j=1}^{N}\left[W\left(i,j\right)\right]^{2}} \qquad (8.63)$$

The watermarking method is robust against different attacks when the value of *NC* approaches 1. Experiments were performed where the detailed results for *NC* and *BER* are presented in Tables 8.4 and 8.5 respectively.

Table 8.4 clearly shows that the extracted binary watermark images using the QPHTs, QLFMs, QRSCMs, QRHFMs and QEMs watermarking methods are very close to the original binary images which ensure the accuracy and the robustness of these watermarking methods. The extracted binary watermark images using the QZMs, QPZMs, and QOFMMs are completely damaged due to low accuracy, numerical instability and the sensitivity to the different attacks.

Based on the size of binary watermark, 32×32, the L value is 1024 and in order to compute the QZM, QPZMs and QOFMMs, the maximum order must cover the total information watermark, L. Therefore, we need a *pmax* > 44 for QZMs, *pmax* > 23 for QPZMs and *pmax* > 20 for QOFMMs where these methods are numerically instable.

Additional experiment was performed where another watermark binary image of size 10×10 is embedded in the host color images using watermarking methods based on different quaternion moment. The watermarked color images are generated and then each watermark is extracted under different attacks such as, different kinds of noise, median filtering, and rotation, scaling, translation. The BER values of the extracted watermarks are shown in Table 8.6.

Table 8.4 The extracted binary watermark under common attacks

Attacks		QZMs [68]	QPZMs [69]	QOFMMs [70]	QLFMs [65]	QRSCMs [72]	QPHT [63] QPCET	QPCT	QPST	QRHFMs [77]	QEMs [61]
Rotation angle	5										
	15										
	25										
	35										
	45										
Scaling factor	0.75										
	1.25										
	1.75										
	2										
Translation	(H 15,V5)										
	(H5, V15)										
Scaling 1.5 +JPEG (90%)											
Rotation 90 + JPEG (90%)											
JPEG compression	50										
	70										
	90										

(continued)

Table 8.4 (continued)

Salt and Peppers Noise	(0.01)									
	0.03									
Gaussian noise	0.01									
	0.03									
Gaussian Filtering	(3*3)									
	(5*5)									
Median Filtering	(3*3)									
	(5*5)									

Bold values indicate the extracted watermark

The obtained results clearly show that QPHTs, QLFMs, QRSCMs QRHFMs and QEMs watermarking methods are robust against the different attacks. Again, the QZMs, QPZMs, and QOFMMs watermarking algorithms show very bad performance.

The robustness against scaling attack is evaluated for various scaling factors. The watermarks are extracted using the tested watermarking methods where the BER values were computed, plotted and displayed in Fig. 8.7. These results and the previously obtained results are consistent where the QPHTs, QLFMs, QRSCMs, QRHFMs and QEMs watermarking methods are outperformed the QZMs, QPZMs, and QOFMMs watermarking methods.

The watermarked images are rotated with angles 5° to 45° with step 10°. The watermarks are extracted from the rotated images using the tested watermarking methods. The computed BER values were computed, plotted and displayed in Fig. 8.8. The obtained results ensure the robustness of QPHTs, QLFMs, QRSCMs, QRHFMs and QEMs and the weakness of the QZMs, PZMs, and QOFMMs watermarking methods against rotation attacks. To evaluate the robustness of the different quaternion moment-based watermarking methods against compression, experiments were conducted where the watermarked color images are compressed using the JPEG compression technique with different compression ratios, 30 to 90. The watermarks are extracted from the compressed images where the computed BER values are plotted and displayed in Fig. 8.9. A similar conclusion was reached.

Additional experiments were performed where the watermarked color images were attacked by different attacks and the watermarks were extracted. The computed

Table 8.5 The BER values for the extracted watermark under different attacks

Attacks		QZMs [68]	QPZMs [69]	QOFMMs [70]	QLFMs [65]	QRSCMs [72]	QPHTs [63]			QRHFMs [77]	QEMs [61]
							QPCET	QPCT	QPST		
Rotation angle	5	0.4971	0.4902	0.4971	0.0195	0.0146	0.0156	0.0146	0.0107	0.0238	0.0313
	15	0.4717	0.4629	0.4824	0.0361	0.0332	0.0117	0.0137	0.0098	0.0186	0.0195
	25	0.4912	0.4824	0.4990	0.0234	0.0166	0.0186	0.0088	0.0117	0.0303	0.0352
	35	0.4854	0.4756	0.4873	0.0332	0.0303	0.0137	0.0098	0.0127	0.0195	0.0244
	45	0.4951	0.4678	0.4990	0.0303	0.0146	0.0146	0.0107	0.0146	0.0225	0.0303
Scaling factor	0.25	0.5000	0.4932	0.5283	0.4541	0.3193	0.5137	0.4795	0.4941	0.4639	0.5029
	0.5	0.4912	0.4756	0.5049	0.1436	0.1738	0.0156	0.0107	0.0117	0.0732	0.0771
	0.75	0.4883	0.4668	0.5039	0.0205	0.0439	0.0107	0.0068	0.0088	0.0156	0.0195
	1.25	0.4668	0.4658	0.4912	0.0098	0.0176	0.0078	0.0049	0.0059	0.0176	0.0186
	1.75	0.4707	0.4697	0.4922	0.0098	0.0205	0.0088	0.0068	0.0068	0.0156	0.0176
	2	0.4854	0.4795	0.5146	0.0068	0.0186	0.0098	0.0068	0.0078	0.0205	0.0225
Trans.	(H15,V5)	0.4981	0.4975	0.5000	0.0078	0.0088	0.0078	0.0049	0.0059	0.0107	0.0137
	(H5,V15)	0.4990	0.4756	0.4932	0.0088	0.0098	0.0059	0.0078	0.0068	0.0098	0.0117
Scaling 1.5 + JPEG (90%)		0.4854	0.4678	0.4707	0.0098	0.0107	0.0088	0.0049	0.0039	0.0156	0.0186
Rotation 45+ JPEG (90%)		0.4824	0.4756	0.4883	0.0342	0.043	0.0127	0.0107	0.0117	0.0322	0.0332

JPEG compression	10	0.4805	0.4697	0.5107	0.3643	0.4033	0.3721	0.4561	0.4775	0.4990	0.4932
	30	0.4863	0.4688	0.5000	0.1230	0.1387	0.1272	0.126	0.123	0.0459	0.0439
	50	0.4834	0.4766	0.4902	0.0527	0.0547	0.0391	0.0254	0.0342	0.0283	0.0313
	70	0.4941	0.4902	0.5088	0.0195	0.0391	0.0107	0.0039	0.0078	0.0244	0.0303
	90	0.4961	0.4668	0.5107	0.0098	0.0303	0.0078	0.0078	0.0068	0.0146	0.0225
Salt & Peppers Noise	0.01	0.4834	0.4714	0.4798	0.0117	0.0127	0.0068	0.0049	0.0059	0.0186	0.0195
	0.03	0.5000	0.4975	0.5107	0.0195	0.0205	0.0107	0.0098	0.0107	0.0225	0.0234
Gaussian noise	0.01	0.4602	0.4576	0.4782	0.0107	0.0137	0.0107	0.0078	0.0088	0.0225	0.0244
	0.03	0.4834	0.4688	0.4902	0.0186	0.0234	0.0156	0.0098	0.0107	0.0303	0.0313
Gaussian filtering	3*3	0.4668	0.4658	0.4912	0.0117	0.0156	0.0107	0.0088	0.0098	0.0176	0.0137
	5*5	0.4980	0.4975	0.5000	0.0166	0.0195	0.0137	0.0107	0.0127	0.0293	0.0303
Median filtering	3*3	0.4704	0.4694	0.4918	0.0098	0.0117	0.0039	0.0059	0.0049	0.0137	0.0186
	5*5	0.4804	0.4697	0.4987	0.0195	0.0225	0.0049	0.0088	0.0078	0.0244	0.0283

Table 8.6 Average BER values of the watermarking methods for various attacks

Attacks		QZMs [68]	QPZMs [69]	QOFMMs [70]	QLFMs [65]	QRSCMs [72]	QPHTs [63]			QRHFMs [77]	QEMs [61]
							QPCET	QPCT	QPST		
Rotation angle	5o	0.2301	0.3518	0.4021	0.0039	0.0074	0.0029	0.0023	0.0045	0.0020	0.0049
	15o	0.3801	0.2473	0.3583	0	0	0	0	0	0	0
	25o	0.2941	0.3402	0.3383	0	0	0	0	0	0	0
	35o	0.2504	0.2685	0.2858	0	0	0	0	0	0	0
	45o	0.2463	0.2317	0.2753	0	0	0	0	0	0	0
Scaling factor	0.5	0.3572	0.3361	0.3235	0.0233	0.0294	0.02	0.0107	0.0205	0.0267	0.0274
	0.75	0.2872	0.3015	0.2800	0	0	0	0	0	0	0
	1.25	0.2364	0.2402	0.2205	0	0	0	0	0	0	0
	1.75	0.2609	0.2682	0.2585	0	0	0	0	0	0	0
	2.0	0.2742	0.2801	0.2704	0	0	0	0	0	0	0
Translation	(H2,V15)	0.4023	0.4301	0.4217	0.0002	0	0	0	0	0	0
	(H20,V20)	0.5204	0.5291	0.5247	0.0039	0.0074	0.0020	0.0020	0.0020	0.0020	0.0020
	(H15,V2)	0.4201	0.4421	0.4461	0.0088	0.0039	0.0034	0	0.0021	0.003	0.0048
	(H50,V0)	0.5140	0.5294	0.5278	0.0074	0.0094	0.0029	0.0029	0.0029	0.0029	0.0029
	(H0,V50)	0.4914	0.4715	0.4997	0.0088	0.0068	0.0039	0.0039	0.0039	0.0039	0.0039

JPEG compression ration	30	0.045	0.05	0.062	0.0098	0.0085	0.0068	0.0074	0.01	0.0201	0.015
	40	0.031	0.023	0.043	0	0	0	0	0	0	0
	50	0.043	0.050	0.046	0	0	0	0	0	0	0
	70	0.028	0.010	0.014	0	0	0	0	0	0	0
	90	0.015	0.030	0.020	0	0	0	0	0	0	0
Shearing (0%–1%)		0.1925	0.2032	0.2106	0.0205	0.02	0.0102	0.0098	0.010	0.0105	0.02
Scaling 1.5 + JPEG (90%)		0.3612	0.3201	0.3342	0	0	0	0	0	0.	0.
Gaussian noise (0.01) + JPEG (90%)		0.2715	0.2801	0.2702	0.0020	0.0033	0.001	0		0.0033	0.0020
Rotation 45 + JPEG (90%)		0.2593	0.2605	0.2685	0	0.0033	0.01	0	0	0.0033	0.0048
Translation (H5,V15) + Salt & peppers noise (0.01)		0.5394	0.5483	0.5464	0.0098	0.010	0.0098	0.0039	0.0058	0.0088	0.0074
Salt and peppers noise (0.01)		0.1642	0.1733	0.1648	0	0	0.	0	0	0	0
Gaussian noise (0.01)		0.2103	0.1957	0.2144	0.0020	0.0025	0.0015	0.0002	0.0039	0.0049	0.0039
Median filtering (3 × 3)		0.20	0.1821	0.1704	0.0020	0.0039	0.0020	0.0013	0.0029	0.0039	0.0049

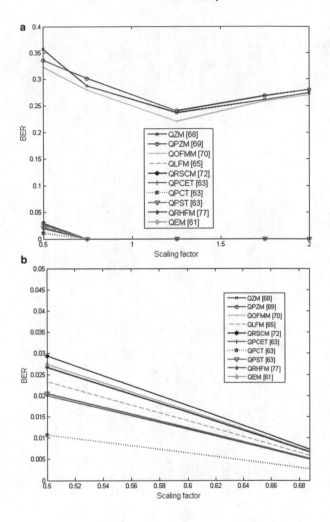

Fig. 8.7 Watermark robustness to scaling

NC values were shown in Table 8.7. It is observed that the NC values of the QPHTs, QLFMs, QRSCMs, QRHFMs and QEMs watermarking methods are very close to 1 which ensure their robustness against different attacks while the NC values of the other watermarking methods, QZMs, QPZMs, and QOFMMs, are close to 0.52 which reflects their poor performance.

In order to ensure the obtained results in Table 8.7, the watermarked image is attacked by a combination of scaling, rotation and JPEG compression. The watermarks are extracted using the quaternion moment-based watermarking methods where the NC values are computed for each extracted watermark. The obtained values are plotted and displayed in Figs. 8.10, 8.11 and 8.12 respectively. The NC values for the QPHTs, QLFMs, QRSCMs, QRHFMs and QEMs are very close to 1 while the corresponding values of QZMs, QPZMs and QOFMMs are deviated from the ideal value, 1.

Fig. 8.8 Watermark
robustness against the rotation

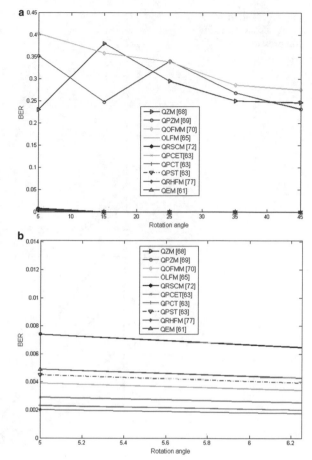

8.4.3   The CPU Times

Fast watermarking methods are very important in many applications such
telemedicine, e-health, online social network, and e-governance. The CPU times are
used as a quantative metric which measure the swift of the watermarking methods
where low CPU times reflects the efficiency of the different watermarking methods.
Experiments were performed with different color images where these images are
watermarked using different quaternion moment-based watermarking methods with
orders 10, 20, and 30. The experiments are repeated 10 times where average CPU
times in seconds are shown in Table 8.8.

Fig. 8.9 Watermark
robustness against JPEG
compression

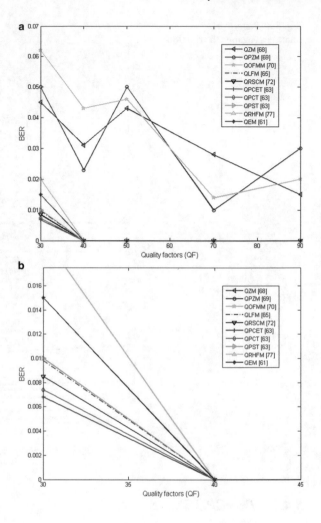

From Table 8.8, we can show that the quaternion moment-based watermarking methods which utilize accurate kernel-based method required much smaller CPU times in computing moments where these kernels are image-independent.

Table 8.7 Average NC values of the extracted watermarks

Attacks		QZMs [68]	QPZMs [69]	QOFMMs [70]	QLFMs [65]	QRSCMs [72]	QPHTs [63]			QRHFMs [77]	QEMs [61]
							QPCET	QPCT	QPST		
Rotation	5	0.5931	0.5862	0.5931	0.9816	0.9862	0.9853	0.9862	0.9899	0.9691	0.9715
	15	0.6084	0.6256	0.6072	0.9659	0.9685	0.9918	0.9872	0.9908	0.9825	0.9816
	25	0.5950	0.6027	0.5931	0.9695	0.9844	0.9825	0.9918	0.989	0.9716	0.9666
	35	0.5953	0.6088	0.6080	0.9687	0.9716	0.9872	0.9908	0.9881	0.9816	0.9769
	45	0.5948	0.6146	0.5946	0.9716	0.9862	0.9862	0.9899	0.9862	0.9795	0.9716
Scaling factor	0.25	0.5810	0.5864	0.5599	0.5162	0.6530	0.4646	0.5214	0.4908	0.5177	0.4687
	0.5	0.5973	0.6058	0.5897	0.8646	0.8350	0.9853	0.9899	0.9890	0.9299	0.9270
	0.75	0.6069	0.6172	0.5902	0.9807	0.9591	0.9899	0.9936	0.9918	0.9853	0.9818
	1.25	0.6184	0.6187	0.6011	0.9908	0.9834	0.9936	0.9954	0.9945	0.9834	0.9825
	1.75	0.6103	0.6137	0.6006	0.9908	0.9808	0.9918	0.9936	0.9936	0.9853	0.9834
	2.0	0.6044	0.6152	0.5674	0.9936	0.9825	0.9908	0.9936	0.9927	0.9809	0.9795
Trans.	(H15, V5)	0.5931	0.5962	0.5810	0.9927	0.9918	0.9927	0.9954	0.9945	0.9899	0.9872
	(H5, V15)	0.9716	0.5959	0.5093	0.9918	0.9936	0.9945	0.9927	0.9936	0.9936	0.989
Scaling 1.5 + JPEG compression 90%		0.5953	0.6146	0.6103	0.9908	0.9899	0.9918	0.9954	0.9963	0.9853	0.9825
Rotation 45 + JPEG compression 90%		0.6027	0.6058	0.6069	0.9679	0.9591	0.9881	0.9853	0.9890	0.9694	0.9685

(continued)

Table 8.7 (continued)

Attacks		QZMs [68]	QPZMs [69]	QOFMMs [70]	QLFMs [65]	QRSCMs [72]	QPHTs [63]			QRHFMs [77]	QEMs [61]
							QPCET	QPCT	QPST		
JPEG compression	10	0.5370	0.5575	0.5198	0.6476	0.6290	0.6343	0.5609	0.5444	0.5299	0.5864
	30	0.5313	0.5652	0.5093	0.8840	0.8691	0.8835	0.8824	0.8836	0.9562	0.9591
	50	0.5252	0.5490	0.5250	0.9506	0.9475	0.9629	0.9762	0.9678	0.9732	0.9715
	70	0.5264	0.5403	0.5011	0.9816	0.9629	0.9899	0.9963	0.9927	0.977	0.9716
	90	0.5019	0.5502	0.5167	0.9908	0.9716	0.9927	0.9927	0.9936	0.9862	0.9795
Salt & peppers noise	(0.01)	0.5252	0.6084	0.6152	0.989	0.9881	0.9936	0.9954	0.9945	0.9825	0.9818
	(0.03)	0.5093	0.5962	0.5198	0.9818	0.9808	0.9853	0.989	0.9918	0.9795	0.9695
Gaussian noise	(0.01)	0.5862	0.5502	0.5382	0.9853	0.9872	0.9853	0.9927	0.9918	0.9795	0.977
	(0.03)	0.5252	0.5962	0.5862	0.9825	0.9695	0.9853	0.9890	0.9853	0.9716	0.9715
Gaussian filtering	(3*3)	0.6184	0.6187	0.5950	0.989	0.9853	0.9899	0.9918	0.9908	0.9835	0.9871
	(5*5)	0.5931	0.5962	0.5093	0.9844	0.9818	0.9871	0.9899	0.9881	0.9722	0.9716
Median filtering	(3*3)	0.6107	0.6137	0.6056	0.9816	0.989	0.9963	0.9945	0.9954	0.977	0.9825
	(5*5)	0.5379	0.5594	0.5215	0.9853	0.9795	0.9954	0.9918	0.9927	0.9769	0.9732

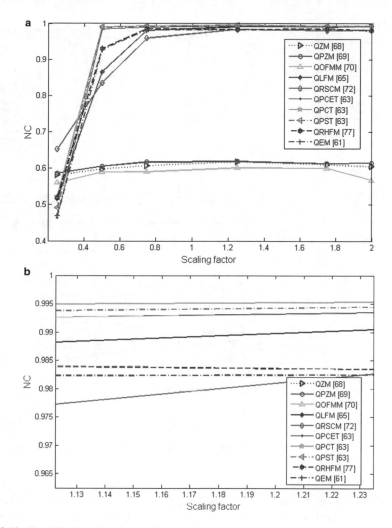

Fig. 8.10 The NC values based on scaling attack

8.5 Conclusion

A comparative study of the different quaternion moment-based watermarking methods for color image is presented. Based on the accurate computation of quaternion moments, the watermark information is embedded into the host image

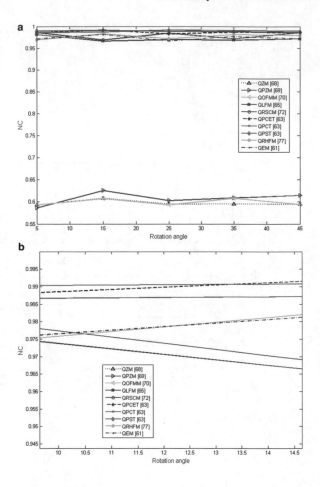

Fig. 8.11 The NC values based on rotation attack

by modifying their invariant QMs magnitudes using dither modulation function, then the embedded watermark information is extracted from the attacked images using the same process. Different attacks such as rotation, scaling, translation, JPEG compression and noise are applied to the color watermarked images. Experiments are performed to test the invisibility, robustness against to various attacks, capacity and computational complexity. Generally, the performance of the QPHT, QLFMs, QRSCMs, QRHFMs, and QEMs-based color watermarking methods show better watermark robustness, embedding capacity, and imperceptibility than QZMs, QPZMs and QOFMMs-based color watermarking methods.

Fig. 8.12 The NC values based on JPEG compression

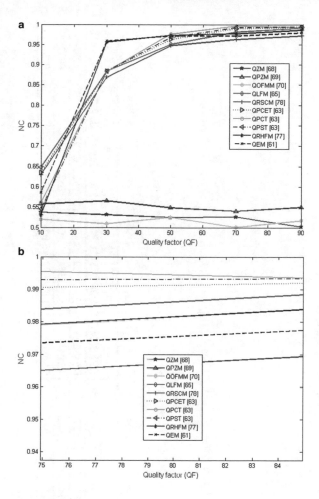

Table 8.8 Average CPU times for the watermarking methods

| Moment Order | QZMs [68] | QPZMs [69] | QOFMMs [70] | QLFMs [65] | QRSCMs [72] | QPHT [63] | | | QRHFMs [77] | QEMs [61] |
						QPCET	QPCT	QPST		
10	2.0356	1.5034	3.0367	0.5376	0.6482	1.2729	0.4537	0.3493	0.8023	1.2932
20	12.0243	11.2490	17.4793	2.3921	3.2981	5.1364	2.1034	1.9652	3.4801	7.0932
30	31.0215	24.0456	26.2046	5.3982	6.3982	10.6972	5.0214	4.8370	6.8651	12.035

References

1. Sun ZZ, Zhang QX, Li YA, Tan YZ (2016) DPPDL: a dynamic partial-parallel data layout for green video surveillance storage. IEEE Trans Circuits Syst Video Technol. doi:10.1109/TCSVT.2016.2605045
2. J. Yu, B. Zhang, Z. Kuang, D. Lin, J. Fan, I "privacy: image privacy protection by identifying sensitive objects via deep multi-task Learning:, IEEE Trans. Inf. Forensics Secur. 12 (5) (2017) 1005-1016.
3. A. Khan, A. Siddiqa, S. Munib, S.A. Malik, A recent survey of reversible watermarking techniques, Inf Sci (NY) 279 (2014) 251-272.
4. Atawneh S, Almomani A, Al Bazar H et al (2016) Secure and imperceptible digital image steganographic algorithm based on diamond encoding in DWT domain. Multimedia Tools and Applications. doi:10.1007
5. Memos VA, Psannis KE (2016) Encryption algorithm for efficient transmission of hevc media. J Real-Time Image Proc 12(2):473-482
6. Shih FY et al (2008) Digital Watermarking and Steganography: Fundamentals and Techniques, Taylor & Francis Group. CRC Press., Inc., Boca Raton
7. W.H. Ren, X. Li, and Z.M. Lu, "Reversible Data Hiding Scheme based on Fractal Image Coding," Journal of Information Hiding and Multimedia Signal Processing, vol. 8, no. 3, pp. 544-550, May 2017.
8. Z. Shokrollahi and M. Yazdi, "A Robust Blind Watermarking Scheme Based on Stationary Wavelet Transform," Journal of Information Hiding and Multimedia Signal Processing, vol. 8, no. 3, pp. 676-687, May 2017.
9. S.C. Chu, H.C. Huang, Y. Shi, S.Y. Wu, and C.S. Shieh, "Genetic Watermarking for Zerotree-based Applications," Circuits, Systems, and Signal Processing, vol. 27, no. 2, pp. 171-182, Apr. 2008.
10. A.K. Singh, B. Kumar, M. Dave, A. Mohan Robust and imperceptible dual watermarking for telemedicine applications. WirelPersCommun 80(4): (2014) 1415–1433
11. D.S. Chauhan, A.K. Singh, B. Kumar, J.P. Saini (2017) Quantization based multiple medical information watermarking for secure e-health, multimedia tools and applications, pp 1–13. https://doi.org/10.1007/s11042-017-4886-4
12. A. K. Singh, "Improved Hybrid Technique for Robust and Imperceptible Multiple Watermarking using Medical Images, Multimedia Tools and Applications, Vol. 76, Issue 6, pp 8881-8900 Springer US, 10.1007/s11042-016-3514-z.
13. A.K. Singh, B. Kumar, A. Mohan, "Medical image watermarking: techniques and applications", book series on multimedia systems and applications. Springer, USA, 2017.
14. A. Zear, A.K. Singh, P. Kumar, A proposed secure multiple watermarking technique based on DWT, DCT and SVD for application in medicine, Multimedia Tools Appl. (2016) https://doi.org/10.1007/s11042-016-3862-8.
15. S. Thakur, A. K. Singh, S. P. Ghrera, A. Mohan, Chaotic based secure watermarking approach for medical images, Multimedia Tools and Applications, Springer DOI: 10.1007/s11042-018-6691-0.
16. A. K. Singh, B. Kumarb, S. K. Singh c, S.P. Ghrera, A. Mohan, Multiple Watermarking Technique for Securing Online Social Network Contents using Back Propagation Neural Network, Future Generation Computer Systems, pp.1-16 DOI: 10.1016/j.future.2016.11.023
17. C. Kumar, A. K. Singh, and P. Kumar, "A recent survey on image watermarking techniques and its application in e-governance", Multimedia Tools and Applications, Springer DOI: 10.1007/s11042-017-5222-8.
18. K.-L. Chung, C.-Y. Chiu, T.-Y. Yu, P.-L. Huang, "Temporal and spatial correlation-based reversible data hiding for RGB CFA videos, Inf Sci (NY) 420 (Sup- plement C) (2017) 386–402.
19. R. Srivastav, B. Kumar, A. K. Singh and Anand Mohan, "computationally efficient joint imperceptible image watermarking and JPEG compression: A green computing approach, Multimedia Tools and Applications, Springer US DOI: 10.1007/s11042-017-5214-8

20. L. Singh, A. K. Singh, P. K. Singh, "Secure data hiding techniques: A survey", Multimedia Tools and Applications, Springer DOI: 10.1007/s11042-018-6407-5.
21. T. Huynh-The, O. Banos, S. Lee, Y. Yoon, T. Le-Tien, "Improving digital image watermarking by means of optimal channel selection", Expert Syst. Appl. 62 (2016) 177–189.
22. E. Tsougenis, G. Papakostas, D. Koulouriotis, E. Karakasis, "Adaptive color image watermarking by the use of quaternion image moments", Expert Syst. Appl. 41 (14) (2014) 6408–6418.
23. C. Kumar, A.K. Singh, P. Kumar, R. Singh, S. Singh, "SPIHT based multiple image watermarking in NSCT domain", Concurrency and Computation: Practice and Experience, Wiley, DOI:10.1002/cpe.4912.
24. A.M. Abdelhakim, H.I. Saleh, A.M. Nassar, "A quality guaranteed robust image watermarking optimization with artificial bee colony", Expert Syst. Appl. 72 (2017) 317–326
25. P.-Y. Lin, J.-S. Lee, and C.-C. Chang., "Protecting the content integrity of digital imagery with fidelity preservation". ACM Trans. Multimedia Comput. Commun. Appl., Article 15, Vol. 7 (3), 20 pages, 2011.
26. M. Yu, J. Wang, G. Jiang, Z. Peng, F. Shao, T. Luo, "New fragile watermarking method for stereo image authentication with localization and recovery". AEU Int. J Electron Commun., Vol. 69(1), p. 361–370, 2015.
27. 12. Petitcolas F, Anderson R, Kuhn M (1998) Attacks on copyright marking systems, LNCS, 218–238
28. Masoud Alghoniemy and Ahmed H. Tewfik, "Geometric invariance in image watermarking," IEEE Transactions on Image Processing, vol. 13, no. 2, pp. 145-153, 2004.
29. Y. Xin, S. Liao, and M. Pawlak, "Circularly orthogonal moments for geometrically robust image watermarking", Pattern Recognition, Vol. 40, p. 3740–3752, 2007.
30. I. A. Ismail, M. A. Shouman, K. M. Hosny, H. M. Abdel-Salam "Invariant image watermarking using accurate Zernike moments", Journal Computer Science, 2010, 6, (1), pp. 52–59
31. H. Q. Zhu, M. Liu, and Y. Li, "The RST invariant digital image watermarking using Radon transforms and complex moments," Digital Signal Processing, vol. 20, no. 6, pp. 1612–1628, 2010.
32. H. Zhang, H. Shu, G. Coatrieux, Affine Legendre moment invariants for image watermarking robust to geometric distortions, IEEE Trans. Image Process., Vol. 20(8), p. 2189–2199, 2011.
33. L. Li et al., "Geometrically invariant image watermarking using Polar Harmonic Transforms," Inform. Sci. 199, 1–19 (2012).
34. Papakostas GA, Koulouriotis DE, Tourassis VD. "Performance evaluation of moment-based watermarking methods: a review. J SystSoftw 2012;85(8):1864–84.
35. E.D. Tsougenis, G.A. Papakostas, D.E. Koulouriotis, V.D. Tourassis, "Towards adaptivity of image watermarking in polar harmonic transforms domain", Optics & Laser Technology, Vol. 54, p. 84-97, 2013.
36. H.Y. Yang, X.Y. Wang, P. Wang, P.P. Niu, "Geometrically resilient digital watermarking scheme based on radial harmonic Fourier moments magnitude", AEU - Int. J. Electron. Commun., Vol. 69, p. 389–399, 2015.
37. Wang Chun-peng, Wang Xing-yuan, Xia Zhi-qiu, "Geometrically invariant image watermarking based on fast Radial Harmonic Fourier Moments", Signal Processing: Image Communication, Vol. 45, p. 10–23, 2016.
38. Qi M, Li BZ, Sun H. "Image watermarking using polar harmonic transform with parameters in SL(2, R). Signal Processing: Image Communication 2015; 31:161–73
39. K. M. Hosny and M. M. Darwish, "Invariant image watermarking using accurate Polar Harmonic transforms", Computers and Electrical Engineering, Vol.62, p.429-447, 2017.
40. T.K. Tsui, X.P. Zhang, D. And routsos, "Color image watermarking using multidimensional Fourier transforms", IEEE Trans. Inform. Forensics Secur., Vol. 3 (1), p.16–28, 2008.
41. J.A. Hussein, "Luminance-based embedding approach for color image watermarking", Int. J. Image Graph. Signal Process., Vol. 4 (3), p.49–56, 2012.
42. H. Peng, J. Wang, W.X. Wang, Image watermarking method in multi-wavelet domain based on support vector machines, J. Syst. Softw., Vol. 83(8), p. 1470–1477, 2010.
43. P.P. Niu, X.Y. Wang, Y.P. Yang, M.Y. Lu, "A novel color image watermarking scheme in non-sampled contourlet domain", Expert Syst. Appl., Vol. 38(3), p. 2081–2098, 2011.

44. Liu. Kuo-Cheng, "Wavelet-based watermarking for color images through visual masking", AEU-Int. J. Electron. Commun., Vol. 64 (2), p. 112–124, 2010.
45. C.H. Chou, K.C. Liu, "A perceptually tuned watermarking scheme for color images", IEEE Trans. Image Process., Vol. 19 (11), p. 2966–2982, 2010.
46. A. Basso, D. Cavagnino, V. Pomponiu, "Blind watermarking of color images using Karhunen–Loève transform keying", Comput. J. 54 (7) (2011) 1076–1090.
47. Q. Su, Y. Niu, X. Liu, "A blind dual color images watermarking based on IWT and state coding, Opt. Commun. 285 (7) (2012) 1717–1724.
48. S. Roy, A. K. Pal, "A blind DCT based color watermarking algorithm for embedding multiple watermarks, Int. J. Electron. Commun. (AEÜ) 72 (2017) 149–161
49. Q. Su and B. Chen, "A novel blind color image watermarking using upper Hessenberg matrix", Int. J. Electron. Commun. (AEÜ) 78 (2017) 64–71.
50. FindIk O, Babaoglu I, Ülker E. A color image watermarking scheme based on artificial immune recognition system. Expert SystAppl 2011;38(3):1942–6.
51. Niu PP, Wang XY, Yang YP, Lu MY. A novel color image watermarking scheme in non-sampled contourlet-domain. Expert SystAppl 2011;38(3):2081–98.
52. Vahedi E, Zoroofi RA, Shiva M. Toward a new wavelet-based watermarking approach for color images using bio-inspired optimization principles. Digital Signal Process 2012;22(1):153–62.
53. Wang X, Wang C, Yang H, Niu P. A robust blind color image watermarking in quaternion Fourier transform domain. J SystSoftw 2013;86(2):255–77.
54. Shao Z, Duan Y, Coatrieux G, Wu J, Meng J, Shu H. Combining double random phase encoding for color image watermarking in quaternion gyrator domain. OptCommun 2015; 343:56–65.
55. Su Q, Niu Y, Zou H, Zhao Y, Yao T. A blind double color image watermarking algorithm based on QR decomposition. Multimedia Tools App 2014;72 (1):987–1009.
56. Chen B, Coatrieux G, Chen G, Sun X, Coatrieux JL, Shu H. Full 4-D quaternion discrete Fourier transform based watermarking for color images. Digital Signal Process 2014;28(5):106–19.
57. B. Chen, C. Zhou, B. Jeon3, Y. Zheng, J. Wang, Quaternion discrete fractional random transform for color image adaptive watermarking, Multimed Tools Appl (2017)
58. Tsougenis ED, Papakostas G A, Koulouriotis DE, Karakasis EG, "Adaptive color image watermarking by the use of quaternion image moments", Expert Syst Appl., Vol. 41(14), p.6408–6418, 2014.
59. Wang XY, Niu PP, Yang HY, Wang CP, Wang AL, "A new robust color image watermarking using local quaternion exponent moments". Inf. Sci. Vol. 277, pp.731–754, 2014.
60. H. Yang, Y. Zhang, P. Wang, X. Wang, C. Wang, "A geometric correction based robust color image watermarking scheme using quaternion Exponent moments", Optik, Vol.125, pp.4456–4469, 2014.
61. X.Y. Wang, H.Y. Yang, P.P. Niu, C.P. Wang, "Quaternion exponent moments based robust color image watermarking", J. Comput. Res. Dev., Vol. 53, p. 651–665, 2016.
62. P. Niu, P. Wang, Y. Liu, H. Yang, X. Wang, "Invariant color image watermarking approach using quaternion radial harmonic Fourier moments", Multimed. Tools Appl. (2015).
63. H.Y. Yang, X.Y. Wang, P.P. Niu, A.L. Wang, "Robust color image watermarking using geometric invariant quaternion polar harmonic transform", ACM Trans. Multimed Comput. Commun. Appl. 11 (3) 1-26, 2015.
64. Wang XY, Liu YN, Han MM, Yang HY, "Local quaternion PHT based robust color image watermarking algorithm", J. Vis Commun Image Represent, Vol. 38, pp.678–694, 2016.
65. Khalid M. Hosny and Mohamed M. Darwish, "Robust Color Image Watermarking Using Invariant Quaternion Legendre-Fourier Moments", Multimedia Tools and Applications, Vol. 77, Issue 19, pp 24727–24750, 2018.
66. W.R. Hamilton, "Elements of Quaternions", Longmans Green, London, U.K., 1866.
67. T.A. Ell, S.J. Sangwine, "Hypercomplex Fourier transforms of color images", IEEE Transaction of Image Process, Vol. 16, p. 22–35, 2007.
68. B. J. Chen, H. Z. Shu, H. Zhang, G. Chen, C. Toumoulin, J. L. Dillenseger, and L. M. Luo, "Quaternion Zernike moments and their invariants for color image analysis and object recognition", Signal Processing, Vol. 92 (2), p. 308-318, 2012.

69. Chen, B.-J., et al., Color face recognition using quaternion representation of color image. ACTA AutomaticaSinica, 2012. 38(11): p. 1815-1823.
70. L.Q. Guo, M. Zhu, Quaternion Fourier Mellin moments for color images, Pattern Recognit. 44 (2011) 187–195.
71. B. Xiao, G. Wang, W. Li, "Radial Shifted Legendre Moments for Image Analysis and Invariant Image Recognition", Image and Vision Computing, Vol.32 (12), p. 994-1006, 2014.
72. Khalid M. Hosny and Mohamed M. Darwish, "New Set of Quaternion Moments for Color Images Representation and Recognition", Journal of Mathematical Imaging and Vision, Vol. 60, p. 717–736, 2018.
73. P. Yap, X. Jiang and A.C. Kot, "Two Dimensional Polar Harmonic Transforms for Invariant Image Representation," IEEE Transaction Pattern Analysis and Machine Intelligence, 32(7):1259-1270, 2010.
74. Xiang-yang Wang, Wei-yi Li, Hong-ying Yang, Pei Wang, and Yong-wei Li, "Quaternion polar complex exponential transform for invariant color image description", Applied Mathematics and Computation, Vol. 256, p. 951–967, 2015.
75. K. M. Hosny and M. M. Darwish, "Accurate computation of quaternion polar complex exponential transform for color images in different coordinate systems," Journal of Electronic Imaging 26(2), 023021 (2017).
76. K. M. Hosny and M. M. Darwish, "Highly accurate and numerically stable higher order QPCET moments for color image representation," Pattern Recognition. Letters, 97, 29–36 (2017)
77. X. Y. Wang, W. Y. Li, H. Y. Yang, P. P. Niu, Y. W. Li, "Invariant quaternion radial harmonic Fourier moments for color image retrieval", Optics and Laser Technology, Vol. 66, pp. 78–88, 2015.
78. K. M. Hosny, M. A. Shouman, and H. M. Abdel-Salam, "Fast computation of orthogonal Fourier-Mellin moments in polar coordinates", Journal of Real-Time Image Process., Vol. 6(2), pp. 73–80, 2011.
79. K. M. Hosny, M. M. Darwish, "A Kernel-Based method for Fast and accurate computation of PHT in polar coordinates", Journal of Real-Time Image Process., J Real-Time Image Proc, DOI 10.1007/s11554-016-0622-y, 2016, p.1-13 (Online first).
80. Y. Xin, M. Pawlak, S. Liao, "Accurate computation of Zernike moments in polar coordinates", IEEE Trans. Image Process., Vol. 16 (2), pp. 581–587, 2007.
81. J. D. Faires, R. L. Burden, "Numerical Methods", Brooks Cole Publication, 3rd edn., 2002.
82. C. Camacho-Bello et al., "High precision and fast computation of Jacobi-Fourier moments for image description," J. Opt. Soc. Am. A 31(1), 124–134 (2014).
83. C. Camacho-Bello et al., "Reconstruction of color biomedical images by means of quaternion generic Jacobi-Fourier moments in the framework of polar pixel," J. Med. Imaging 3(1), 014004 (2016).
84. Z. Wang, A. C. Bovik, H. R. Sheikh, and E. P. Simoncelli, "Image quality assessment: From error visibility to structural similarity," IEEE Transactions on Image Processing, vol. 13, no. 4, pp. 600-612, Apr. 2004.

Chapter 9
Security of Biometric and Biomedical Images Using Sparse Domain Based Watermarking Technique

Rohit Thanki, Surekha Borra, and Deven Trivedi

9.1 Introduction

The rise in the utilization of human related pictures over online networking poses genuine difficulties to the picture security. The watermarking system can be utilized for different applications, for example, copyright assurance, ownership identification, and secure correspondence [1–3]. The human related images are isolated into two kinds: biometric images and biomedical images. The biometric images reflect the conduct and/or physical attributes of human and hence are utilized as unique ID in different organizations. On the other hand, the biomedical images speak about wellbeing related data. Along these lines, the security of such images is vital when it is transmitted over a correspondence channel.

The many watermarking techniques in spatial and transform domain are proposed for the security of images [1–4] in the literature. Many researchers proposed transform domain techniques to result higher robustness and security. Hybrid watermarking techniques are also proposed by combining various image transforms [1, 2, 5]. In these techniques, cover image is converted into its transform coefficients before being modified by watermark image to get modified coefficients. In this chapter, compressive sensing (CS) theory is combined with sparsity property of DWT to propose a secure method for watermarking of human related images. The proposed technique is tested and analyzed using different kind of biomedical images and biometric images. The performance of the technique is further verified

R. Thanki (✉)
C. U. Shah University, Wadhwan City, Gujarat, India

S. Borra
K. S. Institute of Technology, Bangalore, Karnataka, India

D. Trivedi
G. H. Patel College of Engineering and Technology, Vallabh Vidyanagar, Gujarat, India

© Springer Nature Switzerland AG 2019
A. K. Singh, A. Mohan (eds.), *Handbook of Multimedia Information Security: Techniques and Applications*, https://doi.org/10.1007/978-3-030-15887-3_9

against various types of attacks and are compared with two recently proposed spread spectrum based medical image watermarking techniques in terms of peak signal to noise ratio (PSNR) and normalized coefficient (NC). The performance of the proposed technique is also compared with two more biometric image watermarking techniques [8, 9] in the literature.

9.2   Related Work

Watermarking techniques are widely used for securing/copyright protection of human related images in the literature and they differ in choice of different cover images, watermark embedding process, watermark extraction process and processing domains. The literature survey in this section is limited to two different human related images: biometric image watermarking and biomedical image watermarking [6–45].

9.2.1   Biomedical Image Watermarking

Many researchers [6, 7, 11–22] developed various medical image hiding techniques for telemedicine applications by combining different image processing transforms and their hybridizations. It is observed that many existed techniques had less imperceptibility and payload capacity. In last 2 years, many techniques were proposed by various researchers for biomedical images. A few of these techniques are reviewed below [5, 16–28].

Singh et al. [5] have proposed Singular Value Decomposition (SVD)—Discrete Cosine Transform (DCT) based technique in Non-subsampled contourlet domain (NSCT) for biomedical images. Here, the singular values of hybrid coefficients (DCT coefficients of Contourlet coefficients) of secret watermark logo or image are inserted into singular values of hybrid coefficients (DCT coefficients of Contourlet coefficients) of cover medical image to generate watermarked medical image. Very less imperceptibility was achieved for watermarked medical image using this technique. Thanki et al. [16] have proposed Fast Discrete Curvelet Transform (FDCuT)—Discrete Cosine Transform (DCT) based blind biomedical image watermarking.

Kaya and Elbasi [17] have gave comparison of various biomedical watermarking techniques which are robust in nature. They used techniques that involve Least Significant Bit (LSB) substitution, DCT, Discrete Wavelet Transform (DWT), and Discrete Fourier Transform (DFT). Priyanka and Maheshkar [18] have proposed hybrid domain biomedical image watermarking technique. In this technique, cover medical image is divided into two regions: region of interest (ROI) and region of non-interest (RONI). Then, two LSBs of ROI are taken for tamper localization and tamper detection. The multiple watermarks information's is embedded into RONI of biomedical image using integer wavelet transform (IWT)-SVD based hybrid watermarking technique. This technique provides robustness as well as tamper detection and localization.

Selvam et al. [19] have proposed reversible and hybrid domain watermarking technique for color biomedical images. This technique is designed using IWT and Discrete Gould Transform (DGT). Singh and Dutta [20] have proposed reversible biomedical watermarking technique in spatial domain. In this technique, neighborhood estimation of biomedical image pixel method is used for embedding watermark into medical image. Thakkar and Srivastava [21] have proposed blind biomedical image watermarking technique using DWT and block wise SVD. This technique is only applicable on Region of Interest (ROI) of biomedical image. Parah et al. [22] have proposed two transform domain watermarking techniques for medical image. In the first technique, watermark logo and EPR is embedded into ROI and RONI of cover biomedical image using DCT based approach. In the second technique, watermark logo and EPR are inserted into RONI of cover medical image. In both these techniques, two DCT coefficients from each 8×8 DCT block of cover biomedical image are used for watermark embedding. The researchers [23–28] have proposed various watermarking techniques using advanced machine learning algorithm, hybrid approaches for biomedical images.

After reviewing the existing techniques, it is indicated that most of the biomedical image watermarking is performed either in transform domain or in spatial domain. This chapter aims at overcoming the limitations of some existing techniques which are based on Spread Spectrum (SS) approach, in particular, Kumar technique [6] and Singh technique [7]. In these techniques, watermark or encrypted watermark information is inserted into cover biomedical image to generate watermarked biomedical image. The major limitation of these techniques is that the visibility of the watermarked biomedical image and recovered watermark gets degraded with increased gain factor.

9.2.2 Biometric Image Watermarking

In the last 10 years, researchers were proposed different watermarking techniques for the security of biometric data using various image processing transforms and other methodologies. The researchers [8, 9, 29–36] proposed various watermarking techniques using DWT, SVD, and other advanced image processing operations for the security of facial, fingerprint, speech, and signature features. The researchers [37–40, 45] proposed various watermarking techniques using DCT, Phase Congruency Model, and Principal Component Analysis (PCA) for the security of facial, fingerprint, and iris features. After reviewing these papers, it is proven that most of the existing techniques are defined and implemented using face and fingerprint characteristics of human. Also, these techniques explored transform coefficients or pixel information of cover biometric image to generate secure watermarked biometric image. This provided motivation for proposing a watermarking technique in sparse domain for securing ear biometric images.

The proposed technique is a combination of CS theory [46–48] based encryption process and spread spectrum-based approach which is based on correlation of PN sequences [4, 49]. In this technique, first, DWT is applied on the cover image to get its wavelet coefficients. The sparse measurements of cover image in terms of encrypted data are generated from its wavelet coefficients using CS theory. A secure watermark mask is generated using two uncorrelated noise sequences and watermark image. This mask is inserted into sparse measurements of cover image to get watermarked sparse measurements. The watermarked sparse coefficients of cover image are then obtained using CS theory reconstruction algorithm from watermarked sparse measurements. Finally, inverse DWT is applied to watermarked sparse coefficients to obtain watermarked cover image. The watermark extraction is in turn performed using the correlation of noise sequences. In extraction process, the correlation between noise sequences and sparse measurements of watermarked image is performed, and based on the correlation result, watermark image is recovered.

Rest of the chapter is organized as follows; in Sect. 9.3, preliminaries used in the design of the proposed technique are given. Section 9.4 gives the proposed watermarking technique, whereas experimental results and discussions are given in Sect. 9.5. Finally, the conclusions of the chapter are given in Sect. 9.6.

9.3 Technical Background

In this section, various theories and operations used for implementation of proposed technique are given.

9.3.1 Compressive Sensing (CS) Theory

The compressive sensing (CS) theory [46–48] converts an image into its sparse data representation. These coefficients of image f are represented as

$$x = \Psi \times f \times \Psi' \quad (9.1)$$

where, x represents sparse coefficients, Ψ represents basis matrix of image transform, and Ψ' the inverse basis matrix.

The sparse measurements y of input image f is generated using the equation:

$$y = A \times x \quad (9.2)$$

where, A is the measurement matrix, y represents sparse measurements of the image, and x being sparse coefficients.

To recover an image from its sparse measurements, various reconstruction algorithms are used [46–48]. These algorithms are divided into two types: L1 minimization-based algorithms and greedy based algorithms. In this chapter, greedy based OMP algorithm [48] is used for extraction of watermarked sparse coefficients from watermarked sparse measurements.

9.3.2 Digital Watermarking

Digital watermarking is a process that inserts secret information into cover digital content [1–4, 49]. The watermarking is designed for various types of multimedia data such as digital images, digital videos, and digital audio signals. These techniques are generally designed in two domains: spatial and transform [1–4, 41, 49]. The pixels information of cover content is modified in spatial domain technique while in the transform domain technique, frequency coefficients of cover content are modified according to the secret information.

The sparse domain-based watermarking approach is designed such that sparse data of cover content is modified according to the secret information. This approach is recently introduced by researchers using sparsity property of image transform and L1 minimization technique for the standard image [10, 50]. In this approach, watermark image is inserted into sparse measurements of standard image using simple addition operation. The security of watermark image is not measured in this approach.

9.3.3 Wavelet Basis Matrix

In this chapter, a wavelet basis matrix-based method [51, 52] is used for generation of sparse coefficients of a biomedical image where all wavelet coefficients of medical image are considered as sparse coefficients. The steps for generation of this matrix in MATLAB were in detail described by Thanki et al. [29].

In this chapter, Haar wavelet basis matrix is used. The Haar basis matrix is given as below [53]:

$$
\Psi = \begin{bmatrix} h_{1,1} & h_{1,2} & \cdots & h_{1,N} \\ h_{2,1} & h_{2,2} & \cdots & h_{2,N} \\ \vdots & \vdots & \ddots & \vdots \\ h_{N,1} & h_{N,2} & \cdots & h_{N,N} \end{bmatrix}, \quad h_{x,y}(i) = \begin{cases} 1 \, for \, i \in \left[\frac{T}{L}, \frac{T+0.5}{L} \right] \\ -1 \, for \, i \in \left[\frac{T+0.5}{L}, \frac{T+1}{L} \right] \\ 0 \end{cases} \tag{9.3}
$$

where, $L = 2^j, j = 0, 1, 2, \ldots N$ is the level of the wavelet and $T = 0, 1, 2, \ldots L\text{-}1$ is the translation parameter.

The other reason behind choosing Haar wavelet matrix [53] in the proposed technique is that (1) this wavelet transform has sparse data compared to another transform such as Walsh. (2) The size of the input data and output data of matrix is same and it is power of 2. (3) The wavelet analyses the local feature of image due to its orthogonality property.

9.4 Proposed Watermarking Technique

In this section, the procedure of proposed watermarking technique is described. This proposed technique has two processes such as embedding of watermark information into cover image and extraction of watermark information from the watermarked image.

9.4.1 Watermark Embedding Process

In this process, watermark bits are inserted into sparse measurements of cover image using noise sequences. The block diagram of watermark embedding process is depicted in Fig. 9.1. The steps of embedding of watermark bits into the cover image are given below:

Step 1: Calculate the size of watermark image w and convert it into the vector of bits.

Step 2: Take a cover image C and calculate its size. Generate wavelet basis matrix Ψ with the equal size of cover image.

Step 3: The sparse coefficients Cx of cover image is obtain using below equation:

$$Cx = \Psi \times C \times \Psi'$$ (9.4)

where, Cx denotes sparse coefficients of cover image, Ψ is the wavelet basis matrix, and Ψ' is inverse wavelet basis matrix.

Step 4: The measurement matrix A is generating using Gaussian distribution with equal size of cover image.

Step 5: The sparse measurements Cy of cover image is obtained using below equation:

$$Cy = A \times C_x$$ (9.5)

where, Cy denotes sparse measurements of cover image.

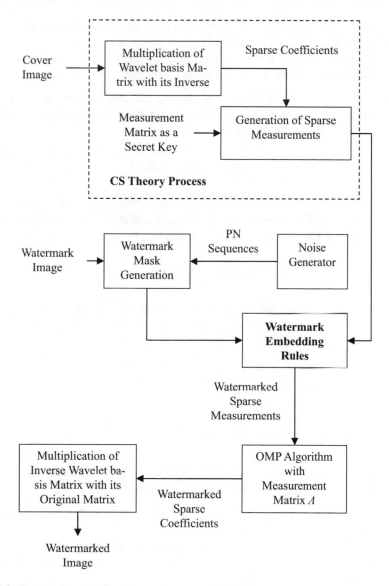

Fig. 9.1 Watermark embedding process in proposed technique

Step 6: The generated sparse measurements Cy of cover image are divided into non-overlapping blocks with size of 8×8.

Step 7: Two noise sequences are generate using Pseudo noise generator. Where, one noise sequence is used for watermark bit 0 and second noise sequence is used for watermark bit 1.

Step 8: The watermark mask *WM* is generated using below procedure:

   a. If watermark information has zero bit then noise sequence for this bit is added to that portion of mask.
   b. Other portion of mask is filled with noise sequence of one bit.
   c. This procedure is repeated for every block of cover image.

Step 9: This generated watermark mask WM is added with sparse measurements C_y of cover image using gain factor k to get watermarked version of sparse measurements WC_y of cover image.

$$WCy = Cx + k \times WM \tag{9.6}$$

Step 10: The CS recovery (CSR) algorithm along with measurement matrix A is applied on watermark WC_y to obtained modified sparse coefficients WC_x (in watermarked version) of the cover image.

$$WCx = CSR(WCy, A) \tag{9.7}$$

Step 11: Finally, inverse procedure of step 2 is applied on modified sparse coefficients (in watermarked version) of the cover image to get watermarked image C^*.

$$C^* = \Psi' \times WCx \times \Psi \tag{9.8}$$

9.4.2 Watermark Extraction Process

The block diagram of extraction of watermark bits from watermarked image is depicted in Fig. 9.2. The steps for this process is given below:

Step 1: The embedding steps no. 3–6 is applied on watermarked image to its sparse measurements with block size 8×8.
Step 2: Two noise sequences are generate using Pseudo noise generator. Where, one noise sequence is used for watermark bit 0 and second noise sequence is used for watermark bit 1.
Step 3: The watermarks bits are recovered using below equations:

$$Seq\_1 = corr2(Cy^*, PNSeq\_1) \tag{9.9}$$

$$Seq\_2 = corr2(Cy^*, PN\_Seq\_0) \tag{9.10}$$

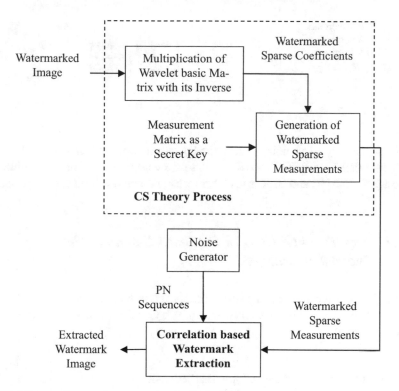

Fig. 9.2 Watermark extraction process in proposed technique

Step 4: If seq_1 < seq_2, then watermark bit is set as zero bit. Else, seq_1 > seq_2 then watermark bit is set as one bit.

Step 5: Reshape recovered vector of watermark bits to get recovered watermark image $w*$.

9.5 Experimental Results and Discussion

The proposed technique is analyzed by various types of biometric and biomedical images. The test biomedical images are obtained from the MedPix™ Medical Image Database [54] and test biometric images are obtained from AMI ear database [55]. A set of two watermark images (which are 8-bit binary images) are used for analysis of technique. The dimensions of watermark image 1 and watermark image 2 are 50 × 20 pixels and 32 × 32 pixels, respectively (shown in Fig. 9.3).

This proposed technique is implemented on MATLAB software while performance of this technique is analysed by standard watermarking quality measures

Fig. 9.3 Test watermark images (**a**) Watermark 1 (WM1) (**b**) Watermark 2 (WM2)

(a)   (b)

such as peak signal to noise ratio (PSNR), normalized correlation (NC) and bit error rate (BER) [56]. The PSNR is used for measurement of imperceptibility of technique while NC and BER is used for measurement of robustness of technique.

9.5.1 Experiment Results of Proposed Technique for Biomedical Images

The experimental results and analysis of proposed technique for biomedical images is covered in this section. The comparison of this technique with existing biomedical image is also given.

9.5.1.1 Information of Test Biomedical Images

The test biomedical images chosen are 8-bit grayscale images of size 256×256 pixels and are shown in Fig. 9.4.

9.5.1.2 Imperceptibility Test

An imperceptibility test of proposed technique is performed using different biomedical images. This test verifies how much distortion introduce by watermark data into biomedical image when it is inserted into it. Figure 9.5 shows generated watermarked biomedical image and recovered watermark image using proposed technique.

Figure 9.6 shows quantitative results of proposed technique for different biomedical images and various gain factor values. Results indicate that when gain factor increases, the perceptual quality of watermarked biomedical images decreases but at the same time the perceptual quality of recovered watermark images increases.

The performance of embedding procedure of proposed technique effects by the value of gain factor k. Thus, performance of this technique is verified for biomedical images by various gain factor values. These values vary from 15 to 60. The corresponding quality measures are given in Table 9.1. The values in Table 9.1 indicated than perceptual quality of recovered watermark images is good for high value of gain factor. The performance of proposed technique is compared with

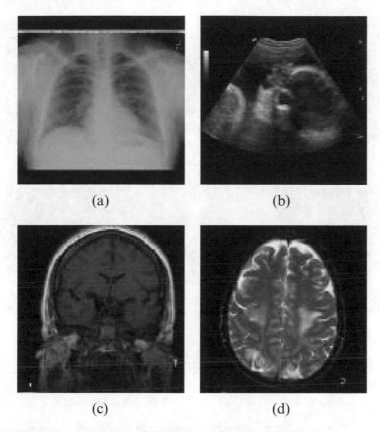

Fig. 9.4 Test cover biomedical images (**a**) X-ray (**b**) US (**c**) MRI (**d**) CT

Kumar et al. [6] and are given in Table 9.2. The comparison of techniques is done using value of gain factor $k = 60$ and Watermark image 2. For better comparison of techniques, same database is used for generation of results of existing technique, i.e. Kumar et al. [6]. The comparison of techniques indicate that the proposed technique provides better imperceptibility and better-recovered watermark images compared to Kumar et al. [6].

9.5.1.3 Robustness Test

The robustness of proposed technique is tested by different kind of watermarking attacks. The robustness of this technique measures using NC and BER. The quality measure values of this technique are also compared with quality measure values of the Kumar et al. [6] for the same set of medical images. Figure 9.7 shows the recovered watermark images under various watermarking attacks.

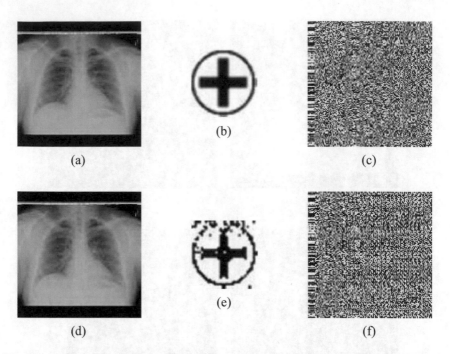

Fig. 9.5 (**a**) Original biomedical image (**b**) Watermark image (**c**) Sparse measurements of biomedical image (**d**) Watermarked biomedical image (**e**) Recovered watermark image (**f**) Watermarked measurements of biomedical image

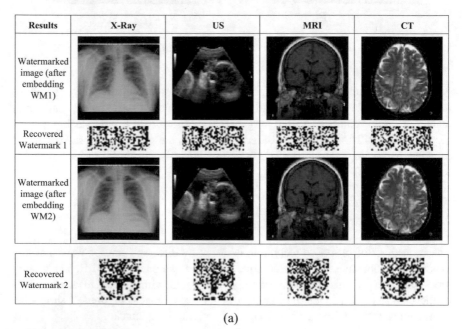

Fig. 9.6 Experiment results of proposed technique for different biomedical images and various gain factor values. (**a**) For $k = 15$, (**b**) For $k = 30$, (**c**) For $k = 60$

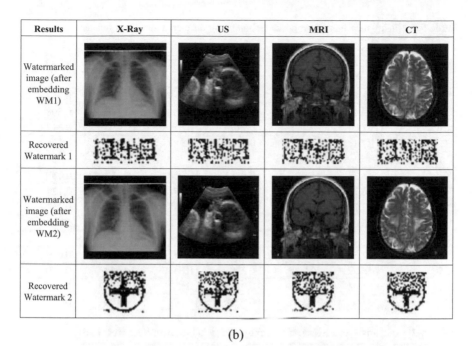

(b)

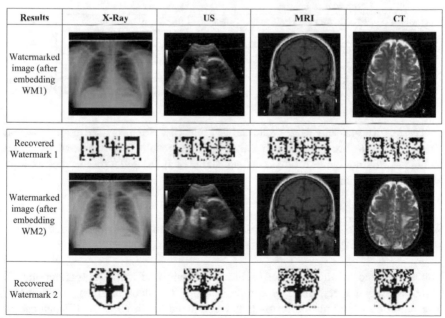

(c)

Fig. 9.6 (continued)

Table 9.1 Quality measures of proposed technique for different biomedical images

Test image	PSNR (dB)		NC		BER	
	WM1	WM2	WM1	WM2	WM1	WM2
(a) For $k = 15$						
X-ray	43.16	42.98	0.7332	0.7397	0.262	0.254
US	39.43	39.61	0.6860	0.6860	0.304	0.308
MRI	37.60	37.66	0.7129	0.6708	0.280	0.317
CT	37.34	36.93	0.7129	0.6873	0.297	0.296
(b) For $k = 30$						
X-ray	41.33	41.26	0.8383	0.8209	0.157	0.155
US	38.79	38.39	0.7884	0.7713	0.210	0.229
MRI	37.13	37.17	0.7830	0.7507	0.222	0.251
CT	36.63	36.69	0.7561	0.7700	0.237	0.224
(c) For $k = 60$						
X-ray	37.34	37.33	0.9272	0.9311	0.074	0.069
US	36.52	36.39	0.8598	0.8540	0.154	0.150
MRI	35.04	35.37	0.8356	0.8320	0.169	0.152
CT	35.07	35.01	0.8248	0.8099	0.180	0.178

Table 9.2 Comparison of performance of proposed technique with Kumar et al. [6]

Test image	Proposed technique			Kumar et al. [6]		
	PSNR (dB)	NC	BER	PSNR (dB)	NC	BER
X-ray	37.33	0.9311	0.069	5.84	0.4690	0.538
US	36.39	0.8540	0.150	4.87	0.4780	0.528
MRI	35.37	0.8320	0.152	5.24	0.4640	0.537
CT	35.01	0.8099	0.178	5.13	0.4770	0.538

The quality measure values such as NC and BER for proposed technique and Kumar et al. [6] are tabulated in Table 9.3. The results indicated that proposed technique provides better robustness than Kumar et al. [6] under these watermarking attacks for high gain value.

9.5.1.4 Comparison of the Proposed Technique with Existing Biomedical Image Watermarking Techniques

The performance of the proposed technique is compared with Singh technique [7] based on spread spectrum. The comparison of NC values is given in Table 9.4. The proposed technique performs better compared to Singh et al. [7] against all mentioned manipulations except for the JPEG (Q = 70).

The proposed technique is also compared with the Kumar et al. [6] and Singh et al. [7] by various features in Table 9.5. The average comparison results indicate that the imperceptibility and robustness of the proposed technique is better than the existing techniques.

Attacks	Kumar et al. [6]	Proposed Technique	Attacks	Kumar et al. [6]	Proposed Technique
JPEG Compression (Q = 90)			Speckle Noise (Variance =0.0004)		
JPEG Compression (Q = 80)			Median Filter (3×3)		
JPEG Compression (Q = 70)	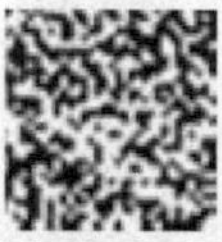		Median Filter (5×5)		
Blurring			GLP Filter (3×3)		
Sharpening	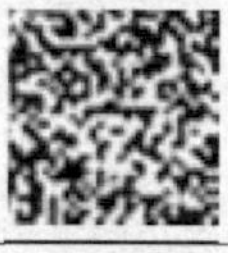		GLP Filter (5×5)		
Gaussian Noise (Variance = 0.0001)	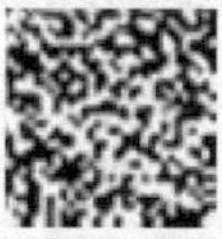		Cropping		
Salt & Pepper Noise (Variance = 0.0005)			Histogram Equalization		

Fig. 9.7 Recovered watermark images for proposed technique and Kumar et al. [6] for various watermarking attacks

9.5.2 Experiment Results of Proposed Technique for Biometric Images

The experimental results and analysis of proposed technique for biometric images is covered in this section.

Table 9.3 NC values and BER values of proposed technique and Kumar et al. [6] under various watermarking attacks

Type of attacks	Kumar et al. [6]		Proposed technique	
	NC	BER	NC	BER
JPEG (Q = 90)	0.4725	0.538	0.8691	0.135
JPEG (Q = 80)	0.4669	0.539	0.7493	0.261
JPEG (Q = 70)	0.4752	0.538	0.6763	0.328
Blurring	0.4972	0.494	0.6515	0.350
Sharpening	0.4725	0.531	0.9366	0.059
Gaussian noise ($\sigma = 0.0001$)	0.4725	0.536	0.9146	0.082
Salt & Pepper Noise ($\sigma = 0.0005$)	0.4821	0.523	0.9270	0.079
Speckle noise ($\sigma = 0.0004$)	0.4835	0.522	0.8953	0.087
Median filter (3×3)	0.5014	0.509	0.8361	0.161
Median filter (5×5)	0.5096	0.493	0.7879	0.221
GLPF (3×3)	0.4876	0.522	0.9091	0.095
GLPF (5×5)	0.4862	0.523	0.9050	0.093
Cropping	0.4752	0.532	0.8967	0.098
Histogram equalization	0.4752	0.525	0.9242	0.066

Table 9.4 Comparison of performance of proposed technique with Singh et al. [7] in terms of NC values

Type of attacks	Singh et al. [7]	Proposed technique
JEPG (Q = 90)	0.7394	0.8691
JPEG (Q = 70)	0.7394	0.6763
Sharpening	0.7364	0.9366
Median filter (3×3)	0.2162	0.8361
Histogram equalization	0.7402	0.9242

Table 9.5 Comparison of techniques for biomedical images

Features	Kumar et al. [6]	Singh et al. [7]	Proposed algorithm
Watermarking domain	DWT	DWT	Sparse measurements
Used encryption	Not used	Bose-Chaudhuri-Hocquenghem (BCH) code	CS theory-based encryption
Maximum PSNR (dB)	8.99	31.92	43.16
NC_{max}	0.5096	0.7544	0.9366
BER_{min}	0.493	0.0472	0.069

9.5.2.1 Description of the AMI Ear Database

The test biometric cover images are obtained from AMI ear database [55] and are shown in Fig. 9.8. The AMI (Mathematical Analysis of Images) ear database was created by Esther Gonzales during her Ph.D. research work at University of las Palma de Gran Canaria (ULPGC), Las Palmas, Spain [55]. In the proposed

Fig. 9.8   Test ear image

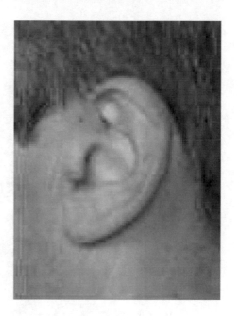

technique, left ear images are considered for analysis, converted into gray scale and resized to 300×400 pixels.

For better application of proposed technique on these ear images, first, ear image is segmented form the cropped face image. The snake model-based image segmentation technique [57, 58] is used to segment ear image from the cropped face image and is shown in Fig. 9.9. The image resizing is applied on these images to get ear images of size 256×256 pixels, to ease the further application of watermarking technique (shown in Fig. 9.9b).

9.5.2.2   Imperceptibility Test

The performance of the proposed technique for ear image in terms of imperceptibility is given in this section. Figure 9.10 shows (a) the watermarked ear image after inserting watermark image 2 in its sparse measurements, (b) the recovered watermark image 2 from watermarked ear image. These results are generated using a gain factor $k = 150$.

The performance of embedding procedure of proposed technique effects by the value of gain factor k. Thus, performance of this technique is verified for biomedical images by various gain factor values. These values vary from 50 to 150. The corresponding quality measures are given in Table 9.6. The results indicated than quality of recovered watermark images is good for high value of gain factor.

Fig. 9.9 (**a**) Segmented ear
image (**b**) Resized ear image

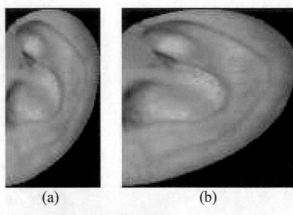

(a)   (b)

Fig. 9.10 Watermarked ear
image and recovered
watermark image

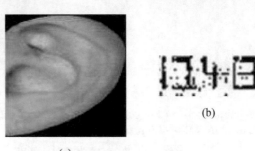

(b)

(a)

Table 9.6 Quality measure
values of proposed technique
for biometric image

	PSNR (dB)		NC	
Test image	WM1	WM2	WM1	WM2
(a) For $k = 50$				
Ear image	36.50	36.56	0.8693	0.8659
(b) For $k = 100$				
Ear image	30.92	31.19	0.9232	0.9083
(c) For $k = 150$				
Ear image	28.74	28.82	0.9340	0.9275

9.5.2.3 Robustness Test

For robustness test, the watermarked ear image generated by inserted watermark
image 2 using gain factor k value $= 150$ is subjected to various watermarking. Figure
9.11 shows recovered watermark images from modified watermarked ear image.
The NC values tabulated in Table 9.7 shows that this proposed technique is not
robust against attacks such as blurring, mean filtering, flipping, and rotation.

Fig. 9.11 Recovered watermark images 2 from watermarked ear image under various watermarking images: (**a–c**) for JPEG compression with Q = 90, 80, 70, respectively, (**d**) Blurring, (**e**) Sharpening, (**f**) Gaussian noise (μ = 0, σ = 0.0001), (**g**) Salt & pepper noise (σ = 0.0005), (**h**) Speckle noise (σ = 0.0004), (**i, j**) Median filter (Size = 3 × 3, 5 × 5), (**k, l**) Mean filter (Size = 3 × 3, 5 × 5), (**m, n**) GLPF (Size = 3 × 3, 5 × 5), (**o**) Flipping, (**p**) Rotation (90°), (**q**) Cropping (20%), (**r**) Histogram equalization

9.5.2.4 Comparison of the Proposed Technique with Existing Biometric Image Watermarking Techniques

The proposed watermarking technique is compared with the existing techniques, i.e., Rege et al. [8], Inamdar et al. [9] by various features in Table 9.8. The results indicated that the performance of the proposed watermarking technique is better than the existing biometric image watermarking techniques in terms of quality of watermarked image and security.

Table 9.7 Robustness checking of proposed technique for watermarked ear image against various watermarking attacks using NC values

Sr. No.	Type of watermarking attacks	Watermarked ear image
1	JPEG (Q = 90)	0.9313
2	JPEG (Q = 80)	0.9232
3	JPEG (Q = 70)	0.8518
4	Blurring	0.7480
5	Sharpening	0.9515
6	Gaussian noise ($\mu = 0$, $\sigma = 0.0001$)	0.9272
7	Salt & pepper noise ($\sigma = 0.0005$)	0.9394
8	Speckle noise ($\sigma = 0.0004$)	0.9205
9	Median filter (3×3)	0.8706
10	Median filter (5×5)	0.8235
11	Mean filter (3×3)	0.5714
12	Mean filter (5×5)	0.5081
13	GLPF (3×3)	0.9232
14	GLPF (5×5)	0.9191
15	Flipping	0.5782
16	Rotation (90°)	0.5000
17	Cropping (20%)	0.9447
18	Histogram equalization	0.9677

Table 9.8 Comparison of proposed technique with existing watermarking techniques for biometric images

Feature	Rege et al. [8]	Inamdar et al. [9]	Proposed technique
Biometric data	Face image, signature image, speech signal	Signature image	Ear image
Watermarking domain	Wavelet	Wavelet	Sparse
Security achieved	Gain factor	Gain factor + PN sequences	CS theory
Maximum PSNR (dB)	35.18	36.32	36.56

9.6 Conclusions

A Novel blind watermarking technique for biomedical images and biometric images is presented in this chapter. This technique is designed using Compressive Sensing (CS) theory hypothesis and sparsity property of wavelet transform. In this technique, biomedical or biometric images are considered as cover images and a monochrome watermark is inserted into sparse measurement of cover image. By changing the gain factor values, the quality measure values of proposed technique vary. Results proved that this proposed technique provides high security to cover image and better transparence. Furthermore, this proposed technique is robust in nature and perform better than many existing techniques in the literature. On the flip side, this technique is not robust against manipulations such as blurring, mean filtering, flipping and rotation.

References

1. Borra, S., Lakshmi, H., Dey, N., Ashour, A., Shi, F.: Digital Image Watermarking Tools: State-of-the-Art. Frontiers in Artificial Intelligence and Applications **296**, 450 – 459 (2017).
2. Thanki, R., Kothari, A.: Digital Watermarking: Technical Art of Hiding a Message. Intelligent Analysis of Multimedia Information, 431 – 466 (2016).
3. Borra, S., Swamy, G.: Sensitive Digital Image Watermarking for Copyright Protection. International Journal of Network Security **15**(2), 95 – 103 (2013).
4. Langelaar, G., Setyawan, I., Lagendijk, R.: Watermarking of Digital Image and Video Data – A State of Art Review. IEEE Signal Processing Magazine. 20 – 46 (2000).
5. Singh, S., Singh, R., Singh, A. K., & Siddiqui, T. J.: SVD-DCT Based Medical Image Watermarking in NSCT Domain. In Quantum Computing: An Environment for Intelligent Large Scale Real Application (pp. 467-488). Springer, Cham (2018).
6. Kumar, B., Kumar, S. B., and Chauhan, D. S.: Wavelet based imperceptible medical image watermarking using spread-spectrum. Telecommunications and Signal Processing (TSP), 2015 38th International Conference on (pp. 1-5). IEEE (2015).
7. Singh, A. K., Kumar, B., Singh, G., & Mohan, A.: Secure Spread Spectrum Based Multiple Watermarking Technique for Medical Images. Medical Image Watermarking (pp. 125–157). Springer, Cham (2017).
8. Rege, P., Inamdar, V.: Dual watermarking technique with multiple biometric watermarks. Sadhana © Indian Academy of Science 29(1), 3 – 26 (2014).
9. Inamdar, V., Rege, P. and Arya, M.: Offline Handwritten Signature based Blind Biometric Watermarking and Authentication Technique using Biorthogonal Wavelet Transform. International Journal of Computer Applications 11(1), 19 – 27 (2010).
10. Yamac, M., Cagatay, D. and Sankur, B.: Hiding Data in Compressive Sensed Measurements" A Conditionally Reversible Data Hiding Scheme for Compressively Sensed Measurements', Digital Signal Processing **48**, 188 – 200 (2016).
11. Priya, S., Santhi, B., Swaminathan, P., Raja Mohan, J.: Hybrid Transform Based Reversible Watermarking Technique for Medical Images in Telemedicine Applications. Optik – International Journal for Light Electron Optics, https://doi.org/10.1016/j.ijleo.2017.07.060 (2017).
12. Yassin, N.: Digital Watermarking for Telemedicine Applications: A Review. International Journal of Computer Applications **129**(17) (2015).
13. Singh, A.: Some New Techniques of Improved Wavelet Domain Watermarking for Medical Images. Ph.D. Thesis (2015).
14. Singh, A., Kumar, B., Dave, M. and Mohan, A.: Multiple Watermarking on Medical Images using Selective Discrete Wavelet Transform Coefficients. Journal of Medical Imaging and Health Informatics **5**(3), 607 – 614 (2015).
15. Singh, A., Dave, M. and Mohan, A.: Hybrid Technique for Robust and Imperceptible Dual Watermarking using Error Correcting Codes for Application in Telemedicine. International Journal of Electronics Security and Digital Forensics **6**(4), 285 – 305 (2014).

16. Thanki, R., Borra, S., Dwivedi, V., & Borisagar, K.: An efficient medical image watermarking scheme based on FDCuT–DCT. Engineering Science and Technology, an International Journal, **20**(4), 1366–1379 (2017).
17. Kaya, V. and Elbasi, E.: Robust Medical Image Watermarking Using Frequency Domain and Least Significant Bits Algorithms. World Academy of Science, Engineering and Technology, International Journal of Computer and Information Engineering **4**(8) (2017).
18. Priyanka and Maheshkar, S.: Region-based Hybrid Medical Image Watermarking for Secure Telemedicine Applications. Multimedia Tools and Applications **76**(3), 3617 – 3647 (2017).
19. Selvam, P., Santhi, B., Swaminathan, P. and Rajamohan, J.: Hybrid Transform based Reversible Watermarking Technique for Medical Images in Telemedicine Applications. Optik-International Journal for Light and Electron Optics **145**, 655 – 671 (2017).
20. Singh, A. and Dutta, M.: A Reversible Data Hiding Scheme for Efficient Management of Tele-Ophthalmological Data. Ophthalmology: Breakthroughs in Research and Practice, pp. 172 (2018)
21. Thakkar, F. and Srivastava, V.: A Blind Medical Image Watermarking: DWT – SVD based Robust and Secure Approach for Telemedicine Applications. Multimedia Tools and Applications **76**(3), 3669 – 3697 (2017).
22. Parah, S., Javaid, S., Ahad, F., Loan, N. and Bhat, G.: Information Hiding in Medical Images: a Robust Medical Image Watermarking System for E-healthcare. Multimedia Tools and Applications **76**(8), 10599 – 10633 (2017).
23. Dey, N., Ashour, A. S., Chakraborty, S., Banerjee, S. and Gospodinova, E., Gospodinov, M., & Hassanien, A. E.: Watermarking in Biomedical Signal Processing. In Intelligent Techniques in Signal Processing for Multimedia Security (pp. 345–369), Springer International Publishing (2017).
24. Dey, N., Biswas, D., Roy, A., Das, A. and Chaudhuri, S.: DWT-DCT-SVD based Blind Watermarking Technique of Gray Image in Electrooculogram Signal. 2012 12th International Conference on Intelligent Systems Design and Applications (ISDA), 680 – 685 (2012).
25. Dey, N., Das, P., Roy, A., Das, A. and Chaudhuri, S.: DWT-DCT-SVD based Intravascular Ultrasound Video Watermarking. 2012 World Congress on Information and Communication Technologies (WICT), 224 – 229 (2012).
26. Chakraborty, S., Samanta, S., Biswas, D., Dey, N. and Chaudhuri, S. S.: Particle swarm optimization-based parameter optimization technique in medical information hiding. In Computational Intelligence and Computing Research (ICCIC), 2013 IEEE International Conference on (pp. 1–6). IEEE (2013).
27. Biswas, D., Das, P., Maji, P., Dey, N. and Chaudhuri, S. S.: Visible watermarking within the region of non-interest of medical images based on fuzzy C-means and Harris corner detection. Computer Science & Information Technology, 161 – 168 (2013).
28. Dey, N., Bose, S., Das, A., Chaudhuri, S. S., Saba, L., Shafique, S. ... and Suri, J. S.: Effect of watermarking on diagnostic preservation of atherosclerotic ultrasound video in stroke telemedicine. Journal of medical systems **40**(4), 91 (2016).
29. Thanki, R. M., Dwivedi, V. J. and Borisagar, K. R.: Multibiometric Watermarking with Compressive Sensing Theory: Techniques and Applications. Springer (2018).
30. Tamijeselvy, P., Palanisamy, V., Elakkiya, S.: A novel watermarking images based on wavelet based contourlet transform energized by biometrics. WSEAS Transactions on Computers **12**(3), 105 – 115 (2013).
31. Inamdar, V., Rege, P.: Face features based biometric watermarking of digital image using singular value decomposition for fingerprinting. International Journal of Security and Its Applications **6**(2), 47 – 60 (2012).
32. Jundale, V. and Patil, S.: Biometric Speech Watermarking Technique in Images Using Wavelet Transform. IOSR Journal of Electronics and Communication Engineering (IOSR-JECE). 33 – 39 (2010).

33. Vatsa, M., Singh, R. and Noore, A.: Feature Based RDWT Watermarking for Multimodal Biometric System. Image and Vision Computing **27**(3), 293 – 304 (2009).
34. Noore, A., Singh, R., Vatsa, M. and Houck, M.: Enhancing Security of Fingerprints through Contextual Biometric Watermarking. Forensic Science International **169**(2), 188 – 194 (2007).
35. Noore, A., Singh, R., Vatsa, M., Houck, M. and Morris, K.: Robust Biometric Image Watermarking for Fingerprint and Face Template Protection. IEICE Electronics Express **3**(2), 23 – 28 (2007).
36. Vatsa, M., Singh, R. and Noore, A.: Improving Biometric Recognition Accuracy and Robustness Using DWT and SVM Watermarking. IEICE Electronics Express **1**(12), 362 – 367 (2005).
37. Paunwala, M. and Patnaik, S.: Biometric Template Protection with DCT Based Watermarking. Machine Vision and Applications **25**(1), 263 – 275 (2014).
38. Behera, B. and Govindan, V.: Improved Multimodal Biometric Watermarking in Authentication Systems Based on DCT and Phase Congruency Model. International Journal of Computer Science and Network **2**(3), 123 – 129 (2013).
39. Isa, M. and Aljareh, S.: Biometric Image Protection based on Discrete Cosine Transform Watermarking Technique. Proceeding of International Conference on Engineering and Technology (ICET). 1 – 5 (2012).
40. Zebbiche, K., Khelifi, F. and Bouridane, A.: Region Based Watermarking of Biometric Images: Case Study in Fingerprint Images. International Journal of Digital Multimedia Broadcasting, 1 – 13 (2008).
41. C. Kumar, A. K. Singh and P. Kumar: A Recent Survey on Image Watermarking Techniques and its Application in E-governance. Multimedia Tools and Applications, 1 – 26 (2017).
42. R. Srivastava, B. Kumar, A. K. Singh and A. Mohan: Computationally Efficient Joint Imperceptible Image Watermarking and JPEG Compression: A Green Computing Approach. Multimedia Tools and Applications, 1 – 13 (2017).
43. D. S. Chauhan, A. K. Singh, A. Adarsh, B. Kumar and J. P. Saini: Combining Mexican Hat Wavelet and Spread Spectrum for Adaptive Watermarking and its Statistical Detection using Medical Images. Multimedia Tools and Applications, 1 – 15 (2017).
44. A. Zear, A. K. Singh and P. Kumar: A Proposed Secure Multiple Watermarking Technique based on DWT, DCT and SVD for Application in Medicine. Multimedia Tools and Applications, 1 – 20 (2016).
45. R. Pandey, A. K. Singh, B. Kumar and A. Mohan: Iris based Secure NROI Multiple Eye Image Watermarking for Teleophthalmology. Multimedia Tools and Applications, **75**(22), 14381 – 14397 (2016).
46. Donoho, D.: Compressed Sensing. IEEE Transaction on Information Theory **52**(4), 1289 – 1306 (2006).
47. Candes, E.: Compressive Sampling. Proceedings of the International Congress of Mathematicians. 1 – 20 (2006).
48. Tropp, J. and Gilbert, A.: Signal Recovery from Random Measurements via Orthogonal Matching Pursuit. IEEE Transactions on Information Theory **53**(12), 4655 – 4666 (2007).
49. Cox, I. J., Kilian, J., Leighton, F. T., and Shamoon, T.: Secure spread spectrum watermarking for multimedia. IEEE transactions on image processing **6**(12), 1673 – 1687 (1997).
50. Zhang, Z., Wu, L., Gao, S., Sun, H., and Yan, Y.: Robust Reversible Watermarking Algorithm Based on RIWT and Compressed Sensing. Arabian Journal for Science and Engineering **43**(2), 979 – 992 (2018).
51. B. Vidakovic: Statistical Modelling by Wavelets. Wiley, pp. 115–116 (1999).
52. J. Yan: Wavelet Matrix. Department of Electrical and Computer Engineering, University of Victoria, Victoria, BC, Canada (2009).
53. P. Saxena, Y. Khandelwal and R. Khandelwal: Haar Transform for The Numerical Solutions of Ordinary Differential Equations and Boundary Value Problem with Maple. International Journal of Engineering, Management and Sciences, **4**(4), 8 – 12 (2017).

54. MedPix^{TM} Medical Image Database available at http://rad.usuhs.mil/medpix/medpix.html, https://medpix.nlm.nih.gov/home
55. **For AMI Ear Database. Available:**http://www.ctim.es/research_works/ami_ear_database/
56. Kutter, M. and Petitcolas, F.: Fair Benchmark for Image Watermarking Systems. Security and Watermarking of Multimedia Contents **3657**, 226 – 239 (1999).
57. Jarjes, A., Wang, K, Mohammed, G.: Improved greedy snake model for detecting accurate pupil contour. In Proceedings of 3rd International Conference on Advanced Computer Control (ICACC). 515 – 519 (2011).
58. Anwar, A., Ghany, K., Elmahdy, H.: Human ear recognition using geometrical features extraction. Procedia Computer Science **65**, 529 – 537 (2015).

Chapter 10
Performance Analysis of Image Encryption Methods Using Chaotic, Multiple Chaotic and Hyper-Chaotic Maps

T. Gopalakrishnan and S. Ramakrishnan

10.1 Introduction

Encryption is used to develop the sensitive information in unreadable form through the insecure public networks so that it is accessed only by the intended receiver only. The information transmitted is not only in text form, but also in the form of audio, image and other multimedia files. Hence, the study on security of image attracts immediate priority in the present global context. Since the network is thrown open to public, the risks of cyber crimes have come to the surface, which warrants the need to study matters related to image encryption. Cryptography with chaos based image encryption has become more popular in the recent past. Symmetric key streams are used for encryption and decryption algorithm. The cryptographic property relies on chaotic systems which are very sensitive in the initial conditions which make the systems more ideal for encrypting images. The image encryption using chaos is based on permutation and diffusion is also known as confusion and substitution. This encryption algorithm is repeated to a number of rounds to encrypt the plain image.

The chaos and hyper-chaos based image encryption techniques are used in order to encrypt the image. The pseudo-random numbers are generated by using chaotic maps for image encryption [1–5]. Chaos is a fool-proof system and possesses the ability to produce sequence of numbers which are random in nature [6–8]. Hyper-Chaos is defined as a chaotic behaviour with at least two positive Lyapunov exponents along with one zero and one negative Lyapunov exponents. The higher-

T. Gopalakrishnan (✉)
Department of Electrical and Electronics Engineering, Karpagam College of Engineering, Coimbatore, Tamil Nadu, India

S. Ramakrishnan
Department of Information Technology, Dr. Mahalingam College of Engineering and Technology, Pollachi, Tamil Nadu, India

© Springer Nature Switzerland AG 2019
A. K. Singh, A. Mohan (eds.), *Handbook of Multimedia Information Security: Techniques and Applications*, https://doi.org/10.1007/978-3-030-15887-3_10

dimensional chaotic maps are used to encrypt the image. Permutation is repeated for number of rounds to shuffle the image. The image is diffused by symmetric block cipher method. Permutation and diffusion requires less number of rounds to encrypt the image. A symmetric key is used for encryption and decryption algorithm [9–11]. Chaotic maps with 1D sequence are used for image, document and data encryption applications. A cryptographic system with chaos based scheme is proposed by "Baptista" [12]. The Logistic map is used for the cryptographic scheme for encryption [13, 14]. In Baptista-type chaotic cryptosystem there are some variants. Similar to cryptographic schemes, attempts to crack the original Baptista-type chaotic cryptosystem and its variants are made [15–18]. The causes of weakness are investigated and remedial operations are proposed.

The random number generation is based on initial condition. The author has introduced unique modifications in the pseudo random number generation by using chaotic map [19–21]. They tested the pseudo-random number generator through various models like NIST SPP 800-22 and performance analysis test in the encrypted image. The permutation and diffusion method presents a strong image encryption algorithm [22, 23]. To introduce irregular and pseudo-random sequence, an optimized treatment with a cross-sampling model is introduced. A scheme with two iterative stages in permutation and diffusion is proposed for image encryption [24]. A fast chaotic system is also introduced with dynamic lookup table for encrypting the images [25, 26]. An image encryption by using two chaotic maps such as standard and logistic maps is developed for substitution-diffusion process [27]. In this encryption algorithm, the standard map is used to encrypt the image. The whole encryption is sequentially executed by preliminary permutation to fix several rounds of substitution. The main permutation of 2D matrix is obtained by 3D matrix and permutation is carried out row-by-row and column-by-column to increase the speed of the algorithm. Each substitution is initiated with an initial vector for different rows, columns and pixels are mixed with pseudo-random number generated by standard map.

An image encryption using chaotic maps for encryption and authentication method [28] is proposed using a hash key. The encryption and decryption of the image is done by using hash keys as a secret key. The generated hash keys are used to authenticate and decrypt the image. A modified confusion and diffusion architecture is developed [29]. This encryption method requires less number of rounds only to achieve its security. For secret keys, the hash function is used as a key for encryption architecture [30, 31]. The image encryption by using canonical transforms and chaotic maps are developed for multiple encryptions [32, 33]. An iterative based image encryption for confusion and diffusion is introduced to yield better encryption scheme [34–36]. Chaotic standard maps are used for permutation and diffusion [37]. Different chaotic maps are used to develop the confusion and diffusion process. The standard map is used for encryption which can be implemented in the integer domain, as it reduces the computational complexity. A bit-level permutation with high-dimension chaotic map is proposed in this image encryption [38, 39]. It is used for color image encryption and its values are converted into a gray scale image to transform into a binary matrix. It is permuted at bit-level by using Piece

Wise Linear Chaotic Mapping (PWLCM) to scramble the image. The hyper-chaotic Chen's system is used to confuse and diffuse the RGB components simultaneously. The performance analysis shows that the scheme achieves larger key space to resist and withstand against common attacks.

An image encryption in bit level by using chaotic maps and a novel permutation is introduced for encryption [40, 41]. The plain image is encrypted by PWLCM and transformed into two binary sequences. These two sequences are generated by chaotic maps in substitution stage to encrypt the images with a single round for encryption. The statistical properties of (PWLCM) chaotic maps and the chaotic cryptography with pseudo-random coding are introduced [42–45]. The performances analyses of the chaotic ciphers are secured in this algorithm and it has good statistical properties. The multiple chaotic pseudo-random number generators are developed for image encryption.

The image encryption algorithms are based on chaos theory and its advantages are proved to be sensitive for the initial conditions. A dynamical system may be classified as chaos, if it satisfies the following conditions namely, sensitive to initial conditions, topologically in mixing state and dense periodic orbits. The confusion and substitution elements are used to analyze the cryptosystems. Confusion is a process which makes the secret key of the cryptosystem to relate the plain image in a complex way. To make it complex, the process should depend upon relationship between the cipher image and the secret key. Many cryptosystems are introduced with different chaotic maps to encrypt the image with both confusion and substitution methods. To replace the order and change the pixel value, the encryption method is repeated to a number of rounds with a combination of confusion and substitution.

The issues diagnosed in the literature reviews and the chaotic maps developed to avoid periodic window problems, key generation process, and to improve the image encryption with lesser number of rounds. The periodic window problems are addressed by using multiple chaotic maps. The key streams are generated by developing a built-in internal key generator process. Multiple chaotic maps are used to improve the randomness in the cipher image for diffusion. The image encryptions with lesser number of rounds are developed with chaotic and hyper-chaotic maps. The hyper-chaotic maps are used for permutation and diffusion to encrypt the image. The hyper chaotic map has an ability to encrypt the image in a single round with large key space [46, 47]. It has larger key space and less computational complexity. Image encryption applications are used in the areas of medical image authentication, identification, patient report identity which needs to be maintained confidently. The chaos based encryption algorithm on watermarking approach is applied for tele-health applications [48]. The watermarking based encryption method gives better multi-level security in performance on the quality of watermarked image.

10.2   Image Encryption Techniques

The image encryption method using permutation and diffusion is widely used as an encryption method as shown in Fig. 10.1. The image is encrypted by using the chaotic, hyper-chaotic and multiple chaotic maps.

In permutation stage, the pixel positions are modified by using chaotic maps. In the diffusion, the pixel values are modified by using chaotic maps. The initial value of chaotic map is taken as a secret key and it is iterated in accordance to the size of the image. The encrypted image is taken as input and it is repeated for number of rounds. Different keys are selected for every round in permutation and diffusion process. The performance analyses tests are carried out to analyze the encrypted image. The same procedure is repeated to decrypt the original plain image.

10.2.1   Chaotic, Multiple Chaotic and Hyper-Chaotic Maps for Image Encryption

Chaos is a dynamic system which produces sequence of numbers that are random in nature. These random sequences are applied to encrypt and decrypt the images. The sequences are purely based on initial condition. A small variation in initial condition may lead to a different sequence of generation. This chaotic behaviour facilitates to develop image encryption methods. The image encryption is carried out by chaotic mapping for scrambling the image pixel to various locations with changes in pixel values. The image encryption techniques are exposed through built-in internal key generator for image encryption process.

Hyper-Chaos is defined as a chaotic behaviour with at least two positive Lyapunov exponents along with one zero and one negative Lyapunov exponents. In this method, image encryption is done by using 2D hyper-chaotic map for permutation and multiple hyper-chaotic maps are developed for diffusion. The image encryption is done by multiple chaotic maps. The periodic window problems of one-dimensional chaotic maps are addressed by multiple chaotic maps. The multiple chaotic maps are (1) Logistic-Sine Map (LSM) (2) Logistic-Tent Map

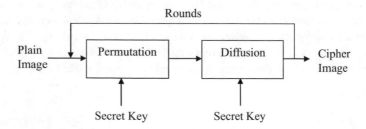

Fig. 10.1 Image encryption based on permutation and diffusion

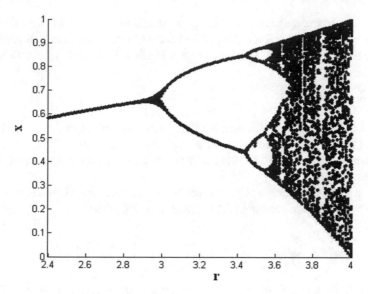

Fig. 10.2 Bifurcation diagram of logistic map

(LTM) and (3) Tent-Sine Map (TSM). The multiple chaotic map exhibit uniform chaotic distribution in the range 0–4.

10.2.2   Chaotic Maps for Image Encryption

The chaos based encryption techniques chaotic maps are used for encrypting images. The commonly used chaotic maps are logistic map, Tent map, Piecewise linear chaotic map, Bernoulli's map, Sine map, Cat map, Henon map and Standard map.

10.2.2.1   Logistic Map

In mathematics, chaotic map can be defined as a model that exhibits chaotic behaviour. The logistic map is a simple dimensional map which is equated below,

$$x_{n+1} = r x_n (1 - x_n) \tag{10.1}$$

where, $X_n \in [0, 1]$ is known as phase space of the logistic map. The control parameter 'r' controls the behaviour of the map [49]. Let X_n be the initial value for the function of logistic map and it is iterated according to the size of the image. The Fig. 10.2 shows the bifurcation diagram of logistic map.

Let 'r' be in the range of 3.57 and above, it behaves chaotic. In almost all initial condition, any oscillations for finite period cannot be observed. A small variation in the initial value of chaotic map yields to a dramatic difference in results [30].

10.2.2.2 Tent Map

It is an iterated process which is in the shape of a tent, forming a discrete dynamical system [5]. It starts from a point x_n on the real line and maps it to another end. This map is aligned from two straight lines, which entails the analysis simpler than nonlinear systems.

It is a form of equation with certain control parameter (μ) value. It is highly complex with chaotic behaviour. The tent map is defined as,

$$x_{n+1} = f_\mu = \begin{Bmatrix} \mu x_n & for\, x_n < \frac{1}{2} \\ \mu\,(1 - x_n) & for\, \frac{1}{2} > x_n \end{Bmatrix} \qquad (10.2)$$

where, μ is in the range [0, 2] and it is a positive real constant. Figure 10.3 shows the bifurcation diagram of tent map.

10.2.2.3 Piecewise Linear Chaotic Maps (PWLCM)

The Piecewise Linear Chaotic maps (PWLCM) form part of discrete dynamic systems. It behaves chaotic for all control parameter and bears a positive Lyapunov exponent. The PWLCM is defined as,

$$x_{n+1} = \begin{cases} x_n/p & if\ 0 \le x_n \le p \\ \frac{(1-x_n)}{(1-p)} & if\ p \le x_n \le 1 \end{cases} \qquad (10.3)$$

where, p is in the range [0, 1] and x_0 is the initial value.

Fig. 10.3 Bifurcation diagram of tent map

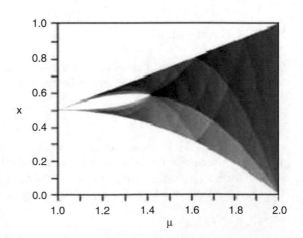

10.2.2.4   Bernoulli's Map

It is another chaotic map. Bernoulli's map recursive equation is represented as,

$$x_{n+1} = (b^* x_n) \bmod 1 \tag{10.4}$$

where, b > 1, x ϵ [0, 1]. The control parameter b is in the range of [1, 5].

10.2.2.5   Sine Map

The sine map is also yet another chaotic map and it is similar to logistic map. It is defined as,

$$x_{n+1} = r \sin (\pi x_n) / 4 \tag{10.5}$$

where, parameter 'r' is in the range of (0–4). The chaotic behaviour of the sine map is almost similar to that of the logistic map. The sine function provides good randomness behaviour.

10.2.2.6   Cat Map

Cat map, otherwise known as Arnold's cat map and it is of one-to-one transformation. It is depicted as,

$$\begin{pmatrix} x' \\ y' \end{pmatrix} = \begin{pmatrix} 1 & p \\ q & pq + 1 \end{pmatrix} \begin{pmatrix} x \\ y \end{pmatrix} (\bmod N) \tag{10.6}$$

where, 'p' and 'q' are its parameters and N is the length. It is invertible as its determinant value is 1. Due to its integer entries, cat map appears to be area preserving. One of its features is that the image can be evidently randomized. It returns to its original position after a number of processing steps.

10.2.2.7   Henon Map

It is yet another form of chaotic map. Let (x_n, y_n) be in the plane with a point and map it into a new point. It depends on two parameters 'a' and 'b' due to 2D map and its values are 1.4 and 0.3, respectively.

It is illustrated as,

$$x_{n+1} = y_n + 1 - ax_n^2,$$
$$y_{n+1} = bx_n$$

(10.7)

10.2.2.8 Standard Map

A standard map is proposed in algorithm [34] and it is specified as,

$$x_{i+1} = (x_i + y_i) \bmod N,$$
$$y_{i+1} = \left(y_i + k \sin \frac{x_{i+1}N}{2\pi}\right) \bmod N$$

(10.8)

where, (x_i, y_i) and (x_{i+1}, y_{i+1}) is the original pixel position, permuted pixel position and K is a positive integer of standard map.

10.2.3 Multiple Chaotic Maps

The periodic window problems of one-dimensional chaotic maps are addressed by multiple chaotic maps [50, 51]. A robust hybrid method is also developed for image encryption by using neural network [52, 53]. The proposed models employ the following multiple chaotic maps to mitigate the periodic window problems. The multiple chaotic maps are (1) Logistic-Sine Map (LSM) (2) Logistic-Tent Map (LTM) and (3) Tent-Sine Map (TSM).

The bifurcation diagram and Lyapunov exponent of all LSM, LTM and TSM are presented in Figs. 10.4 and 10.5 respectively. The multiple chaotic map exhibit uniform chaotic distribution in the range 0–4.

In the similar line, Lyapunov exponent of multiple chaotic maps in Fig. 10.5 shows positive values in the entire range (0, 4) whereas, Lyapunov exponent of one-dimensional map shown in Fig. 10.6 has number of non positive values of Logistic map, Tent map and Sine map.

Hence, multiple chaotic maps namely LSM, LTM and TSM have good chaotic property (positive Lyapunov exponent and uniform distribution) in a wide range (0, 4) as proposed in this work.

Logistic-Sine Map Logistic-Sine Map (LSM) is represented as,

$$x_{n+1} = \left\{\left(rx_n\,(1 - x_n) + (4 - r)\sin\,(\pi x_n)\,/4\right\} \bmod 1$$

(10.9)

where, x_n be the initial condition and 'r' be the parameter in the range (0–4).

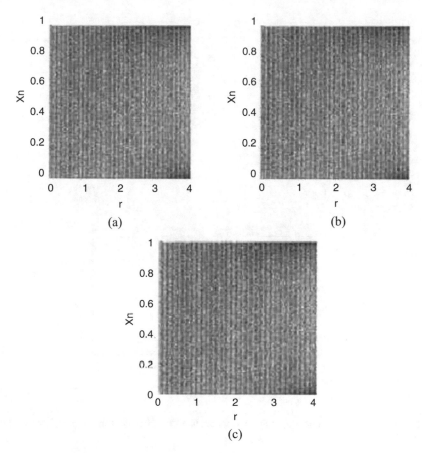

Fig. 10.4 Bifurcation diagrams of multiple Chaotic maps. (**a**) Logistic-Tent map (**b**) Logistic-Sine map (**c**) Tent-Sine Map

Logistic-Tent Map   The Logistic-Tent map (LTM) is inferred by,

$$y_{n+1} = \begin{cases} (ry_n (1 - y_n) + (4 - r) y_n/2) \bmod 1 & y_i < 0.5 \\ (ry_n (1 - y_n) + (4 - r) (1 - y_n) /2) \bmod 1 & y_i \geq 0.5 \end{cases} \quad (10.10)$$

where, the parameter 'r' is in the range of (0–4) and y_n is the initial condition for the map.

Tent-Sine Map   The Tent-Sine map (TSM) is defined as,

$$z_{n+1} = \begin{cases} rz_n/2 + (4 - r) \sin (\pi z_n) /4 & z_i < 0.5 \\ r (1 - z_n) /2 + (4 - r) \sin (\pi z_n) /4 & z_i \geq 0.5 \end{cases} \quad (10.11)$$

where, the parameter 'r' is in the range of (0–4) and Z_n is the initial condition.

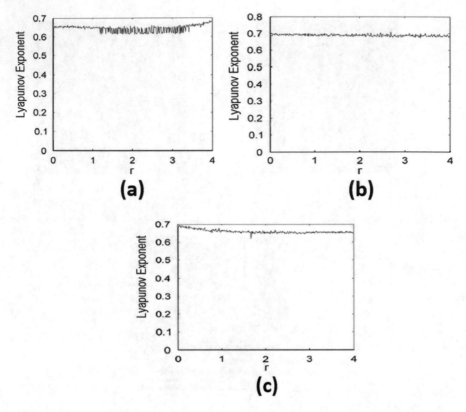

Fig. 10.5 Lyapunov exponent of multiple Chaotic maps. (**a**) Logistic-Tent Map (**b**) Logistic-Sine Map (**c**) Tent-Sine Map

10.2.4 Hyper-Chaotic Maps for Image Encryption

2D Hyper-Chaos 2D hyper-chaos with discrete nonlinear dynamic system [54] is derived by,

$$x_{n+1} = a_1 + a_2{}^*x_n + a_4 y_n$$
$$y_{n+1} = b_1 + b_3{}^*x_n^2 \qquad\qquad (10.12)$$

where, $a_1 = 0.2$; $a_2 = 0.3$; $a_4 = 0.5$; $b_1 = -1.7$; $b_3 = 3.7$

4D Hyper-Chaotic Lorentz System The 4D hyper-chaotic Lorentz's system is specified as,

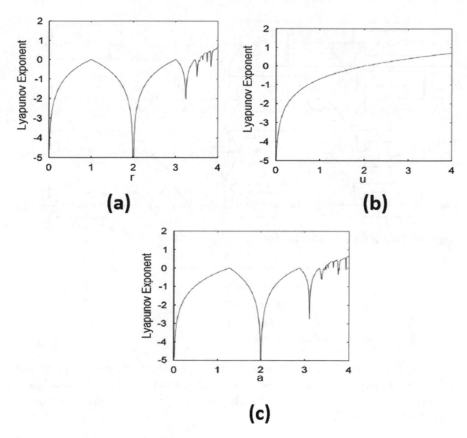

Fig. 10.6 Lyapunov exponent of single Chaotic maps. (**a**) Logistic map (**b**) Tent map (**c**) Sine map

$$
\begin{aligned}
\bar{x}_1 &= a\,(x_1 - x_2)\,, \\
\bar{x}_2 &= cx_1 - x_1 x_3 - x_2 + ex_4, \\
\bar{x}_3 &= x_1^4 - x_2^4 - bx_3, \\
\bar{x}_4 &= -dx_2
\end{aligned}
\tag{10.13}
$$

where, x_1, x_2, x_3, x_4 are state variables and a $= 10$, b $= 8/3$, c $= 46$, d $= 2$, e $= 12$, respectively.

The four Lyapunov exponents of Lorentz system are $\lambda_1 = 0.60613$, $\lambda_2 = 0.28066$, $\lambda_3 = 0$, $\lambda_4 = -11.489$ and its Lyapunov exponent sum is less than zero.

4D Hyper-Chaotic Chen's System The hyper-chaotic is developed by Chen's chaotic system. The system is derived as,

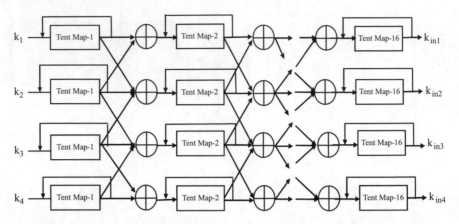

Fig. 10.7 Internal key generation process

$$\begin{aligned}
\overline{x}_1 &= a\,(x_2 - x_1)\,, \\
\overline{x}_2 &= -x_1 x_3 + d x_1 + c x_2 - x_4, \\
\overline{x}_3 &= x_1 x_2 - b x_3, \\
\overline{x}_4 &= x_1 + k
\end{aligned} \tag{10.14}$$

where a, b, c, d and k are the parameters, x_1, x_2, x_3, x_4 are the state variables and when $a = 36$, $b = 3$, $c = 28$, $d = -16$ and $-0.7 \le k \le 0.7$, the system gets hyper-chaotic. For the hyper-chaotic attractor, the four Lyapunov exponents should be λ_1, $\lambda_2 > 0$, $\lambda_3 < 0$, $\lambda_4 = 0$.

10.3 Image Encryption with Chaotic Maps

The image encryption algorithms are based on chaos theory and its advantages are proved to be sensitive for the initial conditions. A dynamical system may be classified as chaos, if it satisfies the following conditions such as, sensitive to initial conditions, topologically in mixing state and dense for periodic orbits. The initial keys for the chaotic maps are generated using the internal key generator. The external keys are given to the internal seed generator to develop the initial keys for chaotic maps in permutation and diffusion process as shown in Fig. 10.7.

The image is encrypted for four rounds and for each round, the keys are selected as follows:

Round 1—k_1, k_2, k_3, k_4;
Round 2—k_2, k_3, k_4, k_1;
Round 3—k_3, k_4, k_1, k_2;
Round 4—k_4, k_3, k_2, k_1;

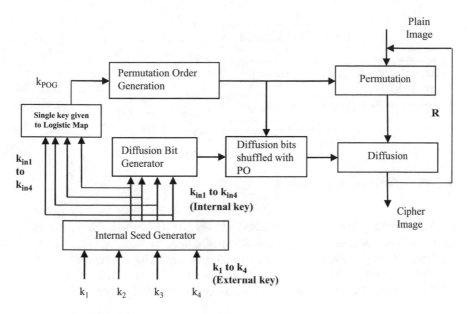

Fig. 10.8 Image encryption with internal key generator

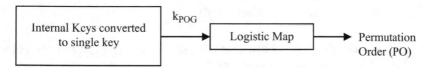

Fig. 10.9 Permutation order generation

The permutation order is already generated using key generator and permuted. In diffusion process, multiple chaotic maps are selected to generate diffusion bits for image encryption.

10.3.1 Image Encryption and Decryption Algorithm

The proposed image encryption process is shown in Fig. 10.8, its key generation process, permutation order generation, and diffusion bit generation are discussed below [55].

The Permutation Order (PO) generation for this method is shown in Fig. 10.9. The permutation order is generated with four internal keys which are used by converting it into a single key for logistic map [15]. The generated sequence is used to permute the image. Then the permuted image is further diffused in the diffusion stage for encryption.

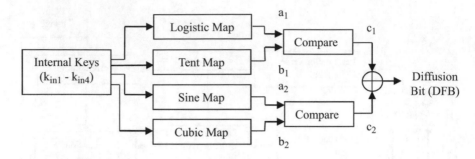

Fig. 10.10 Diffusion bit generation

The diffusion bit generations are shown in Fig. 10.10. The initial key for logistic, tent, sine and cubic maps are generated from the internal keys (k_{in1}–k_{in4}). A single diffusion bit is generated in the diffusion bit generator. The permutation order and the diffusion bits are XORed to generate the encrypted image. The image encryption and decryption steps are discussed below for the proposed algorithm.

10.3.2   Encryption Algorithm Steps

A chaotic bit wise function is integrated into encryption and decryption algorithm. The detailed processing steps are as follows

Step 1: The plain image is converted to 1D binary sequence. The size of the sequence is m = $8 \times N \times M$ for gray level image.

Step 2: The external keys (k_1, k_2, k_3, k_4) are given to the internal seed generator for generating the internal keys (k_{in1}, k_{in2}, k_{in3}, k_{in4}).

Step 3: The external keys (k_1, k_2, k_3, k_4) has an initial key for tent map using the Eq. (10.15) with 100 iterations and it is repeated for 16 steps to strengthen the internal keys (k_{in1}, k_{in2}, k_{in3}, k_{in4}).

Step 4: The tent map with parameter μ is the real-valued function f_μ defined by,

$$x_{n+1} = f_\mu = \left\{ \begin{array}{ll} \mu x_n & for \ x_n < \frac{1}{2} \\ \mu\left(1 - x_n\right) & for \ \frac{1}{2} > x_n \end{array} \right\} \tag{10.15}$$

where 'μ' is the control parameter in the range of 1.7–2

Step 5: The internal seeds are given to PO and DFB block to generate the PO and DFB bits.

Step 6: PO is generated using logistic map sequence with the internal keys given by,

$$x_{n+1} = rx_n (1 - x_n) \tag{10.16}$$

where, $X_n \in [0, 1]$ and r is in the range of $[0, 4]$.

Step 7: The four internal keys (k_{in1}, k_{in2}, k_{in3}, k_{in4}) are obtained using the Eq. (10.17). An initial key for logistic map and permutation order is generated.

$$k_{POG} = F (k_{in1}, k_{in2}, k_{in3}, k_{in4})$$

$$k_{POG} = \frac{\sum\limits_{i=1}^{4} n_i k_{ini}}{\sum\limits_{i=1}^{4} n_i} \tag{10.17}$$

where $n_i > 0$, and it is a non-integer value.

Step 8: For DFB generation, two maps are selected. The output of logistic and tent map are taken as a_1 and b_1. If ($a_1 > b_1$), the value '0' is allocated and if ($a_1 < b_1$), the value '1' is allocated in c_1. The same procedure is repeated for other two maps, the values of (a_2 and b_2) 0 and 1 is allocated in c_2. Then c_1 and c_2 values are XORed and diffusion bits are generated.

Step 9: PO is generated with a internal key to permute the image and DFB is generated to diffuse the image in this algorithm.

Step 10: The generated PO bit and DFB bits are XORed and converted to integer form for a cipher image.

Step 11: Internal keys (k_{in1}, k_{in2}, k_{in3}, k_{in4}) are given to four different maps to generate the diffusion bits (DFB) for first round. Internal key order is rotated as (k_{in2}, k_{in3}, k_{in4}, k_{in1}) for further rounds.

Step 12: Similarly, for PO generation for second round, internal keys are XORed as (k_{in2}, k_{in3}, k_{in4}, k_{in1}) in order to obtain an initial key for logistic map.

Step 13: PO and DFB Internal keys for third round are in the order (k_{in3}, k_{in4}, k_{in1}, k_{in2}).

Step 14: For the plain image of size (256×256), four external keys are used to generate four internal keys. Similarly for an image size of (512×512) and with larger size images, eight external keys are used to generate eight internal keys.

Step 15: The permutation and diffusion process are repeated for R rounds with internal key rotation to get the highly uncorrelated cipher image.

Step 16: Decryption is achieved by reverse process of encryption.

A key generation process is based on the one dimensional chaotic map, which iterates the external keys to generate initial seeds for the next tent map. The output of tent map is further manipulated to strengthen the internal keys according to the structure. To increase the sensitivity of the key this type of configuration is designed. Each block tent map is fed with an initial seed i.e., external keys (k_1, k_2, k_3, k_4) and it is iterated for hundred times. The obtained final values are fed to the next block of tent map and continued. Finally the internal keys (k_{in1}, k_{in2}, k_{in3}, k_{in4}) are obtained. This type of feeding will increase the key sensitivity.

10.3.3 Decryption Algorithm Steps

Step 1: The cipher image is converted to 1D binary sequence. The size of the sequence is m $= 8 \times$ N $\times$ M for gray level image.

Step 2: The third round cipher image is taken and for which the sequence of keys are selected and internal keys are generated.

Step 3: The internal keys are generated for the initial conditions of PO and DFB.

Step 4: For each round, different keys are selected for PO generation.

Step 5: The generated DFB bit and PO bits are XORed and converted to integer form for the second round cipher image.

Step 6: The second round cipher image is taken as input and converted to 1D binary sequence. The same procedure is repeated for another round.

Step 7: The internal key, chaotic map and its iterations are repeated in reverse order for another three rounds to achieve the original plain image.

10.4 Image Encryption Using Multiple Chaotic Maps

The image encryption by a single key generation using hash function [56]. Permutation is done by multiple chaotic map and in diffusion stage, the diffusion bits are generated by two multiple chaotic maps as shown in Fig. 10.11.

A bit-level manipulation is performed in permutation and in diffusion stage the permuted pixel bits are diffused with the generated random bits. SHA algorithm is used to generate symmetric secret key for encryption and decryption process. In the permutation process, permutation order is done in bitwise using chaotic maps.

In diffusion process, diffusion bits are generated by LTM and TSM. Figure 10.11 shows the block diagram of the proposed encryption algorithm and Fig. 10.12 illustrates about the key generator [55]. The encryption and decryption steps are given below.

10.4.1 Encryption Algorithm Steps

The encryption and decryption procedure is explained in step by step procedure.

Step 1:   The plain image pixel positions are changed using the Logistic-sine map in permutation process.

Step 2:   The Hash keys are generated using SHA-256 and converted to decimal value as Key 1, Key 2, Key 3 and Key 4.

Step 3:   The keys are selected as initial condition for the Logistic-sine map to generate the Permutation Order(PO) and it is given by,

$$x_{n+1} = \left\{ \left(rx_n \left(1 - x_n\right) + (4 - r) \sin \left(\pi x_n\right) / 4 \right\} \bmod 1 \right. \tag{10.18}$$

The relation makes initial condition for the Logistic-Sine Map (LSM) which is given by,

$$sub\_key1 = (key1 \times key2)$$
$$sub\_key1 = (key3 \div key4) \tag{10.19}$$

$$perm\_int = (sub\_key1 + sub\_key2) \bmod 1 \tag{10.20}$$

sub_key1, sub_key2 are calculated from the given formula and using these keys, the permutation order initial condition (perm_int) is calculated.

Step 4:   The LSM is iterated for $(8 \times N \times N)$ times, then by sorting the iterated values the random indices are generated by,

$$Ind = sort \, (logistic - sine) \tag{10.21}$$

Step 5:   Ind is the random index, produced by sorting the LSM values. These indices are non-repeated values. Using these indices, the original image is permuted in bit level.

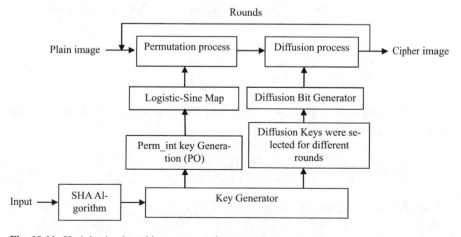

Fig. 10.11 Hash keying based image encryption process

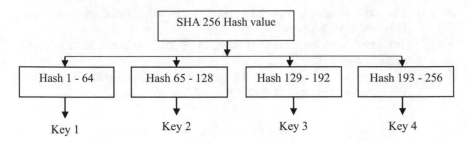

Fig. 10.12 Key generator

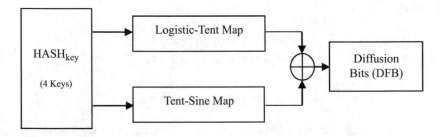

Fig. 10.13 Diffusion bit generator

Step 6: The permutation in bit level increases the encryption quality and also the correlations among the pixels are modified.

$$PO = ind\,(Bin\_img) \tag{10.22}$$

Step 7: PO is the permuted image pixel bits using the random index pixel bits which are relocated from its original locations.

Step 8: The Diffusion Bits (DFB) as shown in Fig. 10.13 is generated by using Logistic-Tent Map (LTM) and Tent-Sine Map (TSM). LTM is given by,

$$y_{n+1} = \begin{cases} (ry_n\,(1-y_n) + (4-r)\,y_n/2)\,\mathrm{mod}\,1 & y_i < 0.5 \\ (ry_n\,(1-y_n) + (4-r)\,(1-y_n)\,/2)\,\mathrm{mod}\,1 & y_i \geq 0.5 \end{cases} \tag{10.23}$$

where, the parameter 'r' is in the range (0–4) and y_n is the initial condition of the map. The TSM is defined by,

$$z_{n+1} = \begin{cases} rz_n/2 + (4-r)\sin(\pi z_n)\,/4 & z_i < 0.5 \\ r\,(1-z_n)\,/2 + (4-r)\sin(\pi z_n)\,/4 & z_i \geq 0.5 \end{cases} \tag{10.24}$$

where, the parameter r in the range of (0–4) and Z_n is the initial condition of the map.

Step 9: The DFBs are generated by LTM and TSM. If TSM generated value greater than LTM value, '0' is generated otherwise '1' is generated by the following relation:

$$DFB = LTM \text{ value} \oplus TSM \text{ value} \qquad (10.25)$$

Step 10: For DFB key generation, different keys are selected as initial key for the LTM and TSM. The selected keys for each round are Round 1—Key4, Key 2; Round 2—Key 1, Key 3; Round 3—Key 3, Key 4; Round 4—Key 2, Key 3.

Step 11: In each round, different DFB is generated by updating the key value which prevents the cipher from chosen plain text attack.

The encrypted image is obtained by PO and DFB using the equation,

$$ENC = PO \oplus DFB \qquad (10.26)$$

Step 12: The encrypted image (ENC) is generated for the round one. The produced cipher image is taken as input and the same procedure is repeated for the rest of four rounds.

10.4.2 Decryption Algorithm Steps

Step 1: The generated hash is securely transmitted to the receiver side.

Step 2: First, the received cipher is converted to binary form.

Step 3: Diffusion bits are manipulated with the cipher pixel bits and using random index PO.

Step 4: DFB are generated by LTM and TSM.

Step 5: The decryption process is repeated for four rounds to perform the encryption process.

Step 6: The original plain image is recovered.

10.5 Image Encryption Using Hyper-Chaotic Maps

The image encryption consists of hyper-chaotic maps for permutation and diffusion. In the permutation process, 2D hyper-chaotic map is used to permute the image. For diffusion, hyper-chaotic Chen's system is used as a key. The combined hyper-

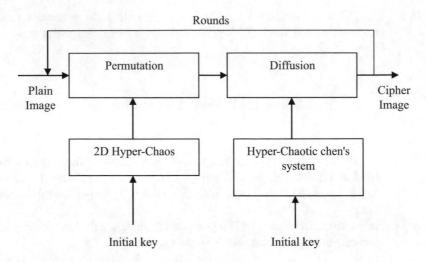

Fig. 10.14 Hyper-chaotic maps for Image Encryption

chaotic diffusion process entails larger key space for the proposed algorithm. The proposed image encryption architecture with hyper-chaotic maps is shown in Fig. 10.14.

10.5.1 2D Hyper-Chaotic System

The 2D hyper-chaotic map is used to shuffle the pixel position of the plain image [54]. The 2D hyper-chaos discrete nonlinear dynamic system is represented as,

$$
\begin{aligned}
x_{n+1} &= a_1 + a_2{}^* x_n + a_4 y_n \\
y_{n+1} &= b_1 + b_3{}^* x_n^2
\end{aligned}
\tag{10.27}
$$

where, $a_1 = 0.2$; $a_2 = 0.3$; $a_4 = 0.5$; $b_1 = -1.7$; $b_3 = 3.7$

The generalized form of the system is furnished below;

$$
\begin{aligned}
x_{n+1} &= f\,(x_n, y_n) \\
y_{n+1} &= g\,(x_n, y_n)
\end{aligned}
\tag{10.28}
$$

where,

$f\,(x_n, y_n) = a_1 + a_2 x_n + a_3 x_n^2 + a_4 x_n + a_5 x_n^2 + a_4 x_n y_n,$
$a_i \in R, i = 1, 2, \ldots, 6$
$g\,(x_n, y_n) = b_1 + b_2 x_n + b_3 x_n^2 + b_4 x_n + b_5 x_n^2 + b_4 x_n y_n,$
$b_i \in R, i = 1, 2, \ldots, 6$

The Lyapunov exponent of the system is transformed in to (x_n, y_n)

$$\begin{pmatrix} \delta x_{n+1} \\ \delta y_{n+1} \end{pmatrix} = \begin{pmatrix} g_{11} & g_{12} \\ g_{21} & g_{22} \end{pmatrix} \begin{pmatrix} \delta x_n \\ \delta y_n \end{pmatrix}$$ (10.29)

where,

$g_{11} = \frac{\delta f}{\delta x} = a_2 + 2a_3 x_n + a_6 y_n$,

$g_{12} = \frac{\delta f}{\delta y} = a_4 + 2a_5 y_n + a_6 x_n$,

$g_{21} = \frac{\delta f}{\delta x} = b_2 + 2b_3 x_n + b_6 y_n$,

$g_{22} = \frac{\delta f}{\delta x} = b_4 + 2b_5 x_n + b_6 x_n$.

Then by numerical computations, Lyapunov exponent of the nonlinear dynamic system is calculated with 2D hyper-chaos discrete nonlinear dynamic systems.

10.5.2 Hyper-Chaotic Chen's System

A hyper-chaotic system generated from generalized Chen's chaotic system is used as key scheming for this encryption method. The system is defined as follows [7],

$$\begin{aligned} \overline{x}_1 &= a(x_2 - x_1) \\ \overline{x}_2 &= -x_1 x_3 + d x_1 + c x_2 - x_4 \\ \overline{x}_3 &= x_1 x_2 - b x_3 \\ \overline{x}_4 &= x_1 + k \end{aligned}$$ (10.30)

where a, b, c, d and k are parameters, x_1, x_2, x_3, x_4 are state variables and when $a = 36, b = 3, c = 28, d = -16$ and $-0.7 \leq k \leq 0.7$, the system is hyper-chaotic. For the hyper-chaotic attractor, the four Lyapunov exponents are as follows $\lambda_1 = 1.552$, $\lambda_2 = 0.023, \lambda_3 = 0, \lambda_4 = -12.573$. The Chen's hyper-chaotic system as shown in Eq. (10.30) is pre-iterated for $N_0 = 3000$ times to overcome the adverse effect. The system is used for diffusing the permuted image to construct the cipher image for better results. Here the initial conditions are randomly selected. The four key stream elements from the current state are calculated and shown in equation given below,

$$K S_i = \mod \left(\left(|x_i| - floor(|x_i|) \right) \times 10^{14}, 256 \right), i = 1, 2, 3, 4$$ (10.31)

These four values act as diffusion key for diffusion and its decimal fractions of this variable is 10^{14}. The Key Stream (KS) is obtained and four values are generated as KS_i, where $i = 1, 2, 3, 4$. The permuted key stream (PKS) is generated by circularly shifted with Per_{mxn} bits, as illustrated in Fig. 10.15.

Fig. 10.15 Circular shift of
key stream

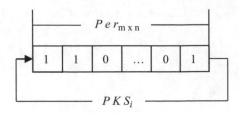

The Permuted Key Stream (PKS) values are modified by using the equation,

$$PKS_{m \times n} = \text{mod}\,(Per_{m \times n}, 4) \tag{10.32}$$

The permuted key stream value in the range of (0, 1, ... 4) are circularly right shifted according to the generated value. If the permuted key stream value is 2, then the key stream is circularly shifted two times to obtain PKS (new)$_i$ in the step of four value. The diffusion key value K_1 is generated by bit XOR with key stream KS_1. Similarly K_2 is bit XORed with key stream KS_2 against its previous value and Again, the next two K_3 and K_4 key values are generated in a step of four values for hyper-chaotic Lorenz's and Chen's system. The diffusion key values $K_{4 \times (n-1)+i}$ are generated in accordance to the image size. Then the diffused pixel is calculated as,

$$D_{4 \times (n-1)+(i+1)} = \left[Per_{m \times n} \oplus PKS_{4 \times (n-1)+(i+1)} \oplus K_{4 \times (n-1)+i} \right] \tag{10.33}$$

where, i = 0, 1, 2, 3 and $m \times n$ is size of the image.

Thus, the diffusion key stream is continued for each step, value wise with respect to the input image. This cryptosystem resists some common attacks such as chosen and known plain text attacks. The decryption is done by the equation,

$$Per_{m \times n} = \left[D_{4 \times (n-1)+(i+1)} \oplus PKS_{4 \times (n-1)+(i+1)} \oplus K_{4 \times (n-1)+i} \right] \tag{10.34}$$

where, i = 0, 1, 2, 3 and $m \times n$ is size of the image.

The diffused values are generated from Eq. (10.34) to perform the permutation process. While performing permutation and diffusion, same keys are used to decrypt the plain image. The decryption procedure is similar to the encryption procedure but in a reverse manner.

10.5.3 Encryption and Decryption Algorithm

The steps of encryption and decryption algorithm for the proposed scheme are detailed below.

Encryption Algorithm Steps

Various steps in the image encryption and decryption procedure are;

Step 1:   The algorithm involves the permutation process by the 2D hyper-chaotic discrete non-linear dynamic system as furnished in Eq. (10.27). With initial value (x_0, y_0), iterations are made for M $\times$ N times in order to get two new sequences; $\{x'_1, x'_2 \ldots \ldots\}$ and $\{y'_1, y'_2 \ldots \ldots\}$.

Step 2:   The pixel values are arranged in ascending order and indexed sequence wise. These indexed sequences are applied to permute pixel positions of the image.

Step 3:   The hyper-chaotic chen's system discussed in Eq. (10.30) is pre-iterated for N_0 times. Fourth-order Runge-Kutta method is used to solve the system equation.

Step 4:   Four key stream elements from the current state are calculated from Eq. (10.31). These four values act as a key for diffusion to generate the Key Stream (KS).

Step 5:   The permuted image is generated in $P_{m \times n}$ and it gets diffused by the continuous hyper-chaotic Chen's system.

Step 6:   The differential equation is iterated for N_0 times by Runge-Kutta algorithm to evade the harmful outcome of transient procedure. Here, the initial conditions are randomly selected in four variables. The key streams are calculated and highlighted in Eq. (10.32).

Step 7:   The permuted image is circularly shifted repeatedly to obtain the new value (PKS). The four keys derived from hyper-chaotic Chen's system for diffusion.

Step 8:   The Chen's system key value K_1 is obtained from bit XOR of key stream KS_i. The new key value $K_{4 \times (n-1) + i}$ is calculated for multiple hyper-chaotic maps in line with the image size.

Step 9:   The encrypted image is obtained using the Eq. (10.33) and the diffusion key stream is continued for each step for four values with respect to the input image.

   The permuted image $Per_{m \times n}$, PKS_i and key K_1 are taken in an array to diffuse the entire image for encryption.

Decryption Algorithm Steps

Step 1:   The encrypted image is diffused with key value K_1, PKS_i and permuted image.

Step 2:   The diffusion key stream is generated for each step of four values with respect to the input image.

Step 3:   The permuted key stream (PKS) values are obtained by using the Eq. (10.32) by circularly shifting left.

Step 4:   The diffused image is obtained vide Eq. (10.34).

Step 5:   The derived image is permuted by the 2D hyper-chaotic map to gain the original plain image.

10.6 Performance Comparison of the Proposed Image Encryption Techniques

The developed image encryption algorithms using multiple chaotic maps give better performance and their results are further analyzed. The algorithms are as follows,

1. Image encryption using chaotic maps.
2. Image encryption using multiple chaotic maps.
3. Image encryption using Hyper-chaotic maps.

These algorithms are tested for performance analysis such as histogram analysis, correlation coefficient analysis, and information entropy analysis are analyzed in order to strengthen the proposed algorithm. The image encryption is compared with the proposed algorithm and also compared with the other existing algorithms.

10.6.1 Key Space Analysis

The key space acts as a measurement of encrypted image towards security. The keys used in this proposed algorithm require one chaotic map for permutation and four chaotic maps for diffusion to encrypt the image. The initial conditions of all the chaotic maps are the secret keys which are set at 14 decimals. The total key space of chaotic map based image encryption algorithm is 10^{70} which are larger than 2^{128}. The total key space is 10^{84} which are larger than 2^{128} for multiple chaotic map based image encryption. For multiple chaotic map based image encryption has the key space of 10^{140} which are larger than 2^{128}. These algorithms have satisfactorily larger key space to resist the possible brute-force attack.

10.6.2 Histogram Analysis

Histogram is a test to showcase the distribution of pixels in the image. It also examines the possible contrast between the plain image and cipher image distribution in histogram. The cipher image histogram is widely uniform and flat in distribution as shown in Figs. 10.16, 10.17 and 10.18 for various image encryptions. The plain image histogram has some peaks and it is unevenly distributed. Even if another image is considered it would also be subjected to a difference in distribution.

The algorithms for the three methods are compared and tabulated as shown in the Table 10.1. Thus test is conducted by using Intel(R) Pentium(R) i5 Processor 2.3 GHz and simulated in MATLAB (R2010a).

The image encryption using chaotic maps with its key generation process provides better results in four rounds. The computation time is 95 ms and its key space is 10^{280} for four rounds. The correlation coefficient is -0.0019, 0.0023 and 0.0018, NPCR is 99.65% and UACI is 33.54% for four rounds, respectively.

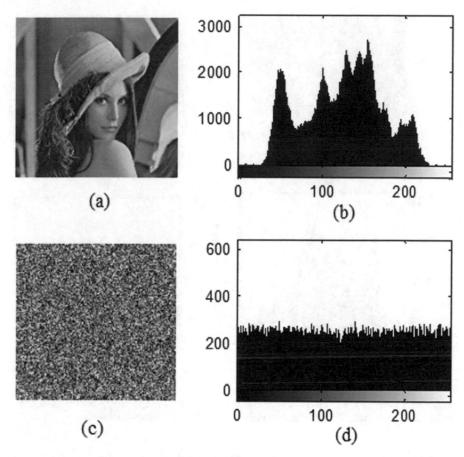

Fig. 10.16 Histogram analysis of chaotic map based image encryption. (a) Lena plain image (b) Histogram of plain image (c) Cipher image (d) Histogram of cipher image

The chaotic permutation and diffusion architecture using multiple chaotic maps with hash key as the key generator provides better results in four rounds. The computation time is 90.5 ms and key space is 10^{336} for four rounds. The correlation coefficient is -0.0001, -0.0075 and 0.0004, NPCR is 99.72% and UACI is 33.60% for four rounds, respectively. To reduce number of rounds and longer key space, the algorithm is extended to hyper-chaos based encryption.

The method based on permutation and diffusion using multiple hyper-chaotic maps requires only one round for encryption. The computation time is 312 ms and the key space is 10^{140} for one round. The correlation coefficient is -0.0113, -0.0150 and -0.0035, NPCR is 99.62% and UACI is 33.71%, respectively. The encryption is achieved in single round whereas it is time consuming. The proposed algorithm performance analysis tests are compared with the existing algorithm and tabulated from Table 10.2 to Table 10.4.

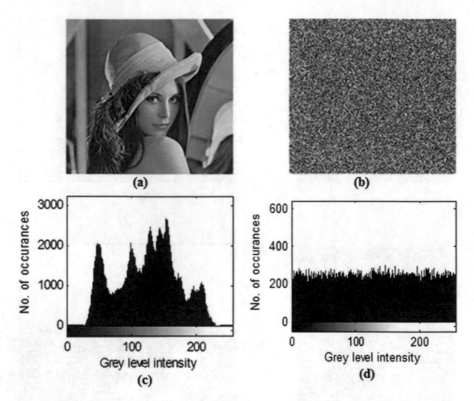

Fig. 10.17 Histogram analysis for multiple chaotic map based image encryption (**a**) Lena plain image (**b**) Cipher image (**c**) Histogram of plain image (**d**) Cipher image histogram

Table 10.2 shows the correlation coefficient of the proposed three methods and their comparison with existing algorithm. It is observed that Zhou's algorithm has better performance as it is almost zero, but multiple chaotic map based algorithm and hyper-chaotic based algorithm have the correlation almost near to zero.

The multiple chaotic map based encryption algorithm requires four rounds to encrypt the image. Hyper-Chaotic maps for image encryption correlation is almost zero but its computation time is longer than the other algorithms. Hyper-chaotic based algorithm has better performance than Gao's Algorithm, its correlation is near to zero and it requires single round to encrypt the image.

Table 10.3 shows the differential attack analysis of proposed three methods compared with existing algorithms. It is observed that NPCR and UACI of multiple chaotic based algorithm has better performance than the other proposed algorithms of 99.72% and 33.60%, respectively. Hyper-chaotic based image encryption has NPCR of 99.62% and UACI of 33.71% which is little lower than the hash keying based algorithm and better than the Gao's algorithm.

Table 10.4 shows the comparison of information entropy analysis of the plain image and encrypted image. From the table, it is observed that the entropy of the

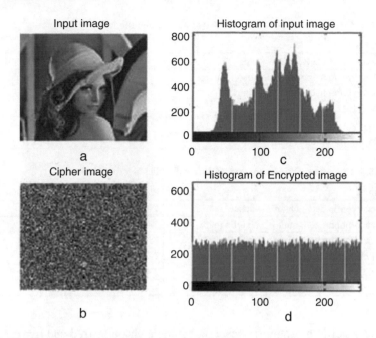

Fig. 10.18 Histogram analysis of Lena image for multiple hyper-chaotic map. (**a**) Lena image (**b**) Cipher image (**c**) Histogram of the plain image (**d**) Histogram of the cipher image

Table 10.1 Comparison of performance analysis test

Proposed algorithms	Correlation coefficients			NPCR	UACI	Information entropy
	Horizontal	Vertical	Diagonal			
Image encryption using chaotic maps	−0.0019	0.0023	0.0018	0.9965	0.3354	7.9970
Image encryption using multiple chaotic maps	−0.0001	−0.0075	0.0004	0.9972	0.3360	7.9976
Image encryption using hyper-chaotic maps	−0.0113	−0.0150	−0.0035	0.9962	0.3371	7.9972

Table 10.2 Comparison of correlation coefficients with other algorithms

Algorithms	Correlation coefficients		
	Horizontal	Vertical	Diagonal
Image encryption using chaotic maps	−0.0019	0.0023	0.0018
Image encryption using multiple chaotic maps	−0.0001	−0.0075	0.0004
Image encryption using hyper-chaotic maps	−0.0113	−0.0150	−0.0035
Zhou et al. [51]	−0.00009	−0.00005	0.00072
Gao and Chen [57]	−0.0142	−0.0074	−0.0183
Tedmori and Al-Najdawi [58]	0.0023	0.0042	0.0053

Table 10.3 Comparison of NPCR and UACI with other algorithms

Algorithms	NPCR	UACI
Image encryption using chaotic maps	0.9965	0.3354
Image encryption using multiple chaotic maps	0.9972	0.3360
Image encryption using hyper-Chaotic maps	0.9962	0.3371
Zhou et al. [51]	0.9971	0.3353
Gao and Chen [57]	0.9953	0.3341
Tedmori and Al-Najdawi [58]	0.9910	0.3624

Table 10.4 Comparison of information entropy with other algorithms

Algorithms	Plain image	Cipher image
Image encryption using chaotic maps	7.4288	7.9970
Image encryption using multiple chaotic maps	7.4288	7.9976
Image encryption using hyper-chaotic maps	7.4143	7.9972
Zhou et al. [51]	7.4378	7.9970
Gao and Chen [57]	7.4593	7.9965
Tedmori and Al-Najdawi [58]	7.4455	7.9980

proposed algorithm is almost near to 8. Multiple chaotic based and hyper-chaotic based algorithm has better performance than the existing algorithms whose value is 7.9976. Hyper-chaotic based encryptions have entropy of 7.9972. The proposed methods of multiple chaotic maps based algorithm have the entropy level almost near to the Zhou's algorithm. From this analysis, the hyper-chaotic based image encryption out performs all the above performance analysis compared with other existing algorithm in a single round.

10.6.3   Randomness Test with SP800-22 Test Suite

NIST recommends the strategies to perform the analysis for 16 statistical tests to identify the binary sequence randomness of encrypted images of the three methods. Its distribution is based on P-value computed from binary sequence. Null and alternative hypothesis sequence in random or non-random behaviour is computed by the equations.

The following equation is used to compute χ^2,

$$\chi^2 = \sum_{i=1}^{10} \frac{(F_i - N/10)}{N/10} \tag{10.35}$$

where, F_i is the number of occurrences that the P- value is in the ith interval and N is the sample size (N = 100).

Table 10.5 NIST statistical test analysis for image encryption using chaotic maps

Statistical test	P-value
Frequency	0.6543
Block frequency	0.5256
Runs	0.8919
Long runs of one's	0.4230
Binary matrix rank	0.8913
Spectral DFT	0.4616
Non-overlapping templates	0.7939
Overlapping templates	0.4350
Universal	0.9862
Linear complexity test	0.7532
Serial test-1	0.5645
Serial test-2	0.9387
Approximate entropy	0.1087
Cumulative sums	0.7349
Random excursions	0.0945
Random excursions variant	0.7681

The P-values are calculated by using,

$$P - value = igamc \left(\frac{9}{2}, \frac{\chi^2}{2} \right) \tag{10.36}$$

where, 'igamc' is the incomplete Gamma function.

The conditions are if P-values are greater than or equal to 0.01 then the P-values are found to be random and uniformly distributed. If the P-values work out to zero, its generated sequence would be non-random with uneven distribution. From Table 10.5, it is observed that NIST test suite succeeds in all the tests of the encrypted image using chaotic maps.

It is found from all the methods if P-values are greater than or equal to 0.01 then, the P-values are found to be random and uniformly distributed. If the P-values work out to zero, its generated sequence would be non-random with uneven distribution. From Tables 10.5, 10.6 and 10.7, it is observed that NIST test suite succeeds in all the test of the encrypted images. This algorithm is more secure and robust for image transmission.

10.7   Conclusion

The multiple chaotic based image encryptions provide better encryption than the chaotic based image encryption methods. In this algorithm, permutation is performed in bit-level, whereas in diffusion the permuted pixel bits are shuffled with generated random bits. To encrypt the image in every round, the secret key gets

Table 10.6 NIST statistical test analysis for image encryption using multiple chaotic maps

Statistical test	P-value
Frequency	0.8431
Block frequency	0.3560
Runs	0.7290
Long runs of one's	0.5268
Binary matrix rank	0.9900
Spectral DFT	0.3025
Non-overlapping templates	0.8932
Overlapping templates	0.2469
Universal	0.8832
Linear complexity test	0.8532
Serial test-1	0.2648
Serial test-2	0.9346
Approximate entropy	0.1259
Cumulative sums	0.7349
Random excursions	0.0945
Random excursions variant	0.5639

Table 10.7 NIST statistical test analysis for image encryption using hyper-chaotic maps

Statistical test	P-value
Frequency	0.6837
Block frequency	0.1876
Runs	0.6195
Long runs of one's	0.8762
Binary matrix rank	0.8991
Spectral DFT	0.4776
Non-overlapping templates	0.7890
Overlapping templates	0.2637
Universal	0.8698
Linear complexity test	0.9215
Serial test-1	0.2894
Serial test-2	0.9719
Approximate entropy	0.1028
Cumulative sums	0.7861
Random excursions	0.2897
Random excursions variant	0.7417

updated in diffusion bit generator. The secret key updation offers different random bits generation for every round in the diffusion process. The performance analysis is carried out and the correlation coefficient vertical, horizontal and diagonal components are works out to -0.0001, 0.0075, and 0.0004, respectively which is nearer to zero. This proposed algorithm has less correlation in the encrypted image. The differential analysis related to NPCR is 99.72% and UACI is 33.60% which is resistive for differential attacks. The key space is 10^{84} which is greater than 2^{128} ($\approx 10^{39}$) to withstand the possible brute force attack.

The hyper-chaotic based image encryption entails better encryption than the other two chaotic based methods. The correlation coefficient of vertical, horizontal and diagonal component works out to -0.0113, -0.0150 and -0.0035, respectively is near to zero and this proposed algorithm has less correlation in the encrypted image. The differential analysis related to NPCR is 99.62% and UACI is 33.71% resistive for differential attacks. The key space is 10^{140} which are greater than 2^{128} ($\approx 10^{39}$) to withstand the possible brute force attack. The hyper-chaotic based image encryption evidences better results in single round itself with larger key space. The tests conducted guaranteed a negligible correlation in the cipher image. The NIST test suits have been conducted and it is proved to be completely random for all the proposed encrypted images. The performance analyses of all the tests show that the hyper-chaotic based image encryption is robust for secured image transformation.

References

1. Blum, L, Blum, M & Shub, M, 'A simple unpredictable pseudo-random number generator', SIAM Journal on computing, vol. 15, no. 2, pp. 364-383, 1986.
2. Dachselt, F & Schwarz, W, 'Chaos and cryptography', IEEE Transactions on Circuits and Systems I: Fundamental Theory and Applications, vol. 12, no. 48, pp. 1498-1509, 2001.
3. Menezes, AJ, Van Oorschot, PC & Vanstone, SA, Handbook of applied cryptography, CRC press, 1996.
4. Palacios, A & Juarez, H, 'Cryptography with cycling chaos', Physics Letters A, vol. 303, no. 5, pp. 345-351, 2002.
5. Parker, TS & Chua, LO, 'Chaos: A tutorial for engineers', Proceedings of the IEEE, vol. 75, no. 8, pp. 982-1008, 1987.
6. Chen, G, Chen, Y & Liao, X, 'An extended method for obtaining S-boxes based on three-dimensional chaotic Baker maps', Chaos, solitons & fractals, vol. 31, no. 3, pp. 571-579, 2007.
7. Forouzan, BA & Mukhopadhyay, D, Cryptography and Network Security (Sie), McGraw-Hill Education, 2011.
8. Stallings, W, Cryptography and network security: Principles and practices, 5th edition, Prentice hall, New Delhi, 2011.
9. Zhang, G & Liu, Q, 'A novel image encryption method based on total shuffling scheme', Optics Communications, vol. 284, no. 12, pp. 2775-2780, 2011.
10. Zhang. X, Zhao. Z, Wang. J, 'Chaotic image encryption based on circular substitution box and key stream buffer', Signal Process.: Image Communication. Vol.29, No.8, pp.902–913, 2014.
11. Schneier, B, 'A self-study course in block-cipher cryptanalysis', Cryptologia, vol. 24, no. 1, pp. 18-33, 2000.
12. Baptista, M 1998, 'Cryptography with chaos', Physics Letters A, vol. 240, no. 1, pp. 50-54.
13. Pecora, LM & Carroll, TL, 'Synchronization in chaotic systems', Physical review letters, vol. 64, no. 8, p. 821, 1990.
14. Gligoroski, D, Dimovski, D, Kocarev, L, Urumov, V & Chua, L, 'A method for encoding messages by time targeting of the trajectories of chaotic systems', International Journal of Bifurcation and chaos, vol. 6, no. 11, pp. 2119-2125, 1996.
15. Wong, K-W, 'A combined chaotic cryptographic and hashing scheme', Physics Letters A, vol. 307, no. 5, pp. 292-298, 2003.
16. Safwan El Assad, Mousa Farajallah, 'A new chaos-based image encryption system', Signal Process.: Image Communication. Vol.41, pp.144-157, 2016.

17. Alvarez, G, Montoya, F, Romera, M & Pastor, G, 'Cryptanalysis of an ergodic chaotic cipher', Physics Letters A, vol. 311, no. 2, pp. 172-179, 2003.
18. Alvarez, G, Montoya, F, Romera, M & Pastor, G, 'Cryptanalysis of dynamic look-up table based chaotic cryptosystems', Physics Letters-A, vol. 326, no. 3, pp. 211-218, 2004.
19. Rukhin, A, 'A statistical test suite for random and pseudorandom number generators for cryptographic applications', NIST special publication, Revision 1a, 2010.
20. Castro, JCH, Sierra, JM, Seznec, A, Izquierdo, A & Ribagorda, A, 'The strict avalanche criterion randomness test', Mathematics and Computers in Simulation, vol. 68, no. 1, pp. 1-7, 2005.
21. Forré, R, 'The strict avalanche criterion: spectral properties of Boolean functions and an extended definition', in Proceedings on Advances in cryptology, pp. 450-468, 1990.
22. Wang, Y, Wong, K-W, Liao, X & Chen, G, 'A new chaos-based fast image encryption algorithm', Applied soft computing, vol. 11, no. 1, pp. 514-522, 2011.
23. Ye, R, 'A novel chaos-based image encryption scheme with an efficient permutation-diffusion mechanism', Optics Communications, vol. 284, no. 22, pp. 5290-5298, 2011.
24. Zeghid, M, Machhout, M, Khriji, L, Baganne, A & Tourki, R, 'A modified AES based algorithm for image encryption', International Journal of Computer Science and Engineering, vol. 1, no. 1, pp. 70-75, 2007.
25. Wong, K-W, 'A fast chaotic cryptographic scheme with dynamic look-up table', Physics Letters A, vol. 298, no. 4, pp. 238-242, 2002.
26. Kwok, H & Tang, WK, 'A fast image encryption system based on chaotic maps with finite precision representation', Chaos, solitons & fractals, vol. 32, no. 4, pp. 1518-1529, 2007.
27. Patidar, V, Pareek, N, Purohit, G & Sud, K, 'A robust and secure chaotic standard map based pseudorandom permutation-substitution scheme for image encryption', Optics Communications, vol. 284, no. 19, pp. 4331-4339, 2011.
28. Yang, H, Wong, K-W, Liao, X, Zhang, W & Wei, P, 'A fast image encryption and authentication scheme based on chaotic maps', Communications in Nonlinear Science and Numerical Simulation, vol. 15, no. 11, pp. 3507-3517, 2010.
29. Wong, K-W & Yuen, C-H, 'Embedding compression in chaos-based cryptography', IEEE Transactions on Circuits and Systems II: Express Briefs, vol. 55, no. 11, pp. 1193-1197, 2008.
30. Dong, Ce, 'Color image encryption using one-time keys and coupled chaotic systems', Signal Processing: Image Communication, vol. 29, no. 5, pp. 628-640, 2014.
31. Yuen, C-H & Wong, K-W, 'A chaos-based joint image compression and encryption scheme using DCT and SHA-1', Applied soft computing, vol. 11, no. 8, pp. 5092-5098, 2011.
32. Singh, N & Sinha, A, 'Chaos based multiple image encryption using multiple canonical transforms', Optics & Laser Technology, vol. 42, no. 5, pp. 724-731, 2010.
33. Tang, Z, Song, J, Zhang, X & Sun, R, 'Multiple-image encryption with bit-plane decomposition and chaotic maps', Optics and Lasers in Engineering, vol. 80, pp. 1-11, 2016.
34. Lian, S, Sun, J & Wang, Z, 'A block cipher based on a suitable use of the chaotic standard map', Chaos, solitons & fractals, vol. 26, no. 1, pp. 117-129, 2005.
35. François, M, Grosges, T, Barchiesi, D, Erra, R, 'A new image encryption scheme based on a chaotic function', Signal Processing: Image Communication, vol. 27, no. 3, pp. 249-259, 2012.
36. Ahmad, J, Hwang, SO, 'Chaos-based diffusion for highly autocorrelated data in encryption algorithms', Nonlinear Dynamics, vol. 82, no. 4, pp. 1839-1850, 2015.
37. Wong, K-W, Kwok, BS-H & Law, W-S, 'A fast image encryption scheme based on chaotic standard map', Physics Letters A, vol. 372, no. 15, pp. 2645-2652, 2008.
38. Liu, H & Wang, X 2011, 'Color image encryption using spatial bit-level permutation and high-dimension chaotic system', Optics Communications, vol. 284, no. 16, pp. 3895-3903.
39. Norouzi, B, Seyedzadeh, SM, Mirzakuchaki, S & Mosavi, MR, 'A novel image encryption based on row-column, masking and main diffusion processes with hyper chaos', Multimedia Tools and Applications, vol. 74, no. 3, pp. 781-811, 2015.
40. Xu, L, Li, Z, Li, J & Hua, W, 'A novel bit-level image encryption algorithm based on chaotic maps', Optics and Lasers in Engineering, vol. 78, pp. 17-25, 2016.

41. Abd-El-Hafiz, SK, Abd-El-Haleem, SH & Radwan, AG 2016, 'Novel permutation measures for image encryption algorithms', Optics and Lasers in Engineering, vol. 85, pp. 72-83, 2016.
42. Zhang, Y-Q, Wang, X-Y, Liu, J & Chi, Z-L, 'An image encryption scheme based on the MLNCML system using DNA sequences', Optics and Lasers in Engineering, vol. 82, pp. 95-103, 2016.
43. Li Shujun, LI, Qi, LI, Wenmin 2001, 'Statistical properties of digital piecewise linear chaotic maps and their roles in cryptography and pseudo-random coding', Lecture notes in computer science, vol.2260, pp.205-221, 2001.
44. Li Shujun, Guanrong Chen, Xuanqin Mou, 'On the dynamic degradation of digital piecewise linear chaotic maps', International Journal of Bifurcation and Chaos, vol.15, no.10, pp.3119-3151, 2005.
45. Lozi, Rene, 'Emergence of randomness from chaos', International Journal of Bifurcation and Chaos, vol.22, no.2, pp.3119-3151, 2012.
46. Gopalakrishnan, T., Ramakrishnan, S., Dhivya, N.: 'An Image Encryption-Compression Algorithm Based on Hyper-Chaos and Number theory', Proceedings of National Conference RTCSP-2014, Amrita Vishwa Vidyapeetham, Coimbatore, pp 88-91, 2014.
47. Gang-Quan, Si., Cao Hui., Zhang Yan-Bin, 'A new four dimensional hyperchaotic Lorenz system and its adaptive control', Chinese Phys.B, 20(1), pp 1-9, 2011.
48. Sriti Thakur, Amit Kumar Singh, Satya Prakash Ghrera, Mohamed Elhoseny, 'Multi-layer security of medical data through watermarking and chaotic encryption for tele-health applications', Multimedia Tools and Applications, first online, pp 1-14, Jun 2018.
49. Wai-Kit Wong, Lap-piu, & Wong, K-w, 'A modified chaotic cryptographic method', Computer Physics Communications, vol.138, no.3, pp. 234-236, 2001.
50. Zhou, Y, Bao, L & Chen, CP, 'Image encryption using a new parametric switching chaotic system', Signal Processing, vol. 93, no. 11, pp. 3039-3052, 2013.
51. Zhou, Y, Bao, L & Chen, CP, 'A new 1D chaotic system for image encryption', Signal Processing, vol. 97, pp. 172-182, 2014.
52. Wang, X-Y, Yang, L, Liu, R & Kadir, A, 'A chaotic image encryption algorithm based on perceptron model', Nonlinear Dynamics, vol. 62, no. 3, pp. 615-621, 2010.
53. Bigdeli, N, Farid, Y & Afshar, K, 'A robust hybrid method for image encryption based on Hopfield neural network', Computers & Electrical Engineering, vol. 38, no. 2, pp. 356-369, 2012.
54. Zhu, H, Zhao, C & Zhang, X, 'A novel image encryption–compression scheme using hyper-chaos and Chinese remainder theorem', Signal Processing: Image Communication, vol. 28, no. 6, pp. 670-680, 2013.
55. Gopalakrishnan, T & Ramakrishnan, S, 'Image Encryption in Bit Wise and Key Generation using Multiple Chaotic Maps', Australian Journal of Basic and Applied Sciences, ISSN: 1991-8178, vol. 9, no. 27, pp. 200-208, Aug 2015.
56. Gopalakrishnan, T., Ramakrishnan, S, 'Chaotic image encryption with Hash keying as key generator', IETE Journal of Research, 63(2), pp 172-187, 2017.
57. Gao, T & Chen, Z, 'A new image encryption algorithm based on hyper-chaos', Physics Letters A, vol. 372, no. 4, pp. 394-400, 2008.
58. Tedmori, S & Al-Najdawi, N, 'Image cryptographic algorithm based on the Haar wavelet transform', Information Sciences, vol. 269, pp. 21-34, 2014.

Chapter 11
Perceptual Hash Function for Images Based on Hierarchical Ordinal Pattern

Arambam Neelima and Kh. Manglem Singh

11.1 Introduction

Users are generating digital media in huge amount each day. The amount of data generated is increasing day by day as the Internet grows. With a growth like this, there arises the need to store and transmit large volume of digital data. Traditional indexing methods are time consuming and inefficient for retrieval of multimedia data. An efficient indexing and retrieval method for multimedia data is required. Another issue is to authenticate the integrity of digital multimedia. Digital media can be easily manipulated using image processing tools. Objects can be easily either inserted or removed. It is almost impossible to subjectively distinguish which are the original and which have been manipulated. Copyright protection is also one of the issues that arises due to advancement of digital communication. Everyone can download any images/videos uploaded by another person in public website without any restrictions or authorization. So, there is a need to identify perceptually identical images or videos even if they suffer some distortions or tampering and prevent illegal usage of the digital media.

A hashing function or a hash function may be defined as any algorithm that maps data of variable length to a data of fixed length called as hash value [1]. A hashing function takes data of finite variable bit length as input and produces a value of fixed size as output. The output of such a function is called hash value, hash or message digest. A hashing function (H) should have the following properties [2].

A. Neelima (✉)
Department of Computer Science and Engineering, NIT Nagaland, Dimapur, Nagaland, India
e-mail: neelima@nitnagaland.ac.in

K. M. Singh
Department of Computer Science and Engineering, NIT Manipur, Imphal, Manipur, India

© Springer Nature Switzerland AG 2019
A. K. Singh, A. Mohan (eds.), *Handbook of Multimedia Information Security: Techniques and Applications*, https://doi.org/10.1007/978-3-030-15887-3_11

- Uniqueness: Hash value should be unique, if the input message is distinct. This will prevent forgery since same hash value for another message will not be found.

$H(M) \neq H(M')$, if messages M and M' are not similar

- Procedure Compactness: The size of the hash value should be smaller than the size of the original input data.

$H(M) < size(M)$

- Perceptual Robustness: Hash value should be same, if the input messages are similar.

$H(M) \approx H(M')$, if M and M'' are similar

- One way function: The hash generation should be invertible. This property will ensure that it is practically impossible to generate the message from a given code, but easy to generate the code given a message.

In addition to the above requirements, a hashing function should also be applicable to a block of data of any size. It should produce a fixed length output. Lastly, it should be relatively easy to compute for any given data.

The most well-known method for building a hashing function is Merkle-Damgard construction [3] named after its inventor the American Ralph C. Merkle and the Danish Ivan Damgard.

The main components are discussed below:

Initialization Vector: It is the fixed value which is set for the first iteration. It is used as a chaining variable.

Compression Function (CF): Compression function acts like a one way hashing function. It is mainly a block based hashing function. The generated hash value is collision resistant if the compression function is collision resistant. It takes two inputs for each iteration, a block of message and a chaining variable.

The step by step generic framework for generating a fixed length value is given in [3]. The process is depicted in Fig. 11.1. The entire message to be hashed is divided into blocks of same length. Message padding can be done for equal partitioning of the message block. Every block is then passed through the compression function. The variable in the initialization vector is used as a chaining variable for the first iteration. The output of the first compression is then used as the chaining variable for the next compression function and so on till the last iteration.

Some of the traditional hashing functions are Secure Hash Algorithm (SHA), MD, Whirpool, Research and Development in Advanced Communications Technologies (RACE) Integrity Primitives Evaluation Message Digest (RIPEMD) [4–6] etc. SHA was developed by National Institute of Standards and Technology (NIST). Different versions of SHA are available such as SHA-1, SHA-256, SHA-384, SHA-512 with hash values of lengths 160, 256, 384 and 512 bits respectively. They follow the same structure, same type of modular arithmetic and logical binary operations. However, the maximum length of the input message varies for each version [5, 6]. MD2, MD4 and MD5 are the published versions of MD. SHA

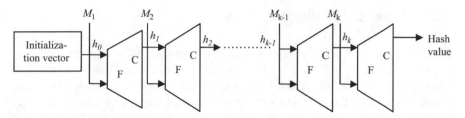

Fig. 11.1 Merkle-Damgard construction

and MD families follow the same general structure like initializing the constants, buffer and compression function, and creation of chaining value that is fed back into the next block. These hashing functions are sensitive to every single bit of input data. Change in even one bit of the original data will result in a different hash value. A traditional hashing function provides authentication and integrity, but it is not suitable for all the types of data. Traditional hashing functions will not work properly for multimedia data like image, audio and video. The sensitivity in traditional hashing will prevent their use on image or video data since various operations like compression, scaling, cropping and enhancement will not alter the perceptual content of the image or video frame but will change the digital representation of the data. It is almost impossible to distinguish subjectively which images and videos are original and which have been manipulated. The main aim is to develop a perceptual image hashing function, which can withstand against legitimate modifications but at the same time have discriminative capability.

A perceptual hashing function should satisfy all the requirements stated above for traditional hashing function but apart from these, some additional properties are also required which are listed below [2].

- Perceptual Similarity/Robustness

Perceptual image hashing algorithm has to be robust, i.e. incidental and legitimate post processing operations on the media must not render an entirely different hash value. Hence, perceptually similar respectively indistinguishable media objects have to exhibit the same or a similar hash value.

- Distinction

The property "distinction" predicates the computational/practical infeasibility of determining two perceptually different media data exhibiting the same or a similar hash value.

11.2   Types of Hashing Functions

A hashing function can be categorized into two types depending on whether a key
is used or not while designing the hashing function. These are keyed and unkeyed
hashing function. A keyed hashing function generates a hash value from an arbitrary
input using a secret key. A keyed hashing function will accept a message of arbitrary
finite length and a fixed length key. Any third party without the knowledge of
the key will not be able to forge the message. It can be considered as Message
Authentication Code (MAC).Most of the earlier hashing functions were unkeyed
hashing function. As the name suggests, an unkeyed hashing function does not
need a key. An unkeyed hashing function is designed only to provide data integrity.
However, a keyed hashing function will also provide authentication in addition to
data integrity.

11.3   Applications of Hashing Functions

Cryptographic hashing functions have many applications like data integrity, data
authentication etc. The applications are explained in details in the following
subsections.

11.3.1   Data Integrity

Data integrity ensures that, the data has not been altered in an unauthorized manner
since the time it was created, transmitted, or stored by the source. Since two distinct
messages are extremely unlikely to generate identical hash value, hashing functions
can be used to determine data integrity. One takes a message or file, computes the
hash value and stores it as a baseline value. Later, the hash value can be recomputed
on the message as shown in Fig. 11.2. If the new value differs from the original
value, then one can be assured that the file has been altered in some way. Therefore,
we see that the properties of cryptographic hashing functions can be used to verify
that files have not been altered.

11.3.2   Data Authentication

Data authentication is the process which enables to verify the source of the data. If
a data is sent along with its hash value, the recipient can check the hash value and
verify the integrity of the message. However, if a secret key is used which is known
only to the sender and the recipient, and then the recipient can determine the source

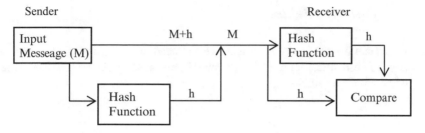

Fig. 11.2 Data integrity using hash function

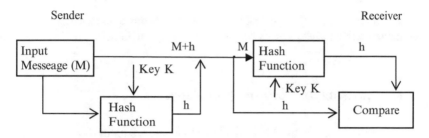

Fig. 11.3 Data authentication using hash function

identity by independently computing the hash value using the same key and compare it with the hash value received. Figure 11.3 illustrates the data authentication process using hash function.

11.3.3   Digital Signature

Digital signature is an electronic signature used to validate the identity and integrity of a document or message. A hashing function is used to generate hash value of a message to be signed. The document or a message to be signed is first transformed to a hash value. The hashing function will convert any arbitrary input into a fixed length value, which is smaller than the input. The sender then converts the hash value into a digital signature using a secret key. The created digital signature is then sent along with the message. As the hash value is unique to the hashed data, any change in data will result in different value. Verification of the created digital signature can be done by computing the hash value of the received message using the same hashing function. Then using the key and the hash value generated, the receiver can verify whether the message is generated by the sender and the message was unaltered.

11.3.4   Password Tables

Passwords can be stored as a message digest instead in the form of text to improve security. To authenticate a user, the password presented by the user is hashed and compared with the stored hash.

11.3.5   Pseudorandom Generation and Key Derivation

Hashing functions can be used to generate psudorandom bits. A new key can also be generated from a given password using a hashing function.

11.3.6   Indexing and Information Retrieval

Hashing functions can be used in hash tables to locate a data in short time.

11.3.7   Finding Duplicate Records

While storing data in a large unsorted file, a hashing function can be used to determine duplicate data or record. An index table can be maintained for the hash values of the data. So, data with the same hash values can be identified as a duplicate data.

11.3.8   Image Watermarking

Image watermark is an invisible signature embedded inside an image for copyright protection, ownership assertion and integrity verification. A hash value of the image can be embedded as a watermark. This can be helpful as the watermark image will be resistant against intentional and unintentional attacks.

11.3.9   Biometric Template Security

With the widespread popularity of biometric system, there arises the increase in concern about the storage, privacy and security of biometric data. These data can

Fig. 11.4 Framework of
perceptual hashing

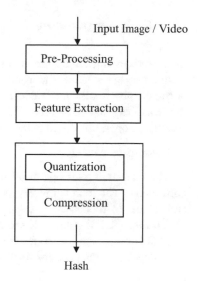

be protected using a robust hashing function. The biometric data can be stored as a
hash value instead of storing it as a biometric image.

11.4 Framework of a Perceptual Hash Function

Most of the perceptual hashing functions try to extract features of the digital image
and video, which are invariant under significant modification in order to meet the
above desired properties. A robust image hashing function normally consists of a
pre-processing stage, feature extraction, and post processing as shown in Fig. 11.4.
But it is not compulsory to have all these stages for perceptual image hashing
function. The main purpose of pre-processing is to enhance the robustness of the
features by reducing the effects of some distortions like additive noise. It also
converts the data into a general format. Some techniques used in pre-processing
stage are color space conversion, image resizing, filtering, image normalization
etc. Transformation stage transforms each partitioned block or the whole image
into some frequency domain as they may be sensitive to modification. Feature
extraction stage extracts meaningful and content relevant features of the image.
Some of the features are coefficients in the transformed domain, mean or variance
of the image frame pixels, local feature pattern like edges etc. Post processing stage
consists of quantization of the extracted features in order to gain more robustness
against distortion, discretized the randomized features and reduces the memory
requirement.

11.4.1 Pre-processing

In pre-processing stage, the input image and video frame undergo some transformations to enhance the robustness. Some uses the pre-processing stage to normalize the image and video frame into standardized format. It also decreases the sensitivity against minor distortion like additive noise. Some common pre-processing operations used at the time of perceptual hashing are discussed below.

a. Color space conversion

The most common operation used in digital image processing is color space conversion. The color images and frames are converted to greyscale images and frames to reduce the computational time or sometimes converted from Red Green Blue (RGB) color space to Luminance Chrominance blue Chrominance red (YCbCr) or Hue Saturation Intensity (HSI) or Hue Saturation Value (HSV) [9]; each component are then used for further processing.

b. Filtering

Filtering improves the robustness of the extracted features against noise addition. Filters such as median filter or Gaussian filter is applied on input image and frame to reduce the noise. However, these filters may sometimes generate blurred image by deleting some details of the image and the frame content.

c. Resizing

The input image or frame is resized to a standard size, since in real life, the size of digital images and video frames may vary from one another and the length of the hash value generated from these images and videos should be same. Also the features extracted from a standardized size are more robust against the aspect ratio change. Resizing also reduces the computational cost of feature extraction. So, it helps in efficient hash generation, fast indexing and retrieval applications.

d. Illumination normalisation

Illumination normalisation process such as gamma correction, histogram equalisation etc. is also used as a pre-processing function. It will make the extracted features invariant to illumination changes.

e. Partitioning

Some hashing partitions the image and frame into blocks of sub-images to reduce the computational cost. Random tiling of the input image also leads to efficiency in security aspect.

11.4.2   Feature Extraction

The second step is feature extraction. Feature extraction is the most important step in the image and video hashing. The features which are unique to an image or a video are extracted thereby making the hashing resistant against certain distortion and geometric attacks. If two images are perceptually similar then the extracted features and thus the hash value generated should be same even under geometrical attacks like rotation, scaling, additive noise, blurring, filtering, cropping etc. In general, the two dimensional image and frame is mapped to a one dimensional feature vector. Some commonly used techniques for robust feature extraction are discussed below.

a. Invariant feature transform

The image and frame undergo some transformation (spatial or frequency). Frequency transformations such as Discrete Cosine Transform (DCT), Discrete Wavelet Transform (DWT) and Fourier Mellin Transform (FMT) are applied to the image and frame as the coefficients in transformed domain are unique and distinctive enough for content identification and at the same time robust against attacks and distortion.

b. Matrix decomposition

As we know that the image and video are actually matrix data, matrix decomposition is also used as a method for feature extraction. Singular Value Decomposition (SVD) and Non- Negative Matrix Factorization (NMF) are the most commonly used matrix decomposition methods for hashing. The singular values obtained from the SVD and the non-negativity constraint from the NMF are used for the hash value generation. The features obtained after matrix decomposition are robust against noise addition, blurring and compression attack.

c. Statistical information

The features are extracted by computing the pixel values of the image and frame in the spatial domain. Statistical information like mean, median, variance, entropy, contrast etc. are extracted as the robust features. However, these features are not distinctive enough for content identification.

d. Local feature

Local feature patterns like edges, corners, blobs etc. are also extracted as invariant features. They are sensitive to noise, blurring and compression, but robust against geometric attacks like rotation, cropping etc.

11.4.3 Quantization

The extracted features are converted to some finite discrete value in quantization stage. Binary quantization using a threshold is one of the popular quantization schemes. This step is one of the popular quantization schemes. Quantization increases the randomness to minimise the collision property.

a. Compression

Compression results in compact hash value. The quantized features or the extracted features are compressed to get a short value or short binary sequence. Error Correcting Code (ECC) [7], Reed-Muller Code (RMC) [8] etc. are used as compression techniques. Clustering is also one of the methods for compression. The feature space is divided and similar features are mapped to the same centroid of clusters. Computational cost for clustering is a little higher than other methods. Conventional cryptography techniques like Ron Shamir Adleman (RSA) algorithm [9], MD5, Data Encryption Standard (DES) [10] are sometimes used for generating shorter hash value.

11.4.4 Similarity Measurement

Distance metrics are used to evaluate the robustness and discriminative capability of its hashing method. It helps in measuring the similarity between image and video hashes. Normally the distance is inversely proportional to similarity, i.e. lesser the distance, higher will be the similarity of the image and video. Different distance metrics are available for the calculating the similarity. For any two hash values $H_1 = \{h_1(1), h_1(2), \ldots, h_1(k),\}$ and $H_2 = \{h_2(1), h_2(2), \ldots, h_2(k),\}$ of length k for the images or video I_1 and I_2, the different distance metrics are discussed below.

a. Hamming Distance (HD)

Hamming distance [11] between two binary strings of equal length is given by number of positions at which the corresponding bits are different. It can be calculated by the following equation.

$$HD(H_1, H_2) = \sum_{i=1}^{k} |h_1(i) \oplus h_2(i)| \qquad (11.1)$$

b. Normalized Hamming Distance (NHD)

The normalized Hamming distance is equal to Hamming distance normalized by the length of the binary string. The distance will result in the range [0 1]. Distance between similar images will be closer towards 0. It can be computed using the following equation.

$$NHD\left(H_1, H_2\right) = \frac{1}{k} \sum_{i=1}^{k} |h_1(i) \oplus h_2(i)| \qquad (11.2)$$

c. Euclidean Distance (ED)

Euclidean distance is suitable for comparing real valued features. It is defined as the square root of the sum of the squares of the differences between hash values [12]. It can be calculated using the following equation.

$$ED\left(H_1, H_2\right) = \sqrt{\sum_{i=1}^{k} (h_1(i) - h_2(i))^2} \qquad (11.3)$$

d. Manhattan distance

Manhattan distance is also called as $L2$ norm distance [7]. It is suitable for comparing discrete integer values. It can be calculated using the following equation.

$$MD\left(H_1, H_2\right) = \sum_{i=1}^{k} |h_1(i) - h_2(i)| \qquad (11.4)$$

e. Bit Error Rate (BER)

Bit error rate is the rate of mismatched bits [8]. It can be combined as an approximate estimate of the bit error probability.

$$BER = \frac{\text{no. of mismatched bit}}{\text{total length of hash}} \qquad (11.5)$$

11.5 Related Work

Primitive image hashing are usually based on color features, histogram, Discrete Cosine Transform (DCT), Discrete Wavelet Transform (DWT), Fourier Transform etc.

Tang et al. developed a perceptual hashing function based on invariant moments [13]. They convert the input image into a normalized image. The invariant moments were extracted from each component of the color spaces and were used to form the image hash, i.e. concatenate all the invariant moment. This method was found to be less robust against rotation attack of larger angle. In [14], Tang et al. later developed another hash method based on color features. They extracted the color features of the input image after resizing it to a standard size and obtained a color feature vector. Sahana and Veena developed a hashing techniques based on color features [15]. The input image was divided into non-overlapping blocks. Mean was calculated for each block. All the means were considered as an extracted feature. The extracted features were then quantized to form an intermediate hash value. The intermediate hash value was compressed and encrypted by the traditional cryptographic hash function SHA-1. The output of the encryption forms the hash value. Tang et al. introduced another hashing based on color vector angle [16]. It has got high computational cost as angles were calculated between the reference pixel and the remaining pixel.

Choi and Jung Park proposed an image hashing scheme based on hierarchical histogram [17]. It hierarchically changes the width of the bins by merging several bins and empowers a weighting factor into the hash at each level. The proposed method was found to be robust againstattacks like noise additions, rotation and cropping attacks, but still shows weakness to histogram equalization attack. Setyavan and Timotius developed a perceptual hashing method based on local histogram of oriented gradients [18]. The local histogram of oriented gradient descriptor using orientation bins was calculated. The descriptors were then normalized into six cells and only the innermost cell was selected for further processing. Tang et al. proposed a technique based on multiple histograms [19]. The input image was converted into a square image by bi-cubic interpolation. The square image was blurred by a Gaussian low pass filter. The blurred image was further converted into YCbCr followed by histogram equalization. The histogram equalized image was divided into several rings. Histograms were calculated for each ring and 1D DWT was applied to the generated histograms. The low frequency component obtained after DWT was divided into two segments and variance was computed for each segment. All the variances were concatenated to generate the hash value. They considered L2 norm similarity matrix as a distance metric for comparing the hash values.

Tang et al. generated a hash value by combiningcolor vector angle with DWT [20], the color vector angle was calculated between the RGB vector and the reference point. The matrix formed by the color vector angle was divided into non overlapping blocks. Another matrix was formed by calculating the mean of each block. A single level 2D DWT was applied to the newly formed matrix and the coefficients in the lowest level sub-band were selected as the lowest level sub-band contains most information of the input matrix. These coefficients were randomly permuted using a secret key to finally generate the hash value. Later, Tang et al. developed another image hashing based on weighted three level DWT. At each level, DWT was applied on non-overlapping blocks of images. However, the method is less resistant to rotation attack due to block processing.

Jie [21] tried to integrate the color histogram and low frequency DCT coefficients as perceptual features for the image. The input image was divided into 64 blocks, and color histograms were calculated for each block and at the same time, DC coefficients and 7 AC coefficients were selected from each block. These two features were then compressed using Principal Component Analysis (PCA) to form the final hash value. Image hash function based on Dominant DCT was proposed by Tang et al. [22]. The luminance component was extracted and divided into non overlapping block of size 64×64. DCT was applied to each block and the first row of DC coefficient was generated to form the feature matrix. These coefficients were then compressed to form the final hash value.

In [23], the input image was resized and converted into YCbCr. A Low Rank Representation (LRR) was applied to the luminance component of the image to generate a low rank feature matrix. The final hash value was generated by encryption and compression of DWT coefficients generated after applying DWT to the low rank feature matrix from LRR.Davarzani et al. proposed image hashing based on the Local Binary Pattern (LBP) [24]. Neelima and Manglem developed an image hash function [25] based on Scale Invariant Feature Transform (SIFT), which was later extended for generating hash value from videos [26]. Khalid et al. had proposed an image hashing using Quaternion Polar Complex Exponential Transform (QPCET) moments [27]. Both global and local features were extracted as hash value in the hashing function proposed by Ram et al. [28]. However, the method fails to detect small tampering in the images.Chuanet. al. developed a hash function based on texture and structure features [29]. Textual features and structural featured were extracted from DCP coded maps and sampled blocks with richest corner respectively. Ding et al. developed a hash function for integrity authentication [30] of High Resolution Remote Sensing image. The method wasbased on edge feature and PCA. Ghardeet. al. proposed an image hash function based on fuzzy color histogram [31]. CIE L*a*b* color space was used for generating the histogram.

Many issues are still unresolved, even though various perceptual hash function has been developed in the recent years. Many of the functions can't resist image rotation attack and there is less visibility between robustness and discrimination. A tradeoff is required between discrimination and robustness.

11.6 Proposed Method

Figure 11.5 illustrates the block diagram of the proposed hashing method. It consists of a pre-processing stage and feature extraction based on ordinal pattern. Detailed algorithm for the proposed image hashing is provided in A1.

11.6.1 Pre-processing

An input image is resized to a standard size $m \times m$ using bilinear interpolation. The resized image is then converted into aYCbCrcolor plane, if the input image is greyscale. Luminance component (Y) is then extracted for further processing. Y is passed through a low pass Gaussian filter to remove the noise.

Fig. 11.5 Block diagram of
proposed hash function

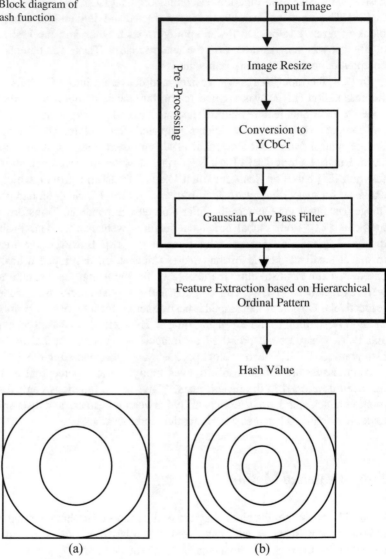

Fig. 11.6 Hierarchical ring generation: (**a**) $i = 1$ and (**b**) $i = 2$

11.6.2 Feature Extraction

The filtered image is then partitioned into rings for feature extraction. Ring processing will be used instead of block processing thereby making it more robust against rotation attack. Ordinal pattern is extracted from each ring in hierarchical manner.

Figure 11.6 depicts how the rings are generated hierarchically. At each level i, The number of ring nr is calculated as 2^i, where, $1 \leq i \leq n$. n can be any positive integer. Average color intensity of each ring is then considered for generation of Ordinal Pattern. All the Ordinal pattern generated from each level is then concatenated to form the final hash value.

A1: Algorithm

Input: Image I, $l=$ no. of level
Output, Hash value HV

Steps:

1. Resize the image to standard size, $M \times M$ to generate RI
2. Convert RI into YCbCr color plane and extract the Luminance component (Y), if RI is in color scale, otherwise set $Y = RI$.
3. Pass Y through a Gaussian low pass filter
4. Repeat step 5–9 for $i = 1$ to l,
5. Initialize number of rings, $n = 2^i$, radius of largest, $r_{ni} = M/2$, center pixel, $x_c = \lceil M/2 \rceil$, $y_c = \lceil M/2 \rceil$.
6. Area of the inscribed circle, $A' = \pi r^2$
7. Area of each concentric ring, $A = \lfloor A'/n \rfloor$ and radius of the first ring at level i, $r_{1i} = \sqrt{A/\pi}$
8. For $j = 2$ to $n - 1$, determine the radius of jth ring at level i

$$r_{ji} = \sqrt{\left(A + \pi r_{(j-1)i}^2\right)/\pi}$$

9. Calculate the average intensity of the pixels present in each concentric ring and assign them a rank depending on the average value. Obtain a pattern code P_i from each the rank assigned to each concentric ring at level i.
10. Concatenate all the Pattern code to form the final hash value. $HV = [P_1 P_2 \ldots \ldots P_l]$.

11.7 Experimental Result

To validate the proposed hash function, the method was tested using various standard color images such as Lena, Airplane, Baboon, Barbara, Goldhill, Pepper etc. Each image was resized to a standard size of 512×512. Each image was hierarchically partitioned into rings and ordinal pattern were generated to form the final hash value of length 127 integer (at level $i = 6$).

Table 11.1 Parameter values for geometric attacks

Attacks	Parameters description	Parameters value
Impulse noise	Impulse noise ratio	0.1, 0.2, 0.3, 0.4, 0.5
Median filter	Window size	2, 3, 4, 5
Scaling	Scaling factor	0.3, 0.2, 1, 2, 3
Rotation	Angle in degree	−30, −20, 20, 30, 50
Sharpening	Sharpening value, alpha	0.1, 0.2, 0.3, 0.4, 0.5
Gamma correction	Gamma value	0.5, 0.1, 0.2, 1, 1.5, 2

11.7.1 Perceptual Robustness

To evaluate the perceptual robustness of the proposed hash function, various geometric attacks such as rotation, sharpening, scaling, Gamma Correction etc. were performed on the images. Table 11.1 gives the detailed parameters used for various attacks.

Canberra distance was then calculated between the hash value generated from the original image and attacked image. Canberra distance can be calculated using the following equation.

$$Distance = \frac{|H1 - H2|}{|H1| + |H2|} \tag{11.6}$$

where, $H1$ and $H2$ are hash value of original image and attacked image respectively.

Figure 11.7 show some of the standard images used. Figure 11.8 show the results of various attack on five standard color images (Airplane, Baboon, Barbara, Lena and Pepper).

It is observed that, the distance between the hash value generated from the original image and attacked images is very less (less than 0.03). Thus, the proposed hash function is robust against the geometric attack.

Distance between the hash value obtained from original image and various attacks are shown in Table 11.2.

It can be clearly observed that, the maximum distance obtained after applying various geometrical attacks is found to be very minimal. Thus, the perceptually similar images can be identified as identical images with high accuracy.

11.7.2 Discriminative Capability

Fifty perceptually different images were considered for validating the discriminative capability of the proposed method. The size of the image ranges from 64 × 64 to 1024 × 1024. Hash values were generated from these images and difference between the generated hash values were calculated leading to a total of 2450 differ-

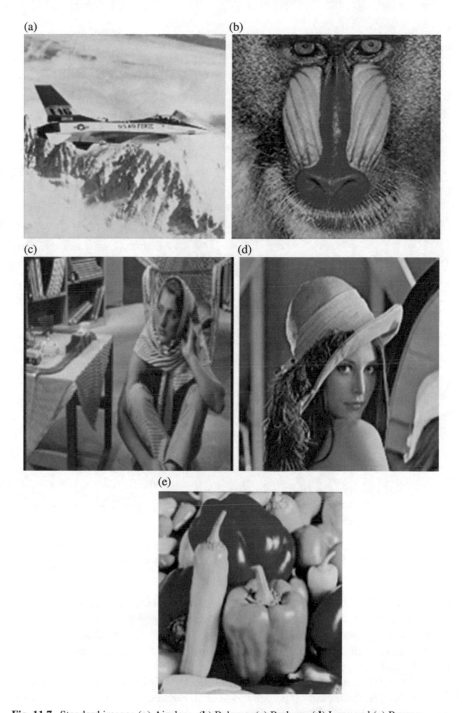

Fig. 11.7 Standard images (**a**) Airplane, (**b**) Baboon, (**c**) Barbara, (**d**) Lena and (**e**) Pepper

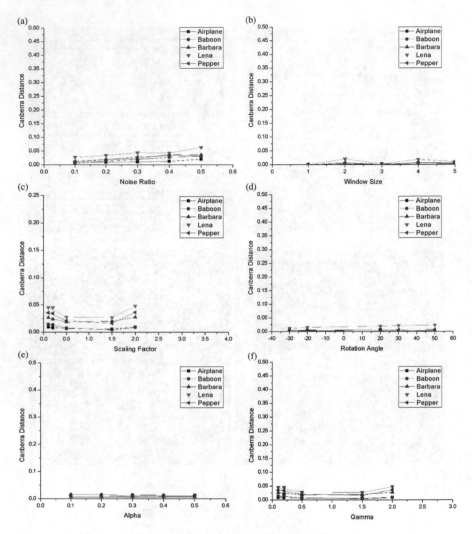

Fig. 11.8 Results for different attacks on five standard images: (**a**) Impulse noise, (**b**) Median filter, (**c**) Scaling, (**d**) Rotation, (**e**) Sharpening and (**f**) Gamma correction

ences. Inter hash statistics are calculated from the normalized Hamming distances between hash values of perceptually different images to represent the discriminative capability. There should be a healthy difference between the maximum intra hash distance and minimum inter hash distance so that perceptually different videos can be distinguished properly.

Figure 11.9a gives the histogram of the normalized frequencies of the Hamming distance derived from pairs of perceptually similar images and Fig. 11.9b gives the histogram of the normalized frequencies of the Hamming distance derived from pairs of different images. It can be observed from Fig. 11.9 that, a threshold value

Table 11.2 Distance between the hash values of original and attacked images

Attack	Maximum distance	Minimum distance	Average distance
Impulse noise	0.06	0.007	0.026
Median filter	0.02	0.001	0.006
Scaling	0.01	0	0.002
Rotation	0.02	0.0009	0.005
Sharpening	0.01	0.0006	0.008
Gamma correction	0.09	0.0005	0.027

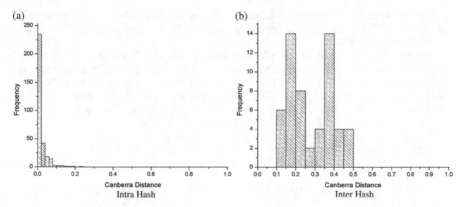

Fig. 11.9 Normalized histogram

Table 11.3 Details of the distance obtained between the hash values

Type	Maximum	Minimum	Average
Inter hash	0.4661	0.1021	0.27875
Intra hash	0.099	0	0.01597

can be selected from the range [0.03, 0.1] to distinguish perceptually similar and dissimilar images. The histogram of intra hash distance lies completely below the threshold range and the histogram of inter hash lies completely above the threshold range, which indicates that the proposed method is robust against all the geometrical attacks under consideration and at the same time capable of discriminating perceptually different videos.

Details of the maximum distance, minimum distance and average distance, which were obtained are shown in Table. 11.3.

11.8 Conclusion

Many image hashing functions were proposed in literature by different authors for authenticating the multimedia data. These techniques were robust against various geometric attacks but also associated with issues like large hash value, less discriminative capability etc.The proposed hashing function is quite robust to geometric attacks such as impulse noise, rotation, sharpening, Gamma correction, scaling etc. In future work, the hierarchical ordinal pattern can be combined with some temporal information for video hashing.

References

1. Stalling, W. (2006). *Cryptography and Network Security* (4 Edition). Pearson Education: India.
2. Canova, B. (2011). *A Survey of Security Mechanisms to Verify the Integrity and Authenticity of Multimedia–based Data.*
3. Damgård, I. (1990). A design principle for hash functions. In *LNCS, CRYPTO*, 435: 416–427.
4. Xiaoyun, W., Xuejia, L., Dengguo, F., Hui, C. and Xiuyuan, Y. (2005). Cryptanalysis of the Hash Functions MD4 and RIPEMD. *Advances in Cryptology – Eurocrypt*, 3494: 1–18.
5. Hans, D. (1996). Cryptanalysis of MD4. *Fast Software Encryption*, 1039: 53–69.
6. Yuliang, Z., Josef, P. and Jennifer, S. (1993). HAVAL – A One Way Hashing Algorithm with Variable Length of Output. *Advances in Cryptology*, 718: 83–104.
7. Ben–Gal, I., Herer, Y. and Raz, T. (2003). Self–correcting inspection procedure under inspection errors. *IIE Transactions on Quality and Reliability*, 34(6): 529–540.
8. David, S. and Gayathree, K. (2014). A comparative study of various correcting code. *IJCMSC*, 3(8): 196–200.
9. Rivest, R., Shamir, A. and Adleman, L. (1978). A Method for Obtaining Digital Signatures and Public–Key Cryptosystems. *Communications of the ACM*, 21(2): 120–126.
10. Coppersmith, D. (1994). The Data Encryption Standard (DES) and its strength against attacks at the Wayback Machine. *IBM Journal of Research and Development*, 38(3): 243–250.
11. Kekre, H.B. and Mishra, D. (2011). Content based image retrieval using weighted Hamming distance image hash value. *Think Quest,* DOI https://doi.org/10.1007/978–81–8489–989–4_53.
12. Wang, L., Zhang, Y. and Feng, J. (2005). On the Euclidean distance of images. *IEEE transactions on Patttern analysis and machine intelligence*, 27(8): 1334–1339.
13. Tang, Z., Dai, Y. and Zhang, X. (2012). Perceptual hashing for color images using invariant moments. *Applied Math. Inf. Sci.* 6(2): 643S–650S.
14. Zhenjun, T., Xianquan, Z., Xuan, D., Jianzhong, Y. and Tianxiu, W. (2013). Robust Image Hash Function using local color features. *Int. J. Electron. Comm. (AEU)*, 67(8): 717–722.
15. Sahana, M.S. and Veera, S.K. (2015). Analysis of Perceptual hashing system for Secure and Robust hashing. *IRJET*, 2(3): 26–30.
16. Tang, Z., Li, X., Zhang, X., Zhang, S. and Dai, Y. (2018). Image hashing with color vector.*Neurocomputing*. 308: 147-158.
17. Choi, Y. S. and Park, J.H. (2012). Image hash generation method using hierarchical histogram. *Multimedia Tools and Applications, Springer*, 61(1): 181–194.
18. Setyawan, I. and Timotius, I.K. (2014). Digital Image hashing using local Histogram of Oriented Gradients. In *Proc. International Conference on Information Technology and Electrical Engineering (ICITEE)*, October 7–8, 2014, pp. 1–4.
19. Tang, Z., Huang, L., Dai, Y. and Yang, F. (2012). Robust Image Hashing Based on Multiple Histograms. *International Journal of Digital Content Technology and its Applications*, 6(23): 39–47.
20. Tang, Z., Dai, Y., Zhang, X., Huang and Yang, F. (2014). Robust image hashing via colour vector angles and DWT. *Image Processing, IET*, 8(3): 142–149.
21. Jie, Z. (2013). A novel block DCT and PCA based image perceptual hashing algorithm. *International Journal of Computer Science Issues*, 10(1): 399–403.

22. Tang, Z.,Yang, F., Huang, L. and Zhang, X. (2014). Robust image hashing with dominant DCT co–efficients, *Optik*, 125(18): 5102–5107.
23. Liu, H., Xiao, D., Xiao, Y. and Zhang, Y. (2015). Robust image hashing with tampering recovery capability via low rank and sparse representation. *Multimedia Tools and Application*, 74: 1–16.
24. Davarzani, R., Mozaffri, S. and YashmaieKh. (2015). Image authentication using LBP based perceptual image hashing. *Journal of AI and Data Mining*, 3(1): 20–29
25. Neelima, A. and Manglem, Kh. (2016). Perceptual Hash Function based on Scale Invariant Feature Transform and Singular Value Decomposition. *The Computer Journal.* 59 (9): 1275-1281
26. Neelima, A. and Manglem, Kh. (2017). Collusion and Rotation Resilient Video Hashing based on Scale Invariant Feature Transform. *The Imaging Science Journal.* 65 (1): 62-74
27. Khalid, M.H., Yasmeen, M.K., Walid, I.K. and Ehab, R.M. (2018). Robust Image hashing using quaternion Polar Complex Exponential Transform for Image Authentication. *Circuit System Signal Process.* https://doi.org/10.1007/s00034-018-0822-8
28. Ram, K.K., Arunav, S. and Rabul, H.L. (2018). Image Authentication based on robust image hashing with geometric corrections. *Multimedia Tools Application.* 77(19): 25409- 25429.
29. Chuana, Q., Xueqin, C, Xiangyang, L, Xinpeng, Z. and Xingming, S. (2018). Perceptual image hashing via dual-cross pattern encoding and salient structure detection. Information Sciences 423: 284-302.
30. Ding, K., Meng, F., Liu, Y., Xu, N., and Chen, W. (2018). Perceptual Hashing Based Forensics Scheme for the Integrity Authentication of High Resolution Remote Sensing Image. Information, 9(9): 229-246.
31. Gharde, N.D., Thounaojam, D.M., Soni, B. (2018). Robust perceptual image hashing using fuzzy color histogram, Multimedia Tools and Application. 77: 30815 https://doi.org/10.1007/s11042-018-6115-1

Chapter 12
Hash Function Based Optimal Block Chain Model for the Internet of Things (IoT)

Andino Maseleno, Marini Othman, P. Deepalakshmi, K. Shankar, and M. Ilayaraja

12.1 Introduction

Internet of Things (IoT) is a type of network that is being utilized by wireless sensor associations and radio frequency identification (RFID) via network topology [1] to accomplish high reliability in transmission as well as intelligent processing [2]. IOT comprises three layers: the sensing layer, transport layer, and application layer. IOT has made a tremendous change in different areas such as business, agriculture, pharmacy, also in nuclear reactors [3]. To receive the IoT innovation, it is important to assemble the certainty among the clients about its security and privacy that it won't make any risk to their data integrity and authority [4]. In secure systems, the secrecy of the information is kept up, and it is ensured that at the processing of message exchange the information holds its inventiveness and no modification by the system [5]. Although the IoT can encourage the digitization of the data itself, the dependability of such data is as yet a key challenge by Bitcoin [6]. It's upheld by a protocol that points of interest the infrastructure responsible for guaranteeing that the data remains unchanging after some time [7]. Benefiting from blockchains power and versatility, in this work, propose an effective decentralized verification system [8]. The principle motivation behind network security data insurance is to accomplish secrecy as well as integrity. Security issues are of extraordinary significance in amplifying the size of network and gadgets [9]. Different cryptographic algorithms have been produced that tends to the said issue.

A. Maseleno (✉) · M. Othman
Institute of Informatics and Computing Energy, Universiti Tenaga Nasional, Kajang, Malaysia
e-mail: andino@uniten.edu.my; marini@uniten.edu.my

P. Deepalakshmi · K. Shankar (✉) · M. Ilayaraja
School of Computing, Kalasalingam Academy of Research and Education, Krishnankoil, Tamil Nadu, India
e-mail: deepa.kumar@klu.ac.in; ilayaraja.m@klu.ac.in

© Springer Nature Switzerland AG 2019
A. K. Singh, A. Mohan (eds.), *Handbook of Multimedia Information Security: Techniques and Applications*, https://doi.org/10.1007/978-3-030-15887-3_12

However, their use in IoT is questionable as the equipment we deal in the IoT is not appropriate for the execution of computationally costly encryption algorithms [10].

A blockchain is a database that stores every processed transaction—or information—in the subsequent request, in an arrangement of PC recollections that are carefully designed to foes. All users then share these exchanges by Minoli et al. in 2018 [11], More significantly, we talk about, how blockchain, which is the basic innovation for bitcoin, can be a key empowering agent to tackle numerous IoT security issues by Minhaj Ahmad Khan and Khaled Salah in 2018 [12]. It's additionally distinguished open research issues and difficulties for IoT security. One of the real issues of a clustering protocol is choosing an optimal group of sensor nodes as the group heads to isolate the network by Bennani et al. 2012 [13]. In any case, optimum clustering is an NP-Hard issue and solving it includes searches through large spaces of conceivable solutions. Two major periods of optimization, exploration, and exploitation, are structured by the social interaction of dragonflies in exploring, hunting foods, and keeping away from foes while swarming powerfully or factually by Mirjalili in 2015 [14]. In Emanuel Ferreira Jesus et al. in 2018 [15] the ideas about the structure and task of Blockchain and, mostly, investigate how the utilization of this innovation can be utilized to give security and privacy in IoT.

12.2   Security Issues in IoT Multimedia Information

Security approaches that depend greatly on encryption are not a solid match for these constrained gadgets since they are not equipped for performing complex encryption and decryption rapidly enough to have the capacity to transmit information safely in a progressive manner [16]. Some security challenges in IoT security are tag attack, Sybil attack, wormhole attack and, etc. [17–20]. Regardless, with traditional encryption procedures, before dealing with some sensitive data from customers, the third party administration (cloud) would decrypt this information and after that find that data [21–23]. Data that is very sensitive to bank account details, usernames, passwords need to encrypt with at least two-factor authentication procedures to guarantee security [24–26]. For enhancing the security in IoT data, BC is utilized. Now, the header turns out to be a piece of a cryptographic riddle which must be comprehended by the block chain's network of clients via a trial and error procedure, from trillions of opportunities—before it is included to the blockchain.

12.3   Methodology for IoT Information Security

The IoT visualizes a completely associated world, where things can convey estimated information and connect with one another. For enhancing the security dimension of the multimedia data's in IoT, optimal Block Chain (BC) security model is utilized, Its behinds the bitcoin concept a permanent open record of data secured by a network of distributed members, its strategy that to enables exchanges to be confirmed by a gathering of untrustworthy on-screen characters. The fundamental of this proposed strategy is, enhance the secrecy as well as the reliability of the IoT data, Moreover, this BC, every block contains the number of transactions. For every transaction, the parameters are stored in the neighborhood BC. The objective of optimization (DA) in this safe procedure is, to select the group Head for IoT data. CH would have coordinate proof about CH if it confirmed a block created by different squares of data. The details of optimal CH with BC mechanisms explained in the below section.

12.3.1   Security and Privacy Analysis in IoT

Security in IoT is difficult because of low asset abilities of the vast majority of devices, huge scale, heterogeneity among the gadgets, and absence of standardization. Besides, a considerable lot of these IoT gadgets gather and offer a lot of information from our own spaces, in this way opening up noteworthy privacy concerns. Security and privacy risk analysis for a commonplace shrewd home engineering that depends on existing and promptly available market IoT gadgets and stages. As opposed to existing security and threat investigation of IoT situations, we focus on a genuine IoT smart home condition sent in our tested concentrating on the interactions among the diverse IoT parts.

12.3.2   IoT Information Generation

The new invention of IoT and multimedia data applications is necessary to address specific business solutions which require needs, for example, predictive maintenance, loss prevention, asset utilization, inventory tracking, disaster planning, and recovery, downtime minimization, energy usage optimization, device performance effectiveness. These datasets are particular in information structures, volume, get to procedures, and some unusual perspectives; they can scarcely be stored and gotten as well, its shows in Fig. 12.1. IoT applications have quite certain qualities; they produce extensive volumes of data and require network and power for significant time periods.

12.3.3   Pre-Processing

This underlying preprocessing IoT data are separated to choose the sensitive or quality information for security, the purpose behind preprocessing is diminishing the computational time. Moreover, the goal is to ensure strong security and improve

Fig. 12.1 IoT components

the performance of the model, and we secure sensitive data only. IoT data clustering using optimization Information is clustered by utilizing irregular clustering model with optimization. The weights of its cluster associations assess each data. Finally, among various nodes and as indicated by their weights a node is elected as the cluster head, for optimal cluster head selection dragonfly optimization is proposed. Finally, among various nodes and as shown by their information a node is elected as the cluster head.

12.3.4   Dragonfly Optimization Algorithm

The primary objective of any swarm is survival, so all of the individuals should be attracted towards food sources and distracted outward enemies. Considering these two behaviors, there are five main factors in position in swarms. This optimization technique based on the exploration and exploitation phases for cluster head selection for security model.

The primary goal of any swarm is survival, so the majority of the individuals ought to be pulled in towards food sources and distracted outward enemies. Considering these two behaviors, there are five principle factors in position updating of individuals in swarms, and this is done based on the exploration and exploitation phases for cluster head selection for security model.

12.3.4.1   Behavior of Dragonflies

The behavior of dragonflies can be composed as the combination of five stages, in particular, separation, alignment, cohesion, attraction towards a food source and distraction outwards an enemy.

12.3.4.2   Objective Function

To estimate the fitness of a solution, it is essential to design a target function to quantify the execution of every solution. In this part, the target work is figured as:

$$objective = \max(accuracy) \tag{12.1}$$

12.3.4.3   Updating New Cluster Head

Separation: Alludes to the static collision shirking of the individuals from other individuals in the area. *Alignment:* On account of the velocity matching of each dragonfly in the specific area, alignment is done. *Cohesion:* Cohesion implies the tendency of individuals towards the point of convergence of the mass of neighborhood; it's trailed by beneath conditions.

$$New\ centriod_{t+1} = (a_1 S_i + a_2 A_i + a_3 C_i + a_4 F_i + a_5 E_i) + w_i\ centroid_t \tag{12.2}$$

By the use of optimization strategy, distinctive explorative and exploitative behaviors can be accomplished. When there is no neighboring solution, the location of dragonflies is updated by methods for a random walk (Levy flight). For updating the position of the above equation, using the behavioral procedure that is

$$\textbf{Separation}\ \ S_i = \sum_{k=1}^{N} C - C_k \tag{12.3}$$

$$\textbf{\textit{Alignment}}:\ \ A_i = \frac{\sum_{k=1}^{N} V_k}{N} \tag{12.4}$$

$$\textbf{\textit{Cohesion}}:\ \ C_i = \frac{\sum_{k=1}^{N} C_k}{N} - C \tag{12.5}$$

$$\textbf{\textit{Attraction towards a food Source}}:\ \ Food_i = C^+ - C \tag{12.6}$$

$$Distraction\ outwards\ an\ enemy: \quad Enemy_i = C^- + C \quad\quad (12.7)$$

Based on the above condition, the term C indicates the current position of the individual C_k denotes the position of a k-th individual, N is the total number of neighboring individual in the search space. Alignment of dragonflies occurs dependent on the velocity V coordinating of individuals to that of different individuals in the area and a_1, a_2, a_3, a_4 and a_5 coefficient parameters. After the alignment procedure of individuals among the dragonflies, cohesion process is performed which implies the inclination of individuals towards the focal point of the mass of the area. The new position refreshed by utilizing the following condition

$$C_{t+1} = C_t + Levy\,(distance) * C_t \quad\quad (12.8)$$

Food source and the enemy is selected over best and the most exceedingly terrible solutions obtained in the whole swarm at any minute. In light of above process choose optimal cluster head for IoT data clustering model. After that, the clustered data are secured by utilizing the BC technique.

12.3.5 Security Model: A Blockchain Model

In a BC, each transaction in the set that contains a block is hashed to produce a hash value. Hashes are combined into a Merkle Tree. Generally, the BC indicated a consistently maintained and controlled database considering developing variables and gathered information test sets. The key components of BC are a member made transactions and the recorder blocks of such exchanges. Here, the block checks whether transaction details were sustained in the correct grouping or not and this does not permit any altering of the data accessible.

12.3.5.1 Bitcoin

Bitcoin is cryptographic money and a digital payment system, in view of a public BC, each block of the Bitcoin blockchain. In Bitcoin, transactions are processed to check their integrity, authenticity, and accuracy by a gathering of creative network nodes called "Miners." Specifically, rather than mining a single transaction, the miners package various transactions that are waiting for the network to get processed in a single unit called "block."

12.3.5.2   Blockchain Hash Function

A cryptographic hash function maps the data of arbitrary size to a settled size string. A cryptographic hash function is a precise mapping for which it is computationally difficult to find a data object that maps to a given hash result or to find two information protests that map to a similar hash result. The yield of this hashing procedure is added to the block's header, along with a hash of the previous block's header and a timestamp. The new header is a contribution to a cryptographic procedure to create a nonce, and this hash function appears in Fig. 12.2. Normal employment of hashing is one-path to secure PC passwords retained in storage or to deliver cryptographic condensations of IoT data. The procedure of blockchain is characterized in the following condition (12.9).

Encryption
Encryption system function as given a message and a key, it creates a ciphered message to be transmitted over unprotected channels, without any risk being comprehended by other people who don't have the decryption key. For the security purpose, the key generation dependent on the two sets, one public and one private. The first to encrypt and the second to decrypt and the vice versa; this is conceivable because of the utilization of some mathematical functions that have the property of being irreversible.

For encrypted and decrypted information

$$Enc = hash \ (info \ group, hash, publickey, IP) \qquad (12.9)$$

Each block of data encrypted by $E \Rightarrow m^k \ | \ \mathrm{mod} \inf o \ | \qquad (12.10)$

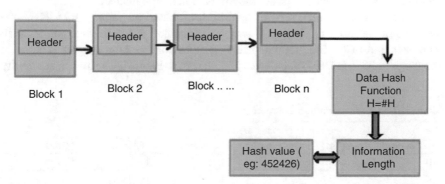

Fig. 12.2   Hash function model

Encrypted data are decrypted by $D \Rightarrow \left(\left(m^k \right) \mid \bmod \ \inf o(E) \mid \right) * Private\ key$

$$(12.11)$$

Hash function proficiently changes over a finite input string to an output string with a fixed length known as hash value. Based on this value, the IoT multimedia information is secured by the end to end BC mechanism, the private keys with restricted randomness can be exploited to compromise the BC accounts. Helpful mechanisms yet should be characterized to guarantee the privacy of transactions at the same time avoid race attack.

12.4 Results and Analysis

Our proposed IoT, information security model, is executed in the Java programming language with the JDK 1.7.0 in a windows machine enclosing the configurations such as the Intel (R) Core i3 processor, 1.6 GHz, 4 GB RAM, and the operating system platform is Microsoft Window7 Professional. This proposed security analysis is compared with other techniques.

Table 12.1 shows the result of the proposed clustering model. Here we select the number of clusters based on the size of the database. We take the size of the database depends on kilobytes, for example, we choose 10–50 kb. For 10 kb, the proposed model achieves cluster 1 as 3, cluster 2 as 4, cluster 4 as 0 and cluster 5 as 3. Similarly, the other databases produce the best selection in the DOA model. The above-said procedures are visualized in below Fig. 12.4.

Table 12.2 and Fig. 12.3 shows the result of proposed parameters which obtains in the study. Depends on file size, we find encryption size, decryption size, memory and execution time. The result depicts that encryption size and decryption increases if the file size increased, the execution time also increased. But compared to other techniques proposed model secure the IoT data in a high manner.

Figure 12.4 shows the graph of security level based on some blocks. Here, we compare the security result with the proposed method to existing techniques such as bitcoin and ECC. The graph depicts that blockchain reaches optimal security in the range of 82–91.23% compared to the other two. Figure 12.5 shows the security

Table 12.1 Results for Proposed clustering analysis

Size of the database (kb)	Number of clusters (kb)			
	Cluster 1	Cluster 2	Cluster 4	Cluster 5
10	3	4	0	3
20	6	7	2	5
30	10	14	4	2
40	16	8	10	6
50	13	11	16	10

Table 12.2 Proposed (blockchain) Security analysis results

File size	Encryption size	Decryption size	Memory (byte)	Execution time (ms)
10	23	10	1,242,488	94,523
20	34	20	374,528	105,481
30	44	30	312,458	98,450
40	49	40	412,141	112,345
50	56	50	423,412	112,482

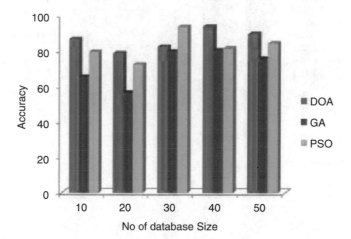

Fig. 12.3 Comparison of clustering accuracy

level based on the database size. The hash blockchain performs an optimal security level for every database size. The security level reaches a maximum at 90% in hash blockchain function.

12.5   Conclusion

In this chapter, the IoT multimedia information's security model with help hash function based blockchain was discussed. Like this, the advantages of applying BC to the IoT ought to be examined precisely and taken with caution. Also, this chapter provided an analysis of the main difficulties that blockchain and IoT must address for them to effectively cooperate. This blockchain technology can help to improve IoT applications and also this data clustering cluster head selection by DOA, and its give better accuracy. However, it is still in the beginning periods of creating block chains, and these obstructions will be defeated, opening the best approach to numerous potential outcomes. One of the principle concerns about blockchain, and especially cryptocurrencies, resides in its volatility which has also been exploited

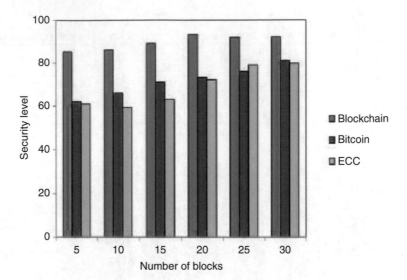

Fig. 12.4 Number of blocks Vs. hash value

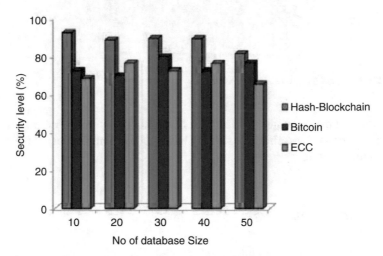

Fig. 12.5 Security Level comparative analysis

by individuals to take unfair advantage of this situation. The incorporation of the IoT and blockchain will extraordinarily increase the security level.

References

1. Alshehri, M.D., Hussain, F.K. and Hussain, O.K., 2018. Clustering-Driven Intelligent Trust Management Methodology for the Internet of Things (CITM-IoT). Mobile Networks and Applications, pp.1-13.
2. Safi, A., 2017. Improving the Security of the Internet of Things Using Encryption Algorithms. World Academy of Science, Engineering and Technology, International Journal of Computer, Electrical, Automation, Control and Information Engineering, 11(5), pp.546-549.
3. Lo'ai, A.T., and Somani, T.F., 2016, November. More secure Internet of Things using robust encryption algorithms against side channel attacks. In Computer Systems and Applications (AICCSA), 2016 IEEE/ACS 13th International Conference of (pp. 1-6). IEEE.
4. Sundaram, B.V., Ramnath, M., Prasanth, M. and Sundaram, V., 2015, March. Encryption and hash based security in internet of things. In Signal Processing, Communication and Networking (ICSCN), 2015 3rd International Conference on (pp. 1-6). IEEE.
5. Bhatia, S. and Patel, S., 2015. Analysis on different Data mining Techniques and algorithms used in IOT. Int. J. Eng. Res Appl, 2(12), pp.611-615.
6. Wang, C., Shen, J., Liu, Q., Ren, Y. and Li, T., 2018. A Novel Security Scheme Based on Instant Encrypted Transmission for Internet of Things. Security and Communication Networks, 2018.
7. Chhabra, A., Vashishth, V., Khanna, A., Sharma, D.K. and Singh, J., 2018. An Energy Efficient Routing Protocol for Wireless Internet-of-Things Sensor Networks. arXiv preprint arXiv:1808.01039.
8. Xingmei, X., Jing, Z. and He, W., 2013, October. Research on the basic characteristics, the key technologies, the network architecture and security problems of the internet of things. In Computer Science and Network Technology (ICCSNT), 2013 3rd International Conference on (pp. 825-828). IEEE.
9. Srinidhi, N.N., Kumar, S.D. and Venugopal, K.R., 2018. Network optimizations in the Internet of Things: A review. Engineering Science and Technology, an International Journal.
10. Reyna, A., Martín, C., Chen, J., Soler, E. and Díaz, M., 2018. On blockchain and its integration with IoT. Challenges and opportunities. Future Generation Computer Systems.
11. Minoli, D. and Occhiogrosso, B., 2018. Blockchain mechanisms for IoT security. Internet of Things, 1, pp.1-13.
12. Khan, M.A. and Salah, K., 2018. IoT security: Review, blockchain solutions, and open challenges. Future Generation Computer Systems, 82, pp.395-411.
13. Bennani, K. and El Ghanami, D., 2012, November. Particle swarm optimization based clustering in wireless sensor networks: the effectiveness of distance altering. In Complex systems (ICCS), 2012 international conference on (pp. 1-4). IEEE.
14. Mirjalili, S., 2016. Dragonfly algorithm: a new meta-heuristic optimization technique for solving single-objective, discrete, and multi-objective problems. Neural Computing and Applications, 27(4), pp.1053-1073.
15. Jesus, E.F., Chicarino, V.R., de Albuquerque, C.V. and Rocha, A.A.D.A., 2018. A Survey of How to Use Blockchain to Secure Internet of Things and the Stalker Attack. Security and Communication Networks, 2018.
16. K. Shankar, Mohamed Elhoseny, E. Dhiravida chelvi, SK. Lakshmanaprabu, Wanqing Wu, An Efficient Optimal Key Based Chaos Function for Medical Image Security, IEEE Access, November 2018. https://doi.org/10.1109/ACCESS.2018.2874026
17. Mohamed Elhoseny, K. Shankar, S. K. Lakshmanaprabu, Andino Maseleno, N. Arunkumar, Hybrid optimization with cryptography encryption for medical image security in Internet of Things, Neural Computing and Applications - Springer, October 2018. https://doi.org/10.1007/s00521-018-3801-x
18. Lakshmanaprabu SK, K. Shankar, Ashish Khanna, Deepak Gupta, Joel J. P. C. Rodrigues, Plácido R. Pinheiro, Victor Hugo C. de Albuquerque, "Effective Features to Classify Big Data using Social Internet of Things", IEEE Access, Volume.6, page(s):24196-24204, April 2018.

19. T. Avudaiappan, R. Balasubramanian, S. Sundara Pandiyan, M. Saravanan, S. K. Lakshmanaprabu, K. Shankar, Medical Image Security Using Dual Encryption with Oppositional Based Optimization Algorithm, Journal of Medical Systems, Volume 42, Issue 11, pp.1-11, November 2018. https://doi.org/10.1007/s10916-018-1053-z

20. K.Shankar and P.Eswaran. "RGB Based Multiple Share Creation in Visual Cryptography with Aid of Elliptic Curve Cryptography", China Communications, Volume. 14, Issue. 2, page(s): 118-130, February 2017.

21. Nur Aminudin, Andino Maseleno, K. Shankar, S. Hemalatha, K. Sathesh kumar, Fauzi, Rita Irviani, Muhamad Muslihudin, "Nur Algorithm on Data Encryption and Decryption", International Journal of Engineering & Technology, Volume. 7, Issue-2.26, page(s): 109-118, June 2018.

22. K. Shankar and P. Eswaran. "RGB Based Secure Share Creation in Visual Cryptography Using Optimal Elliptic Curve Cryptography Technique", Journal of Circuits, Systems, and Computers, Volume. 25, No. 11, page(s): 1650138-1 to 23, November 2016.

23. K. Shankar, Lakshmanaprabu S. K, "Optimal key based homomorphic encryption for color image security aid of ant lion optimization algorithm", International Journal of Engineering & Technology, Volume. 7, Issue. 9, page(s): 22-27, 2018.

24. K. Shankar and P.Eswaran. "A Secure Visual Secret Share (VSS) Creation Scheme in Visual Cryptography using Elliptic Curve Cryptography with Optimization Technique". Australian Journal of Basic and Applied Sciences. Volume: 9, Issue.36, Page(s): 150-163, 2015.

25. K. Sathesh Kumar, K. Shankar, M. Ilayaraja, M. Rajesh, "Sensitive Data Security in Cloud Computing Aid of Different Encryption Techniques", Journal of Advanced Research in Dynamical and Control Systems, Volume. 9, Issue. 18, page(s): 2888-2899, December 2017.

26. K. Shankar and P.Eswaran. "ECC Based Image Encryption Scheme with aid of Optimization Technique using Differential Evolution Algorithm", International Journal of Applied Engineering Research, Volume: 10, No.5, pp. 1841–184, 2015.

Chapter 13
An Adaptive and Viable Face Identification for Android Mobile Devices

Tehseen Mehraj, Burhan Ul Islam Khan, Rashidah F. Olanrewaju, Farhat Anwar, and Ahmad Zamani Bin Jusoh

13.1 Introduction

There has been a massive development in the field of mobile phones past 25 years as of which mobile phones are no longer used for just making call or texting. The advancement of computing power on mobile phone devices in terms of processing capabilities and storage led to their colossal approval among people for simplifying and speeding up different processes [12, 28, 29, 38–40]. Smartphones are being increasingly used for performing precarious and sensitive financial transactions apart from enjoying access to personal data. As per a study in [7], 82% of the population with age-group of 25–35 prefer mobile phones to perform their online banking transactions. This makes smart phones vulnerable to numerous contemporary threats as strong security solutions were not developed while considering devices with limited resources like mobile phones in mind [11, 35, 38, 39, 45]. As such, maintenance of privacy and security are significant issues for current users [1, 11, 17, 18, 22, 41, 52]. Apart from the existing security challenges, mobility also exposes the mobile phones to several additional risks. The mobile phones are susceptible to intentional or unauthorized physical access followed by stolen or missing mobile phones. Further, secure connectivity risks to unknown networks, phones or systems via Wi-Fi, Bluetooth or USB besides threats appearing from mobile operating systems and applications also persists. Furthermore, a variety of facilities exist like cloud technology, which aim at offering numerous services to its customers. However, the data sharing approach utilized by the cloud technology

T. Mehraj
Department of ECE, Islamic University of Science and Technology, Awantipora, Kashmir, India

B. Ul I. Khan (✉) · R. F. Olanrewaju · F. Anwar · A. Z. B. Jusoh
Department of ECE, Kulliyyah of Engineering, International Islamic University Malaysia, Kualalumpur, Malaysia

© Springer Nature Switzerland AG 2019
A. K. Singh, A. Mohan (eds.), *Handbook of Multimedia Information Security: Techniques and Applications*, https://doi.org/10.1007/978-3-030-15887-3_13

uncovers many flaws and hence results in its susceptibility to numerous attacks [21, 33, 37–39]. A need for such a security solution persists that is capable of delivering strong security without compromising user convenience [10, 13, 27, 55].

Numerous security schemes are available in the form of password-based and biometrics-based approaches which can be implemented either as a dedicated hardware device or require specially featured devices to operate, eventually proving inconvenient for users. Moreover, password-based approaches are widely used for managing access to present day digital services. People are required to manage multiple accounts each demanding them to remember specific credentials to enjoy the facilities. This eventually leads to the selection of easily memorable passwords, which can be easily exploited by intruders using numerous password hacking technologies while being vulnerable to dictionary and rainbow table attacks [2, 14, 15, 34, 36, 54]. Humans constitute the weakest link in any security mechanism, thus breaching the systems offering the highest security. Such human failures can be considerably reduced by using biometrics schemes. World Economic Forum (WEF) in a report [30], suggested that biometrics can be seen as a potential contender offering a strong, secure yet user adoptable solution in the financial sector.

Biometrics based schemes offer unparalleled user convenience since they offer advantages like universality, uniqueness, ease-of-use and permanence [19, 23, 46, 48]. With the rise of hardware as well as software capabilities on mobile phone devices, biometric solutions are being implemented on them. However, application of schemes exploiting fingerprint or facial features is limited merely to device unlocking. Such schemes deliver lower accuracy which impedes their adoption among users. Moreover, such systems can be breached at multiple points which involve vulnerability to smudge, replay and spoofing attacks [3, 5, 6, 8, 20, 24, 26, 42–44, 47, 50, 51]. Thus, biometrics can't be used alone as a basis to form a strong security system. Hence, integrating the biometric system with that of a non-biometric system will result in a much secure system offering strong security without compromising user convenience. Further, as per NIST recommendations, widely employed SMS based two-factor access management is no longer suggested [9, 31]. There exists a need to eradicate the dependency on additional insecure channels while stressing on implementing a security model on the mobile phone itself, offering security with continued existence while retaining user convenience. Combining biometrics with non-biometric security models will deliver results to reach this goal. For this purpose, proper selection of biometric trait followed by developing a feasible biometric scheme for mobile phones capable of handling realistic uncontrollable situations is desired.

13.2   Review Work

In [16], a face recognition scheme for Android platform entitled XFace has been proposed. The presented scheme has employed Local Binary Patterns-LBP for face detection followed by exploiting FisherFace and EigenFace algorithms for recognition. The region of interest algorithm has been considered to improve the accuracy of the overall system. However, a static and smaller dataset has been contemplated for training, which eventually leads to poor performance in real-world conditions.

In [4], heart sound has been considered as a biometric trait to achieve continuous access management. The proposed scheme has been developed for medical life support equipments. Body Area Network (BAN) technology has been incorporated to take precise information from heart sonic signals. However, continued authentication can't be achieved by the proposed system since humans' heartbeat condition changes with aging. Further, the system being implemented on BAN results in complex implementation hindering user adoptability while facing the risk of assault during data transmission.

The authors [12] presented a multimodal biometric scheme on mobile phones based on facial feature and iris. An additional step to safeguard against spoofing has been incorporated. However, acquisition of iris needs to be done in extremely controlled conditions besides calling for a high-resolution camera, which eventually impedes user adoptability.

In [32], a multimodal access management scheme founded by combining biometric and non-biometric approaches has been proposed. The system offers an enhanced user adoptability and security. However, the touch dynamics utilized in the scheme as biometric features requires high accuracy and performance, which is difficult to attain with mobile phones. Further, the schemes face threats due to touch-logger attacks.

The authors [54] have addressed two prime complications associated with implicit authentication. The first issue being the selection of best retaining frequency followed by the second issue, which concentrates on handling situations arising due to false negatives. The scheme aids in providing enhanced user experience. Privileges are being assigned to a user depending on their current behavior. Additionally, the scheme proves to be successful in handling authentications due to false negatives. However, evaluation on mobile phones has not been performed while at the same time weaker modalities have been considered by the system. Further, the presented scheme appears to be susceptible to sensor-sniffing, synthetic and timing attacks.

In [53], a scheme merging physiological and behavioral fingerprint has been proposed. Continuous transparent authentication is being offered during the complete process even in case of fingerprint loss. However, the scheme requires the user to retain the sequence for authentication which eventually hampers user acceptability. Further, for acquisition a primary sensor is necessary which comes under additional hardware requirements.

Face has emerged as a biometric trait to be manipulated in this study due to its higher acceptability among users; as it doesn't require any physical touch unlike fingerprints, while at the same time delivering higher performance than other biometric features [12, 25].

13.3 Problem Formulation

From the contemplation of numerous security schemes in the previous section, a lack of comprehensive or standard security scheme forming a feasible solution on mobile phones persists. Several weaknesses were identified from the review, ranging from user adoptability to computational complexity, to susceptibility to attacks. Some of the weaknesses identified (depicted in Fig. 13.10) are as follows:

1. *Additional hardware requirements*

Due to additional hardware needs (specially featured hardware, smart cards), reduced user adoptability perseveres [4, 12, 16].

2. *Processing power and storage constraints*

Conspicuous execution time and processing power exist [4, 32], hindering operation on mobile phones.

3. *Lack of realistic data sets*

Schemes like [16] train with static databases, which does not represent the actual data that one encounters in real life situations. These schemes claim increased accuracy; however when tested using a realistic dataset, the accuracy drops sharply. The quality of training dataset also plays a crucial role in the attainment of better performance.

4. *Rapid variation in behavioral biometrics*

Supreme user convenience is offered when considering behavioral biometrics [53, 54]. Nevertheless, the inverse behavior of user results in an abrupt drop in accuracy of such schemes.

5. *Susceptibility to attacks*

Schemes [4, 12, 32, 53] are unable to provide security against various contemporary threats including replay attacks, touch logger attack, timing and sensor sniffing attacks etc.

6. *Need for appropriate feature set selection in multi-modal systems*

Selection of proper biometric trait in case of multimodal schemes [12, 32] is a grave issue. Scheming a reliable security arrangement skilled in choosing suitable biometric set emerges as an open challenge.

7. *Need for standard performance evaluation on mobile platform*

On a mobile platform, a lack of benchmark exists since performance evaluation of schemes has not been conducted [16, 53, 54]. Thus, hindering the application of such systems on generic mobile phones (Fig. 13.1).

Thus, the study reveals that biometric solutions fail to operate in real life situations, which comprise dynamic backgrounds and varying face angles. The low

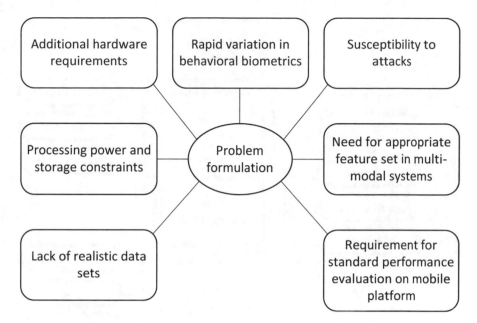

Fig. 13.1 Problem formulation

accuracy offered by such solutions results in the low user acceptance and limits their use in other security solutions. Precisely, the accuracy of the existing biometric security solutions is the prime reason which is holding them back. Therefore, it is evident that the identification accuracy has to be inspected and improved to deal with the real-world situations.

13.4   Methodology

The proposed system offers a much suitable solution than the earlier approaches by employing realistic data portraying the real-world conditions of varying lighting and face orientations. The system implements LBP for face detection known for it's high-speed together with eye detection modules enabling better results. Face detection stage is followed by a pre-processing step which eliminates or diminishes numerous issues like lighting, face angles and expressions affecting the face identification process in general. This stage involves usage of histogram equalization, background cropping followed by face alignment. These steps are performed not only to achieve better accuracy in real-world situations but also to provide data that requires minimal processing as the system considered is a resource-constrained device, i.e. mobile phone. The face alignment is achieved using flandmark library which offers better results in real life situation than the one obtained from the orientation of eyes. The cause behind is the flandmark, which uses

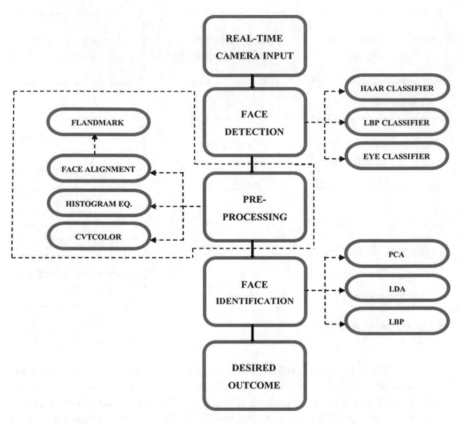

Fig. 13.2 Proposed system

several features of the face and considers the distance between them to conclude the results. Consequently, if one feature is missing, e.g. one eye than other features can be used to reach a decision. However, this is not the case if eye orientation approach is considered. Accordingly, in this study various feature extraction algorithms viz. local Binary Patterns (LBP), Principal Component Analysis (PCA) and Local Discriminant Analysis (LDA) related to the popular biometric trait, i.e. face has been implemented on the mobile phone device. The proposed work is implemented on an Android platform alongside utilizing the OpenCV framework and Flandmark library support. The proposed work has been built and tested on Android, which is gaining popularity among the users globally as compared to tablet PCs and other smart-phones. 87.9% of the market share is held by Android, which is highest than any other mobile OS's market shares [49].

The approach followed to achieve the objectives is discussed in the following section. Figure 13.2 reveals the general stages involved in the system. However, the complete process can competently be envisioned with the assistance of modules which have been described as follows.

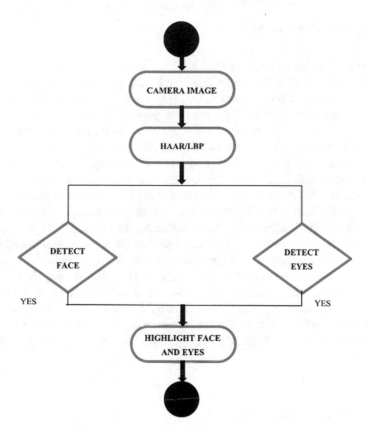

Fig. 13.3 Face detection module

13.4.1 Face Detection Module

The face detection modules perform the crucial step of detecting facial features while ignoring anything else like landscapes, objects, etc. The stage is concerned only about detecting a human face and its location. It doesn't concern with the identity of the user. Further, the face detection stage helps to eliminate the irrelevant information in the later stages to identify a person efficiently.

This module has implemented two distinctive approaches for face detection in the form of Haar based face detector and LBP based detector as displayed in Fig. 13.3. The system captures the live image in the form of frames, which are fed to the classifiers that conclude the face detection process by placing red coloured rectangle around the face. The eye classifier is applied in parallel to further improve the result by reducing the false positive detections indicated by drawing yellow rectangles around the detected eyes within the red rectangle.

13.4.2   Pre-Processing

Once the face has been detected within a frame, the processing of face within the red rectangle can be done in this stage. This step is performed so that the identification system will provide better accuracy. This step deals with diminishing factors like lighting condition and face orientation that primarily affects the accuracy rate. Further, this step is much needed so that the processing power of mobile devices is not overwhelmed, and real-time face identification can be attained.

The activities included in this stage include scaling, greyscale conversion, histogram equalization followed by face alignment. Scaling is required to reduce the amount of information to be processed to suit the processing capability of mobile phones by eliminating the irrelevant background information. Scaling to some extent also enables attaining images of standard size as the picture is not always taken from the same distance. The next sub-step involves greyscale conversion, where the additional colour information is eliminated to reduce the amount of information to be processed. This step is supported by the fact that the algorithms contemplated does not consider colour data. The following step uses histogram equalization, which reduces the variations of light in an image by standardizing the contrast and brightness. The next step involves face alignment to deal with different face orientations. These steps help to reduce the false positives in the system to a great extent.

13.4.3   Feature Extraction

This stage forms the core of the face identification module, by allowing it to acquire information from the image. The information obtained involves relevant data from the face image which constitutes the features, thus proving to be valuable during the identification phase. The various phases within this stage involve extraction followed by the selection of features. The feature extraction obtains the features by transforming the original data. While the feature selection deals with the selection of relevant or optimum feature subset from the input features set. A vital phenomenon called dimensionality reduction can be viewed as an outcome of these two sub-stages. Dimensionality reduction determines to a large extent the performance of the algorithms by reducing the number of features to be considered resulting in light and faster classifiers. If a large number of features are considered, it will lead to an increase in false positives when redundant features exist, eventually degrading performance. In this chapter, three algorithms are considered namely PCA (Principal Component Analysis), LDA (Linear Discriminant Analysis) and LBP (Linear Binary Patterns). These three approaches represent the mathematical procedure and form the statistical techniques from which the template is constructed and eventually stored in the database so that when an input image appears, it is compared with a stored template.

13.4.4   Prediction

This stage deals with face identification by comparing the similarity distance between the input image and the template. The Euclidean distance classifier is used because it is computationally less expensive and offers a simple solution. Euclidean distance attempts to measure the least distance between the input image and the template. The outcome is guarded by a threshold depicting the maximum allowable distance between the two. If the distance calculated exceeds the threshold, then the image is revealed as an unknown face else the identity of the person is revealed.

13.5   Design Implementation

The implementation details have been highlighted in this section including the necessary requirements and corresponding installations. For writing the Android application, the primary needs include: Android SDK, the Java Development Kit (JDK), an editor or an Integrated Development Environment for Android (Android Studio) for making the development process easier. Moreover, a plug-in for Android Studio in the form of Android Development Tools (ADT) is also necessary for providing added support. Further, installing OpenCV library version 3.1.0 successfully to the project is a prime concern, which comprises of optimized C++/C code whilst taking full advantage of multi-core processors, along with the (NDK)-Native Development Kit and JavaCV enabling the use of native class.

In Fig. 13.4, the flowchart of the system is presented. The Fig. 13.4 apart from capturing live camera feed indicates the face identification module, which keeps on updating the training set to make the scheme compatible over time. After grabbing a live frame from camera, the system checks whether the face is a known face or an unknown face. If the face is known, then the system will display the label associated with that face together with the ability to further train the system. On the contrary, if an unknown face is detected, the system will show an option for labelling such face and continue training as such.

The prototype application initially captures the frame from the camera, which will be used to display the camera preview on full screen followed by making rectangles around faces in each frame in upcoming stages. The final findings of this stage are highlighted by drawing a rectangle around the face detected and eyes as shown in Fig. 13.5 below.

The aim of adding eye detection is to decrease the number of false positives. When a face is detected by drawing a rectangle around it, if the eyes are detected as well within it then only the detection is considered valid. Otherwise, if only eyes are detected or more than two eyes are detected, it does not constitute a valid result.

The next phase involves applying the pre-processing steps to improve the accuracy of the system. To allow the system to run in a reasonable amount of time the information reduction needs to be done, which can be achieved by resizing the

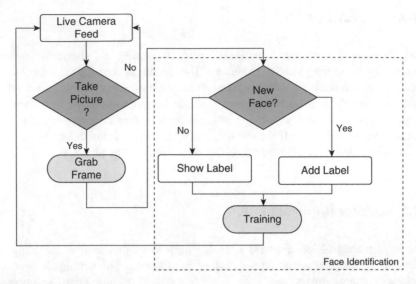

Fig. 13.4 System block diagram

Fig. 13.5 Face and eye detection module

image and by performing the grayscale conversion. Hence, reducing the amount of data to be processed to one-fourth as compared to coloured images. The image is scaled as a separate image of 200×150 resolution by counting pixel coordinates from bottom-left or top-left. Followed by grayscale conversion, which is followed by histogram equalization where lighting distortions are evenly confiscated.

Figure 13.6 highlights the pre-processing stage followed in the system. Then, the flandmark library is imported and applied on the image that passed through the various pre-processing stages. The flandmark is an open source library employing DPM (Deformable Parts Model), which contemplates numerous features and manipulates distances among them to identify other features once one of the features has been detected.

The landmarks hold the individual coordinates for face features such as nose, mouth and eyes. The face alignment is achieved by manipulating these coordinates. Then, the final image obtained from the pre-processing stage is labelled followed by Euclidean distance calculation and storing it in the internal application directory.

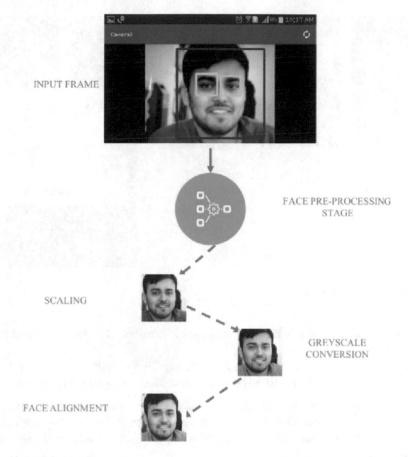

Fig. 13.6 Pre-processing stage

The face identification stage implements three algorithms namely PCA, LDA and LBP. Whenever, a new image inputs the system, the input images undergo all the above-mentioned stages, and its distance is calculated. If the distance calculated is within the threshold, then the label of the image having smallest distance is shown in output toast message along with the minimum face distance. Figure 13.7 highlights the identification process, which involves the enrollment phase where a label is being assigned to a new subject and training under varying environments. Further, once trained, the system returns the minimum distance to face space.

Concisely, the selection choice of algorithms together with the option of threshold values is provided in the navigation menu. Once the algorithm is chosen and the image has been taken, the particular algorithm runs and one of the four probable notifications are shown:

- Unknown Face: if the image is not close to any known face but close to face space

Fig. 13.7 Face identification

- Face detected with label: if the image is close to both the face class and face space.
- Image is not a face: if no face has been detected in the image
- False recognition: if the image is close to face class but apart from face space

The system keeps itself updated by adapting or training with the images, whenever a successful identification is made. Further, the maximum number of images for each subject is also customized which when exceeded, the oldest image of that subject gets deleted.

13.6 Result Evaluation

In this section, the performance evaluation of the proposed system is done. The evaluation approach begins with unit testing of face detection module providing performance and accuracy measures followed by system testing. The results obtained from unit testing of face detection module guides the selection of the detection approach to be followed by the system. Eventually, the system testing is performed by conducting experiments considering varying threshold levels and training dataset sizes.

Fig. 13.8 Face images in varying environments

13.6.1 Real Time Dataset

The face images considered for evaluating the system has been acquired in real-world conditions, which vary in lighting, direction of the light and shadows along with background and emotion of the person and so on, as shown in Fig. 13.8. A total of ten subjects have been considered for evaluating the system.

13.6.2 Analysis of Face Detection Module

The face detection module has considered two algorithms Haar and LBP along with usage of eye detection to decrease the false positives. The module is evaluated in terms of detection speed indicated in milliseconds (ms) followed by detection accuracy. A total of 256 test images acquired in real-time are utilised to evaluate the detection module; 128 test images for each algorithm. Five hardware devices were utilized for testing and analysis of the system. The respective devices and their configuration are mentioned in Table 13.1 below:

A graph for face detection module in Fig. 13.9 has been plotted by considering time in milliseconds (ms) and the respective average time for face and eye detection. From the graph, it is quite evident that the face detection module when integrating LBP for face detection consumes less time than the Haar approach. The face detection module takes 5 ms while employing LBP and 11 ms with Haar in place.

Table 13.1 Hardware
Configuration

Hardware	Configuration
Micromax canvas	1.3 GHz quad-core processor
	512 MB RAM
	Android OS-KitKat
Samsung Core 2	1.2 GHz quad-core processor
	768 MB RAM
	Android OS-KitKat
Samsung Prime J2	1.6 GHz octa-core processor
	3 GB RAM
	Android OS-nougat
Sony Xperia C3	1.2GHz quad-core processor
	1 GB RAM
	Android OS-lollipop
Sony Xperia XA1	1.6 GHz octa-core processor
	3 GB RAM
	Android OS nougat

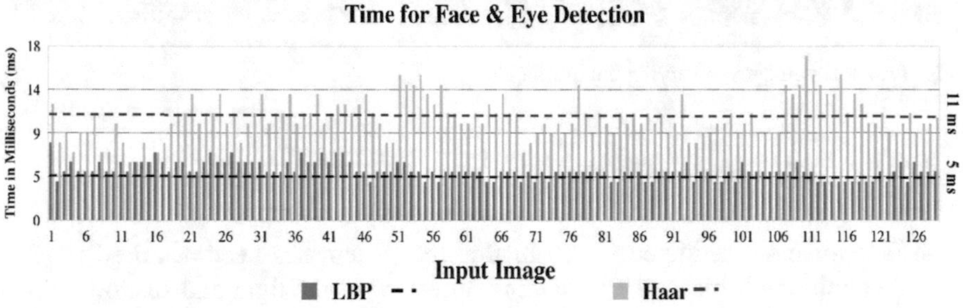

Fig. 13.9 Comparison between Haar and LBP

Table 13.2 Accuracy of
Haar and LBP

Algorithm	No face detected	Face detected
Haar	5	95
LBP	9	91

The reason for such behaviour exhibited by Haar can be understood by the fact that Haar implements 20 cascade stages. Furthermore, LBP performs manipulation of data in integers, resulting in faster processing rather than Haar involving double values.

Further, in order to evaluate the face detection module in terms of accuracy of detecting faces, 100 test images are utilised. The results obtained are tabulated in Table 13.2 highlighting Haar in achieving higher detection accuracy 95% than LBP 91%.

The accuracy of Haar indicated in Table 13.2 can be dedicated to the 20 cascade stages followed by it, unlike LBP which uses three cascade stages. In terms of accuracy, Haar detected more faces than LBP while LBP proved significantly

Table 13.3 Result analysis with varying threshold

Threshold	PCA			LDA			LBP		
	FA	FR	Correct	FA	FR	Correct	FA	FR	Correct
0.100	8	24	28	6	25	29	7	23	30
0.200	**9**	**19**	**32**	**7**	**17**	**36**	**8**	**15**	**37**
0.300	23	7	29	15	10	35	17	13	36
0.400	23	7	30	19	9	32	20	6	34
0.500	29	6	25	25	5	30	23	5	32

Boldface signifies at threshold level 0.200 highest correct results are obtained apart from having lower false acceptance

faster than Haar. Since LBP offers much speedier detection in the face detection module and does not lag much far behind in accuracy while being tolerant against illumination changes, forms a better choice to be incorporated in real-world applications approximating the proposed system.

13.6.3   Analysis of the System with Varying Threshold Levels

The system has considered varying threshold levels ranging from 0.000 to 0.500 indicating the maximum closest distance (Euclidean distance) above which the inputs with higher closest distance will be discarded. The experimental setup has considered ten subjects, where 400 samples captured from the camera at different environments and face angles has been contemplated. In total, the dataset comprises 400 images, where 100 images for training; ten for each subject followed by testing the system at each threshold level by 60 test images. Table 13.3 records the results obtained from varying threshold levels incrementing by 0.100 at each level, in terms of false acceptance, false rejection and correct identification. False acceptance suggests the wrong face where the threshold is greater than the distance calculated. Whereas, false rejection indicates correct face where threshold is less than the distance calculated.

A graph has been plotted in Fig. 13.10 with False Acceptance Rate (FAR) and False Rejection Rate (FRR) for the system incorporating the three schemes.

From Table 13.3, it has been concluded that at threshold level 0.200 highest correct results are obtained apart from having lower false acceptance. The three methods behaved differently at each threshold level. At lower levels, the false rejection rate was higher reason being the distance calculated was higher than the specified threshold. At higher levels, the false acceptance is higher reason being the distance calculated between different faces fall within the threshold. The LDA performs better reason being it considers the class scatter as a prime parameter. Further, PCA degrades after exceeding 0.200 and remains constant providing higher False Acceptance Rate (FAR). The reason for such behaviour could be that the PCA is concerned only about the direction in which maximum change occurs and not

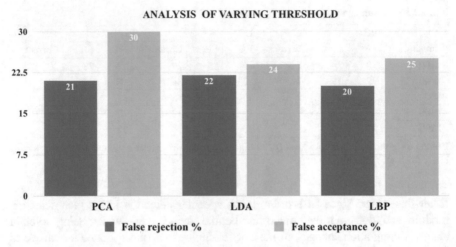

Fig. 13.10 Analysis of varying threshold levels

about the scatter among the classes. From this analysis, a threshold of 0.200 delivers acceptable results in terms of LDA and PCA, as marginally higher FRR is acceptable when lower FAR is being offered.

13.6.4 Analysis of the System with Varying Training Dataset

From the latter experiment conducted, an appropriate threshold level has been specified. However, the size of the training set also plays a significant role in determining the accuracy of the system. This test has been considered with varying number of training images for a subject. In this analysis, a dataset of 50 images is considered. Starting with five training images and increasing successively to 35 and accordingly utilising test images for each subject.

From the graph plotted in Fig. 13.11 with data values from Table 13.4, it is being indicated that increasing the number of trained images considerably increase the accuracy of the algorithms, however not at the same rate for all. This is because having too many trained samples introduces a higher amount of variance in the dataset which has a negative effect on the overall identification procedure.

Further from the graph, it can be concluded that the system performs well when LBP is under consideration. However, in terms of processing time per image the system takes 264 ms when employing LBP; which involves face detection, pre-processing and identification time. Apart from the time inquired by face detection and pre-processing, which is the same for all, PCA and LDA involve loading of face vector and Eigen vector files. Hence, inquiring more time than LBP which is a CPU intensive function making the system suitable for both old and modern devices alike. However, the timing can be an issue when implemented for strictly time constrained schemes like security systems.

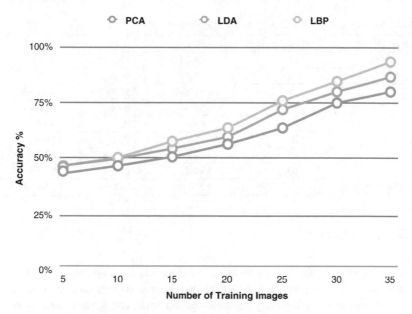

Fig. 13.11 Graph depicting analysis with varying training dataset size

The face detection module has successfully revealed LBP together with eye detection, as a better suited face detection approach than Haar for real-time applications on resource-constrained devices like mobile phones. The system is suitable for data ranging from small to large involving varying number of subjects owing to the three methods considered. Moreover, facial landmark feature detection employed in the system delivers exclusive opportunities to achieve tasks that no former algorithms are presently able to. A realistic dataset considering real-world situations has been utilised for evaluating the system. The effect of training on each algorithm has also been noted down, revealing the impact on the system at different rates. The time taken by the system indicates the overall processes and its direct proportionality to the size of the data. When the training set is increased, LBP works better at smaller datasets. Depending on the requirement, the system is capable for use in diverse scenarios like mobile applications demanding verification in the form of authentication where a one-to-one comparison is required; when the number of subjects is less, then LBP would be a better choice than PCA. While for systems, where there exist a large number of subjects and large training data set LDA can be a better choice than PCA.

Table 13.4 Result analysis with varying training dataset size

Training images	Test images	PCA	LDA	LBP
5	45	44.44%	46.66%	46.66%
10	40	47.5%	50%	50%
15	35	51.43%	54.28%	57.14%
20	30	56.66%	60%	63.33%
25	25	64%	72%	76%
30	20	75%	80%	85%
35	15	80%	86.66%	93.33%
40	10	85%	87%	90%
Identification time		274 ms	281 ms	264 ms

13.7 Conclusion

In this chapter, a fully adaptive and automatic face identification system has been developed, which works in real-time on resource-constrained Android mobile devices while considering varying illumination and face angles. The system is constituted of three phases: face detection, pre-processing and face identification. For face detection phase, eye detection together with LBP has turned out to be a better choice than the Haar for real-time applications on resource-constrained devices like mobile phones. Similarly, the pre-processing phase has been added for handling the real-world data. Finally, the identification phase involves performing of feature extraction and matching processes on data obtained under uncontrollable situations. The system evaluation in terms of varying threshold levels together with varying numbers of trained images has been performed. The system is suitable for data ranging from small to large involving varying number of subjects owing to the three methods considered. Moreover, Facial landmark feature detection employed in the system offers distinctive opportunities to achieve tasks that no other algorithms are presently able to. A realistic dataset considering real-world situations has been utilised for evaluating the system. The effect of training on each algorithm has also been noted down, revealing the impact on the system at different rates. The time taken by the system indicates the overall processes while being directly proportional to the size of the data. However, when the number of subjects is increased greater than ten, the system deteriorates in terms of total time taken and often behaves abnormally on low processor mobile devices. From the analysis, the system is found capable for use in different scenarios like mobile applications requiring real-time identification. When the number of subjects is less LBP would be a better choice than PCA, while for systems, where there exist a large number of subjects and large training data set LDA can be a better choice than PCA in terms of accuracy but not in speed.

13.8   Future Opportunities

Humans constitute the weakest link in any security mechanism, thus breaching the systems offering the highest security. Such human failures can be considerably reduced by using biometrics scheme to ease the user adoptability. However, biometrics itself suffers from shortcomings such as vulnerability to various attacks like replay attacks and presentation attacks, thus can't be used alone as a basis to form a strong security system. Hence, integrating the biometric system with that of a non-biometric system will result in a much secure system offering strong security without compromising user convenience. Furthermore, the presented system has a huge scope in the future due to its applicability in diverse fields like smart cameras, sleep detection on vehicles, online banking security, entertainment besides being capable to act as fully automated face detection and identification system (with an eye detection system) for simple surveillance applications such as ATM user security, etc. The biometrics can be incorporated on the web in place of captcha for detecting humans. However, the security of biometric features while in transit in the network has not yet been studied thoroughly. It is an evolving research topic that needs the attention of the researchers.

Acknowledgments This work was partially supported by Ministry of Higher Education Malaysia (Kementerian Pendidikan Tinggi) under Research Initiative Grant Scheme number: RIGS16-334-0498.

References

1. Abbas, N., Zhang, Y., Taherkordi, A. and Skeie, T., 2018. Mobile edge computing: A survey. *IEEE Internet of Things Journal*, 5(1), pp. 450-465.
2. Adhikary, N., Shrivastava, R., Kumar, A., Verma, S.K., Bag, M. and Singh, V., 2012. Battering keyloggers and screen recording software by fabricating passwords. *International Journal of Computer Network and Information Security*, 4(5), p.13.
3. Ambalakat, P., 2005, April. Security of biometric authentication systems. In *21st Computer Science Seminar* (p. 1).
4. Andreeva, E., 2012, September. Secret sharing in continuous access control system, using heart sounds. In *Problems of Redundancy in Information and Control Systems (RED), 2012 XIII International Symposium on* (pp. 5-6). IEEE.
5. Aviv, A.J., Gibson, K.L., Mossop, E., Blaze, M. and Smith, J.M., 2010. Smudge Attacks on Smartphone Touch Screens. *Woot*, 10, pp. 1-7.
6. Bao, W., Li, H., Li, N. and Jiang, W., 2009, April. A liveness detection method for face recognition based on optical flow field. In *Image Analysis and Signal Processing, 2009. IASP 2009. International Conference on* (pp. 233-236). IEEE.
7. Buriro, A., Gupta, S. and Crispo, B., 2017. Evaluation of Motion-based Touch-typing Biometrics for online Banking.
8. Chingovska, I., Anjos, A. and Marcel, S., 2012. On the effectiveness of local binary patterns in face anti-spoofing. In *Proceedings of the 11th International Conference of the Biometrics Special Interes Group* (No. EPFL-CONF-192369).

9. Coldewey D. NIST declares the age of SMS-based 2-factor authentication over [Online]. TechCrunch. 2018. https://beta.techcrunch.com/2016/07/25/nist-declares-the-age-of-sms-based-2-factor-authentication-over/ [Accessed 30 April 2018].

10. Conklin, A., Dietrich, G. and Walz, D., 2004, January. Password-based authentication: a system perspective. In *System Sciences, 2004. Proceedings of the 37th Annual Hawaii International Conference on* (pp. 10-pp). IEEE.

11. Darwaish, S.F., Moradian, E., Rahmani, T. and Knauer, M., 2014. Biometric identification on Android smartphones. *Procedia Computer Science*, *35*, pp.832-841.

12. De Marsico, M., Galdi, C., Nappi, M. and Riccio, D., 2014. Firme: Face and iris recognition for mobile engagement. *Image and Vision Computing*, *32*(12), pp.1161-1172.

13. Elftmann, P., 2006. Secure alternatives to password-based authentication mechanisms. *Lab. for Dependable Distributed Systems, RWTH Aachen Univ.*

14. Goel, C.K. and Arya, G., 2012. Hacking of passwords in windows environment. *International Journal of Computer Science & Communication Networks*, *2*(3), pp.430-435.

15. Grahakseva, Online fraud happened hacking my icici bank credit card [Online]. 2013 http://www.grahakseva.com/complaints/130310/online-fraud-happened-hacking-my-icici-bank-credit-card [Accessed 30 April 2018].

16. Hu, J., Peng, L. and Zheng, L., 2015, August. XFace: a face recognition system for Android mobile phones. In *Cyber-Physical Systems, Networks, and Applications (CPSNA), 2015 IEEE 3rd International Conference on* (pp. 13-18). IEEE.

17. Hussain, S., Khan, B.U.I., Anwar, F. and Olanrewaju, R.F., 2018. Secure annihilation of out-of-band authorization for online transactions. *Indian Journal of Science and Technology*, *11*(5), pp.1-9.

18. Islam, S.H. and Biswas, G.P., 2011. A more efficient and secure ID-based remote mutual authentication with key agreement scheme for mobile devices on elliptic curve cryptosystem. *Journal of Systems and Software*, *84*(11), pp.1892-1898.

19. Jain, A.K., Ross, A. and Pankanti, S., 2006. Biometrics: a tool for information security. *IEEE transactions on information forensics and security*, *1*(2), pp.125-143.

20. Jee, H.K., Jung, S.U. and Yoo, J.H., 2006. Liveness detection for embedded face recognition system. *International Journal of Biological and Medical Sciences*, *1*(4), pp.235-238.

21. Khan, B.U.I., Baba, A.M., Olanrewaju, R.F., Lone, S.A. and Zulkurnain, N.F., 2015, August. SSM: Secure-Split-Merge data distribution in cloud infrastructure. In *Open Systems (ICOS), 2015 IEEE Conference on* (pp. 40-45). IEEE.

22. Khan, B.U.I., Olanrewaju, R.F., Baba, A.M., Langoo, A.A. and Assad, S., 2017. A compendious study of online payment systems: Past developments, present impact, and future considerations. *International Journal of Advanced Computer Science and Applications*, *8*(5), pp.256-71.

23. Kizza, J.M., 2007. *Ethical and social issues in the information age* (Vol. 999). Springer.

24. Kumar, S., Singh, S.K., Singh, R.S., Singh, A.K. and Tiwari, S., 2017. Real-time recognition of cattle using animal biometrics. *Journal of Real-Time Image Processing*, *13*(3), pp.505-526.

25. Lovisotto, G., Malik, R., Sluganovic, I., Roeschlin, M., Trueman, P. and Martinovic, I., 2017. *Mobile biometrics in financial services: A five factor framework*. Technical Report CS-RR-17-03, Oxford University.

26. Määttä, J., Hadid, A. and Pietikäinen, M., 2011, October. Face spoofing detection from single images using micro-texture analysis. In *Biometrics (IJCB), 2011 international joint conference on* (pp. 1-7). IEEE.

27. Marshall, B.K., 2007. Tips for Avoiding Bad Authentication Challenge Questions. *White Paper*.

28. Masihuddin, M., Khan, B.U.I., Mattoo, M.M.U.I. and Olanrewaju, R.F., 2017. A survey on e-payment systems: elements, adoption, architecture, challenges and security concepts. *Indian Journal of Science and Technology*, *10*(20), pp. 1-19.

29. McQuiggan, S., McQuiggan, J., Sabourin, J. and Kosturko, L., 2015. *Mobile learning: A handbook for developers, educators, and learners*. John Wiley & Sons.

30. McWaters R. 2016. *A Blueprint for Digital Identity*. World Economic Forum.

31. Mehraj, T., Rasool, B., Khan, B.U.I., Baba, A. and Lone, A.G., 2015. Contemplation of effective security measures in access management from adoptability perspective. *International*

Journal of Advanced Computer Science and Applications, *6*(8), pp.188-200.

32. Meng, W., Wong, D.S., Furnell, S. and Zhou, J., 2015. Surveying the development of biometric user authentication on mobile phones. *IEEE Communications Surveys & Tutorials*, *17*(3), pp.1268-1293.

33. Mir, M.S., Suhaimi, M.B.A., Khan, B.U.I., Mattoo, M.M.U.I. and Olanrewaju, R.F., 2017. Critical Security Challenges in Cloud Computing Environment: An Appraisal. *Journal of Theoretical & Applied Information Technology*, *95*(10), pp 2234-2248.

34. Narayanan, A. and Shmatikov, V., 2005, November. Fast dictionary attacks on passwords using time-space tradeoff. In *Proceedings of the 12th ACM conference on Computer and communications security* (pp. 364-372). ACM.

35. Nguyen, N.C., Bosch, O.J., Ong, F.Y., Seah, J.S., Succu, A., Nguyen, T.V. and Banson, K.E., 2016. A systemic approach to understand smartphone usage in Singapore. *Systems Research and Behavioral Science*, *33*(3), pp.360-380.

36. Ockenden W. AM - eBay suffers catastrophic data breach in hack attack 22/05/2014 [Online]. Abc.net.au. 2014. http://www.abc.net.au/am/content/2014/s4009539.htm [Accessed 30 April 2018].

37. Olanrewaju, R.F., Khan, B.U.I., Baba, A., Mir, R.N. and Lone, S.A., 2016, July. RFDA: Reliable framework for data administration based on split-merge policy. In *SAI Computing Conference (SAI), 2016* (pp. 545-552). IEEE.

38. Olanrewaju, R.F., Khan, B.U.I., Mattoo, M.M.U.I., Anwar, F., Nordin, A.N.B. and Mir, R.N., 2017a. Securing electronic transactions via payment gateways–a systematic review. *International Journal of Internet Technology and Secured Transactions*, *7*(3), pp.245-269.

39. Olanrewaju, R.F., Khan, B.U.I., Mattoo, M.M.U.I., Anwar, F., Nordin, A.N.B., Mir, R.N. and Noor, Z., 2017b. Adoption of Cloud Computing in Higher Learning Institutions: A Systematic Review. *Indian Journal of Science and Technology*, *10*(36), pp.1-19.

40. Osseiran, A., Monserrat, J.F. and Marsch, P. eds., 2016. *5G mobile and wireless communications technology*. Cambridge University Press.

41. Pampori, B.R., Mehraj, T., Khan, B.U.I., Baba, A.M. and Najar, Z.A., 2018. Securely eradicating cellular dependency for e-banking applications. *International Journal of Advanced Computer Science and Applications (IJACSA)*, *9*(2), pp.385-398.

42. Pan, G., Sun, L., Wu, Z. and Lao, S., 2007. Eyeblink-based anti-spoofing in face recognition from a generic webcamera.

43. Ratha, N.K., Connell, J.H. and Bolle, R.M., 2001, June. An analysis of minutiae matching strength. In *International Conference on Audio and Video-Based Biometric Person Authentication* (pp. 223-228). Springer, Berlin, Heidelberg.

44. Rathgeb, C. and Uhl, A., 2011. A survey on biometric cryptosystems and cancelable biometrics. *EURASIP Journal on Information Security*, *2011*(1), p.3.

45. Reid, A.S., 2018. Financial Crime in the Twenty-First Century: The Rise of the Virtual Collar Criminal. In *White Collar Crime and Risk* (pp. 231-251). Palgrave Macmillan, London.

46. Ross, A.A., Nandakumar, K. and Jain, A.K., 2008. Handbook of biometrics. *US: Springer*.

47. Sadeghi, A.R., Schneider, T. and Wehrenberg, I., 2009, December. Efficient privacy-preserving face recognition. In *International Conference on Information Security and Cryptology* (pp. 229-244). Springer, Berlin, Heidelberg.

48. Smith, D.F., Wiliem, A. and Lovell, B.C., 2015. Face recognition on consumer devices: Reflections on replay attacks. *IEEE Transactions on Information Forensics and Security*, *10*(4), pp.736-745.

49. Statista, Smartphone OS market share forecast 2014-2022 | Statistic, 2018. [Online]. Available: https://www.statista.com/statistics/272307/market-share-forecast-for-smartphone-operating-systems/. [Accessed: 30- April- 2018].

50. Singh, A.K., Kumar, B., Dave, M., Ghrera, S.P. and Mohan, A., 2016. Digital image watermarking: techniques and emerging applications. In *Handbook of research on modern cryptographic solutions for computer and cyber security* (pp. 246-272). IGI Global.

51. Singh, A.K., Kumar, B., Singh, G. and Mohan, A. eds., 2017. *Medical image watermarking: techniques and applications*. Springer.

52. Téllez, J. and Zeadally, S., 2017. *Mobile Payment Systems: Secure Network Architectures and Protocols*. Springer.
53. Teo, C.C. and Neo, H.F., 2017, May. Behavioral Fingerprint Authentication: The Next Future. In *Proceedings of the 9th International Conference on Bioinformatics and Biomedical Technology* (pp. 1-5). ACM.
54. Yang, Y., Sun, J.S., Zhang, C. and Li, P., 2015, October. Retraining and Dynamic Privilege for Implicit Authentication Systems. In *Mobile Ad Hoc and Sensor Systems (MASS), 2015 IEEE 12th International Conference on* (pp. 163-171). IEEE.
55. Zhao, Z., Dong, Z. and Wang, Y., 2006. Security analysis of a password-based authentication protocol proposed to IEEE 1363. *Theoretical Computer Science*, *352*(1-3), pp.280-287.

Chapter 14
Realization of Chaos-Based Private Multiprocessor Network Via USART of Embedded Devices

Siva Janakiraman, K. Thenmozhi, John Bosco Balaguru Rayappan,
V. Moorthi Paramasivam, and Rengarajan Amirtharajan

14.1 Introduction

Encryption is one among the essential strategies utilised for anchoring the classified information. The job of encryption is to change the delicate data into a frame convoluted to appreciate. Cryptosystems chiefly take a shot at making the mystery extreme to comprehend and unravel. In fact, cryptography uses a key to change over a plaintext into ciphertext. With the quickened section of gate crashers, by and by the need of cryptography is expanding each day. A decent number of conventions have been produced and institutionalised for information security applications including encryption. The property of haphazardness is one of the widely used determinations for the key and convention structure to yield a highly scrambled output by an encryption algorithm.

As said by Rinne et al. [1], the encryption procedures which are solely intended for extremely asset compelled implanted devices such as microcontrollers are designated as LightWeight Cryptography (LWC) schemes. Data manipulation procedures involving less complexity, restricted memory and moderate code measure with consideration on execution time for time-basic applications warrant the regular lightweight property displayed by these algorithms. Numerous lightweight plans have been proposed before to encrypt data in text [2] and picture [3] format. Encryption approaches for text information have been executed on a wide assortment of constrained devices like microcontrollers.

S. Janakiraman · K. Thenmozhi · J. B. B. Rayappan · R. Amirtharajan (✉)
Faculty, School of Electrical & Electronics Engineering, SASTRA Deemed University,
Thanjavur, Tamilnadu, India
e-mail: amir@ece.sastra.edu

V. M. Paramasivam
Cyber Security and Risk Services, Wipro Technologies Ltd., Bengaluru, Karnataka, India

© Springer Nature Switzerland AG 2019
A. K. Singh, A. Mohan (eds.), *Handbook of Multimedia Information Security:
Techniques and Applications*, https://doi.org/10.1007/978-3-030-15887-3_14

Tanougast et al. [4] used reconfigurable embedded devices like FPGAs for applications the uses data in picture format. Contrasted with microcontrollers, FPGAs are outfitted with expanded memory space, rationale units, multipliers and PLLs for fulfilling superior prerequisites. While breaking down the tradeoff among expense and execution time, devices like microcontrollers are found in real-time applications giving low power dissemination and less cost [5].

This chapter manages the implementation and examinations of a chaotic scheme to encrypt text information. The proposed work on encryption utilises baud rate as a significant parameter to build up a protected asynchronous private correspondence interface between the linked microcontrollers. Usage of this proposed content encryption conspire was completed utilising the asynchronous on-chip USART module of 8-bit Advanced Versatile RISC (AVR) microcontroller, ATmega8. Chaos-based techniques have taken the middle phase of encryption field because of their ability to broaden huge keyspace, key sensitiveness and haphazardness. Chaotic plans have been widely used just in software implemented algorithms due to their demand for the use of composite floating point calculations.

The following are the major contribution of this chapter:

- Microcontroller based peer to peer cryptosystem for text encryption has been proposed
- It utilises baudrate as a major parameter to build up a protected asynchronous private correspondence interface between the linked microcontrollers
- Chaotic Duffing map has been adopted for a key generation where session keys have been produced to vary the baud rate
- On-chip USART module of ATmega8 has been utilised for establishing the communication between multiprocessor nodes
- This multiblock encryption scheme provides the variable speed of transmission through baudrate of the USART which inherently offers encryption

14.2   Related Work

14.2.1   Chaotic Functions for Cryptography on Microcontrollers

According to Gonze [6], using one dimensional (1D) discrete logistic map a chaotic system in uncomplicated form can be attained. Chaotic systems utilise an underlying partial key input to generate floating point output with randomness during iterations. These chaotic maps are highly sensitive to deliver arbitrary output for a fragmentary change in its underlying input conditions.

Systems with Chaotic properties are widely appreciated in designing crypto applications [7, 8]. Aboul et al. [9] showed the feasibility for implementing 1D logistic map on a microcontroller with 16-bit AVR core. Serna and Joshi [10] realised the same on 8-bit AVR microcontroller. Managing the floating point rep-

Table 14.1 Illustration of IEEE 754 floating-point format with 32-bit accuracy

Field significance	Sign bit	Exponent value	Mantissa value
Position	D_{31}	D_{30} to D_{23}	D_{22} to D_0
Size (bits)	1	8	23

resentation is the principle challenge in utilising such chaotic maps as a substantial area of memory is expected to administer the mantissa and exponent part of each value. Software library with floating point functions facilitates arithmetic operations on floating point numbers in all advanced embedded devices appropriate from a simple 8-bit microcontroller with AVR core till the complex 32-bit devices with ARM core.

Table 14.1 shows the binary representation of floating point number as per standard IEEE 754 format with 32-bit accuracy [11]. Zapateiro et al. [12] realized chaotic digital function on the microcontroller and used it as key security means in the data encryption process.

14.2.2 Serial Data Encryption with USART

Exclusive on-chip features of embedded hardware are highly adequate to encrypt text information. Universal Synchronous Asynchronous Receiver Transmitter (USART) is such a standout feature amongst the most prevalent and regularly utilised one exists in embedded devices to accomplish serial data correspondence asynchronously. This serial protocol expects the receiver to match itself with the concern transmitter to gather the appropriate data. Here a crucial parameter known as baudrate is required for the organised correspondence between the recipient and transmitter. Baud rate is the main parameter at the recipient that exists to coordinate its data gathering activity called data bit sampling. Bits Per Second (bps) is the link data rate when each symbol is represented with a single bit.

Rhitvik and Gaurav [13] suggested the concept of varying the baudrate in between the asynchronous transmission of data via on-chip USART of microcontrollers for secured private communication of serial data between a pair of the microcontroller. This process can be strengthened by continuously changing the baudrate of the USART at an arbitrary interval based on a randomly generated key.

14.2.3 Auto Baud Rate Detection

While baudrate can be utilised as a parameter to upgrade security, the correspondence will be ensured just until the point at which a malicious user identifies the particular baudrate. In this unique circumstance, encryption is proficient by assuming the baudrate performing the job of a particular key. Amid the procedure of information exchange between the gadgets, it is additionally workable for the recipients to distinguish the baudrate by estimating the duration of each bit after the entry of a start bit.

A component called auto baudrate identification encourages the recognition of this rate at which the frames are communicated between the proposed gadgets. This kind of auto baudrate recognition exists these days as an inbuilt component in embedded devices that contains on-chip USART. Baudrate identification is executed with the utilisation of a known interesting synchronisation byte that comprises of alternate ones and zeros. ASCII character 'U' with equivalent hex value 0×55 (0101 0101) is used for initial synchronisation in PIC24H family of microcontrollers from Microchip [14]. Like-wise ultra-low-power microcontroller MSP 430 from Texas Instruments (TI) [15] uses carriage return 'CR' with hex value $0 \times 0D$ (00001101) to detect auto baud rate. With no mechanism to oppose the detection of auto baudrate; using baudrate alone as a key may be a factor that crumbles the security of the information being communicated.

In vast majority of embedded microcontrollers, this USART is an on-chip peripheral that has added a different kind of user configurable features. The embedded software running at sender and receiver is the main consideration in upholding the selection of appropriate frame format and baudrate committed for the data correspondence. Any disparity in settling the baudrate or frame structure between the sender and recipient USART may prompt loss or damage in the communicated data. Considering the above details, the algorithm proposed in this chapter uses chaotic keys to select the frame format, baud rate and a few other parameters to be used in the process of encryption. Thus the proposed method enhances the security by making the decryption process dependent on multiple parameters of a specific embedded device.

14.2.4 Need for Serial Data Security in a Multiprocessor Network

The frame format used in asynchronous data communication with USART [16] is shown in Fig. 14.1. The frame starts with a default state of logic high that indicates null data or idle condition. The duration of the frame begins with a start bit having logic 0 to make a transition from idle state to active state. The valid data in a

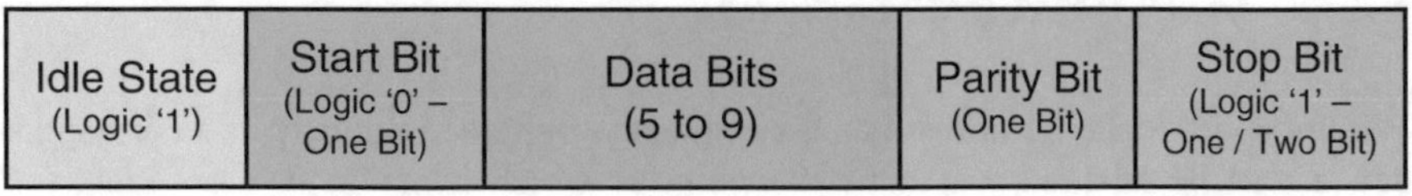

Idle State (Logic '1')	Start Bit (Logic '0' – One Bit)	Data Bits (5 to 9)	Parity Bit (One Bit)	Stop Bit (Logic '1' – One / Two Bit)

Fig. 14.1 USART asynchronous frame format

data frame may vary between 5 and 9 bits in length following which the user can optionally insert a parity bit based on the requirement. The required bit value of odd or even parity may be obtained from the Eqs. (14.1) and (14.2) correspondingly. Again based on a decision by the user, end of each frame may contain 1 or 2 stop bit(s) with logic 1.

$$P_{Even} = b_{n-1} \oplus \cdots \oplus b_2 \oplus b_1 \oplus b_0 \oplus 0 \qquad (14.1)$$

$$P_{Odd} = b_{n-1} \oplus \cdots \oplus b_2 \oplus b_1 \oplus b_0 \oplus 1 \qquad (14.2)$$

where b_n represents the nth data bit of the asynchronous USART frame with $1 \leq n \leq 9$.

The capacity to build up a USART based private connection between a master and one among multiple slave devices in a network system is encouraged through multiprocessor mode. In this method of correspondence, each slave device in the network is allotted an exclusive 8-bit number as device address, and it concurs between the master and slave. Also, a single bit identifier bit is utilised to recognise an Address Frame (AF) and a Data Frame (DF). The sender uses a frame with 9-bit character length where logic 1 in MSB signifies address frame while logic 0 indicates a data frame. The transmitting node chooses a recipient device in the network by broadcasting the address of the destination device to all slave USART present in the system. USART can configure itself as a slave in multiprocessor mode by using a bit in its control register. Any device when operated in this mode is allowed to accept the address frames sent from Master and refuses to take the data frame content to its receive register. The slave device that receives a matching address frame from the master can legitimately change its own internal reconfiguration to start accepting the data frames from the master. In this manner, the address frame is used to match and pair the devices to share a limited number of data frames between them. After the arrival of the final data frame, the embedded software of the slave device at the receiving end has to make its USART come back to multiprocessor mode again.

This sort of existing private data link between a transmitting master and any recipient slave node in a multiprocessor network is sender driven one. In practical situation, disavowal of getting the data frame is chosen by the software configurations that are made at the accepting device. In this way, any unapproved device encroached into a multiprocessor network might have the capacity to cheat the transmitter by changing the setup of its internal USART to accept data frames corresponds to any slave node in the network. Consequently, the confidentiality of any information correspondence between the paired devices in a multiprocessor system will never again exist. Thus to secure the exchange of serial data frames between the paired nodes a unique mechanism is to be incorporated in the multiprocessor USART network.

14.3 Materials and Methods

14.3.1 Cryptic USART Multiprocessor Network Using Microcontrollers

The traditional multiprocessor network for USART does not support master-slave configuration. Hence this book chapter proposes the following steps to create a USART based cryptic multiprocessor network to establish a secured asynchronous serial private communication link between the master and a slave microcontroller.

- Designate a device in the multiprocessor network as a master node
- Configure all the nodes in the system except the master as slaves via embedded software
- Build a network in a star topology by connecting each slave node with the master node via a direct serial link as depicted in Fig. 14.2a
- All slave nodes in the network will wait for the arrival of the address frame from the master
- The master initiates the communication in the network by broadcasting the 9-bit character frame containing a 7-bit slave address
- The device is configured as either transmitter or receiver based on the LSB value of the address frame being logic 1 or 0
- Figure 14.3 shows the structure of the address frame used to select the slave node
- Figure 14.4 shows the structure of the data frame used to communicate encrypted data the master-slave pair

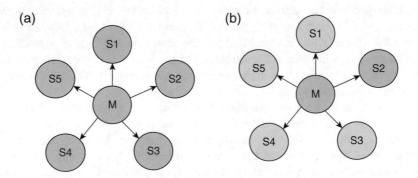

Fig. 14.2 Multiprocessor network topology, (**a**) Broadcast of address frame from master and (**b**) exchange of data frame between paired master-slave nodes

Start	D_8	D_7	D_6	D_5	D_4	D_3	D_2	D_1	D_0	Stop
0	1	Device Address (7-bit)							T_X/R_X (1/0)	1

Fig. 14.3 Address frame (slave selection process)

Start	D$_8$	D$_7$	D$_6$	D$_5$	D$_4$	D$_3$	D$_2$	D$_1$	D$_0$	Stop
0	0	Encrypted data (8-bit)								1

Fig. 14.4 Data frame (encrypted datatransfer)

- At the time of exchanging data frames among the paired master-slave nodes, there is no logical link between the master and other un-paired slave nodes in the network as given in Fig. 14.2b
- Each data frame sent through the network carries the 8-bit character encrypted by the 16-bit symmetric key produced using a chaotic map
- The arrival of the last data frame or a reserved Terminating Character (TC) sets the paired slave node back to multiprocessor mode
- Consequently, the master broadcasts next address frame which brings back the ability for the slave nodes to accept frames to establish a new link for secured data transfer among the master and a slave

14.3.2 Chaotic Key Generation

Attaining improvement in randomness was proposed with the use of chaotic system referred as Duffing map [17]. Equations (14.3) and (14.4) are the digitised version of a differential equation with non-linear properties called the Duffing equation.

For Eq. (14.4), literature results suggests 2.75 and 0.2 as common values for the control parameters a and b respectively with initial conditions x and y (n = 0) close to zero in Eqs. (14.3) and (14.4) to deliver exceeding chaotic behavior in the range of −2 to +2 [17, 18].

$$x_{n+1} = x_n \tag{14.3}$$

$$y_{n+1} = -bx_n + ay_n - y_n^3 \tag{14.4}$$

Once the slave selection is done by the master, both the sender and the receiver generate a symmetric key of 16-bit in length. This work utilises Duffing map to accomplish randomness in the key generation process by implementing it on 8-bit AVR microcontroller (ATmega8). In this multiprocessor network, the embedded software on the microcontrollers uses the trusted values for control parameter as a constant while keeping the values of initial conditions a variable one.

After an iteration of the Duffing map, the present and previous output values are compared to obtain the bit value 'h' in pseudo-random manner by applying Eq. (14.5).

$$h = \begin{cases} 1; \ y_{n+1} > x_n \\ 0; \ y_{n+1} < x_n \end{cases} \quad (14.5)$$

The procedure proceeds until a binary stream is produced to form a 16-bit key. In order to generate a symmetric key for the proposed encryption procedure, matching Duffing map values for threshold and initial parameter are agreed between the communicating master-slave pair and kept consistently. The determination of various initial and threshold parameter among the slaves guarantees the uniqueness of 16-bit chaotic symmetric key produced by the slaves.

This method freezes the parameter values for key generation in master and every slave device at the time of building the multiprocessor network. The code memory area in master and slave have stored with unique key parameter values as constants while the algorithms for encryption and decryption processes. Thus, the need for the exchange of keys or related parameters between the paired master-slave devices is eliminated in this method.

14.3.3   Pseudo Code for Symmetric Key Generation Process

```
Initialize Duffing map control parameters 'a=2.75' and 'b=0.2';
 Assign values for initial conditions x(0) and y(0);
Initialize bit period 'P';
Do Forever
{
 Initialize Key length to zero;
for(Key length=0;Key length < 16; Key length++)
{     while( P> 0)
      { Compute x_{n + 1}and y_{n + 1}using Duffing map;
          P=P-1;
      }
      If(y_{n + 1}>x_n) then
      {        pseudo random bit, h=1;     }
      Else
      { pseudo random bit, h=0;     }
   Collect bit value 'h' to form key 'K' ;
}
   Obtain the 16-bit Chaotic Symmetric key 'K' produced from the
pseudo-random bits of Duffing map;
   Wait till all the data frame for the present link is exchanged;
}
```

14.3.4   Description of Symmetric Key

To maintain the uniqueness of the keys used by each master-slave pair, the input parameters for the evaluation of Duffing map are kept confidential between the master and the relevant slave device. In any security algorithm, key length is the essential component in deciding its strength. To strengthen the security for serial data exchange among the devices with a short key length of 16-bit, the proposed algorithm utilizes baudrate as the vital factor along with further bit level reordering and byte manipulation operations. Baudrateduring the serial exchange of data frames is continued changing in an arbitrary manner coordinated by the key. This extra element upgrades the security of serial data exchange by avoiding the secret data access from unapproved/malevolent users.

The 16-bit symmetric key (Fig. 14.5) is split into two bytes with lower byte as Right Hand Side (RHS) and upper byte as Left Hand Side (LHS). The bits D_7 to D_5 of RHS indicate the Baudrate Fixing (BF) factor that selects the baudrate between 2400 and 115.2 K for the exchange of encrypted serial data frames. The bits D_2 to D_0 of RHS signify Block Size (BS) that defines the amount of data bytes to be encrypted using the present key. The bits D_4 and D_3 in RHS of symmetric key point to the Transform Operation (TO) that manipulates the plain text (secret data) bytes. The single byte key value used to carry out the chosen operation is obtained from the LHS part of the 16-bit symmetric key.

Based on the direction of data transfer, a master and slave node chooses to either send or to stay till the entry of data frames. Effectively, the baud rate to be used for further data correspondence between the master-slave nodes is determined by the

D7	D6	D5	D4	D3	D2	D1	D0	
BF < 2.0 >			TO < 1.0 >		BS < 2.0 >			RHS
Transform Key " (TK) < 7.0 >								LHS

"The Transform Key (TK) is used when performing the selected transform operation with the data byte as a part of encryption / decryption process

Baudrate Fixing (BF)

BF	Baudrate
000	2400
001	4800
010	9600
011	14.4K
100	19.2K
101	38.4K
110	57.6K
111	115.2K

Transform Operation (TO)

TO	Operation	
	Encryption	Decryption
00	Modulo 8 Addition	Modulo 8 Subtraction
01	Circular shift right	Circular shift left
10	Modulo 8 Subtraction	Modulo 8 Addition
11	Circular shift left	Circular shift right

Block Size (BS)

BS	Block size
000	1
001	2
010	4
011	8
100	16
101	32
110	4
111	8

Fig. 14.5 Description of symmetric key

symmetric key. In addition to data manipulation operations, the number of plaintexts bytes selected for the encryption process is determined by the key. Thus the block size becomes a key dependent one. The repeated variation of block size and baudrate introduces random deviation in the payload used by this approach while satisfying the payload requisite on embedded systems.

14.3.5 Encryption by Sender and Decryption at Receiver

Operating modes for on-chip peripherals like USART and I/O pins used for serial data transfer are configured during the initialisation phase of the algorithm. After initialisation, all the slave nodes will stay idle until the entry of an address frame at a baudrate of 9600. The data correspondence in the network can commence only from the master. A pre-designed identifier (node address) sent as broadcast information via address frame at a preset baudrate of 9600 is used to choose a particular node among the multiple slave nodes present in the multiprocessor network. The received node address is compared against its address by every slave node. The address matched slave node is paired with the master node which enables the generation of a symmetric key in the master-slave nodes. At this point, the generated key triggers a new set of configuration in the USART of the master-slave pair. Figure 14.6 depicts the flowchart for the encryption process at the transmitting USART.

Subsequent to the generation of every symmetric key, the sender inserts a pre determined amount of delaypreceding the transmission of its first data frame to the network. This delay duration is essential for the communicating nodes to fix their baudrate based on the key value specifically when master node acts as transmitter. Although the proposed algorithm is a block cipher, it encrypts each plain text byte and instantaneously transmits it similar to a stream cipher.

On instances when the block size to be encrypted is more than the available data bytes, the proposed algorithm inserts a data frame with a default Terminating Character (TC) as final data byte. The TC may be a reserved special character agreed between the sender and receiver at the time of device initialization. The proposed algorithm also involves a cipher text chaining process during the encryption of data bytes insidethe chosen block. This process strengthens the security of the algorithm by introducing data integrity along with confidentiality.

14.3.6 Pseudo Code for Enciphering of Plaintext Block (Transmitter)

```
Obtain 16-bit Symmetric Key, S_K from key generation unit;
Get8-bit Transform Key, T_K from LHS part of S_K;
Fix the baudrate for USART from RHS part of S_K;
Find Block Size from RHS part of S_K;
Initialize count for transmission, Cnt_T_X= i = 0;
```

```
Set PTi-1= CTi-1= 0;
for(Cnt_Tx=0; Cnt_Tx< Block Size; Cnt_Tx++,i++)
{
    If(Transform Operation, TO == 0)
        CTi= CTi-1 ⊕ [8-bit Modulo Addition (PTi, TK)] ⊕PTi-1;
    else if(Transform Operation, TO == 1)
        CTi= CTi-1⊕[Circular Right Shift of PTifor (TKmod 8)
                    times]⊕PTi-1;
    else if(Transform Operation, TO == 2)
        CTi= CTi-1 ⊕ [8-bit Modulo Subtraction (PTi, TK)]⊕PTi-1;
    else if(Transform Operation, TO == 3)
        CTi= CTi-1 ⊕[Circular Left Shift of PTifor (TKmod 8)
                    times]⊕PTi-1;
    Serially Transmit, CTi;
}
```

The termination of established private link between master and a slave is informed to all other slaves in the network by the broadcast of next address frame by the master node. Acquiring the reserved Terminating Character (TC) during decryption process informs the slave node to re-enter multiprocessor mode. At this stage, the slave node starts searching for another matching address frame from master to re-establish its private link. The termination of data frame exchange in the private link when happens abruptly due to the arrival of TC, the byte count on the decrypted of final sub-block will be less than the block size decided by the key.

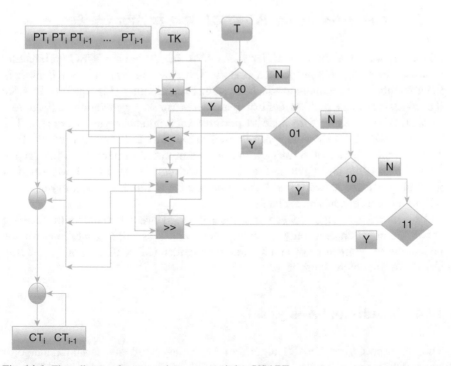

Fig. 14.6 Flow diagram for encryption at transmitting USART

14.3.7 Pseudo Code for Deciphering of Ciphertext Block (Receiver)

```
Obtain 16-bit Symmetric Key, S_K from key generation unit;
Get 8-bit Transform Key, T_K from LHS part of S_K;
Fix the baudrate for USART from RHS part of S_K;
Find Block Size from RHS part of S_K;
Initialize count for reception, Cnt_R_X= i = 0;
Set PT_i-1= CT_i-1= 0;
for(Cnt_R_X=0; Cnt_R_X< Block Size; Cnt_R_X++,i++)
{
    Serially Receive CT_i;
  If(Transform Operation, TO == 0)
      PT_i= CT_i-1 ⊕ [8-bit Modulo Subtraction (CT_i, T_K)] ⊕PT_i-1;
  If(Transform Operation, TO == 1)
      PT_i= CT_i-1 ⊕ [Circular Left Shift of CT_i for (T_K mod 8)
                      times]⊕PT_i-1;
  If(Transform Operation, TO == 2)
      PT_i= CT_i-1 ⊕ [8-bit Modulo Addition (CT_i,T_K)]⊕PT_i-1;
  If(Transform Operation, TO == 3)
      PT_i= CT_i-1 ⊕ [Circular Right Shift CT_i for (T_K mod 8)
                      times]⊕PT_i-1;
}
```

14.3.8 Realization of the Proposed Work in AVR Platform

ATmega8, an 8-bit microcontroller from AVR family having RISC architecture was used to realize the proposed work. In ATmega8, the available 8 KB on-chip flash memory is programmed via In-System Programming (ISP) facility to store the constant values such as control parameters for key generation and address of slave devices along with code to perform encryption/decryption process. The internal 1 KB of SRAM data space is used to the store the plain text information. The internal modules of ATmega8 that are mainly used to implement the cryptic USART algorithm are shown in Fig. 14.7. The circuit in Fig. 14.7 shows a part of the multiprocessor network that forms a private serial link between a master-slave pair for asynchronous data exchange.

Proper data exchange between the chosen master-slave pair in the multiprocessor network can be ensured only by using same values as initial conditions for the generation of symmetric key and by maintaining identical configuration for on-chip USART of the microcontrollers.

14.4 Results and Analysis

The proposed cryptic USART algorithm for the asynchronous serial exchange of secret data bytes in the multiprocessor network has been realised using ATmega8

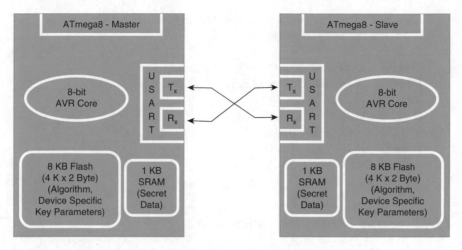

Fig. 14.7 Cryptic USART link between master-slave pair using microcontrollers

microcontrollers. The performance of the proposed serial cryptic system, when implemented on the 8-bit AVR platform, has been evaluated using the parameters such as serial throughput, code size and execution cycles. The input parameters and the result analysis are given below.

14.4.1   Sample Input and Output

The parameters mentioned below were taken as sample inputs for the encryption process.

Inputs:

Controlparametersas constants for Duffing map(Decimal):a = 2.75, b = 0.2
Initial conditions assumed for Duffing map (Decimal):x(0)=0.1, y(0)=−0.06
Interval for Duffing map (Decimal):50
Plaintext data 16 Bytes(ASCII): UART ENCRYPTION!
   or
(Hex): 0×55, 0×41, 0×52, 0×54,
   0×20, 0×45, 0×4E, 0×43,
   0×52, 0×59, 0×50, 0×54,
   0×49, 0×4F, 0×4E, 0×21

Outputs:

Generated 16-bit Duffing Key (Hex): 0×4EDC
Extracted 8-bit Transform key (Hex): 0×4E
Obtained 8-bit Symmetric key (Hex): 0×DC

Parameters derived from the 8-bit symmetric key using Fig. 14.5.

Block size in Bytes (Decimal): 16

Baudrate: 57600

Transform Operation: Modulo eight subtraction

Obtained Ciphertext 16 Bytes (ASCII):Úï"ÐÚíôô.ñ.MÊ

or

(Hex): 0×05, 0×0D, 0×0E, 0×DA,

  0×EF, 0×93, 0×D0, 0×DA,

  0×ED, 0×F5, 0×F4, 0×85,

  0×F1, 0×87, 0×4D, 0×CA

14.4.2   Serial Throughput Calculation

As per our algorithm, the data frame to be communicated by the USART requires 1 bit each to represent the start and stop of the frame in addition to the 9-bit data. This brings the total frame length to become 11 bits. As the 9-bit data includes a 1-bit value for frame type identification, the actual data communicated by the 11-bit data frame reduces to 8 bits. Thus the parameter called serial throughput can be given by Eq. (14.6) to find the useful number of data bits sent by a data frame. Figure 14.8 shows the linear rise in the value of serial throughput for the increase in baud rates chosen for the USART.

$$\text{Serial Throughput (bits/s)} = \frac{\text{Baudrate} \times \text{Actual number of data bits}}{\text{Total number of bits present in the data frame}}$$

(14.6)

Fig. 14.8 Serial throughput against USART baudrate

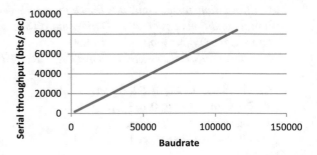

14.4.3   Lightweight Parameter Analysis of the Encryption Algorithm

Embedded C language used to create the proposed cryptic USART encryption algorithm. An open-source GCC compiler was used to compile the code for the chosen AVR microcontroller. Open-Source software development and debugging tool is known as Atmel studio [19] version 7.0 was used to analyse the memory footprint and execution cycles consumed by the embedded software to complete the encryption process. The time and size optimisation option supported by the GCC compiler was also utilised in analysing the developed embedded software for the proposed chaotic text encryption algorithm. The lightweight parameter results are given in Table 14.2. In addition to the change in execution cycles due to the selection of different optimisation options on the compiler, the transform operation determined by the chaotic symmetric key also contributes to the change in execution cycles taken to complete the encryption process.

A tradeoff has to be made between the degree of randomness in the keys generated by the Duffing map and time taken to generate the keys. Selecting larger values as intervals to improve the randomness in the keys linearly rises the time for key generation as shown in Fig. 14.9.

The execution time for encryption can be minimised by operating the microcontroller at higher frequencies. On the other hand, operating USART at high baudrate shrinks the duration of serial frames. Thus, maintaining the time for encryption lower than the frame duration to keep the next cipher byte ready before the completion of ongoing serial transmission is a mandatory requirement for this

Table 14.2 Device performance analysis

Optimisation	Encryption cycles		Code size (bytes)
	Modulo addition/subtraction	Rotation	
None	135	210	2699
Code size	109	168	2258
Execution time	69	119	2539

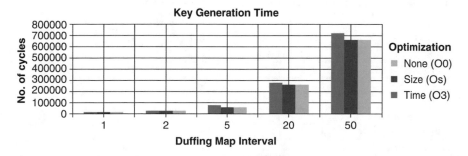

Fig. 14.9 Impact of Duffing map interval on key generation time

algorithm. An appropriate selection of microcontroller's operating frequency based on the maximum baudrate to be chosen for the USART satisfies the above-said restriction of the algorithm.

14.5 Discussions

Table 14.3 makes a comparison of the parameters considered in the implementation of the proposed work with the results available in earlier works [12, 13]. In contrast to the variable baudrate based serial data encryption by Rhitvik and Gaurav [13] and chaotic digital key based encryption by Zapateiro et al. [12], the proposed method provides security in the dual fold by using a chaotic key to vary the baudrate.

One of the future challenges to be addressed will be replacing the use of Terminating Character with an appropriate solution to indicate the final character of the last data block. This will give the freedom for the user to utilise any unique character as a part of their secret data. Further, the issues concerned with data loss at the receiver side should also be addressed.

14.6 Conclusions and Future Directions

Baudrate based encryption algorithm for serial data exchange between a pair of embedded devices connected in a multiprocessor network through USART is presented in this chapter. The algorithm uses 2D discrete Duffing map to generate chaotic keys and ensures intrinsic security by providing garbage data to the receiver that fails to set its USART with the appropriate baudrate instantaneously as indicated in the key. Further, the user-defined block sizes strengthen the algorithm by its random byte interval between generation and usage of subsequent keys. Although the results were analysed for text encryption, the proposed method is suitable for

Table 14.3 Comparison of the proposed method with previous work

Parameters	Proposed method	Previous work	
		Ref. [13]	Ref. [12]
Target device	AVR (ATmega8)	AVR	AVR (ATmega328)
Variable baudrate	✓	✓	✗
Chaotic key	✓	✗	✓
Timing analysis	✓	✗	✓
Code size analysis	✓	✗	✗
Throughput analysis	✓	✗	✗
Optimization analysis	✓	✗	✗

securing the exchange of any multimedia data in serial form. The obtained results confirm the betterment of the proposed scheme over earlier works.

The future work may be the identification of a novel parameter to extend this security feature for other on-chip serial protocols such as Serial Peripheral Interface (SPI) and Two-Wire Interface (TWI) supported by microcontrollers.

References

1. Rinne, S., Eisenbarth, T. and Paar, C., 2007. Performance analysis of contemporary lightweight block ciphers on 8-bit microcontrollers. In Ecrypt Workshop SPEED, 33-43.
2. Noura, H., Chehab, A., Sleem, L., Noura, M., Couturier, R. and Mansour, M.M., 2018. One round cipher algorithm for multimedia IoT devices. Multimedia Tools and Applications. 77:1-31.
3. Janakiraman, S., Thenmozhi, K., Rayappan, J. B. B., and Amirtharajan, R., 2018. Lightweight chaotic image encryption algorithm for the real-time embedded system: Implementation and analysis on the 32-bit microcontroller. Microprocess. Microsyst. 56:1–12.
4. Tanougast, C., Dandache, A., Azzaz, M.S. and Sadoudi, S., 2012. Hardware Design of Embedded Systems for Security Applications. INTECH Open Access Publisher.
5. Stanescu, D., Stangaciu, V., Ghergulescu, I. and Stratulat, M., 2009. Steganography on embedded devices. In IEEE 5th International Symposium onApplied Computational Intelligence and Informatics, SACI'09, 313-318.
6. Gonze, D., 2013. The logistic equation [Available Online] http://homepages.ulb.ac.be/~dgonze/TEACHING/logistic.pdf
7. Rajagopalan, S., Sivaraman, R., Upadhyay, H.N., Rayappan, J.B.B. and Amirtharajan, R., 2018. ONChip peripherals are ON for chaos–an image fused encryption. Microprocessors and Microsystems. 61: 257-278.
8. Ramalingam, B., Ravichandran, D., Annadurai, A.A., Rengarajan, A. and Rayappan, J.B.B., 2018. Chaos triggered image encryption-a reconfigurable security solution. Multimedia Tools and Applications, 77: 11669-11692.
9. Aboul-Seoud, A.K., El-Badawy, E.S.A., Mokhtar, A., El-Masry, W., El-Barbry, M. and Hafez, A.E.D.S., 2011. A simple 8-bit digital microcontroller implementation for chaotic sequence generation. In IEEE National Radio Science Conference (NRSC), 1-9.
10. Serna, J.D. and Joshi, A., 2012. Visualizing the logistic map with a microcontroller.Physics Education, 47: 736-740.
11. Kahan, W., 1997. IEEE Standard 754 for Binary Floating-Point Arithmetic [Available Online] http://www.eecs.berkeley.edu/~wkahan/ieee754status/IEEE754.PDF
12. Zapateiro De la Hoz, M., Acho, L. and Vidal, Y., 2015. An experimental realization of a chaos-based secure communication using Arduino microcontrollers. Scientific World Journal, 123080: 1-10. https://doi.org/10.1155/2015/123080
13. Rhitvik, K. and Gaurav, J., 2016. Serial communication encryption in embedded system. Proceedings of ASAR-IJIEEE, 23-27.[Available Online] http://ww1.microchip.com/downloads/en/DeviceDoc/70188E.pdf
14. PIC24H Family Data sheet [Available Online] https://www.alliedelec.com/m/d/7233b39102e5973a203de8d684cd3f3f.pdf
15. Application Report, 2004. Automatic Baud Rate Detection on the MSP430. [Available Online] https://nanopdf.com/download/automatic-baud-rate-detection-on-the-msp430_pdf
16. Atmega8 Datasheet, 2013. [Available Online] https://ww1.microchip.com/downloads/en/DeviceDoc/Atmel-2486-8-bit-AVR-microcontroller-ATmega8_L_datasheet.pdf

17. Mishra, M. and Mankar, V., 2012. Chaotic cipher using arnolds and duffings map. Advances in Computer Science, Engineering & Applications,529-539. Springer, Berlin, Heidelberg.
18. Stoyanov, B. and Kordov, K., 2014. Novel image encryption scheme based on Chebyshev polynomial and Duffing map. Scientific World J., 2014: 1-11.
19. Getting Started with Atmel Studio 7, 2018. [Available Online] http://ww1.microchip.com/downloads/en/DeviceDoc/Getting-Started-with-Atmel-Studio7.pdf

Chapter 15
Robust and Secure Hiding Scheme for Open Channel Transmission of Digital Images

Harsh Vikram Singh and Purnima Pal

15.1 Introduction

In the recent era with the development of computer technology and multimedia, images, audio, text and video can be more produced easily, processed and stored by digital devices in recent years. Watermarking technique is introduced to protect the secret data from the copying [1]. The main objectives of watermarking are embed information without any distortion of cover image, perceptual degradation should be minimum and without any loss extraction of information [2]. In image watermarking technique various transformations are used and they are DFT (Discrete Fourier Transform), DCT (Discrete Cosine Transform), DWT (Discrete Wavelet Transform) and spatial Domain transformations (Figs. 15.1, 15.2, 15.3, 15.4, 15.5, 15.6, 15.7, 15.8, 15.9, 15.10, 15.11, 15.12, 15.13 and 15.14).

DWT is partial transform and have ability of multi scale analysis. Decomposition of the original image is done into four sub-band images by DWT technique in which three high frequency parts (HL, LH and HH, named detail sub images) and one low frequency part (LL, named approximate sub image) [3].

In Singular Value Decomposition a image is consider as a real matrix I, which can be decomposed as [4] $I = USV^T$ which is known as singular value decomposition of I. Where U is m*m unitary matrix, S is a m*n matrix with non negative numbers on the diagonal and zeros on the off diagonal, and V^T denotes the conjugate transpose of V, an n*n unitary matrix.

H. V. Singh (✉) · P. Pal
Department of Electronics, Kamla Nehru Institute of Technology (KNIT), Sultanpur, Uttar Pradesh, India

© Springer Nature Switzerland AG 2019
A. K. Singh, A. Mohan (eds.), *Handbook of Multimedia Information Security: Techniques and Applications*, https://doi.org/10.1007/978-3-030-15887-3_15

341

Fig. 15.1 Cover image, KNIT watermark and watermarked image

Watermarked Image.

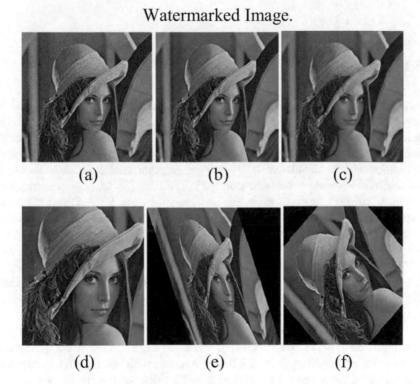

(a)   (b)   (c)

(d)   (e)   (f)

Fig. 15.2 Watermarked Lena image after various attacks: (**a**) salt and pepper attack, (**b**) mean attack, (**c**) median attack, (**d**) crop attack, (**e**) shear attack, (**f**) rotation attack

15.2 Proposed Methodology

Initially, the process of decomposition is applied on the original (cover) image by using 2-D DWT technology into four sub-bands, and then we apply the SVD

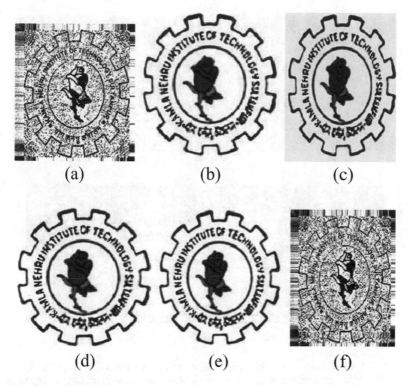

Fig. 15.3 Extracted KNIT watermark image after various attacks on Lena image (**a**) salt and pepper attack, (**b**)mean attack, (**c**) median attack, (**d**) crop attack, (**e**) shear attack, (**f**) rotation attack

Fig. 15.4 Cover Lena image, JAVA watermark and watermarked image

on each band by modifying singular values of each sub bands. After treating the watermarked image from various attacks like rotation, crop, mean, filtering, median filtering, shear, salt and pepper, we extract inserted originally watermark image from the bands and evaluate the values of PSNR, SSIM and NC.

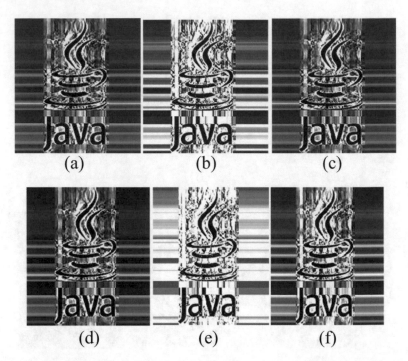

Fig. 15.5 Extracted JAVA watermark images after various attacks on Lena watermarked image: (**a**) crop attack, (**b**) rotation attack, (**c**) mean attack, (**d**) median attacks, (**e**) salt and pepper attack, (**f**) shear attack

Fig. 15.6 Cover Lena image, quotation watermark and watermarked image

15.2.1 Embedding Process

1. Consider the cover image and convert the colour image into gray scale image.
2. Decompose the cover image into four sub-bands. Haar transformation is used in this paper for original image (I) decomposition into four sub-bands.
3. After DWT, SVD is performed to the sub-band images.

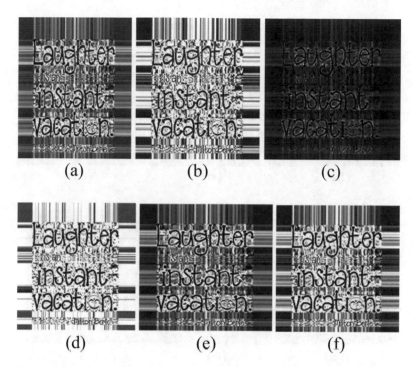

(a)   (b)   (c)

(d)   (e)   (f)

Fig. 15.7 Extracted quotation watermark images after various attacks on Lena watermarked image: (**a**) crop attack, (**b**) rotation attack, (**c**) mean attack, (**d**) median attacks, (**e**) salt and pepper attack, (**f**) shear attack

Fig. 15.8 Cover Mandrill image, KNIT watermark and watermarked image

$$I^k = U_a^J S_a^J V_a^{JT}$$

where $J = 1, 2, 3, 4$ where J denotes LL, LH, HL and HH sub-bands and XXXXXXXXX$_i^J$, i = 1, . . . , n.

4. Apply SVD on the Watermark Image i.e.

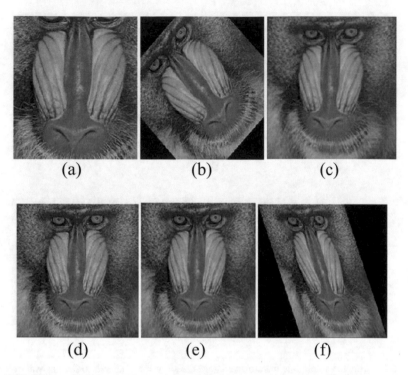

Fig. 15.9 Watermarked image after various attacks image: (**a**) crop attack, (**b**) rotation attack, (**c**) mean attack, (**d**) median attacks, (**e**) salt and pepper attack, (**f**) shear attack

$$W = U_W S_W V_W^T \lambda_{wi}, i = 1, \ldots, n$$

5. Modification of the singular values of cover image in each sub-band with the singular values of watermark image,

$$\lambda_i^{*J} = \lambda_i^J + \alpha_J \lambda_{wi}$$

where i = 1, 2, ..., n and J = 1, 2, 3, 4

6. After the above step we obtain four sets of modified DWT coefficients, i.e.

$$I^{*J} = U_a^J S_a^{*J} V_a^{JT}$$

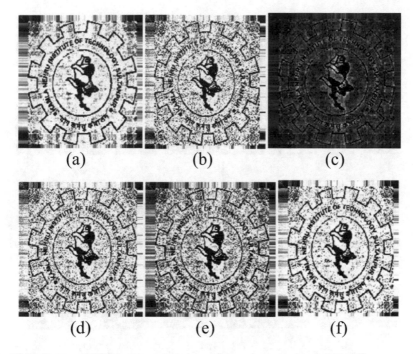

Fig. 15.10 Extracted KNIT watermark images after various attacks on Mandrill watermarked image: (a) crop attack, (b) rotation attack, (c) mean attack, (d) median attacks, (e) salt and pepper attack, (f) shear attack

Fig. 15.11 Cover Mandrill image, JAVA watermark and watermarked image

where $J = 1, 2, 3, 4$

7. After performing the IDWT on the subbands we obtained a watermarked image I_W.

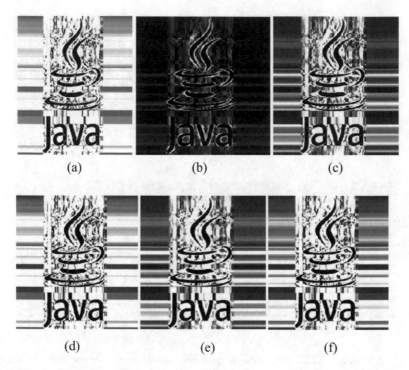

Fig. 15.12 Extracted JAVA watermark images after various attacks on Mandrill watermarked image: (**a**) crop attack, (**b**) rotation attack, (**c**) mean attack, (**d**) median attacks, (**e**) salt and pepper attack, (**f**) shear attack

Fig. 15.13 Cover Mandrill image, quotation watermark and watermarked image

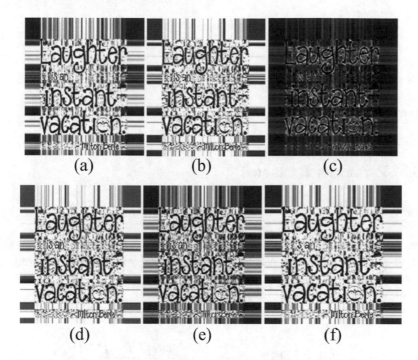

Fig. 15.14 Extracted quotation watermark images after various attacks on Mandrill watermarked image: (**a**) crop attack, (**b**) rotation attack, (**c**) mean attack, (**d**) median attacks, (**e**) salt and pepper attack, (**f**) shear attack

15.2.2   Extraction Process

1. Decompose the Watermarked image (I^{*j}) which is distorted by various attack into four sub-bands by using Haar transformation.
2. Then SVD is apply to the sub-bands i.e.

$$I^{*J} = U_a^J S_a^{*J} V_a^{JT}$$

$J = 1, 2, 3, 4$, where J denotes the attacked sub-band.

3. Extract the singular values from each sub-bands.

$$\lambda_{wi}{}^j = \left(\lambda_i^{*j} - \lambda_i^j \right) / \alpha j$$

where $i = 1, 2, \ldots, n, j = 1, 2, 3, 4$.

4. Construct the watermark using the singular values i.e.

$$W^j = U_W S_W V_W{}^T$$

where j = 1, 2, 3, 4.

15.3 Parameter Evaluated

15.3.1 PSNR

The PSNR value is considered for the distortion measure of original image after hiding information. The original data is considered as signal and the error introduced by various attack is considered as noise. Where I is the original carrier image and I_W is watermarked image [7–13].

$$PSNR = 10 \log \left[\frac{512^* 512^* \max \left[I\left(i, j\right) \right]^2}{\sum_{i=1}^{512} \sum_{j=1}^{512} \left[I\left(i, j\right) - I_w\left(i, j\right) \right]^2} \right]$$

15.3.2 Normalized Correlation Coefficient

The difference between the extracted watermark image and the original watermark image is evaluated by using normalized correlation coefficient (NC) [14–18].

$$NCC = \frac{\sum_{i=1}^{32} \sum_{j=1}^{32} w_i\left(i, j \times w_i^*\left(i, j\right)\right)}{\sum_{i=1}^{32} \sum_{j=1}^{32} w_i\left(i, j \times w_i\left(i, j\right)\right)}$$

15.3.3   SSIM

Measures of the perceptual difference between two similar images is established by SSIM. For the prediction of quality of Image is depend on a reference image that is distortion free image [19–23].

$$SSIM\,(x,\,y) = \frac{\left(2\mu_x\mu_y + c_1\right)\left(2\sigma_{xy} + c_2\right)}{\left(\mu_x^2 + \mu_y^2 + c_1\right)\left(\sigma_x^2 + \sigma_y^2 + c_2\right)}$$

15.4   Results

15.4.1   Conclusion

A proposed algorithm Study and Analysis of Robust Watermarking Scheme Using DWT-SVD Techniques for Digital Images provides the better imperceptibility of the watermark without adequate resilience to various attacks types and provides robustness against various types of attacks which is implemented to degraded perceptual quality of cover image. In this, cover image is decomposed into LL, LH, HL, HH sub bands using the discrete wavelet transform and the Singular value Decomposition is applied on the each sub bands. The modification is performed on the coefficients of the singular value decomposition ant then by using Inverse Discrete Wavelet Transform we obtain Watermarked Image. Proposed algorithm undergoes through subjective judgments of image quality check and extracted watermark reconstruction. The watermarked images were evaluated for robustness by using PSNR, NC, and SSIM. The results show that, if used appropriately, the distortion caused by the watermarking embedding is perceptually low. This was concluded from the high values of PSNR and SSIM as shown in Tables 15.1, 15.2, 15.3, and 15.4. Similarities between original watermark and the recovered watermark were evaluated using the normalized cross correlation values (NC). Comparisons of new algorithm against the earlier established algorithm confirmed that it offered better performance to the quality of the watermarked image and robustness against various attack is shown in Tables 15.5 and 15.6. Values of NC were almost high the implemented algorithms are robust against common watermarking attacks which proves that the quality was improved using the DWT AND SVD algorithm.

Table 15.1 PSNR value of various extracted watermark images on Lena image

Attacks	KNIT logo	JAVA logo	Quotation
Salt and pepper	26.1089	27.3814	26.3442
Mean	22.1293	23.8954	21.4968
Median	25.1591	23.3851	23.8014
Rotation	25.9333	25.0789	24.7584
Shear	26.1097	24.3329	24.5414
Crop	25.5689	23.8954	24.4409

Table 15.2 SSIM value of various extracted watermark image on Lena image

Attacks	KNIT logo	JAVA logo	Quotation
Salt and pepper	0.1226	0.4087	0.2778
Mean	0.4828	0.2254	0.0982
Median	0.4838	0.1839	0.1129
Rotation	0.2784	0.1301	0.1196
Shear	0.3862	0.2118	0.1125
Crop	0.4522	0.2254	0.1509

Table 15.3 PSNR value of various extracted watermark images on Mandrill image

Attacks	KNIT logo	JAVA logo	Quotation
Salt and pepper	28.0139	27.8795	29.491
Mean	22.8341	21.5105	22.3369
Median	26.8462	24.3859	25.9973
Rotation	27.6601	27.1268	28.1371
Shear	29.0077	26.3377	28.0456
Crop	29.3055	25.2823	27.3376

Table 15.4 SSIM value of various extracted watermark images on Mandrill image

Attacks	KNIT logo	JAVA logo	Quotation
Salt and pepper	0.1807	0.4245	0.4411
Mean	0.1065	0.0973	0.1872
Median	0.1326	0.1778	0.2482
Rotation	0.1731	0.3771	0.4031
Shear	0.2562	0.3054	0.3789
Crop	0.2906	0.2433	0.3328

Table 15.5 Comparative values of PSNR of literature [5] and proposed work of watermarked image

Attacks	PSNR of literature [5]	PSNR of proposed work							
		Lena image				Mandrill image			
		KNIT logo	JAVA logo	Quotation		KNIT logo	JAVA logo	Quotation
Mean	22.9708	28.1472	23.9671	27.2861		25.9233	26.1089	23.8954
Salt and pepper	35.2672	25.1716	29.8119	23.4522		28.5414	24.5414	25.9333
Median	22.6924	34.5239	31.2642	29.3862		28.3851	27.3829	26.5689
Rotation	30.9875	30.4283	28.9915	31.5689		30.1089	31.3329	29.3329

Table 15.6 Comparative values of NC of literature [6] and proposed work of watermarked image

Attacks	NC of literature [6]	NC of proposed work					
		Lena image			Mandrill image		
		KNIT logo	JAVA logo	Quotation	KNIT logo	JAVA logo	Quotation
Mean	0.9081	0.9675	0.9126	0.9435	0.9742	0.9218	0.9125
Salt and pepper	0.9969	0.9501	0.9357	0.9528	0.9748	0.9548	0.9218
Median	0.9905	0.9915	0.9814	0.9917	0.9874	0.9244	0.9876
Rotation	0.9950	0.9650	0.9125	0.9384	0.9567	0.9984	0.9839

References

1. Mei Jiansheng1, Li Sukang1 and Tan Xiaomei "A Digital Watermarking Algorithm Based on DCT and DWT", International Symposium on Web Information Systems and Applications (WISA) 2009, pp. 104-107.
2. W. Zeng and B Liu, "On Resolving Rightful Ownership of Digital Images by Invisible Watermarks", Proc. IEEE 1997 Intrenational Conference on Image Processing, ICIP-97, Vol. 1, pp 552-555.
3. Chandra Munesh, Pandey Shikha," A DWT Domain Visible Watermarking Techniques for Digital Images" International Conference on Electronics and Information Engineering (ICEIE), Volume 2,2010,pp-421-427.
4. Asna Furqan, Munish Kumar, "Study and Analysis of Robust DWT-SVD Domain Based Digital Image Watermarking Technique Using MATLAB", IEEE International Conference on Computational Intelligence & Communication Technology, 2015 pp 638-644.
5. Saira Mudassar, Munazah Jamal, Farkhand Shakeel Mahmood, Nouman Shah, Hamza Bin Tahir, Hassan Malik, "Hybrid DWT-SVD Digital Image Watermarking", International Journal of Computer (IJC), 2017, pp 105-109
6. Xueyi Ye, Xueting Chen, Meng Deng, Shuyun Hui, Yunlu Wang, "A Multiple-Level DCT Based Robust DWT-SVD Watermark Method",10th International Conference on Computational Intelligence and Security, IEEE, 2014, pp 479-483.
7. Neha Chauhan, Akhilesh A. Waoo and P. S. Patheja, "information hiding watermarking detection technique by psnr and rgb intensity", Journal of Global Research in Computer Science, Volume 3, No. 9, September 2012 PP 18-22.
8. Wang Y., Doherty J.F., Dyck V.R.E., "A wavelet-based watermarking algorithm for ownership verification of digital images", IEEE Transactions, Image Processing, 11 pp. 77-88, 2002.
9. Evelyn Brannock, Michael Weeks, Robert Harrison, "Watermarking with Wavelets: Simplicity Leads to Robustness", Computer Science Department Georgia State University, South eastcon, IEEE, 2018, pp 587 – 592.
10. N. Chandrakar and J. Baggaa, "Performance Comparison of Digital Image Watermarking Techniques: A Survey", International Journalof computer Application Technology and Research, vol. 2, issue 2,(2013), pp. 126-130.
11. Parag Havaldar, Gerard Medioni, "Watermarking Techniques" in Multimedia Systems, Algorithms, Standards, and Industry Practices, Boston, USA, Course Technology, Cengage Learning, 2010, ch.13, sec.2.1, pp. 414-415.
12. Vinita Gupta, "A Review on Image Watermarking and Its Techniques", International Journal of Advanced Research in Computer Science and Software Engineering,Volume 4, Issue 1, 2014
13. Emir Ganic, and Ahmet M. Eskicioglu, "Robust DWT-SVD Domain Image Watermarking: Embedding date in All Frequencies", CiteSeerX, MM&SEC'04, 2004, pp 20-21.
14. Chandra Munesh, Pandey Shikha," A DWT Domain Visible Watermarking Techniques for Digital Images" International Conference on Electronics and Information Engineering (ICEIE), Volume 2,2010,pp-421-427.
15. Harsh Vikram Singh, Sonam Tyagi, Raghav Agarwal Sandeep Kumar Gangwar, "Digital Watermarking Techniques for Security Applications", International Conference on Emerging Trends in Electrical, Electronics and Sustainable Energy Systems (ICETEESES) 2016, pp 379-382.
16. M.M Yeung et al. "Digital Watermarking for High-Quality Imaging",1997 IEEE First Workshop on Multimedia Signal Processing, J Princeton, New Jersey, 1997, pp 357-362.
17. Munesh Chandra, Shikha Pandel, Rama Chaudhary, "Digital watermarking technique for protecting digital images" Third IEEE International Conference on Computer and Information Science and Technology (ICCSIT 2010), pp.226-233.
18. Mei Jiansheng1, Li Sukang1 and Tan Xiaomei "A Digital Watermarking Algorithm Based on DCT and DWT", International Symposium on Web Information Systems and Applications (WISA) 2009, pp. 104-107.

19. Harsh Vikram Singh, "Information Hiding Techniques for Image Covers," LAP LAMBERT Academic Publishing GmbH & Co. KG, Ddudweiler Landstr. 99, 66123 Saarbrücken, Germany, ISBN-10: 3843377537 ISBN-13: 978-3843377539
20. Harsh Vikram Singh, Raghav Agrawal "Diagnosis of Carious Legions Using Digital Processing of Dental Radiographs" Scopus Indexed Springer Book Series "Computational Vision and Bio Inspired Computing", pp 864-882, 2018. (ISBN: 978-3-319-71766-1)
21. Harsh Vikram Singh, Ankur Rai "Medical Image Watermarking in Transform Domain" Accepted in Scopus Indexed Springer Book Series "Advances in Intelligent Systems and Computing". April 2018 (ISBN: 978-3-319-45991-2)
22. Harsh Vikram Singh and Arun Kumar Singh "DCT and DWT based Intellectual Right Protection in Digital Images" Accepted in Scopus Indexed Springer Book Series "Advances in Intelligent Systems and Computing". May 2018 (ISBN: 978-3-319-45991-2)
23. Harsh Vikram Singh, Ankur Rai, "Machine Learning Based Robust Watermarking Technique for Medical Image Transmitted over LTE Network", Journal of Intelligent Systems (JISYS), De Gruyter, Scopus, Vol. 27 (1), pp.105-114 (2018) (ISSN2191-026X)

Part II
Multimedia Processing

Chapter 16
Image Processing Based Automated Glaucoma Detection Techniques and Role of De-Noising: A Technical Survey

Sima Sahu, Harsh Vikram Singh, Basant Kumar, Amit Kumar Singh, and Prabhat Kumar

16.1 Introduction

Glaucoma is a retinal disorder that results the narrowing of visual field. It is caused due to the degeneration of retinal nerve fibers. Increase in Intra Ocular Pressure (IOP) within the eye causes glaucoma. It is the primary cause of blindness and it would affect 80 million people in 2020 [1]. Prior detection may stop the progression of this disease. There are some conventional diagnostic techniques such as Tonometry, Perimetry, Ophthalmoscopy, Gonioscopy and Pachymetry for glaucoma detection. These diagnostic methods are tiresome, time consuming and expensive. New diagnostic approaches should be developed that would enable early detection of glaucoma. Glaucoma can be detected by applying intelligent algorithms for extracting diagnostic features from different imaging modalities. Image modalities used for the detection of glaucoma are fundus, ultrasound, optical coherence tomography (OCT) and Heidelberg Retinal Tomography (HRT), which are generated by using different sources [2–6]. The OCT has a similar working principle as ultrasound imaging, but the difference is that, ultrasound imaging uses sound whereas OCT uses light to capture the high resolution retinal structure. So

S. Sahu (✉)
Dr. A. P. J. Abdul Kalam Technical University, Lucknow, Uttar Pradesh, India

H. V. Singh
Department of Electronics, Kamla Nehru Institute of Technology (KNIT), Sultanpur, Uttar Pradesh, India

B. Kumar
Department of ECE, Motilal Nehru NIT Allahabad, Prayagraj, India
e-mail: singhbasant@mnnit.ac.in

A. K. Singh · P. Kumar
Department of Computer Science and Engineering, NIT Patna, Patna, India
e-mail: prabhat@nitp.ac.in

© Springer Nature Switzerland AG 2019
A. K. Singh, A. Mohan (eds.), *Handbook of Multimedia Information Security: Techniques and Applications*, https://doi.org/10.1007/978-3-030-15887-3_16

OCT has the advantage over ultrasound imaging in processing speed because light travels faster than sound. HRT uses laser scanning system and captures the three-dimensional retinal image. Quantitative assessment data of the ocular structure and topographical changes can be viewed on this imaging system. Digital fundus camera produces fundus image. These images are generally stored in digital form and can be demonstrated on a monitor. Different features are considered for diagnosis the glaucoma. These features are complete field of vision, color and shape of the optic nerve, inner eye pressure, angle between iris and cornea and thickness of the cornea [7]. These features are used to check the abnormalities in the retinal image. Severity of the glaucoma disease can be tested through the field of vision. Glaucoma disease results tunnel vision in patients. The optic nerve in glaucoma patients generally termed as cupped nerve and this disease causes the nerve to look pale. The normal eye pressure is 12–22 mm Hg and when it increases beyond the normal range, causes glaucoma. Normally, the angle between iris and cornea is 40–45°. For a primary angle—closer glaucoma patient, the angle decreases to less than 20°. Central Corneal Thickness (CCT) is an important measurement of glaucoma risk. CCT has the inverse relation with the glaucoma damage [8].

Noise may degrade the quality of medical images and hence the performance. This chapter has reviewed de-noising methods for reducing speckle noise which is a main issue in OCT and ultrasound retinal image. By using efficient de-speckling method in image processing, the accuracy of the glaucoma detection has been increased. The de-speckling methods are used as preprocessing step in glaucoma detection.

In this chapter, different image modalities along with diagnostic parameters used in glaucoma detection are discussed in Sect. 16.2. Different steps of detection are briefly discussed in this section. Existing de-speckling methods are summarized in Sect. 16.3. A mapping between de-noising and detection is also reviewed in this section. Section 16.4 concludes the chapter.

16.2 Digital Image Processing Based Glaucoma Detection

Digital image processing (DIP) supports the ophthalmologist in glaucoma detection. Glaucoma detection through computer-aided diagnostics plays an important role in medical science and supports an ophthalmologist to diagnosis glaucoma through DIP. Computer-aided screening analyses the glaucomatous image through pattern recognition techniques that supports the ophthalmologist to diagnosis glaucoma through DIP. This section provides the current progress in digital image processing techniques for automatic glaucoma diagnosis.

Table 16.1 Diagnostic features for the detection of glaucoma

Image modalities	Diagnostic parameters
Fundus image	(a) Glaucoma risk index (GRI)
	(b) Optic nerve head(ONH)
	(c) Cup to disk ratio(CDR)
OCT image	(a) Ganglion cell complex (GCC) thickness
	(b) Retinal nerve fiber layer (RNFL) thickness
Ultrasound image	(a) Angle opening distance (AOD) calculation
	(b) Location of the apex point
HRT image	(a) Mean height contour
	(b) Rim area

16.2.1 Medical Image Modalities and Diagnostic Parameters

Recently digital image processing methods are preferred than the existing methods in the detection of eye diseases. Intelligent algorithms are applied for extracting diagnostic features from different imaging modalities. Different features are considered for diagnosis the glaucoma. Different diagnostic parameters, those are used for the early detection of the glaucoma are given in Table 16.1.

Glaucoma risk index, Optic Nerve Head (ONH) and cup-to-disc ratio (CDR) are the key parameters used in fundus image modality for the detection of glaucoma. Bock et al. [2] proposed a method for automatic glaucoma detection, where the authors compressed and combined the generic features of image like pixel intensity values, FFT coefficients and B-spline coefficients of the image to form Glaucoma Risk Index (GRI). Cup-to-disk ratio also plays a key role in the detection process. It is defined as the ratio of cup area to the disc area. ONH normalization is an important process for observing glaucomatous characteristics. Thickness of Retinal Nerve Fiber Layer (RNFL) and Ganglion Cell Complex (GCC) are used for glaucoma detection in case of OCT image modality. Measurement of Angle Opening Distance at 500 μm (AOD 500) and the angle apex point are parameters used in ultrasound image for diagnosis of glaucoma. HRT image uses mean height contour and rim area parameters for diagnosis glaucoma. Rim area is the area which is enclosed by the contour line and Mean height contour is measured as the height along the contour line.

16.2.2 Key Steps for Glaucoma Detection Using Digital Image Processing

Figure 16.1 shows various steps involved in glaucoma detection using digital image processing. The steps are preprocessing, image segmentation, feature extraction, classification and performance analysis.

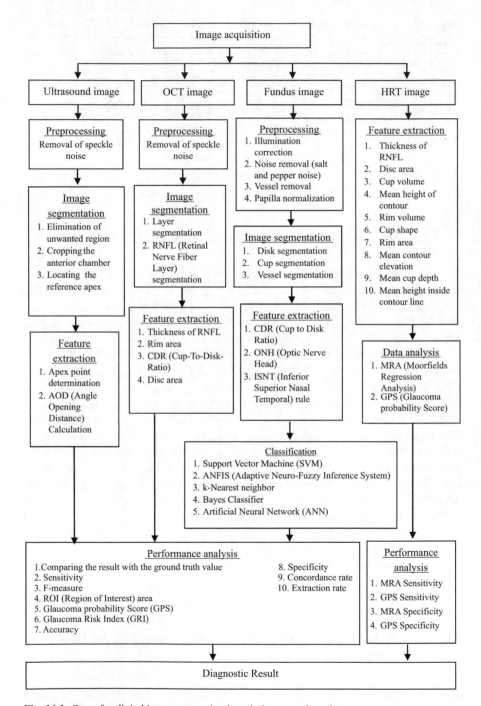

Fig. 16.1 Steps for digital image processing based glaucoma detection

16.2.2.1 Image Preprocessing

Image preprocessing step improves the recognition of data in images and transfers the image into suitable one for further processing. This step removes the inherent noise present in the image and eliminates the disease independent variations like inhomogeneous illumination and blood vessels. Image enhancement is the ultimate goal of the preprocessing step. The retinal image is generally corrupted by noise in its acquisition or transmission. The different sources of noise are due to the use of charge coupled device (CCD) and some outer effects such as space radiation can have the negative effect on the obtained data. Impulsive noise is found in sensors and transmission channel during the acquisition and transmission of the digital fundus images. Salt and pepper noise is a classic kind of impulsive noise that affects the fundus image [9]. Speckle noise affects more to OCT image. It degrades the fine details and makes it difficult for the proper diagnosis. Apart from OCT other imaging modalities such as ultrasound image is also affected by speckle noise [10]. Speckle occurs in images whose fundamental structures are too small. The transducer in ultrasound imaging system produces ultrasonic waves and these waves are passed through human body tissues. The return sound waves are collected and vibrated the transducer that transforms again to electrical pulses. These pulses are processed by ultrasonic scanner which converts electrical pulses to digital image. In this case higher frequencies are required for better resolution of the image but it limits the depth of penetration. In this technique, noise occurs due to the air gap present or improper contact between the body and transducer probe. It is very hard to identify small and narrow contrast lesion in our body due to the speckle noise [11].

Various algorithms have been proposed for preprocessing of retinal image and proved to be useful in the glaucoma diagnosis. Meier et al. [12] verified the effect of preprocessing on the detection of glaucoma eye diseases. Three preprocessing steps were applied by them in fundus retinal image. They are illumination correction, vessel inpainting and region of interest (ROI) normalization. The accuracy of detection was 79% for normal image and 81% for preprocessed image. The accuracy of preprocessed image was better than the normal image in glaucoma diagnosis.

16.2.2.2 Image Segmentation

The image segmentation step transfers the image into more suitable and simplest one for further analysis. This step simplifies the image and makes it more meaningful for further processing steps. Vascular structures, specific organs, tissues and organs are extracted in this step. Segmentation targets accurate extraction of glaucoma abnormalities. Glaucoma detection using fundus eye image requires the segmentation of disk, vessel and optic cup. OCT retinal image requires segmentation of different eye layers. In ultrasound eye image, segmentation is required for locating the apex point.

Ishikawa et al. [13] proposed a method for segmenting macular Nerve Fiber layer (mNFL) in OCT image. In this method mNFL thickness was compared with the inner retinal complex. The authors concluded this method as a powerful method that can be used for glaucoma diagnosis. Morales et al. [14] proposed a segmentation method for the disc contour. The method was based on principal component analysis (PCA). Five public databases were used to validate the method. Different parameters like Jaccard's Coefficient (JC), Dice's coefficient, true positive fraction and false positive fraction were used for validation. The detection accuracy of the proposed method was 0.9947. A super pixel classification method was proposed by Cheng et al. [15] for optic disc and cup segmentation in retinal fundus image. The proposed method classified each pixel as disc or non disc. They applied this method on 650 retinal images. The result was compared with the manually marked cup and disc boundary by the trained professionals. The calculated average overlapping error was 9.5% and 24.1% for optic cup and disc segmentation respectively.

16.2.2.3 Feature Extraction

Feature extraction step extracts the specific features (or diagnostic parameters), which determines whether the patient is having glaucoma or not. It is the fundamental step in automatic detection of glaucoma. This step converts the image into its reduced form. This step makes the diagnosis easier during classification. Many efforts have been made to extract features from the retinal image. Different features are apex point, Angle Opening Distance (AOD), CDR, thickness of RNFL, Inferior Superior Nasal Temporal (ISNT) ratio, rim area, Disc area, cup shape, rim volume, cup volume, and mean height of contour. The most important feature used to determine glaucoma is CDR [16]. CDR specifies the change in cup area due to glaucoma. Wong et al. [17] proposed a method to calculate CDR for determining glaucoma progression. A level set technique was used to detect the boundary of the optic cup and disc in fundus image. The proposed method was validated in 104 retinal images. CDR of the images were calculated and found to be within the range of ±2, which is also the range for manually calculated CDR values. The accuracy of the method was 96%. A canny edge detection filter was proposed by Hatanaka et al. [18] to determine the edges of the optic disc. They calculated CDR using vertical profile of the disc. They implemented zero crossing method to find out the cup area. The concordance rate of the proposed method was 85%, which was compared to the cup area determined by ophthalmologist. The Area Under Curve (AUC) of the proposed method was 0.974. Khan et al. [19] proposed a method to detect glaucoma by extracting two features of retinal image. These features are CDR and area ratio of Neuro Retinal Rim (NRR) in ISNT quadrants. The proposed method achieved an accuracy of 94%. Ahmad et al. [20] proposed a method to extract features such as CDR, ratio of NRR in inferior, superior, temporal and nasal quadrants. Their method was validated over 80 retinal images and the accuracy was 97.5%.

16.2.2.4 Classification

Classification step calculates the probability of glaucoma disease and based on the probability, classifies as glaucoma or not glaucoma. The classification procedure is based on the features extracted from the retinal image. Turpin et al. [21] used the support vector machine (SVM) classifier in their proposed method. The authors have proposed a data mining technique for checking glaucoma progression in fundus image. Visual field measurements were taken for detecting the progression. Nayak et al. [22] proposed Artificial Neuro Network (ANN) classifier for automatic detection of glaucoma in fundus retinal image. Different features like CDR, ratio of the distance between optic disc center and optic nerve head to diameter of optic disc and the ratio of blood vessels area in inferior superior side to area of blood vessels in the nasal temporal side were validated by using the ANN classifier. The specificity and sensitivity of the method was 100% and 80% respectively. An automated classifier based on Adaptive Neuro Fuzzy Inference System (ANFIS) was developed by Huang et al. [23] to distinguish between normal eye and glaucomatous eye in OCT retinal image. The classification accuracy was 90% for training set and 85.6% for testing set. In this technique, the Region of Interest (ROI) area was 0.925. Bock et al. [24] proposed a two stage classification method by combining features of glaucomatous fundus image. The authors compared the detection accuracy of SVM, Bayes and K-Nearest neighbor classifiers. The classification accuracy was 86% for SVM classifier, which was better than other two classifiers. The F-measure for the SVM classifier was 0.83 for healthy eye and 0.88 for glaucomatous eye.

16.2.2.5 Performance Analysis

The purpose of performance analysis step is to estimate the accuracy of the glaucoma detection algorithm. There are two potential methods used in analyzing the results. They are statistical method and ground truth method. Statistical method uses statistical calculations for the performance assessment. In ground truth method, the results are compared to the ground truth values obtained from the ophthalmologist for performance assessment. Different statistical performance parameters used in glaucoma diagnosis are sensitivity, specificity, F-measure, ROI area, Glaucoma Risk Index (GRI), Moorfields Regression Analysis (MRA), Glaucoma Probability Score (GPS), accuracy, concordance rate and extraction rate. Nyul [25] proposed a glaucoma detection method by evaluating the GRI parameter of a retinal fundus image. The authors designed a SVM classifier by combining the features of FFT coefficients, pixel intensity and B-spline coefficients of the digital image. Glaucoma Risk Index (GRI) was calculated from the values of the classifier and based on the GRI value, glaucoma was identified. Bock et al. [2] used specificity, sensitivity and GRI parameters to show the accuracy of detection. F-measure was used by Bock et al. [24] to show the detection performance. Ferreras et al. [26] used GPS and MRA parameters to discriminate glaucomatous eye from healthy eye in HRT image.

16.3   Role of De-Noising in Glaucoma Detection

De-noising is the crux in glaucoma detection, as it gives meaningful data for further processing. Imaging techniques based on the detection of coherent waves are affected by speckle noise such as ultrasound image and OCT image. Noise in these images affects the accuracy of detection [60]. In this section the existing de-speckling (i.e., speckle de-noising) techniques are described. The effect of speckle de-noising in glaucoma detection is also reviewed.

16.3.1   De-Speckling Techniques

Speckle noise has granular structure and is multiplicative in nature. Speckle noise is multiplied with the original image, which results degradation of the image. The characteristics of speckle noise may be understood from the Eq. (16.1). Let X is the image degraded by the speckle noise N, results noisy image Y. The noisy image can be written as

$$Y = XN \qquad (16.1)$$

Equation (16.1) shows the modeling of speckle noise as multiplicative noise. Speckle noise degrades the quality of Ultrasound image and OCT image, which affects the glaucoma diagnosis. In OCT, speckle occurs due to the interference signal, which has limited spatial-frequency bandwidth. The reflected laser beam which is mutually coherent forms dark and bright granular structure, whenever reflected from a rough surface. This structure causes speckle noise. The speckle degrades the images or signals acquired using narrow band detection systems like ultrasound image. The other sources of speckle in OCT image are motion of target image, coherence and size of light source and detector aperture. The undesirable granular structure in ultrasound image is called speckle noise. Speckle in ultrasound image generated in a similar way as OCT. If the length of ultrasound pulse is more than carrier signal, the phases of the wavelets acts as coherent waves, thus generates speckle in the image.

Existing speckle de-noising techniques can be categorized as design change approach, algorithmic approach and statistical modeling approach. The classification of de-noising methods to remove speckle noise is shown in Fig. 16.2. Design change approach applies post processing to the acquired signal and improves the signal-to-noise ratio of the recorded image. But this approach suffers from limitations, are given in Table 16.2. Due to these limitations algorithmic approach is preferred.

Algorithmic approach uses different types of filter to enhance the speckle affected image. This approach can be classified as filtering approach and transform domain approach. Filtering approach can be classified as spatial domain filtering and fre-

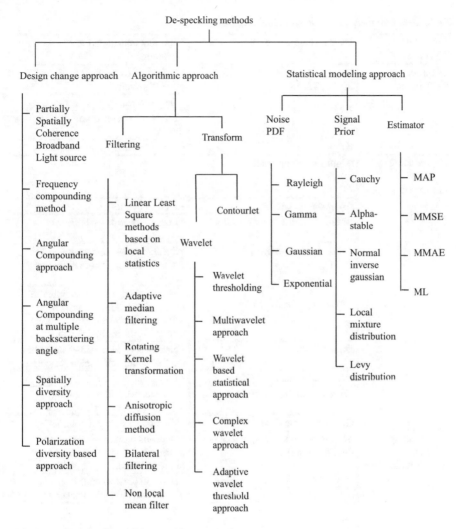

Fig. 16.2 Classification of de-speckling methods

quency domain filtering. Spatial domain filtering approach uses spatial information for filtering the noise while frequency domain filters use frequency information for filtering the noise. Several filtering approached methods are adaptive median filtering, linear least square methods based on local statistics, Rotating Kernel transformation, anisotropic diffusion method, non local mean filter and bilateral filtering. Transform domain approach use wavelet transform or contourlet transform in filtering the noise. Different techniques using wavelet transform approach are wavelet thresholding, wavelet based statistical approach, multiwavelet approach, complex wavelet approach and adaptive wavelet threshold approach.

Table 16.2 Summary of the De-speckling methods

Proposed objective	Used technique to achieve objective	Important consideration or limitations
De-speckling OCT image	Design change approach [28, 29, 30, 31, 32, 33]	• It is required to change the design of OCT system
		• Data acquisition time is more.
		• Effect of speckle de-noising is limited
		• Increases the system complexity
De-speckling OCT and ultrasound image	Algorithmic approach	
	Adaptive median [34]	• Loss of details
	Rotating Kernel transformation [35]	• Loss of structural details.
	Anisotropic diffusion [36, 37, 55]	• Speckle noise suppression is limited under high contamination of noise.
		• This method uses less number of pixels, which does not provide sufficient information for accurate estimation of original signal.
	Bilateral filter [38]	• Narrow spatial windows may filter out the useful small scale structures
	Non local mean filter [39]	• Computational complexity is high.
	Wavelet transform [40]	• Introduce artifacts. Filtering depends on the threshold value.
	Contourlet transform [41, 42]	• High computational complexity.
De-speckling OCT and ultrasound image	Statistical modeling approach [43, 44, 56, 57, 58]	• Depends on the noise and signal distribution models and efficiency of the estimator.
		• Less effective when the distribution model is inaccurate.

Statistical modeling approach is based on the statistical modeling of the true coefficients and noisy coefficients. The general block diagram of the statistical modeling approached filter is presented in Fig. 16.3. For making the statistical approached filters simpler and easier, the speckle noise is converted to additive noise by use of logarithmic transformation. Speckle noise is a multiplicative noise, so a homomorphic approach is used to convert it into additive noise [27]. Multi-resolution approach is used to find the wavelet coefficients of image. The log-transformed image is converted to coefficients by performing wavelet transform.

Wavelet transform is a multiscale or multiresolution approach which decomposes the two-dimensional image into four subbands. The subbands are LL, LH, HL and HH. LL is the low frequency approximation and most of the information is available

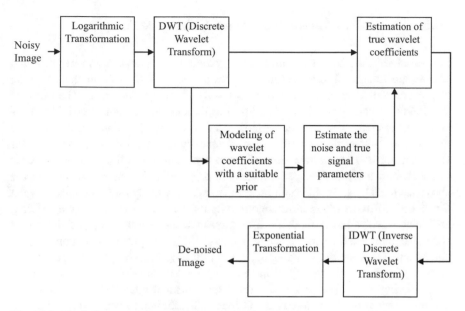

Fig. 16.3 Block diagram of de-speckling methods using statistical properties of image and noise

in this subband. LH and HL subbands contain the horizontal and vertical details respectively. HH contains diagonal detail and gives information of noisy data.

By use of Bayesian approach, it is possible to remove the noisy coefficients. Bayesian approach needs a prior or distribution function, used for modeling the wavelet coefficients. The modeling of wavelet coefficients can be described by a probability density function (PDF). Different PDFs have been implemented in literature for modeling wavelet coefficients like Cauchy, Alpha-stable, Inverse Normal Gaussian and Levy PDF [59]. Suitable priors are assumed for true coefficient and noisy coefficients. The wavelet coefficients are modeled using the statistical prior and thus collect the necessary signal information and noise information. The information includes signal parameters, signal variance ($\hat{\sigma}_x^2$) and noise variance ($\hat{\sigma}_n^2$).

By using the statistical characteristics (variance information) of the noise and prior, a suitable estimator is designed which estimates noise free coefficients. Estimators use Bayes statistics for generating a decision rule that minimizes the loss function of the expected value and maximizes the posterior expectation. Further, inverse discrete wavelets transform (IDWT) and exponential transformation, are performed to recover the de-noised image. Filtering based on statistical approach is the current research issue in de-speckling. The summary of de-speckling methods is tabulated in Table 16.2.

16.3.2   Current State-of-the-Art de-Noising Techniques

Several algorithms have been proposed for removing speckle noise in OCT and Ultrasound images. These imaging modalities play a great role in the detection of glaucoma disease. Both the modalities suffer from speckle noise. The intrinsic speckle noise causes problem in identifying the diagnostic parameters. The diagnostic parameters provide a quantitative tool to the ophthalmologist to diagnose the disease. Spatial domain filters and frequency domain filters are suitable for Gaussian noise. These filters suffer from decrease in resolution problem in case of speckle noise. Adaptive spatial filters are proposed as an improvement over the above methods [34]. But these filters failed to preserve many useful details. Wavelet filters and diffusion filters have become popular for their edge preserving ability. Different wavelet based methods like wavelet thresholding [45], wavelet based statistical approach [46], multiwavelet approach [47], complex wavelet domain [43] and adaptive wavelet thresholding approach [48] have been proposed in past years. Anisotropic diffusion filters [37] have also gained popularity as it prevents from over filtering. De-noising methods based on statistical characterization of signal and noise, are current research issue. Different distribution functions used to model speckle noise are Gamma distribution [44], Rayleigh, Gaussian distribution, Cauchy distribution [38] and Log normal distribution. Bayesian estimators are proved to recover signal from the noise more effectively. A number of speckle removal methods have been developed that make use of the estimators like Maximum Likelihood (ML), Maximum a Posteriori (MAP), Minimum Mean Absolute Error (MMAE), Minimum Mean Square Error (MMSE), and Mixture ratio estimator [49, 50, 51, 43].

Speckle filtering is a critical preprocessing step for retinal image analysis, recognition and feature extraction in medical science. The above discussed de-speckling algorithms are applied in the preprocessing step of glaucoma detection to improve the accuracy of detection. Speckle filtering algorithms are proved in the performance improvement. A method proposed by Anantrasirichai et al. [38] for de-noising and enhancement of OCT retinal image. Further the authors processed the de-speckled image for glaucoma detection. The authors found the classification accuracy of glaucoma detection increased from 72.95% (for original OCT image) to 84.13% (for de-speckled OCT image) and 85.15% (for de-speckled and enhanced OCT image). RNFL segmentation is required to find the thickness of the RNFL. And it is an important diagnostic parameter in the detection of glaucoma. Fernadez et al. [52] proposed a method for de-noising and enhancement of OCT retinal image. They applied the layer segmentation on the de-speckled OCT image and detected the RNFL, Inner Plexiform Layer (IPL), Ganglion cell layer (GCL), Outer Plexiform Layer (OPL), Inner Nuclear Layer (INL), Outer Nuclear Layer (ONL) and Inner/Outer Segment Layer effectively. Garvin et al. [53] proposed a method for inter retinal layer segmentation to detect eye diseases. They applied anisotropic diffusion filter for speckle noise reduction in OCT retinal image. The method correctly classified the retinal layer and provides a better assessment factor for early glaucoma detection. An automated segmentation method was proposed by Xu et al. [42] to detect early retinal diseases. The authors applied bilateral filtering for speckle removal that enhances the accuracy of segmentation. Segmentation provides a quantitative analysis of features of glaucoma eye disease. Ghafaryasl et al. [54] developed a structure oriented smoothing filter to reduce speckle noise from OCT image. From the preprocessed OCT image, the authors estimated the orientations of Retinal Nerve Fiber Bundles (RNFBs). Combination of visual field data and RNFB trajectories may be used for diagnosis and detection glaucoma.

16.4 Conclusion

This chapter presented a study of glaucoma detection techniques and de-noising methods to increase the efficiency of detection. Early diagnosis prevents the development of the disease and progression of the condition. Image modalities and their diagnostic parameters were discussed. Different image processing steps for the detection of glaucoma were given. Recently, ophthalmologists work with these steps to identify glaucoma by its signs, symptoms, and from the results of various diagnostic parameters. Image de-noising has a great role in the image processing system. Retinal ultrasound and OCT images are affected by speckle noise. Methods to de-noise the speckle noise in retinal image and their impact on the detection also discussed.

The primary purpose of this survey is to aware about the different available speckle de-noising techniques. In future, the survey summary will help the researchers to develop hybrid filtering approach that combines the features from different filtering approaches.

In future, this study might be helpful in automatic detection of diseases other than glaucoma like diabetic retinopathy, skin diseases and dental defects and cracks, which will reduce the cost of disease screening programs. The improvement and practical advancement in this area of glaucoma detection will grow in the coming years.

Acknowledgement This chapter is a part of my Ph.D. thesis which has been submitted to AKTU, Lucknow.

References

1. Quigley, H. A., & Broman, A. T. (2006). The number of people with glaucoma worldwide in 2010 and 2020. *British Journal of Ophthalmology*, 90(3), 262-267.
2. Bock, R., Meier, J., Nyul, L. G., Hornegger, J., & Michelson, G. (2010). Glaucoma risk index: automated glaucoma detection from color fundus images. *Medical image analysis*, 14(3), 471-481.

3. Garcia-Feijoo, J., Mendez-Hernandez, C. De la Casa, J. M. M., Saenz-Frances, F., Sanchez-Jean, R., & Garcia-Sanchez, J. (2016). Ultrasound Biomicroscopy in Glaucoma. In *Glaucoma Imaging* (pp. 97-121), Springer International Publishing.

4. Huang, M. L., & Chen, H. Y. (2005). Development and comparison of automated classifiers for glaucoma diagnosis using stratus optical coherence tomography. *Investigative Ophthalmology and Visual Science*, 46(11), 4121-4129.

5. Radhakrishan, S., Goldsmith, J., Huang, D., Westphal, V., Dueker, D. K., Rollins, A. M., Izatt, J. A., & Smith, S. D. (2005). Comparison of optical coherence tomography and ultrasound biomicroscopy for detection of Narrow Anterior Chamber Angles. *Archives of Ophthalmology*, 123(8), 1053-1059.

6. Swindale, N.V., Stjepanovic, G., Chin, A., & Mikelberg, F. S. (2000). Automated analysis of normal and glaucomatous optic nerve head topography images. *Investigative ophthalmology and visual science*, 41(7), 1730-1742.

7. Sivalingam, E. (1995). Glaucoma: an overview'. *Journal of ophthalmic*. Nursing & technology, 15(1), 15-18.

8. Budenz, D. L., Anderson, D. r., Varma, R., Schuman, J., Cantor, L., Savell, J., ... & Tielsch, J. (2007). Determinants of normal retinal nerve fiber layer thickness measured by stratus OCT. Ophthalmology, 114(6), 1046-1052.

9. Yu, W., Ma, Y., Zheng, L., & Liu, K. (2016). Research of Improved Adaptive Median Filter Algorithm. In *Proceedings of the 2015 international conference on Electrical and Information Technologies for Rail Transportation* (pp. 27-34), Springer, Berlin, Heidelberg.

10. Cheng, J., Duan, L., Wong, D. W. K., Tao, D., Akiba, M., & Liu, J. (2014, September). Speckle reduction in optical coherence tomography by image registration and matrix completion. In *International Conference on Medical Image Computing and Computer- Assisted Intervention* (pp.162-169), Springer International Publishing.

11. Benzarti, F., & Amiri, H. (2013). Speckle noise reduction in medical ultrasound images. *arXiv preprint* arXiv:1305.1344.

12. Meier, J., Bock, R., Michelson, G., Nyul, L. G.,& Hornegger, J. (2007, August). Effects of preprocessing eye fundus images on appearance based glaucoma classification. In *International Conference on Computer Analysis of Images and Patterns* (pp. 165-172). Springer Berlin Heidelberg.

13. Ishikawa, H., Stein, D. M., Wollstein, G., Beaton, S., Fujimoto, J.G., & Schuman, J.S. (2005). Macular segmentation with optical coherence tomography. *Investigative ophthalmology & visual science*, 46(6), 2012-2017.

14. Morales, S., Naranjo, V., Angulo, J., & Alcaniz, M. (2013). Automatic detection of optic disc based on PCA and mathematical morphology. *IEEE transactions on medical Imaging*, 32(4), 786-796.

15. Cheng, J., Liu, J., Xu, Y., Yin, F., Wong, D. W. K., Tan, N. M., Tao, D., Cheng, C. Y., Aung, T., & Wong, T. Y. (2013). Superpixel classification based optic disc and optic cup segmentation for glaucoma screening. IEEE *Transaction on Medical Imaging*, 32(6), 1019-1032.

16. Joshi, G. D., Sivaswami, J., & Krishnadas, S.R. (2011). Optic disk and cup segmentation from monocular color retinal images for glaucoma assessment. *IEEE Transaction on Medical Imaging*, 30(6), 1192-1205.

17. Wong, D.W.K., Liu, J., Lim, J. H., Jia, X., Yin, F., Li, H., & Wong, T. Y. (2008, August). Level-set based automatic cup-to-disc ratio determination using retinal fundus images in ARGALI. In *Engineering in Medicine and Biology Society, 2008. 30th Annual International Conference of the IEEE* (pp. 2266–2269), IEEE.

18. Hatanaka, Y., Noudo, A., Maramatsu, C., Sawada, A., Hara, T., Yamamoto, T., & Fujita, H. (2011, August). Automatic measurement of cup to disc ratio based on line profile analysis in retinal images. In *Engineering in Medicine and Biology Society, EMBC, 2011 Annual International Conference of the IEEE* (pp. 3387-3390), IEEE.

19. Khan, F., Khan, S.A., Yasin, U.U., ul Haq, I., & Qamar, U. (2013, October). Detection of glaucoma using retinal fundus images. In *Biomedical Engineering International Conference (BMEiCON), 2013 6th* (pp. 1-5), IEEE.

20. Ahmad, H., Yamin, A., Shakeel, A., Gillani, S. O., & Ansari, U. (2014, April). Detection of glaucoma using retinal fundus images. In *Robotics and Emerging Allied Technologies in engineering (iCREATE), 2014 International Conferences on* (pp. 321-324), IEEE.

21. Turpin, A., Frank, E., Hall, M., Witten, I. H., & Johnson, C. A. (2001, April). Determining progression in glaucoma using visual fields. In *Pacific-Asia Conference on Knowledge Discovery and Data Mining* (pp.136-147), Springer, Berlin, Heidelberg.

22. Nayak, J., Acharya, R., Bhat, P. S., Shetty, N., & Lim, T. C. (2009). Automated diagnosis of glaucoma using digital fundus images. *Journals of medical systems*, 33(5), 337-346.

23. Huang, M. L., Chen, H. Y., & Huang, J. J. (2007). Glaucoma detection using adaptive neuro-fuzzy inference system. *Expert systems with applications*, 32(2), 458-468.

24. Bock, R., Meier, J., Michelson, G., Nyul, L., & Hornegger, J. (2007). Classifying glaucoma with image-based features from fundus photographs. *Pattern Recognition*, 355-364.

25. Nyul, L. G. (2009, October). Retinal Image Analysis for Automated Glaucoma Risk Evaluation. In *6th International Symposium on Multispectral Image Processing and Pattern Recognition* (pp. 74971C-74971C), International Society for optics and photonics.

26. Ferreras, A., Pajarin, A. B., Polo, V., Larrosa, J. M., Pablo, L.E., & Honrubia, F.M. (2007). Diagnostic ability of Heidelberg Retinal Tomograph 3 Classifications: glaucoma probability score versus Moorfields regression analysis. *Ophthalmology*, 114 (11), 1981-1987.

27. Atlas, L., Li, Q., & Thompson, J. (2004, May). Homomorphic modulation spectra. In *Acoustics, Speech, and Signal Processing, 2004, Proceedings. (ICASSP'04), IEEE International Conference on* (Vol. 2, pp.761-764), IEEE.

28. Desjardins, A. E., Vakoc, B.J., Oh, W. Y., Motaghiannezam, S. M. R., Tearney, G. J., & Bouma, B.E. (2007). Angle-resolved optical coherence tomography with sequential angular selectivity for speckle reduction. *Optics Express*, 15(10), 6200-6209.

29. Iftimia, N., Bouma, B. E., & Tearney, G. J. (2003). Speckle reduction in optical coherence tomography by path length encoded angular compounding. *Journal of Biomedical Optics*, 8(2), 260-263.

30. Jorgensen, T. M., Thrane, L., Mogensen, M., Pedersen, F., & Andersen, P. E. (2007, June). Speckle reduction in optical coherence tomography images of human skin by a spatial diversity method. In *European Conference on Biomedical Optics* (p. 6627-22), Optical Society of America.

31. Kim, J., Miller, D. T., Kim, E., Oh, S., Oh, J., & Milner, T. E. (2005). Optical Coherence Tomography Speckle Reduction by a Partially Spatially Coherent Source. *Journal of Biomedical Optics*, 10(6), 064034-064034.

32. Kobayashi, M., Hanafusa, H., Takada, K., & Noda, J. (1991). Polarization-independent interferometric optical-time-domain reflectometer. *Journal of Lightwave Technology*, 9(5), 623-628.

33. Pircher, M., Go, E., Leitgeb, R., Fercher, A. F., & Hitzenberger, C. K. (2003). Speckle reduction in optical coherence tomography by frequency compounding. *Journal of Biomedical Optics*, 8(3), 565-569.

34. Loupas, T., McDicken, W. N., & Allan, P.L. (1989). An adaptive weighted median filter for speckle suppression in medical ultrasound images. *IEEE Transactions on Circuits and Systems*, 36(1), 129-135.

35. Rogowska, J., & Brezinski, M. E. (2000). Evaluation of the adaptive speckle suppression filter for coronary optical coherence tomography imaging. *IEEE Transaction on Medical Imaging*, 19(12), 1261-1266.

36. Aja, S., Alberola, C., & Ruiz, A. (2001). Fuzzy Anisotropic diffusion for speckle filtering. *In Acoustics, Speech, and Signal Processing Proceedings, 2001.Proceedings, (ICASSP'01), 2001 IEEE International Conference on* (Vol. 2, pp.1261-1264), IEEE.

37. Ramos-Llorden, G., Vegas-Sanchez-Ferrero, G., Martin-Fernandez, M., Alberola-Lopez, C., & Aja-Fernandez, S. (2015). Anisotropic diffusion filter with memory based on speckle statistics for ultrasound images. *IEEE Transaction on Image Processing*, 24(1), 345-358.

38. Anantrasirichai, N. Nicholson, L., Morgan, J. E., Erchova, I., Mortlock, K., North, R. V., Albon, J., & Achim, A. (2014). Adaptive-weighted bilateral filtering and other pre-processing

techniques for optical coherence tomography. *Computerized Medical Imaging and Graphics*, 38(6), 526-539.

39. Yang, J., Fan, J., Ai, D., Wang, X., Zheng, Y., Tang, S., & Wang, Y. (2016). Local statistics and non-local mean filter for speckle noise reduction in medical ultrasound image. *Neurocomputing*, 195, 88-95.

40. Habib, W., Sarwar, T., Siddiqui, A. M., & Touqir, I. (2016). Wavelet denoising of multiframe optical coherence tomography data using similarity measures. *IET Image Processing*, 11(1), 64-79.

41. Gupta, A., Tripathi, A., & Bhateja, V. (2013). Despeckling of SAR images in contourlet domain using a new adaptive thresholding. In *Advance Computing Conference (IACC), 2013 IEEE 3rd International* (pp.1257-1261), IEEE.

42. Xu, J., Ou, H., Lam, E. Y., Chui, P. C., & Wong, K. K. Y. (2013). Speckle reduction of retinal optical coherence tomography based on contourlet shrinkage. *Optic Letters*, 38(15), 2900-2903.

43. Rabbani, H., Vafadust, M., Abolmaesumi, P., & Gazor, S. (2008). Speckle noise reduction of medical ultrasound images in complex wavelet domain using mixture priors. IEEE *Transactions on Biomedical Engineering*, 55(9), 2152-2160.

44. Sudeep, P.V., Niwas, S. I., Palanisamy, P., Rajan, J., Xiaojun, Y., Wang, X., Luo, Y., & Liu, L. (2016). Enhancement and bias removal of optical coherence tomography images: An iterative approach with adaptive bilateral filtering. *Computers in Biology and Medicine*, 71, 97-107.

45. Sudha, S., Suresh, G. R., & Sukanesh, R. (2009). Speckle noise reduction in ultrasound images by wavelet thresholding based on weighted variance. *International Journal of Computer Theory and Engineering*, 1(1), 1793-8201.

46. Gupta, S., Chauhan, R. C., & Sexana, S. C. (2004). Wavelet-based statistical approach for speckle reduction in medical ultrasound images. *Medical and Biological Engineering and Computing*, 42(2), 189-192.

47. Fablet, R., Augustin, J.M., & Isar, A. (2005, June). Speckle Denoising Using a Variational Multi-wavelet Approach. In *Oceans 2005-Europe* (Vol. 1, pp. 539-544).IEEE.

48. Andria, G., Attivissimo, F., Lanzolla, A. M., & Savino, M. (2013). A suitable threshold for speckle reduction in ultrasound images. *IEEE Transaction on Instrumentation and Measurement*, 62(8), 2270-2279.

49. Bhuiyan, M. I. H., Ahmad, M. O., & Swamy, M. N. S. (2009). Spatially adaptive thresholding in wavelet domain for despeckling of ultrasound images. *IET Image Processing*, 3(3), 147-162.

50. Bibalan, M. H., & Amindavar, H. (2016). Non-Gaussian amplitude PDF modeling of ultrasound images based on a novel generalized Cauchy-Rayleigh mixture. EURASIP Journal on Image and video Processing, 2016(1), 48.

51. Jafari, S., & Ghofrani, S. (2017). Using Heavy-Tailed Levy model in non subsampled shearlet transform domain for ultrasound image despeckling, Jounal of Advances in Computer Research. 8(2), 53-66.

52. Fernadez, D. C., Salinas, H. M., & Puliafito, C. A. (2005). Automated detection of retinal layer structures on optical coherence tomography images. *Optic Express*, 13(25), 10200-10216.

53. Garvin, M. K., Abramoff, M. D., Kardon, R., Russell, S. R., Wu, X., & Sonka, M. (2008). Intraretinal layer segmentation of macular optical coherence tomography images using optimal 3-D graph search. *IEEE Transaction on Medical Imaging*, 27(10), 1495-1505.

54. Ghafaryasl, B., Baart, R., de Boer, J. F., Van Vliet, L.J., & Vermeer, K. A. (2017, February). Automatic estimation of retinal nerve fiber bundle orientation in SD-OCT images using a structure-oriented smoothing filter. In SPIE medical Imaging (pp. 101330C-101330C). International Society for Optics and Photonics.

55. Yu, Y., & Acton, S. T. (2002). Speckle Reducing Anisotropic Diffusion. *IEEE Transactions on Image Processing*. 11(11), 1260-1270.

56. Sahu, S., Singh, H. V., Kumar, B., & Singh, A. K. (2018). A Bayesian Multiresolution Approach for Noise Removal in Medical Magnetic Resonance Images. *Journal of Intelligent Systems*. https://doi.org/10.1515/jisys-2017-0402

57. Sahu, S., Singh, H.V., Kumar, B. and Singh, A.K., (2018). Statistical Modeling and Gaussian-ization Procedure based de-speckling algorithm for Retinal OCT images, Journal of Ambient Intelligence and Humanized Computing (AIHC), 1-14.
58. Sahu, S., Singh, H. V., Kumar, B., & Singh, A. K. (2019). De-noising of ultrasound image using Bayesian approached heavy-tailed Cauchy distribution. Multimedia Tools and Applications, 78(4), 4089–4106.
59. Sahu, S., Singh, H.V. and Kumar, B., 2017, December. A heavy-tailed levy distribution for despeckling ultrasound image. *Fourth IEEE International Conference on Image Infor-mation Processing (ICIIP),* Himachal Pradesh, India, December 21-23, 2017, pp. 1-5. https://doi.org/10.1109/ICIIP.2017.8313674
60. Sonali, Sahu, S., Singh, A.K., Ghrera, S.P. and Elhoseny, M., 2018. An approach for de-noising and contrast enhancement of retinal fundus image using CLAHE. *Optics & Laser Technology, an International Journal of Elsevier.* https://doi.org/10.1016/j.optlastec.2018.06.061

Chapter 17
A Study on Dictionary Learning Based Image Reconstruction Techniques for Big Medical Data

Shailendra Tiwari, Kavkirat Kaur, and K. V. Arya

17.1 Introduction

In today's world, Computed Tomography (CT) has been widely used for analyzing the internal structures of the human body. During the CT scan diagnosis, quality of reconstructed images is directly propositional to the number of photon counts and the amount of ionizing radiation dose.Higher the X-ray dose increase the ionizing radiation which causes the harmful impact on the soft-tissues and generate some biological changes such as failure of organs (lungs, kidney), risk of genetic disorder and cancer etc. Therefore, the major challenge is to minimizing the radiation dose without compromising with the diagnostic accuracy. Iterative Image reconstruction algorithms is a mathematical technique that produced the tomographic CT images with the help of measured projection data acquired from the different view angles around the patient or any objects. Generally, our focus is to reconstruct an acceptable image from the noisy and incomplete data collected from the different projection views around the object (patient). To fulfil this desire an efficient reconstruction method is required. The common problems associated with reconstruction method is that the region-of-interest (ROI) is not directly available from the scanning devices. Therefore, this problem is mathematically called as an inverse problem or ill-possed problem.

In literature, there are various methods of image reconstruction are introduced over the last few decades. Basically, they are classified into two main categories analytical techniques [5, 10, 22, 45] and iterative techniques [2, 5, 16–19, 22, 44,

S. Tiwari (✉) · K. Kaur
Department of Computer Science and Engineering, Thapar Institute of Engineering and Technology, Patiala, India
e-mail: shailendra@thapar.edu

K. V. Arya
Computer Science & Engineering (CSE), Institute of Engineering & Technology, Lucknow, India

© Springer Nature Switzerland AG 2019   377
A. K. Singh, A. Mohan (eds.), *Handbook of Multimedia Information Security: Techniques and Applications*, https://doi.org/10.1007/978-3-030-15887-3_17

45, 48]. The analytical techniques were depending upon transformation techniques such as Radon transform [5, 23, 45]. Filtered back-projection algorithm (FBP) [10] is one of the most commonly used techniques in this category because of its ability to provide an adequate image quality on the basis of faster, simpler, and computationally efficient manner. Despite, its overall acceptable performance, CT studies that the reconstructed images with FBP can be still affected by poor visual quality, stair-casing artifacts and less SNR (signal-to-noise ratio) value due to the limited projection sets.

On the contrary, iterative reconstruction methods have the capability to handle the noisy data and reconstruct a better quality image. Iterative Reconstruction methods have shown a great potential to replace the traditional analytical methods like FBP that was taken into account of statistical properties, which have shown to be superior in suppressing the noise and streak artifacts. In iterative methods, multiple steps have been performed iteratively to form a better quality image. Further, the iterative methods can be divided into algebraic iterative methods and statistical iterative methods. Solving the linear equations is the basic fundamental of algebraic iterative methods. The classical Algebraic reconstruction technique (ART) [18] method repeatedly changes the structure until it satisfies with the original image. Simultaneous iterative reconstructive technique (SIRT) [16] is the advancement of ART method, the densities are altered with respect to all the angles of projections which help in improving the results. Andersen and Kak [2] proposed an algorithm which can consider being the best combination of ART and SIRT termed as statistical algebraic reconstruction technique (SART) [2]. As it is imposing the higher convergence rate property of ART and noise-reducing property of SIRT. In SART all the acquired pixels updates for only one view at a time. Hence, the convergence rate of SART is much better in their ART's family but it provides unsatisfactory visual results at the end. Recently, image restoration using sparse representations has been an emerging techniques for low-dose image reconstruction [4, 6, 11, 20, 26, 43, 54].

Iterative Reconstruction (IR) Algorithms have used from a long time since for Low-dose Image Reconstruction. IR algorithms provides enhanced results but have more computational time. So to get better of it Dictionary Learning (DL) came into existence in 2004 [34]. Dictionary learning is an unsupervised learning method to learn and extract various features of a(n) signal/image. DL approach is an efficient way to summarize and present the sparse data or huge amount of training images/signals into a compressed form without amplify the noise or other factors that distorted the data. The training data is used to train the dictionary model, i.e., a large database of images with an arbitrary size. The goal of dictionary learning is to represent the input signals/images as a homogeneous vector which is an approximation of linearly weighted signals by combining the small number of features or unknown basis elements. Moreover, these basis elements also called as elements of the dictionary that can further be classified into the high-level patterns or features from the training data-sets. Hence, the DL have become an efficient and robust techniques to remove the irrelevant features.

As the technology grows rapidly, Sparse reconstruction techniques have been extensively used for analyzing the Big medical databases of signals and images to build an intelligent Health-care management system [4, 6, 11, 52]. In the classical framework for the sparse reconstruction problem, the dictionaries are fixed and predefined. Examples of such dictionaries are Fourier, Curvelets and Wavelets bases. For instance, Fourier are the powerful tools used in image and signal processing to solve the ordinary and partial differential equations (ODEs and PDEs), Wavelets are used in a Bayesian regularization formulation [27] and Curvelets are used for sparse regularization in X-ray computed tomography [54]. Methods using learned dictionaries are computationally more expensive than using pre-computed dictionaries in solving the inverse problem regularization with sparsity constraints. It perform better in promoting sparsity while fitting the measurement data, because the dictionary is customized using the statistical approach to optimized the training data-set. This concept is commonly used for tomographic image reconstruction. If the unknown image is sparse representation in a specific dictionary, the remaining task is to estimate the exact coefficients that reconstruct the original image from the given noisy data.

The role of DL in medical imaging applications has been a hot topic in the last few years. Generally, it is categorized into two different approaches, either constructing the dictionary from the intermediate solutions using an joint learning iterative reconstruction algorithm [7, 25, 33, 34, 46] or constructing the dictionary from the training images separately before starting the process of sparse reconstruction [14, 39, 51, 56, 64]. The simultaneous learning and reconstruction is a non-convex optimization problem. Furthermore, it violates the elementary principle of inverse problems that a data-adaptive prior must be incorporated in the problem formulation to eliminate unrealistic solutions that may fit into the data.

To obtain a sparse representation, the dictionaries are typically overcomplete, i.e., dictionaries have more basis functions that necessary to span the solution space. Such a sparse representation of natural images has been proposed by Olshausen and Field in 1996 [3]. It is often interested in approximating an image as a linear combination of a few (aka sparse) elements of the dictionary. Once an unknown signal is sparse in a specific dictionary, the main challenge is to find the representation coefficients that reconstruct the original full signal from the given data. We should note that when a signal is said to be sparse in an engineering sense, it means that the signal is compressible, i.e., it can be expressed either with a small number of dictionary elements or with significantly decaying expansion coefficients. Therefore, the DL method has been used to solve the problem of optimization and extracted the desired results from Big and complex medical data-sets. It also provides the optimal techniques to classify or discriminate into the classes that contain millions of training images and signals. The general flowchart for image reconstruction using DL is described in Fig. 17.1.

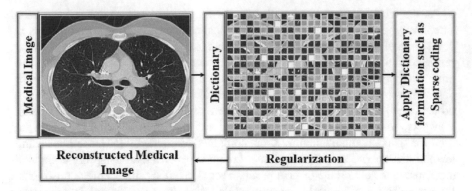

Fig. 17.1 Flowchart for image reconstruction using dictionary learning

17.2 Dictionary Representation

Suppose that $\mathcal{R}, N, M$ be real numbers and integers respectively. Let us define dictionary matrix $\mathcal{D} \in \mathcal{R}^{N \times M}$ with columns $c_i \in R^{N \times 1}$ for $i = 1, \ldots, M$. This N dimension vector is known as atom. Normally N is very small compared to M. Image patch of size $\sqrt{N} \times \sqrt{N}$ is defined using $x \in \mathcal{R}^{N \times 1}$. Let x is defined using linear sparse combination of columns of $\mathcal{D}$ for $\epsilon \geq 0$ error, $\alpha \in \mathcal{R}^{M \times 1}$ is a sparse vector, then

$$\|D\alpha - x\|_2^2 \leq \epsilon \tag{17.1}$$

Now $M \gg N \gg \|\alpha\|_0$ with l_0-norm. Length of atom is lesser than number of atoms which implies the duplication of dictionary. Solving the objective function can be written as:

$$\min\|\alpha\|_0 \text{s.t.}\|D\alpha - x\|_2^2 \leq \epsilon \tag{17.2}$$

will yield the sparse description of $\alpha \in \mathcal{R}^{M \times 1}$ for a patch $x \in \mathcal{R}^{N \times 1}$ w.r.t. D. Now using Lagrangian polynomial, one can derive a no constrained version of this objective. Suppose k is Lagrangian multiplier defined as:

$$\min\|D\alpha - x\|_2^2 + k\|\alpha\|_0 \tag{17.3}$$

Here l_0-norm is often substituted by l_1-norm to get the convex version of the problem. Let the training be consists of P patches, then each patch has sparse representation by dictionary atoms. Let $x_P \in \mathcal{N} \times \infty$ where $s \in [1, P]$ is a column vector. Then the column vector $\alpha \in R^{M \times P}$ for $\alpha \in \mathcal{R}^{M \times P}$ and $\alpha_P \in \mathcal{R}^{M \times 1}$. Now the objective function represents as:

$$\min_{[D,\alpha]} \sum_{i=1}^{P} \left(\|D\alpha_i\|_2^2 + k_i \|\alpha_i\|_0 \right) \tag{17.4}$$

Let ϵ and L_0 be the precision and sparsity. In other words, it can be stated that

$$\min_{[D,\alpha]} \|D\alpha - X\|_2^2 \text{s.t.} \forall s, \ \|\alpha_i\|_0 \leq L_0 \tag{17.5}$$

or the following objective is also consistent with the previous one

$$\min_{[D,\alpha]} \|\alpha_i\|_0 \text{s.t.} \forall s, \ \|D\alpha - X\|_2^2 \leq \epsilon \tag{17.6}$$

Let $M = H \times W$ and non overlapping patches are defined as $P = (H - \sqrt{N} + 1) \times (W - \sqrt{N} + 1)$. Now suppose $z \in \mathcal{R}^{M \times 1}$ is a vector for noisy image and $x \in \mathcal{R}^{M \times 1}$ is its filtered form. These extracted patches can be defined in the form of dictionary such that the filtered version is almost identical to the noisy image. The mathematical formulation of objective function for image restoration (denoising) can be written as:

$$\min_{[D,\alpha,x]} \|z - x\|_2^2 + \mu \sum_{i=1}^{P} \left(\|D\alpha_i - E_i x\|_2^2 + k_i \|\alpha_i\|_0 \right) \tag{17.7}$$

Here $E_i \in R^{N \times M}$ matrix segments a patch out of an image x and μ is just a variable for regularization for the level of low-dose in z. Now D can be derived in two ways: (a) construct D during denoising process and (b) during the training set D can be constructed while containing structures representing the image targeted for filtering. In the following subsection, there is a discussion on objective function reconstruction based upon statistics.

17.3 Dictionary Learning Problem

The term dictionary learning refers to methods of inferring, given a data matrix Y, an overcomplete dictionary that will perform good at sparsely encoding the data in Y i.e., modeling data matrix as sparse linear combinations of the dictionary. A dictionary learning problem can be formulated as follows: Given a data matrix $Y = [y_1, y_2, \ldots, y_t] \in R^{\xi \times t}$ and a number of entries to find the two matrices $D = [d_1, d_2, \ldots, d_s] \in R^{\xi \times t}$ and $H \in R^{s \times t}$, which factorize Y in such a manner that: $Y \approx DH$ or in other words $Y = DH + E$, where the matrix $E \in R^{\xi \times t}$ represents the approximation error. This standard generative model assumes that the factorization error is distributed as a zeromean Gaussian distribution with covariance $\sigma^2 I$. The problem of learning a basis set (dictionary) can be formulated as a matrix factorization problem.

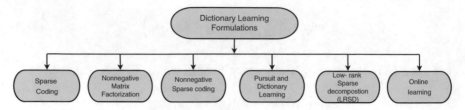

Fig. 17.2 Different dictionary learning formulations

The classical Dictionary Learning (DL) problem can be defined using minimization of the objective function as:

$$\min_{D,H} \mathcal{L}_{dic}(Y, DH) + \Phi_{dic}(D) + \Phi_{rep}(H) \qquad (17.8)$$

where the value of misfit loss function is estimated using the factorization approximation method, while the prior knowledge of the dictionary patch D, as well as the system (representation) matrix H, were measured by the regularization functions. However, at the time of implementation some basic constraints is strictly followed in unsupervised learning such as non-negativity constraints over the data elements of dictionary D, similarly the sparsity constraints on the representation (system) matrix H. We also note that the Bayesian methods presented in, e.g. [28, 65] is based on maximum likelihood (ML) and maximum a-posteriori (MAP) probability which are designed to estimate the desired outputs from the noisy or incomplete training data.

However, dictionary learning formulations as shown in Fig. 17.2, are classified into standard sparse coding, non-negative matrix factorization, and non-negative sparse coding, are discussed in this work. The other classification of DL such as Pursuit Dictionary Learning, Low-rank sparse decomposition (LRSD) and Online Learning are not consider in this work due to the lack of reliable data source and limitations of prior research study on this topics. It will give an opportunity to describe the need for future research scope.

17.3.1 Sparse Coding

The term Sparse Coding (SC)comes from the classic paper [3] in which it is shown that a coding strategy that maximizes the sparseness is sufficient to account for capturing natural image features. In sparse coding the problem of discovering the underlying dictionary is often formulated in terms of vector representations, i.e., each input vector y_j is characterized and denoted using basis vectors $[d_1, d_2, \ldots, d_s]$ and a weighted sparse vector is represented as $h_j \epsilon \Re^s$, $j = 1, \ldots, t$ such that $y_j \approx Dh_j$. In its simplest form, the sparsity of the coefficients h_j is measured by its cardinality number. The cardinality is sometimes called the l_0 pseudo-norm, although the cardinality function is not a norm. The cardinality is denoted by $\| \cdot \|_0$, defined as:

$$\|h_j\|_0 = \{i \epsilon \{1, \ldots \ldots \xi\} : h_{i,j}\}, \quad \forall j = 1, \ldots, t \tag{17.9}$$

Commonly, an optimization problem of the following form is written as:

$$\min_{D, \{h_j\}_{j=1}^t} \sum_{j=1}^t \|y_j - Dh_j\|_2^2, \quad s.t. \|h_j\|_0 \leq k_0, \quad j = 1, \ldots, t \tag{17.10}$$

where, every representation has at most k_0 non-zero entries. Let the spark of a matrix D be defined as the smallest number of columns from D that are linearly dependent. In terms of uniqueness, for the case when $y_j = Dh_j$, if D exists such that $h'_j s \, for \, j = 1, \ldots, t$ are defined by using $k_0 < spark(D)/2$ at most atoms; after we apply the re-scaling and permutation method simultaneously on the column vector D in an iterative manner until not achieved the desired unique dictionary from the large and sparse training database. Dictionary learning algorithms for Eq. (17.10) based on such strategy has been proposed for instance in Method of Optimal Directions (MOD) proposed by Engan et al. [13] and K-SVD by Aharon et al. [1]. Recent modifications and improvements of the MOD and K-SVD dictionary learning algorithms are also discussed in [47].

However minimizing $\| \cdot \|_0$ is known to be a NP-hard problem [52], instead commonly in the formulation it is replaced by the l_1 regularization, leading to a convex relaxation of the sparse coding problem in Eq. (17.10), when the dictionary D is fixed. Therefore to favor sparse coefficients, the sparsity regularization technique is commonly used to provide the sparse coefficient value, also increase the robustness by reducing the irrelevant features. To prevent the dictionary D from the smaller random noisy values that would lead to the large impact on the value of in h_j), or vise versa, one can introduce constraints on the l_2-norm of the matrix columns

$$D_1 \equiv \{D \epsilon \mathbb{R}^{\xi \times s} | \|d_j\|_2^2 \leq \xi, \quad \forall j \epsilon \{1, \ldots, s\}\}. \tag{17.11}$$

Then the search for a sparse code can be formulated as an optimization problem by constructing the following cost function to be minimized:

$$\min_{D \epsilon D_1, h_j \epsilon R^s} \frac{1}{2} \|y_j - Dh_j\|_2^2 + \lambda \|h_j\|_1, \quad for \, j = 1, \ldots, t \tag{17.12}$$

The emphasis on minimizing the sparsity induced on the elements h_j, is controlled by the regularization parameter $\lambda \geq 0$. Similar to the problem of Eq. (17.10), the non-convex optimization problem defined in Eq. (17.12) is solved alternatively for D and h_j for all $j = 1, \ldots, t$. The h_j updating step is a sparse linear problem which we will describe in the next section and the D update is a norm constrained least squares problem. Most of the current methods such as coordinate descent (gradient descent) using soft thresholding are used for solving these problems. For examples of sparse coding algorithms based on problem formulation Eq. (17.12), we refer to [30] and the online dictionary learning method [36].

Using the definition of the l_1-*norm* and the Frobenius norm of a matrix [58], lead the problem definition in Eq. (17.12), to a more general representation. More specifically, given a training set of t signals $Y = [y1, \ldots, yt]$ in $\mathbb{R}^{\xi \times t}$, where each signal y_j declare as a sparse decomposition of Dictionary matrix D:

$$\min_{D \in D, H \in \mathbb{R}^{s \times t}} \frac{1}{2} \|Y - DH\|_F^2 + \lambda \sum_{i,j} |H_{i,j}| \tag{17.13}$$

Note that the problem formulation Eq. (17.13) is proper since the columns of the representation matrix H are independent and separable. Note that the problem Eq. (17.13) is an example of the generic problem formulation (3.1). The optimization problem Eq. (17.13) is not jointly convex in (D, H) and hence there is no guarantee to obtain the global minimum, but, each variable of D and H follows the convex properties where others remain fixed.

17.3.2 Nonnegative Matrix Factorization (NMF)

The study shows that most of the real world data are based on non-negativity constraints and their corresponding basis elements physically satisfied these constraints. The concept of non-negative matrix factorization was first given by Lee and Seung [29], to find the state of basis functions used to represents non-negative data. It is shown in [29] that the basis vectors displayed as images, appear as a collection of parts and localized features, so one can say that NMF leads to patch based model. NMF follow only additive combination, whereas zero-element means the miss value and positive elements mean as the hit value of the basis part of the dictionary.

In principle NMF explore to discriminate the non-negative matrix into the low rank matrix form. Lets a non-negative matrix $Y \in \mathbb{R}_+^{\xi \times t}$, NMF searches for non-negative factors D and H that approximate Y (i.e., $Y \in DH$) where all the entries of D and H are nonnegative.

The NMF problem is commonly reformulated as the following optimization problem:

$$\min_{D \in \mathbb{R}^{\xi \times s}, H \in \mathbb{R}^{s \times t}} \frac{1}{2} \|Y - DH\|_F^2 \quad s.t. D \geq 0 \quad and \quad H \geq 0, \tag{17.14}$$

where D is a basis matrix and H is a coefficient matrix. The non-negative elements of the matrices are represented by D and H parameter that may encourage into the sparsity [59]. We note that even in situations where $Y = DH$ holds exactly, the decomposition is not be unique [59].

A simple way to present the energy or cost function in the non-convex optimization problem (3.5) is another way to present the minimization method between the matrix D and H, such that one should remain stable and optimized for the other and vice-versa. Numerous methods are proposed in literature for solving the NMF problem. One can mention the multiplicative iterative techniques as a substitute of the least-square optimization method and gradient descent methods. A detailed summary of the NMF and its application has been presented in [23]. Projected gradient approaches are better suited in solving the overcomplete non-negative matrix factorization problems (i.e., $\xi < s \subset t$) [63].

17.3.3   Nonnegative Sparse Coding

In the standard sparse coding method, the raw-data is simply represented as a collection of basic features coupled with both positive and negative elements. It can also eliminate the irrelevant features. As per the previous section, we have noticed that whatever the solutions provided by the NMF methods may neither be unique nor stable. Therefore some additional constraints such as sparsity are further required to resolve the issues. Moreover, the constraint matrix factorization techniques are widely used for the parameter estimation of the structured dictionary learning as compared to the others [24].

However, it is also observed that inducing both the non-negativity and sparsity constraints simultaneously may lead to degrading the variance value. It means, there is a proper balancing must be needed to maintain the interpret-ability, promoting sparsity and data/statistical fidelity.

For these reasons we prefer to consider the dictionary learning problem which represents both the constraints sparse coding [50] matrix Y as:

$$\min_{D,H} \frac{1}{2}\|Y - DH\|_F^2 s.t. D \epsilon D and H \epsilon \mathbb{R}_+^{s \times t}, \tag{17.15}$$

where the set D is convex and $\lambda \geq 0$ is a regularization term that balance the sparsity constraints P $\Sigma_{i,j}|h_{i,j}|$.

A nonnegative dictionary D with s elements refers to a collection of basis image carrying image features and a nonnegative H represents conic combinations of dictionary elements when approximating a nonnegative data matrix Y . A sparse H refers to the approximation of training images with a small number of dictionary elements.

17.4 Related Work

In 2006, Elad and Ahron [12] firstly, proposed the solution of image denoising problem using the combination of the dictionary learning (DL) and the sparse reconstruction techniques. By using K-SVD method they first trained the dictionary from the noise-free images [1] and then merged with the model of adaptive DL that is based on the patches of the noisy image. It is shown in [12] that both dictionaries perform very well in the denoising process. Since then, the dictionary learning approach has been explored in areas such image denoising [9, 31], image deblurring [34], image restoration [38] and image classification [37]. The dictionary learning approach in tomographic imaging is likewise beginning to emerge recently, e.g., X-ray tomography [56], spectral computed tomography [64], magnetic resonance imaging (MRI) [46], ultrasound tomography [51], electron tomography [34], positron emission tomography (PET)[7] and phase-contrast tomography [39].

For better identification of low-construct structures, iterative CT reconstruction algorithm is implemented with edge preserving total variation regularization (EPTV)[50]. EPTV only smooths the non-edge area of images to enhance the visibility. Wang et al. [53] have used sinogram affirmed iterative reconstruction (SAFIRE) to investigate the image quality of low-dose CT coronary angiography (CTCA). They reduced 50% of radiation dose as compared to standard dose CTCA which used the filtered back-projection (FBP) in obese patients. Bulla et al. [62] have utilized the iterative reconstruction technique to reduce the dose radiations in low-dose CT of the paranasal sinus. This technique has reduced 60% of radiation dose as compared to FBP, without a deterioration in image quality. Dictionary learning is implemented by Xu et al. [56] in statistical iterative reconstruction framework to reduce the dose of radiations in X-ray CT. Dictionary learning produces better images as compared to FBP- and total variation (TV)-based reconstructions.

Takx et al. [49] compared SAFIRE method with FBP using coronary CT Angiography (cCTA) datasets. Results showed that SAFIRE improves the image quality with dose reduction of 80%. The role of iterative reconstructions in low-dose CT with their advantages and disadvantages has been explained in Refs. [55] and [57]. Iterative reconstructions improve the quality of images with dose reduction from 23% to 76%. However, iterative reconstructions suffer from high reconstruction time. Chen et al. [8] enhanced the quality of low-dose CT images. They used dictionary learning process to suppress the amplified metal noise staircase artifacts without introducing the blurring effects. Zhang et al. [61] also reduced the noise in low-dose CT images by using non-local mean (NLM) based regularization in statistical image reconstruction (SIR) methods. This technique is much better than SIR with Gaussian MRF regularization and the conventional FBP approach in terms of quality. Li et al. [32]. used impainting singnogram technique with K-SVD Dictionary learning technique. This method provides better results with comparision to the FBP method. Oda et al. [42] used a knowledge-based iterative model reconstruction (IMR) with FBP to improve the quality of low-dose cardiac CT images. This method has reduced the radiation up to 80% as compared to conventional FBP. Fang et al. [15] reconstructed the low-dose CT images with tensor total-variation regularization (TVR) method. The method has fast convergence and low computation complexity. Greffier et al. [21] brought optimization in diagnostic medical imaging. They designed a software in which radiologists can obtain required image quality with a reduction in dose and with an adequate combination of parameters. Nagata et al. [41] compared the iterative low-dose CT colonography (CTC) reconstruction (ICTR) with routine-dose CTC reconstruction. They found that iterative reconstruction can reduce the radiation dose from 48.5% to 75.1% as compared to routine-dose with FBP without compromising the image quality. Zhang et al. [60] introduced spatial adaptivity to improve the characteristics of low-dose CT images. This method needs more manual tuning and high computational complexity. Lu et al. [35] presented a manifold regularized sparse learning, which results in High Resolution Images. This methods provides better results than the iterative methods.

Yuki et al. [57] have designed a fast reconstruction method based on model type iterative reconstruction for low-dose chest CT. This method has acceptable speed, but still is slower than some techniques. Greffier et al. [20] studied the effect of noise on circular structures due to dose reduction in CT. They studied only those circular structures which have the density in the range of soft tissues. Murphy et al. [40] examined the affect of radiation dose CT in testicular cancer patients using the pure model- based iterative reconstruction (PMIR). The reconstruction time of model-based iterative method is more as compared to hybrid iterative reconstruction methods. Kang et al. [26] proceeded in a new direction by using deep learning framework in low-dose CT reconstruction field. This method used convoluted neural networks with a directional wavelet method to enhance the image quality. The main benefit of this approach is its reconstruction time which is faster than model-based iterative reconstruction methods. Zhang et al. [58] reduced the over-smoothing effect using iteratively reweighted least squares (IRLS) in dictionary learning process. Still, its reconstruction time is significantly more than other methods.

Zhang et al. [63] used Gamma regularization along with Sparse representation for CT images. This technique is capable of handling streak artifacts and preserving edges. Zonoobi et al. [66] proposed a dictionary learning approach for MR Images. In this method both the global and patch-based sparsity information is used and patch grouping is also used. This method outperforms the existing method visually as well in terms computational time. Soltani et al. [47] used regularized nonnegative matrix factorization (NMF)for forming a dictionary and is further regularized with help of regularized least squares fit. This method leads to reduction of streak artifacts, noisy. Pathak et al. [43] designed an integrated low-dose CT reconstruction technique which has used GDSIR- and ADSIR-based reconstruction techniques. In case the dictionary (D) is predetermined, then GDSIR can be used, and if D is adaptively defined then ADSIR is an appropriate choice. The gain intervention-based filter is also used as a post-processing technique for removing the artifacts from low-dose CT reconstructed images. Experiments have been done by considering the proposed technique and other low-dose CT reconstruction techniques on well-known benchmark CT images. Extensive experiments have demonstrated that the proposed technique outperforms the available approaches.

In the Double-Sparsity model the dictionary update is represented by the number of non-zeros elements into the columns of A. The similar approach is presented in called as sparse K-SVD. In literature, various methods have been presented to solve this approach one of them is known as a batch method that updates the data elements in a sequential manner. Another double-sparsity approach has modified the model into sparse-coding constraints and estimated the solution using OMP method. Generally, maintaining the large sparse data may require the sufficient training data set and efficient algorithms that may reduce the computational load. Despite, Big-data concept gain a feasible benefit to solving the constraint optimization and sparse coding problems. Further, dimensionality reduction is also the advanced and fast optimization technique to resolve that issue by suppressing the amount of training data in a less number of iterations. Similarly, in the case of extreme online learning, processing each online data is a tedious and time-consuming process, therefore we processed the data only once treated as new data. Hence, storing all the online processed data is almost impossible and wastage of resources. This motivation leads to the development of another optimization techniques called as Online Sparse Dictionary Learning (OSDL) method based on widely used numerical gradient descent algorithm that effectively solves the specific online learning Problem. We should note that online dictionary learning, and specifically SGD, have been already applied to the dictionary-learning task. The special setting analyzed here is different for two main reasons: The dimensions involved are different, as we will be handling up to 4000 entries in a typical example. The double-sparsity structure imposes a tailored approach.

The overcomplete dictionary D plays the central role in the sparsity-based processing. It can be defined either in a descriptive manner, via some analytical formula, or learned in some way from training data. There are many prescribed dictionaries that work well for natural signals—curvelets, contourlets, steerable wavelet filters, short time Fourier transforms, and more. Such transforms have the advantage of computational speed over an explicit matrix multiplication, usually by factor of $n/\log(n)$; for high-dimensional signals, the difference may become decisive. However, a dictionary specially tailored to the given signal family may have much better sparse coding properties and, as a result, serve to improve the algorithm performance. The problem of signal dimensionality can be solved by passing to local processing: large images are treated by working on small overlapping 2-D patches. Often, this approach is the correct one also because the small pieces of the image are much more likely to be efficiently encoded than the entire image.

17.5   Conclusion

In this work, we presented a comprehensive study of Dictionary Learning (DL) based image reconstruction algorithms used in Computed Tomography (CT) for the clinical diagnosis on the big-medical data. The basic principles, to reconstruct an acceptable image from the noisy and incomplete projection data acquired from the different projection views around the object (patient). Generally, a large and sparse representation data have collected during the acquisition process. The problem associated with this big sparse medical data, the region-of-interest (ROI) is not directly available from the scanning devices is called as an inverse problem or ill-posed problem. To solve this problem, estimate the desired output for accurate clinical diagnosis, an efficient and robust reconstruction method is required. In this work, we discussed in details the DL problem and their solutions with some exhaustive literature survey in the field of DL based CT image reconstruction for analyzing the big medical sparse data with some conclusive remarks.

References

1. Aharon, Michal and Elad, Michael and Bruckstein, *rmk*-SVD: An algorithm for designing overcomplete dictionaries for sparse representation. IEEE Transactions on signal processing (2006). https://doi.org/10.1109/TSP.2006.881199.
2. Andersen, Anders H and Kak, Avinash C, Simultaneous algebraic reconstruction technique (SART): a superior implementation of the ART algorithm. Ultrasonic imaging (1984). https://doi.org/10.1016/0161-7346(84)90008-7.
3. Brono, A and Osshausen, BA, Emergence of simple-cell receptive field properties by learning a sparse code for natural image. Nature (1996). https://doi.org/10.1038/381607a0.
4. Bruyant, Philippe P, Analytic and iterative reconstruction algorithms in SPECT. Journal of Nuclear Medicine (2002) 1;43(10):1343–58.
5. Bruyant, Philippe P, Analytic and iterative reconstruction algorithms in SPECT, Journal of Nuclear Medicine, Soc Nuclear Med (2002) https://doi.org/10.1016/j.patcog.2016.09.038.
6. Chen, Scott Shaobing and Donoho, David L and Saunders, Michael A, Analytic and iterative reconstruction algorithms in SPECT. SIAM review (2001). https://doi.org/10.1137/S003614450037906X.
7. Chen, Scott Shaobing and Donoho, David L and Saunders, Michael A, Sparse representation and dictionary learning penalized image reconstruction for positron emission tomography. Physics in Medicine Biology, IOP Publishing (2015). https://doi.org/10.1088/0031-9155/60/2/807.
8. Chen, Yang and Shi, Luyao and Feng, Qianjing and Yang, Jian and Shu, Huazhong and Luo, Limin and Coatrieux, Jean-Louis and Chen, Wufan, Artifact suppressed dictionary learning for low-dose CT image processing. IEEE transactions on medical imaging (2014). https://doi.org/10.1109/TMI.2014.2336860.
9. Chen, Yang and Yin, Xindao and Shi, Luyao and Shu, Huazhong and Luo, Limin and Coatrieux, Jean-Louis and Toumoulin, Christine, Improving abdomen tumor low-dose CT images using a fast dictionary learning based processing. Physics in Medicine & Biology, IOP Publishing (2013). https://doi.org/10.1088/0031-9155/58/16/5803.
10. Devaney, Anthony J, A filtered backpropagation algorithm for diffraction tomography. Ultrasonic imaging, Elsevier (1982). https://doi.org/10.1016/0161-7346(82)90017-7.

11. Elad, Michael, From exact to approximate solutions. Sparse and Redundant Representations, Springer (2010).
12. Elad, Michael and Aharon, Michal, Image denoising via sparse and redundant representations over learned dictionaries. IEEE Transactions on Image processing, Springer (2006). https://doi.org/10.1109/TIP.2006.881969.
13. Engan, Kjersti and Aase, Sven Ole and Husy, John Hkon, Multi-frame compression: Theory and design. Signal Processing, Elsevier (2000). https://doi.org/10.1016/S0165-1684(00)00072-4.
14. Etter, Vincent and Jovanovic, Ivana and Vetterli, Martin, Use of learned dictionaries in tomographic reconstruction. Wavelets and Sparsity XIV, International Society for Optics and Photonics, Elsevier (2011), vol. 8138, pp. 81381C.
15. Fang, Ruogu and Zhang, Shaoting and Chen, Tsuhan and Sanelli, Pina C, Robust low-dose CT perfusion deconvolution via tensor total-variation regularization. IEEE transactions on medical imaging (2015), https://doi.org/10.1109/TMI.2015.2405015.
16. Gilbert, Peter, Iterative methods for the three-dimensional reconstruction of an object from projections. Journal of theoretical biology, Elsevier (1972). https://doi.org/10.1016/0022-5193(72)90180-4.
17. Gopi, Varun P and Palanisamy, P and Wahid, Khan A and Babyn, Paul and Cooper, David, Iterative computed tomography reconstruction from sparse-view data. Journal of Medical Imaging and Health Informatics, American Scientific Publishers (2016). https://doi.org/10.1166/jmihi.2016.1579.
18. Gordon, Richard and Bender, Robert and Herman, Gabor T, Algebraic reconstruction techniques (ART) for three-dimensional electron microscopy and X-ray photography. Journal of theoretical Biology, Elsevier (1970). https://doi.org/10.1016/0022-5193(70)90109-8.
19. Green, Peter J, Bayesian reconstructions from emission tomography data using a modified EM algorithm. IEEE transactions on medical imaging, IEEE (1990). https://doi.org/10.1109/42.52985.
20. Greffier, J and Macri, F and Larbi, A and Fernandez, A and Pereira, F and Mekkaoui, C and Beregi, J-P, Dose reduction with iterative reconstruction in multi-detector CT: what is the impact on deformation of circular structures in phantom study? Diagnostic and interventional imaging, Elsevier (2016). https://doi.org/10.1016/j.diii.2015.06.019.
21. Greffier, J and Macri, F and Larbi, A and Fernandez, A and Khasanova, E and Pereira, F and Mekkaoui, C and Beregi, JP, Dose reduction with iterative reconstruction: optimization of CT protocols in clinical practice. Diagnostic and interventional imaging, Elsevier (2015). https://doi.org/10.1016/j.diii.2015.02.007.
22. Hansen, Per Christian and Saxild-Hansen, Maria, AIR tools: a MATLAB package of algebraic iterative reconstruction methods. Journal of Computational and Applied Mathematics, Elsevier (2012). https://doi.org/10.1016/j.cam.2011.09.039.
23. He, Qian and Huang, Lihong, Penalized maximum likelihood algorithm for positron emission tomography by using anisotropic median-diffusion. Mathematical Problems in Engineering, Hindawi (2014). https://doi.org/10.1155/2014/491239.
24. Hoyer, Patrik O, Non-negative matrix factorization with sparseness constraints. Journal of machine learning research, (2004), vol 5, Pages 1457–1469.
25. Huang, Yue and Paisley, John and Lin, Qin and Ding, Xinghao and Fu, Xueyang and Zhang, Xiao-Ping, Bayesian nonparametric dictionary learning for compressed sensing MRI. IEEE Transactions on Image Processing, IEEE (2014). https://doi.org/10.1109/TIP.2014.2360122.
26. Kang, Eunhee and Min, Junhong and Ye, Jong Chul, A deep convolutional neural network using directional wavelets for low-dose X-ray CT reconstruction. Medical physics, Wiley Online Library (2017). https://doi.org/10.1002/mp.12344.
27. Kolehmainen, Ville and Lassas, Matti and Niinimäki, Kati and Siltanen, Samuli, Sparsity-promoting Bayesian inversion. Inverse Problems, IOP Publishing, vol 28, no. 2, pp. 025005 (2012).

28. Kreutz-Delgado, Kenneth and Murray, Joseph F and Rao, Bhaskar D and Engan, Kjersti and Lee, Te-Won and Sejnowski, Terrence J, Dictionary learning algorithms for sparse representation. Neural computation, MIT Press (2003). https://doi.org/10.1162/089976603762552951.
29. Lee, Daniel D and Seung, H Sebastian, Learning the parts of objects by non-negative matrix factorization. Nature, Nature Publishing Group (1999). https://doi.org/10.1038/44565.
30. Lee, Honglak and Battle, Alexis and Raina, Rajat and Ng, Andrew Y, Efficient sparse coding algorithms, Advances in neural information processing systems, Proceedings of the 2006 Conference, pp. 801–808 (2007).
31. Lee, Daniel D and Seung, H Sebastian, An efficient dictionary learning algorithm and its application to 3-D medical image denoising. Nature, IEEE Transactions on Biomedical Engineering (2012). https://doi.org/10.1109/TBME.2011.2173935.
32. Li, Si and Cao, Qing and Chen, Yang and Hu, Yining and Luo, Limin and Toumoulin, Christine, Dictionary learning based sinogram inpainting for CT sparse reconstruction, Optik-International Journal for Light and Electron Optics, Elsevier (2014). https://doi.org/10.1016/j.ijleo.2014.01.003.
33. Liao, Hstau Y and Sapiro, Guillermo, Sparse representations for limited data tomography, 5th IEEE International Symposium on Biomedical Imaging: From Nano to Macro (2008). https://doi.org/10.1109/ISBI.2008.4541261.
34. Liu, Baodong and Yu, Hengyong and Verbridge, Scott S and Sun, Lizhi and Wang, Ge, Dictionary-learning-based reconstruction method for electron tomography, Scanning, Wiley Online Library (2014). https://doi.org/10.1002/sca.21121.
35. Lu, Xiaoqiang and Huang, Zihan and Yuan, Yuan, MR image super-resolution via manifold regularized sparse learning, Neurocomputing, Elsevier (2015). https://doi.org/10.1016/j.neucom.2015.03.065.
36. Mairal, Julien and Bach, Francis and Ponce, Jean and Sapiro, Guillermo, Online learning for matrix factorization and sparse coding, Journal of Machine Learning Research, vol. 11, pp.19–60 (2010). arXiv:0908.0050.
37. Mairal, Julien and Bach, Francis and Ponce, Jean and Sapiro, Guillermo and Zisserman, Andrew, Discriminative learned dictionaries for local image analysis, Computer Vision and Pattern Recognition, 2008. CVPR 2008. IEEE Conference on IEEE (2008). https://doi.org/10.1109/CVPR.2008.4587652.
38. Mairal, Julien and Sapiro, Guillermo and Elad, Michael, Learning multiscale sparse representations for image and video restoration, Multiscale Modeling & Simulation SIAM (2008). https://doi.org/10.1137/070697653.
39. Mirone, Alessandro and Brun, Emmanuel and Coan, Paola, A dictionary learning approach with overlap for the low dose computed tomography reconstruction and its vectorial application to differential phase tomography, PloS one, Public Library of Science (2014). https://doi.org/10.1371/journal.pone.0114325.
40. Murphy, Kevin P and Crush, Lee and O Neill, Siobhan B and Foody, James and Breen, Micheál and Brady, Adrian and Kelly, Paul J and Power, Derek G and Sweeney, Paul and Bye, Jackie and others, Feasibility of low-dose CT with model-based iterative image reconstruction in follow-up of patients with testicular cancer, European journal of radiology open, Elsevier (2016). https://doi.org/10.1016/j.ejro.2016.01.002.
41. Nagata, Koichi and Fujiwara, Masanori and Kanazawa, Hidenori and Mogi, Tomohiro and Iida, Nao and Mitsushima, Toru and Lefor, Alan T and Sugimoto, Hideharu, Evaluation of dose reduction and image quality in CT colonography: comparison of low-dose CT with iterative reconstruction and routine-dose CT with filtered back projection, European radiology, Springer (2015). https://doi.org/10.1007/s00330-014-3350-3.
42. Oda, Seitaro and Utsunomiya, Daisuke and Funama, Yoshinori and Katahira, Kazuhiro and Honda, Keiichi and Tokuyasu, Shinichi and Vembar, Mani and Yuki, Hideaki and Noda, Katsuo and Oshima, Shuichi and others, A knowledge-based iterative model reconstruction algorithm: can super-low-dose cardiac CT be applicable in clinical settings? Academic radiology, Elsevier (2014). https://doi.org/10.1016/j.acra.2013.10.002.

43. Pathak, Yadunath and Arya, KV and Tiwari, Shailendra, Low-dose CT image reconstruction using gain intervention-based dictionary learning, Modern Physics Letters B, World Scientific (2018). https://doi.org/10.1142/S0217984918501488.
44. Perona, Pietro and Malik, Jitendra, Scale-space and edge detection using anisotropic diffusion, IEEE Transactions on pattern analysis and machine intelligence, IEEE (1990). https://doi.org/10.1109/34.56205.
45. Qi, Jinyi and Leahy, Richard M, Iterative reconstruction techniques in emission computed tomography, Physics in Medicine & Biology, IOP Publishing (2006). https://doi.org/10.1088/0031-9155/51/15/R01.
46. Ravishankar, Saiprasad and Bresler, Yoram, MR image reconstruction from highly undersampled k-space data by dictionary learning, IEEE transactions on medical imaging, IEEE (2011). https://doi.org/10.1109/TMI.2010.2090538.
47. Soltani, Sara and Andersen, Martin S and Hansen, Per Christian, Tomographic image reconstruction using training images, Journal of Computational and Applied Mathematics, Elsevier (2017). https://doi.org/10.1016/j.cam.2016.09.019.
48. Strohmer, Thomas and Vershynin, Roman, A randomized Kaczmarz algorithm with exponential convergence, Journal of Fourier Analysis and Applications, Springer, vol. 15, no. 2, pp. 262 (2009).
49. Takx, Richard AP and Schoepf, U Joseph and Moscariello, Antonio and Das, Marco and Rowe, Garrett and Schoenberg, Stefan O and Fink, Christian and Henzler, Thomas, Coronary CT angiography: comparison of a novel iterative reconstruction with filtered back projection for reconstruction of low-dose CT a initial experience, European journal of radiology, Elsevier (2013). https://doi.org/10.1016/j.ejrad.2012.10.021.
50. Tian, Zhen and Jia, Xun and Yuan, Kehong and Pan, Tinsu and Jiang, Steve B, Low-dose CT reconstruction via edge-preserving total variation regularization, Physics in Medicine & Biology, IOP Publishing (2011). https://doi.org/10.1088/0031-9155/56/18/011.
51. Tošić, Ivana and Jovanović, Ivana and Frossard, Pascal and Vetterli, Martin and Durić, Neb, Ultrasound tomography with learned dictionaries, Acoustics Speech and Signal Processing (ICASSP), 2010 IEEE International Conference on IEEE (2011). https://doi.org/10.1109/ICASSP.2010.5495211.
52. Tropp, Joel A and Wright, Stephen J, Computational methods for sparse solution of linear inverse problems, Proceedings of the IEEE, IEEE (2010). https://doi.org/10.1109/JPROC.2010.2044010.
53. Wang, Rui and Schoepf, U Joseph and Wu, Runze and Reddy, Ryan P and Zhang, Chuanchen and Yu, Wei and Liu, Yi and Zhang, Zhaoqi, Image quality and radiation dose of low dose coronary CT angiography in obese patients: sinogram affirmed iterative reconstruction versus filtered back projection, European journal of radiology, Elsevier (2012). https://doi.org/10.1016/j.ejrad.2012.04.012.
54. Wieczorek, Matthias and Frikel, Jürgen and Vogel, Jakob and Eggl, Elena and Kopp, Felix and Noël, Peter B and Pfeiffer, Franz and Demaret, Laurent and Lasser, Tobias, X-ray computed tomography using curvelet sparse regularization, Medical physics, Wiley Online Library (2015). https://doi.org/10.1118/1.4914368.
55. Willemink, Martin J and Leiner, Tim and de Jong, Pim A and de Heer, Linda M and Nievelstein, Rutger AJ and Schilham, Arnold MR and Budde, Ricardo PJ, Iterative reconstruction techniques for computed tomography part 2: initial results in dose reduction and image quality, European radiology, Springer (2013). https://doi.org/10.1007/s00330-012-2764-z.
56. Xu, Qiong and Yu, Hengyong and Mou, Xuanqin and Zhang, Lei and Hsieh, Jiang and Wang, Ge, Low-dose X-ray CT reconstruction via dictionary learning, IEEE Transactions on Medical Imaging, IEEE (2012). https://doi.org/10.1109/TMI.2012.2195669.
57. XYuki, Hideaki and Oda, Seitaro and Utsunomiya, Daisuke and Funama, Yoshinori and Kidoh, Masafumi and Namimoto, Tomohiro and Katahira, Kazuhiro and Honda, Keiichi and Tokuyasu, Shinichi and Yamashita, Yasuyuki, Clinical impact of model-based type iterative reconstruction with fast reconstruction time on image quality of low-dose screening chest CT, Acta Radiologica, SAGE Publications Sage UK: London, England (2016). https://doi.org/10.1177/0284185115575537.

58. Zhang, Cheng and Zhang, Tao and Li, Ming and Peng, Chengtao and Liu, Zhaobang and Zheng, Jian, Low-dose CT reconstruction via L1 dictionary learning regularization using iteratively reweighted least-squares, Biomedical engineering online, BioMed Central (2016). https://doi.org/10.1186/s12938-016-0193-y.

59. Donoho, David and Stodden, Victoria, When does non-negative matrix factorization give a correct decomposition into parts? Advances in neural information processing systems (2004). https://doi.org/10.1186/s12938-016-0193-y.

60. Zhang, Cheng and Zhang, Tao and Li, Ming and Peng, Chengtao and Liu, Zhaobang and Zheng, Jian, Statistical image reconstruction for low-dose CT using nonlocal means-based regularization. Part II: An adaptive approach, Computerized Medical Imaging and Graphics, Elsevier (2015). https://doi.org/10.1016/j.compmedimag.2015.02.008.

61. Zhang, Hao and Ma, Jianhua and Wang, Jing and Liu, Yan and Lu, Hongbing and Liang, Zhengrong, Statistical image reconstruction for low-dose CT using nonlocal means-based regularization, Computerized Medical Imaging and Graphics, Elsevier (2014). https://doi.org/10.1016/j.compmedimag.2014.05.002.

62. Bulla, Stefan and Blanke, Philipp and Hassepass, Frederike and Krauss, Tobias and Winterer, Jan Thorsten and Breunig, Christine and Langer, Mathias and Pache, Gregor, Reducing the radiation dose for low-dose CT of the paranasal sinuses using iterative reconstruction: feasibility and image quality, European journal of radiology, Elsevier (2012). https://doi.org/10.1016/j.ejrad.2011.05.002.

63. Zhang, Junfeng and Hu, Yining and Yang, Jian and Chen, Yang and Coatrieux, Jean-Louis and Luo, Limin, Sparse-view X-ray CT reconstruction with Gamma regularization, Neurocomputing, Elsevier (2017). https://doi.org/10.1016/j.neucom.2016.12.019.

64. Zhao, Bo and Ding, Huanjun and Lu, Yang and Wang, Ge and Zhao, Jun and Molloi, Sabee, Dual-dictionary learning-based iterative image reconstruction for spectral computed tomography application, Physics in Medicine & Biology, IOP Publishing (2012). https://doi.org/10.1088/0031-9155/57/24/8217.

65. Zhou, Mingyuan and Chen, Haojun and Paisley, John and Ren, Lu and Li, Lingbo and Xing, Zhengming and Dunson, David and Sapiro, Guillermo and Carin, Lawrence, Nonparametric Bayesian dictionary learning for analysis of noisy and incomplete images, IEEE Transactions on Image Processing, IEEE (2012). https://doi.org/10.1109/TIP.2011.2160072.

66. Zonoobi, Dornoosh and Roohi, Shahrooz F and Kassim, Ashraf A and Jaremko, Jacob L, Dependent nonparametric bayesian group dictionary learning for online reconstruction of dynamic mr images, Pattern Recognition, Elsevier (2017). https://doi.org/10.1016/j.patcog.2016.09.038.

Chapter 18
Quantum Image Processing and Its Applications

J. J. Ranjani

18.1 Introduction

A mathematical framework used for the constructing physical theories is called quantum mechanics. The study of information processing accomplished using mechanical systems is termed as quantum computation and quantum information. Quantum computation has opened the doors of exciting aspects for processing and communication of information. In the broader sense, quantum computation has demonstrated that any physical theory can be used for processing information. Quantum bit or qubit is analogous to the bit in classic computation and information [2]. A classical bit has two states—0 and 1, similarly, qubit also has two possible states i.e., $|0\rangle$ and $|1\rangle$. The major difference between qubits and bits is a linear combination of states is possible in qubits, which is often stated as superposition:

$$|\psi\rangle = \alpha|0\rangle + \beta|1\rangle$$

where α and β can be real or complex numbers. The qubit can also be represented in terms of a unit vector in 2D Hilbert space as,

$$|\psi\rangle = \begin{pmatrix} \alpha \\ \beta \end{pmatrix} = \alpha \begin{pmatrix} 1 \\ 0 \end{pmatrix} + \beta \begin{pmatrix} 0 \\ 1 \end{pmatrix}$$

J. J. Ranjani (✉)
Department of Computer Science and Information Systems, Birla Institute of Technology and Science, Pilani, Rajasthan, India

© Springer Nature Switzerland AG 2019
A. K. Singh, A. Mohan (eds.), *Handbook of Multimedia Information Security: Techniques and Applications*, https://doi.org/10.1007/978-3-030-15887-3_18

Fig. 18.1 Bloch sphere

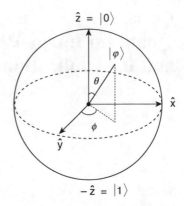

The next difference with classical bit is qubits cannot be examined to determine its state as 0 or 1. When the qubits are measured, the result 0 or 1 is obtained with a probabilities $|\alpha|^2$ and $|\beta|^2$ respectively. Since $|\alpha|^2 + |\beta|^2 = 1$,

$$|\psi\rangle = \cos\frac{\theta}{2}|0\rangle + \exp^{i\phi}\sin\frac{\theta}{2}|1\rangle$$

where θ and ϕ are real numbers defined on a unit three dimensional sphere, called as the *Bloch sphere* (Fig. 18.1).

Four possible states in case of two classical bits are $00, 01, 10,$ and 11, correspondingly two qubits has $|00\rangle, |01\rangle, |10\rangle,$ and $|11\rangle$ computational basis states. The two qubit state vector can be denoted as

$$|\phi\rangle = \alpha_{00}|00\rangle + \alpha_{01}|01\rangle + \alpha_{10}|10\rangle + \alpha_{11}|11\rangle$$

Section 18.2 discusses several quantum image representation algorithms like Flexible representation, novel enhanced quantum representation and multi channel representation of quantum images. Section 18.3 presents Quantum processing algorithms such as Quantum filtering, Quantum Boolean image processing, Quantum edge detection, and Quantum Hilbert image scrambling.

18.2 Image Representation

18.2.1 Flexible Representation of Quantum Images [3]

The flexible representation of Quantum Images (FRQI) is proposed to represent the colors and its respective positions of an image on quantum computers. The quantum image in the FRQI representation integrates the image information into a quantum state as

$$|I(\theta)\rangle = \frac{1}{2^n} \sum_{i=0}^{2^{2n}-1} (cos\theta_i |0\rangle + sin\theta_i |1\rangle) \otimes |i\rangle \qquad (18.1)$$

where $\theta_i \in \left[0, \frac{\pi}{2}\right]$, and $i = 0, 1, \ldots, 2^{2n} - 1$

Here, $\otimes$ denote the tensor product, $|i\rangle$, $i = 0, 1, \ldots, 2^{2n} - 1$ are the computational basis quantum states and $\theta = \left(\theta_0, \theta_1, \ldots \theta_{2^{2n}-1}\right)$ is the angular vector used for encoding the colors.

18.2.2   Novel Enhanced Quantum Representation [4]

The image pixels are stored in FRQI using normalized superposition, in which all the pixels can be processed simultaneously. Thus, FRQI is faster and can be used in real time applications. However, FRQI uses a single qubit to store the grayscale information of each pixel in an image, which might not be ideal for certain complex operations. A novel enhanced quantum representation (NEQR) is then proposed [4] to improvise the FRQI representation, which uses two entangled qubit sequences. NEQR have the following advantages over the FRQI representation: (1) Quadratic decrease in time complexity of preparation of the Quantum image. (2) 1.5 times increased compression ratio when using minimization of Boolean expressions (3) Retrieval of the original image is accurate whereas it is probabilistic in case of FRQI. (4) Ease in performing image operations.

For a $2^n x 2^n$ quantum image with gray range 2^q, NEQR requires $q + 2n$ bits to store the information of a grayscale image. The quantum image can be represented in the NEQR as:

$$|I\rangle = \frac{1}{2^n} \sum_{y=0}^{2^n-1} \sum_{x=0}^{2^n-1} |f(y,x)\rangle |yx\rangle = \frac{1}{2^n} \sum_{y=0}^{2^n-1} \sum_{x=0}^{2^n-1} \otimes_{i=0}^{q-1} |C_{yx}^i\rangle |yx\rangle \qquad (18.2)$$

The Quantum Computing Functions (QCF) for Matlab is used for demonstration [1].

```
function Qi = neqr(I)
// text Matlab function to represent images using NEQR

[m n] = size(I);
k = 1;

// no of bits to represent the graylevel
g = ceil(log2(256));

// no of bits to denote position
p = ceil(log2(m*n));
```

```
Qi = zeros(2^q*2^n,1);

for i = 1 : m
    for j = 1 : n

        phI(:,k) = dec2vec(I(i,j),g);
        phi(:,k) = dec2vec(k-1,p);
        Qi = Qi+(kron(phI(:,k),phi(:,k)));
        k = k+1;

    end
end

Qi = 0.5 * Qi;
```

18.2.3 Multi Channel Representation of Quantum Images [5]

The RGB information of color images can be captured in quantum states simultaneously using multi-channel representation of quantum images, as

$$|I(n)_{mc}\rangle = \frac{1}{2^{n+1}} \sum_{i=0}^{2^n-1} |C^i_{RGB\alpha}\rangle \otimes |i\rangle \tag{18.3}$$

$|C^i_{RGB\alpha}\rangle$ encodes the color information of the RGB channels as

$$|C^i_{RGB\alpha}\rangle = cos\theta^i_R|000\rangle + cos\theta^i_G|001\rangle + cos\theta^i_B|010\rangle + cos\theta_\alpha|011\rangle +$$
$$sin\theta^i_R|000\rangle + sin\theta^i_G|001\rangle + sin\theta^i_B|010\rangle + sin\theta_\alpha|011\rangle \tag{18.4}$$

The RGB color channel of the ith pixel are encoded using the three angles $\{\theta^i_R, \theta^i_G, \theta^i_B\} \in [0, \pi/2]$ and θ_α is set to zero.

The normalized state of MCQI is given by,

$$\||I(n)_{mc}\rangle\| = \frac{1}{2^n + 1} \left(\sum_{i=0}^{2^{2n}-1} cos^2\theta^i_R + sin^2\theta^i_R \right.$$

$$\left. + cos^2\theta^i_G + sin^2\theta^i_G + cos^2\theta^i_B + sin^2\theta^i_B + cos^2 0 + sin^2 0 \right)^{\frac{1}{2}}$$

$$= 1 \tag{18.5}$$

Advantages of MCQI representation are

- It uses less number of qubits in normalized quantum states to code information in RGB channels.
- It enables to design lower complexity color image operators.
- It provides a possibility to devise watermarking algorithms for quantum color images.

18.3 Quantum Preprocessing

Traditional digital image processing has operators for performing various fundamental operations like pixel manipulation, transformation, and shifting etc. Whereas with quantum image processing it is not feasible to perform classical operations like convolution because quantum computing does not satisfy the invertible property.

18.3.1 Optimal Estimation of Quantum States [7]

According to the Pole-to-pole Axis only (PAO) principle, each color in an image can be represented by considering the $z-$ axis projection values only. According to the PAO criteria

$$\mu = 1 - \alpha$$

The quantum counterpart of the PAO criteria is represented as

$$|\mu\rangle = |0\rangle - |\psi\rangle \tag{18.6}$$

where $|0\rangle = \begin{bmatrix} 1 \\ 2 \end{bmatrix}$, $|\psi\rangle = \begin{bmatrix} \alpha \\ \beta \end{bmatrix}$ and $\begin{bmatrix} \mu_\alpha \\ \mu_\beta \end{bmatrix} = \begin{bmatrix} 1 \\ 0 \end{bmatrix} - \begin{bmatrix} \alpha \\ \beta \end{bmatrix} = \begin{bmatrix} 1 - \alpha \\ -\beta \end{bmatrix}$

The first and the last pixel values in an 8-bit quantum image can be represented as

$$|00000000\rangle = \begin{pmatrix} 1 \\ 0 \\ \cdot \\ \cdot \\ \cdot \\ \cdot \\ 0 \end{pmatrix}$$

and

$$|11111111\rangle = \begin{pmatrix} 0 \\ 0 \\ . \\ . \\ . \\ 1 \end{pmatrix}$$

These numbers can also be represented as $|0\rangle$ and $|2^B - 1\rangle = |255\rangle$ where $B = 8$ bits.

Thus, the classic converter can be represented as

$$\mu = \left(2^B - 1\right) - \alpha \tag{18.7}$$

and its quantum counterpart as

$$|\mu\rangle = |0\rangle - |\psi\rangle \tag{18.8}$$

The logic operations on quantum computational basis states $|0\rangle, |1\rangle$ are tabulated in Table 18.1. Here $\overline{(.)}$ refers to $NOT(.)$

Here,

$$\overline{|\psi_i\rangle} = NOT\left(|\psi_i\rangle\right) = NOT\begin{pmatrix} \alpha_i \\ \beta_i \end{pmatrix} = \begin{pmatrix} \beta_i \\ \alpha_i \end{pmatrix} \tag{18.9}$$

and

$$XOR\left(|\psi_1\rangle, |\psi_2\rangle\right) = \left(|\psi_1\rangle AND\overline{|\psi_2\rangle}\right) OR\left(\overline{|\psi_1\rangle}AND|\psi_2\rangle\right) \tag{18.10}$$

Generally, the four quantum logical operations i.e. AND, OR, XOR, NOT are implemented using the Toffoli or Control-NOT (CNOT) gates. Table 18.2 shows the impact of α and μ on the computational basis states.

From the Table 18.3, we can infer that the logical operations with respect to μ is similar to the Boolean operations on binary numbers. The AND operation results in $|0\rangle$, when the value of either one of the two $\mu = 0$, and is denoted by the North Pole, whereas the AND operation results in $|1\rangle$, when both the $\mu = 1$, and is denoted by

Table 18.1 Logical operations on quantum basis states

$|\psi_1\rangle$	$|\psi_2\rangle$	AND	OR	$\overline{|\psi_1\rangle}$	$\overline{|\psi_2\rangle}$	XOR
$|0\rangle$	$|0\rangle$	$|0\rangle$	$|0\rangle$	$|1\rangle$	$|1\rangle$	$|0\rangle$
$|0\rangle$	$|1\rangle$	$|0\rangle$	$|1\rangle$	$|1\rangle$	$|0\rangle$	$|1\rangle$
$|1\rangle$	$|0\rangle$	$|0\rangle$	$|1\rangle$	$|0\rangle$	$|1\rangle$	$|1\rangle$
$|1\rangle$	$|1\rangle$	$|1\rangle$	$|1\rangle$	$|0\rangle$	$|0\rangle$	$|0\rangle$

Table 18.2 Impact of α and μ on the computational basis states

α_1	α_2	μ_1	μ_2	AND	OR	XOR
1	1	0	0	$|0\rangle$	$|0\rangle$	$|0\rangle$
1	0	0	1	$|0\rangle$	$|1\rangle$	$|1\rangle$
0	1	1	0	$|0\rangle$	$|1\rangle$	$|1\rangle$
0	0	1	1	$|1\rangle$	$|1\rangle$	$|0\rangle$

Table 18.3 Logical operations regarding μ

μ_1	μ_2	AND_μ	OR_μ	XOR_μ
0	0	0	0	0
0	1	0	1	1
1	0	0	1	1
1	1	1	1	0

the South Pole. Likewise, the OR operation results in $|0\rangle$, when both $\mu = 0$ i.e. North Pole and when the result of the OR is $|1\rangle$, then only one of the two $\mu = 1$. Thus, according to the PAO criteria, AND and the OR operations denotes the minimum and maximum between the $|\psi\rangle$, i.e.,

$$|\psi_1\rangle \wedge |\psi_2\rangle = min\,(|\psi_1\rangle, |\psi_2\rangle) \tag{18.11}$$

$$|\psi_1\rangle \vee |\psi_2\rangle = max\,(|\psi_1\rangle, |\psi_2\rangle)$$

$$|\psi_1\rangle \underline{\vee} |\psi_2\rangle = max\left(min\left(|\psi_1\rangle, \overline{|\psi_2\rangle}\right), min\left(\overline{|\psi_1\rangle}, |\psi_2\rangle\right)\right)$$

where $\wedge$, $\vee$, and $\underline{\vee}$ refers to AND, OR and XOR operations respectively.

18.3.2 Quantum Image Filtering [6, 8]

Quantum Fourier Transform (QFT) is the process of applying Discrete Fourier transform to the vector amplitudes of the quantum states.

On a basis state $|x\rangle$, QFT is given by

$$|x\rangle \xrightarrow{QFT_N} \frac{1}{\sqrt{N}} \sum_{k=0}^{N-1} e^{2i\pi xk/N} |k\rangle \tag{18.12}$$

Inverse QFT is given by

$$|x\rangle \xrightarrow{QFT_N^{-1}} \frac{1}{\sqrt{N}} \sum_{k=0}^{N-1} e^{-2i\pi xk/N} |k\rangle \tag{18.13}$$

```
function m = qft(q)

// Create QFT matrix with q rows and cols
w=exp(2*pi*i/q);

s = zeros(q);

row=0:q-1;

for r=1:q
    m(r,:)=row*(r-1);
end

m = w.^m;

m = m/sqrt(q);
```

It is well known that the computational complexity of fast Fourier transform (FFT) is $O(NlogN) = O(n2^n)$ whereas for QFT it is $O(log^2n) = O(n^2)$ and is exponentially faster.

Using [3], the spectrum $|F\rangle$ of the image can be easily obtained as

$$|F\rangle = \frac{1}{2^n} \sum_{i=0}^{2^{2n}-1} (cos\theta_i|0\rangle + sin\theta_i|1\rangle) \otimes QFT (|i\rangle)$$

$$= \frac{1}{2^n} \left[\sum_{i=0}^{2^{2n}-1} c_l|0l\rangle + \sum_{i=0}^{2^{2n}-1} s_l|1l\rangle \right]$$

where

$$c_l = \frac{1}{2^n} \sum_{i=0}^{2^{2n}-1} e^{\frac{2\pi jil}{2^{2n}}} cos\theta_i$$

$$s_l = \frac{1}{2^n} \sum_{i=0}^{2^{2n}-1} e^{\frac{2\pi jil}{2^{2n}}} sin\theta_i$$

$$l = 0, 1, \ldots 2^{2n} - 1$$

Pixels in a specific range of frequencies can be removed by adaptively selecting a frequency band or by using pre-defined threshold. The quantum circuits designed so far are not suitable for an adaptive method, thus pre-defined thresholds are to be used.

The processed spectrum map can be obtained as

$$\xi = \frac{1}{2^n}\{ \sum_{\substack{0 \le x \le 2^n-1 \\ 0 \le y \le 2^n-1 \\ \theta \le T}} \left(cos\theta_{xy}|0\rangle + sin\theta_{xy}|1\rangle\right) \otimes |x\rangle|y\rangle + \sum_{\substack{0 \le x \le 2^n-1 \\ 0 \le y \le 2^n-1 \\ \theta \ge T}} |0\rangle \otimes |x\rangle|y\rangle\}$$

Using inverse QFT, the filtered quantum image stored in FRQI model can be represented as

$$|I_{filtered}\rangle = IQFT \left(\frac{1}{2^n} \left[\sum_{i=0}^{2^{2n}-1} c_l|0l\rangle + \sum_{i=0}^{2^{2n}-1} s_l|1l\rangle \right] \right)$$

$$= \frac{1}{2^n} \sum_{i=0}^{2^{2n}-1} \left(cos\theta_i'|0\rangle + sin\theta_i'|1\rangle \right)$$

where

$$c_l = \frac{1}{2^n} \sum_{i=0}^{2^{2n}-1} e^{\frac{2\pi jil}{2^{2n}}} cos\theta_i'$$

$$s_l = \frac{1}{2^n} \sum_{i=0}^{2^{2n}-1} e^{\frac{2\pi jil}{2^{2n}}} sin\theta_i'$$

$$l = 0, 1, \ldots 2^{2n} - 1$$

18.3.3   Quantum Boolean Image Processing [9]

The steps involved in Quantum Boolean Image Processing are detailed below in the following subsections

18.3.3.1   Decomposition and Bit-Plane Slicing

The RGB color components are decomposed using bit-plane slicing. For a 24-bit color image, each color component is decomposed into 8 planes where the 7th slice is called as the most significant bit (MSB) plane which contains most information regarding the original image. In the following subsections image refers to the MSB.

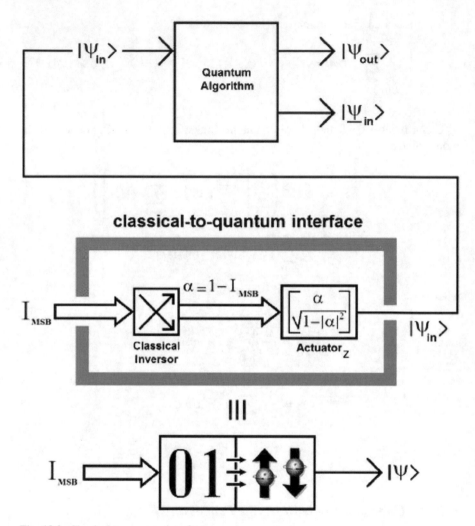

Fig. 18.2 Classical to quantum interface

18.3.3.2   Classical to Quantum Interface

The traditional inversor determines $\alpha = 1 - I_{MSB}$. The wave function component can be obtained as $|\beta| = \sqrt{1 - |\alpha|^2}$ for any ϕ. An actuator performs this task by building a wave function ψ_{in}. The classical to quantum interface is shown in Fig. 18.2. α and I_{MSB} are inverted to each other i.e. if $\alpha = 1$ and $|\psi\rangle = |0\rangle$ then $I_{MSB} = 0$ and if $\alpha = 0$ and $|\psi\rangle = |1\rangle$ then $I_{MSB} = 1$. This infers that only $z-$axis of the Bloch's sphere is required.

18.3.3.3 Image Denoising Using Quantum Boolean Mean Filter (QBMF)

Similar to the traditional kernel, the quantum kernel can be of any odd dimension with an equal number of rows and columns. The basic steps involved in Quantum convolution are

```
function Out_MSB = qbmf(In_MSB)

// w window or kernel
// h half the number of elements in the kernel
// n number of 1s in each kernel
// In_MSB incoming Quantum Boolean MSB for each color
// Out_MSB outgoing Quantum Boolean MSB for each color

Out_MSB = In_MSB;
[ROW,COL] = size(In_MSB);
w = input('w = ');
h = round(w*w/2);

for r = 1 + floor(w/2) : ROW - floor(w/2)
        for c = 1 + floor(w/2) : COL - floor(w/2)

        W = In_MSB(r - floor(w/2):r + floor(w/2),
                        c - floor(w/2):r + floor(w/2));

        n = sum(sum(W));
        if(n >= h)
                Out_MSB (r,c) = 1;
        else
                Out_MSB (r,c) = 0;
        end
        end
end
```

18.3.3.4 Quantum to Classical Interface

The denoised $|\psi\rangle$ from the QBMF is subjected to the quantum to classical interface to the yield the denoised MSB of each color. The denoised MSB along with the other bitplanes can be combined to construct the denoised color component of the image.

Table 18.4 displays the states before and after the quantum measurement. As mentioned before an automatic and direct correspondence exist between [0, 1] and [$|0\rangle$, $|1\rangle$]. Likewise an inverse correspondence exists between [$|0\rangle$, $|1\rangle$] and [0, 1].

Table 18.4 Measurement outcome with computational basis and generic states

Before quantum measurement	After quantum measurement
$|0\rangle$	$|0\rangle$
$|1\rangle$	$|1\rangle$
$|\psi\rangle$	$|\psi\rangle_{pm} = \dfrac{\hat{M}_m|\psi\rangle}{\sqrt{\langle\psi|\hat{M}_m^\dagger \hat{M}_m|\psi\rangle}}$

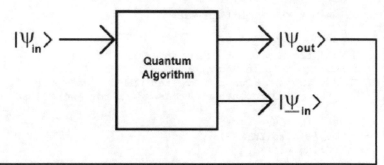

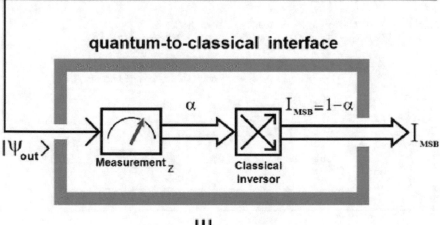

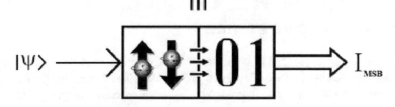

Fig. 18.3 Quantum to classical interface

18.3.3.5 Bit Reassembling and Color Recomposition

The processed image can be recomposed by reassembling the denoised I_{MSB} and the remaining unprocessed bitplanes for each color component (Fig. 18.3).

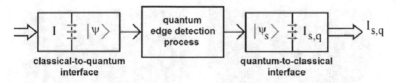

Fig. 18.4 Quantum edge detector

18.3.4   Quantum Edge Detection [10]

The MSB of the image is considered for detecting the edges using the quantum edge detection. Quantum edge detector follows the similar steps as that of the quantum Boolean mean filter as shown in Fig. 18.4. A kernel of size 3×3 (but it could be of any odd dimension) is considered for the edge detection process.

The Boolean edge detection algorithm comprises of three major stages,

1. The elements in 3×3 local neighbourhood of the image is converted into a row vector
2. The max of the elements in row vector except the center element is computed
3. The center element is XORed with the maximum element obtained in the previous step and is replaced with the original center element.

The core part of the Boolean edge detector is listed below. It follows the same convolution logic as that of the quantum Boolean mean filter.

```
function E_MSB = edge(I_MSB)

// w window or kernel
// I_MSB incoming Quantum Boolean MSB for each color
// E_MSB outgoing Quantum Boolean MSB for each color

E_MSB = I_MSB;
[ROW,COL] = size(I_MSB);
w = input('w = ');

for r = 1 + floor(w/2) : ROW - floor(w/2)
        for c = 1 + floor(w/2) : COL - floor(w/2)

        W = I_MSB(r - floor(w/2):r + floor(w/2),
                        c - floor(w/2):r + floor(w/2));
        M = W(:)';
        M(5) = [];
        E_MSB(r,c) = xor(max(M),W(5));

        end
end
```

The quantum Boolean mean filter and the quantum edge detector are applied on the 'Rice' image in Fig. 18.5a. The bit planes are sliced and the bitplane 7 i.e. MSB is portrayed in Fig. 18.5b. The quantum Boolean mean filter is applied on the MSB and is displayed in Fig. 18.5c. The quantum edge detector might result in

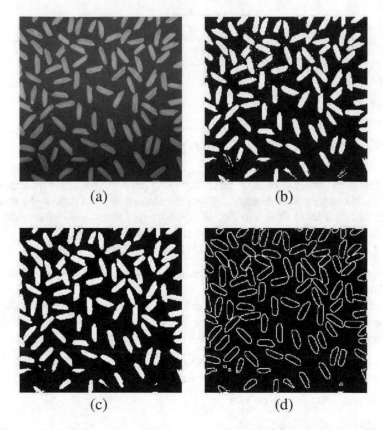

(a)   (b)

(c)   (d)

Fig. 18.5 (**a**) Original 'Rice' image (**b**) bitplane 7 (MSB) (**c**) filtered image using QBMF (**d**) Boolean edge detection

spurious output. Hence, the Boolean image is processed using the mean filter before it undergoes the edge detection process and is demonstrated in Fig. 18.5d.

The Quantum edge detector uses the PAO criteria on μ instead of α.

18.3.5   Quantum Hilbert Image Scrambling [11]

The process of transforming a meaningful image into a disordered or meaningless image is often utilized for transmitting data digitally, for storing data confidentially or for protecting the integrity of the images through watermarking. Several scrambling algorithms are available in the literature which uses Fibonacci transform, Hilbert transform, Magic square transform or Arnold transform etc. [12–17]. Hilbert curve is used to obtain Hilbert Matrix, is a popular transformer among the other scrambling algorithms. Figure 18.6, display a Hilbert curve when $n = 4$. A recursive algorithm is presented in [11] comprises of three stages of operation: initialization, odd and even.

Fig. 18.6 Hilbert curve when
$n = 4$

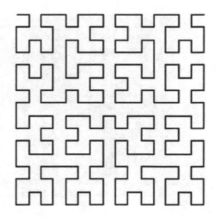

In the following subsection, k refers to the sub-image index and it varies from 0 to $n - 1$.

18.3.5.1 Module *PARTITION*(k)

The *PARTITION*(k) is used for dividing $2^n \times 2^n$ input image into $2^{n-k-1} \times 2^{n-k-1}$ number of sub-images each of $2^{k+1} \times 2^{k+1}$ size. This circuit swaps x_{k+1} with x_{k+2}, x_{k+2} with $x_{k+3}, \ldots$, and x_{n-2} with x_{n-1}. It also swaps x_{n-1} with y_k.

18.3.5.2 Module O(k)

Let us consider four matrices A, B, C, D of dimensions $2^{k-1} \times 2^{k-1}$ and k is odd. The module O(k) converts $\begin{pmatrix} A & B \\ C & D \end{pmatrix}$ into $\begin{pmatrix} A & D^{PP} \\ B^T & C^T \end{pmatrix}$

The module O(k) swaps x_k with y_k using a C-NOT Gate, where x_k acts as a control qubit and y_k as target qubit. The CSWAP gates are used to swap x_0 with y_0, x_1 with y_1 etc. using y_k as a control qubit. 01-NOT Gates are used to reverse $x_{k-1}, x_{k-2}, \ldots x_0$ and $y_{k-1}, y_{k-2}, \ldots y_0$ using y_k as 0-control and x_k as 1-control qubit respectively.

18.3.5.3 Module E(k)

This module is used to convert $\begin{pmatrix} A & B \\ C & D \end{pmatrix}$ into $\begin{pmatrix} A & B^T \\ D^{PP} & C^T \end{pmatrix}$ when k is even.

The module E(k) uses a C-NOT Gate by setting y_k acts as a control qubit and x_k as target qubit. The CSWAP Gates are used to swap x_0 with y_0, x_1 with y_1 etc. using x_k as a control qubit. 01-NOT Gates are used to reverse $x_{k-1}, x_{k-2}, \ldots x_0$ and $y_{k-1}, y_{k-2}, \ldots y_0$ using x_k as 0-control and y_k as 1-control qubit respectively.

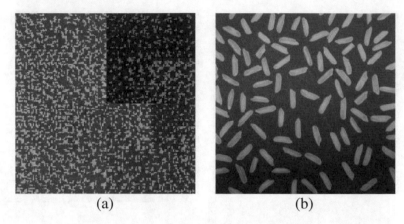

(a)   (b)

Fig. 18.7 Quantum Hilbert image scrambling. (**a**) Scrambled Image. (**b**) Re-scrambled Image

A MATLAB implementation of [11] is available online at [18]. Figure 18.7 shows the 'Rice' Image scrambled and re-scrambled using Quantum Hilbert transform. A 256×256 image takes approximately 30 s and 61 s for scrambling and re-scrambling process.

18.4 Conclusion

Image processing with quantum mechanics is one of the vital approaches to address the computationally high real-time requirements of traditional image processing. In this chapter, the basics of Quantum computing is discussed. The main focus of this chapter is on the applications of quantum computing in image processing. Initially, quantum representation of images is discussed. It is found that the novel enhances quantum representation has the following advantages such as [4]:

1. Less computational complexity for preparing the image.
2. The compression ratio of NEQR is improved over the FRQI by at least 1.5 times.
3. Quantum measurements can be accurately obtained from NEQR, whereas in FRQI it is obtained probabilistically.
4. NEQR can perform all kinds of color operations conveniently.

Quantum Boolean version of the image is utilized for many applications such as mean filtering, edge detection etc. The Boolean image can be obtained using bit plane slicing and a classical to quantum interface. The advantage of Quantum Boolean image processing is that the algorithms are devised based on simple quantum-based logical operations. One more application of Quantum computing is also discussed i.e. Quantum scrambling for cryptography applications. Hilbert image scrambling is a recursive algorithm for scanning the image matrix and to convert it into a scrambled image using quantum circuits.

The future scope of this work is to devise algorithms for complex image processing applications like classification, segmentation, object recognition using quantum circuits.

References

1. Fox C. (2003) QCF: Quantum Computing Functions for MATLAB. https://sourceforge.net/projects/qcf/
2. Nielsen M. A., Chuang I. L. (2002) Quantum Computation and Quantum Information. 10th edn., Cambridge University Press, UK.
3. Le P., Dong F., Hirota K. (2011) A Flexible Representation of Quantum Images for Polynomial Preparation, Image Compression, and Processing Operations. Quantum Inf. Process, **10**,63–84.
4. Zhang Y., Lu K., Gao Y., Wang M. (2013) NEQR: A Novel Enhanced Quantum Representation of Digital Images. Quantum Inf. Process., **12**,2833–2860.
5. Yan F., Iliyasu A. M., Jiang A. (2014) Quantum Computation-based Image Representation, Processing Operations and their Applications. Entropy, **16**, 5290–5338.
6. Caraiman S., Manta V. I. (2013) Quantum Image Filtering in the Frequency Domain. Advances in Electrical and Computer Engineering, **13**, 77–84.
7. M. Mastriani (2014) Optimal Estimation of States in Quantum Image Processing. ArXiv:1406.5121[quant-ph]
8. Liu K., Zhang Y., Wang X.-p., and Lu K. (2016) A Strategy of Quantum Image Filtering in Frequency Domain. In the International Conference on Applied Mechanics, Electronics and Mechatronics Engineering, Article no. 5763, May 28–29, China.
9. Mastriani M. (2015) Quantum Boolean Image Denoising. Springer Quantum Inf. Process. **14**, 1647–1673.
10. Mastriani M. (2014) Quantum Edge Detection for Image Segmentation in Optical Environments. arXiv:1409.2918[cs.CV]
11. Jiang N., Wang L., Wu W.-Y. (2014) Quantum Hilbert Image Scrambling. International Journal of Theoretical Physics. **53**, 2463–2484.
12. M. -Y. Hu, X. -L. Tian, S.-W. Xia. (2010) Image Scrambling based on 3D Hilbert Curve. In: 3rd International Congress on Image and Signal Processing. **1**, 147–149.
13. J.-M. Guo, Y. Yang, N. Wang. (2011) Chaos-based Gray Image Watermarking Algorithm. In: International Conference on Uncertainty Reasoning and Knowledge Engineering. **1**, 158–160.
14. X.-H. Lin, L.-D. Cai. (2004) Scrambling Research of Digital Image based on Hilbert Curve. Chinese J. Stereology Image Anal. **9**(4), 224–227.
15. Z. Shang, H. Ren, J. Zhang. (2008) A block location scrambling algorithm of digital image based on Arnold transformation. In: 9th International Conference for Young Computer Scientists. 2942–2947.
16. W.-G. Zou, J.-Y. Huang, C.-Y. Zhou. (2010) Digital image scrambling technology based on two dimension Fibonacci transformation and its periodicity. In: 3rd International Symposium on Information Science and Engineering. 415–418.
17. M.-G. Wen, S.-C. Huang, C.-C. Han. (2010) An information hiding scheme using magic squares. In: IEEE International Conference on Broadband, Wireless Computing, Communication and Applications. 556–560.
18. E. Farzadnia. (2017) A MATLAB simulation for the Quantum Hilbert Image Scrambling Technique (Version 1.1) [Source code] https://www.researchgate.net/publication/318761544_A_MAT-LAB_simulation_for_the_Quantum_Hilbert_Image_Scrambling_Technique. https://doi.org/0.13140/RG.2.2.23279.33449.

Chapter 19
3-D Shape Reconstruction Based CT Image Enhancement

Manoj Diwakar and Pardeep Kumar

19.1 Introduction

Computed Tomography has become the diagnostic tool of choice in a wide variety of situations. Computed Tomography images show organ of interest at selected levels of the body. They are the visual equivalent of bloodless slices of anatomy, with each scan being a single slice. CT examinations produce detailed organ studies by stacking individual images. To analyze CT scanned images in depth, three-dimensional (3-D) image surface reconstruction has been an important research area in computer vision. For minimizing the cost function of CT scanning and analyzing in depth, 3D image reconstruction method has a great potential to improve the image quality with noise reduction [1].

2-D image reconstruction is an effective tool for medical specialist to analysis the medical scientific organs [2], which can help to improve the medical diagnostic accuracy greatly. Three dimensional tomography improves the sensitivity of the scanner in terms of shape reconstruction in such a way that photons traverse several slices and 3D reconstructed shape are also recovered [3, 4]. Another way to deal is use projection-based techniques to improve image quality [5]. In this case problems are reduced by improving 2D projection images obtained directly from the scanning device. Projections are processed in a way to reduce the problems in the resulting 3D volume. For that, reconstruction algorithm is applied to provide corrected projections in a 3D volume with reduced problems [6]. Analytic reconstruction

M. Diwakar
Department of CSE, DIT University, Dehradun, Uttarakhand, India

P. Kumar (✉)
Department of CSE and IT, Jaypee University of Information Technology, Solan, Himachal Pradesh, India

© Springer Nature Switzerland AG 2019
A. K. Singh, A. Mohan (eds.), *Handbook of Multimedia Information Security: Techniques and Applications*, https://doi.org/10.1007/978-3-030-15887-3_19

methods have traditional understanding that incomplete data reconstruction implies some type of approximation of the object to be reconstructed [7, 8].

This paper deals direct 3d surface reconstruction where shading technique is used to reconstruct the image with the help of fast marching method. These methods can be problem from image reconstruction by interpreting an image as the propagating interface to the final position [9, 10].

19.1.1 Radon Transform

CT image reconstruction is one important mathematical representation where CT images are generated via a mathematical model. This mathematical model is known as Radon transform which is only help to generate the CT images. The mathematical model of Radon transform is used to collect all the raw data from n number of angels. These raw data are collected from detectors which were absorbed via X-Ray transmission [11]. The radon transform is an integral transform whose inverse is used to reconstruct the CT images.

In Fig. 19.1, Radon transform is applied over the phantom image with 180° angels. The middle of Fig. 19.1 shows the results of radon transform which indicates the sine waves and it is impossible to understand these sine waves. Hence to understand the meaning of sine waves, inverse Radon transform is applied with same number of angels. Last of Fig. 19.1 shows the results of inverse radon transform. This is the process of CT image reconstruction.

With the help of the Dirac "function" δ, which is zero for every argument except to 0 and its integral is one, $g(0, \theta)$ is expressed as:

$$g(0, \theta) = \iint f(x, y) \cdot \delta(x \cos \theta + y \sin \theta) \, dxdy$$

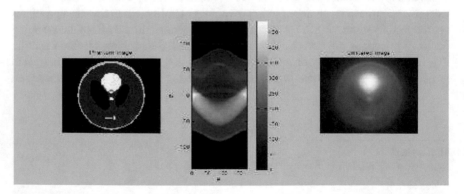

Fig. 19.1 The Radon transform computation over the phantom image: (**a**) Phantom Image, (**b**) Sinogram and, (**c**) Unfiltered reconstructed image

The inverse of Radon transform is calculated by the following equation:

$$f(x, y) = \int_{-\pi/2}^{\pi/2} \rho \cdot R_\theta \left(s\left(x, y\right)\right) d\theta$$

19.2   Fast Marching Method

To generate the CT images, CT image reconstruction is a big tool to underhand the processing of reconstruction. Similarly Shape from Shading [12–16] is one other important tool to enhance the shape of images in terms of shape which can be applied via curve analysis. For shape from shading there are number of methods to provide the edges in terms of shape. One of major methods is Fast Marching Method which is introduced by Sethian [11]. There are various problems in CT image reconstructions such as blurring, noise, artifacts and so on, but many solutions are also provided to solve it [18–27]. The main concept of Fast Marching method is to identify the pixels and their neighborhood pixels and give a speed function to identify the curve or line [28–31].

This method is to move the curve from one pixel in a progressive manner according to the speed function while preserving the nature of the implicit function [12]. The Fast Marching method can be defined as follows:

Algorithm
- Definition:

    - Label the set of all grid points as Alive for values which has been reached and will not be changed;
    - Label the set of next grid points (6-connexity neighbors) as Trial for examined and estimate of surface grid;
    - Label the set of all other grid points as Far for which surface grid can't estimate;

- Loop:

    - Let $A(i_{min}, j_{min}, k_{min})$ be the Trial point with the smallest Value;
    - Move it from the Trial to the Alive set
    - For each neighbor (i, j, k) (6-connexity in 3D) of $(i_{min}, j_{min}, k_{min})$

    If (i, j, k) is Far, add it to the Trial set and compute T using Loop;

    If (i, j, k) is Trial, recomputed the value of T, and update it.

19.3   Results and Discussion

Synthetic phantom image has been created with the help of ellipse and geometric methods on the MATLAB as Fig. 19.2a. To get the synthetic image in the form of 2D-CT scanned data, some pre-processing methods are applied. After applying radon transform over the synthetic image, the image is filtered with the help of Ram-Lak Kernel. Ram-Lak kernel which acts as high pass filter is recommended for filtered back projection. To obtain the intensities at each pixel in the surfaces should be projected orthographically on $z = 0$ plane. The obtained shaded image of phantom image is in Fig. 19.2b. These shaded images are used as the input FMM algorithms for the possible 3D shape reconstruction. Since the images are synthetic and we have the true depth values corresponding to them, the true depth values are assigned on the minimum singular points. The minimum singular points are chosen by the visualization of image, which are basically the brightest points in the local

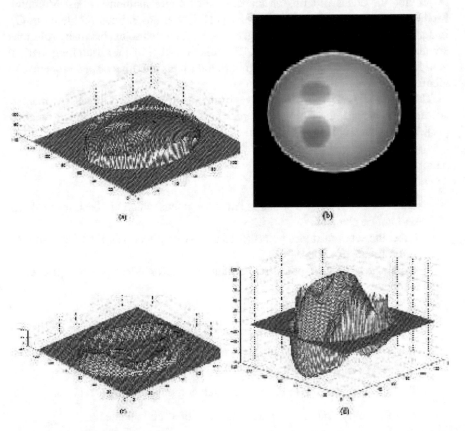

Fig. 19.2 (a) True 3D map from simulated image; (b) Simulated image; (c) Reconstructed 3D map; (d) Error map

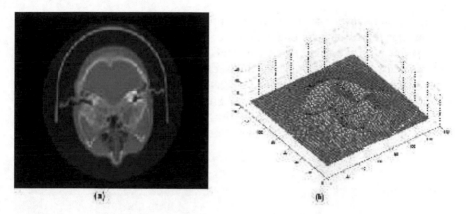

Fig. 19.3 (a) Real CT image; (b) 3D map from real image

regions of the images. The reconstructed surface is shown in Fig. 19.2c. The error maps corresponding to the synthetic image are shown in the Fig. 19.2d where, we get the value of mean error is 6.88.

We have tested the scheme on real CT scanned images. The original CT image has obtained in the format of DICOM. The size of the image is 128 × 128. We set two minimum singular points in CT scanned image. The reconstructed depth map of CT scanned image is shown in the Fig. 19.3a. The shaded image from the reconstructed depth maps is shown in Fig. 19.3b.

The algorithm for 3d shape reconstruction is coded in C++ and MATLAB is used as a tool to draw the images. The computational time for all synthetic and real images is recorded in milliseconds.

19.4 Conclusion

We have tested CT image reconstruction based on 3D fast marching method for produces significant improvements over direct analytical methods in terms of noise, and resolution. The fast marching is used to extract rough boundaries. The level set is used to fine tune the rough contour. This is because though the level set can smooth the contour, some details can also be lost. Using the level set with no fast marching presumably yields similar results, but takes much longer computation time. As the reconstruction technique remains independent from the exact form of the forward model, Fast Marching Method is applicable to any geometry and is particularly well suited to the reconstruction problem [17]. The orthographic projection and most widely used Lambertian reflectance map are used in SfS problem formulations. For the simplicity of the problem, the light source direction is considered as vertical to the image plane. In this case, Fast Marching Method is applied and shown that it solves the problem in less memory space and less computation time. Computational time varies according to images and their sizes.

Experiments are conducted on synthetic image and real CT scanned image. The qualitative results are found to be excellent. In case of synthetic data, there constructed shapes are closely matched with the true data, computed errors are also small and in case of real data, the shaded images obtained from the reconstructed depth values are quite similar to the original images. This work can supports for clinical application by providing further control over image quality and analysis.

References

1. J-B.Thibault, K. Sauer, C. Bouman, and J. Hsieh, "A three-dimensional statistical approach to improved image quality for multi-slice helical CT," in *Journal on Med. Phys.*, vol. 34, pp. 4526–44, 2007.
2. RenJingying and Chen Shuyue, "Research on interpolation methods for cross-sections slice image,"in *Journal onComputer Measurement and Control*, vol. 13, pp. 729-733, 2005.
3. W. Withayachumnankul, C. Pintavirooj, M. Sangworasilp and K. Hamamoto, "3D shape recovery based on tomography,"in Proceedings IEEE Signal Processing, August, 2002.
4. M. Defrise. "A short reader's guide to 3D tomographic reconstruction,"in *Journal onComputerized Medical Imaging and Graphics*, Vol. 25, pp. 113–6, 2001.
5. ArtemAmirkhanov, ChristophHeinzl, Michael Reiter, Johann Kastner, and M. Eduard Groller, "Projection-Based Metal-Artifact Reduction for Industrial 3D X-ray Computed Tomography," *in IEEE Transactions on visualization and computer graphics*, vol. 17, no. 12, December 2011.
6. R.Clackdoyle and M.Defrise, "Tomographic reconstruction in the 21st century. region-of-interest reconstruction from incomplete data," in *Journal onIEEE Signal Processing*, vol. 60, pp. 60–80, 2010.
7. Y. Zhou, K. Panetta, and S. Agaian, "3D CT baggage image enhancement based on order statistic decomposition," in *Proceedings IEEE Inter. Conf.* on, 2010, pp. 287-291.
8. SangtaeAhn, Abhijit J Chaudhari, Felix Darvas, Charles A Bouman and Richard M Leahy," Fast iterative image reconstruction methods for fully 3D multispectral bioluminescence tomography," in *Journal* on Phys. Med. Biol., Vol. 53 pp. 3921, 2008.
9. Edward J. Ciaccioa, Christina A. Tennysona, GovindBhagata, b, Suzanne K. Lewisa and Peter H.R. Greena, "Use of shape-from-shading to estimate three-dimensional architecture in the small intestinal lumen of celiac and control patients," in *Journal on Computer Methods and Programs in Biomedicine,* Volume 111, pp. 676–684, 2013.
10. J. Sethian and A. Popovici, "3-D traveltime computation using the fast marching method," in *Journal onGEOPHYSICS*, vol. 64, pp. 516–523, 1999.
11. S. Venturras and I. Flaounas," Study of Radon Transformation and Application of its Inverse to NMR", Paper for " Algorithms in Molecular Biology" Course Assoc Prof. I. Emiris, 4 July, 2005.
12. Firas Wada and Mohamed Ali Hamdi, "3D Segmentation of Intravascular Ultrasound Images: A Fast-Marching Method," in *Journal on Radiology and Diagnostic Imaging*, Vol. 1, pp. 29-36, 2013.
13. Mai BabikerAdm andAbasMd Said, "3D Reconstruction using Interactive Shape from Shading," in *Journal onInternational Journal of Computer Applications*vol. 28, pp. 20-24, August 2011.
14. A. Patel and W.A.P. Smith, "Shape-from-shading driven 3D Morphable Models for Illumination Insensitive Face Recognition".*In Proc. BMVC*, 2009.

15. W. M. Sheta, M. F. Mahmoud and E. H. Atta, "Evolutionary Computation Approach for Shape from Shading,"*in Journal on IJICIS*, vol. 5, 2005.
16. I. Kemelmacher-Shlizerman and R. Basri, "3D Face Reconstruction from a Single Image Using a Single Reference Face Shape"*In IEEE Transactions on Pattern Analysis and Machine Intelligence*, vol. 33, 2011.
17. Vikram Appia and Anthony Yezzi, "Symmetric Fast Marching Schemes for Better Numerical Isotrophy," *in IEEE Transactions on Pattern Analysis and Machine Intelligence,* vol. 35, pp. 2298-2304, 2013.
18. M. Diwakar, M. Kumar, CT image noise reduction based on adaptive Wienerfiltering with wavelet packet thresholding, in: 2014 InternationalConference on Parallel, Distributed and Grid Computing (PDGC), IEEE, 2014,pp. 94–98.
19. M. Diwakar, M. Kumar, Edge preservation based CT image denoising usingWiener filtering and thresholding in wavelet domain, in: 2016 FourthInternational Conference on Parallel, Distributed and Grid Computing(PDGC), IEEE, 2016, pp. 332–336.
20. M. Diwakar, M. Kumar, A hybrid method based CT image denoising usingnonsubsampled contourlet and curvelet transforms, in: Proceedings ofInternational Conference on Computer Vision and Image Processing,Springer, 2017, pp. 571–580.
21. M. Diwakar, M. Kumar, et al., CT image denoising based on complex wavelettransform using local adaptive thresholding and bilateral filtering., in:Proceedings of the Third International Symposium on Women in Computingand Informatics, ACM, 2015, pp. 297–302.
22. M. Kumar, M. Diwakar, CT image denoising using locally adaptive shrinkagerule in tetrolet domain, J. King Saud Univ. Comput. Inf. Sci. (2016).
23. M. Kumar, M. Diwakar, Edge preservation based CT image denoising usingwavelet and curvelet transforms, in: Proceedings of Fifth InternationalConference on Soft Computing for Problem Solving, Springer, 2016, pp.771–782.
24. M. Kumar, M. Diwakar, A new exponentially directional weighted functionbased CT image denoising using total variation, J. King Saud Univ. Comput.Inf. Sci. (2016).
25. M. Kumar, M. Diwakar, A new locally adaptive patch variation based CT image denoising, Int. J. Image Graph. Signal Process. 8 (1) (2016) 43.
26. M. Diwakar, M. Kumar, A review on CT image noise and its denoising, Biomedical Signal Processing and Control, Elsvier, 2018, 42(1) pp. 73–88.
27. M. Diwakar, M. Kumar, CT image denoising using NLM and correlation based wavelet packet thresholding." IET Image Processing, , 2018, 12(5) pp. 708 - 715.
28. S. Sahu, A.K. Singh, S.P. Ghrera, and M. Elhoseny, "An approach for de-noising and contrast enhancement of retinal fundus image using CLAHE" Optics & Laser Technology, 2018.
29. Sahu, Sima, Harsh Vikram Singh, Basant Kumar, and Amit Kumar Singh. "Statistical modeling and Gaussianization procedure based de-speckling algorithm for retinal OCT images." Journal of Ambient Intelligence and Humanized Computing (2018): 1-14.
30. Sahu, Sima, Harsh Vikram Singh, Basant Kumar, and Amit Kumar Singh. "De-noising of ultrasound image using Bayesian approached heavy-tailed Cauchy distribution." Multimedia Tools and Applications (2017): 1-18.
31. Sahu, Sima, Harsh Vikram Singh, Basant Kumar, and Amit Kumar Singh. "A Bayesian multiresolution approach for noise removal in medical magnetic resonance images." Journal of Intelligent Systems (2018).

Chapter 20
A Segmentation-Less Efficient Alzheimer Detection Approach Using Hybrid Image Features

Sitara Afzal, Mubashir Javed, Muazzam Maqsood, Farhan Aadil, Seungmin Rho, and Irfan Mehmood

20.1 Introduction

Alzheimer's disease (AD) is the type of dementia, which damages the brain's cells and causes memory loss. This ultimately results that a patient is not able to do simple daily errands [1]. There is no appropriate medical remedy has been found yet and the reason of AD is insufficiently comprehended [2, 3]. As per an approximation, in 2015 about 5.3 million American is going through the AD. In 2050, the digit is probably going high up to 16 million [4]. The life quality of AD patients can be improved by early identification of this disease. At present time for medical diagnosis, MRI is extensively utilized in hospitals for the AD because of its remarkable resolution, good contrast and high availability [5, 6]. The region of interest (ROI), Volume of interest (VOI) [7–9], the medial temporal lobe, Gray matter (GM) voxels in the image segmentation [10], and hippocampus measurement and morphometric methods, structural MRI has been utilized for the extraction and classification of AD features [11–13]. Regardless of the enhancement in Initial Identification of AD, structural MRI remains a challenging task for the prediction of progression of ailment and needs further exploration.

A cautious medical assessment is needed for the finding of the AD. This includes physical, neuro-biological exams, and clinical dementia rating (CDR)

S. Afzal · M. Javed · M. Maqsood · F. Aadil
Department of Computer Science, COMSATS University Islamabad, Attock, Pakistan

S. Rho (✉)
Department of Software, Sejong University, Seoul, Korea
e-mail: smrho@sejong.edu

I. Mehmood
School of Media Design and Technology, Faculty of Engineering and Informatics, University of Bradford, United Kingdom

© Springer Nature Switzerland AG 2019
A. K. Singh, A. Mohan (eds.), *Handbook of Multimedia Information Security: Techniques and Applications*, https://doi.org/10.1007/978-3-030-15887-3_20

which is a 5-point scale used to characterize six domains of cognitive and functional performance and mini-mental state examination (MMSE) questionnaire. Moreover, examining structural and functional variation in the cerebrum, non-invasive approaches like resting-state functional MRI (rs-fMRI) and structural MRI have been utilized [14, 15]. The tasks including reminiscence, preparation, thinking, and ruling gets effect because of the changes in the brain and hippocampus. The stage of diseases progression changes the number of different cerebrum areas. Essentially expanded ventricles and an extreme volume decrease of the hippocampus and cerebral cortex can be easily detected using MRI images.

Developing an algorithm, which can distinguish between an AD patient and normal person is of extraordinary significance to the clinicians [16]. In this work, we present a statistical-based analysis, in which MRI images are divided into three different sections Axial, Coronal, and Sagittal. Histogram of oriented gradient (HOG) descriptor, local binary pattern, and Gray-level co-occurrence matrix method (GLCM) techniques are utilized without segmentation MRI images to extract features. For AD diagnosis, multiclass classification is performed by providing these enhanced features as an input to classifiers. Our contribution to this chapter has described in the following points:

- Features based classification methods are proposed using statistical features
- Using the whole image without segmentation and produces enhanced results in multiclass classification.

The remaining chapter is structured as Sect. 20.2 presents related work, Sect. 20.3 shows methodology and Sect. 20.4 shows results section followed by a conclusion.

20.2   Related Work

Many contributions have been done by the researcher in the detection of Alzheimer's disease. Ateeq et al. [17] proposed an efficient approach for the detection of cerebral microbleeds (CMB) in brain MRI, as this CMB is the essential indicator for the detection of dementia. This approach is comprised of three phases including brain extraction, extraction of the initial candidate based on the threshold and the last one is feature extraction and classification using Support Vector Machine, Quadric Discriminant Analysis (QDA) and ensemble methods. They attained the best sensitivity of 93.7% by utilizing QDA classifier.

In [1], five phases were used, wherein the first stage images were pre-processed, and segmentation was used to divide the image into a gray and cerebrospinal fluid and white matter. The second phase is to build similarity, the GM segmented ROIs were utilized through features and separated in the next phase. To categorize ADs patients and healthy subjects, 3-Dimensional displacement field was utilized in [2]. Features were extracted using three approaches i.e. Bhattacharya distance, Welch's t-test. Voxel-based morphometry (VBM) is used to find Global and Local atrophy in AD patients vs normal subjects [18].

In [19], Sections having remarkable GM atrophy variations were chosen as the volume of interest (VOIs) and GM volume was perceived by using VBM for the AD and normal subjects. The voxel values separated from the sections that were perceived as raw features are next assessed using seven distinct features grading approaches i.e. Fisher's criterion, T-test score, statistical dependency, mutual information, information gain, the Gini-index, and Pearson correlation coefficient. SVM was used for classification and achieved 92.4% accuracy. To classify the AD a Laplace Beltrami eigenvalue form descriptor was utilized in [20]. Segmenting T1 weighted MRI scans, the shape change of corpus callosum were examined through reaction diffusion level set technique. Information gain ranking was used to select the significant features and then subjected to classification using SVM and K-nearest neighbor (KNN). KNN classifier gives 93.37% accuracy. On the other hand, the difficulty of quantifying differences in the micro arrangements of corpus callosum makes this the technique less beneficial.

In [21], an outline for the extraction of features from low aspect sub-spaces was proposed. To build the manifold sub-space, Data-driven ROI were used. To learn these regions, MMSE score with sparse regression was used. For performing the variable selection, the sampling bias was abridged accompanied by resampling arrangement using sparse regression. The accuracy of classification achieved was 71%. A classification technique for the AD and cognitively normal (CN) classification, named sulcal medial surface was also proposed [22]. To take out 24 different sulci from every individual subject, Brain-VISA sulcal identification pipeline was utilized and SVM was used to classify AD and CN and attained 87.9% accuracy. To make a bio-marker, different dimensions like hippocampus texture, cortical thickness, and shape were combined, that utilized information from MRI data [23]. The accuracy of multiclass classification using LDA was 62.7% for ADNI [24].

In [25], a deep learning-based method was proposed to classify AD subjects. To foresee the output classes as AD patients and healthy, auto-encoders were used together with a convolutional neural network (CNN) and reported an accuracy of 98.7%. CNN has been used to excerpt discriminative features for classification of the AD and healthy persons [26, 27]. In big data analysis, deep learning methods have attained remarkable outcomes. However, a lot of training and a large number of computational power is required for gathering useful information from a large collection of unstructured data [28]. This is also a difficult task to select optimal-hyper parameters and best structural design.

Most strategies reported in the literature highlights that the limitation in classification is due to features taken out directly from the brain images. Both binary and multiclass classification is still an open research problem. In this study, the binary and multiclass classification performance is improved by using clinical information along with features.

20.3   Proposed Methodology

Three main segments are proposed in this method, specifically the preprocessing
phase, feature, and results. The complete process is shown in Fig. 20.1.

20.3.1   Preprocessing

In this phase, MR images are firstly sliced to get three different angles of that
image—Axial, Coronal, and Sagittal. Features of all these three angles are extracted
separately to make a feature vector.

20.3.2   Feature Extraction

20.3.2.1   Gray-Level Co-occurrence Matrix

The Gray-level co-occurrence matrix (GLCM) was firstly analyzed by Haralick in
1973 [1]. The algorithm then analyzed and fourteen texture based features were
proposed known as Gray-level co-occurrence features [2]. Normally in images,
pixels are highly correlated because of the same levels of gray in a specific region.
In a specified area, the frequency of pixels that occur with value 'j' having spatial
relation with pixels value 'p' was computed by GLCM [3, 4].

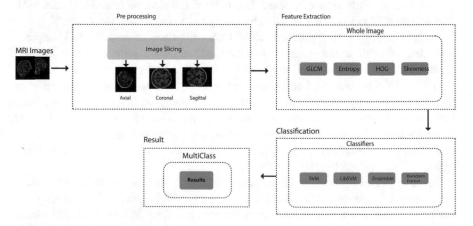

Fig. 20.1 The proposed methodology for segmentation less Alzheimer detection

Contrast

The contrast measures the local difference in GLCM and calculated as:

$$\sum_{i,j=0}^{n-1} P\,i,j\,(i-j)\string^2 \tag{20.1}$$

Contrast is the 'sum of square variance'. As $(i-j)$ values increases, the contrast also continues to increase but there is no increase in contrast when the values go equivalent.

Correlation

Correlation measures the joint probability and is calculated as:

$$\sum_{x,y} \cdot \left(\cdot \frac{(x-\mu_1)\,(y-\mu_2\cdot)\,\Pr\theta\,(x,y)}{\sigma_1\sigma_2} \right) \tag{20.2}$$

Images that are correlated have $\mu_1, \mu_2\cdot$ as the means and σ_1, σ_2 as the variance value.

Homogeneity

It measures the closeness of elements i.e. how close the GLCM elements are to its diagonal. The weight of homogeneity value is opposite to the weight of contrast and can be measured as:

$$\sum_{x,y} \cdot \left(\cdot \frac{P\,r\theta\,(x,y)}{1+|x-y|^2} \right) \tag{20.3}$$

Entropy

It measures image disorder, when the image has non-uniform texture, entropy value is high. Entropy is calculated as:

$$-\sum_{x,y}^{n} \Pr\theta\,(x,y)\,\log\Pr\theta\,(x,y) \tag{20.4}$$

20.3.3 Classification

A multiclass classification of ADs without segmentation has been proposed. Different classifiers including the SVM, Ensembles method, and Random Forest were trained to classify the data and to validate the efficiency of the extracted features. All these classifiers are separately trained on normal, very mild, mild and severe AD according to their CDR values.

20.4 Experimental Results and Discussion

In this section, the details for dataset, experimental setup and results are reported in detail.

20.4.1 Dataset

The dataset has been taken from the OASIS database which is openly accessible to be utilized for research objective for AD classifications.

This set contains a total of 416 subject's stage adult (18) to old age (96) years old. For every subject, three to four persons contained MRI (T1-weighted) scans captured in single sessions. We have not used the images with missing information. Around 100 of subjects are found from with very mild to the mild AD. We limited our research to right-handed participants, both men, and women. These participants were categorized based on CDR values i.e. clinical dementia rating, as having normal cognition (CDR = 0) i.e. healthy subject or early-stage AD (CDR = 0.5). The set also has age, sex (male/female), socioeconomic status (SES), mini-mental state examination (MMSE) and estimated total interaction volume (eTIV). Demographic physiognomies of the individuals are presented in Table 20.1.

20.4.2 Result and Discussion

This proposed approach is evaluated using accuracy and precision [5–7, 29–32]. Models were trained and then validated by using fivefold cross-validation. Different classifiers were utilized to evaluate the performance of the obtained features. The

Table 20.1 Demographic physiognomies of the participants

Characteristics	Normal	Early stage
Age (yearly)	75.4 ± 7.8	76 ± 7.5
Gender (M/F)	29/46	20/55
Education (yearly)	3.16 ± 1.2	2.85 ± 1.3
MMSE	28.89 ± 1.2	24 ± 4.0
CDR	0	1
SES	2.5	2.87

Table 20.2 Multiclass classification results i.e. normal vs very mild vs mild vs severe AD with four classifiers i.e. SMO, LibSVM, Adaboost and Random Forest

Classifier name	Accuracy (%)
Random Forest	94.2
SMO	92.9
SMO (RBF kernel)	90.0
LibSVM (polynomial kernel)	92.7
LibSVM (linear)	90.5
Adaboost	83

main classifiers utilized were supported vector machine (SVM), ensemble methods, naïve Bayes, and random forest.

Random Forest was trained with 100 numbers of iterations and gave the best accuracy of 94.2%. Three different SVM kernels—Linear, Poly-linear, and RBF were used to evaluate the results. The output accuracy for polylinear kernel function, linear kernel and RBF is 92.9%, 92.7%, and 90.5% respectively. Ensemble methods were trained by using Adaboost (boosting) technique and attained 83% accuracy.

A good accuracy has been achieved for classification of binary class but multiclass classification is still tough errand as multiclass classification has been a major issue in Alzheimer's subjects. The results for multiclass classification are presented in the table and obtained by using features extracted from MR images. It is evident that from all the classifiers used, Random Forest generated best results.

Table 20.2 shows that the highest classification accuracy was achieved using Random Forest classifier. We compared the computational time for a clustering-based method and our proposed algorithm. The results in terms of computational time are 205 ms and 56 ms respectively.

20.4.2.1 Importance in Multimedia Applications

Multimedia applications are based on both image-based and audio-based applications. Image processing has seen an enormous growth in the last few decades. Medical imaging is one of the important research areas because of its critical nature. The innovations in medical imaging can help to improve computer diagnostic based applications. There is an enormous increase in the volume of medical imaging and diversity in datasets, automated tools are required to analyze the collection of images and do predictions based on information extracted. This study further helps to find the efficacy of multimedia tools. Furthermore, it also helps to build mobile technology to aid patients with Alzheimer decease like memory test applications.

20.5 Conclusion and Future Directions

In this research, statistical based features extraction is proposed to classify Alzheimer's using MRI images automatically. The output has shown that these statistical features produce good results in comparison with other features including texture based. It is evident from the results that the multiclass classification utilizing Random Forest gives best results on publicly available OASIS dataset. By correcting diagnose the AD in patients will enhance the efficiency of treatments. The accuracy of multiclass classification was significantly increased. In the future, we are exploring the effect of class imbalance issue in the available datasets. There is also a need to explore the effect of more sophisticated machine learning approaches like deep learning for Alzheimer detection.

Acknowledgement This research was supported by Basic Science Research Program through the National Research Foundation of Korea (NRF) funded by the Ministry of Education (NRF-2016R1D1A1A09919551).

References

1. Beheshti, I., et al., Histogram-Based Feature Extraction from Individual Gray Matter Similarity-Matrix for Alzheimer's Disease Classification. Journal of Alzheimer's Disease, 2017. **55**(4): p. 1571-1582.
2. Wang, S., et al., Detection of Alzheimer's disease by three-dimensional displacement field estimation in structural magnetic resonance imaging. Journal of Alzheimer's Disease, 2016. **50**(1): p. 233-248.
3. Belleville, S., et al., Detecting early preclinical Alzheimer's disease via cognition, neuropsy-chiatry, and neuroimaging: qualitative review and recommendations for testing. Journal of Alzheimer's disease, 2014. **42**(s4): p. S375-S382.
4. Beheshti, I., H. Demirel, and A.s.D.N. Initiative, Feature-ranking-based Alzheimer's disease classification from structural MRI. Magnetic resonance imaging, 2016. **34**(3): p. 252-263.
5. Zhang, Y., et al., Detection of Alzheimer's disease and mild cognitive impairment based on structural volumetric MR images using 3D-DWT and WTA-KSVM trained by PSOTVAC. Biomedical Signal Processing and Control, 2015. **21**: p. 58-73.
6. Altaf, T., et al. Multi-class Alzheimer disease classification using hybrid features. in IEEE Future Technologies Conference. 2017.
7. Liu, Y., et al. Discriminative MR image feature analysis for automatic schizophrenia and Alzheimer's disease classification. in International conference on medical image computing and computer-assisted intervention. 2004. Springer.
8. Lao, Z., et al., Morphological classification of brains via high-dimensional shape transforma-tions and machine learning methods. Neuroimage, 2004. **21**(1): p. 46-57.
9. Fung, G. and J. Stoeckel, SVM feature selection for classification of SPECT images of Alzheimer's disease using spatial information. Knowledge and Information Systems, 2007. **11**(2): p. 243-258.
10. Klöppel, S., et al., Automatic classification of MR scans in Alzheimer's disease. Brain, 2008. **131**(3): p. 681-689.
11. Chincarini, A., et al., Local MRI analysis approach in the diagnosis of early and prodromal Alzheimer's disease. Neuroimage, 2011. **58**(2): p. 469-480.
12. Westman, E., et al., Sensitivity and specificity of medial temporal lobe visual ratings and multivariate regional MRI classification in Alzheimer's disease. PloS one, 2011. **6**(7): p. e22506.
13. Ahmed, O.B., et al., Classification of Alzheimer's disease subjects from MRI using hippocam-pal visual features. Multimedia Tools and Applications, 2015. **74**(4): p. 1249-1266.
14. Vemuri, P., D.T. Jones, and C.R. Jack, Resting state functional MRI in Alzheimer's Disease. Alzheimer's research & therapy, 2012. **4**(1): p. 2.

15. He, Y., et al., Regional coherence changes in the early stages of Alzheimer's disease: a combined structural and resting-state functional MRI study. Neuroimage, 2007. **35**(2): p. 488-500.
16. Tripoliti, E.E., D.I. Fotiadis, and M. Argyropoulou. A supervised method to assist the diagnosis and classification of the status of Alzheimer's disease using data from an fMRI experiment. in Engineering in Medicine and Biology Society, 2008. EMBS 2008. 30th Annual International Conference of the IEEE. 2008. IEEE.
17. Ateeq, T., et al., Ensemble-classifiers-assisted detection of cerebral microbleeds in brain MRI. Computers & Electrical Engineering, 2018.
18. Beheshti, I., et al., Classification of Alzheimer's disease and prediction of mild cognitive impairment-to-Alzheimer's conversion from structural magnetic resource imaging using feature ranking and a genetic algorithm. Computers in biology and medicine, 2017. **83**: p. 109-119.
19. Beheshti, I., et al., Structural MRI-based detection of Alzheimer's disease using feature ranking and classification error. Computer methods and programs in biomedicine, 2016. **137**: p. 177-193.
20. Ramaniharan, A.K., S.C. Manoharan, and R. Swaminathan, Laplace Beltrami eigen value based classification of normal and Alzheimer MR images using parametric and non-parametric classifiers. Expert Systems with Applications, 2016. **59**: p. 208-216.
21. Guerrero, R., et al., Manifold population modeling as a neuro-imaging biomarker: application to ADNI and ADNI-GO. NeuroImage, 2014. **94**: p. 275-286.
22. Plocharski, M., L.R. Østergaard, and A.s.D.N. Initiative, Extraction of sulcal medial surface and classification of Alzheimer's disease using sulcal features. Computer methods and programs in biomedicine, 2016. **133**: p. 35-44.
23. Sørensen, L., et al., Differential diagnosis of mild cognitive impairment and Alzheimer's disease using structural MRI cortical thickness, hippocampal shape, hippocampal texture, and volumetry. NeuroImage: Clinical, 2017. **13**: p. 470-482.
24. Ahmed, O.B., et al., Alzheimer's disease diagnosis on structural MR images using circular harmonic functions descriptors on hippocampus and posterior cingulate cortex. Computerized Medical Imaging and Graphics, 2015. **44**: p. 13-25.
25. Sarraf, S. and G. Tofighi, DeepAD: Alzheimer's Disease Classification via Deep Convolutional Neural Networks using MRI and fMRI. bioRxiv, 2016: p. 070441.
26. Payan, A. and G. Montana, Predicting Alzheimer's disease: a neuroimaging study with 3D convolutional neural networks. arXiv preprint arXiv:1502.02506, 2015.
27. Farooq, A., et al. Artificial intelligence based smart diagnosis of Alzheimer's disease and mild cognitive impairment. in Smart Cities Conference (ISC2), 2017 International. 2017. IEEE.
28. Chen, X.-W. and X. Lin, Big data deep learning: challenges and perspectives. IEEE access, 2014. **2**: p. 514-525.
29. Mishra, S., et al., Gray level co-occurrence matrix and random forest based acute lymphoblastic leukemia detection. Biomedical Signal Processing and Control, 2017. **33**: p. 272-280.
30. Kalsoom, A., et al., *A dimensionality reduction-based efficient software fault prediction using Fisher linear discriminant analysis (FLDA).* The Journal of Supercomputing, 2018: p. 1-35.
31. Khan, S., et al., Optimized Gabor feature extraction for mass classification using cuckoo search for big data e-healthcare. Journal of Grid Computing, 2018: p. 1-16.
32. Nazir, F., et al., Social media signal detection using tweets volume, hashtag, and sentiment analysis. Multimedia Tools and Applications, 2018: p. 1-34.

Chapter 21
On Video Based Human Abnormal Activity Detection with Histogram of Oriented Gradients

Nadeem Iqbal, Malik M. Saad Missen, Nadeem Salamat, and V. B. Surya Prasath

21.1 Introduction

Automatic human abnormal activity recognition gains vital importance in the field of video analysis and it has become important field of research because of its emerging demands from several applications like video surveillance environments and video analysis etc. and entertainment environments like sports, games etc. and in healthcare environments. All the application domain will have a significant impact on various aspect of daily life. Abnormal activity detection can be used to recognize occasions where further actions are required, for example notifications of criminal activities in surveillance. Potential scenarios include but not limited to are in automatic reporting of person loitering in strategic places like an airport or on a metro station or in a bank. In recent years, proliferation of surveillance cameras in both public and private locations are noticeable. The videos are constantly recorded and being observed by the video operators. Automatic video analysis software can

N. Iqbal · M. M. Saad Missen (✉)
Department of Computer Science and IT, The Islamia University of Bahawalpur, Bahawalpur, Pakistan
e-mail: saad.missen@iub.edu.pk

N. Salamat
Department of Mathematics, Khawaja Fareed University of Engineering and Information Technology (KFUIT), Rahim Yar Khan, Pakistan
e-mail: nadeem.salamat@kfueit.edu.pk

V. B. S. Prasath
Division of Biomedical Informatics, Cincinnati Children's Hospital Medical Center, Cincinnati, OH, USA

Department of Pediatrics, College of Medicine, University of Cincinnati, OH, USA
e-mail: prasatsa@uc.edu

© Springer Nature Switzerland AG 2019
A. K. Singh, A. Mohan (eds.), *Handbook of Multimedia Information Security: Techniques and Applications*, https://doi.org/10.1007/978-3-030-15887-3_21

be useful in reducing the human burden of analyzing these steady stream of video data and can be useful in automatically identifying any abnormal activity.

Detection of abnormal activities of human is normally the requirement of the various surveillance environments. Normal actions and activities of human are periodic like jogging, walking, siting etc. Many activities could be there that are not periodic, the lack of periodicity can be a significant indication of an activity which differentiate it from usual or an ordinary activity. For example, if two persons are exchanging bags with each other and a person who is walking near them swiftly bends and lift the bag and runaway. This activity can be considered as an abnormal activity though an abnormal action or activity of humans can be context dependent and it can be different in different situations. Another example, people in a shopping mall normally walk through so if a person is running there could be considered as abnormal activity, and this could be considered as an event of attentiveness for surveillance purpose.

In an orthodox surveillance system, humans are used as observers and to monitor CCTV and they manually decide it there are the actions and activities in the video.

In these orthodox systems many activities that are actionable are missed due to many reasons by human operators. Some reasons for missing those activities could be following.

- Multiple video screens are to be monitored by a few number of operators, see Fig. 21.1.
- Monitoring an environment can be boring, and it is an exhaustive work due to prolonged monitoring of constant backgrounds on the screens.
- Lack of knowledge what is exactly is looking for, as well abnormal activities occur rarely.
- Attention of an operator can be distracted by various other responsibilities as well as fatigue.

Fig. 21.1 CCTV control room where various complex screens are monitored which places a burden on human observers, who can miss abnormal activities

There are numerous studies which is about the limitations of manual or human based surveillance environments. For instance, a study conducted by the US Sandia National Lab found that the human operators in these environments lost their attention below acceptable levels just after 20 min of monitoring [1], even in an innocuous school surveillance scenario. Detection of abnormality can be hard in important and critical surveillance environments, for e.g., in border surveillance systems or airports management systems. The manual supervision-based methods of video analysis are insufficient to fulfill the requirement for screening timely and searching broadly and comprehensively massive amount of video data, which are produced from the growing number of surveillance cameras at public places. To meet this need, video analysis paradigm is shifting from a complete human operated system to automated or machine assisted model.

In this chapter, we propose a new algorithm for automatic abnormal activity detection system. A fixed camera for video capturing is used, and our automatic system is able to detect human and observe the activity of human in videos. This method has many applications like theft control, fighting in the classrooms or in the streets etc.

21.2 Literature Review

This section of chapter has two sub-section. First section describes the algorithms for feature extractions and second section composed of the algorithms for classification.

21.2.1 Review for Feature Extraction Algorithms

The object detection in particular human detection in images is the most interesting subject for the researcher's community in the computer vision. A review of video based human activity recognition, technology, methods and their applications are discussed by Ke et al. [2]. There are three levels for activity recognition in humans, low, middle, and high levels of the system. The low level consists of features extraction, object segmentation, activity detection algorithms and classification algorithms. In the mid-level, the system performs single people activity detection, crowd behavior and/or multiple interaction of people, and abnormal activity detection. At the highest level, the system needs to be applicable to surveillance, entertainment environments and health care systems [2].

In human detection, the important level is feature extraction and efficient representation of the computed features. Automatic feature extraction, and robust representation have vital influence on the effectiveness of activity recognition model. Therefore, feature selection and their representation in a systematic way is an important task. In space time volume (STV) [3, 4] method, the feature represents the relationship of time and space in videos. In STV, silhouette of a specific object along with the time axis is concatenated. Gesture of body parts attached to human action is captured by 3D (XYT) volumetric feature, where XY is spatial, and T is temporal coordinate. The STV model is restricted to non-periodic events. The Discrete Fourier transform (DFT) is used for representation object geometric [5]. Since, the intensity gray levels of foreground is dissimilar to the background in an image, the DFT of an image is used to find information in the spatial domain. The K-nearest neighbor (KNN) algorithm can then be used to detect the action of an object if the information of the geometric shape is obtained already. The DFT and STV are the global features, and these transformations are limited by occlusion and viewpoints, they are also global features that are noise sensitive. Therefore, some local features are needed which can capture the characteristics of an image by taking patch of an image. The SIFT [6] and HOG [7] local features are widely used in the literature, and they work by taking the part of an image and find the characteristics of that specific part of an image. These features are invariant to scale and rotations of an image, and further these features are also partially invariant to illumination changes and 3D projections.

Lowe [6] presented four steps for detection of scale space extrema in the computation of SIFT features. In first step interest points are detected, which are invariant to scale and orientation. The location and scale in images are computed from the difference of Gaussian (DoG). The stable key points from the interest points are selected in the second step. In next step, the orientation is assigned on the basis of directional gradient. In the final and fourth step, the key points in image gradients are measured on a particular scale. These gradients are then converted into the final representation of the feature points. This computational aspect leads to robustness with respect to illumination as well as local distortions of objects present in the images. The SIFT feature is very popular due to its robustness to affine transformation and illumination changes. However, computing the SIFT features is costly due to dimensionality in the matching step. By accumulating the high dimensional vector which represents the image gradient the distinctiveness of SIFT can be achieved. The SIFT feature are applied to the grey images. Histogram of oriented gradients (HOG) proposed by Dalal et al. [7], divides the image into small spatial areas, for each the particular area gathers a local one-dimensional HOG over cell or pixels. This HOG feature is computed from the histogram of each patch of an image gradient that are dense grids, and utilizes fine scale gradients and orientation bins. The local features are usually extracted from a fixed scale, for example 128×128 or 64×64 etc. These fixed scales can have bad impact on the accuracy of methods that use them, so it is major weakness of local features.

Lin et al. [8] introduce non-parametric weighted feature extraction (NWFE). The method considers the width and distance information of silhouette. In this method histogram vector use the nearest neighbor classifier for recognition of human activity. This method has low computational complexity and high detection rate. This method mainly focus on the outline of body and color information is not considered in it which results in loss of information about the image [9, 10]. Lucas–Kanade-Tomasi (LKT) feature tracker is introduced by Lucas et al. [11], and it is based on the sum of the square intensity differences across frames of videos. These features are generally utilized in tracking body joints of humans, in actual and key frames. These features are difficult to deal with the large motion among frames as they assume the same flow factor in terms of neighbouring pixels of neighbourhood patches [12].

Shape based models are also have importance in the field of object tracking and activity recognition [13]. Shape extraction of human in these models are invariant to rotation and scale and these are robust to errors. As in the shape-based model the silhouette of human is extracted so the internal body parts of human are difficult to find in the silhouette region. Working in the dynamic environment extracting accurate silhouette is a difficult [14]. Appearance based features consists of more information like occlusion, color and other discriminative information so these models are more robust than these shape-based methods. The features based on these models are normally used in human tracking. These models can be used in both, bottom up approach and in top down approaches [15, 16]. These methods can also be useful in discriminative model that looks for the entire body. These methods are sensitive to illumination and clothing [17].

21.2.2   Classification Algorithms

After the extraction of salient features, the next step in generic abnormal activity recognition systems is the choice of a human activity detection algorithm or machine learning classification algorithm. There exist many classification algorithms, and these algorithms can be broadly divided into four major categories: dynamic time wrapping (DTW), generative, discriminative models and fourth is other relevant methods.

21.2.2.1   Dynamic Time Wrapping (DTW)

Dynamic Time Wrapping (DTW) [18] is a classic method and is utilized in measuring the distance, and similarity among two video frames. Despite the method being easy, it has a high computation cost since it uses large number of templates at various situations [19].

21.2.2.2   Discriminative Models

Discriminative models use conditional probability distribution for a specific class in a given observed variable. Artificial neural networks (ANNs), support vector machines (SVMs), and the relevance vector machines (RVMs) are examples of discriminative models. Artificial neural networks (ANNs) [20] consists of neurons which are the directed nodes of the graph. It is a mathematical model that has directed weighted edges and directed graphs. The nodes of directed graphs are called artificial neurons. The weighted directed edges are identified as connection between these artificial neurons. Complex input-output relationships are learned by ANN. These relationships are of non-linear nature, with the ANN model used as an universal approximation as a black box [21].

SVM [22] is the most widely used supervised classifier in the machine learning literature. The margin of two different classes in SVM are separated by an optimal hyperplane, with different data points residing on the boundary of this hyperplane are called the support vectors. The computational time of SVM is high when it is in learning phase due to the higher computational complexity for the associated constrained optimization programming [23].

Relevance Vector Machine (RVM) is a related discriminative model [24], which is similar to SVM probabilistic model, however RVM uses fewer kernel functions than SVM. Full predictive distribution is provided, and it also preserves sparseness which provide SVM by point distribution. RVM furnish sparse sets based on features, however the major drawback of RVM is in its higher computational cost for learning [25]. Note that all these methods support supervised learning as well.

21.2.3   Generative Models

A generative model is a general model for observed and target variables that can only be computed from those observed variables. The hidden Markov model (HMM) proposed by Rabiner et al. [26], is a doubly stochastic process that comprises of an experimental stochastic process with a fundamental stochastic process used to produce a number of observed symbols. The HMM addresses three types of problems, namely, the evaluation, decoding and learning problem.

The drawback of HMM in video activity recognition and analysis is that a cycle of human body movements is not captured and will not be easily modeled by the left-to-right HMM. This drawback can be avoided by introducing using a cyclic HMM proposed by Hoang et al. [27]. Left-to-right HMM of the cyclic HMM is defined with the return transition from the ending state to the beginning state, see [27] for more details.

21.2.4   Graphical Models

The binary tree algorithm consists of a tree structure with two child nodes. These binary trees are used for classification purpose are known as classification tree. The binary tree algorithms can also be used for classification and activity [28]. This algorithm cannot be used for multiclass problems [12]. The K nearest neighbors (KNN) classifier based on the K closet training data points in the feature space in which K is defined as a constant [13]. K-NN can be used for multimodal tasks for classification and it is based on K neighborhood points. The Simplicity with less parameters and computation time is independent from classes are the main advantages of KNN. It is robust in nonlinear separable data, and K sensitive [13, 24].

21.3 Human Activity Recognition Systems

Human activity detection or recognition models can be effectively incorporated into single people activity detection, human abnormal activity recognition system, multiple people activity analysis and crowd behavior etc. Following are the basic definitions used in our work.

21.3.1 Single People Activity Recognition

Trajectory The path or track that a human move in a specific time. The activity of persons are analyzed by corresponding trajectories [29].

Falling Detection Falling detection is a popular topic for detection in a single person activity recognition. It is significantly important topic for safety point of view specially for elderly people [30]. HMM, back-propagation neural network (BPNN) and human-shape-based algorithms are used by different researchers for falling detection [31].

Human Pose Estimation Recognizing the pose is important in designing an automatic human activity recognition system [32] and has been studied widely in computer vision. Based on human pose estimation result, human activity can be easily and efficiently recognized [33].

21.3.2 Multiple People Interaction and Crowd Behavior

Multi people interaction is an important subject of research within activity recognition area. It is very relevant to the topic of security. People counting, people tracking, and crowd behavior analysis are important issues in multiple people interaction and crowd behavior in videos.

21.3.3 Abnormal Activity Recognition

Abnormal activity recognition from videos is an important problem, and defining what is an abnormal activity is not an easy task. Change of position according to some surroundings and environment can be defined as an abnormal activity. Defining the abnormal activity explicitly however is quite difficult. The activities that are not regular can be classified as abnormal activities. Typically, the methodology which is adopted by the researchers is that a normal activity model is prepared and if input data has motion of human or some parameters that are not contained in the training data are then classified as abnormal activity [2]. The motion of human in video which are not usual are classified as abnormal.

21.4   Model Evaluation

The efficiency of the automatic abnormal activity recognition models are evaluated thorough receiver operating characteristic (ROC) and cross validation is used for checking the models.

21.4.1   Receiver Operating Characteristic (ROC)

In the ROC computations, the sensitivity (The True Positive rate) is plotted as a function of Specificity (False Positive rate) for different cutoff points. Each and every point on the ROC curve represent the specificity/sensitivity pair corresponding to the precise threshold. A good discriminator (no overlap in two distributions) will have ROC that passes through the upper left corner (100% specificity, 100% sensitivity) ideally. High accuracy is reflected in the ROC plot to the upper left corner. Following terms are used in this evaluation.

True Positive The number of predictions that positive and the classifier also marked them as positive are known as true positive or TP.

True Negative The predictions which are negative, and the classifier also marked them as negative are called True Negative or TN.

False Positive The actual prediction was negative but it was marked as positive by the classifier is called false positive (FP).

False Negative The case was actually positive but the model marked it was a Negative, such prediction is called False Negative (FN).

Precision The proportion of the total number of positive predictions to the true positive predictions. To calculate the precision expression no (21.1) is used in which PPV means Positive Predictive Values.

$$PPV = \frac{TP}{TP + FP} \tag{21.1}$$

Recall Recall is also known as sensitivity of the Model. The following expression no (21.2) is used to calculate where the TPR stands for True Positive Rate.

$$TPR = \frac{TP}{P} \qquad (21.2)$$

Accuracy Overall performance of the Model is the accuracy. It shows how often the Model is accurate or precise in prediction etc. expression no (21.3) is used to calculate the accuracy of model in which ACC represents accuracy of model, P represents the total positive values and N represents Total negative values.

$$ACC = \frac{TP + TN}{P + N} \qquad (21.3)$$

Specificity True negative Rate is called specificity. If a model predict "False" to the value which is actually "False". The proportion of negative classes to the negative predicted values.

$$SPC = \frac{TN}{N} \qquad (21.4)$$

Miss Rate False Negative Rate is known as the miss rate of a model. This can be described as proportion of negatives values to the values which are accurately predicted as negative.

$$FNR = \frac{FN}{P} \qquad (21.5)$$

False Discovery Rate False Discovery Rate is defined the proportion of false positive with the total positives. These are the values that are predicted as positive, however actually they were not. It can also be calculated as subtracting positive predictive value from 1.

$$FDR = \frac{FP}{FP + TP} = 1 - PPV \qquad (21.6)$$

False Positive Rate Ratio of negative values which are predicted as positive by the model with the total negative is known as False Positive Rate (FPR). FPR is also known as false alarm ratio. Generally, it is false rejection of null hypothesis for a precise test.

$$FPR = \frac{FP}{N} = 1 - SPC \qquad (21.7)$$

21.4.2 Cross Validation

Cross validation, the behavior of the model is checked when data given to the model which is unseen for the model. In training phase, some percentage of data is used and the remaining data set is used for checking the performance of model. Cross validation has three common types: holdout, leave-one-out, and K-fold.

Holdout This is simple way to verify the authentication of the model. In this technique, the dataset is partitioned into two parts, with one used for training and other one used for testing. The final results of this holdout method is sensitive to the partition of dataset.

Leave-One-Out In this technique, the data points are taken to extreme level, The predictor function is trained for every data point except one point. This point is validated through the prediction function.

K-Fold In this technique, the data is separated into K data points. Every K^{th} point is used to test as a test set, and the remining $K - 1$ is used for training.

In this chapter, the tenfold cross validation method is utilized for our model abnormal activity system evaluation. We used 30 test count for each fold. This approach has numerous advantages, it does not depend upon the partition of data points, every data point is tested once, and used as a training set $K - 1$ times.

21.5 The Proposed Human Abnormal Activity Detection Scheme

We describe our human abnormal activity detection method that is based on hisrogram of oriented gradients (HOG), and SVMs. Our proposed method is divided into two phases, first phase consist of the method for human detection and the second phase is the classification of activity as normal and abnormal. In the first phase, the taxonomy developed by Dalal et al. [7] is used. Key frames are taken from a video, each frame is divided into subimages.

Histograms of Oriented gradients (HOG) is computed for each subimages and features are extracted. These extracted features are feed into the SVM classifier to classify the image into negative and positive classes. The images including human are called positive images and without human body are called negative images. The two-point central difference formula as defined as Eq. (21.8) below is used to find the centered gradients of an images,

$$f(x) = \lim_{h \to 0} \frac{f(x+h) - f(x-h)}{2h} \tag{21.8}$$

Masks are filtered in x and y directions after computing gradients. Then the magnitude of oriented gradients are computed by the following Eq. (21.9),

$$S = \sqrt{S_x^2 + S_y^2} \tag{21.9}$$

Every frame of the video is divided into a dense grid of small cells, and these cells are further divided into bins. The orientation angle of these bins are calculated, and are divided into 0–180°. The *arctan* function is used to take the inverse of the tangent of the ratio in the x and y direction.

$$\theta = \arctan\left(\frac{S_y}{S_x}\right) \tag{21.10}$$

We next divide the bins in 0–180°, for example 0, 22.5, 45, 67.5, ... If a centered point occurs in other than these points then the center on the bin is calculated, and assigned to the closet bin. For example, if $\theta = 75$, then the distance from the bin center 60 and 80 is 15 and 5° respectively. So the ratio from the bins are ¾ and ¼ respectively. We truncated the 75–80 on the basis of these particular ratios.

The block diagram of the proposed model is shown in Fig. 21.2. We first use a given video as input into the system utilize standard color normalization, and gamma correction steps. On this preprocessed video frames, we compute gradients of image frames, and votes are assigned to the orientation and spatial bins as per HOG features. In the next step, we perform contrast normalization on the overlapping blocks, and histograms are collected over each of the detection windows. We then apply SVM classification to classify each detection window into a human or non-human class. This complete process is contained inside the model. The model obtains a resultant image frame having humans of interest, and provides an annotation of that specific part of the detection window. The detection window with annotated frame is tracked frame by frame, and then correlation is computed for each of these positively annotated tracked frames. The binary classification is used to classify the activity into normal and abnormal activity. In this method, the value of the correlation is used as a threshold.

21.6 Experimental Results and Disscusions

21.6.1 Human Detection Model

We provide exact specifications of the model proposed here for the optimal human detection. For each frame from the video, the gamma correction, color normalization are performed, and gradients computation is undertaken. The image is then divided into 64 × 128 image parts, see Fig. 21.3 for an example of cell and block structures. Divide the image into 16 × 16 pixels block with 50% of overlapping. When one block of 16 × 16 pixels are taken there will be 105 blocks in total as the size of the image is 64 × 128 and the block size is 16 × 16 with 50% overlapping.

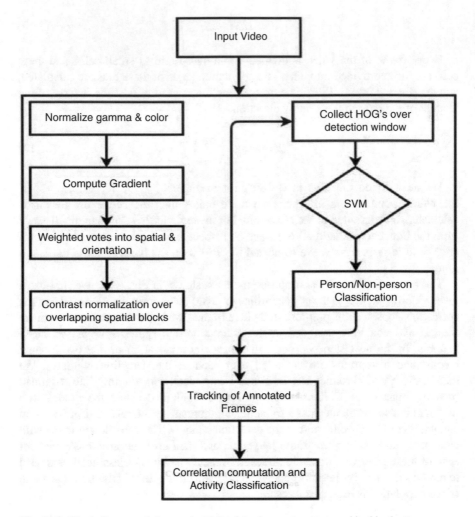

Fig. 21.2 Block diagram of abnormal activity detection system proposed in this chapter

Each block consists of 2×2 cells having size 8×8 of each block, see Fig. 21.4. Next, quantization of the gradient's orientation into 9 bins in 9 dissimilar directions. Histograms are concatenated with resulting feature dimensions of $105 \times 4 \times 9$ $= 3780$. For an image of size 64×128 there will be 105 blocks in total of 16×16 block so there will be 105 histograms in total. After concatenating all these histograms one feature vector is made. Finally, a large feature vector is obtained that is a combination of 105 histograms. In Fig. 21.5a we show an example result of the human detection step, and Fig. 21.5b shows an example histogram computation from an image frame from our dataset.

Fig. 21.3 The dense grid of cells of 64 × 128 image utilized in the human detection step

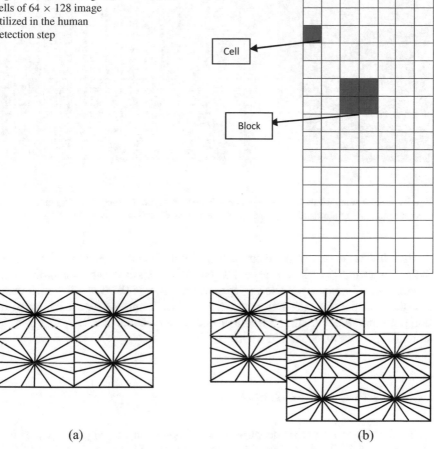

(a)   (b)

Fig. 21.4 Block structures and overlapping used in the human detection step (**a**) Block of 2 × 2 cells divided into bins, and (**b**) overlapping of blocks

21.6.2   Classification of Activity

Once the frames are annotated by the human detection model. The correlation of annotated consecutive frames is computed and a manual threshold of 0.80. an activity is marked as abnormal if the correlation is less than 0.80 otherwise it is a normal activity. Image frame which have low correlation from its previous frame. The correlation of this frame is less than 80% which is set a threshold by the user.

These overlapping blocks are normalized with the equation used by Dalal and Trigs [7] which is described as follow. Let υ is the non-normalized vector which contain histograms in a specific block, $\|\upsilon\|_{\kappa}$ is the k-norm from $k = 1, 2$ and e be the constant then the normalization factor can be following.

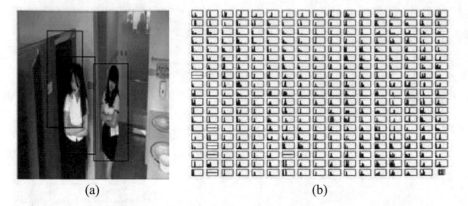

(a)   (b)

Fig. 21.5 (**a**) Example frame our dataset, and (**b**) the histogram of each cell computed from the example frame from our dataset. We also show the human detections as bounding boxes

Each image frame is used to compute the HOG features with this technique and the corresponding blocks are passed to the SVM classifier which classifies each detection window into positive and negative classes. If there is a negative image then the classifier separates it from the overall video frames set, and if it is a positive image the classifier classifies it with a positive index. Figure 21.6 shows an example abnormal activity detected in our dataset.

21.6.3 Results and Discussions

Using the above designed model, our experiments showed significant results in abnormal activity detection in real life videos. Our training dataset consists of 3634 images in total in which 1218 images were positive images and 2416 images are negative images. The proposed HOG-SVM based algorithm is evaluated for this dataset, the results produced by the proposed algorithm for the true positive and false positive are given in Table 21.1.

Our model obtained a precision of 97.95%, and the recall is 96.47%. The overall accuracy of the proposed model is 98.02% showing the promise of our approach. Specificity of the proposed model is 98.79%. Miss rate of the suggested human detection model is considerably low and obtained the value of 0.0355 and the FDR is also considerably low which is 0.024 and the FPR of model is 0.012. These results showed the accuracy and efficiency of the proposed model, and these results are obtained after applying tenfold cross validation method in which 30 test counts are applied.

The results show that our presented human abnormal activity detection system is better to track the humans and detect abnormal activities. However, due to the limited experimental results on our method, we further need to benchmark the

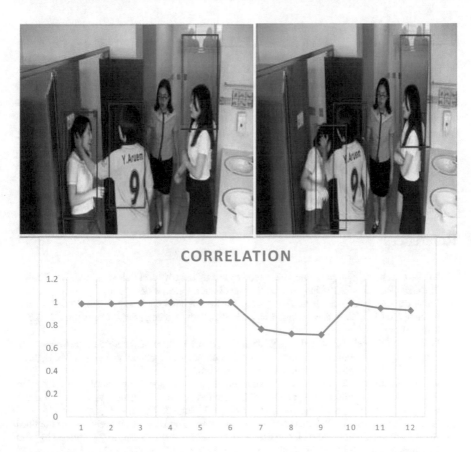

Fig. 21.6 Top row: example of abnormal activity detection from the proposed approach. Two consecutive frames are shown with human detection bounding boxes. Bottom row: Correalation of the two frames indicating the abnormal activity instance

Table 21.1 Experimental results of our proposed human abnormal activity detection on our dataset

Total images	Total positive	Total negative	TP	TN	FP	FN
3634	1218	2416	1175	2387	29	43

method as well as add robust features to make it more accurate and robust. Our proposed method is primarily focused on detection of humans in videos not objects, that is one of the current works along with large-scale benchmarking comparisons.

21.7 Conclusions

In this chapter, an algorithm for video based human abnormal activity detection is proposed. In this algorithm, histograms of oriented gradient (HOG) features, and SVM classifier are used for classification for positive and negative images in terms of human abnormal activity detections. The correlation is used for defining the abnormal activity. Abnormal Activity is context dependent and varies indifferent scenarios, any single system cannot be utilized effectively in multiple scenarios. Our proposed model obtained promising results and further testing on a large scale dataset is required to further validate the model considered here.

References

1. M. W. Green, "The appropriate and effective use of security technologies in U.S. schools." Technical Report NCJ 178265, Sandia National Laboratories, 1999.
2. Shian-Ru Ke, Hoang Le Uyen Thuc, Yong-Jin Lee, Jenq-Neng Hwang, Jang-Hee Yoo, and Kyoung-Ho Choi, "A review on video-based human activity recognition." Computers, 2(2):88–131, 2013.
3. Blank, M.; Gorelick, L.; Shechtman, E.; Irani, M.; Basri, R, "Actions as Space-time Shapes." In Proceedings of the Tenth IEEE International Conference on Computer Vision (ICCV), Beijing, China, 17–21 October 2005; Volume 2, pp. 1395–1402.
4. Ke, Y.; Sukthankar, R.; Hebert, M, "Spatio-temporal Shape and Flow Correlation for Action Recognition." In Proceedings of the IEEE Conference on Computer Vision and Pattern Recognition (CVPR), Minneapolis, MN, USA, 17–22 June 2007; pp. 1–8.
5. Kumari, S.; Mitra, S.K., "Human Action Recognition Using DFT." In Proceedings of the third IEEE National Conference on Computer Vision, Pattern Recognition, Image Processing and Graphics (NCVPRIPG), Hubli, India, 15–17 December 2011; pp. 239–242.
6. Lowe, D.G, "Distinctive image features from scale-invariant keypoints." Int. J. Comput. Vis. 2004, 60, 91–110.
7. Dalal, N,; Triggs, B, "Histograms of oriented Gradients for Human Detection". In proceedings of IEEE Computer Society Conference on Computer vision and Pattern Recognition (CVPR), San Diego, CA, USA, 20-26 June 2005; Volume 1, pp. 886-893
8. Lin, C.; Hsu, F.; Lin, W, "Recognizing human actions using NWFE-based histogram vectors." EURASIP J. Adv. Signal Process. 2010, 2010, 9.
9. Veeraraghavan, A.; Roy-Chowdhury, A.K.; Chellappa, R, "Matching shape sequences in video with applications in human movement analysis." IEEE Trans. Pattern Anal. Mach. Intell. 2005, 27, 1896–1909.
10. Leong, I.; Fang, J.; Tsai, M, "Automatic body feature extraction from a marker-less scanned human body." Comput.-Aided Des. 2007, 39, 568–582.
11. Lucas, B.D.; Kanade, T, "An Iterative Image Registration Technique with An Application to Stereo Vision." In Proceedings of the 7th International Joint Conference on Artificial Intelligence, Vancouver, B.C., Canada, 24–28 August 1981.

12. Ramanan, D.; Forsyth, D.A, "Finding and Tracking People from the Bottom Up." In Proceedings of IEEE Computer Society Conference on Computer Vision and Pattern Recognition, Madison, WI, USA, 16–22 June 2003; Volume 2, pp. II-467–II-474.

13. Prasath, V. B. S., Pelapur, R., Palaniappan, K., and Seetharaman, G. (2014). Feature fusion and label propagation for textured object video segmentation. In *Geospatial InfoFusion and Video Analytics IV; and Motion Imagery for ISR and Situational Awareness II* (Vol. 9089, p. 908904). International Society for Optics and Photonics.

14. Hoang, L.U.T.; Ke, S.; Hwang, J.; Yoo, J.; Choi, K, "Human Action Recognition based on 3D Body Modeling from Monocular Videos." In Proceedings of Frontiers of Computer Vision Workshop, Tokyo, Japan, 2–4 February 2012; pp. 6–13.

15. Ramanan, D.; Forsyth, D.A.; Zisserman, A, "Strike a Pose: Tracking People by Finding Stylized Poses." In Proceedings of IEEE Computer Society Conference on Computer Vision and Pattern Recognition (CVPR), San Diego, CA, USA, 20–26 June 2005; vol. 1, pp. 271–278

16. Hoang, L.U.T.; Ke, S.; Hwang, J; Tuan, P.V.; Chau, T.N, "Quasi-periodic Action Recognition from Monocular Videos via 3D Human Models and Cyclic HMMs." In Proceedings of IEEE International Conference on Advanced Technologies for Communications (ATC), Hanoi, Vietnam, 10–12 October 2012; pp. 110–113.

17. Sempena, S.; Maulidevi, N.U.; Aryan P.R, "Human Action Recognition Using Dynamic Time Warping." In IEEE International Conference on Electrical Engineering and Informatics (ICEEI), Bandung, Indonesia, 17–19 July 2011; pp. 1–5.

18. Rabiner, L.; Juang, B, "Fundamentals of Speech Recognition;" Prentice Hall: Englewood Cliffs, NJ, USA, 1993.

19. Foroughi, H.; Rezvanian, A.; Paziraee, A, "Robust Fall Detection Using Human Shape and Multi-Class Support Vector Machine." In Proceedings of the IEEE Sixth Indian Conference on Computer Vision, Graphics & Image Processing (ICVGIP), Bhubaneswar, India, 16–19 December 2008; pp. 413–420

20. Jain, A.K.; Duin, R.P.W.; Mao, J, "Statistical pattern recognition: A review. IEEE Trans. Pattern Anal." Mach. Intell. 2000, 22, 4–37.

21. Chu, C.; Hwang, J.; Wang, S.; Chen, Y, "Human Tracking by Adaptive Kalman Filtering and Multiple Kernels Tracking with Projected Gradients." In Proceedings of IEEE Fifth ACM/IEEE International Conference on Distributed Smart Cameras (ICDSC), Ghent, Belgium, 23–26 August 2011; pp. 1–6.

22. Schuldt, C.; Laptev, I.; Caputo, B, "Recognizing Human Actions: A Local SVM Approach." In Proceedings of the 17th IEEE International Conference on Pattern Recognition (ICPR), Cambridge, UK, 23–26 August 2004; Volume 3, pp. 32–36.

23. Tipping, M.E, "The relevance vector machine." Adv. Neural Inf. Process. Syst. 2000, 12, 652–658.

24. Tipping, M.E, "Sparse Bayesian learning and the relevance vector machine." J. Mach. Learn. Res. 2001, 1, 211–244.

25. Fiaz, M.K.; Ijaz, B, "Vision based Human Activity Tracking using Artificial Neural Networks." In Proceedings of IEEE International Conference on Intelligent and Advanced Systems (ICIAS), Kuala Lumpur, Malaysia, 15–17 June 2010; pp. 1–5.

26. Rabiner, L.; Juang, B, "An introduction to hidden Markov models." IEE ASSP Mag. 1986, 3, 4–16.

27. J. Black, S. A. Velastin, and B. Boghossian, "A real time surveillance system for metropolitan railways," in Proc. IEEE Conf. Adv. Video Signal based Surveillance, 2005, pp. 189–194.

28. D. Aubert, F. Guichard, and S. Bouchafa, "Time-scale change detection applied to real-time abnormal stationarity monitoring," Real-Time Imaging, vol. 10, no. 1, pp. 9–22, Feb. 2004.

29. Töreyin, B.U.; Dedeoğlu, Y.; Çetin, A.E, "HMM based falling person detection using both audio and video." In Proceedings of the 2005 International Conference on Computer Vision (ICCV) in Human-Computer Interaction, Beijing, China, 17–20 October; pp. 211–220.
30. Shieh, W.; Huang, J. Speedup the Multi-Camera, "Video-Surveillance System for Elder Falling Detection." In Proceedings of IEEE International Conference on Embedded Software and Systems (ICESS), HangZhou, Zhejiang, China, 25–27 May 2009; pp. 350–355.
31. Lee, M.W.; Nevatia, R, "Body Part Detection for Human Pose Estimation and Tracking." In Proceedings of IEEE Workshop on Motion and Video Computing (WMVC), Austin, TX, USA, 23–24 February 2007 ; pp. 23–23.
32. Lee, M.W.; Nevatia, R, "Human pose tracking in monocular sequence using multilevel structured models." IEEE Trans. Pattern Anal. Mach. Intell. 2009, 31, 27–38.
33. Lu, X.; Liu, Q.; Oe, S, "Recognizing Non-rigid Human Actions using Joints Tracking in Space-Time." In Proceedings of the IEEE International Conference on Information Technology: Coding and Computing (ITCC), Las Vegas, NV, USA, 5–7 April 2004; Volume 1; pp. 620–624.

Chapter 22
Enhancement and De-Noising of OCT Image by Adaptive Wavelet Thresholding Method

Sima Sahu, Harsh Vikram Singh, Basant Kumar, Amit Kumar Singh, and Prabhat Kumar

22.1 Introduction

Optical coherence tomography (OCT) is a three-dimensional imaging technique has the property of high resolution and high speed. In biomedicine, OCT plays an important role in the departments of ophthalmology, orthopedic, cardiology, dermatology and dentistry [1]. In the department of ophthalmology, OCT is used for detection and diagnosis of different diseases like glaucoma, diabetic retinopathy (DR), Diabetic Macular Edema (DME) and intra ocular tumor.

Preservation of sharpness and removal of speckle noise are the important preprocessing steps in the analysis of OCT retinal images [2]. These preprocessing steps help in accurate disease diagnosis. A method was proposed by Anantrasirichai et al. [3] for de-noising and enhancement of OCT retinal image. Further the authors processed the de-speckled image for glaucoma detection. The authors found the classification accuracy of glaucoma detection increased from 72.95% (for original OCT image) to 84.13% (for de-speckled OCT image) and 85.15% (for de-speckled and enhanced OCT image).

S. Sahu (✉)
Dr. A. P. J. Abdul Kalam Technical University, Lucknow, Uttar Pradesh, India

H. V. Singh
Department of Electronics, Kamla Nehru Institute of Technology (KNIT), Sultanpur, Uttar Pradesh, India

B. Kumar
Department of ECE, Motilal Nehru NIT Allahabad, Prayagraj, India
e-mail: singhbasant@mnnit.ac.in

A. K. Singh · P. Kumar
Department of Computer Science and Engineering, NIT Patna, Patna, India
e-mail: prabhat@nitp.ac.in

© Springer Nature Switzerland AG 2019
A. K. Singh, A. Mohan (eds.), *Handbook of Multimedia Information Security: Techniques and Applications*, https://doi.org/10.1007/978-3-030-15887-3_22

Speckle de-noising methods can be classified as: de-noising by hardware modification and de-noising by software solution. Hardware methods are implemented before the image acquisition procedure and physically remove the speckle noise. Hardware methods involve spatial compounding [4], frequency compounding [5] and angular compounding [6]. Main drawback of this technique is system complexity, low resolution and speed. De-noising by software solutions are based on filter-based algorithms. Classification of speckle removal techniques are discussed through Fig. 22.1. State-of-the-art OCT de-noising techniques are listed in Table 22.1.

De-noising based on wavelet thresholding method involves the estimation of threshold value, which decides the wavelet coefficients are noisy or not. In literature these techniques show an excellent performance in removing the multiplicative noise and sharpness preservation [29]. In finding the threshold value, variance of the wavelet coefficients in different sub-bands play a major role.

This chapter uses the wavelet coefficient modeling for finding out the variance of the wavelet coefficients in different sub-bands. A modified wavelet threshold method is proposed which provides the wavelet threshold value by accurately finding the wavelet coefficient variance from the sub-band coefficients for different de-composition level. A Cauchy PDF is used to model the wavelet coefficient and thus finding the coefficient variance [30].

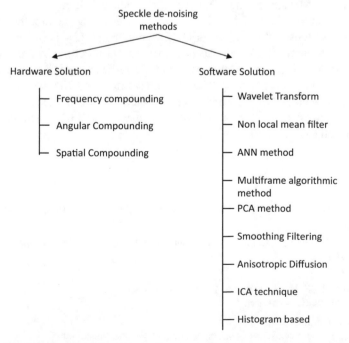

Fig. 22.1 Classification of speckle de-noising methods [*PCA* principal components analysis, *ICA* independent component analysis, *ANN* artificial neural network]

Table 22.1 Review of speckle de-noising methods

Reference	Purpose	Method
Ghafaryasl et al. [7]	• Reduce speckle noise • Estimation of Retinal Nerve Fiber Layer (RNFL) for Glaucoma detection	• Structure oriented smoothing filter
Zhang et al. [8]	• Speckle noise reduction	• Noise pixels are identified • Intensity of the noise pixels is adjusted • Utilizes the phase information • Wavelet shrinkage or contourlet is used
Tang et al. [9]	• Speckle noise reduction	• Low rank representation is used to recover noise free group data matrix
Esmaeili et al. [10]	• Speckle noise reduction	• K-SBD dictionary learning in curvelet transform
Adabi et al. [11]	• Speckle noise for dermatology application	• Clustering method and filtering methods (wiener filter)
Kato et al. [12]	• To reduce speckle and impulse noise	• Locally weighted averaging
Rajabi and Zirak [13]	• Reduction of speckle noise • Correction of motion artifact	• Statistical de-noising and jitter refinement method
Duan et al. [14]	• Reduce speckle noise and segmenting OCT image	• Variational image decomposition model
Baghaie et al. [15]	• Reduction of speckle noise	• Independent component analysis (ICA) technique
Kim al. [16]	• Reduce the ghost artifact noise in OCT image	• Histogram based de-noising method to estimate ghost artifact by polynomial curve fitting
Thapa et al. [17]	• Speckle noise reduction	• Multi-frame weighted nuclear norm minimization method
Aum et al. [18]	• Speckle noise suppression	• Non-local means denoising filters with double Gaussian anisotropic kernel
Duan et al. [19]	• De-noising OCT retinal image	• Decomposition of image by second order total generalized variation model • Used split Bregman algorithm for decomposition

(continued)

Table 22.1 (continued)

Reference	Purpose	Method
Avanaki.et al. [20]	• Reduce speckle noise	• Artificial neural network (ANN) is used to find the noise parameters sigma • Rayleigh distribution is used to model the noise
Bian et al. [21]	• Speckle noise separation and detail preservation	• Multi-frame algorithmic method
Gyger et al. [22]	• Speckle reduction in retinal OCT image	• Film grain removal technique
Cheng et al. [23]	• Speckle noise removal	• Low rank matrix completion using bilateral random projections is utilized to estimate the noise and recover the clean image
Thapa et al. [24]	• Reduce speckle noise in OCT image	• Dictionary and its implementation
Chen et al. [25]	• Reduce speckle noise in OCT image	• Homogeneity similarity based denoising
Xu et al. [26]	• Reduce speckle noise • Overcome the disadvantages of Wavelet shrinkage method (directionality and anisotropy)	• Shrinkage in the contourlet domain • Determine the threshold in the contourlet domain
Guo et al. [27]	• Reduction of multiplicative noise in OCT heart tube image • Preserve edges multi-directional information	• Variance of noise is evaluated in the log domain • A joint Probability Density Function (PDF) is constructed to take the inter-dependency in contourlet domain • Bivariate shrinkage function is used to denoise the image by Maximum a Posteriori (MAP) approach
Luan and Wu [28]	• Reduction of speckle noise	• Robust principle component analysis method • The matrix of transformed OCT image is decomposed as a sum of sparse matrix of speckle noise and low rank matrix of the de-noised image

The organization structure of the chapter is as follows. Basic theory and principles of the proposed method are discussed in Sect. 22.2. Section 22.3 discusses the de-noising methodology. Simulation results are analysed through figures and tables in Sect. 22.4. In Sect. 22.5, concluding remarks of the chapter are given.

22.2 Theory and Principles

This section briefly describes about the basic principles of modified wavelet thresholding method, finding the wavelet coefficient variance and noise variance and concept of histogram mapping.

22.2.1 Modified Wavelet Threshold Approach for De-Noising OCT Image

Wavelet thresholding approach transforms the image from spatial coordinates to wavelet coefficients. The wavelet sub-band coefficients for a three level decomposition of OCT image is shown in Fig. 22.2. In this figure, H_K for $K = 1, 2, 3$ denote the sub-bands consist of horizontal detail coefficients for level K respectively, D_K for $K = 1, 2, 3$ denote the sub-bands consists of diagonal detail coefficients for level K respectively and V_K for $K = 1, 2, 3$ denote sub-band consist of vertical coefficients for level K respectively. In Fig. 22.2, symbol 'A' denotes the sub-band consists of approximation coefficients for level 3. The horizontal coefficients are generated by using a low-pass and then a high-pass filter. The vertical coefficients are generated by using a high-pass and then a low-pass filter. Two high-pass and two low-

Fig. 22.2 Three-level decomposition of OCT image

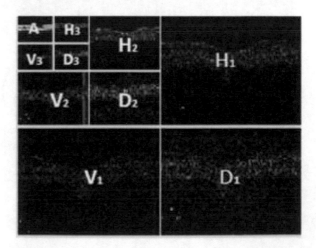

pass filters are used to generate the diagonal detail coefficients and approximation coefficients respectively.

A wavelet threshold value is calculated for each detailed sub-band coefficients which is used to recovery the wavelet coefficients. The threshold value (T_h) is given by [2]:

$$T_h = \frac{\sigma_n^2}{\sigma_s} \tag{22.1}$$

Where, σ_n^2 is the noise variance and σ_s is the standard deviation of noise free signal. A Soft thresholding function given by Eq. (22.2) is applied on each sub-band wavelet coefficient (W). The Soft thresholding function is given by:

$$S_{th} = \begin{cases} 0 & ; & \leq T_h \\ \text{sgn}(W)\left[|W| - T_h\right]; & |W| > T_h \end{cases} \tag{22.2}$$

22.2.2 Calculation of Noise and Wavelet Coefficient Variances

One of the most important steps in the proposed de-noising process is the estimation of noise and wavelet coefficient variances. Wavelet coefficients of different sub-bands are statistically modeled to get the accurate variance information. Orthogonality property of the discrete wavelet transform is used to find the noise variance and it says that the noisy wavelet coefficients in diagonal sub-band have a zero mean Gaussian distribution. The probability density function and cumulative distribution function (CDF) of a Gaussian distributed random variable, N with mean μ and variance σ_n are given by:

$$f_n(N) = \frac{1}{\sigma_n\sqrt{2\pi}} e^{-\frac{(N-\mu)^2}{2\sigma_n^2}} \tag{22.3}$$

$$F_n(N) = \frac{1}{2}\left[1 + \text{erf}\left(\frac{N-\mu}{\sigma_n\sqrt{2}}\right)\right] \tag{22.4}$$

Noise variance is estimated using a Median Absolute Deviation (MAD) estimator applied on the diagonal sub-band of level-1. The approximation of noise variance using MAD estimator is given by [31]:

$$\sigma_n^2 = \left(\frac{median\,(D_1)}{0.6745}\right)^2 \tag{22.5}$$

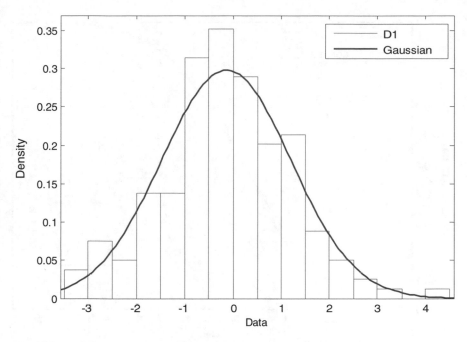

Fig. 22.3 Modeling of wavelet coefficients in D_1 sub-band using Gaussian PDF

Figure 22.3 shows the modeling of wavelet coefficients in D_1 sub-band using Gaussian PDF. Figures 22.4 and 22.5 show the distribution fit plot using CDF and probability plots respectively.

The variance information of the wavelet coefficients is calculated from the local data statistics. In order to obtain the signal parameters a statistical modeling methodology is implemented in this chapter. The distribution of wavelet coefficients of the OCT image is shown in Fig. 22.6. A suitable PDF is required to model the wavelet coefficients to get the signal parameters. As, it is seen that the distribution of wavelet coefficients show a long-tail behavior and peaked at zero, a Cauchy PDF with zero location parameter is used to model the OCT image wavelet coefficients and to find the signal variance. For a Cauchy random variable Z, the Cauchy PDF and CDF are defined as follows:

$$f_z(Z) = \left(\frac{1}{\pi}\right) \left(\frac{b}{(Z-m)^2 + b^2}\right) \tag{22.6}$$

$$F_z(Z) = \frac{1}{2} + \frac{1}{\pi}\tan^{-1}\left(\frac{Z-m}{b}\right) \tag{22.7}$$

Where $Z \in (-\infty, +\infty)$ and the scale and location parameters are denoted by b and m respectively. For $m = 0$, Cauchy PDF and CDF are defined as:

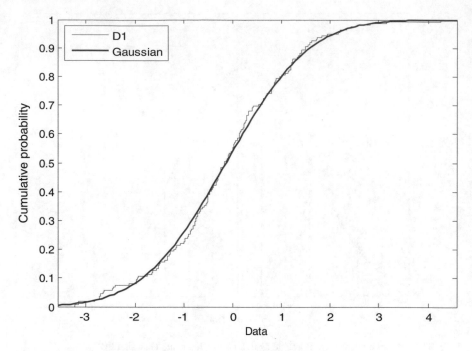

Fig. 22.4 Goodness-of-fit plot through CDF plot for D_1 sub-band

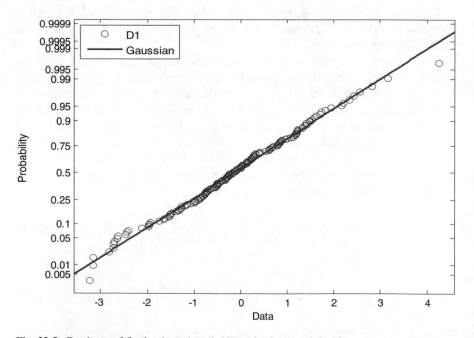

Fig. 22.5 Goodness-of-fit plot through probability plot for D_1 sub-band

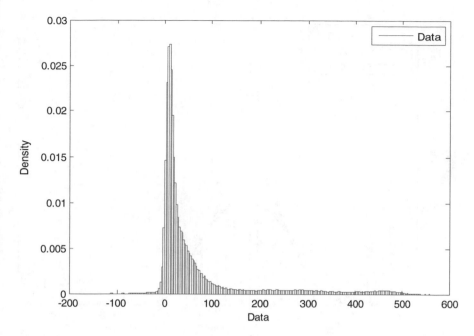

Fig. 22.6 Wavelet coefficients distribution plot for OCT image

$$f_z(Z) = \left(\frac{1}{\pi}\right)\left(\frac{b}{Z^2 + b^2}\right) \tag{22.8}$$

$$F_z(Z) = \frac{1}{2} + \frac{1}{\pi}\tan^{-1}\left(\frac{Z}{b}\right) \tag{22.9}$$

The detailed sub-band wavelet coefficients are modeled by Cauchy PDF to get the signal parameters. The goodness-of-fit comparison plots of H_3, H_2 and H_1 sub-bands in terms of PDF, plots are shown in Figs. 22.7, 22.8 and 22.9 respectively. The goodness-of-fit comparison plots of V_1, V_2 and V_3 sub-bands in terms of PDF plots are shown in Figs. 22.10, 22.11 and 22.12 respectively. In all the sub-bands H_1, H_2, H_3, V_1, V_2 & V_3, Cauchy PDF fits better than the Gaussian PDF.

Let us assume that I is a noisy image, results when an image Q is affected by multiplicative speckle noise, N. It can be written that:

$$I = Q \times N \tag{22.10}$$

Multiplicative noise is converted into additive noise by taking the logarithmic transformation of both the sides of Eq. (22.10) and results:

$$\log I = \log Q + \log N \tag{22.11}$$

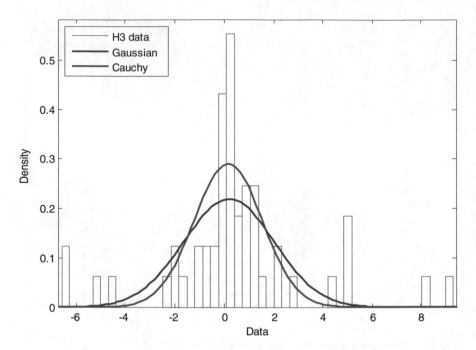

Fig. 22.7 Goodness-of-fit comparison plot of H_3 sub-band

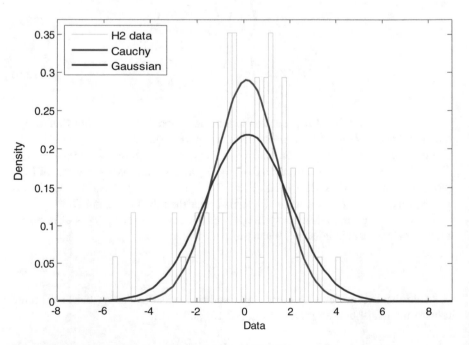

Fig. 22.8 Goodness-of-fit comparison plot of H_2 sub-band

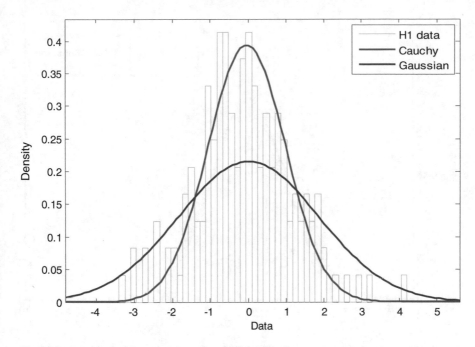

Fig. 22.9 Goodness-of-fit comparison plot of H_1 sub-band

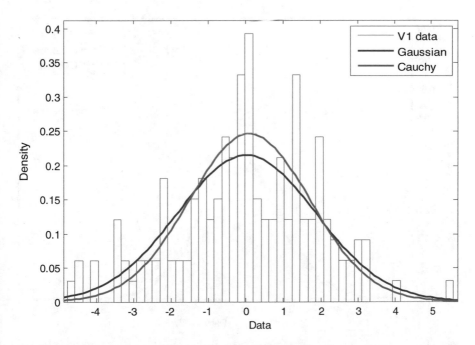

Fig. 22.10 Goodness-of-fit comparison plot of V_1 sub-band

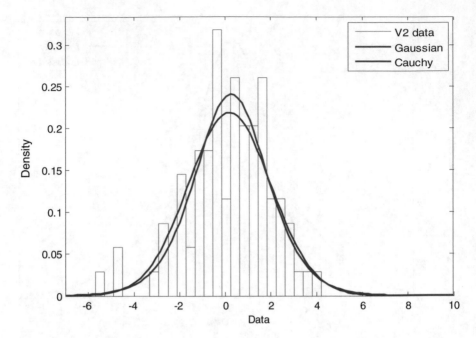

Fig. 22.11 Goodness-of-fit comparison plot of V_2 sub-band

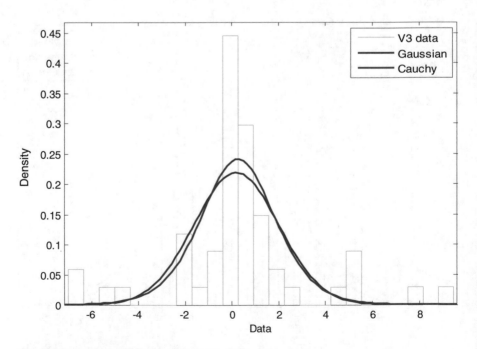

Fig. 22.12 Goodness-of-fit comparison plot of V_3 sub-band

Wavelet transform of Eq. (22.11) results wavelet coefficients are given by:

$$I_x^y = Q_x^y + N_x^y \tag{22.12}$$

Here I_x^y, Q_x^y and N_x^y are assumed as random variables consists of wavelet coefficients for $y = 1, 2, 3$ and $x = 1, 2, 3 \ldots l$. x represents the level of wavelet decomposition and l is the maximum level of decomposition. y represents the orientations of the sub-band. $y = 1$ represents horizontal, $y = 2$ represents vertical and $y = 3$ represents diagonal orientations. The scale parameter b of the wavelet modeled Cauchy density function is found out by minimizing the equation [32]:

$$\int_{-\infty}^{+\infty} \left| \hat{\phi}_I(\omega) - \phi_I(\omega) \right| e^{-\omega^2} d\omega$$

$$= \int_{-\infty}^{+\infty} \left| \hat{\phi}_I(\omega) - \left(\phi_Q(\omega) \, \phi_N(\omega) \right) \right| e^{-\omega^2} d\omega \tag{22.13}$$

The characteristics function of I, Q and N in different sub-band for different orientations are denoted by $\hat{\phi}_I(\omega)$, $\phi_Q(\omega)$ and $\phi_N(\omega)$ respectively. $\phi_I(\omega)$ is defined as:

$$\phi_I(\omega) = \phi_Q(\omega) \times \phi_N(\omega) \tag{22.14}$$

Hermite Gauss Quadrature is applied to solve the Eq. (22.13) and results:

$$\int_{-\infty}^{+\infty} f(\omega) e^{-\omega^2} d\omega = \sum_{j=1}^{k} a_j f(\omega_j) \tag{22.15}$$

Where $f(\omega) = \hat{\phi}_I(\omega) - \left(\phi_Q(\omega) \, \phi_N(\omega) \right)$, a_j denotes weights of Hermite Quadrature polynomial and ω_j denotes roots of the polynomial of order k. Cauchy CDF is calculated using Eq. (22.9) by taking the value of b.

Histogram mapping procedure which is also called Gaussianization transform is applied to obtain the Gaussianized wavelet coefficients W_G to correctly estimate the density of the wavelet coefficients [33]. The fundamental theorem of probability is applied to find the signal variance and is given by:

$$\sigma_s^2 = E\left[W_G^2 \right] - E[W_G]^2 \tag{22.16}$$

Where $E[.]$ represents the expectation operation. Assumption of zero mean PDF, makes $E[W_G]^2$ to become zero value. So Eq. (22.16) can be written as:

$$\sigma_s^2 = E\left[W_G{}^2\right] \qquad\qquad (22.17)$$

22.2.3 Histogram Mapping

Histogram mapping is a non-linear process which maps the wavelet coefficients into gaussianized data. This process equates the assumed empirical CDF '$F_z(Z)$' to Gaussian CDF '$F_{W_G}(W_G)$' and finds the Gaussianized wavelet coefficients. By equating the CDFs, the gaussianized wavelet coefficients are given by [33]:

$$F_{W_G}(W_G) = F_z(Z) = \frac{1}{2}\left[1 + \mathrm{erf}\left(\frac{W_G - \mu_s}{\sigma_s\sqrt{2}}\right)\right] \qquad (22.18)$$

$$W_G = \mu_s + \sqrt{2}\,erfinv\,(2F_z(Z) - 1) \qquad\qquad (22.19)$$

Where, μ_s and σ_s are the mean and standard deviation of gaussianized data. *erf* represents the error function and *erfinv* represents the inverse error function. W_G is the gaussianized random variable of Z and contains the gaussianized data. The Gaussianized PDF is obtained by replacing W_G with N in the Eq. (22.3).

22.3 Methodology

The proposed de-noising method recovered wavelet coefficients using soft threshold method. Generation of threshold value requires the knowledge of noise and signal variances. A Cauchy PDF is used to model the OCT image wavelet coefficients and getting the signal parameters. Histogram mapping is used to accurately estimating the signal variance and MAD estimator applied on the D_1 sub-band is used for estimating noise variance. The algorithm of the proposed method is discussed below and the block diagram is given in Fig. 22.13.

Step 1 Input the retinal OCT image.
Step 2 Logarithmic transformation of the image.
Step 3 DWT of the logarithmic transformed enhanced image.
Step 4 Modeling of the generated wavelet coefficients using Cauchy PDF.
Step 5 Estimation of Cauchy distribution parameters using Eq. (22.15).
Step 6 Application of histogram mapping
Step 7 Estimation of noise and signal variance parameters using Eqs. (22.5) and (22.17) respectively.
Step 8 Generation of threshold value using Eq. (22.1).
Step 9 Recovering the wavelet coefficients in each sub-band using Eq. (22.2)
Step 10 Reconstruction of image using IDWT.
Step 11 Exponential transformation of the reconstructed image.

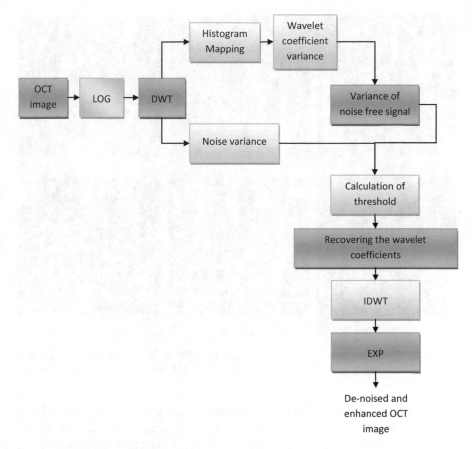

Fig. 22.13 Block diagram of the proposed adaptive wavelet threshold method

22.4 Simulation Results

The effectiveness of the proposed adaptive wavelet threshold method is demonstrated on OCT retinal image collected from the dataset CIRRUS™ HD-OCT (Carl Zeiss Meditec, Inc., SW Ver: "5.1.1.4", Copyright 2010) available at Department of Ophthalmology, Institute of Medical Sciences, Banaras Hindu University (BHU), Varanasi. The size of the image is 459×304. 3rd-level wavelet decomposition in the processing strategy of db8 in Daubechies group is used for simulation of the proposed method. MATLAB environment is used to realize the algorithm both quantitatively and qualitatively. Different state-of-the-art methods, Zaki et al. [2], Cao et al. [29] and Donoho's Soft Threshold [34] are used to compare with the proposed method. The proposed method is also simulated on a synthetic phantom image of size 256×256. Artificial speckle noise of variances of 0.1, 0.2 and 0.3 are added separately to the synthetic image to prove the effectiveness of the

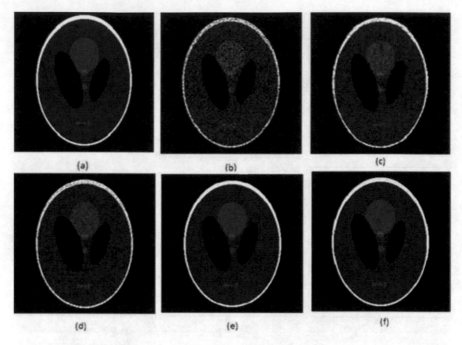

Fig. 22.14 De-noising results in phantom image. (**a**) Original image (**b**) Noisy image with variance 0.2 (**c**) Donoho's Soft Threshold (**d**) Zaki et al. [2] (**e**) Cao et al. [29] (**f**) Proposed method

proposed method. Figures 22.14 and 22.15 show the compared result qualitatively for phantom and retinal OCT image. Performance parameters such as Peak Signal-to-Noise Ratio (PSNR), Structural Similarity (SSIM), Correlation coefficient (CoC), and Edge Preservation Index (EPI) are used for quantitative measurement with the state-of-the-art methods. Tables 22.2, 22.3, 22.4, and 22.5 show the compared results for the synthetic image, for different performance parameters. Table 22.6 shows the comparison of different state-of-the-art methods for retinal OCT image for different performance parameters. Quantitative comparison metrics are defined as follows.

(a) Noise reduction capability is determined by PSNR parameter. It is defined as:

$$PSNR = 20 \log_{10} \left(\frac{M}{\sqrt{\frac{1}{p \times q} \sum_{m=1}^{p \times q} \left(Q_m - \hat{Q}_m \right)^2}} \right) \qquad (22.20)$$

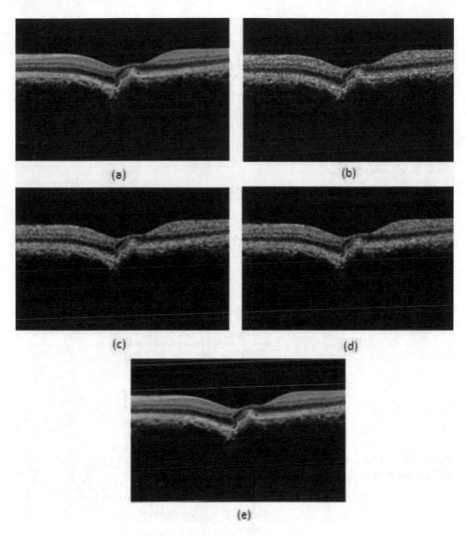

Fig. 22.15 De-noising results in OCT image. (**a**) Original image (**b**) Donoho's Soft Threshold [34] (**c**) Zaki et al. [2] (**d**) Cao et al. [29] (**e**) Proposed method

Where M is the highest value of intensity in the simulated image. $p \times q$ represents the size of the image. Q_m is the intensity of the mth pixel of reference image and $\hat{Q}_m$ is the mth pixel of the de-noised image.

(b) Structural variation between the reference image Q and de-noised image $\hat{Q}$ can be compared using SSIM parameter. It is defined as:

Table 22.2 PSNR (dB) result for phantom image

Methods	Variance (σ_n^2)		
	0.1	0.3	0.5
Noisy	20.12	15.45	13.63
Donoho's soft threshold [34]	25.62	21.36	19.25
Zaki et al. [2]	28.54	24.22	22.34
Cao et al. [29]	31.32	30.42	27.86
Proposed method	33.08	32.91	31.55

Table 22.3 SSIM result for phantom image

Methods	Variance (σ_n^2)		
	0.1	0.3	0.5
Noisy	0.765	0.656	0.582
Donoho's soft threshold [34]	0.831	0.771	0.619
Zaki et al. [2]	0.854	0.821	0.746
Cao et al. [29]	0.952	0.932	0.866
Proposed method	0.986	0.973	0.946

Table 22.4 CoC result for phantom image

Methods	Variance (σ_n^2)		
	0.1	0.3	0.5
Noisy	0.815	0.770	0.635
Donoho's soft threshold [34]	0.923	0.824	0.811
Zaki et al. [2]	0.946	0.858	0.816
Cao et al. [29]	0.978	0.958	0.833
Proposed method	0.989	0.976	0.954

Table 22.5 EPI result for OCT phantom image

Methods	Variance (σ_n^2)		
	0.1	0.3	0.5
Noisy	0.325	0.276	0.188
Donoho's soft threshold [34]	0.545	0.534	0.422
Zaki et al. [2]	0.664	0.585	0.448
Cao et al. [29]	0.751	0.613	0.648
Proposed method	0.776	0.694	0.663

Table 22.6 Image performance parameters for retinal OCT image

Methods	Parameters			
	PSNR(dB)	SSIM	CoC	EPI
Original image	17.39	0.347	0.599	0.250
Donoho's soft threshold [34]	25.65	0.671	0.813	0.493
Zaki et al. [2]	29.34	0.725	0.842	0.538
Cao et al. [29]	30.15	0.856	0.958	0.742
Proposed method	31.63	0.879	0.971	0.819

$$SSIM = \frac{\left(2\overline{Q}\overline{\hat{Q}} + 2.55\right)\left(2\sigma_{Q\hat{Q}} + 7.65\right)}{\left(\overline{Q}^2 + \overline{\hat{Q}}^2 + 2.55\right)\left(\sigma_Q^2 + \sigma_{\hat{Q}}^2 + 7.65\right)} \qquad (22.21)$$

Where $(^-)$ denotes the symbol for finding the mean value or expectation operation. The covariance between reference and de-noised image is represented by $\sigma_{Q\hat{Q}}$. The variance of the reference image is represented by σ_Q^2 and the variance of the de-noised image is represented by $\sigma_{\hat{Q}}^2$.

(c) The interdependence between the images can be measured by the quality parameter CoC. It can be defined as:

$$CoC = \frac{\sigma_{Q\hat{Q}}}{\sigma_Q\sigma_{\hat{Q}}} \qquad (22.22)$$

Where σ_Q represents the standard deviation of the reference image and $\sigma_{\hat{Q}}$ represents the standard deviation of the de-noised image.

(d) Edge preservation capability is determined by EPI parameter. It is defined as:

$$EPI = \frac{\sum_{m=1}^{p\times q}\left(\Delta_Q - \Delta_{\overline{Q}}\right)\left(\Delta_{\hat{Q}} - \Delta_{\overline{\hat{Q}}}\right)}{\sqrt{\sum_{m=1}^{p\times q}\left(\Delta_Q - \Delta_{\overline{Q}}\right)^2\sum_{m=1}^{p\times q}\left(\Delta_{\hat{Q}} - \Delta_{\overline{\hat{Q}}}\right)^2}} \qquad (22.23)$$

Where Laplace operation performed on the reference image is represented by Δ_Q and Laplace operation performed on the de-noised image is represented by $\Delta_{\overline{Q}}$.

From Table 22.2, it is clear that the proposed method has achieved better PSNR result than other state-of-the-art methods. For the proposed de-noising method, the PSNR (dB) result is 33.08, 32.91 and 31.55 for noise variance values of 0.1, 0.3 and 0.5 respectively. For a noise variance value of 0.1, the improvement of the proposed method is 22.55%, 13.72%, and 5.32% than Donoho's Soft Threshold [34], Zaki et al. [2], and Cao et al. [29] methods respectively. For a noise variance value of 0.3, the improvement of the proposed method is 35.09%, 26.40%, and 7.56% than Donoho's Soft Threshold [34], Zaki et al. [2], and Cao et al. [29] methods respectively. For a noise variance value of 0.5, the improvement of the proposed method is 38.98%, 29.19%, and 11.69% than Donoho's Soft Threshold [34], Zaki et al. [2], and Cao et al. [29] methods respectively.

Table 22.3 shows SSIM result of the different state-of-the-art and proposed methods. Higher value of SSIM result has achieved by the proposed method than other state-of-the-art methods and is 0.986, 0.973 and 0.946 for noise variance of 0.1, 0.3 and 0.5 respectively. For noise variance of 0.1, the SSIM improvement of the proposed method is 15.72%, 13.38%, and 3.44% than Donoho's Soft Threshold [34], Zaki et al. [2], and Cao et al. [29] methods respectively. For noise variance of 0.3, the SSIM improvement of the proposed method is 20.76%, 15.62%, and 4.21% than Donoho's Soft Threshold [34], Zaki et al. [2], and Cao et al. [29] methods respectively. For noise variance of 0.5, the SSIM improvement of the proposed method is 34.56%, 21.14%, and 8.45% than Donoho's Soft Threshold [34], Zaki et al. [2], and Cao et al. [29] methods respectively.

Table 22.4 shows the CoC result for different filtering methods. CoC value for the proposed method is 0.989, 0.971, and 0.954 for noise variance value of 0.1, 0.3 and 0.5 respectively. For noise variance of 0.1, the CoC improvement for the proposed method is 6.67%, 4.34% and 1.11% than Donoho's Soft Threshold [34], Zaki et al. [2], and Cao et al. [29] methods respectively. For noise variance of 0.3, the CoC improvement for the proposed method is 15.57%, 12.09% and 1.84% than Donoho's Soft Threshold [34], Zaki et al. [2], and Cao et al. [29] methods respectively. For noise variance of 0.5, the CoC improvement for the proposed method is 14.98%, 14.46% and 12.68% than Donoho's Soft Threshold [34], Zaki et al [2], and Cao et al. [29] methods respectively.

It is verified from Table 22.5 that the proposed method provides de-noising and edge preservation as well. The edge preservation capability of the proposed method is shown through Table 22.5. The EPI index of the proposed method is 0.776, 0.694, and 0.663 for noise variance value of 0.1, 0.3 and 0.5 respectively. For noise variance of 0.1, the EPI improvement of the proposed method is 29.76%, 14.43%, and 3.22% than Donoho's Soft Threshold [34], Zaki et al. [2], and Cao et al. [29] methods respectively. For noise variance of 0.3, the EPI improvement of the proposed method is 23.05%, 15.70%, and 11.67% than Donoho's Soft Threshold [34], Zaki et al. [2], and Cao et al. [29] methods respectively. For noise variance of 0.5, the EPI improvement of the proposed method is 36.34%, 32.42%, and 2.26% than Donoho's Soft Threshold [34], Zaki et al. [2], and Cao et al. [29] methods respectively.

Different performance parameter values are shown in Table 22.6 for retinal OCT image. The improvement of PSNR result for OCT retinal image for the proposed method is 18.9%, 7.23% and 4.67% than Donoho's Soft Threshold [34], Zaki et al. [2], and Cao et al. [29] methods respectively. The improvement of SSIM result for OCT retinal image for the proposed method is 23.66%, 17.51% and 2.61% than Donoho's Soft Threshold [34], Zaki et al. [2], and Cao et al. [29] methods respectively. The improvement of CoC result for OCT retinal image for the proposed method is 16.27%, 13.28% and 1.33% than Donoho's Soft Threshold [34], Zaki et al. [2], and Cao et al. [29] methods respectively. The improvement of EPI result for OCT retinal image for the proposed method is 39.80%, 34.31% and 9.40% than Donoho's Soft Threshold [34], Zaki et al. [2], and Cao et al. [29] methods respectively.

22.5 Conclusion

An adaptive soft thresholding method was proposed in this chapter to remove speckle noise from OCT image. Wavelet threshold value was calculated by statistical modeling the wavelet coefficients. A suitable Cauchy prior was proposed to model the detail sub-band wavelet coefficients to accurately estimate the signal parameters and is proved through goodness-of-fit plots. Histogram mapping procedure was implemented for density estimation. Noise variance was calculated by assuming that wavelet coefficients have a Gaussian distribution in the diagonal sub-band. The superior performance of the proposed de-noising method was demonstrated by vast experimentations by comparing with the state-of-the-art methods both qualitatively and quantitatively. Along with removing the speckle noise, the proposed method preserved the structural information of the OCT image.

In future the proposed method may be implemented for other imaging modality for different types of noise.

References

1. Sahu, S., Singh, H.V., Kumar, B. and Singh, A.K., Statistical Modeling and Gaussianization Procedure based de-speckling algorithm for Retinal OCT images, *Journal of Ambient Intelligence and Humanized Computing (AIHC), an International Journal of Springer*. DOI: https://doi.org/10.1007/s12652-018-0823-2
2. Zaki, F., Wang, Y., Yuan, X. and Liu, X., 2017, June. Adaptive Wavelet Thresholding for Optical Coherence Tomography Image Denoising. In *Computational Optical Sensing and Imaging* (pp. CTh4B-4). Optical Society of America.
3. Anantrasirichai, N., Nicholson, L., Morgan, J.E., Erchova, I., Mortlock, K., North, R.V., Albon, J. and Achim, A., 2014. Adaptive-weighted bilateral filtering and other pre-processing techniques for optical coherence tomography. *Computerized Medical Imaging and Graphics*, 38(6), pp.526-539.
4. Kim, J., Miller, D. T., Kim, E., Oh, S., Oh, J., & Milner, T. E. (2005). Optical Coherence Tomography Speckle Reduction by a Partially Spatially Coherent Source. *Journal of Biomedical Optics*, 10(6), 064034-064034.
5. Pircher, M., Go, E., Leitgeb, R., Fercher, A. F., & Hitzenberger, C. K. (2003). Speckle reduction in optical coherence tomography by frequency compounding. *Journal of Biomedical Optics*, 8(3), 565-569.
6. Iftimia, N., Bouma, B. E., & Tearney, G. J. (2003). Speckle reduction in optical coherence tomography by path length encoded angular compounding. *Journal of Biomedical Optics*, 8(2), 260-263.
7. Ghafaryasl, B., Baart, R., de Boer, J.F., Vermeer, K.A. and van Vliet, L.J., 2017, February. Automatic estimation of retinal nerve fiber bundle orientation in SD-OCT images using a structure-oriented smoothing filter. In *Medical Imaging 2017: Image Processing* (Vol. 10133, p. 101330C). International Society for Optics and Photonics.
8. Zhang, A., Xi, J., Sun, J. and Li, X., 2017. Pixel-based speckle adjustment for noise reduction in Fourier-domain OCT images. *Biomedical optics express*, 8(3), pp.1721-1730.
9. Tang, C., Cao, L., Chen, J. and Zheng, X., 2017. Speckle noise reduction for optical coherence tomography images via non-local weighted group low-rank representation. *Laser Physics Letters*, 14(5), p.056002.

10. Esmaeili, M., Dehnavi, A.M., Rabbani, H. and Hajizadeh, F., 2017. Speckle noise reduction in optical coherence tomography using two-dimensional curvelet-based dictionary learning. *Journal of medical signals and sensors*, 7(2), p.86.

11. Adabi, S., Rashedi, E., Conforto, S., Mehregan, D., Xu, Q. and Nasiriavanaki, M., 2017, February. Speckle reduction of OCT images using an adaptive cluster-based filtering. In *Optical Coherence Tomography and Coherence Domain Optical Methods in Biomedicine XXI* (Vol. 10053, p. 100532X). International Society for Optics and Photonics.

12. Kato, Y., Kuroki, N., Hirose, T. and Numa, M., 2016. Locally weighted averaging for denoising of medical tomographic images. *Journal of Signal Processing*, 20(4), pp.217-220.

13. Rajabi, H. and Zirak, A., 2016. Speckle noise reduction and motion artifact correction based on modified statistical parameters estimation in OCT images. *Biomedical Physics & Engineering Express*, 2(3), p.035012.

14. Duan, J., Lu, W., Tench, C., Gottlob, I., Proudlock, F., Samani, N.N. and Bai, L., 2016. Denoising optical coherence tomography using second order total generalized variation decomposition. *Biomedical Signal Processing and Control*, 24, pp.120-127.

15. Baghaie, A., D'souza, R.M. and Yu, Z., 2016. Application of independent component analysis techniques in speckle noise reduction of retinal OCT images. *Optik-International Journal for Light and Electron Optics*, 127(15), pp.5783-5791.

16. Kim, K.S., Park, H.J. and Kang, H.S., 2015. Enhanced optical coherence tomography imaging using a histogram-based denoising algorithm. *Optical Engineering*, 54(11), p.113110.

17. Thapa, D., Raahemifar, K. and Lakshminarayanan, V., 2015. Reduction of speckle noise from optical coherence tomography images using multi-frame weighted nuclear norm minimization method. *Journal of Modern Optics*, 62(21), pp.1856-1864.

18. Aum, J., Kim, J.H. and Jeong, J., 2015. Effective speckle noise suppression in optical coherence tomography images using nonlocal means denoising filter with double Gaussian anisotropic kernels. *Applied Optics*, 54(13), pp.D43-D50.

19. Duan, J., Tench, C., Gottlob, I., Proudlock, F. and Bai, L., 2015. New variational image decomposition model for simultaneously denoising and segmenting optical coherence tomography images. *Physics in Medicine & Biology*, 60(22), p.8901.

20. Avanaki, M.R., Marques, M.J., Bradu, A., Hojjatoleslami, A. and Podoleanu, A.G., 2014, March. A new algorithm for speckle reduction of optical coherence tomography images. In *Optical Coherence Tomography and Coherence Domain Optical Methods in Biomedicine XVIII* (Vol. 8934, p. 893437). International Society for Optics and Photonics.

21. Bian, L., Suo, J., Chen, F. and Dai, Q., 2015. Multiframe denoising of high-speed optical coherence tomography data using interframe and intraframe priors. *Journal of biomedical optics*, 20(3), p.036006.

22. Gyger, C., Cattin, R., Hasler, P.W. and Maloca, P., 2014. Three-dimensional speckle reduction in optical coherence tomography through structural guided filtering. *Optical Engineering*, 53(7), p.073105.

23. Cheng, J., Duan, L., Wong, D.W.K., Akiba, M. and Liu, J., 2014, August. Speckle reduction in optical coherence tomography by matrix completion using bilateral random projection. In *Engineering in Medicine and Biology Society (EMBC), 2014 36th annual international conference of the IEEE* (pp. 186-189). IEEE.

24. Thapa, D., Raahemifar, K. and Lakshminarayanan, V., 2014, August. A new efficient dictionary and its implementation on retinal images. In *Digital Signal Processing (DSP), 2014 19th International Conference on* (pp. 841-846). IEEE.

25. Chen, Q., de Sisternes, L., Leng, T. and Rubin, D.L., 2015. Application of improved homogeneity similarity-based denoising in optical coherence tomography retinal images. *Journal of digital imaging*, 28(3), pp.346-361.

26. Xu, J., Ou, H., Lam, E.Y., Chui, P.C. and Wong, K.K., 2013. Speckle reduction of retinal optical coherence tomography based on contourlet shrinkage. *Optics letters*, 38(15), pp.2900-2903.

27. Guo, Q., Dong, F., Sun, S., Lei, B. and Gao, B.Z., 2013. Image denoising algorithm based on contourlet transform for optical coherence tomography heart tube image. *IET image processing*, 7(5), pp.442-450.

28. Luan, F. and Wu, Y., 2013. Application of RPCA in optical coherence tomography for speckle noise reduction. *Laser Physics Letters*, *10*(3), p.035603.
29. Cao, J., Wang, P., Wu, B., Shi, G., Zhang, Y., Li, X., Zhang, Y. and Liu, Y., 2018. Improved wavelet hierarchical threshold filter method for optical coherence tomography image denoising. *Journal of Innovative Optical Health Sciences*, *11*(03), p.1850012.
30. Sahu, S., Singh, H. V., Kumar, B., & Singh, A. K. (2017). De-noising of ultrasound image using Bayesian approached heavy-tailed Cauchy distribution. *Multimedia Tools and Applications*, 1-18.
31. Sahu, S., Singh, H. V., Kumar, B., & Singh, A. K. A Bayesian Multiresolution Approach for Noise Removal in Medical Magnetic Resonance Images. *Journal of Intelligent Systems*.
32. Bhuiyan, M. I. H., Ahmad, M. O., & Swamy, M. N. S. (2007). Spatially adaptive wavelet-based method using the Cauchy prior for denoising the SAR images. *IEEE Transactions on Circuits and Systems for Video Technology*, *17*(4), 500-507.
33. Amini, Z., & Rabbani, H. (2016). Statistical modeling of retinal optical coherence tomography. *IEEE transactions on medical imaging*, *35*(6), 1544-1554.
34. Donoho, D. L. (1995). De-noising by soft-thresholding. *IEEE transactions on information theory*, *41*(3), 613-627.

Chapter 23
Quantization Table Selection Using Firefly with Teaching and Learning Based Optimization Algorithm for Image Compression

D. Preethi and D. Loganathan

23.1 Introduction

Image compression is highly essential for effective storage and transmission of images. The need of communication via telecommunication network and accessing the multimedia data using Internet is tremendously increasing. The advancements in the digital camera lead to the generation of larger size images requires more communication bandwidth for transmission and massive amount of memory for storage [1]. It is useful in various applications such as medical imaging, satellite imaging, teleconferencing, etc. For instance, a medium size color image (512×512 pixels) needs a storage area of 0.75 megabytes (MB); 35 mm digital slide with 12 μm resolution consumes a storage area of 18 MB. A 12-bit X-ray image of 2048×2560 pixels requires a storage area of 13 MB. A 16-bit mammogram image of 4500×4500 pixels requires 40 MB of disk storage. The original video for 1 s needs around 20 MB of storage space. So, image compression techniques are developed to effective store and transmit data to utilize the available resources in an efficient manner. Basically, data compression techniques work on the principle of eliminating repeated and unwanted data [2]. As the images are composed of pixels, image compression techniques are based on the idea of removing redundant and irrelevant pixels in an image [3]. For highly correlated images, better compression performance can be achieved when compared to less correlated images. Generally, image compression techniques are classified to lossy and lossless compression techniques [4]. The compression of images with no loss of information comes under lossless compression, which is useful in applications where loss of information is not bearable [5]. Medical imaging and satellite imaging follows the concept of

D. Preethi (✉) · D. Loganathan
Department of Computer Science and Engineering, Pondicherry Engineering College, Puducherry, India
e-mail: preethidpreethi@pec.edu; drloganathan@pec.edu

lossless image compression. By Contrast, sometimes, the loss of information in an image during compression is tolerable in various applications. In multimedia, graphics and browsing internet, lossy compression techniques can be utilized. On the other hand, image compression techniques can be partitioned to predictive and transform coding techniques. In predictive coding, the existing information can be utilized for the prediction of upcoming data, and the obtained difference is encoded. This type of coding is simple, easier to implement and can be adaptable to different local image features. Next, transform coding, converts an image from one kind of representation to another and the transformed values (coefficients) are encoded by compression techniques. The performance of transform coding is much higher than predictive coding but at the cost of high computational complexity. An image compression model under transform coding comprises of three components namely transformer, quantizer and encoder. It is a reversible, liner mathematical transform which maps the pixels to a set of coefficients, which undergoes quantization and encoding process. Transform coding techniques partitions the reference image to sub-images (blocks) of smaller sizes (8*8). Then, the transform coefficients are determined for each block, efficiently transforming the reference 8*8 array of pixel values to an array of coefficients inside which the coefficients at the top left corner contains more information, which needs to be quantized and encoded with less distortion. The resultant coefficients are quantized and symbol encoding methods are employed to achieve output bit stream, which represents the compressed image. During decompression, at the decoder size, the reversible operation takes place. The advantage of transform coding is that most of the resultant coefficients of natural images have smaller magnitude, which can be easily quantized with no distortion in the reconstructed image. A better transform coding technique has the ability to compress images using less number of coefficients. DCT and DWT are the most widely used type of transform coding techniques [6]. DCT is a popular image compression technique used in JPEG. It partitions an image into various portions of distinct frequencies where less significant parts are removed by quantization and significant frequencies are employed to reconstruct the image in the decompression process. DCT has many benefits: easily implemented to an IC, capability to store information in lesser number of coefficients and reduces the blocking artifacts [7].

Quantization is an important source of compression along with some loss of information. An important characteristic of JPEG is that diverse levels of image compression and quality can be achieved by the selection of quantization tables. Consequently, the quality ratio can be altered based on the application requirements. Every coefficient in the 8×8 DCT matrixes is divided by a weight present in the quantization table and less important DC coefficients are eliminates. When all the weights are found to be 1, the transformation process involves zero compression. JPEG suggested quantization table for brightness component, which is available in the information annexure of the JPEG standard. Table 23.1 shows the quality level of 50 quantization matrix which provides better compression with high reconstructed data quality. The user can choose the quantization level ranges between 1 and 100 where 1 implies worst image quality with best compression performance and vice versa.

Table 23.1 Quantization matrix Q50

16	11	10	16	24	40	51	61
12	12	14	19	26	58	60	55
14	13	16	24	40	57	69	56
14	17	22	29	51	87	80	62
18	22	37	56	68	109	103	77
24	35	55	64	81	104	113	92
49	64	78	87	103	121	120	101
72	92	95	98	112	100	130	99

For every application, the quantization table may vary and a universal quantization table applicable for all application is not available. So, the selection of quantization table is a combinatorial optimization problem which can be solved by meta-heuristic algorithms.

Several methods like statistical and meta heuristic algorithms have been proposed to determine the transform coefficients in DCT for image compression [8–11]. Some of the meta heuristic algorithms used in image compression techniques are particle swarm optimization (PSO) [12], quantum particle swarm optimization (QPSO) [13], genetic algorithm (GA) [14], differential evolution (DE) [15], honey bee mating optimization (HBMO) [16], pollination based optimization (PBO) [17], cuckoo search optimization [18] and so on.

The contribution of the chapter is summarized as follows: This chapter presents a Firefly (FF) with Teaching and learning based optimization (TLBO) algorithm termed as FF-TLBL algorithm for the selection of quantization table. The efficiency of the proposed is validated using a set of benchmark images. The obtained results are compared with PBO method in terms of Mean Square Error (MSE), Root mean square error (RMSE), Peak signal to noise ratio (PSNR), structural similarity index (SSIM), compression ratio (CR), compression factor (CF) and compression time (CT).

The succeeding part of the chapter is arranged as follows: Section 23.2 reviews the existing meta-heuristic based image compression techniques in detail. The basic concepts of DCT and FF algorithm are given in Sect. 23.3. Section 23.4 presents the proposed FF-TLBO algorithm with necessary steps and diagrams. The validation of the proposed method and discussion of results takes place in Sect. 23.5. Finally, in Sect. 23.6, the chapter is ended with concluding remarks and future studies.

23.2 Related Studies

Numerous lossless image compression methods are proposed by the utilization of mathematical models and metaheuristic algorithms. As the proposed method employs one of the bio-inspired algorithms, the image compression techniques based on optimization algorithms are reviewed and the comparison is tabulated in Table 23.2. A fast fractal encoding technique using PSO algorithm is presented in

Table 23.2 Comparison of reviewed image compression techniques

Reference	Year	Objective	Algorithm used	Performance measure	Compared with	Merits
[9]	2010	To decrease the amount of time required for fractal encoding process	PSO	Encoding time, PSNR	Full search technique	High speed and preserves image quality
[10]	2011	To build the codebook of VQ	HBMO algorithm	–	LBG, PSO–LBG, QPSO–LBG	Reliable with higher quality
[11]	2012	To build the codebook of VQ	FF algorithm	MSE, PSNR and bit rate	LBG, PSO, QPSO, HBMO	Faster and attain better quality
[12]	2013	To integrate Super-Spatial Structure Prediction with inter-frame coding for better CR	Head code compression	CR	JPEG-LS	Low computation complexity
[13]	2014	To compress images based on multi-level image thresholding	Shannon entropy and DE	PSNR, Weighted PSNR, storage size and standard deviation	PSO and GA	Better CR
[14]	2014	To reduce the fractal encoding time	GA ad DWT	MSE, PSNR, encoding time	GA	100 times faster than full search method
[15]	2015	To perform compression by incorporating IWT with prediction step	Median edge detector	CR	DPCM	Better compression performance

[16]	2015	To propose a compression algorithm by exploiting the relationship between fractional numbers and their quotients	GA	CR	-	Image quality is saved with higher CR
[17]	2015	To perform lossless compression of significant parts by extracting ROI in DICOM images	GA	PSNR	Hybridization of RLE and Huffman coding	Better CR
[18]	2016	To reduce the fractal image encoding time	CIFS	CPU time, GPU time, MSE, PSNR	PSO with Wavelet Classification, GA with RSM	Robust, lower MSE
[19]	2016	To compress image using the fitness value of a DCT block	PBO	MSE, PSNR	JPEG	Better CR
[31]	2018	To develop a A novel hybrid DWT followed by VQ based codec	Hybrid DWT	Hardware complexity, power, memory, and critical path delay	JPEG	High speed architecture with a lower hardware complexity

[19], to decrease the amount of time required for the encoding process. The usage of PSO algorithm increases the fractal encoding speed and also conserves the image quality. This method is tested on medical images and the results are analyzed in terms of encoding time and PSNR. An author in [20] used HBMO algorithm to build the codebook of vector quantization (VQ). It produces reliable results with higher quality when compared to conventional Linde–Buzo–Gray (LBG) [21], PSO-LBG and QPSO-LBG algorithms. The presented HBMO–LBG method resulted to the construction of better codebook with smaller distortions. A firefly (FF) algorithm is also used in [22] to build the codebook of VQ. The author employed LBG algorithm as the initialization of FF algorithm to design VQ algorithm. The presented FF-LBG technique implemented VQ and improves the results of LBG method. The simulation results of FF-LBG is compared with LBG, PSO, QPSO and HBMO algorithms using MSE, PSNR and bit rate. The FF-LBG algorithm is found to be faster and attain better quality than LBG, PSO and QPSO. However, it showed no superior performance than HBMO algorithm. In the year 2013, [23] integrated Super-Spatial Structure Prediction with inter-frame coding to attain better CR. At first, Super-Spatial Structure Prediction algorithm is employed with a fast block-matching process (Diamond Search method). Head code compression algorithm is used to further enhance the CR. The proposed method is evaluated on medical images and found that it outperforms JPEG-LS in terms of CR.A histogram based image compression method using multi-level image thresholding is presented in [24]. The gray scale image is split to crisp group of probabilistic partitions. Shannon's Entropy is utilized to calculate the level of randomness of the crisp grouping. The entropy function is maximized by Differential Evolution (DE) to decrease the computation complexity and standard deviation of optimized objective value. The proposed method is experimented by the use of benchmark images from UC Berkeley and CMU dataset. The simulated results verify that the proposed DE algorithm is efficient when compared to PSO and GA.

Ming-Sheng Wu 2014 presented a GA based DWT model to reduce the fractal encoding time [25]. Initially, at every range blocks, two wavelet coefficients are employed to determine the fittest Dihedral block of the domain block. Next, DWT is embedded to GA to attain fast encoding and maintains better image retrieval quality. This GA method operates at much faster rate than full search technique, but at the cost of relatively acceptable reconstructed image quality. In [26], a lossless image compression approach is presented by incorporating integer wavelet transform (IWT) with prediction step. Initially, the transformation of image takes place and a difference image is produced. Then, the difference image is passed to IWT and computes the transform coefficients employed in the lossless codeword assignment. This method attained better compression performance and the computational complexity is mostly nearer to its competitors. Omari and Salah Yaichi [27] exploited the relativity between fractional numbers and their respective quotient representation. Every individual sub-image is mapped to a fractional number by RGB representation and then decreased to an effective quotient. This technique reported better CR, when the least significant bits of every byte is changed, hence, the image quality is saved with higher CR. Harpeet Karu et al.

devised lossless image compression technique for compressing significant parts by the extraction of a region of interest in DICOM images [28]. Then, Huffman coding is used to compress the extracted region and GA further enhances the compression performance. This presented model involves several steps like ROI extraction, GA, Huffman coding and finally compresses the image.

Mohammed Ismail also reduced the fractal image encoding time by the use of cuckoo inspired fast search (CIFS) technique [29]. CIFS technique makes use of vectors of range blocks which are arranged by the level of resemblance and coordinate distance respectively. The cuckoo search is altered in a way that the searching process takes place on limited nests (maximum six) and initialization of nest selection searching process is done by levy flights strategy. The overall results revealed that the CIFS method is found to be robust and attained significantly less MSE. Priyanka Jindal et al. [30] introduced pollination based optimization (PBO) algorithm in image compression based on the fitness value of a DCT block of image data. By employing PBO algorithm, the local best and global best values of several DCT blocks are determined. Based on global best values, the compression process will be carried out by the use of RLE and Huffman coding. This method is validated by comparing its results with JPEG in terms of MSE and PSNR. In this paper, an improved JPEG compression algorithm for color image is proposed [31]. We mainly focused on the improvement of compressed image quality by modifying luminance quantization table in frequency domain. A novel hybrid DWT followed by VQ based codec have been proposed [32]. In [33], an adjustment of the recent guided fireworks algorithm is proposed from the class of swarm intelligence algorithms for quantization table optimization. The proposed hybrid image codec is compared best of with the existing structure in terms of hardware complexity, power, memory, and critical path delay. Though several image compression techniques have been proposed and found in the literature, we believe that there is more room for enhancement to attain even better compression performance.

23.3 Background Information

23.3.1 *Discrete Cosine Transform (DCT)*

DCT is the fundamental concept of various image processing techniques. DCT is a type of mathematical transformation, intends to transform a signal from one type of representation to another [34]. In general, images are 2D signal which is based on the perception of human visual system (HVS). DCT is defined as the process of converting a signal (spatial information) to numeric data (frequency or spatial information), so that the information of the image exists in a quantitative form which can be manipulated for compression. The general form of 1D-DCT (N data items) is represented in Eq. (23.1).

$$F(u) \triangleq \begin{cases} \sum_{i=0}^{N-1} 2.f(i) . \cos\left[\frac{\pi.u}{2.N}(2i+1)\right], & u \in [0, N-1] \\ 0, & \text{otherwise} \end{cases} \tag{23.1}$$

where $w(i) \triangleq \begin{cases} \frac{1}{\sqrt{2}} & \text{for } i = 0 \\ 1 & \text{otherwise} \end{cases}$. For every N point signal f (i) having support [0,

N − 1], the corresponding inverse DCT (IDCT) can be computed as,

$$f(i) = \begin{cases} \frac{1}{N} \sum_{u=0}^{N-1} w(u) . F(u) \cos\frac{\pi.u}{2N}(2i+1), & i \in [0, N-1] \\ 0, & \text{otherwise} \end{cases} \tag{23.2}$$

Assume that the data has finite rectangular support on $[0, M-1] \times [0, N-1]$. The basic representation of 2D-DCT of images is given in Eq. (23.3).

$$F(u, v) \triangleq \sum_{i=0}^{M-1} \sum_{j=0}^{N-1} 4.f(i, j) . \cos\left[\frac{\pi.u}{2.M}(2i+1)\right] \cos\left[\frac{\pi.v}{2.N}(2j+1)\right] \tag{23.3}$$

For $(u, v) \in [0, M-1] \times [0, N-1]$, otherwise $F(u, v) \triangleq 0$. Next, IDCT also exist and given in Eq. (23.4).

$$f(i, j) \triangleq \sum_{u=0}^{M-1} \sum_{v=0}^{N-1} w(u) w(v) . F(u, v) . \cos\left[\frac{\pi.u}{2.M}(2i+1)\right] \cos\left[\frac{\pi.v}{2.N}(2j+1)\right] \tag{23.4}$$

where $w(i) \triangleq \begin{cases} \frac{1}{\sqrt{2}} & \text{for } i = 0 \\ 1 & \text{otherwise} \end{cases}$. the weight function of 2D-DCT is same as 1D-DCT.

23.3.2   Firefly (FF) Algorithm

FF algorithm was originally introduced by Xin-She Yan in the year of 2007 and 2008 at Cambridge University, inspired by the flashing pattern and behavior of FFs [35]. The flashing pattern of FFs are quite fascinating and there are around 2000 species exists. For every individual FF species, the flashing pattern is different and many FFs show short and rhythmic flashes. These flashlights are caused by the process of bioluminescence and the original reason for those signaling system are still unexplored. There are two basic functions of flashes: attraction of mating partners (communication) and potential preys. Sometimes, it is also used as a protective warning signal from the predators. The rhythmic flash, flashing rate and time period constitute a part of signal system which makes both sexes contact with each other. It is a known fact that light intensity I reduces at some distance r from the light source as it follows the inverse square law, i.e. light intensity I reduces as the distance r increases, $I \propto (1/r^2)$. In addition, when r increases, the absorption of light in the air weakens the brightness of the flashes. These two characteristics limit the visual distance of FFs. During night, FFs can easily communicate over several hundred meters. The pseudo code of FF algorithm is given in Algorithm I. The flashes can be formulated in such a way that it can be integrated with the objective function to be optimized, which makes it possible to formulize new optimization algorithm. FF algorithm follows three ideal rules which are listed below.

- FFs are unisex, they attract with each other independent of their sex
- Attractiveness is related to brightness, the lesser bright FF will move towards a brighter FF
- Brightness of an FF is influenced or calculated by the landscape of the objective function

---

Algorithm I. Firefly Optimization

---

1. **Begin Algorithm**
2. **Step 1: Initialize,** $f(x) \leftarrow$ Objective Function, $x_i \leftarrow$ Initial Population (i=1,2,3 . . . n), $\delta \leftarrow$ Light Intensity, $I \leftarrow$ Formulate Light Intensity *(I α f(x))*, $\gamma \leftarrow$ Absorption Coefficient.
3. **Step 2:Repeat** through step 2.2 **until** $T < Max\_Generation$
4. **Step 2.1:For** $i = 1$ to n do
5. **Step 2.1.1:For** $j = 1$ to n do
6. **Step 2.1.1.1:If** $(I_j > I_i)$
7. **Step 2.1.1.1.1:** Vary attractiveness with distance r
8. **Step 2.1.1.1.2:** Shift Firefly i approaching towards j
9. **Step 2.1.1.1.3:** Assess current solution and update δ
10. **Step 2.1.1.2:End If**
11. **Step 2.1.2:End For**
12. **Step 2.2:End For**
13. **Step 3:** Rank Fireflies and Find the Best cost
14. **Step 4:** Post-Process the solution
15. **End Algorithm**

For maximization problems, flashing brightness is directly proportional to the value of objective function. Basically, there are two issues in FF algorithm: variation in light intensity and formulation of attractiveness. For the sake of simplicity, the attractiveness of an FF is calculated by the brightness, which is integrated with the encoded objective function. In those problems, the brightness I of an FF at specific position x is selected as

$$I(x) \propto f(x) \tag{23.5}$$

Additionally, the attractiveness β is a relativity parameter which is determined by other FFs. Hence, for two FFs i and j, β is varied with respect to the distance r_{ij}. At the same time, light intensity diminishes as the distance from the source increases and is absorbed by the medium. Hence, it is noted that the attractiveness varies with the degree of absorption. In general, light intensity $I(r)$ modifies using the inverse square law as equated in Eq. (23.6).

$$I(r) = \frac{I_s}{r^2} \tag{23.6}$$

where I_s represents the intensity at the source. When the light intensity I changes with distance r, in presence of predefined light absorption coefficient γ, I can be calculated as

$$I = I_0 e^{-\gamma r} \tag{23.7}$$

where I_0 indicates initial light intensity. To eliminate singularity at point $r = 0$ in Eq. (23.6), the Eqs. (23.6) and (23.7) undergo approximation as the Gaussian form given in Eq. (23.8).

$$I(r) = I_0 e^{-\gamma r^2} \tag{23.8}$$

When the FF's attractiveness β is based on the light intensity perceived by neighboring FFs, the value of β is determined as given in Eq. (23.9).

$$\beta = \beta_0 e^{-\gamma r^2} \tag{23.9}$$

where β_0 represents the attractiveness at $r = 0$. Since, it can be easier to compute $\frac{1}{1+\gamma r^2}$ than exponential function, Eq. (23.9) can be rewritten as

$$\beta = \frac{\beta_0}{1 + \gamma r^2} \tag{23.10}$$

The above two equations define a characteristic distance $\Gamma = 1/\sqrt{\gamma}$, where β is significantly changed from β_0 to $\beta_0 e^{-1}$ in Eq. (23.9) or $\beta_0/2$ in Eq. (23.10). For implementation purposes, attractiveness function $\beta(r)$ is monotonically decreasing as given in Eq. (23.11).

$$\beta(r) = \beta_0 e^{-\gamma r^m}, \quad (m \geq 1) \tag{23.11}$$

The characteristic length is computed as

$$\Gamma = \gamma^{\frac{-1}{m}}, \qquad m \to \infty \qquad (23.12)$$

By contrast, for a given Γ in optimization problem, γ is represented as a conventional initial value.

$$\gamma = \frac{1}{\Gamma^m} \qquad (23.13)$$

The Cartesian distance between two FFs i and jx_i and x_j can be computes as

$$r_{ij} = \| x_i - x_j \| = \sqrt{\sum_{k=1}^{d} \left(x_{i,k} - x_{j,k}\right)^2 \frac{1}{\Gamma^m}} \qquad (23.14)$$

where $x_{i,k}$ is the kth component of the spatial coordinate x_i of the ith FF. The r_{ij} in 2D space is calculated in Eq. (23.15).

$$r_{ij} = \sqrt{\left(x_i - x_j\right)^2 - \left(y_i - y_j\right)^2} \qquad (23.15)$$

The movement of a FFi is attracted to a brighter FF and can be equated as

$$x_i = x_i + \beta_0 e^{-\gamma r_{i,j}^2} \left(x_j - x_i\right) + \alpha \epsilon_i \qquad (23.16)$$

where 2nd term represents attraction and 3rd term indicates the randomization. Here, α is the randomized parameter and ϵ_i is a vector of random numbers derived from Gaussian or uniform distribution. As each FF works in an independent way, it can be applicable for parallel implementation. It is superior to GA and PSO due to the nature of FFs aggregation more closely around every optimum.

23.4 The Proposed Lossless Compression Model

23.4.1 Overview

The overall operation of the proposed lossless image compression model is shown in Fig. 23.1. Initially, the reference image needs to be compressed is partitioned into sub-images (8*8 blocks). The blocks of image undergo the quantization process where the proposed FF-TLBO algorithm constructs the quantization table based on the maximization of fitness function. FF-TLBO algorithm is employed to compute the transform coefficients, where the coefficients closer to top left corner holds the most significant information. The resultant coefficients are quantized by the use of quantization table. Next, encoding process takes place where the AC coefficients are encoded by RLE [36] and DC coefficients are encoded by Huffman coding

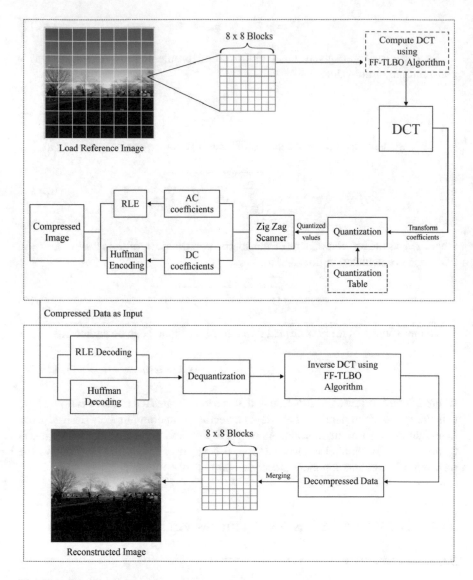

Fig. 23.1 Overall process of the proposed method

[37] technique to generate the compressed image. The proposed method follows
symmetric compression in which the decompression process is exactly same as
compression process, but in the opposite direction.

23.4.2 FF-TLBO Algorithm

As explained above, the input image is partitioned into 8*8 blocks of sub-images which is given as input to DCT. The FF-TLBO algorithm computes the best fitness value for every DCT block. This algorithm determines the best fit value for every block is called as local best whereas the best fitness value for the entire image is considered as global best. The fitness function is defined in Eq. (23.17) assigns a fitness value for transforming the array of coefficients.

$$f(x) = (x_1, x_2, \ldots x_d)^T \tag{23.17}$$

23.4.2.1 Teacher Phase

- Initialization: In this step the initial population x_i, light intensity I_i at x_i and γ are initialized.
- Choose the current best solution: This step chooses the best solution from all the solutions and is defined as x_i^{max},

$$x_i^{max} = \arg \max_i f(x_i) \tag{23.18}$$

- Attractiveness: The movement of FF x_i is attracted to another FF x_j. Every solution x_j calculates the fitness values with respect to the brightness of the FFs as given in Eq. (23.17).
- Termination condition: When the number of iterations exceeded, then the FF algorithm stops its execution and give the best solution.

The FF algorithm performs well when the brighter FF is available in the search space. In some cases, when none of the brighter FF appears in the search space, the FFs start moving randomly. This is the major drawback of the FF algorithm. To resolve this algorithm, we introduce the FF-TLBO algorithm which integrates the TLBO algorithm with FF algorithm to explore the search space efficiently.

The TLBO algorithm is stimulated from the knowledge transfer between the teachers and students in the learning and it depends on the influence of the teacher on the outcome of the learners in the class [38]. The two main phases in TLBO algorithm is 'Teacher Phase' (learns from teacher) and 'Learner Phase' (learns via their interaction).

The nature of the good teacher is they should try to improve the learner's knowledge level to a maximum level or atleast to his/her level. In practical, it is difficult and the teacher can attain the mean of the class to a certain level based on different dimensions. For instance, M_i indicates the mean of the class and T_i is the teacher at any iteration i. The teacher T_i will try to move the mean M_i closer to its own level, therefore the new mean become T_i named as M_{new}. The solution will be updated using the differences between the present and new mean M_{new} as given in Eq. (23.19).

$$\text{Difference\_Mean}_i = r_i (M_{new} - T_F M_i) \tag{23.19}$$

Where T_F denotes a teaching factor which calculates the mean value to be modified and r_i is a random number lies between [0, 1]. The T_F value will be either 1 or 2, which is arbitrarily decided as T_F = round $[1 + \text{rand} (0, 1) \{2 - 1\}]$. This modification will alter the existing solution using Eq. (23.20) as represented below.

$$X_{new,\ i} = X_{old,\ i} + \text{Difference\_Mean}_i \tag{23.20}$$

23.4.2.2 Learner Phase

The learners can improvise the knowledge by the use of two ways: the former one is getting input from the teacher and latter one is their interaction between them. A learner can improve the knowledge by random interaction with other learners. In general, the knowledge of a learner improves once the learner will interact with the more knowledgeable learner. In those situations, the learner modification can be equated as

For $i = 1 : P_n$
    Randomlyselecttwolearners X_i and X_j, where $i \neq j$
      If $f(X_i) < f(X_j)$
          $X_{n,i} = X_{o,i} + r_i(X_i - X_j)$
      Else
          $X_{n,i} = X_{o,i} + r_i(X_j - X_i)$
      End If
End For

Accept X_n when a better function value is obtained.

The TLBO algorithm aims to maximize the fitness function by the construction of the quantization table at desired compression efficiency. At the initial state, the quantization table generated by the FF algorithm is used as the initial point. Every quantization table generated by the FF algorithm denotes a student in the TLBO algorithm. At the end, the optimized quantization table for the applied images has been attained by maximizing the fitness function by the utilization of the phases involved in the TLBO algorithm.

After the execution of the quantization process, the zigzag scanner scans all the quantized coefficients as shown in Fig. 23.2. In the zigzag sequence, the coefficients with lower frequencies (DC coefficients) are encoded first and the higher frequencies (AC coefficients) are encoded. The AC coefficients are encoded using RLE and the DC coefficients are encoded by Huffman coding. Finally, the compressed image with reduced file size from reference image is generated.

When the compressed image is received, decoding process will take place using Huffman decoding and RLE decoding techniques. Next, the decoded image undergoes dequantization process and then IDCT operation is performed. Once the

Fig. 23.2 Zigzag scanner

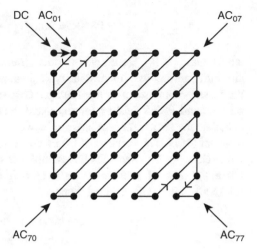

IDCT operation is completed, all the individual sub-images (8*8 blocks) are merged and finally, the reconstructed image is generated.

23.5   Performance Evaluation

To ensure the efficiency of the proposed lossless compression algorithm, it is tested against a set of 40 benchmark images from LIVE database [39]. The obtained results are compared with existing PBO method, which is one of the popular bio-inspired algorithm employed in the area of lossless image compression.

23.5.1   Metrics

MSE, PSNR, SSIM, CR and CT are used as performance measures to validate the results of the proposed and existing methods [40, 41]. MSE is commonly employed to calculate the difference between the reference and reconstructed images. It can be equated as

$$\text{MSE} = \frac{1}{n} \sum_{i=1}^{n} \left(P_i - P_j\right)^2 \tag{23.21}$$

where n represent the total number of pixels in the image, P_i and P_j is the pixel values of the reference and reconstructed images. The value of MSE should be lower to produce better compression performance. Root Mean Square Error (RMSE) is the square root of MSE, which is used to calculate PSNR.

PSNR is the ratio between maximum possible power of signal and power of error signal which influences the fidelity of its representation. It can be computed as

$$PSNR = 20\log_{10}\frac{\max_{i,j} \mid P_{i,j} \mid}{RMSE} \qquad (23.22)$$

where $\max_{i,j} \mid P_{i,j}\mid$ represents the maximum pixel value in the image. For better similarity among two images, the typical value lies in the range of 20 and 40. When the reference and reconstructed images are exactly identical, the value of MSE will be zero and PSNR will be infinity. Next, SSIM is a HVS based measure used to calculate the structural resemblance between two images and the values falls in the range of [0, 1]. The value of SSIM nearer to 1 indicates higher resemblance and the value closer to 0 denotes lesser resemblance between the compared images. Then, CR is the ratio of number of bits in compressed image and number of bits in the reference image. CR can be defined as

$$CR = \frac{\text{No. of bits in the compressed image}}{\text{No. of bits in the original image}} \qquad (23.23)$$

For better compression performance, the value of CR should be as low as possible. When the value of CR exceeds the value of one, it results to negative compression, i.e. compressed file size is larger than the original file size. Finally, CT represents the total amount of time required to compress an image and is usually measured in seconds.

23.5.2   Results and Discussion

Table 23.3 and Fig. 23.3 provides the comparative results of proposed and existing FF algorithms in terms of MSE, PSNR, SSIM, CR and CT respectively. The same set of 40 images is applied to both the existing and proposed methods. The tabulated results revealed that the average MSE of FF method is worse when compared to proposed method. The existing method attains an average MSE of 0.910975 whereas the proposed method achieves an efficient MSE of 0.64205. The obtained results show that the proposed method produces lesser MSE which indicates the better compression performance. Likewise, the average PSNR of FF method is 48.565, but the proposed method attains a PSNR of 53.1322, which is much higher than FF method. In the same way, average SSIM values of the proposed and existing FF methods are 0.86925 and 0.67025 respectively. The higher value of SSIM by proposed method notifies that the better reconstructed image quality of the proposed method when compared to FF method.

On comparing the compression performance in terms of CR, the FF and the proposed method produce a value of 0.3201 and 0.2971 respectively. It implies that the compressed file size of the FF-TLBO method is smaller and consumes less amount of storage space when compared to FF algorithm. In terms of CT, the average CT of FF method is 31.05 s whereas the proposed FF-TLBO algorithm

Table 23.3 Comparison of FF-TLBO algorithm with FF algorithm in terms of MSE, PSNR, SSIM, CR and CT

LIVE Dataset	MSE		PSNR		SSIM		CR		CT	
	FF	FF-TLBO	FF	FF-TLBO	FF	FF-TLBO	FF	FF-TLBO	FF	FF-TLBO
Image 3	0.998	0.581	48.15	52.84	0.69	0.94	0.285	0.281	10.00	8.76
Image 4	0.982	0.697	48.29	51.26	0.68	0.96	0.298	0.280	15.00	13.14
Image 5	0.903	0.680	49.0?	51.47	0.74	0.96	0.378	0.280	23.09	20.23
Image 6	0.901	0.772	49.04	50.38	0.61	0.95	0.384	0.280	28.80	25.23
Image 7	0.893	0.713	49.12	51.07	0.75	0.96	0.456	0.405	41.60	36.44
Image 8	0.818	0.605	49.87	52.50	0.65	0.98	0.367	0.280	70.44	61.71
Image 9	0.882	0.452	49.22	55.02	0.72	0.99	0.478	0.474	11.67	10.22
Image 10	0.838	0.493	49.67	54.28	0.64	0.99	0.434	0.430	18.99	16.64
Image 11	0.890	0.689	49.14	51.37	0.67	0.95	0.411	0.407	27.90	24.44
Image 12	0.895	0.557	49.09	53.22	0.66	0.98	0.397	0.393	31.33	27.45
Image 13	0.801	0.474	50.05	54.62	0.65	1.00	0.386	0.322	44.89	39.32
Image 14	0.965	0.671	48.44	51.59	0.68	1.00	0.377	0.356	75.65	66.27
Image 15	0.848	0.658	49.57	51.77	0.65	0.90	0.331	0.327	13.89	12.17
Image 16	0.974	0.795	48.36	50.12	0.63	0.97	0.314	0.310	19.88	17.41
Image 17	0.985	0.596	48.26	52.62	0.63	0.96	0.308	0.304	29.90	26.19
Image 18	0.855	0.757	49.49	50.55	0.61	1.00	0.305	0.256	33.43	29.28
Image 19	0.978	0.727	48.32	50.9	0.72	0.94	0.301	0.297	46.23	40.50
Image 20	0.902	0.739	49.02	50.76	0.60	0.92	0.302	0.298	76.96	67.42
Image 21	0.923	0.655	48.82	51.81	0.64	1.00	0.289	0.189	10.50	9.19
Image 22	0.855	0.796	49.49	50.12	0.62	0.99	0.286	0.282	16.00	14.02

(continued)

Table 23.3 (continued)

LIVE Dataset	MSE		PSNR		SSIM		CR		CT	
	FF	FF-TLBO	FF	FF-TLBO	FF	FF-TLBO	FF	FF-TLBO	FF	FF-TLBO
Image 23	0.951	0.737	48.56	50.78	0.65	0.97	0.287	0.283	24.89	21.80
Image 24	0.953	0.424	48.55	55.58	0.73	0.96	0.287	0.283	29.90	26.19
Image 25	0.864	0.451	49.40	55.06	0.65	0.99	0.412	0.408	42.78	37.48
Image 26	0.872	0.764	49.32	50.46	0.68	0.95	0.285	0.281	72.87	63.83
Image 27	0.991	0.450	48.21	55.06	0.69	0.95	0.285	0.281	11.20	9.81
Image 28	0.923	0.780	48.82	50.29	0.62	0.92	0.276	0.272	15.10	13.23
Image 29	0.900	0.730	49.05	50.86	0.67	0.93	0.285	0.281	26.50	23.21
Image 30	0.953	0.449	48.55	55.09	0.65	0.96	0.224	0.220	30.10	26.37
Image 31	0.971	0.698	48.39	51.25	0.70	0.95	0.270	0.266	43.60	38.19
Image 32	0.949	0.560	48.59	53.16	0.60	0.99	0.270	0.266	80.50	70.52
Image 33	0.856	0.532	49.48	53.62	0.64	0.97	0.283	0.279	11.05	9.68
Image 34	0.969	0.782	48.40	50.27	0.64	0.98	0.272	0.268	14.10	12.35
Image 35	0.945	0.522	48.62	53.77	0.69	0.98	0.269	0.265	24.60	21.55
Image 36	0.834	0.704	49.71	51.18	0.66	0.97	0.313	0.209	29.10	25.49
Image 37	0.961	0.678	48.47	51.51	0.75	0.98	0.345	0.261	50.20	43.98
Image 38	0.882	0.498	49.23	54.18	0.69	0.91	0.265	0.261	75.30	65.96
Image 39	0.947	0.775	48.60	50.34	0.71	0.96	0.224	0.220	3.51	3.07
Image 40	0.977	0.587	48.33	52.76	0.68	0.90	0.290	0.266	3.52	3.08
Image 41	0.834	0.713	49.71	51.07	0.73	0.96	0.288	0.282	3.52	3.08
Image 42	0.821	0.741	49.85	50.73	0.74	0.99	0.289	0.283	3.52	3.08

Fig. 23.3 Evaluation of LIVE image dataset (**a**) Image 13, (**b**) Image 14, (**c**) Image 18 and (**d**) Image 21

takes a CT of only 27.19 s. From these average results, it is found that the FF-TLBO algorithm performs well than FF algorithm in all the different perspectives.

To further facilitate the highlights of the proposed method, some interesting results of the applied benchmark images are shown in Fig. 23.3. This figure shows the obtained values of four images from LIVE database include Image 13, Image 14, Image18 and Image 21 respectively. From Fig. 23.3a, the results of Image 13 show that the proposed method attains better performance than FF method. It can be shown from the values MSE of 0.474, PSNR of 54.62, SSIM of 1.00, CR of 0.322 and CT of 39.32 seconds respectively. However, the FF method fails to achieve a closest performance, achieved an MSE of 0.801, PSNR of 50.05, SSIM of 0.65, CR of 0.386 and CT of 44.89 respectively. Likewise, in Fig. 23.3b, the results of Image 14 are shown where the proposed method is superior to FF method in all the performance measures involved. It is clearly shown from the values MSE of 0.671, PSNR of 51.59, SSIM of 1.00, CR of 0.356 and CT of 66.27 seconds respectively. However, the FF method fails to attain maximum performance, achieved a MSE of 0.95, PSNR of 48.44, SSIM of 0.68, CR of 0.377 and CT of 75.65 respectively. Similarly, for Image 18 in Fig. 23.3c, the attained values revealed that the existing method outperforms the FF-TLBO method. The existing FF method reported the values of MSE 0.855, NR 49.49, SSIM 0.61, CR 0.305 and CT 33.43 respectively. But, the proposed method produced enhanced results with the values MSE of 0.757, PSNR of 50.55, SSIM of 1.00, CR of 0.256 and CT of 29.28 seconds respectively. Finally, in Fig. 23.3d, the results of existing and FF-TLBO algorithms are shown. The obtained values indicated that the effectiveness of proposed method over FF method. The proposed method attained an MSE of 0.655, PSNR of 51.81, SSIM of 1.00, CR of 0.189 and CT of 9.19 seconds respectively. At the same time, FF method fails to manage maximum compression performance and better reconstructed image quality with the MSE of 0.923, PSNR of 48.82, SSIM of 0.64, CR of 0.289 and CT of 10.20 seconds respectively.

From the results of four images, it is perhaps interesting that the SSIM of four images is found to one. It shows that the proposed FF-TLBO algorithm is reliable and robust for all the applied images. These values depict that maximum reconstructed image quality and better compression performance is produced by the proposed method. The obtained values imply that the proposed method manages to retain the image quality as well as the better compression performance in a reasonable amount of time. Figures 23.4, 23.5, 23.6, 23.7, and 23.8 shows the comparison results of proposed and FF method in terms of MSE, PSNR, SSIM, CR and CT respectively. Figure 23.4 illustrates the comparison results of proposed and existing FF methods in terms of MSE. From this figure, it is noted that the MSE of the FF-TLBO algorithm is significantly better than FF method. As the FF algorithm produces a MSE value closer to 1 in most of the applied images, which indicates the worse performance in the reconstructed image quality. At the same time, the proposed method achieves lower MSE in all the applied images, particularly for Image 9, Image 24, Image 25, Image 27 and Image 30 respectively. Figure 23.5 demonstrates the performance of the proposed and existing FF methods in terms of PSNR. Figure shows that the maximum value of PSNR is achieved

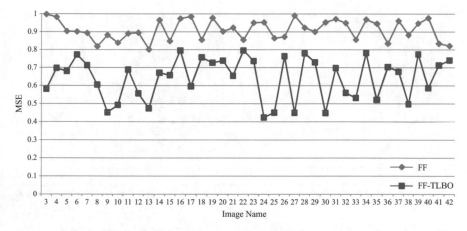

Fig. 23.4 Comparative analysis of proposed method with FF method in terms of MSE

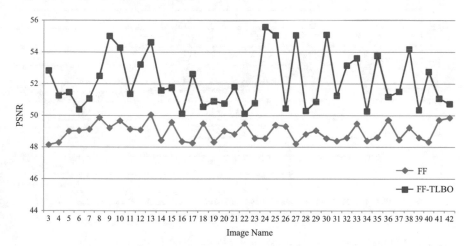

Fig. 23.5 Comparative analysis of proposed method with FF method in terms of PSNR

by proposed method, which reveals the maximum performance of the proposed method. The existing method achieves a minimum PSNR of 48.15 and maximum PSNR of 49.71 whereas the proposed method reported a minimum PSNR of 50.12 and maximum PSNR of 55.58 respectively. The performance of the proposed and compared method in terms of SSIM is depicted in Fig. 23.6. From the figure, it is interesting that the proposed method reaches maximum resemblance with the SSIM of 1.0 for Image 13, Image 14, Image 18 and Image 21 respectively. Also, it leads to the closest resemblance of 0.99 for Images 9 and Image 10. The existing method achieves a minim PSNR of 48.15 and maximum PSNR of 49.71 whereas the proposed method reported a minimum PSNR of 50.12 and maximum PSNR of 55.58 respectively.

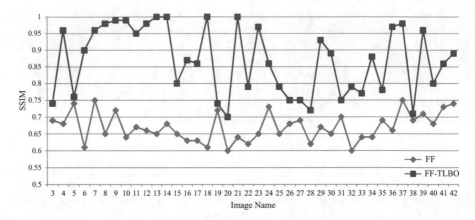

Fig. 23.6 Comparative analysis of proposed method with FF method in terms of SSIM

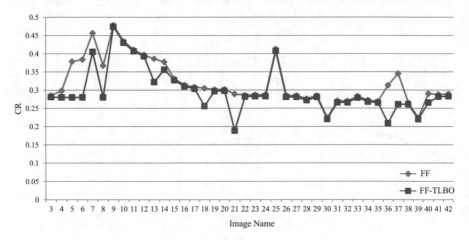

Fig. 23.7 Comparative results of proposed method with FF method in terms of CR

The obtained values of the proposed and compared methods in terms of SSIM are depicted in Fig. 23.6. From this figure, it is interesting that the proposed method reaches maximum resemblance with the SSIM of 1.0 for Image 13, Image 14, Image 18 and Image 21 respectively. Also, it leads to a closer resemblance of 0.99 for Images 9 and Image 10. On basis of the assessment of compression performance, the comparison results in terms of CR is shown in Fig. 23.7. The proposed method obtains lesser value of CR for all the images, which indicates the better compression performance of the proposed method. However, the existing method shows nearly equal performance only for some of the images. Figure 23.8 depicts the results of existing and proposed method in terms of CT. The FF method consumes more CT when compared to the proposed method. From the overall experimentation, it is not

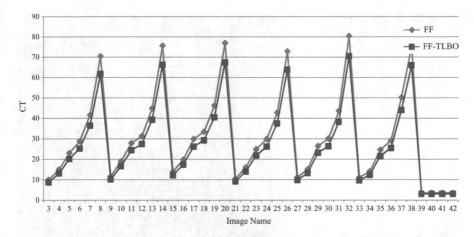

Fig. 23.8 Comparative analysis of proposed method with FF method interms of CT

Fig. 23.9 Original image
"Lena", 512*512

surprising that the FF algorithm based on DCT is superior to the existing method in different perspectives.

For better understanding, an additional experiment is carried out to analyze the visual similarities by comparing the results obtained by FF algorithm and FF-TLBO algorithm. Figures 23.9 and 23.10 shows the original and compressed images with quality coefficient with standard quantization matrix attained by FF algorithm is given in Table 23.4. It is found that the CR is high with degraded image quality. The average pixel intensity distance between the original and compressed image is 11.

Fig. 23.10 FF algorithm

Table 23.4 Quantization matrix by FF

120	56	60	129	190	225	255	255
60	66	76	156	154	255	255	255
78	78	129	198	223	255	255	255
70	86	178	143	255	255	255	255
90	123	185	255	255	255	255	255
126	189	255	255	255	255	255	255
250	255	255	255	255	255	255	255
255	255	255	255	255	255	255	255

The proposed FF-TLBO algorithm obtained the optimal quantization matrix for the same level of compression. This matrix is shown in Table 23.5 and the decompressed image with that quantization matrix is shown in Fig. 23.11. It is found that same level of compression is attained with better reconstructed image quality and the average pixel intensity distance was reduced to 5.1.

From these figures, it is clear that the FF-TLBO algorithm obtained the quantization table with same number of bits for nonzero frequency coefficients. This illustration verifies the significance of meta heuristic algorithms on the selection of quantization tables.

Table 23.5 Quantization matrix by FF-TLBO algorithm

16	26	68	124	96	255	255	255
16	22	124	143	178	255	255	255
16	34	187	165	255	255	255	255
234	228	18	122	255	255	255	255
16	42	65	255	255	255	255	255
245	16	255	255	255	255	255	255
255	255	255	255	255	255	255	255
255	255	255	255	255	255	255	255

Fig. 23.11 FF-TLBO algorithm

23.6 Conclusions

This chapter presented a detailed explanation of how the FF-TLBO algorithm finds useful to construct the quantization table and enhances the performance of the compression techniques. All of the experimentation results reported that the proposed method achieved better compression performance and also increased the reconstructed image quality with respect to compared FF algorithm. This ensures that FF-TLBO algorithm is potentially powerful in achieving ear lossless compression performance which will be concentrated more in future studies.

Additionally, further studies on the application of different meta heuristic algorithm may create an interesting field for upcoming research in image compression.

References

1. Bookstein A, A.Storer J. Data Compression. Inf Process Manag 1992;28.
2. Salomon D. Data Compression The Complete Reference. 4th ed. Springer; 2007.
3. Rehman M, Sharif M, Raza M. Image compression: A survey. Res J Appl Sci Eng Technol 2014;7:656–72.
4. Drost SW, Bourbakis N. A Hybrid system for real-time lossless image compression. Micropro-cess Microsyst 2001;25:19–31. https://doi.org/10.1016/S0141-9331(00)00102-2.
5. Holtz K. The Evolution of Lossless Data Compression Techniques 1999:140–5.
6. Tarek S, Musaddiqa M, Elhadi S. Data compression techniques in Wireless Sensor Networks. Futur Gener Comput Syst 2016;64:151–62. https://doi.org/10.1016/j.future.2016.01.015.
7. Narasimha M, Peterson A. On the Computation of the Discrete Cosine Transform. IEEE Trans Commun 1978;26:934–936.
8. Bonabeau E, Dorigo M, Theraulaz G. Swarm Intelligence: From Natural to Artificial Systems. Oxford University Press; 1999.
9. Deb K. Optimisation for Engineering Design. Prentice-Hall, New Delhi; 1995.
10. Kennedy J, Eberhart R, Shi Y. Swarm intelligence. London: Academic Press; 2001.
11. Shilane D, Martikainen J, Dudoit S, Ovaska SJ. A general framework for statistical per-formance comparison of evolutionary computation algorithms. Inf Sci (Ny) 2008;178:) 2870–2879.
12. Kennedy J, Eberhart RC. Particle swarm optimization. Proc. IEEE Int. Conf. Neural Networks, Piscataway, NJ, 1995, p. 1942–1948.
13. Wang Y, Feng XY, Huang YX, Pu DB, Zhou WG, Liang YC. A novel quantum swarm evolutionary algorithm and its applications. Neurocomputing 2007;70:633–640.
14. Goldberg DE. Genetic Algorithms in Search, Optimization, and Machine Learning. ADDISON-WESLEY PUBLISHING COMPANY, INC.; 1989.
15. Storn R, Price K. Differential Evolution – A Simple and Efficient Heuristic for global Optimization over Continuous Spaces. J Glob Optim 1997;11:341–59. https://doi.org/10.1023/A:1008202821328.
16. Abbasss HA. Marriage in honey-bee optimization (HBO): A haplometrosis Computation, polygynous swarming approach. Congr. Evol., 2001, p. 207–14.
17. Yang X-S. Flower Pollination Algorithm for Global Optimization. Int. Conf. Unconv. Comput. Nat. Comput. UCNC 2012 Unconv. Comput. Nat. Comput., 2012, p. 240–9.
18. Yang XS, Deb S. Engineering optimisation by cuckoo search. Int J Math Model Numer Optim 2010;1:330–43.
19. Muruganandham A, Wahida Banu RSD. Adaptive Fractal Image Compression using PSO. Procedia Comput Sci 2010;2:338–44. https://doi.org/10.1016/j.procs.2010.11.044.
20. Horng MH, Jiang TW. Image vector quantization algorithm via honey bee mating optimization. Expert Syst Appl 2011;38:1382–92. https://doi.org/10.1016/j.eswa.2010.07.037.
21. Linde Y, Buzo A, Gray RM. An algorithm for vector quantizer design. IEEE Trans Commun 1980;28:84–95.
22. Horng MH. Vector quantization using the firefly algorithm for image compression. Expert Syst Appl 2012;39:1078–91. https://doi.org/10.1016/j.eswa.2011.07.108.
23. Ukrit, Mferni. Suresh G. Effective lossless compression for medical image sequences using composite algorithm. Int. Conf. Circuits, Power Comput. Technol., 2013, p. 1122–6.

24. Paul S, Bandyopadhyay B. A Novel Approach for Image Compression Based on Multi-level Image Thresholding using Shannon Entropy and Differential Evolution. Proceeding 2014 IEEE Students' Technol. Symp. A, 2014, p. 56–61.
25. Wu MS. Genetic algorithm based on discrete wavelet transformation for fractal image compression. J Vis Commun Image Represent 2014;25:1835–41. https://doi.org/10.1016/j.jvcir.2014.09.001.
26. Fouad MM. A Lossless Image Compression Using Integer Wavelet Transform With a Simplified Median-edge Detector Algorithm. Int J Eng Technol 2015;15:68–73.
27. Omari M, Yaichi S. Image Compression Based on Genetic Algorithm Optimization. 015 2nd World Symp. Web Appl. Netw., Sousse: 2015, p. 1–5.
28. Kaur H, Kaur R, Kumar N. Lossless compression of DICOM images using genetic algorithm. 2015 1st Int. Conf. Next Gener. Comput. Technol., 2015, p. 985–9. https://doi.org/10.1109/NGCT.2015.7375268.
29. Ismail BM, Eswara Reddy B, Bhaskara Reddy T. Cuckoo inspired fast search algorithm for fractal image encoding. J King Saud Univ - Comput Inf Sci 2016. https://doi.org/10.1016/j.jksuci.2016.11.003.
30. Jindal P, Raj Bhupinder Kaur. Lossless Image Compression for storage reduction using Pollination Based Optimization. Commun. Electron. Syst. (ICCES), Int. Conf., 2016, p. 1–6.
31. Alam, L., Dhar, P.K., Hasan, M.A.R., Bhuyan, M.G.S. and Daiyan GM. An improved JPEG image compression algorithm by modifying luminance quantization table. Int J Comput Sci Netw Secur 2017;17:200.
32. Chandraraju T, Radhakrishnan S. Image encoder architecture design using dual scan based DWT with vector quantization. Mater. Today Proc., vol. 5, 2018, p. 572–7.
33. E. T, M. T, D. S, R J, V. B, R. B. JPEG Quantization Table Optimization by Guided Fireworks Algorithm. Lect Notes Comb Image Anal IWCIA Comput Sci 2017;10256.
34. Watson AB (Nasa ARC. Image Compression Using the Discrete Cosine Transform. Math J 1994;4:81–8. https://doi.org/10.1006/jvci.1997.0323.
35. Yang X-S. Firefly Algorithms for Multimodal Optimization. Proc. 5th Int. Conf. Stoch. Algorithms Found. Appl., 2009, p. 169–78. https://doi.org/10.1007/978-3-642-04944-6_14.
36. Capon J. A probabilistic model for run-length coding of pictures. IRE Trans Inf Theory 1959;100:157–63.
37. Huffman DA. A Method for the Construction of Minimum-Redundancu Codes. Proc IRE 1952;40:1098–102.
38. Rao RV, Savsani VJ, Vakharia DP. Teaching–learning-based optimization: A Comput.-, novel method for constrained mechanical design optimization problems. Aided Des 2011;43:303–315.
39. Sheikh HR, Wang Z, Cormack L, Bovik AC. LIVE image quality assessment database. Http//Live Ece Utexas Edu/Research/Quality 2003. http://live.ece.utexas.edu/research/quality/subjective.htm.
40. Sayood K. Introduction to Data Compression. 2006. https://doi.org/10.1159/000207355.
41. Wang Z, Bovik AC, Sheikh HR, Simoncelli EP. Image quality assessment: from error visibility to structural similarity. EEE Trans Image Process 2004;13:600–12. https://doi.org/10.1109/TIP.2003.819861.

Chapter 24
Wavelet Packet Based CT Image Denoising Using Bilateral Method and Bayes Shrinkage Rule

Manoj Diwakar and Pardeep Kumar

24.1 Introduction

The reconstruction process of Computed tomography (CT) is a typical task to get the CT images. There are certain processes to reconstruct the CT images. X-rays are transmitted to human body; raw data is collected by detectors over the different directions, and finally radon and inverse radon transform has been performed to reconstruct the CT images. The efficiency of whole process is important task. But due to software, hardware and other transmissions and mathematical problems the noise may appears in CT images. The reason of noise appear in CT image is also depend on the X-rays transmission. If the higher amount of X-rays are transmitted over the human body organs, then the quality of CT images are good but it may not good for affect human body organs. With low amount of CT images, human body organs may safe but noise is degraded to the quality of CT images. Hence, if noise can be suppressed from low dose CT images, it will good for the society.

Various research have been already done to reduce noise from the CT images, still it is a challenging task. To suppress noise from CT images, three major techniques are categorized: Projection based denoising, Iterative based denoising and Post-processing based denoising. In projection based denoising, the CT images are filtered when CT images are reconstructed through projected X-ray beams such as filtering of sinogram using bilateral filtering over the low dose CT images [1–3]. In iterative based denoising, CT images are reconstructed using an iterative approach such as iterative CT image reconstruction using shearlet transform [4, 5]. The major

M. Diwakar
Department of CSE, DIT University, Dehradun, Uttarakhand, India

P. Kumar (✉)
Department of CSE and IT, Jaypee University of Information Technology, Solan, Himachal Pradesh, India

© Springer Nature Switzerland AG 2019
A. K. Singh, A. Mohan (eds.), *Handbook of Multimedia Information Security: Techniques and Applications*, https://doi.org/10.1007/978-3-030-15887-3_24

drawback of iterative reconstruction is high cost computation. In post-processing based denoising, CT images are denoised directly after obtained CT reconstructed images through X-ray computed tomography. Various techniques have been proposed to denoised CT images using post-processing methods. In post-processing, CT images are denoised broadly in two domains: spatial and transform domain. In spatial domain, pixels are directly denoised using mathematical optimization and computation. Linear and non-linear methods in spatial domain are very popular to denosied the CT images where non-linear methods are providing good results in compare of linear methods in terms of sharp and smooth images. Non-linear filters such as bilateral and non-local mean (NLM) filters are very helpful to provide edge preserving denoised CT images. Bilateral filter [6] is a non-iterative, local filtering method which provides edge preserved smoothing data but it is dependent on kernel radius. NLM [7] filter provides denoised images in terms of sharp edges based on self-similarity approach. But due to self-similarity concept, the computation cost is high.

In transform domain, wavelet transform is used where images are decomposed into low and high frequency subbands. The noise has a tendency that it affects over the edges or detail parts in most of the cases. Thresholding is one of the popular ways to denoised the images in transform domain. Before thresholding, a threshold value is estimated which helps to denoised the images. Soft and Hard thresholding are two popular methods for thresholding. In hard thresholding, a threshold value is estimated. Below the estimated threshold value, the wavelet coefficients are set as zero and rest of the values will be same. In soft thresholding, below the estimated threshold value, the wavelet coefficients are set as zero same as hard thresholding and rest of the wavelet coefficients are modified by subtracting the estimated threshold value. Both processes are good but soft threholding provides better outcomes in most of the cases [8–10]. VISUShrink [11], SUREShrink [12] and BayesShrink [13] are the popular thresholding methods for image denoising. In most of the cases, BayesShrink provides better outcomes in compare to VISUShrink and SUREShrink [14–18]. In transform domain, wavelet transform is one powerful tools [19–22] but it also has some limitations. To overcome that, many other transforms are used such as, wavelet packet transform, dual-tree complex wavelet transform, curvelet, tetrolet, framelet and so on.

In CT images, every small detail has their own significance and may be used for diagnosis purpose. With this consideration, a method noise concept is included with bilateral filtering. In this paper wavelet packet thresholding is performed so that maximum high frequency coefficients can be collected and thresholded. The main concept of this proposed scheme is to reduce noise and preserve the edges from the noisy CT images. Rest of the paper is organized as: Sect. 24.2 gives a small description of wavelet packet transform and bilateral filter. In Sect. 24.3, a brief description of proposed method has been defined. The result analysis and comparative results are discussed in Sect. 24.4. Finally, conclusions are defined in Sect. 24.5.

24.2 Wavelet Packet Transform

Wavelet transform is one of the major tools in the area of image and signal processing. The best part of wavelet that it divides the information into low and high frequencies. Further decompositions are possible as per the size of images. The extended version of wavelet transform is wavelet packet transform. Wavelet packet gives the information into low and high frequencies. The only difference between discrete wavelet transform (DWT) and wavelet packet transform (WPT) that WPT gives higher information in compare to DWT. WPT decompose both low and high frequency components while DWT decompose only low frequency components.

24.3 Proposed Methodology

CT images are generally corrupted with additive Gaussian noise. Hence noisy CT images are obtained via simulation methods. It can be expressed as:

$$X(m, n) = Y(m, n) + \eta(m, n) \tag{24.1}$$

Where, $\eta(m, n)$ is a noise coefficient, $Y(m, n)$ and $X(m, n)$ are noiseless and noisy images respectively.

The proposed algorithm has been designed using wavelet packet transform (WPT). WPT is using to obtain low and high frequency components. The low frequency components are filtered using Bilateral method. Similarly, high frequency components are denoised using thresholding.

The formulation of bilateral filter [6] is given below:

$$BF[I]_{\mathbf{p}} = \frac{1}{K} \sum_{\mathbf{q} \in S} G_{\sigma_s}(\|\mathbf{p} - \mathbf{q}\|) \ G_{\sigma_r}(|I_{\mathbf{p}} - I_{\mathbf{q}}|) \ I_{\mathbf{q}} \tag{24.2}$$

Where, p and q are two different pixels, K is normalization constant, σ_S and σ_r are control the behavior of bilateral filtering.

It has two filter kernels as shown in Eq. (24.2). The first kernel is used to enhance the edges and works as edge stopping function. The other kernel is works as Gaussian filter which is used for suppressing the Gaussian noise.

To denosie high frequency components, Bayes shrinkage function is used. This function is used to suppress the Gaussian noise from CT images. The method used for estimating threshold value is defined via statistical methods.

The threshold λ can be selected as:

$$\lambda = \left(\frac{\sigma_\eta^2}{\sigma_Y}\right) \tag{24.3}$$

Where the noise variance can be estimated using robust median estimation method [15] as follows:

$$\sigma_\eta^2 = \left[\frac{median\ (|X\,(m,n)\,|)}{0.6745} \right]^2, \tag{24.4}$$

Where, $X(m,n) \epsilon HH_L$, L represents respective level in wavelet decomposition. The standard deviation of noise less image (σ_Y) can be estimated as:

$$\sigma_Y^2 = \max \left(\sigma_X^2 - \sigma_\eta^2,\quad 0 \right) \tag{24.5}$$

Where, $\sigma_X^2 = \frac{1}{N} \sum_{i=1}^{N} X_i^2$, and N represent patch size of an input image.

The thresholding function can be expressed as:

$$\hat{X} := \begin{cases} 0 & if\ |X| \leq \lambda \\ sign(X) & (|X| - \lambda)\ if\ |X| > \lambda \end{cases} \tag{24.6}$$

The proposed method can be expressed with the following major steps:

Step 1: Perform wavelet packet transform on input noisy CT image to obtain low and high frequency subbands.

Step 2: Perform bilateral method on the low frequency subbands using Eq. (24.2).

Step 3: Perform thresholding over high frequency subbands using following steps:

i. Estimate noise variance using Eq. (24.4)
ii. Apply thresholding on high frequency subbands using Eq. (24.6)

Step 4: Apply inverse WPT to obtain denoised image.

24.4 Experimental Results

In the experimental result evaluation, the proposed method is performed over the various standard CT images. The size of CT images are 512×512 with additive Gaussian noise. Experimental evaluation are tested with five different noise level $\sigma \in [10, 15, 20, 25, 30, 35]$. The CT images are obtained from public source database (https://eddie.via.cornell.edu/cgibin/datac/logon.cgi) which are shown in Fig. 24.1. There are six test CT images which are recognized here as CT1, CT2, CT3, CT4, CT5 and CT6, respectively. For result analysis, the noisy CT images are obtained with different noise level. In Fig. 24.2, noisy CT images are obtained with noise level 25. To execute proposed method, values of some parameters are used such as patch size is 10×10, σ_S is 1.2 and σ_r is 0.13.

Fig. 24.1 Input test CT image dataset. (**a**) CT 1 image. (**b**) CT 2 image. (**c**) CT 3 image. (**d**) CT 4 image

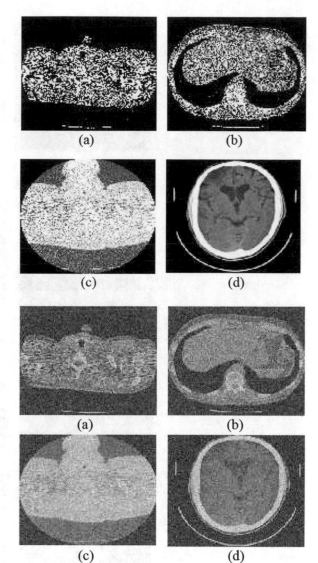

(a)   (b)

(c)   (d)

Fig. 24.2 Noisy CT image dataset ($\sigma = 25$). (**a**) CT 1 image. (**b**) CT 2 image. (**c**) CT 3 image. (**d**) CT 4 image

(a)   (b)

(c)   (d)

The existing methods for comparison are bilateral filtering [6], Surelet [23] and adaptive wavelet transform with Bayes shrinkage [13]. Figures 24.3, 24.4, 24.5 and 24.6 are showing the results of Bilateral filtering, Surelet, Wavelet based denoising using Bayes shrinkage and proposed method respectively. For comparative study and result analysis, some performance metrics are used to show the performance of methods. The performance metrics which are used, PSNR and IQI.

Fig. 24.3 Results of bilateral filtering. (**a**) CT 1 image. (**b**) CT 2 image. (**c**) CT 3 image. (**d**) CT 4 image

Fig. 24.4 Results of Surelet. (**a**) CT 1 image. (**b**) CT 2 image. (**c**) CT 3 image. (**d**) CT 4 image

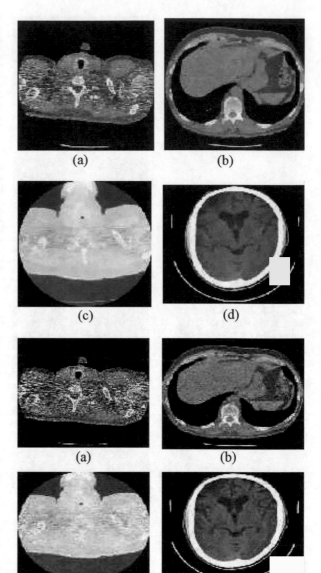

Peak Signal-to-noise Ratio (PSNR) is one major factors to show the performance of methods. Increasing value of PSNR shows that method is good in compare to less PSNR value. The PSNR value can be measured as:

$$PSNR = 10\log_{10}\frac{255^2}{mse} \text{ dB} \tag{24.7}$$

Fig. 24.5 Results of Bayes thresholding. (**a**) CT 1 image. (**b**) CT 2 image. (**c**) CT 3 image. (**d**) CT 4 image

Fig. 24.6 Results of proposed scheme. (**a**) CT 1 image. (**b**) CT 2 image. (**c**) CT 3 image. (**d**) CT 4 image

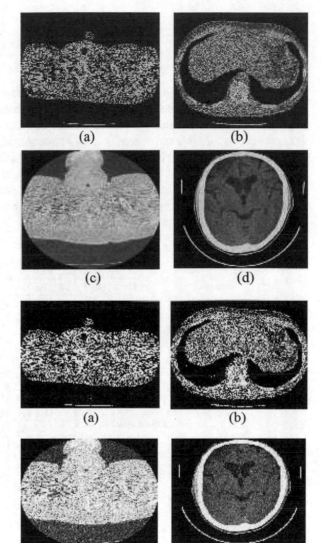

(a)   (b)

(c)   (d)

(a)   (b)

(c)   (d)

Where $mse = \frac{1}{mn} \sum\limits_{i=1}^{m} \sum\limits_{j=1}^{n} [X(i,j) - W(i,j)]^2$

Image quality index (IQI) is other important metric which is used to show the results in terms of edge preservation. For input image (X) and denoised image (W), the IQI can be defined as:

$$IQI = \frac{4\sigma_{XW}\overline{X}\overline{W}}{\left(\sigma_X^2 + \sigma_W^2\right)\left[\left(\overline{X}\right)^2 + \left(\overline{W}\right)^2\right]} \tag{24.8}$$

Where, $\overline{X} = \frac{1}{N}\sum_{i=1}^{N} X_i$, $\overline{W} = \frac{1}{N}\sum_{i=1}^{N} W_i$, $\sigma_X^2 = \frac{1}{N-1}\sum_{i=1}^{N}(X_i - \overline{X})^2$, $\sigma_W^2 = \frac{1}{N-1}\sum_{i=1}^{N}(W_i - \overline{W})^2$ and $\sigma_{XW} = \frac{1}{N-1}\sum_{i=1}^{N}(X_i - \overline{X})(W_i - \overline{W})$.

The results of all existing methods and proposed method indicate that visually, the results of proposed scheme is better in terms of contrast, noise reduction and edge preservation. The values of PSNR and IQI are also indicates that most of the times the results of proposed scheme giving better outcomes.

From Table 24.1, it can be analyzed that proposed method gives minimum value of IQI for different noise level in most of the cases. Similarly, Table 24.2 also indicates that maximum PSNR value is achieved by proposed algorithm in most cases. Hence it can be concluded that proposed algorithm better results in terms noise suppression and edge preservation.

Table 24.1 IQI of denoised images

	σ	TV	Surelet	Bayes	Proposed
CT 1 image	10	0.993	0.9912	0.9924	0.9976
	15	0.9534	0.9856	0.9762	0.9865
	20	0.9312	0.9541	0.9365	0.9597
	25	0.8972	0.9165	0.9174	0.9248
	30	0.8903	0.8954	0.8832	0.8962
	35	0.8894	0.8762	0.8014	0.8747
CT 2 image	0	0.9817	0.9828	0.9751	0.9889
	15	0.9789	0.9794	0.9745	0.9831
	20	0.9421	0.9654	0.9241	0.9521
	25	0.8452	0.8684	0.8922	0.9047
	30	0.8364	0.8361	0.8632	0.8740
	35	0.8189	0.8314	0.8614	0.8694
CT 3 image	10	0.9874	0.9812	0.9914	0.9965
	15	0.9514	0.9614	0.9762	0.9893
	20	0.9423	0.9591	0.9432	0.9614
	25	0.9102	0.9241	0.9397	0.9235
	30	0.8964	0.8931	0.8942	0.9131
	35	0.8831	0.8894	0.8913	0.8941
CT 4 image	10	0.9871	0.9974	0.9954	0.9979
	15	0.9642	0.9831	0.9645	0.9846
	20	0.9409	0.9641	0.9469	0.9698
	25	0.9123	0.9352	0.9231	0.9411
	30	0.8991	0.8978	0.8945	0.9006
	35	0.8647	0.8649	0.8791	0.8771

Table 24.2 PSNR (in dB) of denoised images

	σ	TV	Surelet	Bayes	Proposed
CT 1 image	10	32.14	33.25	31.50	33.9
	15	30.95	31.45	29.96	31.44
	20	29.5	30.10	28.21	30.05
	25	27.98	29.68	28.01	29.85
	30	26.31	28.47	27.25	28.54
	35	25.26	26.19	25.31	26.88
CT 2 image	10	31.54	32.12	30.98	32.47
	15	30.87	30.64	29.42	31.05
	20	28.95	29.08	28.47	29.53
	25	28.48	28.64	27.26	28.96
	30	27.69	28.03	26.17	28.11
	35	25.83	26.96	25.34	26.97
CT 3 image	10	32.33	33.19	31.98	33.89
	15	31.29	31.25	30.67	31.87
	20	29.84	30.98	28.68	30.91
	25	27.15	29.27	28.34	29.31
	30	26.29	28.54	27.52	28.67
	35	24.36	26.65	24.64	26.73
CT 4 image	10	32.65	33.65	31.63	33.79
	15	31.35	31.24	29.26	31.35
	20	29.64	30.19	28.31	30.61
	25	27.45	29.34	28.72	29.36
	30	26.64	28.21	27.37	28.42
	35	25.39	26.94	25.61	26.61

24.5 Conclusions

CT images which are degraded with Gaussian noise are filtered with proposed method and some standard recent existing methods. The utilization of bilateral filter in proposed algorithm gives better results for providing better noise suppression and edge preservation. From results, it was observed that mostly results of proposed scheme are giving better outcomes in terms of noise suppression and edge preservation. The proposed scheme is effectively suppress the noise from CT images as well as also helpful to preserve the edges and structural details.

References

1. A. Manduca, L. Yu, J. D. Trzasko, N. Khaylova, J. M. Kofler, C. M. McCollough and J. G. Fletcher, "Projection space denoising with bilateral filtering and CT noise modeling for dose reduction in CT," International Journal of Medical Physics Research and Practice, Vol. 36, No. 11, pp. 4911–4919, 2009.

2. D. Kim, S. Ramani and J. A. Fessler, "Accelerating X-ray CT ordered subsets image reconstruction with Nesterov's first-order methods" In Proc. Intl. Mtg. on Fully 3D Image Recon. in Rad. and Nuc. Med pp. 22–5, 2013.
3. F. Durand and J. Dorsey, "Fast bilateral filtering for the display of high dynamic range images," ACM Transactions on Graphics, Vol. 21, No. 3, pp. 257–266, 2002.
4. T. Goldstein and S. Osher, "The Split Bregman Method for L1 Regularized Problems," SIAM Journal on Imaging Sciences, Vol. 2, No. 2, pp. 323–34, 2009.
5. A. Chambolle, "An algorithm for total variation minimization and applications," Journal of Matter Image and Visualization', Journal Roy Statistic Society, Vol. 20, No. 1, pp. 89–97, 2004.
6. C. Tomasi and R. Manduchi. Bilateral filtering for gray and color images. In Sixth International Conference on Computer Vision, pages 836–846, Jan 1998.
7. Z. Li, L. Yu, J. D. Trzasko, D. S. Lake, D. J. Blezek, J. G. Fletcher, C. H. McCollough and A. Manduca, "Adaptive nonlocal means filtering based on local noise level for CT denoising," International Journal of Medical Physics Research and Practice, Vol. 41, No. 1, 2014.
8. S. Mallat, "A theory for multiresolution signal decomposition: the wavelet representation," IEEE Trans. on Pattern Anal. Mach. Intell., Vol. 11, No. 7, pp. 674–693, 1989.
9. A. Fathi and A. R. Naghsh-Nilchi, "Efficient image denoising method based on a new adaptive wavelet packet thresholding function," IEEE Trans Image Process, Vol. 21, No. 9, pp. 3981–3990, 1989.
10. D. L. Donoho and I. M. Johnstone, "Ideal spatial adaptation via wavelet shrinkage," Biometrika, Vol. 81, pp. 425–455, 1994.
11. A. Borsdorf, R. Raupach, T. Flohr and J. Hornegger Tanaka, "Wavelet Based Noise Reduction in CT-Images Using Correlation Analysis," IEEE Transactions on Medical Imaging, Vol. 27, No. 12, pp. 1685–1703, 2008.
12. D. L. Donoho, "De-noising by soft-thresholding," IEEE Transactions on Information Theory, Vol. 41, No. 3, pp. 613–627. Signal Process. Vol. 90 no. 8 pp 2529–2539, 2010, 1995.
13. F. Abramovitch, T. Sapatinas, and B. W. Silverman "Wavelet thresholding via a Bayesian approach," Journal Roy Statistic Society, Vol. 60, No. 4, pp.725– 749, 1998.
14. J. Romberg, H. Choi and R. G. Baraniuk, "Bayesian wavelet domain image modeling using hidden Markov models," IEEE Transactions on Image Processing, Vol. 10, pp. 1056–1068, 2001.
15. S. G. Chang, B. Yu and M. Vetterli, "Adaptive wavelet thresholding for image denoising and compression," IEEE Trans. on Image Proc, Vol. 9, No. 9, pp. 1532–1546, 2000.
16. L. Xinhao, M. Tanaka and M. Okutomi, "Single- Image Noise Level Estimation for Blind Denoising," IEEE Transactions on Image Processing, Vol. 22, No. 12, pp. 5226–5237, 2013.
17. H. S. Bhadauria and M. L. Dewal, "Efficient Denoising Technique for CT images to Enhance Brain Hemorrhage Segmentation," International Journal of Digit Imaging, Vol. 25, No. 6, pp. 782–791, 2012.
18. P. Jain and V. Tyagi, "LAPB: Locally adaptive patch-based wavelet domain edge-preserving image denoising," Journal of Information Sciences, Vol. 294, pp. 164–181, 2015.
19. S. Sahu, A.K. Singh, S.P. Ghrera, and M. Elhoseny, "An approach for de-noising and contrast enhancement of retinal fundus image using CLAHE" Optics & Laser Technology, 2018.
20. Sahu, Sima, Harsh Vikram Singh, Basant Kumar, and Amit Kumar Singh. "Statistical modeling and Gaussianization procedure based de-speckling algorithm for retinal OCT images." Journal of Ambient Intelligence and Humanized Computing (2018): 1–14.

21. Sahu, Sima, Harsh Vikram Singh, Basant Kumar, and Amit Kumar Singh. "De-noising of ultrasound image using Bayesian approached heavy-tailed Cauchy distribution." Multimedia Tools and Applications (2017): 1–18.
22. Sahu, Sima, Harsh Vikram Singh, Basant Kumar, and Amit Kumar Singh. "A Bayesian multiresolution approach for noise removal in medical magnetic resonance images." Journal of Intelligent Systems (2018).
23. Luisier, Florian, and Thierry Blu. "SURE-LET multichannel image denoising: interscale orthonormal wavelet thresholding." Image Processing, IEEE Transactions on 17.4 (2008): 482–492.

Chapter 25
Automated Detection of Eye Related Diseases Using Digital Image Processing

Shailesh Kumar, Shashwat Pathak, and Basant Kumar

25.1 Introduction

Around 1.3 billion individuals across the world have some type of distance or near vision impairment. Concerning distance vision, 188.5 million have mild vision impairment, 217 million have moderate to serious vision disability, and 39 million individuals are visually impaired [1]. Concerning near vision, 826 million individuals have near vision impairment [2]. Globally, uncorrected refractive errors are primary reason of moderate and severe visual impairments; cataract remains the leading cause of blindness in middle and low-income countries. According to a study conducted in 2010, cataract contribution to worldwide blindness is around 51%, which represents 20 million people. From a report of WHO, 53.8 million people in the world are suffering from moderate to severe disability caused by cataract, more than 97% of whom are from low and middle income countries [1].

Glaucoma is second leading cause of blindness in the world. As per WHO estimate, approximately 80 million people will be affected by glaucoma by 2020, and its pervasiveness is likely to increase. The number of people assessed to be visually impaired because of essential glaucoma is 4.5 million, which represents more than 12% of all worldwide visual impairment.

Latest assessment says that 6.2 million individuals suffer from macular degeneration globally [3]. In 2013, it was the fourth highest cause of visual deficiency after cataract, pre-term birth, and glaucoma [4]. It most regularly occurs in people with more than 50 years of age and in United States, it is the most broadly perceived reason behind vision adversity in the age 50 years or above [5]. It occurs in 0.7%

S. Kumar · S. Pathak · B. Kumar (✉)
Department of ECE, Motilal Nehru NIT Allahabad, Prayagraj, India
e-mail: shailesh@mnnit.ac.in; singhbasant@mnnit.ac.in

© Springer Nature Switzerland AG 2019
A. K. Singh, A. Mohan (eds.), *Handbook of Multimedia Information Security: Techniques and Applications*, https://doi.org/10.1007/978-3-030-15887-3_25

of people with age 60–70 years, 2.3% of those with age 70–80 years, and relatively 12% of people over 80 years of age [5].

According to WHO, more than 347 million persons are suffering from diabetes and it will be 7th leading cause of death by 2030. Diabetic people are susceptible to retina abnormalities, called diabetic retinopathy (DR). As per WHO estimate, DR contributes 4.8% of the 37 million instances of visual deficiency because of eye illnesses across the world [6].

The retina is a light sensitive layer of tissue that lies inside the eyes and sends visual messages through the optic nerve to the cerebrum. Under retinal detachment (RD), retina is lifted or pulled from its common position. If not treated appropriately, RD can cause permanent vision loss. Retinal detachment influences one out of 10,000 individuals each year. Most of the retinal detachments (80–90%) are related with retinal- break formation at the time of posterior vitreous detachment (PVD). Most of the (70%) retinal tissues break at the time of PVD and viewed as tears in the retina, or as openings with a free-coasting retinal operculum [7]. RD can happen at any age; however, it achieves top pervasiveness in individuals of 60–70 years of age. It influences males more than females, and white individuals more than dark individuals [8].

Diabetic Macular Edema (DME) is the main source of visual impairment in grown-ups in developed nations, which is caused by Diabetic Mellitus One (DM1) and Diabetic Mellitus Two (DM2). The pervasiveness of DME is higher in DM2 patients (28%) than in DM1 (12%) [9]. The yearly occurrence of DME in DM1, ranges from 0.9 to 2.3% [10] and investigations demonstrate that the yearly occurrence in DM2 ranges from 1.25 to 1.40%. In the Wisconsin study, the rate of DME at 25 years in DM1 patients diminished from 2.3% to the current 0.9% rate in patients pursued from years 14 to 25 [10].

The causes of visual impairment varies by demography. For instance, the extent of vision debilitation owing to cataract is higher in low and moderate wage nations than high-wage nations. In high wage nations, illnesses such as, DR, glaucoma and age-related macular degeneration are more typical. Among youngsters, the reason for vision impairments varies significantly from nations to nations. For instance, in low-wage nations, inherent cataract is a main source, whereas in high wage nations it will probably be retinopathy.

25.1.1 Need for Automated Diagnostic Assessment Using Medical Image Processing

Effects of various diseases including eye diseases are more severe in developing or under developed countries due to lack of adequate healthcare infrastructure and the trained medical professionals. Further, in countries like India, where most of the doctors and super speciality hospitals are located in urban areas. Therefore, a large population residing in rural and remote areas are deprived of quality healthcare facilities. Ophthalmoscope is the most common instrument used for recognition of eye ailments. Handling of ophthalmoscope and other imaging gadgets for the diagnosis of eye sicknesses needs more prepared and talented specialists. Evolution of modern medical imaging has enhanced the accurate diagnostic decision-making, based on detailed diagnostic feature detection. Computer-Aided Diagnostic (CAD) has emerged as one of the major research topic in medical imaging and diagnostic radiology. CAD is an idea that combines expertise of doctors and computer, while automated computer analysis is an idea dependent on computer algorithm only.

There are significant advancements in computing and Artificial Intelligence (AI) technology with adaptive learning and big data analytics. In future, radiologists will have a level of clinical decision support that will significantly reduce diagnostic errors.

Computer assisted diagnostics improves speed of diagnostic, speeds up inspection of sickness, and helps in locating the particular area. CAD aided discovery framework has many advantages over manually locating the infected area. A few injuries have a little size and may go unnoticed by even trained ophthalmologist. The objective of automated techniques for screening is to distinguish the requirements of referral for future treatment. The utilization of advanced imaging in ophthalmology has now given the likelihood of handling retinal pictures to help clinical conclusion and treatment. Mechanized conclusion of retinal fundus pictures utilizing computerized picture investigation offers enormous potential advantages. Because of advances in Computer assisted diagnostics innovation, medicinal conclusion can be profited from Computer assisted diagnostics, which will help specialists to investigate therapeutic information and pictures with enhanced precision. Improvement of an automatic framework for examining the picture of the retina will encourage CAD supported conclusion of eye ailments. The enthusiasm towards programmed recognition of glaucoma and diabetic retinopathy has been expanding alongside quick advancement of computerized imaging and CAD control.

25.2   Imaging Systems for the Diagnosis of Eye Diseases

25.2.1   Ultrasound

Ultrasound is the word that portrays sound waves of frequencies surpassing the scope of human hearing. Ultrasound imaging works between 2 and 15 MHz, although even higher frequencies are used in some situations. Ultrasound imaging utilizes pulse echo method to incorporate a gray-scale tomographic picture of tissues dependent on the mechanical communication of short beats of high-recurrence sound waves and their returning echoes. Since, ultrasound pictures are captured progressively; they show the organs and plasma traveling through the veins. In ultrasound test, a transducer is placed directly on the skin. A thin layer of gel is spread over skin with objective that the ultrasound waves are diffused from probe through the gel into organs. The nature of the sound signal and the time it takes for the wave to experience from body give the information to convey an image.

Fig. 25.1 Ultrasound
imaging probe of eye [11]

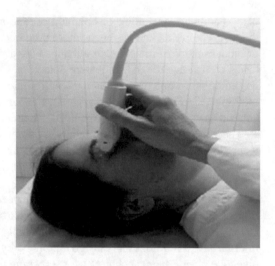

The special type of ultrasound called eye or orbit ultrasound that uses high frequency to measure and create detailed image of our eye. This test gives a considerably more point-by-point perspective of eye than a normal eye exam. This type of ultrasound is a quick and painless procedure. The ultrasound probe for eye imaging is shown in Fig. 25.1. This procedure supports in recognizing impairment within the eyes such as detachment of retina, tumours or neoplasms involving the eye and it helps in diagnosis of diseases.

Ultrasound is widely used to visualize abdominal tissues and organs, bone abnormalities, breast cancer, to see heartbeat, to visualise blood flow through blood vessels, to visualise the pregnancy, and as ophthalmic ultrasound.

25.2.2   Optical Coherence Tomography (OCT)

OCT is another innovation for accomplishment of high-resolution cross sectional imaging of inner tissues of human body. OCT is a non-invasive ocular imaging modality that uses near infrared light to create high-resolution pictures of flesh microstructure. OCT can give cross sectional pictures of organ texture on the micron scale (1–15 μm) in real time [12]. OCT imaging system is shown in Fig. 25.2. OCT functions as a sort of optical biopsy and is an extreme imaging advancement for helpful diagnostics in light of the way that not in any manner like customary histopathology which requires clearing of a tissue model and taking care of little examination [12]. OCT is practically equivalent to two imaging techniques: ultrasound imaging that exploits light rather than sound and Confocal Microscopy. Confocal microscopy is an optical imaging technique with high goals, moving toward 1 μm, constrained by the diffraction of light. Because of optical dispersion, the infiltration is extremely poor. In many cases, just a couple of hundred micrometres of profundity are achievable, which makes confocal microscopy less applicable

Fig. 25.2 Optical coherence
tomography imaging system

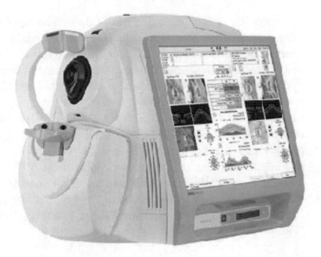

where critical imaging depth is required [13]. Ultrasound can give extraordinary imaging depth of up to around 10 cm, because of the low weakening of sound waves at frequencies commonly utilized in clinical applications. Higher frequencies of around 100 MHz have been utilized to accomplish resolution of micrometres, yet the solid constriction of sound waves at those frequencies in organic tissue restricts the profundity to around 15 mm [13]. Optical coherence tomography combined these two imaging methods. It is an optical imaging technique, with resolution constrained by the bandwidth of the light source utilized—ordinarily, around 1–15 μm—and an infiltration profundity of around 2–3 mm, better in transparent tissue. OCT imaging is used broadly for imaging the inner part of eye including fovea, blood vessels, macula, optic nerve and RNFL, and in inspecting the morphology and enumerating deviations in eye. OCT can also be used for choroidal thickness [14]. Currently, OCT is applicable for diagnosis of many diseases namely age-related macular degeneration, central serous chorioretinopathy, DR, and intraocular tumours.

25.2.3 Fundus Photography

Retinal Fundus Photography customs a fundus camera to acquire colour pictures of the interior part of eye (i.e. fundus), in order to record the event of scatters and screen their change after some time. A retinal fundus camera is a specialized low power microscope with connected camera intended to click photo inside eye, including the optic disc (OD), fovea, macula, retina, retinal veins, and back post.

The retina can be captured straightforwardly as the pupil is utilized as both a passage and departure for camera enlightening and imaging light beams. The person sits at the fundus camera with their button in a jaw rest and their brow beside the bar. An ophthalmic picture taker centres and adjusts the fundus camera. A glimmer fires as the photographic artist presses the screen discharge, making a fundus photo. Ophthalmologists utilize these retinal photos to pursue, analyse, and treat eye infections. The retina is imaged to record instances such as DR, glaucoma, cataract, age related macular degeneration, and retinal detachment.

Fundus camera's optical plan depends on circuitous ophthalmoscope. The optical plan of fundus cameras depends on the guideline of monocular indirect ophthalmoscopy [8, 9]. A fundus camera gives an upstanding, amplified perspective of the fundus. They are depicted by the point of view—the optical edge of acknowledgment of the focal point. A point of 30°, thought about the ordinary edge of view, makes a film picture 2.5 times overwhelming, and permits some change of this relationship through zoom focal points from 15°, which gives multiple times amplification. Wide edge fundus cameras catch pictures somewhere in the range of 45° and 140° and give proportionately less retinal magnification [15]. A thin edge camera has a point of perspective of 20° or less (Fig. 25.3).

25.2.4 Heidelberg Retinal Tomography (HRT)

HRT is a non-invasive diagnostic system, which uses confocal laser scanning microscopy to quantify precisely for exact perception and documentation of the inner part of eye, basic for the determination and administration of eye related diseases [9]. HRT is actually commercial name of confocal scanning laser ophthalmoscopy. The principle of confocality is shown in Fig. 25.4a. HRT innovation

Fig. 25.3 Non-mydriatic fundus camera

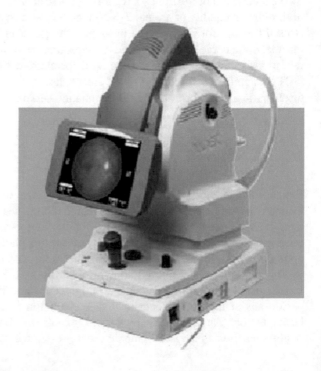

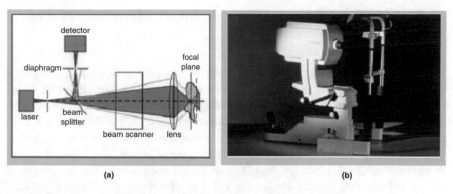

(a)   (b)

Fig. 25.4 (a) The principle of confocality (b) Heidelberg retinal tomography [16]

Table 25.1 Imaging modalities along with diagnostic features for the detection of various eye related diseases

Disease	Imaging technique	Features
Cataract	MRI, fundus photography, ophthalmoscope	Mean intensity, uniformity, standard deviation, entropy
Diabetic retinopathy	OCT, HRT, fundus photography	Microaneurysm, haemorrhages, hard exudates, cotton wools, abnormal new vessels
Glaucoma	OCT, HRT, fundus photography	Cup to disc ratio, neural retinal rim, parapapillary atrophy
Retinal detachment	Ultrasound, OCT, fundus photography, MRI	A thin constant hyperechoic line isolated from the wall of globe, RD looks like isolation of the neurosensory retinal wall from the retinal pigment epithelium Layer floating in the vitreous fluid
Age related Macular degeneration	OCT, fundus photography, fluorescein angiography	Large drusen, confluent drusen and pigment atrophy
Macular edema	OCT, HRT	Retinal thickness measurement

licenses exact, exceptionally reproducible documentation of the back fundus, alongside programming intended for longitudinal investigation of the optic nerve in glaucoma. The HRT uses a unique laser to take 3-dimensional photographs of the optic nerve and encompassing retina. This laser does not damage the eye, is centred on optic nerve and catches picture. The HRT takes pictures of more and more profound layers until the desired point has been achieved. Finally, the instrument takes every one of these photos of the layers and assembles them to shape a 3D picture of the whole optic nerve. HRT is utilised for detection of DR, glaucoma and macular edema.

Table 25.1 presents various imaging systems that can used for detection of each eye disease along with the diagnostic features to be examined.

25.3   DIP Based Techniques for Automated Diagnosis of Eye Diseases

Presently, automated detection and diagnosis of various eye diseases using digital image processing based techniques have acquired immense attention. DIP based diagnosis framework consists of various stages namely acquisition of eye image, pre-processing, segmentation of ROI, feature selection and classification of eye diseases. The block diagram of DIP based framework for automated detection of eye diseases is shown in Fig. 25.5. The images of eye are acquired as per requirement from the various imaging techniques such as ultrasound image for retinal detachment, fundus image for DR and glaucoma, OCT image macular degeneration. MRI and HRT image are widely used for detection of eye disease by ophthalmologist. MRI and HRT imaging are costlier than other imaging techniques. Hence, these imaging techniques are rare in practice in DIP based system for automated detection and diagnosis. Pre-processing is performed with the end goal to

Fig. 25.5 Block diagram of automated detection of eye diseases

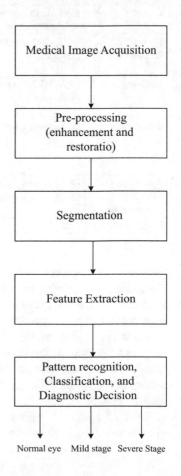

Medical Image Acquisition

Pre-processing (enhancement and restoratio)

Segmentation

Feature Extraction

Pattern recognition, Classification, and Diagnostic Decision

Normal eye   Mild stage   Severe Stage

boost the contrast and remove impulse noise of these pictures. Because these images are picked up from different imaging techniques under diverse circumstances, which may introduce salt and pepper noise and non-uniform illumination. The improvement is mandatory since collected images experience the negative effects of uneven illumination, poor contrast and noise. Due to the existence of noise in the retinal photograph, there are high chances of wrong detection of lesions. Hence, pre-processing is necessary for any detection system. After pre-processing, segmentation is performed in order to achieve region of interest from pre-processed image that contains important information about abnormalities. A variety of features is extracted from segmented image. These features are useful in training parameters of classification model. Artificial intelligence (AI), Pattern Recognition or Computer Vision domains are used for automated detection of diseases. The classification model namely Support Vector Machine (SVM), Artificial Neural Net (ANN), Radial Basis Function Neural Net (RBFNN) are widely used for grading and diagnose the eye diseases. Parameters of extracted features are utilised for training and testing purpose.

25.3.1 Diabetic Retinopathy

Diabetic retinopathy is a kind of eye condition that arises several years of diabetic mellitus. It harms the modest veins inside the retina, subsequently the veins ends up blocked, flawed and develop indiscriminately. DR is asymptomatic, it does not impede with vision until the point when it achieves propel arrange. The risk of completely loss of vision can be lessen by 50% with an prior therapy to avoid the improvement of DR [17, 18]. It generally influences the both eyes and it often has no early warning sign. DR is isolated into two phases to be specific Non-Proliferative Diabetic Retinopathy (NDPR) and Proliferative Diabetic Retinopathy (PDR). NDPR is early phase of DR. At this moment, the veins in the retina turn out to be thin and release retinal liquids prompting microaneurysm (MAs). There are variety of lesions appear in progress of DR. Microaneurysm are earliest sign of diabetic retinopathy, it shows up as little red dabs on retina shaped by expanding out of frail piece of veins [19–21]. Retinal haemorrhages are lesions which come into sight next to MAs, have larger size than MAs and it appears in case of blood leakage [22–24]. The leakage of fat and protein inside of retina is called as hard exudates [25]. Because of veins get swell and fleecy, white patches are called cotton wool spots. Abnormal new blood vessels appear in advance stage of diabetic retinopathy [26–28]. When blood vessels are completely blocked, in order to provide requisite oxygen to the retina, abnormal blood vessels grow, known as PDR [29, 30]. PDR is last phase of DR. In this phase, the vision of eye is completely lost. DR cannot be cured but its pervasiveness can be control by treatment. Hence, regular screening of eye plays very important role in early detection of DR.

There are three imaging techniques which could be used for DR detection namely OCT, HRT and fundus photography. Fundus photography is widely used

Fig. 25.6 Block diagram of
DR detection from fundus
image

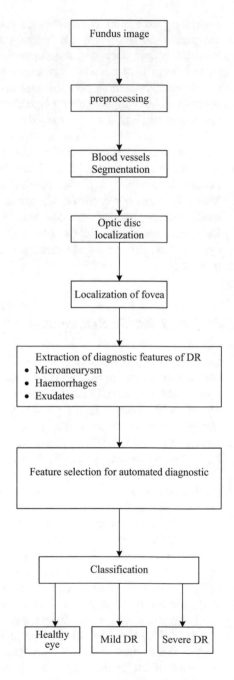

by ophthalmologist for DR detection. Digital fundus images are also used by
automated diabetic retinopathy detection system. The block diagram of automated
DR detection is depicted in Fig. 25.6. First, fundus images are taken with the help

of fundus camera. There are a few techniques proposed by specialists to distinguish DR utilizing DIP on retinal fundus pictures. Pre-processing of fundus picture is performed to enhance the differentiation of these pictures. The upgrade is vital since fundus pictures experience the undesirable effects of uneven enlightenment, poor contrast and clamour. Due to the occurrence of noise in the retinal images, there are high chances of wrong detection of lesions thus all approaches needed pre-processed image. Vascular structures, OD and fovea have to remove from fundus photograph because it causes false positive in detection system [31]. After removal of all these pathologies from fundus images, the diagnostic features namely microaneurysm (MA), haemorrhages, and exudates are remaining. Next, geometrical features namely area, perimeter, major axis length, minor length, and number of MA are extracted from the MA or haemorrhages. These geometrical features are used for training and testing of detection algorithm for classification of DR or non-DR images.

Rasta et al. [32] has proposed a comparative study of pre-processing techniques for illumination correction and histogram equalization diabetic retinopathy digital colour retinal images. They have implemented few illumination correction and contrast enhancement techniques and compared all techniques for best method for optimum image enhancement.

Hani et al. [33] proposed denoising approaches for digital retinal colour fundus photograph which suffered from difficulty of small and diverse contrast. Retinal vasculature was difficult to analyse with noise being present in the image. They have analysed several techniques such as Time Domain Constraint Estimator (TDCE), stationary wavelet transform, least square estimator, and minimum variance estimator for denoising the retinal fundus image. Based on achievement of numerous approaches, it was found that the TDCE shows better achievement in the PSNR upgrading. TDCE was able to maintain more specifics of the image and vascular texture around the macula. Huang et al. [34] proposed efficient method for modify histogram and enhance contrast of digital images. They used adaptive gamma correction with weighting distribution for contrast enhancement.

Thirilogasundari et al. [35] proposed fuzzy based approach for exclusion of impulse noise which occurred due to imperfection in taking images from imaging system, transmission system errors, and faulty memory units. The suggested approach was based on switching median filter, which comprises two phases namely detection phase and filtering phase. Neighbourhood mapping based algorithm detects corrupted pixels in detection phase and fuzzy membership function is utilised for filtering of corrupted pixels. The remaining pixels are retained as original pixels.

Junior and Welfer [36] has suggested an automated recognition of MAs and haemorrhages in colour fundus images. This technique comprised of five strategies: pre-processing, upgrade of low power structure, location of veins, removal of veins, and removal of fovea. Green channel and CLAHE were used for pre-processing. Boosting of low intensity has been accomplished with the support of alternating sequential filtering (ASF), H-minima and RMIN operator. ASF is nothing but sequential application of morphological opening and closing. Detection of blood vessels contains four steps. First, CLAHE image was subtracted form ASF with one iteration. After that, multiscale structuring element was applied for detection of linear structure. Then, reconstruction by dilation followed by RMIN operator was applied for blood vessel detection. Exclusion of vascular structure was executed by subtracting the detected blood vessels from improvement of low intensity texture image. For fovea detection, location of fovea centre was identified [37]. After that, dilation was applied with disc shape structuring element, with 25 pixels radius. MAs and haemorrhages were extracted after subtracting blood vessels and fovea from the pre-processed image.

Niemeijer et al. [38] proposed programmed recognition of microaneurysm (MAs) in fundus photographs. They compared five different detection techniques on same data. Gaussian mixture model for candidate extraction and logistic regression was used for classification in first method. The Waikato microaneurysm detector was used for detection of diabetic retinopathy, which performs top hat transform, and morphology operation in detection of vasculature is used in second method. In third method, it was assumed that microaneurysm could be exhibited with 2D, rotational-symmetric comprehensive Gaussian function. Pattern corresponding in wavelet domain is used to find feature extraction. In fourth method, Bayesian correlation filtering is used for candidate extraction. Thoroughgoing filter response for that specific abrasion was employed for classification. In fifth method, brightness rectification, gamma rectification and contrast enrichment were used for pre-processing. Original double ring filter and modified double ring filter were used for detection of microaneurysm. All these five diverse microaneurysm recognition procedures were tested on similar database.

Antal and Hajdu [39] has suggested an cooperative based scheme for MA detection. They suggested an ensemble-based scaffolding to improve the microaneurysm detection. The blends of pre-processing and competitor extractors were utilized in identification of microaneurysm. Correlation of pre-processing techniques for microaneurysm recognition has been displayed. Walter-Klein contrast enhancement, CLAHE, vascular structures exclusion and extrapolation illumination equalization and no pre-processing has been compared. They have compared different MAs candidate extraction methods and proposed a novel set of pre-processing and candidate extraction pair for MAs detection. MAs removal depends on their perceivability and spatial area. A versatile weighting approach for outfit based MAs location additionally exhibited. (This methodology allocates weights to the competitors in light of their difference and their spatial area).

Bae et al. [24] offered an investigation on haemorrhage recognition expending hybrid scheme in fundus images. Detection of haemorrhages from fundus images consists of different stages such as pre-processing and feature abstraction. The intent of pre-processing was to make the intensity of image undeviating and enhance the disparity between haemorrhages and ground. 3D Gaussian algorithm and Hue Saturation Value (HSV) illumination rectification has been applied to RGB images. For contrast enhancement, CLAHE has been applied on uniform image. After pre-processing, haemorrhages candidate extraction is done using rounded moulded pattern with normalized cross-correlation (NCC). Region growing segmentation has been performed candidate extraction by template matching because. Adaptive Seed Region Growing Segmentation (ASRGS) and Region Growing Segmentation Using The Local Threshold (RGSLT) has been performed for segmentation. Number of big haemorrhages and their area has been considered for calculating sensitivity.

Welikala et al. [30] modified line operator and dual classification for proliferative diabetic retinopathy. They described automated detection method for new vessels in coloured retinal images. Pre-processing of noisy retina images was achieved by selecting inverted green channel and applying median filter, CLAHE, shade correction and morphological top hat transform respectively on it. Vessel segmentation has been performed using standard line operator and modified line operator. After vascular detachment, straight vessel removal is performed for exclusion of normal blood vessels from new vasculature. Quantity of vascular pixels, quantity of vascular segment, quantity of vascular orientation and vascular density have been extracted as features of PDR. SVM classifier was employed for binary classification of novel vascular tree and non-novel vascular tree.

Hussain and Holambe [47] have proposed DR investigation utilizing machine learning that examinations fundus picture with fluctuating brightening field and field of view and creates seriousness review for DR utilizing machine learning. The lessening in quantity of features utilized for abrasion detection using Adaboost was the main objective of this paper. Classifier such as the GMM, KNN, SVM and Adaboost are investigated for classification of DR or non-DR. There were two major contributions of this paper. First significant commitment was recognizing of the best 30 features from the arrangement of 78 features for ordering brilliant and red abrasions. The second commitment was a novel two-advance various levelled parallel characterization technique that rejects the false positive in initial step, brilliant sores were delegated cotton fleece spots and hard exudates and second step, and dull sores were named MAs and haemorrhages. They have investigated verity of trait built classifier, for example, GMM, KNN, SVM, Adaboost and combinational classifiers, and select an ideal classifiers set that guarantees high specificity and affectability with low computational time. They have concluded that GMM was a favoured decision of classifier for identification of bright lesions and KNN was favoured decision for discovery of dark abrasions.

Michael [48] proposed advancement and approval of deep learning algorithm for discovery of DR in retinal fundus photos. The primary target was to apply deep learning figuring out how to make a calculation for computerized recognition of DR and diabetic macular edema in fundus photo. Deep learning was a group of computational strategies that enable a calculation to program itself by gaining from vast arrangement of models. Deep learning was exceptional kind of neural net that comprises four to ten layers roughly. It was enhanced for retinal picture, which were evaluated three to seven times for DR. The sensitivity and specificity of the calculation for discovery of referable DR, characterized as moderate and most severe DR, referable diabetic macular edema or both depend on the reference standard set by ophthalmologist board.

Wang et al. [40] have recommended an integrated methodology for localizing MA in fundus images through singular spectrum analysis (SSA). The aim of this approach was to design a reliable recognition of MAs for developing a DR detection scheme. First, Gaussian-filtering process was applied on feature objects for removing the dark objects. Feature extraction were first situated by applying a multi-layered dark object filtering process. Their cross-section profiles along various directions were prepared through SSA. The correlation coefficient between each prepared profile and a regular MA profile was estimated and utilized as a scale factor to alter the state of the applicant profile. This was to build the distinction in their profiles between MAs and non-MA objects. KNN classifier was utilised for separation of statistical features. MAs were classified precisely from the retinal background. The sensitivity and specificity shows that proposed system was robust clinically.

Seoud et al. [41] proposed red lesion such as MAs and haemorrhages detection using dynamic shape features for DR screening. They have extracted novel shape feature set known as dynamic shape features that do not need exact segmentation of the area to be classified. These features speak to the advancement of the shape during image flooding and permit to distinguish among sores and vessel portions. A number of steps such as pre-processing, optic disc removal, feature extraction were applied for detection of DR. pre-processing was achieved by illumination equalization, denoising method, adaptive contrast equalization, and colour normalization. They have used entropy based approach for OD centre localization. OD radius and position was estimated by multi-scale ring-shaped match filter. They utilized dynamic transform for candidate extraction.

Cao et al. [42] proposed a MA detection system utilising PCA and machine learning. They have analysed utilizing little patches extracted from images. Raw pixel intensities of separated patches served straightforwardly as contributions to the accompanying classifiers namely random forest (RF), ANN, and SVM. There were three sets of features were utilized for classification of MA and non-MA. Raw pixels were considered as first set of features. Hence, PCA was applied for dimension reducibility. They investigated the utilization of two systems PCA and RF for lessening input dimensionality. They explored the utilization of RF feature importance in lessening the dimension. They approved proposed technique on an alternate dataset retinopathy online challenge data set. The execution of the three classifiers and the example with various level of principal component were predictable on both data.

Zhou et al. [43] recently proposed deep multiple instance learning for automatic detection of DR in fundus photograph, which together takes features and classifiers from data and accomplishes a huge enhancement for identifying DR pictures and their inside sores. First of all, pre-processing of retinal image was accomplished by illumination equalization and contrast enhancement. Then image patches were extracted from pre-processed image. These patches were fed into CNN-based patch level classifier to access their DR probabilities and then global aggregation was utilized to make the classification of DR images. They also proposed an end-to-end multi scale scheme for better DR lesions detection. They tested the proposed system on Kaggle dataset.

Dashtbozorg et al. [44] proposed a novel and reliable retinal microaneurysm detection system using local convergence index. At pre-processing stage, Luminosity and contrast variability in the background were estimated and employed for normalizing image. Then, many preliminary MA candidates were extracted utilizing a gradient weighting method namely Gaussian derivative kernel and Gaussian kernel and an iterative thresholding approach. At later stage, a novel feature set was extracted based on local convergences index filters for intensity and shape descriptor for each candidate. As a final point, cooperative feature set was fed to hybrid sampling classifier to categorize the MAs and non-MAs candidate.

25.3.2 Glaucoma

Glaucoma is optic neuropathy, which consequences in dynamic harm to the optic nerve and vision misfortune. Glaucoma is portrayed by increment in the intraocular pressure interior of eyeball. This may affect optic nerve. The main problem with glaucoma, it has no symptoms, no pain, and vision stays normal in its early stages. It becomes noticeable when reached into advanced stage. Glaucoma becomes visible when the patient has lost already 70% of his/her vision. Hence, the regular screening of eye is necessary for glaucoma detection. Glaucoma can be delegated as primary/open angle glaucoma, angle-closure glaucoma, and typical pressure glaucoma. Primary angle glaucoma is most normal sort of glaucoma. In this kind of glaucoma, the seepage arrangement of the eye ends up deficient after some time. This wastefulness of seepage framework results in continuous increment of the weight inside the eye [45]. The harm is moderate and easy. The moderate preventing of the seepage waterways, bringing about increment in eyeball pressure, causes open-angle glaucoma. It has wide and open angle between the iris and cornea. It grows gradually and long lasting condition. Angle-closure glaucoma is less basic type of glaucoma. In this glaucoma, the waste edge of the eye is blocked. It very well may be dynamic slowly or showing up all of a sudden [46]. Physical wounds causes the secondary angle glaucoma. It can also be appear by eye variations from the norm, prescription and eye medical procedure. In ordinary strain glaucoma, the eye weight stays inside the range yet there is harm of optic nerve [46]. There are five tests for glaucoma identification. *Tonometry* computes the pressures inside the eye. During tonometry, eye drop is using to traumatize the eye. *Ophthalmoscopy* causes the specialist to look at the optic nerve for glaucoma harm. Eye drop is utilized to widen the understudy with the goal that specialist can see through the eye. *Perimetry* is pictorial arena test that creates the guide of finish arena of vision. This test causes specialist to choose whether vision is influenced by glaucoma. *Gonioscopy* decides if the point where iris encounters the cornea open or shut. *Pachymetry* is easy test to gauge the thickness of the cornea. It can help analyse, in light of the fact that corneal thickness can impact the eye weight perusing [47].

There are variety of affected parameters of eye due to glaucoma namely Cup To Disc Ratio (CDR), Neural Retinal Rim (NRR), cup-diameter, blood vessels in inferior, superior, nasal, temporal (ISNT) region, Peri-Papillary Atrophy (PPA) [48, 49]. A fundus photograph comprises veins, macula, and Optic Nerve Head (ONH). The ONH is the locale from which the nerve strands leave the eye. The ONH is the most brilliant bit in the fundus photograph can be sub isolated into optic disc and optic cup. A glaucoma-influenced eyeball may comprise decay and optic cup. The PPA is the diminishing of the retinal thickness nearby the optic nerve head locality [50, 51]. At the point when pressure inside eyeball develops, it causes compression at first glance on retina, which makes harm the retinal nerve filaments. This makes compression on ONH and the optic plate begins measuring. This measuring of optic disc consequences in the arrangement of optic cup. The proportions of optic cup concludes the damage of eye typically cup-to-disc ratio value 0.3 for the normal eye [52, 53]. NRR is the ring moulded configuration which is left after cup detaches from the disc [54]. The NRR of healthy disc follows the ISNT rule [55]. For healthy fundus images, it is known that the veins are mostly focused in the inferior and superior portion of the optic disc [46]. When glaucoma affects eye, the blood vessels shift towards nasal side of disc because shift occurs in ONH. This move causes diminish the veins in the inferior and superior area. The vascular area in ISNT is enumerated as proportion of addition of the zone of inferior side and area of superior side to the addition of zone of nasal side and temporal side [55]. The cup diameter is the perpendicular width of the cup. Glaucoma cannot be relieved however; its movement can be back off by early treatment. Henceforth, early recognition of glaucoma is imperative to keep the further harm of vision.

The block diagram of glaucoma detection is depicted in Fig. 25.7. Automated detection of glaucoma consists several phases as shown in block diagram. Firstly, fundus image is taken from eye centre or database, which may consist impulse noise. Green or red channel are used for segmentation purpose as per requirement. Since, fundus image suffers from impulse noise, poor contrast and uneven illumination hence pre-processing is needed. Next, ROI is extracted from pre-processed image. Then, features like as CDR, NRR, ISTN rule and ONH are extracted from ROI area. At last stage, ANN, SVM and KNN are applied for classification and grading of glaucoma.

Pruthi and Mukherjee [56] suggested a CAD system for an automated detection of glaucoma at an earlier stage uses of retinal colour fundus images. Glaucoma detection was achieved in three stages namely pre-processing, feature selection and classification. Pre-processing contained illumination correction, blood vessel removal and region of interest extraction. Green channel was used because it displays maximum disparity between the vascular tree and background. They used anisotropic diffusion filter for noise removal pre-processing. Greyscale image was used for vessel removal because it provided higher magnitude of contrast then segmentation and in painting of vessel tree was carried out. Otsu's thresholding, canny edge map was used for vessel removal. K-means clustering, multi Thresholding, active contour method, fuzzy C-means clustering, ANN, morphological operation were used for feature extraction. Artificial neuro fuzzy inference system (ANFIS), SVM, Back-propagation neural network was employed to classify standard and

Fig. 25.7 Block diagram of
glaucoma detection from
fundus image

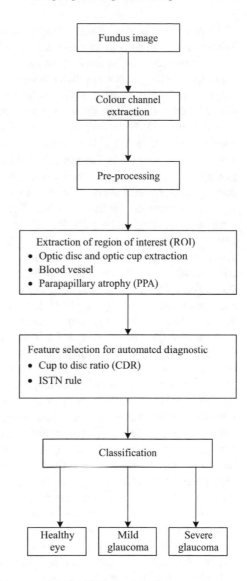

Fig. 25.7 Block diagram of glaucoma detection from fundus image

glaucoma instances. SVM classifier had given better results than ANFIS and Back propagation neural network.

Narasimhan and Vijayarekha [57] has proposed a productive automated framework for glaucoma location utilizing fundus picture. This framework comprised of three phases namely ROI, include extraction and arrangement organize. Green channel was utilized for extraction of optic disc and optic cup. In the wake of investigating the green channel of fundus picture, a square size of 360 × 360 pixels with the most splendid pixels as the inside point considered as ROI. K-mean clustering was assuming a critical job in highlight extraction to figure CDR. ISNT proportion was computed by assessing the territory of veins in ISNT locales.

Neighbourhood entropy thresholding system was utilized for identification of veins in OD locale. Arrangement was finished utilizing K-Nearest neighbour, SVM, and Bayes classifiers. The separation measure utilized in KNN classifier was Euclidean separation. Straight bit was utilized for preparing the information in SVM classifier. Bayes classifier, typical appropriation was utilized to fit the component base. SVM classifier gave best outcomes among three classifiers.

Bock et al. [58] proposed automated discovery of glaucoma identification from shading fundus pictures. Glaucoma risk index has been evaluated in three steps such as pre-processing, feature selection, and classification. Glaucoma specific pre-processing techniques contained Brightness rectification, vascular tree removal and optic nerve head normalization. Illumination correction was accomplished by universal correction techniques [59]. They have combined edge-based [60] and template-matching techniques for vessel removal. Optic nerve head normalization was achieved using circular Hough transform. Appearance-based dimension reduction technique and linear Principal Component Analysis (PCA) was employed for candidate extraction. Pixel intensity value, FFT coefficients and B-spline coefficients were calculated from pre-processed images after that PCA was applied for dimension lessening. A probabilistic two-stage SVM classification technique was used to extricate the glaucoma threat indicator.

Issac et al. [24] proposed a versatile threshold based image-processing procedure for enhance glaucoma identification and grouping. They have used red channel for optic disc segmentation and green channel for optic cup segmentation. They have suggested an adaptive threshold scheme for glaucoma detection, which was helpful for image taken from different sources. Optic disc and optic cup segmentation has been done using histogram smoothing in threshold selection, morphology operation, and calculating SD and mean of the Gaussian window. NRR acquired after by subtracting the cup from disc. The area was attained when the NRR image is multiply with the mask image the corresponding region. Blood vessels in ISNT region are extracted by multiplying the mask with the vascular trees extracted image. ANN and SVM have been used for classification. A verity of kernels of the SVM were used, in which radial basis function (RBF) kernel achieved best accuracy.

Cheng et al. [52] proposed a glaucoma screening technique utilizing super pixel classification which was constructed on cup and disc dissection. They have computed centre surround statistics (CSS) from super pixel and bring together them with histogram for optic disc and optic cup dissection. They used SLIC to aggregate nearby pixel into super pixels in fundus photographs. They have combined HIST and CSS for feature extraction of optic disc from the red channel. LIBSVM with linear kernel was utilised for the classification of optic disc. Super classification based method has also been proposed for cup segmentation which was similar to disc segmentation with minor modification. The combination of HIST and CSS was utilised for feature extraction of optic cup from green channel. LIBSVM with linear kernel employed for the grouping of optic cup and non-cup region. After obtaining the disc and cup, cup to disc was evaluated which they used for glaucoma screening.

Nayak et al. [61] has proposed an automated diagnosis of glaucoma using fundus photograph. Pre-processing, morphological operation, and thresholding were used for feature extraction. Red channel has been used for disc segmentation because optic disc was easily discriminated on red image. Green channel was utilised to distinguish the optic cup from the rest of the image. Morphology operation such as opening, closing, and thresholding operation were applied for optic disc and optic cup localization. Green channel, bottom-hat filtering, thresholding, and morphology closing and opening operation had extracted ONH shift. The area of vessels in the ISNT regions were the important feature for glaucoma detection which was extracting by calculating ratio of area of vascular tree in inferior and superior side to area of vascular tree in nasal and temporal side. Artificial neural network (ANN) classifier was used for classification of glaucoma and normal. Three layers feed forward network with sigmoid activation function was optimized by gradient descent algorithm.

Lu et al. [62] proposed a Parapapillary atrophy and optic disc region assessment (PANDORA) for evaluation of the disc and PPA in retinal colour fundus images. Applied Sobel edge operator on red channel of cropped picture, generating edge gap, performed pre-processing of optic disc. After edge gap produced, the recognition of blood veins was done by applying thresholding techniques on hue image. KNN was used for isolating the OD from the background. DLSFE was applied to estimate the OD boundary. Thresholding techniques, K-Nearest neighbour, and DLSFE were applied for optic disc segmentation. PPA detection was carried out in blue channel. PPA segmentation was done using modified Chan-Vase analysis, multi speed region growing, thresholding, and scanning filter. Three parameters namely dimension of OD, dimension of minor/major OD axis and dimension of PPA were evaluated. The area enclosed by ground estimate was counted pixel by pixel to quantify the dimension of each section.

Cheng et al. [63] proposed sparse dissimilarity constrained (SDC) coding for glaucoma screening. They introduced a novel SDC technique for CDR, which considered both dissimilarity constraint and sparse constraint using fundus images. They also proposed a new method to compute the dissimilarity between images. In this method, first they performed disc localization, segmentation and normalization. OD was segmented using self-assessed disc management method (SADM), which was combination of three approaches such as Active Shape Model (ASM) based method, super pixel classification method, and elliptical Hough transform method. The SADM method selects one of the result based on outputs of all individual methods. After segmentation of OD, disc normalization was performed. Morphological closing process was utilised for blood veins removal. Then uneven brightness correction within disc was achieved by linear mapping. They proposed surface fitting within disc to evaluate the difference between two disc images. The reconstruction coefficients from SDC were used to compute CDR from the testing disc. Result shows that suggested technique achieved much more accurate CDR assessment.

Khalil et al. [64] recently proposed a better detection of glaucoma from fundus photograph utilising textural features and hybrid structural. Since, an eyeball illness for the finding of glaucoma has neglected to recognize all glaucoma cases precisely. They introduced a reliable CAD system dependent on novel arrangement of hybrid structure and textural highlights. The framework enhances the decision making process in the wake of investigating an assortment of glaucoma conditions. It comprised of two fundamental modules Hybrid Structure Feature set (HSF) and Hybrid Texture Feature set (HTF). HSF module could successfully classify a sample utilizing SVM from various basic glaucoma condition and the HTF module investigations. The sample established on different texture, intensity based highlights, and again utilizing SVM settled on a choice.

Zahoor and Fraz [65] in 2017 presented fast optic disc segmentation in retina using polar transform. Optic disc removal from retinal pictures was the fundamental advancement in building up the indicative apparatus for early Glaucoma recognition. They have exhibited a hierarchal system for quick and exact OD segmentation and localization. Blood vessels and other pathologies were depicted and evacuated by utilizing mathematical morphological operation at pre-processing stage pursued by Circular Hough Transform (CHT) for OD confinement. Then, exact boundary of OD is acquired by computing ROI and apply a polar-based transform based adaptive threshold.

Zahoor and Fraz [66] in 2018 presented correction of their previous paper named as 'fast optic disc segmentation in retina using polar transform' which was mentioned earlier. Retinal image examination was considered a vital technique for early detection and diagnosis of glaucoma, which helped in preventing vision impairment. A variety of pre-processing stage occurred in glaucoma detection from retinal pictures incorporated the detection of OD, NRR, and OC segmentation; included calculation from the sectioned OD and OC. In previous paper, they presented only fast and robust OD disc segmentation from fundus image. The segmented OD was pre-processed to highlight the NRR and OC zone. ANN with 12 features were used for pixel characterization based OC removal. Later stage, decision-tree based random subspace ensemble classifier was utilized to classify the glaucoma and non-glaucoma.

25.3.3   Cataract

Cataract is an eye issue, which happens because of obfuscating of focal point in the eye. It is easy eye ailment and created when some of protein at focal point amassed together over an extensive stretch of time. This averts light going plainly through the perspective, causing loss of vision [67–69]. Cataracts are characterized into three kinds in view of the zone where it grows specifically normal cataract, cortical cataract, and sub-capsular cataract [70]. Normal cataract is most regular kind of cataract. It grows somewhere down in the focal zone of the focal point [71, 72]. It is typically finding in more established age individuals. Cortical cataract is because of the focal point cortex (external edge) ends up murky. It happens when variations in the water content in the encompasses of the focal point cause fissuring [73, 74]. Posterior sub capsular arises at the rear of the lens [75]. Individuals with

Fig. 25.8 Block diagram of
cataract detection

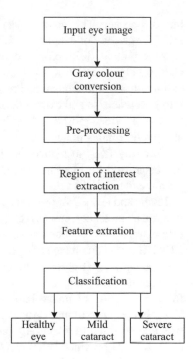

diabetes of those taking high measurements steroid solution have a more serious
danger of building up this kind of cataract [76].

The block diagram of cataract detection is shown in Fig. 25.8. Automatic cataract
detection system consists many stages as depicted in block diagram. Firstly, eye
image is taken from ophthalmoscope or fundus camera which may contains noise
and low contrast. Hence, pre-processing is performed on gray scale image. Next,
ROI is extracted from enhanced image. Then features like as uniformity, mean
intensity, variance, and entropy are extracted for training and testing of classifiers
named as SVM and ANN. Theses classifiers grades eye image into healthy eye,
mild, moderate and severe cataract.

Guo et al. [68] analysed a CAD healthcare system for cataract classification
and grading using fundus images. The system was composed of fundus image pre-
processing, feature extraction, and cataract classification and grading. Non-cataract
fundus image showed more clear organ details such as blood veins and fovea than
the cataract fundus image. For this reason, features associated to high frequency
components such as edges and sudden small peaks were used to select the feature
sensitive to different grading of cataract. Discrete Wavelet Transform (DWT) and
Discrete Cosine Transform (DCT) were used for feature extraction. Haar Wavelet
transform has been used because it could achieve high computation efficiency. PCA
was used for different grading of wavelet transformation coefficient data matrix.
Another process to estimate the high frequency component in the image was sketch

based approach. The feature selection was achieved by sketch method together with DCT for grading of cataract.

Zheng et al. [77] proposed cataract classification based on fundus images. Cataract classification was achieved in three stages such as pre-processing, feature extraction and classification. Pre-processing was achieved by resizing all images into the same size and extracting green channel from fundus images because green channel provided most details of image. 2-D Discrete Fourier Transform (DFT) was applied on fundus image and used the obtained spectrum as the feature of cataract followed by PCA to reduce the dimension. Linear Discriminant Analysis (LDA) has been used for classification into four classes. Ada-Boost algorithm is used to promote the classifier.

Kolhe and Guru [78] proposed automated cataract detection system using fundus images. Cataract detection system consisted four stages namely pre-processing, feature extraction, classification and grading. Pre-processing was completed utilising CLAHE on fundus image of eye. DWT and DCT were used to find the coefficients and later principal component analysis (PCA) was applied on these coefficients for feature extraction. Binary SVM classifier was applied on extracted features for classification of image into two classes i.e. cataract and non-cataract. Multi-Class Fisher Discriminant Analysis (MDA) was used for grading. MDA algorithm was implemented to grade only on cataract images into mild, moderate and severe classes. SVM provided better results than MDA algorithm.

Zhang et al. [79] investigated the performance and efficiency of deep CNN to detect and grade cataract automatically. Cataract classification and grading has been achieved in two steps namely pre-processing and, feature extraction and classification. They have combined the feature selection and classification in one-step to reduce computation burden, which made cataract grading more efficient. The first step of pre-processing was resizing all images taken from different sources and applied illumination correction on resized images. Deep Convolutional Neural Network (DCNN) has been applied for feature extraction and classification of cataract. DCNN is a weight sharing network structure. It is similar to NN, which reduced the complication of model, and reduced the number of weight. DCNN was more useful for multidimensional input; the image was directly used as input, which avoided the complex feature extraction. CNN was specially designed as multi-layer perceptron for recognizing photographs. In this paper, eight layers were used, initial five were convolutional layers and remaining three were fully connected layers. The output of the last layer was fed to a four-way softmax that produced four class labels. Using max pooling, each feature map was sub sampled in the pooling layer.

Pathak and Kumar [80] proposed a cataract detection algorithm using diagnostic opinion based parameter thresholding for telemedicine application. They developed an inexpensive, convenient and robust algorithm, which conjugate with proper gadget, had the capacity to analyse the existence of cataract from the simple image of eyeball. Texture features namely uniformity, intensity and SD were extracted for cataract screening of eye. The extracted features were mapped with ophthalmologist opinion to define the threshold for screening system, later they tested the system on real subjects in eye clinics. Lastly, they had suggested a tele-ophthalmology model using proposed system, which confirmed the telemedicine application of proposed system.

Zisimopoulos et al. [81] analysed that surgical simulation can be utilised to train detection and classification of ANN. Computer aided interventions intend to expand the adequacy, accuracy and repeatability of methods to enhance the surgical results. The presence and movement of surgical devices was considered a key data contribution for CAI careful stage acknowledgment algorithms. Vision-based instrument detection and recognition approaches were considered an alluring arrangement which was exploited for incredible deep learning paradigm which was quickly advancing image recognition and classification. They have used surgical simulation to train tool detection and segmentation based CNN and generative adversarial network. A financially accessible test system was utilized to make a simulated cataract dataset for training models before performing transfer learning on genuine surgical data. They declared it as their first effort to train deep learning models for surgical device detection on simulated data while exhibiting promising outcomes to sum up on genuine information.

Caixinha et al. [82] presented in-vivo automatic nuclear cataract detection and classification in an animal model by ultrasounds. They have proposed ultrasound based technique for early detection of nuclear cataract and grading using machine learning. Total twenty-seven features were extracted in time and frequency domain to train SVM, Bayes classifier, and random forest classifier. Rats were used to train animal model for nuclear cataract. The stiffness of the nucleus of the cortex region was objectively measured on some of rats using Nanotest. Velocity, attenuation and frequency downshift fundamentally expanded with cataract formation. The SVM classifier demonstrated the higher performance for the automatic classification of cataract.

25.3.4 Retinal Detachment

Retinal Detachment (RD) is a visual irregularity in which retina gets disengaged from the choroidal layer underneath it. Separation limits the sustenance gave to the retina and subsequently may prompt the visual impairment. Myopia, cataract medical procedure, diabetes and injury could cause RD in eyeball. Contingent on the film of the withdrew visual globe, detachment are three sorts: RD, choroid detachment and hyaloids detachment. Based on the causes, RD can be additionally arranged into rhegmatogenous, tractional and exudative [83]. Rhegmatogenous is the most well-known type and it happens because of partial blindness. Tractional retinal separation happens because of compression of scratch organs on retina's surface, making retina pull away. Exudative retinal connection is caused because of liquids, plasma or tumour behind retina [84]. Before the fame of ultrasound based analysis, eye doctors used to assess the retina by investigating the eye utilizing an ophthalmoscope, which is yet a priceless instrument in the determination of retinal separation. Different biomedical imaging modalities, for example, OCT, MRI, shading fundus photography and ultrasound imaging are utilized for examination of eye to have better determination of diseases. OCT can give high goals imaging of retina and utilized generally for the recognition of RD. OCT pictures can get influenced because of dispersing of light going through the fringe some portion of the crystalline focal point [85], OCT supplies are over the top expensive. Along these lines, MRI has restricted job in the assessment of the vitreous, retina and choroid [86]. In addition, being speediest, most straightforward, reasonable, bedside accessible and safe, ultrasound imaging can be performed regardless of whether the vitreous is not clear. As retina is behind vitreous liquid, ultrasound imaging is the most reasonable methodology for the RD diagnosis [87, 88]. Ultrasound pictures are commonly noisy which presents challenges in identifying the correct position and seriousness of the RD. Precision of RD recognition is restricted by nature of the visual ultrasound picture, perception error and absence of accessibility of restorative radiologist. In this way, automated detection of RD alongside its exact area and other clinical parameters can be exceptionally helpful in making primer symptomatic ends and choosing conceivable restorative intercessions.

25.3.5   Diabetic Macular Edema (DME)

Diabetic Macular Edema is one of the most complicated and irreversible eye diseases which may lead to permanent blindness and is growing exponentially worldwide. Macular edema (ME) is usual cause of blindness in persons with DR, retinal vein occlusion, and uveitis [89]. If detected and treatment started at an early stage, it will prevent severe vision loss [10]. Increase in retinal thickness with or without exudates and presence of cystoids with or without sub retinal fluid are the basic characteristics of DME. Maculae edema in diabetic patients are two types namely ME and clinically significant ME. ME is frequently characterized by retinal thickening or the nearness of hard exudates inside one disc diameter measurement of the focal point of the macula. To portray the seriousness of macular edema, the term clinically huge macular edema is utilized. ME is clinically significant if any of the below conditions are met [90]

1. Retinal thickness is lesser than or equal to 500 mm of the centre of macula
2. Hard exudates is lesser than or equal to 500 mm of the centre of macula whenever related with thickening of contiguous retina
3. Zonal thickening of retina within one disc diameter of macula centre up to the area of one disk size

DME is grouped into focal or diffuse, based on spillage pattern. In focal DME, discrete purposes of retinal hyper fluorescence are available on the FA because of central spillage of microaneurysm, the reason for retinal thickening. Generally, these microaneurysms are enclosed by round exudates. The variation of these forms is the multifocal macular edema, which at times is mistaken for diffuse macular edema. This form appears under fluorescein angiography as different foci of leakage due to presence of multiple foci of microaneurysm. The executives of DME spillage because of the presence of different foci of microaneurysms. In diffuse DME, there are regions of diffuse spillage on the FA due to intra retinal spillage from enlarged retinal slender bed and additionally Intra Retinal Microvascular Abnormalities (IRMA) as well as from arterioles and venules without foci of spilling microaneurysm. Cystoid Diabetic Macular Edema (CDME) results from the generalized breakdown of the internal blood retinal boundary with liquid aggregation in the external plexiform layer [90]. OCT is widely used for detection of ME. OCT depends on optical reflectivity and can picture retinal thickness and structure delivering cross-sectional and three-dimensional pictures of the focal retina. It is already widely utilized in light of the fact that it gives objective and quantitative appraisal of macular edema not at all like the subjectivity of fundus bio microscopic evaluation, which is routinely utilized by ophthalmologists rather than photography. OCT is likewise utilized for quantitative follow up of the impacts of treatment of CSMO [91].

25.4 Research Challenges in Automated Detection of Eye Diseases

From the literature survey of the research work done in the field of medical imaging and automated detection of digital image processing based various eye diseases, it is evident that the use of computer-aided diagnostic system and artificial intelligence are equally important in detection of eye diseases such as cataract, glaucoma and DR. From the presented review, it is clear that several machine-learning techniques have been explored. Since the requirements of machine learning are different as compared to the other conventional applications, hence special research efforts are required in this area. Fundamentally, there are three stages in detection of eye disease: pre-processing, feature selection and classification or grading of disease. Several pre-processing techniques have been proposed in previous years. We can improve the pre-processing by acquiring the image carefully, and combine the application of AI at suitable fundamental steps.

25.4.1 Research Challenges in Detection of DR

In detection of PDR, occurrence of false positive due to visibility of vascular tree from the layer underneath the retina (choroid) and another cause of false response are dilated capillaries known as intra retinal micro vascular irregularities, which are challenging to distinguish from new vascular tree [30]. Some cases of DR are misclassified due to presence of more DR specific abrasions such as exudates and cotton wools and Large abrasions are always not segmented or detection rate is low

[6, 32]. Semi-supervised learning and active learning into our deep MIL method are used to further accomplish the precise separation of DR abrasions and detection of diabetic retinopathy could be improved by utilizing different pre-processing techniques such as optic disc localization, vessel segmentation and fuzzy CHT [19, 20]. Feature extraction play an important role in detection of diabetic retinopathy. The system could be extended in order to get more details on DR classifications such as healthy eye, mild NDPR, moderate NDPR, severe NDPR and PDR cases based on retinopathy sign [20, 92].

25.4.2   Research Challenges in Detection of Glaucoma

The usual problem in glaucoma detection is the precise localization of OD, which can be affected due to occurrence of PPA. In some cases, CDR < 0.3 is diagnosed due to occurrence of PPA. We can develop an algorithm for detection of PPA [46, 62]. There is problem in glaucoma detection when cup size is too small and too large and presence of some other pathologies affects the glaucoma detection [52, 56]. There is trade-off between sensitivity and specificity. It is difficult to get the highest sensitivity at highest specificity. Detection can be improved by extracting some other features from the fundus images and use another learning algorithm such as ANN, RBFNN and different kernels for SVM classifier [57, 58].

25.4.3   Research Challenges in Detection of Cataract

Most of the research is focused on nuclear cataract and cortical cataract. It can be extended to detect Posterior sub capsular and mixed morphology [76]. Childhood cataract detection is a major challenge. Some detection techniques based on few features and less number of training and testing samples. Hence, these systems are less robust [70]. Cataract detection can be improved by taking more diverse optical image and extract more features of cataract from images [93]. Artificial intelligence technique also helps in automated detection of eye disease. SVM classifier with different kernel might improve the system. Artificial intelligence algorithm such as ANN, RBF ANN, fuzzy inference system, KNN, Bayesian classifier might improve the detection of eye disease [68, 94].

25.5   Chapter Summary

This chapter presented a detailed review of automated detection of eye related diseases through digital image processing. In first section, statistical status of various eye diseases namely cataract, glaucoma, age related macular degeneration,

DR, retinal detachment, and macular edema around the world and India were depicted. It highlighted motivation and need of automated system in detection and diagnosis of eye related diseases. In second section, various eye diseases and their corresponding detection and diagnosis techniques were presented. A brief introduction of imaging techniques for eye diseases was also discussed. Section 25.3 contained broad framework of automated detection system of eye related diseases using DIP. Diabetic retinopathy, glaucoma and cataract were discussed in depth, in subsequent sections. A brief introduction of retinal detachment and macular edema were also discussed in this chapter. Current research gap in detection of ocular diseases through digital image processing was compiled in the last section. We can improve detection by choosing more suitable and extract more features from the fundus eye images. Different feature selection techniques fuzzy K-mean clustering, KNN and GMM might helpful for better detection of DR, glaucoma and cataract. Detection system can also be improved by finding other retinopathy signs, such as exudates, haemorrhages, cotton wool spot, venous bending and abnormal blood vessels. In case of glaucoma, other sign like as NRR, PPA and ONH might improve the detection algorithm. In case of cataract, texture based feature and geometric based feature can improve the detection algorithm. At classification stage, the detection algorithm can improve by acquired more data from different sources for robust training and testing of classifiers. Classification can also be improved using RBF kernel SVM, RBFNN, artificial neuro fuzzy inference system, ANN, decision tree and random forest classifiers for grading of eye image into healthy, mild, moderate and severe diseases.

References

1. R. R. A. Bourne et al., "Magnitude, temporal trends, and projections of the global prevalence of blindness and distance and near vision impairment: a systematic review and meta-analysis," Lancet Glob. Heal., vol. 5, no. 9, pp. e888–e897, 2017.
2. T. R. Fricke et al., "Global Prevalence of Presbyopia and Vision Impairment from Uncorrected Presbyopia: Systematic Review, Meta-analysis, and Modelling," Ophthalmology, vol. 125, no. 10, pp. 1492–1499, 2018.
3. T. Vos et al., "Global, regional, and national incidence, prevalence, and years lived with disability for 310 diseases and injuries, 1990–2015: a systematic analysis for the Global Burden of Disease Study 2015," Lancet, vol. 388, no. 10053, pp. 1545–1602, 2016.
4. T. Vos et al., "Global, regional, and national incidence, prevalence, and years lived with disability for 301 acute and chronic diseases and injuries in 188 countries, 1990–2013: a systematic analysis for the Global Burden of Disease Study 2013," Lancet, vol. 386, no. 9995, pp. 743–800, 2015.
5. R. D. Jager, W. F. Mieler, and J. W. Miller, "Age-Related Macular Degeneration," N. Engl. J. Med., vol. 358, no. 24, pp. 2606–2617, 2008.
6. S. B. J. and D. Welfer2 and Programa, "Automatic Detection of Microaneurysms and Haemorrhages in Color Eye Fundus Images," Int. J. Comput. Sci. Inf. Technol., vol. 5, no. 5, pp. 21–37, 2013.

7. D. Mitry, D. G. Charteris, B. W. Fleck, H. Campbell, and J. Singh, "The epidemiology of rhegmatogenous retinal detachment: Geographical variation and clinical associations," *Br. J. Ophthalmol.*, vol. 94, no. 6, pp. 678–684, 2010.
8. R. Acheson, "Retinal detachment.," *Ir. Med. J.*, vol. 84, no. 2, pp. 45–46, 1991.
9. A. Mistlberger, J. M. Liebmann, D. S. Greenfield, and M. E. Pons, "Heidelberg Retina Tomography and Optical Coherence Tomography in Normal, Ocular- hypertensive, and Glaucomatous Eyes," pp. 2027–2032.
10. R. Klein, M. D. Knudtson, K. E. Lee, R. Gangnon, and B. E. K. Klein, "The Wisconsin Epidemiologic Study of Diabetic Retinopathy XXIII: The Twenty-five-Year Incidence of Macular Edema in Persons with Type 1 Diabetes," *OPHTHA*, vol. 116, no. 3, pp. 497–503, 2008.
11. M. De La Hoz Polo, A. Torramilans Lluís, O. Pozuelo Segura, A. Anguera Bosque, C. Esmerado Appiani, and J. M. Caminal Mitjana, "Ocular ultrasonography focused on the posterior eye segment: what radiologists should know," *Insights Imaging*, vol. 7, no. 3, pp. 351–364, 2016.
12. J. G. Fujimoto, "Optical coherence tomography," vol. 2147, no. 01, pp. 1099–1111, 2001.
13. P. Informatik, M. Author, L. D. Advisor, Y. Z. Medizingruppe, and I. Fakult, "Optical Coherence Tomography," 2011.
14. C. E. Ehrhart, "Delivering Tomorrow Logistics 2050 A Scenario Study," vol. 24, no. 3, p. 184, 2012.
15. N. Fundus, "Monochromatic Ophthalmoscopy The Normal Fundus," 2015.
16. C. Alexandrescu *et al.*, "Confocal scanning laser ophthalmoscopy in glaucoma diagnosis and management," vol. 3, no. 3, pp. 229–234, 2010.
17. P. Adarsh and D. Jeyakumari, "A Novel Method for Micro Aneurysm Detection and Diabetic Retinopathy Diagnosis," *Int. J. Comput. Appl.*, pp. 42–46, 2013.
18. B. Zhang, X. Wu, J. You, Q. Li, and F. Karray, "Detection of microaneurysms using multi-scale correlation coefficients," *Pattern Recognit.*, vol. 43, no. 6, pp. 2237–2248, 2010.
19. K. M. Adal, D. Sidibé, S. Ali, E. Chaum, T. P. Karnowski, and F. Mériaudeau, "Automated detection of microaneurysms using scale-adapted blob analysis and semi-supervised learning," *Comput. Methods Programs Biomed.*, vol. 114, no. 1, pp. 1–10, 2014.
20. S. S. Rahim, V. Palade, J. Shuttleworth, and C. Jayne, "Automatic Screening and Classification of Diabetic Retinopathy Fundus Images," *Commun. Comput. Inf. Sci.*, vol. 459 CCIS, pp. 113–122, 2014.
21. S. S. Rahim, V. Palade, C. Jayne, A. Holzinger, and J. Shuttleworth, "Detection of diabetic retinopathy and maculopathy in eye fundus images using fuzzy image processing," *Lect. Notes Comput. Sci. (including Subser. Lect. Notes Artif. Intell. Lect. Notes Bioinformatics)*, vol. 9250, 2015.
22. R. Inbarathi and R. Karthikeyan, "Detection of Retinal Hemorrhage in Fundus Images by Classifying the Splat Features Using SVM," *2014 Int. Conf. Innov. Eng. Technol.*, vol. 3, no. 3, pp. 1979–1986, 2014.
23. P. Jitpakdee, P. Aimmanee, and B. Uyyanonvara, "A survey on hemorrhage detection in diabetic retinopathy retinal images," *2012 9th Int. Conf. Electr. Eng. Comput. Telecommun. Inf. Technol. ECTI-CON 2012*, pp. 12–15, 2012.
24. J. P. Bae, K. G. Kim, H. C. Kang, C. B. Jeong, K. H. Park, and J. M. Hwang, "A study on hemorrhage detection using hybrid method in fundus images," *J. Digit. Imaging*, vol. 24, no. 3, pp. 394–404, 2011.
25. P. N. N. Gaikwad and P. P. R. Badadapure, "Image Processing Technique for Hard Exudates Detection for diagnosis of Diabetic Retinopathy," *Int. J. Recent Innov. Trends Comput. Commun.*, vol. 3, no. 4, pp. 4–7, 2015.
26. E. Ricci and R. Perfetti, "Retinal blood vessel segmentation using line operators and support vector classification," *IEEE Trans. Med. Imaging*, vol. 26, no. 10, pp. 1357–1365, 2007.
27. K. BahadarKhan, A. A. Khaliq, and M. Shahid, "A morphological hessian based approach for retinal blood vessels segmentation and denoising using region based otsu thresholding," *PLoS One*, vol. 11, no. 7, pp. 1–19, 2016.

28. M. Kaur and R. Talwar, "Automatic Extraction of Blood Vessel and Eye Retinopathy Detection," vol. 2, no. 4, pp. 57–61, 2015.
29. S. S. Rahim, C. Jayne, V. Palade, and J. Shuttleworth, "Automatic detection of microaneurysms in colour fundus images for diabetic retinopathy screening," *Neural Comput. Appl.*, vol. 27, no. 5, pp. 1149–1164, 2016.
30. R. A. Welikala *et al.*, "Automated detection of proliferative diabetic retinopathy using a modified line operator and dual classification," *Comput. Methods Programs Biomed.*, vol. 114, no. 3, pp. 247–261, 2014.
31. B. Kumar, Shailesh and Kumar, "Diabetic Retinopathy Detection by Extracting Area and Number of Microaneurysm from Colour Fundus Image," *2018 5th Int. Conf. Signal Process. Integr. Networks*, pp. 359–364, 2018.
32. S. H. Rasta, M. E. Partovi, H. Seyedarabi, and A. Javadzadeh, "A comparative study on preprocessing techniques in diabetic retinopathy retinal images: illumination correction and contrast enhancement," *J Med Signals Sens*, vol. 5, no. 1, pp. 40–48, 2015.
33. A. F. M. Hani, T. A. Soomro, I. Faye, N. Kamel, and N. Yahya, "Denoising methods for retinal fundus images," *2014 5th Int. Conf. Intell. Adv. Syst. Technol. Converg. Sustain. Futur. ICIAS 2014 - Proc.*, no. 2, 2014.
34. S. C. Huang, F. C. Cheng, and Y. S. Chiu, "Efficient contrast enhancement using adaptive gamma correction with weighting distribution," *IEEE Trans. Image Process.*, vol. 22, no. 3, pp. 1032–1041, 2013.
35. V. Thirilogasundari, V. S. Babu, and S. A. Janet, "Fuzzy based salt and pepper noise removal using adaptive switching median filter," *Procedia Eng.*, vol. 38, pp. 2858–2865, 2012.
36. segio B. Junior and D. Welfer, "Automatic Detection of Microaneurysms Ang Haemorrhages in Color Eye Fundus Images," *Southeast Asian J Trop Med Public Heal.*, vol. 34, no. 4, pp. 751–757, 2003.
37. D. Welfer, J. Scharcanski, and D. R. Marinho, "Fovea center detection based on the retina anatomy and mathematical morphology," *Comput. Methods Programs Biomed.*, vol. 104, no. 3, pp. 397–409, 2011.
38. M. Niemeijer, M. D. Abràmoff, and B. van Ginneken, "Fast detection of the optic disc and fovea in color fundus photographs," *Medical Image Analysis*, vol. 13, no. 6. pp. 859–870, 2009.
39. B. Antal and A. Hajdu, "An Ensemble-Based System for Microaneurysm Detection and Diabetic Retinopathy Gradin," *IEEE Trans. Biomed. Eng.*, vol. 5, no. 1, pp. 70–77, 2012.
40. W. S. *et al.*, "Localizing Microaneurysms in Fundus Images Through Singular Spectrum Analysis," *IEEE Trans. Biomed. Eng.*, vol. 64, no. 5, pp. 990–1002, 2017.
41. L. Seoud, T. Hurtut, J. Chelbi, F. Cheriet, and J. M. P. Langlois, "Red Lesion Detection Using Dynamic Shape Features for Diabetic Retinopathy Screening," *IEEE Trans. Med. Imaging*, vol. 35, no. 4, pp. 1116–1126, 2016.
42. W. Cao, N. Czarnek, J. Shan, and L. Li, "Microaneurysm detection using principal component analysis and machine learning methods," *IEEE Trans. Nanobioscience*, vol. 17, no. 3, pp. 191–198, 2018.
43. L. Zhou, Y. Zhao, J. Yang, Q. Yu, and X. Xu, "Deep multiple instance learning for automatic detection of diabetic retinopathy in retinal images," *IET Image Process.*, vol. 12, no. 4, pp. 563–571, 2018.
44. B. Dashtbozorg, J. Zhang, F. Huang, and B. M. T. H. Romeny, "Retinal Microaneurysms Detection Using Local Convergence Index Features," *IEEE Trans. Image Process.*, vol. 27, no. 7, pp. 3300–3315, 2018.
45. R. N. Weinreb, T. Aung, and F. A. Medeiros, "The Pathophysiology and Treatment of Glaucoma," *Jama*, vol. 311, no. 18, p. 1901, 2014.
46. A. Issac, M. Partha Sarathi, and M. K. Dutta, "An adaptive threshold based image processing technique for improved glaucoma detection and classification," *Comput. Methods Programs Biomed.*, vol. 122, no. 2, pp. 229–244, 2015.

47. S. A. Hussain and A. N. Holambe, "Automated Detection and Classification of Glaucoma from Eye Fundus Images: A Survey," *Int. J. Comput. Sci. Inf. Technol.*, vol. 6, no. 2, pp. 1217–1224, 2015.
48. M. D. Michael, "Optic disc size, an important consideration in the glaucoma evaluation," *Clin. Eye Vis. Care*, vol. 11, no. 2, pp. 59–62, 1999.
49. J. B. Jonas, "Glaucomatous Parapapillary Atrophy," 2015.
50. W. M. Budde and J. B. Jonas, "Influence of cilioretinal arteries on neuroretinal rim and parapapillary atrophy in glaucoma," *Investig. Ophthalmol. Vis. Sci.*, vol. 44, no. 1, pp. 170–174, 2003.
51. M. Seong *et al.*, "Macular and peripapillary retinal nerve fiber layer measurements by spectral domain optical coherence tomography in normal-tension glaucoma," *Investig. Ophthalmol. Vis. Sci.*, vol. 51, no. 3, pp. 1446–1452, 2010.
52. J. Cheng *et al.*, "Superpixel Classification Based Optic Disc and Optic Cup Segmentation for Glaucoma Screening," *Lect. Notes Comput. Sci. (including Subser. Lect. Notes Artif. Intell. Lect. Notes Bioinformatics)*, vol. 8151 LNCS, no. PART 3, pp. 421–428, 2013.
53. Y. For, E. Of, and M. Using, "a N E Fficient D Ecision S Upport S Ystem for D Etection of G Laucoma in F Undus I Mages Using," vol. 2, no. 1, pp. 227–240, 2012.
54. J. B. Li and M. Y. Li, "Neuroretinal rim area in early glaucoma.," *Chin. Med. J. (Engl).*, vol. 106, no. 3, pp. 191–195, 1993.
55. N. Harizman *et al.*, "The ISNT Rule and Differentiation of Normal From Glaucomatous Eyes," *Arch Ophthalmol*, vol. 124, pp. 1579–1583, 2006.
56. J. Pruthi and S. Mukherjee, "Computer Based Early Diagnosis of Glaucoma in Biomedical Data Using Image Processing and Automated Early Nerve Fiber Layer Defects Detection using Feature Extraction in Retinal Colored Stereo Fundus Images," vol. 4, no. 4, pp. 1822–1828, 2013.
57. K. Narasimhan and K. Vijayarekha, "An efficient automated system for glaucoma detection using fundus image," *J. Theor. Appl. Inf. Technol.*, vol. 33, no. 1, pp. 104–110, 2011.
58. R. Bock, J. Meier, L. G. Nyúl, J. Hornegger, and G. Michelson, "Glaucoma risk index: Automated glaucoma detection from color fundus images," *Med. Image Anal.*, vol. 14, no. 3, pp. 471–481, 2010.
59. A. A. A. Youssif, A. Z. Ghalwash, and A. S. Ghoneim, "Comparative Study of Contrast Enhancement and Illumination Equalization Methods for Retinal Vasculature Segmentation," *Cairo Int. Biomed. Eng. Conf.*, no. DECEMBER, p. 5, 2006.
60. B. Al-Diri, A. Hunter, and D. Steel, "An Active Contour Model for Segmenting and Measuring Retinal Vessels," *IEEE Trans. Med. Imaging*, vol. 28, no. 9, pp. 1488–1497, 2009.
61. J. Nayak, R. Acharya U., P. S. Bhat, N. Shetty, and T. C. Lim, "Automated diagnosis of glaucoma using digital fundus images," *J. Med. Syst.*, vol. 33, no. 5, pp. 337–346, 2009.
62. C. K. Lu, T. B. Tang, A. Laude, B. Dhillon, and A. F. Murray, "Parapapillary atrophy and optic disc region assessment (PANDORA): retinal imaging tool for assessment of the optic disc and parapapillary atrophy," *J. Biomed. Opt.*, vol. 17, no. 10, p. 106010, 2012.
63. J. Cheng, F. Yin, D. W. K. Wong, D. Tao, and J. Liu, "Sparse dissimilarity-constrained coding for glaucoma screening," *IEEE Trans. Biomed. Eng.*, vol. 62, no. 5, pp. 1395–1403, 2015.
64. T. Khalil, M. U. Akram, H. Raja, A. Jameel, and I. Basit, "Detection of Glaucoma Using Cup to Disc Ratio from Spectral Domain Optical Coherence Tomography Images," *IEEE Access*, vol. 6, pp. 4560–4576, 2018.
65. M. N. Zahoor and M. M. Fraz, "Fast optic disc segmentation in retinal images using polar transform," *Commun. Comput. Inf. Sci.*, vol. 723, pp. 38–49, 2017.
66. M. N. Zahoor and M. M. Fraz, "A correction to the article fast optic disc segmentation in retina using polar transform," *IEEE Access*, vol. 6, pp. 4845–4849, 2018.
67. R. U. Acharya, W. Yu, K. Zhu, J. Nayak, T. C. Lim, and J. Y. Chan, "Identification of cataract and post-cataract surgery optical images using artificial intelligence techniques," *J. Med. Syst.*, vol. 34, no. 4, pp. 619–628, 2010.

68. L. Guo, J. J. Yang, L. Peng, J. Li, and Q. Liang, "A computer-aided healthcare system for cataract classification and grading based on fundus image analysis," *Comput. Ind.*, vol. 69, no. May, pp. 72–80, 2015.
69. H. Li *et al.*, "Lens image registration for cataract detection," *Proc. 2011 6th IEEE Conf. Ind. Electron. Appl. ICIEA 2011*, pp. 132–135, 2011.
70. H. Shen, H. Hao, L. Wei, and Z. Wang, "An Image Based Classification Method for Cataract," *2008 Int. Symp. Comput. Sci. Comput. Technol.*, pp. 583–586, 2008.
71. tien yin wong li Huiqi, Lim, J. H., paul mitchell, ava grace tan, jie jin wang, "A Computer-Aided Diagnostic System of Neuclear Cataract.".
72. R. Srivastava *et al.*, "Automatic nuclear cataract grading using image gradients," *J. Med. Imaging*, vol. 1, no. 1, 2014.
73. T. Kuroda, T. Fujikado, N. Maeda, T. Oshika, Y. Hirohara, and T. Mihashi, "Wavefront analysis in eyes with nuclear or cortical cataract," *Am. J. Ophthalmol.*, vol. 134, no. 1, pp. 1–9, 2002.
74. C. J. Hammond *et al.*, "The heritability of age-related cortical cataract: The twin eye study," *Investig. Ophthalmol. Vis. Sci.*, vol. 42, no. 3, pp. 601–605, 2001.
75. Y. C. C.; X. G.; H. L.; J. H. L.; Y. S.; T. Y. Wong, "Automatic detection of cortical and PSC cataracts using texture and intensity analysis on retro-illumination lens images.".
76. A. U. Patwari, "Detection, Categorization, and Assessment of Eye Cataracts Using Digital Image Processing," no. June, pp. 1–5, 2011.
77. J. Zheng, L. Guo, L. Peng, J. Li, J. Yang, and Q. Liang, "Fundus image based cataract classification," *IST 2014 - 2014 IEEE Int. Conf. Imaging Syst. Tech. Proc.*, pp. 90–94, 2014.
78. S. Kolhe and S. K. Guru, "Remote Automated Cataract Detection System Based on Fundus Images," pp. 10334–10341, 2016.
79. L. Zhang *et al.*, "Automatic cataract detection and grading using Deep Convolutional Neural Network," *Proc. 2017 IEEE 14th Int. Conf. Networking, Sens. Control. ICNSC 2017*, pp. 60–65, 2017.
80. S. Pathak and B. Kumar, "A Robust Automated Cataract Detection Algorithm Using Diagnostic Opinion Based Parameter Thresholding for Telemedicine Application," *Electronics*, vol. 5, no. 3, p. 57, 2016.
81. O. Zisimopoulos *et al.*, "Can surgical simulation be used to train detection and classification of neural networks?," *Healthc. Technol. Lett.*, vol. 4, no. 5, pp. 216–222, 2017.
82. M. Caixinha, J. Amaro, M. Santos, F. Perdigão, M. Gomes, and J. Santos, "In-Vivo Automatic Nuclear Cataract Detection and Classification in an Animal Model by Ultrasounds," *IEEE Trans. Biomed. Eng.*, vol. 63, no. 11, pp. 2326–2335, 2016.
83. R. Gupta, V. Gupta, and B. Kumar, "A novel method for automatic retinal detachment detection and estimation using ocular ultrasound image," 2018.
84. H. Heimann, "[Retinal detachment].," *Klin. Monatsbl{ä}tter f{ü}r Augenheilkd.*, vol. 229, no. 6, pp. 651–670, 2012.
85. G. J. Jaffe and J. Caprioli, "Optical coherence tomography to detect and manage retinal disease and glaucoma," *Am. J. Ophthalmol.*, vol. 137, no. 1, pp. 156–169, 2004.
86. C. H. Damianidis, D. Konstantinou, V. Kyriakou, M. Arvaniti, and N. Kotziamani, "Magnetic Resonance Imaging and Ultrasonographic Evaluation of Retinal Detachment in Orbital Uveal Melanomas," pp. 329–338, 2010.
87. D. J. Coleman and R. L. Jack, "B-Scan Ultrasonography in Diagnosis and Management of Retinal Detachments," *Arch. Ophthalmol.*, vol. 90, no. 1, pp. 29–34, 1973.
88. M. S. Blumenkranz and S. F. Byrne, "Standardized Echography (Ultrasonography) for the Detection and Characterization of Retinal Detachment," *Ophthalmology*, vol. 89, no. 7, pp. 821–831, 1982.
89. B. Rutledge *et al.*, "Quantitative Assessment of Macular Edema With Optical Coherence Tomography," 2015.
90. P. Romero-aroca, "Managing diabetic macular edema: The leading cause of diabetes blindness," vol. 2, no. 6, pp. 98–104, 2011.

91. G. Virgili, F. Menchini, V. Murro, E. Peluso, F. Rosa, and G. Casazza, "Optical coherence tomography (OCT) for detection of macular oedema in patients with diabetic retinopathy (Review)," no. 7, 2011.
92. D. Marin, M. E. Gegundez-Arias, A. Suero, and J. M. Bravo, "Obtaining optic disc center and pixel region by automatic thresholding methods on morphologically processed fundus images," *Comput. Methods Programs Biomed.*, vol. 118, no. 2, pp. 173–185, 2015.
93. R. Supriyanti, H. Habe, M. Kidode, and S. Nagata, "Compact cataract screening system: Design and practical data acquisition," *Int. Conf. Instrumentation, Commun. Inf. Technol. Biomed. Eng. 2009, ICICI-BME 2009*, 2009.
94. C. Science, E. V. Academy, and T. Thrissur-, "Automatic cataract detection and classification systems: A survey," vol. 3, no. March 2015, pp. 28–36, 2014.

Chapter 26
Detector and Descriptor Based Recognition and Counting of Objects in Real Time Environment

Harsh Vikram Singh and Sarvesh Kumar Verma

26.1 Introduction

Digital image processing uses different computer techniques and algorithms to implement image processing on digital images. As a subdivision or area of digital signal processing, digital image processing has numerous advantages over analog image processing [1]. This field empowers a much vast range of algorithms to be applied on different digital image and can keep away from different problems such like the build-up of noise and signal distortion during processing. Since images are defined over two dimensions digital image processing may be model in the form of multidimensional systems.

Face detection technique is a computer based technology being used in a different of applications which helps in identifies various human faces in digital images and videos. Face detection technique is as similar as human psychological process by which human can identifies different faces in visual scene. Face detection can be considered as a special case of object detection [2].

The primary objective for object detection and recognition systems is to detect and recognize if any object from origin image was known earlier, many computer vision application recently consider the problems arises with this concept because there are problems of different images acquisition methods, the corruption of background image and noise affects. To solve these difficulties one of the best

H. V. Singh (✉) · S. K. Verma
Department of Electronics, Kamla Nehru Institute of Technology (KNIT), Sultanpur, Uttar Pradesh, India

© Springer Nature Switzerland AG 2019
A. K. Singh, A. Mohan (eds.), *Handbook of Multimedia Information Security: Techniques and Applications*, https://doi.org/10.1007/978-3-030-15887-3_26

Fig. 26.1 Flow chart of proposed methodology

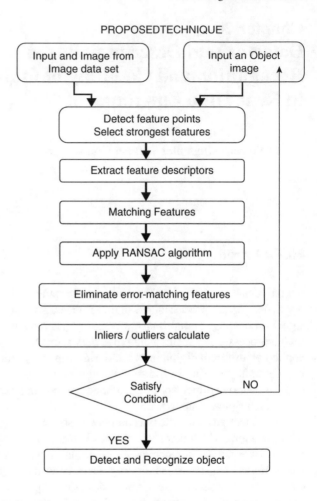

and robust algorithms are consider in many computer vision implementation called Speeded Up Robust Features "SURF" algorithm [3]. Speeded Up Robust Features "SURF" algorithm is a local feature and descriptor algorithm, which will be used in different application such like object recognition, SURF can accurately and in real time detection and recognize objects in input images even in case of clutter and partial occlusion [4].

In Proposed method as shown in Fig. 26.1, Firstly, detection of the interest points for object and input image has done this also called detection of SURF points. The information about different features having by these SURF points also called blob features. We choose only strongest features by using a particular threshold and selection range then we compare all these features are return represent the strongest features for our interest object and origin image [5]. Then in second step, feature descriptor also called features vector are extracted from pixels that surrounding an interest point. Pixels represent match features define single point location and this gives information of a particular (center) location of neighborhood pixels at the end of this step we get strongest feature point (interest point) descriptors also called object representative points because descriptor also having information that has ability to distinguish and recognize object. Third step is a matching step in which matching of features or strongest points from first set of (object image) to second features set (origin image).

In step 4 we use RANSAC algorithm to eliminate the error matched features. Result may include outliers matched features, to remove outliers in matched feature sets, RANSAC (Radom Sample Consensus) algorithm will be used here by establish an initial inliers combination and calculate fundamental matrix by fetch eight matched pairs randomly, Here we are using metrics to calculate the matched pairs points and distinguish the inlier and outliers points based on this we have built our decision if the object is exist or not, and measure matching percent based on it [6–18].

26.2   Result and Discussion

26.2.1   Parameters

The descriptor evaluation employs the following parameters (Fig. 26.2):

Precision (P): Precision parameter is defined as ratio of detected region where are the objects belonging to the database.

$$P = \frac{T_p}{F_p + T_p}$$

Fig. 26.2 Illustrate meaning of false positive (Fp), false negative (Fn) and true positive (Tp)

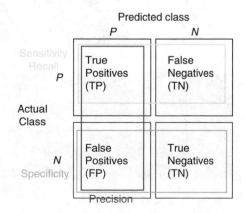

Recall (*R*): Recall parameter is defined as ratio of object region that is detected.

$$R = \frac{T_p}{F_n + T_p}$$

F–Measure (*F*): Measure parameter is defined as the harmonic-mean of *P* and *R*.

$$F = \frac{2PR}{P + R}$$

26.2.2 Performance Evaluation

Object detection and recognition simulation done by using Matlab, Main GUI interface for input the selected image from image data set and entered object image are shown in the Fig. 26.3.

(a)

(b)

Fig. 26.3 (**a, b**) Learning phase objects used for training

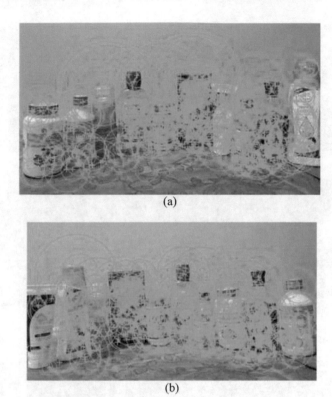

(a)

(b)

Fig. 26.4 (**a, b**) Strongest feature points from scene image

Then find interest points for both images and from these points select strongest points based on threshold, Fig. 26.4 show strongest features for both origin and interest object images.

Feature descriptors for both images has been found, these descriptors are represented in vectors also called representative points which can recognize object in the scene, then matched features from origin image to the object image.

For the purpose of eliminating error-matched features, RANSAC algorithm is being used the result can produce matched features, then we calculate the percentage of matching there, if the matching score does not have enough matching points then that object is not found, the implementation of this step can be shown in the Fig. 26.5.

Here different images are used from image data set and tested against our interest objects, object can be found in these images in different scene (Figs. 26.6, 26.7, 26.8, 26.9, 26.10, 26.11, 26.12, 26.13, 26.14, 26.15, 26.16, and 26.17; Tables 26.1, 26.2, and 26.3).

(a)   (b)

(c)   (d)

Fig. 26.5 (**a–d**) Putatively matched points (including outlier)

(a)   (b)

(c)   (d)

Fig. 26.6 (**a–d**) Matched points (inliers only)

Fig. 26.7 Detected box (**a**) Tedhe Medhe box, (**b**) Kurkure box

Fig. 26.8 Detected objects in setup 1

Fig. 26.9 Detected objects in setup 2

Fig. 26.10 Detected objects in setup 3

Fig. 26.11 Detected objects in setup 4

Fig. 26.12 Detected objects in setup 5

Fig. 26.13 Detected objects in setup 6

Fig. 26.14 Detected objects in setup 7

Fig. 26.15 Detected objects in setup 8

Fig. 26.16 Detected objects in setup 9

Fig. 26.17 Detected objects in setup 10

Table 26.1 Evaluation results obtained for the ten different setups used for system evaluation

Setup	Number of objects	Detected objects	Detection rate (%)
1	8	7	87.5
2	8	6	75
3	10	7	70
4	9	6	66.6
5	9	9	100
6	10	7	70
7	8	8	100
8	9	7	77.7
9	10	6	60
10	10	8	80

Table 26.2 Detection of each object in terms of the parameters recall, precision and measure

Objects	Recall (%)	Precision (%)	Measure
Dabur Amla	7.920	5.405	0.0642
Figaro	32.88	85.17	0.5470
Ayur Cream	69.50	97.69	0.8043
Garnier Oil	47.85	84.93	0.6114
Triphala Churna	23.21	94.53	0.3703
Nucool MPS	38.48	95.58	0.5421
Cofdex	67.11	83.95	0.6269
Chocos box	22.29	31.06	0.1676
Skin Toner	80.66	64.16	0.7147
Cream	37.32	55.42	0.4460

Table 26.3 Comparative values of different parameters of base algorithm and proposed work of object detection

Parameter	SURF	SURF + RANSAC
Precision (%)	68.5	79
Recall (%)	42.5	47.5
F-measure (%)	52.45	59.32
Detection Rate	70	78.02

26.3 Conclusion

Proposed method for detect and recognize object in the scene is based on enhanced speeded up robust feature (SURF) algorithm, the performance of object detection technique is enhanced by selecting the strongest features descriptor, this method detects one or more objects in data set of different images for object in the scene by performing thresholds and accuracy measures on objects detection under various circumstances such as rotation, partial occlusion, orientation and illumination changes by enhanced illumination of image inputs. Most of the real time implementation that uses SURF algorithm can detect or recognize objects by visualize mode, this model can also able to evaluate many statistics that are used across object detection outline, therefore proposed model is very convenient where one can set and changed different parameters that are used for detection and recognition process.

References

1. Rafael C. Gonzalez, Richard E. Woods, Handbook of "Digital Image Processing", 2nd Edition published by Pearson Education (2002).
2. P. Viola, M. Jones, "Rapid object detection using a boosted cascade of simple features", in: Proceedings of Computer Vision and Pattern Recognition (CVPR), pp. 129–185 (2001).
3. H. Bay, A. Ess, T. Tuytelaars, and L. V. Gool, "Speeded-up robust features (SURF)," Computer Vision and Image Understanding, vol. 110, no. 3, pp. 346–359, June 2008.
4. Bassem Sheta, Mohamed Elhabiby, Nase El-Sheimy, "Assessments of different Speeded UP Robust Features SURF algorithm resolution for Pos estimation of UAV", IJCSES, vol. 3, No. 5, pp. 21–22, October 2012.
5. K. Velmurugan, Santhosh Baboo, "Content-Based image retrieval using SURF and colour moment", Global journal of computer science and technology (GJCST), vol. 11, pp. 125–147, (2011).
6. Peng-le, C., "Study over high-precision vision inspection based on RANSAC algorithm", Journal of Convergence Information Technology, vol. 7, no. 20, pp. 33–38, (2012).
7. Kong Jun, Jitang Min, Alimujiang Yiming, "Research on Speeded UP Robust Features with RANSAC", International journal of technical research and applications (IJTRA), vol. 5, pp. 18–24, (2013).
8. Bay, H., Tuytelaars, T., VanGool, L., "SURF: Speeded Up Robust Features", In ECCV (1), pp. 404–417, (2006).
9. E. Rosten, R. Porter, and T. Drummond, "Faster and Better: A Machine Learning Approach to Corner Detection". IEEE Transactions on Pattern Analysis and Machine Intelligence, 32, pp. 105–119, (2010).
10. E. Hsiao and M. Hebert, "Occlusion Reasoning for Object Detection under Arbitrary Viewpoint". IEEE Transactions on Pattern Analysis and Machine Intelligence, 36(9) pp. 1803–1815, (2014).
11. Y. Tian, B. Fan, and F. Wu, "L2Net: Deep learning of discriminative patch descriptor in Euclidean space," in Proceedings of the IEEE Computer Society Conference on Computer Vision and Pattern Recognition, 2017.
12. Z. Wang, B. Fan, and G. W. an Fuchao Wu, "Exploring local and overall ordinal information for robust feature description," IEEE Transactions on Pattern Analysis and Machine Intelligence, vol. 38, no. 11, pp. 2198–2211, 2016.
13. Q. Gu, T. Takaki, and I. Ishii, "A fast multi-object extraction algorithm based on cell-based connected components labeling", IEEE International Conference on Computer Vision (ICCV), vol. E95-D, no. 2, pp. 636–645, (2012).
14. Baugh, G., Kokaram, A., "Feature-based object modeling for visual surveillance", 15th IEEE International Conference on Image Processing, ICIP, pp. 1352–1355, (2008).
15. D. Hoiem, R. Sukthankar, H. Schneiderman, and L. Huston, "Object-Based Image Retrieval Using the Statistical Structure of Images". Journal of Machine Learning Research, 02 pp. 490–497, (2004).

16. L. Liu, P. Fieguth, Y. Guo, X. Wang, and M. Pietikainen, "Local binary features for texture classification: Taxonomy and experimental study," Pattern Recognition, vol. 62, pp. 135–160, 2017.
17. Iscen, Ahmet, et al. "A comparison of dense region detectors for image search and fine-grained classification." Image Processing, IEEE Transactions on (Volume: 24, Issue: 8), pp. 2369–2381, 2015.
18. L. Liu, P. Fieguth, G. Zhao, M. Pietikainen, and D. Hu, "Extended local binary patterns for face recognition," Information Sciences, vol. 358–359, no. 1, pp. 56–72, 2016

Part III
Multimedia Applications

Chapter 27
Role of Multimedia in Medicine: Study of Visual Prosthesis

Parsa Sarosh, Shabir A. Parah, and Rimsha Sarosh

27.1 Introduction

MARC is an acronym for Multiple Artificial Retinal Chipset which is an interfacing device used in the retinal prosthesis. The retinal prosthesis basically replaces the photoreceptor function with an electronic device, which was initiated by Dr. Humayun et al. [10]. According to the basic definition, prosthesis is any device which replaces a body part. In order to do so, it must replicate or mimic the functionality of that part. In case of the visual prosthesis, it is therefore important to have knowledge of anatomy as well as the physiology of the eye. Furthermore, to understand the construction details and working of the MARC system it is imperative to have an in-depth understanding of concepts pertaining to medicine, engineering, communication, material sciences etc. The MARC system successfully integrates the various components ranging from image acquisition devices to the retinal stimulating electrode.

P. Sarosh
Department of Electronics and Instrumentation Technology, University of Kashmir, Srinagar, Jammu and Kashmir, India

S. A. Parah (✉)
Department of Electronics and Instrumentation Technology, University of Kashmir, Srinagar, Jammu and Kashmir, India

Department of Ophthalmology, Government Medical College (GMC), Srinagar, Jammu and Kashmir, India

R. Sarosh
Department of Ophthalmology, Government Medical College (GMC), Srinagar, Jammu and Kashmir, India

© Springer Nature Switzerland AG 2019   559
A. K. Singh, A. Mohan (eds.), *Handbook of Multimedia Information Security: Techniques and Applications*, https://doi.org/10.1007/978-3-030-15887-3_27

GROSS ANATOMY OF THE EYEBALL

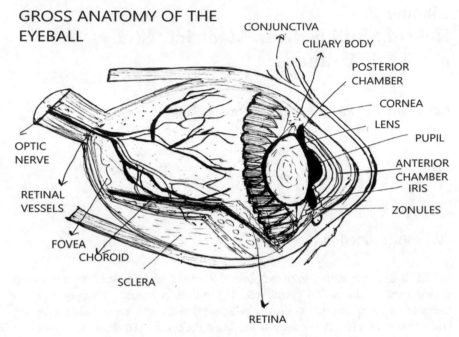

Fig. 27.1 Anatomy of the eye

27.2 Anatomy of the Eye

The eye is present in the orbit, which is a cavity of the skull and is suspended by six extraocular muscles. The eye has the following parts which include the cornea, iris, pupil, lens, choroid, retina among others. It also contains the clear membrane called conjunctiva which covers the surface of the eye. The eye's lacrimal gland present near the eyebrows produces tears and keeps the eyes lubricated [1, 3] (Fig. 27.1).

The Retina is the main layer responsible for the reception of incoming light and conversion into chemical and nervous signals which reach the brain by way of the optic nerve [55]. The retina is composed of 10 layers among which the photoreceptor layer is the most important for the physiology of vision. The photoreceptor layer is mainly composed of two types of cells: the rod cells and the cone cells. The rode cells contain a photosensitive membrane. They subserve the vision of low illumination (scotopic or night vision) and the peripheral vision. The cone cells also have a photosensitive membrane and are required for discriminatory central vision called photopic or bright-light vision. They contribute to the perception of colours [1, 4, 10, 14] (Fig. 27.2).

The centre part of the retina is known as Macula or yellow spot and the central depressed part of the macula is known as the fovea. With careful examination of the retina, it can be seen that the photosensitive cells are unevenly distributed. The rod cells predominate more in the periphery of the retina while the cone cells greatly outnumber the rod cells in the centre and are the only photoreceptor cells in the

Microscopic Structure of Retina

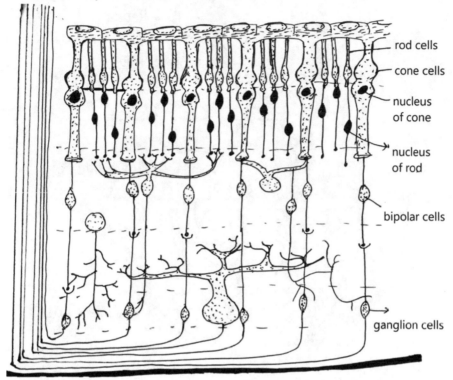

Fig. 27.2 Structure of the retina

fovea having a density of about 150,000 elements per mm2 [4, 10, 14]. The light enters the eye from the cornea and strikes the photoreceptor layer of the retina. The photoreceptor cells are stimulated in the process. There is compression and encoding of the visual information from the 120 million rods and 6.5 million cone cells to about 1 million ganglion cells this compression is mainly carried out by the bipolar cells. The ganglion cells which are actually neurons have axons which combine together to form the optic nerve. The complex visual information is given to the optic nerve which takes it to the primary visual cortex that is the part of the brain which processes the images. It is seen that the visual system is like a transmission chain in which retinal image pixels are encoded into a series of pulses ultimately activating the visual cortex. This is called the visual pathway [2, 4] (Fig. 27.3).

27.2.1 Bindness

Blindness can arise when a portion of the visual pathway is damaged by diseases like Retinitis Pigmentosa, Diabetic Retinopathy, Glaucoma, Genetic Abnormalities,

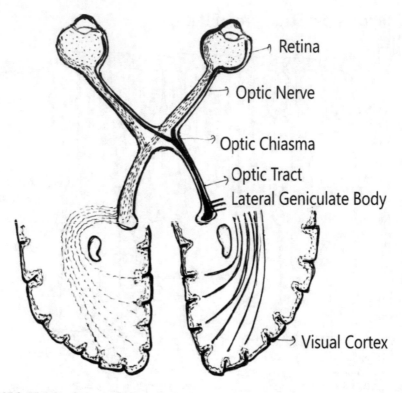

Fig. 27.3 Visual pathway

Infections, Trauma, and Cancer etc. The International Statistics Classification Of Diseases and Related Health Problems of the World Health Organisation (ICD-10) uses codes 1–5 to describe the various levels of visual impairment from moderate to total blindness [2, 4]. Visual acuity (VA) commonly refers to the clarity of vision. The visual acuity is measured by means of a Snellen chart. The Snellen visual acuity measures the pattern recognition acuity as the ratio of 'd/D', where 'D' is the distance at which a sign subtends 5 min of arc (5/60 degree) and 'd' is the distance at which they can be recognised. The top letter of the Snellen chart corresponds to a visual acuity of 20/200 this is legal blindness threshold and there is no implant that has ever been able to achieve that level of visual acuity. The visual acuity has a direct relationship with the number, size and height (pitch) of electrodes. The more the number of electrodes on the implant the better is the visual acuity. The 20/20 or 6/6 visual acuity implies an ability to successfully resolve an angle of 1/60 degree (one arc min which corresponds to normal vision) and 1 degree corresponds to 288 μm of retinal surface therefore 1/60 degree will correspond to 5 μm. Thus for the visual acuity of 20/20 electrode pixel size should be 5 μm while the threshold 20/200 corresponds to 50 μm [2, 4, 5].

27.2.2 Retinitis Pigmentosa and AMD

The patients suffering from diseases like Retinitis Pigmentosa and Age-related Macular Degeneration (AMD) are potential recipients of the retinal prosthesis. The Retinitis Pigmentosa (RP) is a hereditary retinal disorder which leads to degeneration of the rod cells. This disease appears in childhood and is more prevalent in males. RP is a bilateral disease and affects both the eyes equally. RP causes damage to rod photoreceptor cells which results in poor night vision and loss of vision near the periphery progressively leading to tunnel vision. Later the cone photoreceptor cells also get involved and the person is left completely blind [2]. It has been estimated that the prevalence of the RP-like degenerations is about 1:3500 around the world (Haim 2002) [9, 56]. AMD leads to the slow degeneration of the photoreceptor cells. It occurs during the later stage of life and initially affects the cone cells in the fovea. Hence the person suffering from AMD will have some peripheral vision but will have dark spots near the centre of his visual field. There is no treatment for these two diseases but there is some treatment to reduce the pace at which the AMD progresses [2]. In both of these diseases, the photoreceptor cells are partially or completely damaged but, the layers beyond the photoreceptor layer of the retina including the rest of the visual pathway and visual cortex largely remain functional [5].

27.3 Review of the Different Approaches

Some efforts to restore the vision in blind patients include invasive and non-invasive procedures. Several non-surgical systems have been developed to assist the blind person like the GPS [Hub (2006)] [7]. The invasive approaches involve the stimulation of the various areas of the visual pathway. Some prototypes are being developed which explore different regions of the visual pathway to judge whether these areas can be effectively stimulated or not. Based upon the actual location where the visual pathway is stimulated, the visual prosthesis is mainly classified into 8 types. Subretinal, Epiretinal, Transretinal, Hybrid, Optic Nerve, Cortex Surface or Intracortical, Suprachoroidal and LNG Implants [4]. There are many groups around the world that are working on visual prosthetic devices each following a specific approach. A large number of these approaches bypass the eye completely and use a camera and processor to send the signals to the brain. These include the optic nerve implants and the intracortical implants. Brindley and Lewin (1968) were the first to test for direct stimulation of the brain cells [57]. Dobelle (2000) has also been a pioneer in this effort and even tried to connect a television camera to the brain [58]. It has been shown that sensory percepts can be generated in the brain by the stimulating currents using the Utah electrode array (Normann et al. 1999). Generation of phosphenes with cortical stimulation has been reported by Tong (2003) [7, 59, 60]. The work done in the development of cortical implants by Troyk et al. (2005) is also worth noting [61]. The use of chemical release (e.g., neurotransmitters) from the implanted device has also been suggested (Peterman et al. 2004) [62]. It has been proposed that a neural interface can be developed that utilizes multiwalled carbon nanotube pillars as microelectrodes (Wang et al. 2006) [9, 63]. Although at a very early stage of development these prototypes are being developed all over the world. There are some prosthetic prototypes of the suprachoroidal implants as well for example STS developed by Fujikado et al. in Japan. The STS has 49 platinum electrodes [64]. The BVA implant is also an effort to achieve wide-view suprachoroidal vision. The slow development of the optic nerve and cortical implants is because of the fact that optic nerve and visual cortex are part of the central nervous system and hence the implant has to be much more sophisticated as compared to the retinal implants [2, 4, 6, 7]. Apart from the above mentioned sophisticated techniques, there are some common approaches that most researchers follow. These include the implantation of electrodes on or above the retinal surface. When the electrode array is placed under the retina, the implant is known as subretinal implant but when the electrode array is placed above the retinal surface i.e. the ganglion cell layer, it is called the epiretinal implant. In the subretinal approach, Optobionics was the first company to undertake a fully approved clinical trial in the USA by using a micro-photodiode array for retinal stimulation (Peachey and Chow 1999) [9, 65]. The subretinal implant is one in which an array of micro photodiodes are placed between the photoreceptor layer and the pigmented epithelium. This approach is surgically complex thus leading to the possibility of complications. The Optobionics Company (Peachey and Chow 1999) developed the subretinal implant called Artificial Silicon Retina or ASR (Chow et al. 2004) and implanted it in many patients [66]. However, there was no visual perception due to this implant as it was powered by the incoming light only and had no other source of energy [9] (Fig. 27.4).

Apart from ASR some other subretinal implants are also been developed which include 1500 electrode-Alpha IMS (Retina Implant AG, Reutlingen, Germany) and photovoltaic retinal prosthesis developed by Palanker et al. (2005) [8, 67]. In the epiretinal approach, the pioneer is Humayun et al. who along with other scientists in the field like Zrenner (2002); Weiland et al. (2005) have developed and reviewed the functionality and performance of the epiretinal implants at various levels [9, 10, 68, 69]. In an epiretinal implant, an electrode array is used in place of the photodiodes and is placed on the retinal surface. The electrode array directly stimulates the ganglion cells and the bipolar cells and the process completely bypasses the photoreceptor cells. The ganglion cell axons then take the response to the brain through the optic nerve. The implants like EPIRET3 (25 electrodes), IRIS I, IRIS II, ARGUS I (16 electrodes) and ARGUS II (60 electrodes) are epiretinal implants [4]. Another implant called the Boston retinal implant (100 electrodes) is also under development by the Retinal Implant Research Group at the Massachusetts Institute of Technology (MIT) and the Massachusetts Eye and Ear Infirmary (MEEI). The group has now created a company, Bionic Eye Technologies, to commercialize the system [24]. The retinal prosthesis is the only one which has been approved for implantation in patients, therefore, people suffering from diseases pertaining to the

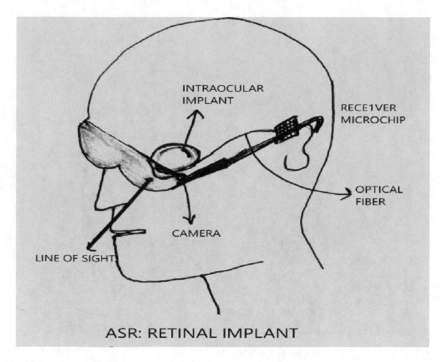

Fig. 27.4 ASR implant

optic nerve or visual cortex have damaged visual pathway beyond the retina and thus cannot benefit from the retinal implants.

27.4 Construction and Working of a MARC System

The MARC system has multiple components which range from the image acquisition device to the electrode array. This electrode array is interfaced with the operative neuronal cells and is used to replace the functionality of the photoreceptor cells of the retina. The MARC system having multiple internal and external components forms the basis of newer retinal implants including ARGUS II [18, 20]. This system has been developed by the effective integration of various fields like medicine, communication, material sciences and image processing among others. The external components include a video camera, video processing chip, RF generator and a primary coil. The internal components include the secondary coil, rectifier, regulator, MARC processing and demultiplexing chips and the electrode array. The figure below shows how the various components are connected to each other [10] (Fig. 27.5).

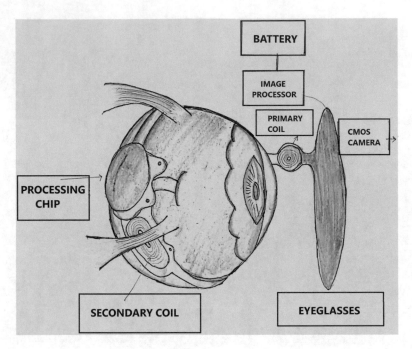

Fig. 27.5 Components of MARC system [10]

27.4.1 Transmission and Reception of Data

Data transmission from the external environment to the implant is called downlink transmission and that from the implant to the external device is known as uplink transmission [25]. The basic process begins with the camera which takes the real-time images of the scene to be viewed. This camera is mounted on the eyeglasses that are worn by the patient at all times. Since the state of the art cameras available are very efficient and can easily outperform the visual prosthesis, the obtained image has to be sub-sampled using the indicial mapping techniques [10]. The image is processed so that the resolution of the image matches that of the electrode array. The silicon photonic devices are generally used for visible detection [28]. The current camera captures images having a resolution of 480×640 at a rate of 30 frames/s. The image needs to be processed so that it is perceived in a better way. The image processing includes edge detection, edge enhancement, decimation and low-pass filtering. Saliency maps are also used for object recognition in the bionic eye. This is done using the image pyramids [27]. These strategies are essential for the conversion of high-resolution image into low-resolution image. Each pixel's intensity value is represented by 8 bits and that bit pattern is converted to a PWM modulated wave that can be done by an OPAMP circuit and is then modulated using ASK modulation [23]. The amplitude shift keying modulation scheme regulates the carrier amplitude. Because the recovered power is derived from this amplitude, the average transferred power would depend on the transmitted bit pattern. To avoid this dependence on

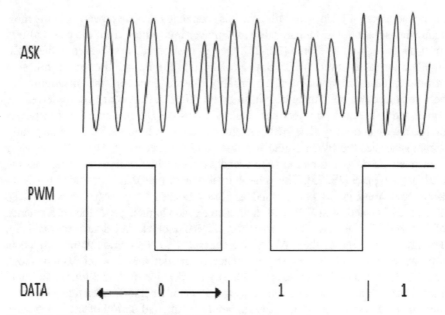

Fig. 27.6 Waveform of ASK and PWM [10]

data, we first encode the transmitted data using the alternate mark inversion pulse width modulation [23]. Then the encoded bit pattern needs to be modulated using the appropriate modulator for wireless transmission. Earlier ASK modulators were mainly used because the receiver and transmitter design was quite simple but now BPSK modulators are employed [25]. This chapter, however, represents the ASK modulation alternative for data transmission (Fig. 27.6).

After the signal is ASK modulated it is given to a gate driver and CLASS E amplifier which amplifies the RF signal. CLASS E amplifier is generally the preferred choice for the RF amplification since it has 100% theoretical efficiency. In this amplifier class, the active device is used as a switch and the voltage and current waveforms are 180 degrees out of phase. This leads to minimum power dissipation and an increase in overall %age efficiency [10, 11]. After being amplified by the CLASS E amplifier the signal is given to the primary coil for the transcutaneous transmission. The primary coil housed in the eye-glasses transmits the wireless signal to the implanted secondary coil and is then processed by the MARC chip. The necessary data is provided by this incoming wireless signal which is required for the generation of appropriate current pulses and power. Carrier frequencies used in the inductive links for the transfer of power should be kept below 15 MHz (Jow and Ghovanloo 2007, 2009) [26, 70]. Both sides of the link are required to be tuned to the same frequency for high efficiency (Sawan et al. 2005; Jow and Ghovanloo 2009) [26, 71, 72]. There are many alternatives that provide power to the implant which include the use of implanted and external antenna or deriving power from the external environment. Some researchers have also suggested that we can use nanogenerators [30]. However, till now it is seen that inductive powering is the most promising solution. For human safety, the power transmitted from the external unit must not exceed 10 mW/cm^2 [22, 25]. One of the sources in this area is the IEEE standard for safety levels (IEEE Std C95.1-2005) [26]. For maximum transmission of power and information from the primary to secondary coil, the misalignments between these two coils must be within limits [10, 11]. Secondary coil receives the signal and passes it to the rectifier which derives the DC power from it to power up the internal circuitry. The ASK envelope is then given to the ASK demodulator which generates the PWM signal for clock and data recovery. The PWM wave is then given to a delay locked loop and decoder circuit which derive the corresponding bits for each pixel [19, 23]. The general overview of the DLL is provided by Chih-Kong Ken Yang in his paper titled as Delay-Locked Loops-An Overview [31]. Thomas H Lee and John F. Bulzacchelli also explain in their paper the performance of a monolithic DLL which is used for 155-MHz clock and data recovery [29]. The ascending edge of the PWM pulse generated by the demodulator is fixed in time periodically and serves as a reference in the derivation of an explicit clock signal [23]. The data, however, is encoded by the position of the falling transition at each pulse. For retinal stimulation, it is experimentally demonstrated that a biphasic current pulse is required with optimum height, width and period of the pulse wave [10]. A configuration protocol frame provides the configuration data, according to which the timing generator circuit specifies the timing of the stimulus waveform [23] (Fig. 27.7).

The current control circuit specifies the full scale amplitude (A) of the biphasic current pulses [23]. This specification is then applied to the current stimulation drivers. Once the configuration process is completed, the chip automatically enters the run mode. By multiplexing, the electrode stimulators drive the desired biphasic current pulses to the electrode array [2, 10, 21, 23]. The current drivers produce the stimulating currents in accordance with the bit pattern they receive. The information encoded needs to be perceived by the patient therefore the frame transmission rate is increased from 30 frames/s as in the case of normal television to 60 frames/s [10]. As the image presentation rate should be 60 Hz, the necessary stimulating current pulses must be generated 60 times a second for each driver or once every 16.6 ms, this will reduce the flicker seen by the patient [10, 12]. There are many circuits that can be used to produce a biphasic current pulse for example the dual supply stimulator and the switched bridge stimulator. The basic dual supply stimulator requires dual power supply rails and positive and negative current sources. The design requiring two power supplies is an inefficient design therefore a switched bridge circuit having a single power supply can be used. The bridge network requires 4 switches and a digital to analog converter (DAC). In the bridge circuit, two switches conduct in one phase and the charge is delivered in one direction through the electrode. In the following phase the other switches conduct and deliver charge in the opposite direction to the electrode. This produces a biphasic current pulse through the electrode which generates spots of light called phosphenes [10, 12]. The current generated is provided to the electrode array placed over the retina and is fastened to it using a retinal tack [36]. These electrodes are fabricated on

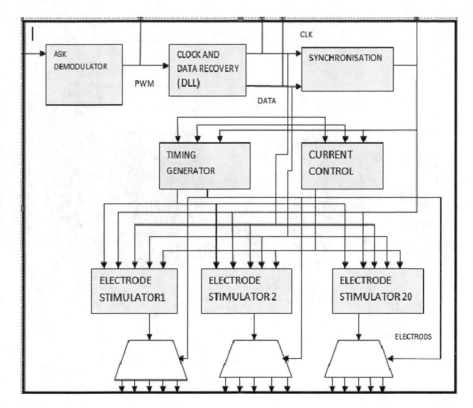

Fig. 27.7 MARC3 CHIP

a biocompatible material like polyamide. Flexible polyamide based electrode arrays are also being developed and their biocompatibility evaluated [13, 33]. The different types of electrodes developed for the retinal, optic nerve and cortical implants are described by Mohamad Sawan et al. [34]. A review of the design and challenges of implementation is also presented by BaharehGhane-Motlagh, Mohamad Sawan [35]. This stimulating current is used to elicit percepts into patients but the inherent differences between the stimulating technology and the underlying neurophysiology results in distortions of perceptual experience [32]. Nonetheless, these percepts can provide some form of rudimentary vision to the blind (Fig. 27.8).

27.5 The ARGUS II Retinal Prosthesis

As stated earlier, the ongoing research is directed at developing and improving the different visual prosthesis. For this purpose, it is imperative that one must have knowledge of the basic anatomy of the complete human visual system [37–39]. The retinal prosthesis has been developed to a fairly large extent mainly

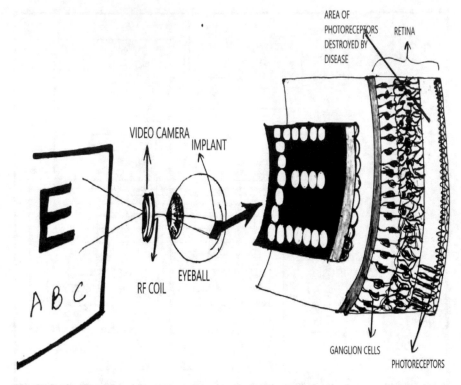

Fig. 27.8 The MARC system [10]

because the human eye is more accessible than the brain. Many epiretinal implants have been developed but the only FDA approved implant is ARGUS II epi-retinal implant [17]. The name of this device is similar to the name of a Greek mythical creature ARGUS, who had 100 eyes and was believed to be all seeing. This is a sophisticated device which is based upon years of scientific research and the latest technology. The ARGUS II product has been developed by Second Sight Medical Products, Inc [47]. This implant was FDA approved for sale in the United States as the Humanitarian Device Exemption on February 14, 2013. The humanitarian device can be used for the treatment of fewer than 4000 patients a year [16]. The MARC system is the underlying technology upon which the ARGUS II has been built. Although the major components are the same for example the camera, video processor, electrode array etc, there are some additional components included in the end product. These components include patient kit, clinician fitting components and surgical components etc. Therefore the retinal prosthesis system is composed of the following [15]:

1. ARGUS II IMPLANT
2. ARGUS II GLASSES Fig. 27.9 is the diagrammatical representation of the eyeglasses.

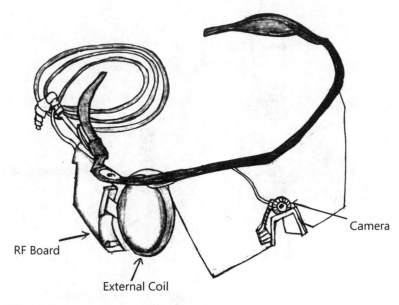

Camera

RF Board

External Coil

Fig. 27.9   ARGUS II eyeglasses an RF board [15]

3. ARGUS II OPERATING (OR) COIL
4. ARGUS II VIDEO PROCESSOR UNIT (VPU)
5. ARGUS II CLINICIAN FITTING SYSTEM (CFS) (Fig. 27.9). The clinician fitting system is not shown in the diagram.

The working of the ARGUS II implant is the same as the basic MARC system. The prosthetic system has a camera which collects the image data and sends it to the video processor for image processing. The processed image is given back to the eyeglasses and the information is transmitted to the secondary coil placed near the cornea. This information is then decoded and the corresponding currents are generated and are given to the electrode array. The array consists of 60 platinum gray electrodes, each electrode is 200 μm in diameter, the horizontal and vertical pitch is 525 μm [15, 16, 40]. It is stimulated according to the information captured by the camera. This information is then transmitted to the brain through optic nerve for perception (Fig. 27.10).

The available pulse rates in the Argus II are 3–60 Hz [40]. In terms of the visual acuity, the best result from ARGUS II was 1.8 logMAR (equivalent to Snellen 20/1262) (Humayun et al. 2012; da Cruz et al. 2016) [73, 74]. The performance of the device is best evaluated by using the Berkeley Rudimentary Vision Test (BRVT) Grating Acuity cards. BRVT allow calculation of visual acuity in patients unable to read the standard Snellen chart [41]. In order to evaluate the performance of the device several functional vision tasks are performed which include the square localisation, direction of motion and mobility tasks among others. The tests also include staying on a crosswalk, locating windows and doors, following lines,

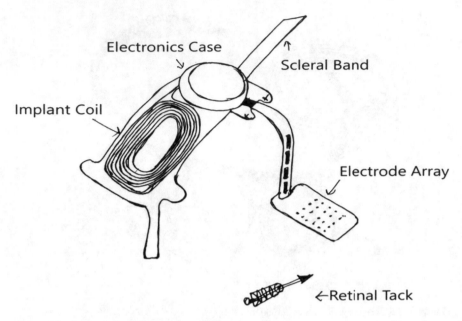

Fig. 27.10 ARGUS II implant and tack [15]

avoiding obstacles, locating people just to name a few [42]. Functional Low-Vision Observer-Rated Assessment (FLORA) (Geruschat et al. 2015, 2016) shows that there is a positive impact of ARGUS II on the subjects [40–42, 75]. Questionnaires assessing the improvement in the quality of life have shown that 67% of the participating Argus II subjects (26 out of 30) experienced some positive effect of the Argus II system [40].

27.6 Issues and Future Work

Advancements are required in the device in order to improve the various aspects. The camera size, for example, needs to be reduced so that it is placed in the lens of the patient and not in the eyeglasses. This will avoid the unusual head scanning done by the patient. The electrode array needs to be miniaturized so that more electrodes are fabricated on the same area. This will improve the resolution of the device. Nonetheless, the success of the Argus II has become an inspiration all around the world and as such many new research endeavours are being initiated. These aim at improving the existing hardware as well as developing novel devices to enhance the quality of life enjoyed by recipients of these implants [42]. With the success of the ARGUS II device, many countries around the world are slowly warming up to its idea and will eventually approve the device for implantation [43–46].

27.7   Conclusion

This chapter presents a brief review of the various visual prosthetics being developed around the world. The various approaches taken in the visual prosthesis is reviewed. The working and principle of operation of the MARC system is described in detail. As this technology forms the basis of the state of the art retinal prosthesis called ARGUS II. The ARGUS II implant is discussed to some extent and the impact it has on the subject's lives. It is clear from the above discussion that, the visual prosthesis is a ray of hope for the blind people who are suffering from diseases that have no treatment and ARGUS II is a pioneering effort in this regard that will pave the way for future initiatives [48–54].

References

1. Boyd, K. (2016). Parts-of-Eye. Retrieved from https://www.aao.org/.
2. Weinland, J.D. and Humayun, M.S. (2008). "Visual Prosthesis," *Proceedings of the IEEE, 96* (07). pp. 1076-1084. https://doi.org/10.1109/JPROC.2008.922589.
3. Aao. (2016-2017). Basic-Clinical-Science-Course. Retrieved from https://ebooks.aao.org/.
4. Delbeke J, Veraart C (2006) Visual Prostheses. In: John W (ed) Encyclopedia of medical devices and instrumentation. Brussels John Wiley and Sons, pp. 530–549.
5. Ha, S., Khraiche, M.L., Akinin, A., Jing Y., Damie, S., Kuang, Y., Bauchner, S., Lo, Y. H., Freeman, W.R., Silva, G. A. and Cauwenberghs, G. (2016). "Towards high-resolution retinal prosthesis with direct optical addressing and inductive telemetry," *Journal of Neural Engineering., 13.* 056008. https://doi.org/10.1088/1741-2560/13/5/056008.
6. Wyatt, J.L. (2015) "Development of a wireless Retinal Implant for Chronic Human Implantation," *The Retinal Implant Project-RLE at MIT.*
7. F. Robert-Inacio, E. Kussener, G. Oudinet and G. Durandau. (March 16th 2012). Image Analysis for Automatically-Driven Bionic Eye, *Advanced Topics in Neurological Disorders, Ken-Shiung Chen, IntechOpen*, DOI: https://doi.org/10.5772/31585. Available from: https://www.intechopen.com/books/advanced-topics-in-neurological-disorders/image-analysis-for-automatically-driven-bionic-eye.
8. Wang, L., Mathieson, K., Kamins, T.I., Loudin, J.D., Galambos, L., Goetz, G, Sher, A., Mandel, Y., Huie, P., Lavinsky, D., Harris, J.S. and Palanker, D.V. (2012). "Photovoltaic retinal prosthesis: implant fabrication and performance," *J.Neural Eng., 9* , 11 pp.
9. Chader, G. J., Weiland, J. and Humayun, M. S., (2009). "Artificial vision: needs, functioning, and testing of a retinal electronic prosthesis," *Progress in brain research*, 175, pp. 317-32.
10. Liu, W., McGucken, E., Clements, M., DeMarco, C., Vichienchom, K., Hughes, C., Humayun, M., Weinland, J., Greenberg, R., Jaun, E.D. (2018). "Multiple-unit Artificial Retinal Chipset System to Benefit the Visually Impaired".
11. H. Ali, T. J. Ahmad and S. A. Khan. (2009). "Inductive link design for medical implants," IEEE Symposium on Industrial Electronics & Applications, Kuala Lumpur, pp. 694-699. doi: https://doi.org/10.1109/ISIEA.2009.5356376.
12. Li, X., Zhong, S. And Morizio, J. (2017). "16 Channel biphasic current-mode programmable charge balanced neural stimulation," *Biomedical Engineering Online.* 16. https://doi.org/10.1186/s12938-017-0385-0.
13. Krisch I., Hosticka B.J. (2007). "Restoring visual perception using microsystem technologies: engineering and manufacturing perspectives," *In: Sakas D.E., Simpson B.A. (eds) Operative Neuromodulation. Acta Neurochirurgica Supplements*, vol 97/2. Springer, Vienna.

14. Rafael, G. C., Woods, R. E. (2008). "Digital Image Processing," (3rded.). *Upper Saddle River, N.J.: Prentice Hall.*
15. Second Sight, "Surgeon Manual and Device Fitting Manual." *ARGUS II retinal prosthesis system.*
16. Zhou, D. D., Dorn, J. D, Greenberg, R.J. (2013). "The ARGUS II Retinal Prosthesis System: An Overview," IEEE International Conference on Multimedia and Expo Workshops (ICMEW), San Jose, CA, pp. 1-6.
17. Gareth, L. (2014). "Restoration of sight: Argus II Retinal Prosthesis," *Foundation Fighting Blindness Vision Walk Organising Reception.*
18. Weinland, J.D., Humayun, M.S. (2014). "Retinal Prosthesis," *IEEE transactions on biomedical engineering,* 61 (5), pp. 1412-1424.
19. Woogeun, R., Herschel, A., Sergey, R., Alexander, R., Michael, B., Daniel, F., Sudhir, G. and Mehmet, S. (2003). "A 10-Gb/s CMOS clock and data recovery circuit using a secondary delay locked loop," *Proceedings of the IEEE 2003 Custom Integrated Circuits Conference,* pp. 81-84.
20. Michelle, B. (2014). "Bionic Eyes," *Biomedical engineering.*
21. Ngamkham, W., van Dongen, M. N., Serdijn, W. A., Bes, C. J., Briaire, J. J., Frijns, J. H. M. (2015). "A 0.042mm2 programmable biphasic Stimulator for cochlear implants suitable for a large number of channels," *In:*ArXiv.org, pp. 1-13.
22. Abbas, S. M., Hannan, M. A., Samad, S. A., Hussain, A., (2012). "Transcutaneous inductive powering links based on ASK modulation techniques," *International journal of computer and systems engineering,* 6 (8), pp. 862-866.
23. Teodorescu, H. N. (Ed) Jain, L. (Ed.), et. al. (2000). "A retinal prosthesis to benefit the visually impaired," *Intelligent Systems and technologies inrehabilitation engiuneering.* Boca Raton: CRC Press LLC.
24. Mertz, L. (2012). "Sight Restoration Comes Into Focus: Versions of Visual Prostheses," IEEE pulse. 3(5), pp. 10-6. https://doi.org/10.1109/MPUL.2012.2208024.
25. Kiourti, A. (2010). "Biomedical telemetry: Communication between implanted devices and the external world," *Opticon,* 1826 (8), pp. 1-7.
26. Asgarian, F. and Sodagar, A.M. (2011). "Wireless Telemetry for Implantable Biomedical Microsystems," *Biomedical Engineering, Trends in Electronics Anthony N. Laskovski, IntechOpen,* DOI: https://doi.org/10.5772/12997. Available from: https://www.intechopen.com/books/biomedical-engineering-trends-in-electronics-communications-and-software/wireless-telemetry-fior-implantable-biomedical-microsystems.
27. Sharmili, N., Ramaiah, P. S., Swamynadhan, G. (2011). "Image Compression and Resizing for Retinal Implant in Bionic Eye," *International Journal of Computer Science & Engineering Survey (IJCSES).* 2.https://doi.org/10.5121/ijcses.2011.2204.
28. Smith, B. T., Feng, D., Lei, H., Zheng, D., Fong, J. And Asghari, M. (2011). "Fundamentals of Silicon Photonic Devices," *in Engineer IT.*
29. Lee, T. H., Bulzacchelli, J. F. (1992). "A 155-MHz Clock Recovery Delay- and Phase-Locked Loop," *IEEE Journal of solid-state circuits,* 27 (12). pp. 1736-1746.
30. Narayanan, P., Senthil, G. (2011). "Bionic eye powered by nanogenerators," *International conference on life science and technology,* 3, pp. 91-95.
31. Behzad Razavi, "Delay Locked Loops An Overview," in Phase-Locking in High-Performance Systems: From Devices to Architectures, IEEE, 2003, pp. 13-22 doi: https://doi.org/10.1109/9780470545492.ch2.
32. Fine, I. and Boynton, G. M. (2015). "Pulse trains to Percepts: the challenge of creating a perceptually intelligible world with sight recovery technologies," *Philosophical transactions of the Royal Society of London.* Series B, Biological sciences. 370. https://doi.org/10.1098/rstb.2014.0208.
33. Rousche, P. J., Pellinen, D. S., Pivin, D. P., Williams, J. C., Vetter, R. J. and Kipke D. R. (2001). "Flexible polyimide-based intracortical electrode arrays with bioactive capability," in IEEE Transactions on Biomedical Engineering. 48 (3), pp. 361-71.

34. Sawan, M. et al. (2013). "Electrodes – Part II," *GBM8320 Dispositifs Médicaux Intelligents.* pp. 1-23.
35. Motlagh, B. G. and Sawan, M. (2013). "Design and Implementation Challenges of Microelectrode Arrays: A Review," *Materials Sciences and Applications, Scientific Research*, 4(8), pp. 483-495.
36. Seo J. M., Paik, S. J., Kim, E. T., Byun, S. W., Lee, A. R., Cho, D., Kim, S. J., Yu, H. G., Yu, Y. S., Chung, H. (2006). "Silicon retinal tack for the epiretinal fixation of the polyimide electrode array," *Current Applied Physics, 6(4), pp. 649-653.*
37. Bron, A. J., Tripathi, R. C. and Tripathi, B. J. (1997). "Wolff's Anatomy of the Eye and Orbit," *Chapman & Hall medical.*
38. Pasquale, L. R., Cepko, C. L., and Kloek, C. E. (2014) "The Eyes Have It: Why and how you see," *The Longwood Seminars, Harvard Medical School.*
39. Fact Sheet. (2017). "Bionic Eye," *Bionics Institute.* Retrieved from www.bionicsinstitute.org.
40. Stronks, H. C. and Dagnelie, G. (2014). "The functional performance of the Argus II retinal prosthesis," *Expert Reviews medical devices*, 11(1), pp. 23-30.
41. Humayun, M. S. and Koo, L. C. O.D. (2018). "Retinal Prosthesis," *Springer International Publishing*, doi: https://doi.org/10.1007/978-3-319-67260-1.
42. Reddy, V., Maldonado, R. S., Humayun, M. S., Hahn, P. (2015). "Bionic Eye: A Glance at the Argus II retinal prosthesis," *Adv Ophthalmol Vis Syst,* 2(3): 00041. DOI: https://doi.org/10.15406/aovs.2015.02.00044.
43. Markowitz, M., Rankin, M., Mongy, M., Patino, B. E., Manusow, J., Devenyi, R. G., Markowitz, S. N. (2018). "Rehabilitation of lost functional vision with the Argus II retinal prosthesis,"*Can J Ophthalmol*, 53(1), pp. 14-22.
44. Argus II Retinal Prosthesis System Visual Rehabilitation Guide. *Second Sight, Inc.* Accessed: (2017). Retrieved from http://www.secondsight.com.
45. Devenyi, R. G., Manusow, J., Patino, B. E., Mongy, M., Markowitz, M., Markowitz, S. N. (2017). "The Toronto experience with the Argus II retinal prosthesis, new technology, new hopes for patients," Canadian Journal of Ophthalmology, 53(1), pp. 9-13.
46. Jeter, P. E., Rozanski, C., Massof, R., Adeyemo, O., Dagnelie, G. (2017). "Development of the Ultra Low Vision Visual Functioning Questionnaire (ULV-VFQ)," *Trans Vis Sci Technol.* 6(11), doi:https://doi.org/10.1167/tvst.6.3.11.
47. Lin, T. C., Yue, L. and Humayun, M. S. (2018). "Retinal prosthesis: The ARGUS system," *Technology and Innovation,* 19, pp. 605-611.
48. Daschner, R., Rothermel, A., Rudorf, R., Rudorf, S., and Stett, A. (2018). "Functionality and performance of the subretinal implant chip Alpha AMS," *Sensors and Materials,* 30(2), pp. 179-192.
49. Caspi A, Roy A, Wuyyuru V, et al. (2018). "Eye movement control in the Argus II retinal-prosthesis enables reduced head movement and better localization precision," *Investigative Ophthalmology and Visual Science*, 59(2), pp. 792–802.
50. Finn, A. P., Tripp, F., Whitaker, D., Vajzovic, L. (2018). "Synergistic visual gains attained using Argus II retinal prosthesis with OrCamMyEye," *Ophthalmol Retin*, 2(4), pp. 382–384.
51. Finn, A. P., Viehland, C., Zevallos, O. M. C., Izatt, J. A., Toth, C. A., Vajzovic, L. (2018). "Four-dimensional microscope-integrated OCT use in Argus II placement," *Ophthalmol Retin*, 2(5), pp. 510–511.
52. Delyfer, M.N, Gaucher, D., Govare, M., et al. (2018). "Adapted surgical procedure for Argus II retinal implantation: feasibility, safety, efficiency, and postoperative anatomic findings," *Ophthalmol Retin,* 2(4), pp. 276–287.
53. Yoon, C. K., and Yu, H. G. (2018). "Ganglion cell-inner plexiform layer and retinal nerve fibre layer changes within the macula in retinitis pigmentosa: a spectral domain optical coherence tomography study," *Acta Ophthalmol*, e180–e188.
54. Finn, A. P., Grewal, D. S. and Vajzovic, L. (2018). "Argus II retinal prosthesis system: a review of patient selection criteria, surgical considerations, and post-operative outcomes," *Clinical Ophthalmology,* 12, pp. 1089–1097

55. Definition retina, Accessed (2018). Retrieved from https://www.merriam-webster.com/dictionary/retina.
56. Haim, M. (2002), "The epidemiology of retinitis pigmentosa in Denmark," Acta Ophthalmologica Scandinavica, 80, pp. 1-34. doi:https://doi.org/10.1046/j.1395-3907.2002.00001.x
57. Brindley, G. S., & Lewin, W. S. (1968). "The sensations produced by electrical stimulation of the visual cortex," The Journal of physiology, 196(2), pp. 479–493.
58. H. Dobelle, Wm. (2000). "Artificial Vision for the Blind by Connecting a Television Camera to the Visual Cortex," ASAIO journal (American Society for Artificial Internal Organs : 1992). 46. pp 3-9. https://doi.org/10.1097/00002480-200001000-00002.
59. Normann et. al., (1999) "A neural interface for a cortical vision prosthesis," Vision Research, 39(15), pp. 2577-2587, ISSN 0042-6989, https://doi.org/10.1016/S0042-6989(99)00040-1.
60. Tong, F. (2003). "Primary visual cortex and visual awareness," Nature reviews. Neuroscience. 4. pp. 219-29. https://doi.org/10.1038/nrn1055.
61. P.R. Troyk, et. al. (2005). "Intracortical Visual Prosthesis Research - Approach and Progress," IEEE Engineering in Medicine and Biology Society, Conference. 7, 7376-9. https://doi.org/10.1109/IEMBS.2005.1616216.
62. C Peterman et. al., (2004). "Localized chemical release from an artificial synapse chip," Proceedings of the National Academy of Sciences of the United States of America. 101. 9951-4. https://doi.org/10.1073/pnas.0402089101.
63. Wang et. al., (2006). "Neural Stimulation with a Carbon Nanotube Microelectrode Array," Nano letters. 6. 2043-8. https://doi.org/10.1021/nl061241t.
64. Fujikado T. et. al., (2016) "One-Year Outcome of 49-Channel Suprachoroidal-Transretinal Stimulation Prosthesis in Patients With Advanced Retinitis Pigmentosa," Invest Ophthalmol Vis Sci. Nov 1;57(14), pp. 6147-6157. doi: https://doi.org/10.1167/iovs.16-20367. PubMed PMID: 27835711.
65. N. Peachey & A. Chow, (1999). "Subretinal implantation of semiconductor-based photodiodes: Progress and challenges," Journal of rehabilitation research and development. 36. pp. 371-6.
66. A. Y. Chow et. al. (2004) "The artificial silicon retina microchip for the treatment of vision loss from retinitis pigmentosa," Arch Ophthalmol. 122(4), pp. 460-9. PubMed PMID: 15078662
67. Palanker et. al. (2005). "Design of a high-resolution optoelectronic retinal prosthesis," Journal of neural engineering. 2. pp. 105-20. https://doi.org/10.1088/1741-2560/2/1/012.
68. E. Zrenner, (2002). "Will Retinal Implants Restore Vision?," Science (New York, N.Y.). 295. pp. 1022-5. https://doi.org/10.1126/science.1067996.
69. D. J . Weiland et. al., (2005), "Retinal Prosthesis," Annual Review of Biomedical Engineering 7:1, pp. 361-401
70. U. Jow and M. Ghovanloo, (2007), "Design and Optimization of Printed Spiral Coils for Efficient Transcutaneous Inductive Power Transmission," in IEEE Transactions on Biomedical Circuits and Systems, 1(3), pp. 193-202. doi: https://doi.org/10.1109/TBCAS.2007.913130
71. Sawan et. al., (2005). "Wireless smart implants dedicated to multichannel monitoring and microstimulation," Circuits and Systems Magazine, IEEE. 5. pp. 21 - 39. https://doi.org/10.1109/MCAS.2005.1405898.
72. U. Jow and M. Ghovanloo, (2009),"Modeling and Optimization of Printed Spiral Coils in Air, Saline, and Muscle Tissue Environments," in IEEE Transactions on Biomedical Circuits and Systems, 3(5), pp. 339-347, doi: https://doi.org/10.1109/TBCAS.2009.2025366
73. M. S. Humayun et. al., (2012) "Interim results from the international trial of Second Sight's visual prosthesis," Ophthalmology. Apr;119(4), pp. 779-88. doi: https://doi.org/10.1016/j.ophtha.2011.09.028.
74. L. da Cruz et. al., (2016) "Five-Year Safety and Performance Results from the Argus II Retinal Prosthesis System Clinical Trial", Ophthalmology, 123(10), pp. 2248-2254, ISSN 0161-6420, https://doi.org/10.1016/j.ophtha.2016.06.049.
75. Geruschat DR, et al., (2016), "An analysis of observer-rated functional vision in patients implanted with the Argus II Retinal Prosthesis System at three years," Clin Exp Optom. 99(3), pp. 227-32. doi: https://doi.org/10.1111/cxo.12359.

Chapter 28
Finger Biometrics for e-Health Security

Gaurav Jaswal, Aditya Nigam, and Ravinder Nath

28.1 Security Trends

In the last few years, it has been noticed that security and privacy of personal information has become an important concern of everyone due to day to day identity theft and credit card frauds in society. As per the latest reports on identity fraud released by various agencies, the variety of microchip enabled debit or credit cards like Visa, Discover, American Express etc confronted billions of U.S. dollars in fraud losses [19]. It is found that about 2–5 card holders in America have been an identity theft victim. In another study, after recognizing a large number of duplicate PAN (Permanent Account Number) cards, the government of India deactivated around 11.44 lakh PAN cards by July 2017. It thus demands at least some level of security to ensure the personal identity in various social and commercial applications [18]. The conventional knowledge (e.g., PIN or password) or token (e.g., driving license) based identity mechanisms require to remember long or repetitive passwords [18, 19]. On the contrary, biometric authentication refers to recognition of an individual by his/her unique characteristics, namely physiological and behavioral traits or both [18].

Role of Biometric Technology in e-Health The electronic health (e-Health) schemes has proved to be very riveting for the health industry due to the many advantages it imparts to the society. The world health organization (WHO) defined E-Health as the use of Information and Communication Technology (ICT) in

G. Jaswal (✉) · A. Nigam
Indian Institute of Technology, Mandi, Mandi, India
e-mail: gaurav_jaswal@projects.iitmandi.ac.in; aditya@iitmandi.ac.in

R. Nath
National Institute of Technology, Hamirpur, Hamirpur, India
e-mail: nath@nith.ac.in

© Springer Nature Switzerland AG 2019
A. K. Singh, A. Mohan (eds.), *Handbook of Multimedia Information Security: Techniques and Applications*, https://doi.org/10.1007/978-3-030-15887-3_28

health sector [44]. In India, Government has begun plenty of e-Gov startups in public health care sectors, the branch is called as e-Health division [5]. E-Health enhances the quality of health care by several means. It provides easy access to patient health data, improves efficiency, and reduces the total cost of health service delivery [44]. Despite the above mentioned advantages of e-Health scheme, it still come across various security challenges that need to be handled. The patient data privacy and security are one of major challenges due to which health companies are facing difficulties, and to which they still looking for solutions. The main security requirements for E-Health schemes are based on the basic principles of information security. In addition, user authentication and authorization are another important issues in relation to the security requirements of e-Health scheme [44]. Figure 28.1 depicts architecture of e-health security with the use of biometrics. Therefore to achieve reliable user authentication forms the basis for all other measures to be achieved. In this context, the conventional recognition approaches such as knowledge or token are not suitable in the e-Health due to the possibility of being lost, stolen, forgotten, or misplaced [19]. Since possession and knowledge are not intrinsic human characteristics, thereby tough to manage. The pictorial example of conventional methods of authentication is depicted in Fig. 28.2.

It thus proves that biometrics has a larger scope in e-health and its counterparts. In particular, biometric is an image recognition system which comprises of various pre-processing and post-processing techniques such as collecting a biometric image

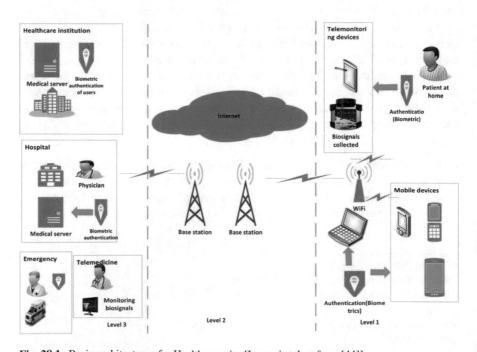

Fig. 28.1 Basic architecture of e-Health security [Image is taken from [44]]

Fig. 28.2 Examples of traditional authentication methods

from a person, ROI extraction and enhancement, robust feature extraction and feature matching with the stored templates in the database [42]. Biometrics is a fundamental security mechanism that assigns a unique identity to an individual according to some physiological or behavioral characteristics [18]. The advantages of such biometric characteristics are:

- These characteristics are inherently related to users.
- One cannot easily manipulate, misplace, steal, or share them. Hence, they are easy to manage.
- There is a need of physical presence of the trait for authentication.
- Hard to spoof.
- Features properties are unique.

Ideally, any human biological feature cannot be a biometric trait unless it satisfies the characteristics like universality, accessibility, uniqueness, permanence etc [18, 19].

- Universality: The biometric trait should be present in all who access the application.
- Uniqueness: The feature should be as unique as possible, so that the same feature does not appear in any two different individuals even in case of identical twins.
- Permanence: The biometric feature should be invariant to any environmental change.
- Collectability: It should be easily collectible in terms of acquisition, digitization, and feature extraction.
- Acceptability: It refers to the willingness of an individual to provide his/her biometrics to the device.
- Circumvention: The biometric feature cannot be easily imitated using artifacts.
- Performance: The feature should be robust and capable to achieve highest recognition at high speed.

28.1.1   Historical Background: Biometrics

According to the historical narrative, the term biometricsis derived from Greek words: bio (life) and metric (to measure). In literature, the first reference found for the term biometrics was in a 1981 article in The New York Times [12]. However, proofs suggest that biometric patterns were used even thousands of years ago in old caves where humans had signed their pictures by fingerprints. Over the years various types of non-automated biometrics methods used but automated biometric technologies came into existence with the expansion of computers. The first known reference to non-automated biometrics was found in prehistoric picture of a hand with ridge patterns that was discovered in Nova Scotia [28]. Fingerprint recognition represents the oldest method of biometric identity mechanism; with its history going back as far as at least 6000 B.C. [38]. The first recorded use of fingerprints was in the form of stamps by the ancient Babylonians, Chinese, Japanese, and Assyrians, for the signing of legal documents and business transactions. Almost a same technique was used in China by stamping children palm prints and footprints on paper with ink to distinguish the children from each other. The use of palm and fingerprints was started in India in past 1858, when Sir William Herschel pressed hand prints on the backs of contracts. Likewise, in late 1980's, the police force in India, started using fingerprints to identify lawbreakers [28]. In early 1990's, development of biometric technology revolutionized the field of digital human identity management as it led to the possibility of designing efficient automated authentication. Nowadays, several financial as well as security related applications, require an automated, and accurate access for recognition of individuals. Security forces deploy various human identifications systems to discern potential wrongdoers [12]. Modern definition of biometrics refers to automatic recognition or verification of an individual by his/her unique biological characteristics which can be measured. In 1985, the Naval Postgraduate School in US utilized first retinal scanning system for securing access to department facility. The first biometric industry organization, the International Biometrics Association (IBA) was founded in 1986 [12]. Iris recognition technology was developed in the 1980s by Dr. John Daugman at the University of Cambridge. In 1998, the International Biometric Industry Association (IBIA) was founded in Washington, DC, as a non-profit industry trade association to flourish the biometric industry [28]. In 1997, Central research institute at Hitachi Ltd. had designed first ever touch less finger vein recognition device and approximately 80% of the banks, in Japan, Korea, Poland, use this facility for user verification [19]. In 1996, the first commercial hand geometry biometric scanner i.e., Immigration and Naturalization Service Passenger Accelerated Service System (INSPASS) was used at airports/lands in USA to facilitate passage through entry barriers [23]. In 1989, first time researchers revealed about the novelty of finger knuckle texture and found its utility in forensic identification [29].

28.1.2 Biometric Traits and Characteristics

In the past 2–3 decades, several biometric traits have been investigated, including fingerprint, face, ear, iris, palm print, and gait for reliable security solutions. However, there does not exist any biometric trait which strictly satisfies all desired properties strictly. Each of these has its own specific challenges that do not allow its usages in all application scenarios. For example, facial features are not permanent throughout the life span, fingerprints are not visible for manual workers etc.

In particular, biometric traits can be divided into three main categories based on one of the following biological characteristics of human beings [18, 19]:

- Behavioural characteristics: The behavioural biometric traits are acquired due to the repeated action of a person such as typing rhythm, voice, gait, handwriting etc.
- Physiological characteristics: The physiological characteristics are inherent characteristics of human body in which biometric sample is obtained directly. Some well known physiological traits are fingerprint, iris, ear, etc. Physiological and behavioural biometrics are clubbed and named hard biometrics [19]. These characteristics do not vary much over sufficient duration of time and are highly distinctive in nature. Figure 28.3 shows an example of biometric characteristics. Further, there are few more features which provide some information about a person and may be used as biometric identifiers.

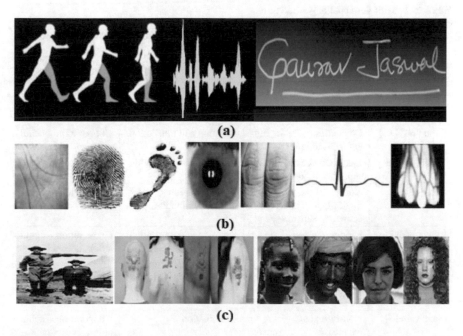

(a)

(b)

(c)

Fig. 28.3 Biometric characteristics for personal authentication. (**a**) Behavioral characteristics, (**b**) physiological characteristics, (**c**) soft characteristics

- Soft Biometrics: The soft characteristics includes age, height, weight, colour of eye/skin/hair, scars, gender, marks, and tattoos, etc. which can be used to identify human beings. The soft biometrics is unable to distinguish between large populations of individuals, as they are not unique and stable. However, it has been observed that soft biometrics work well when used in conjunction with hard biometric traits [19].

Therefore, biometrics based authentication solution is more reliable than traditional authentication approaches for differentiating between an authorized person or an imposter [7]. Biometric traits cannot be lost or forgotten; they are difficult to duplicate, share, or distribute. Moreover, it requires person to be present at the time of authentication; it is hard to copy, and unlikely for a user to repudiate [18] (Table 28.1).

28.1.3   Design of an Automated Biometric System

Depending upon the application, any biometric system is commonly a part of enrollment, verification or identification, as depicted in Fig. 28.4 [42]. Firstly, every individual is instructed to provide samples of her/or his biometric trait to the system for ensuring registration. A specific resolution sensor is deployed to capture the

Table 28.1 Trait-wise challenges and issues

Trait	Motivation	Challenges	Issues
Fingerprint [9]	Easy collection, unique, economic sensor, less cooperative	Rotation and translation	Acceptance
Iris [40]	Highly discriminative and unique, expensive sensor, well protected	Segmentation, Motion blur, illumination, rotation	Cooperation, acquisition
Palm print [15]	Contactless sensor, bigger ROI, unique	Rotation and translation	Cooperation, acquisition, acceptance
Hand geometry [46]	Easy collection, cheap sensor, less cooperative	Rotation and translation	Acceptance
Face [13]	Non-intrusive, most obvious, universal, economic sensor	Pose, rotation expression, illumination, ageing	Acquisition
Finger knuckle-print [29]	Unique, cheap sensor discriminative, well protected,	Rotation and translation	Cooperation, acquisition, acceptance
Ear [32]	Non-intrusive, cheap sensor, universal, robust shape	Scale, rotation translation, illumination	Cooperation, acquisition, acceptance
Hand vein [8]	Non-intrusive, expensive sensor, universal, robust shape	illumination	Cooperation, acquisition, acceptance

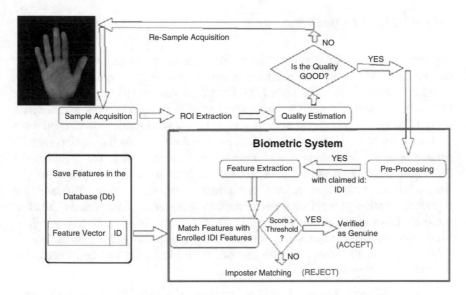

Fig. 28.4 Architecture for verification system

biometric sample from the user. Further, important image attributes are extracted from the given sample and is saved in the database to create the template. In practice, biometric systems are employed in following modes [19, 42]:

- Enrollment: In the first stage, an individual registers her or him to the current database and system creates a biometric template that is linked with the user. But the quality of sample needs to be ensured before subsequent processing because quality has a significant impact on the system performance. The user is asked to provide sample again if the quality is found below the empirically set threshold. After this, features are extracted and a unique identification ID is linked to it.
- Verification: It allows one to one matching to determine whether the claim is true or not. In this mode, the user claims an identity and the biometric system validates the correctness of the claim against the earlier stored samples of the same individual. For this, features are extracted from the input biometric sample provided by the user and compared with the features of the earlier collected templates in the database. The claim is said to be verified if the similarity matching score between them is more than a pre-decided threshold, else the claim is rejected.
- Identification: It is described as one to all matching. In this mode of operation, the system may not have any clue about the stored templates of other individuals. The biometric system strives to recognize the true identity of the user among all the enrolled users in the database; hence it is called as identification. As mentioned above, it follows the similar procedure to pre-process the ROI image and then extracts the important image features. But in this case, the feature vector of user's biometric sample is compared with feature vectors of all individuals enrolled in the database and the top best genuine matches are considered.

28.1.4   Multi Biometric System

The performance of any unimodal biometric system, i.e., system which uses only one biometric trait is usually confined in unrestricted image acquisition situations as well as unaccommodating users [18]. Broadly, such confounding factors include lack of robustness in changing background conditions, non-universality, vulnerability to spoof attacks, sensor accuracy as well as several traits specific challenges such as bad sample quality and lesser social acceptance for the fingerprint. As with limited biometric information, a single modality cannot satisfy the requirements for higher recognition accuracy, especially for large population applications [8]. Hence, fusion of two or more than two biometric samples or algorithms can be a righteous solution to meet high performance requirements [19]. This is called as multi biometrics [18]. A multi-biometric system is capable of dealing with a large number of registered subjects and provide strong anti spoofing capabilities.

According to the source of information, multi-biometrics can be divided into following six categories [18, 42]:

- Multiple Sensors System: It utilizes samples of a same biometric trait where images are acquired by virtue of multiple compatible sensors. An imaging sensor uses different electronic technologies such as ultrasonic, thermal, optical to capture data and hence the qualities, as well as discriminative features of their samples, are significantly different.
- Multiple Algorithms System: It considers multiple matching algorithms to improve the performance of the system. Samples of the selected trait are captured using the single imaging sensor. One fingerprint algorithm may be using some local minutia point features while another one may use global singular point or ridge orientation features. Grouping of these classifiers takes the advantage to improve the performance of any of the individual algorithms.
- Multiple Instances System: It considers multiple image samples of the same trait per individual.
- Multiple Modalities System: It considers multiple biometric traits for authentication. The features derived from different biometric traits are combined to achieve better performance. Also, it makes the system more vigorous against spoofing attacks as it becomes immensely tough to replicate all associated traits at once. It is mostly termed as multi modal system. In particular, multi modal systems are more applicable when the number of registered users are very large. The system error rates like false acceptance grows immediately with the increase in the size of the database; hence multiple traits are used to achieve better performance. Also multi-modal systems can enable us to deal with missing trait.

Biometric fusion is the key to multi-biometrics as it consolidates the different information given by more than one biometric trait [19]. There are several ways that can be used to fuse various characteristics in a multi biometric system. In particular, information fusion can be classified into two broad categories which are discussed below:

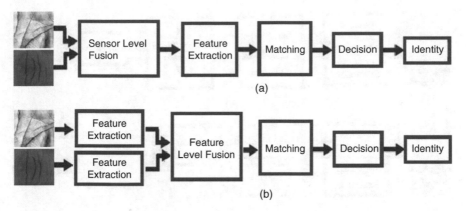

Fig. 28.5 Pre-classification fusion. (a) Sensor level fusion. (b) Feature level fusion

Pre-classification Information Fusion It refers to integration of information prior to matching algorithm such as; sensor level, feature level fusion. An example of sensor and feature level fusion using palm print and finger knuckle biometric traits is shown in Fig. 28.5.

Post-classification Information Fusion It is related to clubbing of information after decision of classifier. The combination can be mainly done using score level, decision level, or rank level fusion. An example of score, decision, and rank level fusion using palm print and finger knuckle biometric traits is shown in Fig. 28.6.

There are, however, a few limitations of using a multi biometric system. First, a multi-biometric system is more expensive and requires more computational and storage resources [8]. Secondly, such systems generally require more time for enrollment and verification, causing some inconveniences to the user [8]. Nevertheless, these are considerably insignificant in comparison to the gain achieved in terms of performance (Figs. 28.7 and 28.8).

28.1.5 Performance Analysis Parameters

Any identification or verification algorithm is tested for evaluating its performance on a database to determine whether it has capability to be used in variety of applications or not. Generally, a few important performance metrics such as Correct Recognition Rate (CRR), Equal Error Rate (EER), False Acceptance Rate (FAR), False Rejection Rate (FRR), Cumulative Match Characteristics (CMC), Receiver Operating Characteristic (ROC), Verification Accuracy, Decidability Index (DI), Area under ROC Curve (AUC) and Computation Time are used for evaluation of biometric system [19]. Further, there are some instances in which samples are not captured properly, and user is unable to enroll in a system due to absence of physical

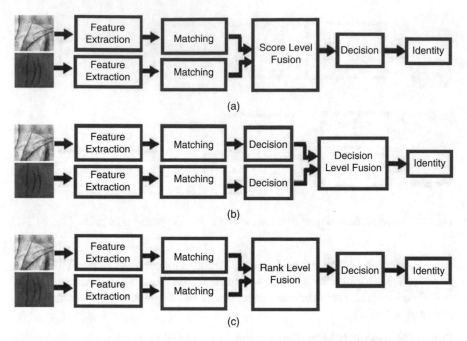

Fig. 28.6 Post-classification fusion. (**a**) Score level fusion, (**b**) decision level fusion, (**c**) rank level fusion

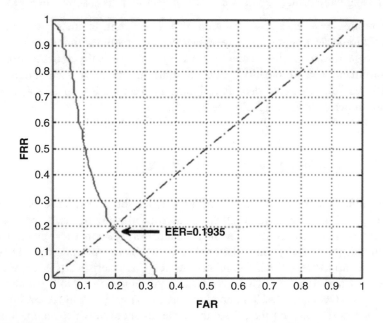

Fig. 28.7 ROC graph for biometric verification [Image is taken from [19]]

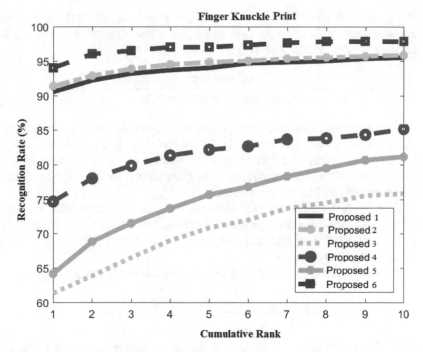

Fig. 28.8 CMC graph for biometric identification [Image is taken from [8]]

trait or poor quality of sample. So, these acquisition errors are quantified in terms of Failure To Capture (FTC) and Failure To Enroll (FTE) which deteriorates the overall performance of the system [42]. These terms are described below:

- FAR: The probability that a system incorrectly matches the user input to non-matching template in database. It measures the percentage of invalid matches which are incorrectly accepted. It is also sometimes termed as False Match Rate (FMR).

$$FAR = \frac{\text{Proportion of impostor match scores accepted wrongly}}{\text{Total number of impostor matches}} \times 100$$

(28.1)

- FRR: The probability that a system fails to detect a match between user input and matching template in database. It measures the percentage of valid matches being rejected. It is also referred as False Non-Match Rate (FNMR).

$$FRR = \frac{\text{Proportion of genuine match scores rejected wrongly}}{\text{Total number of genuine matches}} \times 100 \quad (28.2)$$

However, FAR and FRR are not the exact synonyms for FMR and FNMR but somehow they have been considered equivalent. One more possibility for authorized users is described as genuine acceptance rate.

$$GAR = \frac{\text{Proportion of genuine match scores accepted}}{\text{Total number of genuine matches}} \times 100 \qquad (28.3)$$

Beside the performance measures, graphical methods like DET (Detection Error Trade off) curve (graph of FAR vs FRR) and Receiver Operating Characteristics (ROC) which plots (1-FRR) against various FARs are used to assess the performance of verification systems [19]. Each point on a ROC or a DET curve relates with a specific decision threshold.

- EER: A predetermined threshold at which FAR linearly varies with respect to FRR in ROC plot, then the common value is called as EER. It means, EER is a point of intersection of FAR and FRR curves. The lower value of EER provides better system performance.
- Verification Accuracy: This defines the performance of verification algorithm.

$$Accuracy = 100 - \frac{\text{Sum of FAR and FRR}}{2} \times 100 \qquad (28.4)$$

- CRR: The probability of correctly identifying a person from total number of individuals available in dataset. Besides, comparing the training and test images, it also arranges them on the basis of matching scores. This is also termed as rank-1 recognition rate.

$$Accuracy = \frac{\text{Proportion of top} - 1 \text{ genuine matches}}{\text{Total number of test matches performed}} \times 100 \qquad (28.5)$$

- CMC: This plots the rank-k recognition rate (number of genuine matches that occurred in top k matches) against k.
- FTE and FTC, the acquisition errors are defined as:

$$FTC = \frac{\text{Number of attempts fail to capture}}{\text{Total No of attempts}} \times 100 \qquad (28.6)$$

$$FTE = \frac{\text{Total Number of users fail to enroll}}{\text{Total No of users}} \times 100 \qquad (28.7)$$

- DI: This measures separability between imposter and genuine matching scores and is defined as:

$$DI = \frac{|\mu_g - \mu_i|}{\sqrt{\frac{\sigma_g^2 + \sigma_i^2}{2}}} \qquad (28.8)$$

where μ_g, μ_i represent mean of genuine and imposter scores whereas σ_g, and σ_i represent variance of genuine and imposter scores.

- Computation Time: This describes the average execution time for pre-processing as well as verification/identification tasks.
- AUC: It estimates the amount of error incurred while decision making between genuine and imposter matching. Ideally, its value should have to be 0 or as much close to zero (28.8).

28.1.6 Motivation: Biometric Traits

Among the most usable biometric traits such as ear, palm print, face, iris, fingerprint, gait etc., human finger patterns are the most successful and accepted modalities due to their high user acceptance. Fingerprint is one of the most accepted biometric features used in the recognition system. Fingerprint systems have a very high accuracy in matching. They have been used in different commercial and forensic applications for years. Although the use of fingerprints is the most common approach, this method is vulnerable to forgery as the fingerprints are easily exposed to others. Moreover, it also requires physical contact, which is not desirable from a hygienic viewpoint and may cause problems with the device. Also, they require high resolution sensors for better image quality. Finger knuckle and vein traits, on the other hand, offer a promising solution to these disadvantages. Unlike a fingerprint, finger knuckle print is difficult to scrap because they concentrate on the deep surface of the finger and it can be clearly captured in a contact-less manner. Likewise, the vein patterns of a individual are unique just like fingerprint and remain unchanged due to aging. Also finger vein images are relatively stable and can be captured with a low-resolution camera. In addition to this, finger knuckle and finger vein biometric traits do not require much user cooperation and can be simultaneously captured. Despite the advantages mentioned, finger knuckle and vein authentication system does have some weaknesses. Their performance is seriously affected by the condition of the external factors like sensor types, illumination conditions, finger orientations etc. To enhance the performance of single modality based finger biometric, a multimodal biometric system including finger knuckle and vein patterns is introduced. It is more robust than the unimodal system as it takes advantage of multiple biometric traits to improve recognition performance in many aspects including accuracy, noise-resistance, universality and reduce chances of spoof attack.

Finger Knuckle Print The convex shape lines like skin patterns on finger dorsal surface specifically at Proximal Inter Phalangeal (PIP) joint is called as finger knuckle print (FKP) [29]. Such line features can be easily captured through touch-less manner using visible light cameras and do not need much user efforts. Also the size of the capturing device is small and hence reduces space complexity. The sample FKP images are shown in Fig. 28.9a.

Finger Vein The inter-connected blood vessel network collected from palmer side of finger is called as finger vein (FV) patterns [45]. The touchless acquisition procedures are convenient and hygienic than other biometric traits. Also, vein patterns are collected under infrared light source with wavelengths of 700–1000 nm. Finger vein authentication technique is also known for its fast capturing speed and its compact size. Near infrared light can only penetrates through the body tissue with a certain thickness. Otherwise, the captured vein pattern is not clear or no vein pattern can be observed from the captured image. The sample infrared FV images are shown in Fig. 28.10a.

Figures 28.9 and 28.10 shows two types of finger sensors which can be used to build a finger biometric system based on finger knuckle and finger vein traits. These two sensors use different technologies to acquire data and hence the quality as well as discriminative features of their samples are significantly different.

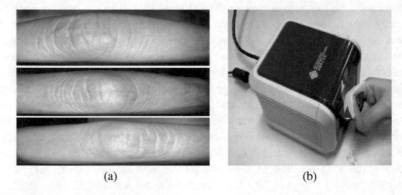

(a)   (b)

Fig. 28.9 Finger knuckle print acquisition. (**a**) Sample finger knuckle images [4]. (**b**) Ordinary sensor [53]

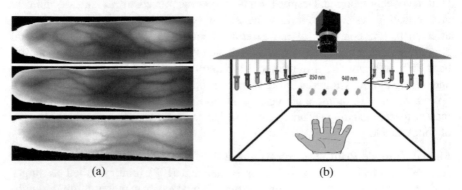

(a)   (b)

Fig. 28.10 Finger vein acquisition. (**a**) Sample finger vein images [3]. (**b**) Infrared sensor [8]

28.2 Related Work: Finger Biometrics

Here in this section we are discussing in detail about the various state-of-art studies on finger knuckle print and finger vein as a biometric identifier.

The research in finger knuckle has received significant considerations in early 2009. After that numerous state-of-art techniques have been proposed for finger knuckle image biometrics. But still, no commercial finger knuckle image-based biometric system is available so far [19]. Recently, to alleviate hygiene concerns and to provide a user-friendly environment for finger acquisition devices (like fingerprint scanners), a platform-free, non-contact or touch-less formats have been considered [22]. But overall, these devices are more convenient to the user than the guiding platforms and improve the scope of application. The first time in 1989, authors exposed about the significance of knuckle texture for forensic applications [24]. In [6], a scale, and rotation invariant descriptor was used for finger knuckle texture representation. In [30], authors proposed a multi-algorithmic approach based on matching score fusion of three subspace methods and achieved an EER of 1.39%. The well known study named as competitive code [51], focused to use major knuckle near PIP joint employed 2D Gabor filter to extract orientation information. The similar coding approaches include improved CompCodeMagCode [26], knuckle code [34], Adaptive Steerable Orientation Coding (ASOC) [37], monogenic code (based on phase and orientation information of knuckle images) [52] etc. In [47], authors computed the Gabor filter response and applied dimension reduction by projecting PCA weights into LDA. In [27], authors applied two-stage classification using Gabor filter and SURF methods and obtained EER of 0.22% and 0.218% respectively. In [31], the authors considered recovered minutiae of knuckle samples for template matching using a data-set of 120 subjects. In [29], authors made an attempt to highlight minor lower finger knuckle patterns (MCP joint) between proximal and the metacarpal phalanx bones of fingers. In [33], efforts were made to explore the overall information present on hand dorsal surface. The lower minor knuckle and palm dorsal texture were fused using two separate data-sets and the results proved the significance of dorsal texture in biometric applications. In [43], authors proposed a multi-texture fusion for finger knuckle patterns and obtained very superior recognition results. In [22] authors proposed a novel Deep-Matching algorithm to classify the extracted gradient features from bubble ordinal pattern.

On the other hand, most of the studies in vascular biometrics extract the line and curvature based information in the vessel structures present in the images. In [10], authors used local maximum curvatures in cross-sectional profiles of a vein image. In [39], authors applied line tracking method. In [11], the mean curvature of the vein image intensity was computed and it showed remarkable performance improvement in comparison with the line-tracking. In [35], a finger vein extraction method was presented which applied gradient normalization, principal curvature calculation, and binarization to compute robust vein features. In [36], authors used an image restoration model that can account for optical blur and skin scattering to improve the finger-vein matching accuracy. Another approach to improve finger-vein recognition accuracy was presented to develop a finger-vein image synthesis model [16]. This work was based on enhanced vein pattern which incorporated realistic imaging variations to synthesize finger-vein images. In a latest study [48], authors proposed a finger vein authentication using the CNN and supervised discrete hashing.

Apart from single modality finger biometrics, a number of multimodal finger based biometrics are being developed. These combinations include finger vein and finger geometry [25], fingerprint and finger vein [49], finger vein, finger print and geometry [26], finger vein and finger knuckle print [50] etc. In [8], authors presented fusion of finger vein and palm vein modalities acquired from a single sensor based imaging setup. Also the latest studies have started to explore deep learning based solutions to extract and match the deep features [20, 48].

28.3   Finger Based Multimodal Biometric System

The various studies on validation of commercial usages of biometric traits have reveled that individuals like laborers and workers in rural areas does not have good quality fingerprints. So, the fingerprint based biometric system is not very useful in such conditions to check the loopholes that are present in the transfer of payments to rural people through various levels of financial inclusion projects initiated by government or organization. The use of finger knuckle images can provide a promising alternative in such situations. A typical finger biometric system consist of sample acquisition, quality estimation, ROI extraction, pre-processing, feature extraction, matching and finally fusion of multiple traits. In this work, we suggest an idea of multimodal finger biometric system based on the fusion of finger vein and finger knuckle print traits which can be extracted from the same finger.

28.3.1   Finger Knuckle Print Biometrics

The non-rigid and weakly textured regions of knuckle patterns provide intricacies to FKP recognition. They are the major contributor towards false rejection in FKP based matches. To handle such non-rigid deformation and large displacement in FKP image, there are many well known approaches exist in literature but a quad tree patch subdivision based Deep-matching algorithm can be seen as an ultimate solution. In this study, the analysis of FKP system is shown over two publicly available datasets Hong Kong Polytechnic University (PolyU) FKP database [4] and PolyU Contactless FKI Dataset [2]. Before extracting the robust knuckle features, three important pre-processing techniques are applied to raw knuckle images, which are described as follows.

28.3.1.1 Quality Estimation

System performance is highly dependent on the quality of the input image. The images acquired from different types of sensors have varied quality parameters [41]. Hence quality assessment should be done as early as possible during data acquisition to achieve better results. In general, finger-knuckle-print images are of poor quality mainly because of reflection, poor uniformity, out of focus and due to camera reflection [22]. To deal with finger knuckle image quality, a trained network namely FKQNet is used which comprises of two CNN models [20]. The objective of this network is to first estimate the quality of given image and then classify this into one of the three categories based on quality score.

FKONet [20] The network for quality estimation of finger knuckles is trained in two levels. In the first level, a fine tuned ResNet model is trained for each of the single quality parameters. In the second level, each of the feature vector extracted from quality parameters is taken, combined and some classification layers are included at the end. Then, the entire model is trained in an end to end mode. As discussed above, state-of-art ResNet model is selected as the base model for quality estimation of finger knuckles and this model is chosen because it has achieved state of the art results in the ImageNet classification challenge. Specifically, feature vector of 2048 neurons is extracted from the 'Flatten' layer of the ResNet model and the rest of the classification layers are chopped off. This is done because the lower classification layers of the ResNet model learn more about global features related to the ImageNet database but in this problem basic features like edges and blobs are required thus we chop off these layers. Finally, it is dropped to two neurons gradually through a series of fully connected layers. After each layer, a dropout of 0.3 is applied to avoid over-fitting. These dense layers include six layers with 1000, 500, 250, 100, 50 and 20 neurons respectively. Relu activation is applied over each of these dense layers to impart regularization and to introduce non-linearity. Finally, a classification layer consisting of two neurons is added over it with a softmax classification to classify a particular image as good or bad based on that particular quality trait. The above model is trained only starting from the second last convolution layer of the Resnet model and all the layers till the 'Activation47' layer of the Resnet model are freezed because the basic local features is already learned by the ResNet model and now the requirement is only to learn the global features of the knuckle images. Hence such a network is trained for each of the quality parameters individually. The model is then trained with the ground truth generated by performing k means clustering of the values computed for the individual parameters. The optimizer used is Adam with a learning rate of 0.001 and the loss considered is sparse categorical cross entropy.

Model Description The feature vector of each of single quality parameters are taken from the trained ResNet which consist of 20 neurons and then merged to construct a feature vector of 120 neurons. This is then dropped to 3 classes through a series of 5 dense layers with number of neurons 100, 50, 30, 15 and 3 respectively.

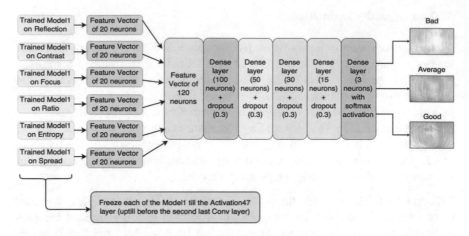

Fig. 28.11 Combined model for quality estimation of knuckle images [Image is taken from [20]]

Relu activation is applied to the output of the first four dense layers to provide regularization and Softmax activation is applied to the last classification layer for finding the class probabilities. Following each of the first four dense layers is a dropout of 0.3 to avoid over-fitting. Adam optimizer with a learning rate of 0.003 is used to optimize the sparse categorical Cross entropy loss. Each of the ResNets are freezed till the 'Activation47' layer. As shown in Fig. 28.11, the combined model is then trained in an end to end fashion with the ground truth obtained by performing k-means clustering based on the fused quality attribute which took into account all the six individual quality parameters. The quality of finger knuckle image is computed with six main attributes [41]: Focus (F), Clutter (C), Spread (S), Entropy (E), Reflection (R), and Contrast (C). The selected quality parameters specifically tend to analyze the quality of longitudinal features as they are more prominent in finger knuckle image. Finally, sobel kernel (3×3) is used to estimate the vertically strong edges over finger knuckle image.

1. Focus The defocus in an image acquisition procedure describes the dislocation of focal point of the sensor's lens at the reference object. In a de-focused image, it is observed that the frequency spectra is not fine towards high frequencies while it appears uniform for focused image. In case of FKP, the amount of well focused area is considered for quality assessment. To compute this, an input image is convolved with given (6×6) kernel that can well approximate the band pass characteristics. With this, we have a set of pixels that are well focused, means the convolved value of those pixels is more than empirically set threshold. Therefore, the set of well focused pixels are used to constitute the most significant region for quality assessment. Finally, focus (F) as a quality parameter is defined as the number of well focused vertically aligned long edge pixels.

2. Contrast Often the large illumination variation can reduce the discriminative line features in FKP and result into degradation of overall uniqueness and quality of the image. The contrast (C) describes about the dynamic gray level range present in the image. In this work, it is used to estimate the uniformity in illumination in the overall FKP image. The entire intensity level is grouped into three parts (0; 75); (76; 235); (236; 255). Hence, contrast as a quality attribute (C) is defined as the number of gray scale pixels that lie in the intermediate range of intensities (i.e (76; 235)).

3. Reflection It is very important to remove reflection from the image that is caused by camera flash or lighting source. High reflection usually creates a bright patch of very high intensity gray values. The unique lines and creases lying over this patch in FKP images are almost collapsed resulting in serious quality degradation. To control the effects of high reflection, a sample FKP image is thresholded again and again until the most accurate reflection patch is estimated. The thresholding procedure gets terminated when the count of number of pixels gets saturated (i.e when the difference in the count before and after thresholding is less than an empirically selected value). After termination the full reflection patch is identified as shown in Fig. 28.12. The reflection (R) as quality attribute is defined as the number of pixels belonging to the reflection patch hence it is inversely proportional to the image quality.

4. Entropy To compute the amount of information in any gray scale image (I), the most common parameter is the entropy (E). In this work, the input FKP image is first partitioned into blocks of size 5×5 and the entropy is calculated block wise (as shown in Fig. 28.12). One can observe that all these blocks are not equally important, therefore the blocks with well focused and long vertically aligned edge pixels are considered as significant blocks. Hence, the entropy (E) as a quality attribute is obtained by summing up the all the entropies of significant blocks as shown in Fig. 28.12.

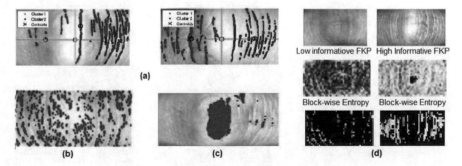

Fig. 28.12 Computation for reflection, entropy, spread and clutter [Image is taken from [41]]. (**a**) Non-uniform vs uniform texture, (**b**) clutter, (**c**) reflection, (**d**) entropy

5. Spread It has been noticed that well focused structure exists only in left or right half of most of the FKP images as shown in Fig. 28.12. However, the texture should have to be distributed uniformly through out the whole image. The spread (S) is defined as a quality attribute which is directly proportional to the uniformity in texture distribution as shown in Fig. 28.12. In this work, the set of well focused pixels are clustered using K-Means algorithm using K = 2, because FKP images are well aligned horizontally. Then cluster point ratio and cluster deviation standard ratio of the two clusters are used to compute the value of S.

6. Clutter As it is clear that the vertical features in FKP images are well defined. But, there are a few short vertical edge pixels as well that are usually present due to abrupt discontinuity in the edge structure. These pixels can degrade the quality of the image. It basically creates false features that can confuse any recognition algorithm. The clutter (C) as quality parameter is defined as the ratio of long vertically aligned strong edge pixels to the shorter ones. It is inversely proportional to the image quality.

7. Fused Quality Attribute The values of all the above described six quality parameters are computed and then normalized using maxmin normalization.The likelihood ratio based fusion is used to find a fused score for all the six quality parameters which can then be used to estimate the overall quality of the image.

Finally, the quality attributes from the randomly selected finger-knuckle-images along with their respective true quality label are used to train the deep Learning model. The initial classification results using reflection, ratio, and output are shown in Fig. 28.13.

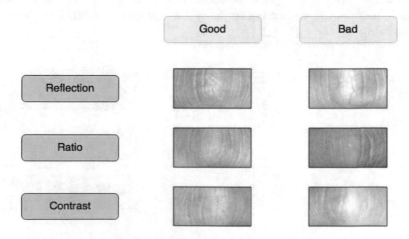

Fig. 28.13 Classification results for quality parameters [Image is taken from [20]]

28.3.1.2 Knuckle ROI Extraction

The ROI extraction is one of the major stages in an automated biometric system because the accuracy of feature extraction and matching algorithms completely dependent on its consistent segmentation. The poor ROI segmentation deteriorates the performance of biometric system which limits its usages in various modern security applications [22]. In literature, most of algorithms share a common viewpoint for ROI extraction of major finger knuckle when tested on publicly available PolyU FKP database [4]. These methods are based on local convexity characteristics of the skin patterns near major finger joint (PIP).

1. Convex Coding [53] In this method, authors encoded the pixels $(1, -1)$ over curved lines and considered convexity magnitude to locate the center of the finger joint. The various steps involved in it are shown in Fig. 28.14.

2. Curvature Gabor Filter [43] In this method, authors used Gabor filter response to locate middle knuckle line at the major finger joint. The various steps involved in it are shown in Fig. 28.15.

3. Major-Minor Coarse Segmentation [29] In this method, authors proposed ROI segmentation framework for utilizing rough information of major and minor

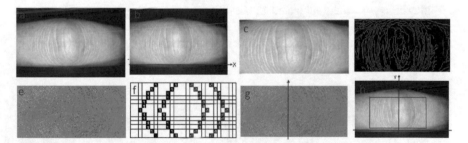

Fig. 28.14 FKP ROI extraction. (**a**) Original, (**b**) binary sample, (**c**) boundary, (**d**) FKP area, (**e**) Knuckle filter, (**f**) filter response, (**g**) localized ROI, (**h**) final ROI [Images are taken from [53]]

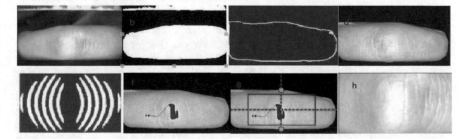

Fig. 28.15 FKP ROI extraction. (**a**) Original, (**b**) binary sample, (**c**) boundary, (**d**) FKP area, (**e**) Knuckle filter, (**f**) filter response, (**g**) localized ROI, (**h**) final ROI [Images are taken from [43]]

finger joints w.r.t. finger. The experiments are performed on publicly available finger knuckle image contact-less database. The various processing stages involved in ROI extraction are shown in Fig. 28.16.

28.3.1.3 ROI Enhancement and Transformation

The textured region of the knuckle print can be used for identification as it is unique for every individual. The finger dorsal signifies a fairly deformable surface, which results in uncertain reflections and illuminations [22].

1. Contrast Limited Adaptive Histogram Equalization In this method, the estimated illumination of every cell is divided from the corresponding cell of the major FKP ROI and get a uniformly brightened ROI sample, as shown in Fig. 28.17c. Now, the resulting ROI image is enriched using CLAHE, which improves the contrast in the texture without adding noise and increases the discriminative strength as shown in Fig. 28.17d. Further, the blocking effect is reduced using bi-linear interpolation [22]. Finally, Weiner filtering is applied to smooth the boundaries between image blocks, and to minimize the additive noise as depicted in Fig. 28.17e.

2. Histogram Equalization In this method, the estimated illumination is subtracted from the minor knuckle image to remove the uneven illuminations. The resulting image is then subjected to the histogram equalization operation which generates enhanced minor finger knuckle images [29]. Figure 28.18b shows image samples after the image enhancement operations.

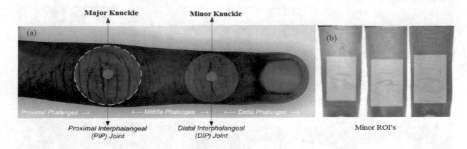

Fig. 28.16 FKP ROI extraction. (**a**) Original, (**b**) ROI samples [Images are taken from [29]]

Fig. 28.17 (**a**) I_{ROI}, (**b**) Steady Ill., (**c**) En. (Additive), (**d**) En. (Multiplicative), (**e**) de-noised [Images are taken from [22]]

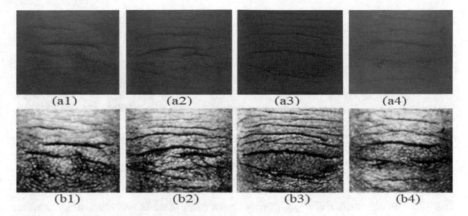

Fig. 28.18 (**a**) Minor Knuckle ROI Images (a_1–a_4), (**b**) enhanced ROI images (b_1–b_4) [Images are taken from [29]]

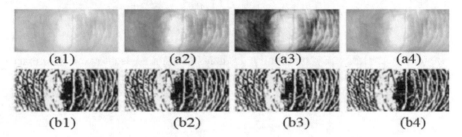

Fig. 28.19 (**a**) Major Knuckle ROI Images (a_1–a_4), (**b**) enhanced ROI images (b_1–b_4) [Images are taken from [43]]

3. Local Gradient Binary Pattern (LGBP) The major knuckle images can be enhanced using robust representations (vcode and hcode) that can ensure small change of illumination variation [43]. The type of image encoding scheme is called LGBP transformation. In Fig. 28.19, one raw FKP image is considered under varying illumination and is shown along with the corresponding vcode.

4. Bubble Ordinal Pattern (BOP) The BOP computes the ordinal relationship of two adjacent pixel gradient values, specifically when neighbors have similar values [22]. The longitudinal and transverse derivatives of its eight neighbors as shown in Fig. 28.20a. The gradient of any pixel will be +ve or −ve that is encoded into a bit either 1 or 0 coding value. Hence, such ordinal relationship encodes the type of edge that is passing trough the corresponding pixels. The BOP encoding mechanism utilizes Sobel longitudinal kernel to assign an 8-bit code (l_{BOP}) to every pixel based on the derivatives of eight neighbors. It has been observed that the obtained transverse derivatives are not very robust primarily due to the prominent longitudinal features present in the FKP images, as shown in Fig. 28.20b. Hence, after rigorous experiments, we have dropped transverse gradient (t_{BOP}) and other derived features

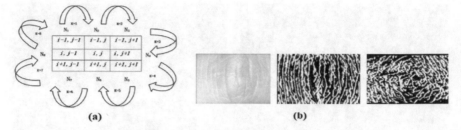

Fig. 28.20 (a) Neighborhood pattern, (b) enhanced ROI images (original image, longitudinal BOP image, transverse BOP image) [Images are taken from [22]]

from it. The obtained BOP_{Code} response for each pixel is an 8-bit binary number whose kth bit is stipulated in Eq. (28.9):

$$BOP_{Code}(u, v)[k] = \begin{cases} 1, \text{if} G_k > G_{k+1} \\ 0, \text{otherwise} \end{cases} \tag{28.9}$$

where, G_K, k=1,2,3....8 represent the gradients of eight adjacent pixels positioned around $E_{u,v}$ with the use of transverse or longitudinal Sobel kernels. Therefore, l_{BOP} or t_{BOP} are basically BOP_{Code} based representation of entire pixels in a ROI sample as computed in step 2 of Algorithm 1.

Algorithm 1 BOP algorithm [22]

Require:

    The image gradient (I_g) of size $w \times h$.

Ensure:

    Encoded images I_{BOP} of size $(w - 2) \times (h - 2)$.

 1: **for** u=1 to w-1 **do**

 2:    **for** v=1 to h-1 **do**

 3:        **for** k=1 to 8 **do**

 4:            **if** $G_k > G_{(k+1)\%8}$ **then**

 5:                $BOP(u, v)[k] = 1$

 6:            **else**

 7:                $BOP(u, v)[k] = 0$

 8:            **end if**

 9:        **end for**

10:    **end for**

11: **end for**

28.3.1.4 Feature Extraction and Matching

Feature extraction and matching are two main steps involved in biometric recognition task. For this, first image features are extracted from pre-processed enhanced image which we get from the image ROI extraction step [19]. Extracted image features can be local or it can be global features, depend upon the type of feature extraction algorithm is used [19, 22]. In this section, some of well known FKP feature extraction and matching algorithms are presented.

1. Multiple Orientation and Texture Feature Matching In this method [14], a FKP image is processed by the following steps: (1) An input FKP ROI image is transformed to obtain multiple Gabor filtering responses by applying multi-orientation Gabor filters; (2) Histograms are evaluated to obtain optimal multi-thresholds. For orientation feature extraction, the histogram is calculated directly on Gabor filter responses. For texture feature extraction, each Gabor response is first converted to local binary pattern (LBP) map, then histogram is evaluated based on these LBP maps; (3) Multilevel image thresholding based coding is performed on Gabor responses and LBP maps based on the optimal multi-thresholds respectively. Finally, modified Hamming distance is used to compute distance between two two Moricode (MtexCode) maps. The various processing steps involved for multi-orientation feature extraction are shown in Fig. 28.21.

2. SIFT and SURF Matching In SIFT matching [6], an input FKP image is matched with the knuckle print features present in the database. The SIFT detector basically extracts a collection of key points from an image and builds a descriptor with scale, orientation, and translation invariant properties. Exactly an eight-bin orientation histogram is determined for each region of the 4×4 spatial grid around every key point. Finally, nearest-neighbour-ratio is used for calculating the matching scores between corresponding feature vectors. When FKP images of the same user is matched it is known as the genuine matching whereas different user sample matching is known as an imposter matching. However, one of the major drawback

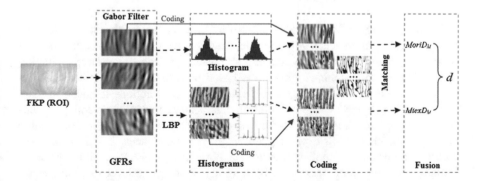

Fig. 28.21 Multiple orientation feature extraction [Images are taken from [14]]

Fig. 28.22 SIFT matching: (**a**) SIFT key-points detected, (**b**) genuine matching of SIFT key-points, (**c**) imposter matching of SIFT key-points [Images are taken from [6]]

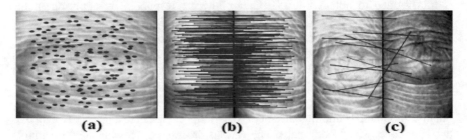

Fig. 28.23 SURF matching: (**a**) SURF key-points detected, (**b**) genuine matching of SURF key-points, (**c**) imposter matching of SURF key-points [Images are taken from [6]]

of using SIFT is that, SIFT fails to match non-rigid deformable regions, image patches with weak or repetitive textures. An example of SIFT matching is shown in Fig. 28.22.

On the other hand, SURF [6] goes a little further and approximates Laplacian of Gaussian with Box Filter. One big advantage of this approximation is that, convolution with box filter can be easily calculated with the help of integral images. And it can be done in parallel for different scales. Also the SURF rely on determinant of Hessian matrix for both scale and location. An example of SIFT matching is shown in Fig. 28.23.

3. DeepMaching: A Multi Scale Pyramidal Approach In contrast to descriptor based matching approaches a multi scale, hierarchical algorithm to compute point wise correspondence between images is introduced, known as Deep-Matching (DM) [21]. Deep Matching algorithm is based on a multi-stage architecture with 6 layers (depending on the image size), interleaving convolutions and max-pooling, a construction similar to deep convolution nets. Here, convolution is done at patch-level, which proceeds in a multi-layer fashion. This method can perform reasonable non-rigid matching with explicit pixel-wise correspondences, if it is applied in recursive nature, which motivates to use Deep Matching in FKP matching problem. Initially, the algorithm works in a bottom-up fashion (fine level to coarse-level) which include convolution, max-pooling and sub-sampling. An example of bottom-up approach is shown in Fig. 28.24. It starts with the computation of correlation

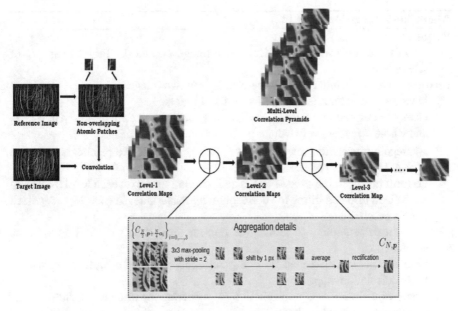

Fig. 28.24 Deep-matching bottom up approach [Images are taken from [22]]

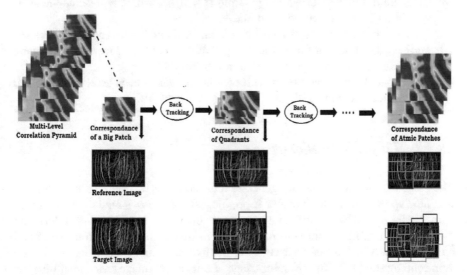

Fig. 28.25 Deep-matching top down approach [Images are taken from [22]]

maps of small sized patches and proceeds up to larger patches by aggregating the smaller patches. Finally, a top-down method is implemented to estimate the motion of atomic patches starting from top level correlation maps. An example of bottom-up approach is shown in Fig. 28.25. A matching algorithm based on correlations at patch-level for comparison between two images I_g and I_p is given in Algorithm 2.

Algorithm 2 Deep-Matching [22]

Require:

Two FKP sample images, (a) Reference image I_g, and (b) Target Image I_p of size $m \times n$.

Ensure: Return a Similarity score between given two images.

1: Divide I_g into atomic patches of size 4×4 pixels.

2: Compute correlation map $C_{4,p} = I_{g(4,p)} * I_p$ between each atomic patch in I_g and whole I_p recursively, where p= N > 4, is a power of 2.

3: Aggregate correlation maps of four $\frac{N}{2} \times \frac{N}{2}$ sized atomic patches to create a $N \times N$ size larger patch.

4: Perform max-pooling over $M \times N$ sized correlation map at each level by sliding 3×3 sized grid and filling the corresponding max-values in each $N_1 \times N_2$ sized atomic patch.

5: Perform sub-sampling to reduce the non-maximal values as well as the time complexity.

6: Shift each correlation map by one pixel and compute the shifted average of those correlation map.

7: Apply non- linear mapping function (γ rectification) to increase the range of correlation values at each level.

8: Compute multilevel correlation pyramid $(C_{N,p})_{N,p}$ which represents the average similarity score between two images.

9: Set a tolerating scaling factor (0.5 to 2.5) and rotation in the range (-26 to $+26$)

10: Perform backtracking for undoing aggregation so as to recover corresponding matching points of atomic-patches at lower level.

11: Find local maxima (M_1) from each correlation map at each level and then find the next local maxima (M_2) in the neighborhood of M_1.

28.3.2 Finger Vein Biometrics

The usage of extrinsic biometrics generate some concerns on privacy and security in real time applications. On the other hand, intrinsic biometrics modalities are much harder to forge as they are difficult to acquire without user knowledge [35]. Vascular biometrics traits, like palm vein or finger vein images have the strong structural characteristics which make it extremely difficult to surgically change the underneath vein configuration [8]. Moreover, the usage of finger vein image based identification lies in the enhanced anonymity during personal authentication as the subsurface vascular patterns are largely hidden underneath and difficult to imaged under visible illumination. There are two publicly available finger vein datasets on which most of work is done in literature: CASIA Multispectral Palm print Dataset [1] and PolyU Contactless Finger Vein Dataset [3]. Thus, in this section we will describe some important pre-processing and feature extraction techniques used so far for finger vein recognition.

28.3.2.1   Finger Vein ROI Extraction

The ROI extraction is a very early step and one can easily infer that its performance plays an important role in the overall system performance as all subsequent levels has to work over the region currently extracted. Since, the acquired finger images are noisy with rotational and translational variations resulting from unconstrained image acquisition. Therefore, the consistent ROI extraction of acquired images are very important.

1. Finger Vein Coarse ROI Extraction In this method [35], two main steps are performed for accurate segmentation of finger vein ROI by using PolyU contactless dataset [3]: (a) segmentation of ROI, (b) translation and orientation alignment. At first, the acquired finger vein images is binarized using a fixed threshold value to localize the coarse finger shape. But, it is observed that a small portions of background still appears connected to the bright finger regions. Thus to eliminate the isolated and loosely connected regions in the binarized images, the following two steps are performed: First,the Sobel edge detector is applied to the entire image and the resulting edge map is subtracted from the binarized image. Next,the isolated blobs in the resulting images are eliminated from the area thresholding, i.e., the eliminating number of connected white pixels being less than a threshold. The resulting binary mask is used to segment the ROI from the original finger vein image. The finger-vein ROI extraction is shown in Fig. 28.26a–e.

2. Finger Vein ROI Extraction In this method [8], efforts are made to extract ROI from the finger-vein images taken from CASIA MS palmprint database [1] to improve the performance. The thumb is excluded since the orientation of the thumb is such that only the lateral part of the thumb is visible which has very little vascular information. In order to segment the finger ROIs from the binarized images, three points on each finger contour are identified including the fingertip denoted by T and two points on the base of the finger. Next, the valley between any two fingers is identified but it is not necessarily a single point which depend on the location of the reference point. Thus in order to correctly identify the valley points, one of the fingertips is considered as the reference point and the other fingertip as the end point or vice versa. The valley point is identified as the maxima on the radial distance function curve plotted for the points on the contour between the reference

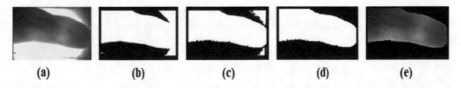

(a)   **(b)**   **(c)**   **(d)**   **(e)**

Fig. 28.26 Finger Vein ROI extraction: (**a**) original image, (**b**) binarized image, (**c**) edge map, (**d**) ROI mask, (**e**) ROI finger vein image [Images are taken from [35]]

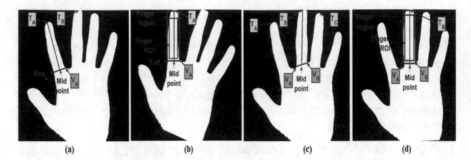

Fig. 28.27 Finger Vein ROI extraction: (**a**, **c**) Tip and Valley detection, (**b**) Index finger ROI extraction, (**d**) Middle finger ROI extraction [Images are taken from [8]]

and the end points. On this assumption, ROI of inner (middle and ring), and outer (index and little) are extracted. The finger-vein ROI for index and middle finger is shown in Fig. 28.27b, d.

28.3.2.2 Finger Vein ROI Enhancement and Transformation

The normalized finger-vein ROIs contain several curvilinear vessel structures of varying shapes and sizes. In order to effectively characterize these structures, the following main enhancement approaches are applied:

1. CS-LBP Center-symmetric local binary pattern (CS-LBP) [8], a computationally efficient and illumination invariant feature representation used in the literature for image region description. It captures the image gradient information by comparing the gray levels of pixels in a local image neighbourhood. CS-LBP is a more compact form of LBP since instead of comparing the intensities with center pixel, pixels located symmetrically about the center are compared and thresholded based on a preset value T, which is typically set to 1% of the range of the pixel intensities. Most commonly, a neighborhood of 8 pixels ($N = 8$ and radius $R = 2$) are considered centered at the current pixel. Figure 28.28 shows the CS-LBP feature templates extracted for finger-vein ROIs taken from CASIA MS palmprint Dataset. The difference between the pixel intensities of the ith and $(i + \frac{N}{2})$th pixels, denoted by g_i and $g_{i+(\frac{N}{2})}$, respectively, is considered and a binary code is assigned to each pixel in the enhanced ROI $I(x, y)$ based on Eq. (28.10). This generates the CS-LBP image which is an encoded template with values ranging from 0 to 16 and can be used for matching.

$$CS - LBP_{R,N,T}(x, y) = \sum_{i=0}^{(\frac{N}{2})-1} s(g_i - g_{i+(\frac{N}{2})})2^i, \text{ where} \qquad (28.10)$$

$$s(p) = \begin{cases} 1, & \text{if } p > T \\ 0, & \text{otherwise} \end{cases}$$

Fig. 28.28 Image
enhancement by CS-LBP
[Images are taken from [8]]

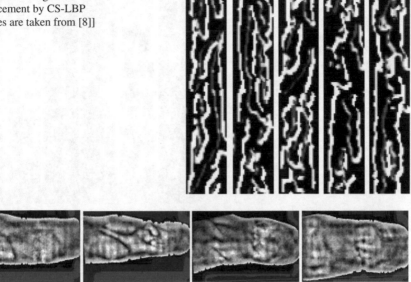

Fig. 28.29   Image enhancement by histogram equalization [Images are taken from [35]]

2. Histogram Equalization Instead of having permanent vein texture, the poor contrast and varying illumination conditions necessitates the need of nonlinear image enhancement. In this process, the original vein images are first partitioned into fixed size (30×30) sub-cells, and the mean gray level from every such cell is measured. Bicubic interpolation is then used to generate mean background image by the use of mean gray level computed in last step. However, finger-vein image consist of a filled background region that does not provide meaningful content. Therefore, the criteria of original image partitioning into sub-cells result into biased prediction of background illumination. In order to obtain the enhanced vein image, local histogram equalization is applied [35]. Figure 28.29 shows the enhanced finger-vein ROIs taken from PolyU Finger Vein Dataset.

28.3.2.3   Feature Extraction and Matching

In order to extract robust finger vein patterns from the challenging vein images, various methods including hand crafted and deep learning mechanisms are proposed. In this section, some of well known approaches are discussed.

1. Line Tracking and Curvature Extraction Methods The repeated line tracking (RLT) [39] method is based on an idea to trace the veins in the image by selected directions according to predefined probability in the horizontal and vertical orientations. In this method, initial seed is randomly selected and the whole process

Fig. 28.30 Feature templates extracted from Finger vein ROIs using (**a**) WLD, (**b**) Hessian, (**c**) LBP, (**d**) MPC, (**e**) NMRT, and (**f**) RLT [Images are taken from [8]]

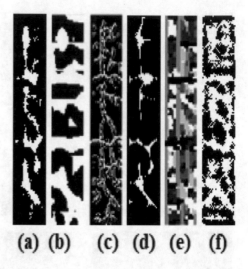

(a) (b)   (c)   (d)   (e)   (f)

is repeatedly done for a certain number of times. In case of maximum principal curvature (MPC) method [10], the image pattern position that owns the maximum curvature from the image is selected, and then image profile is captured in multiple directions while all feature points are extracted. In addition, neighborhood matching radon transform (NMRT) [35], Hessian phase [35], and wide line descriptor (WLD) [17] approaches are well discussed in literature and shown promising results for vein biometrics. Figure 28.30 shows the feature templates extracted for finger-vein ROIs using the above-mentioned feature extraction techniques.

In general, patch based similarity measure like hamming distance is used for matching of NMRT and Hessian phase based features.

2. CNN Based Matching N/W Several CNN models have been developed to learn useful feature representation for the finger vein image matching. A brief introduction to various CNN architectures such as light CNN, VGG-16 etc., considered for vein representation and matching is provided here [48].

In light CNN (LCNN) architecture [48], the complexity of network is maintained low by introducing a max feature map (MFM) operation between convolutional layers and it result into a light CNN model. For finger vein matching, it contains 9 convolutional layers, 4 pooling layers, and 2 fully connected layers. Here an image is referred as positive sample if it is choosen from same class, otherwise image which is from a different class referred to as negative sample. The main objective of this framework is to maximize the similarity between random and negative features and minimize the distance between random and positive features by computing triplet similarity loss.

On the other side, the most common Visual Geometry Group (VGG) [48] architecture with sixteen layers is modified for the CNN to retrieve the match scores directly. The main aim of this framework is to cover the extracted finger vein ROI images without adding the noise. To perform such operation, a pair of

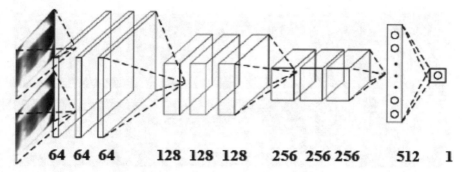

64 64 64   128 128 128   256 256 256   512   1

Fig. 28.31 VGG-16 for finger vein matching [Image is taken from [48]]

images is given as the input in conventional VGG-16 since it is required to compute the similarity between finger vein images using cross-entropy loss function. The pictorial view of VGG-16 network architecture is shown in Fig. 28.31.

28.4 Experimental Analysis

In particular, the performance of any biometric authentication approach is computed in either verification or identification mode. In this section, we have presented a performance comparison among several existing feature extraction/matching techniques that are found to be effective for finger vein and finger knuckle biometrics in the literature.

28.4.1 Database Description

In this section we have discussed different biometric datasets which have been used for finger vein and finger knuckle research and available in public domain.

1. PolyU FKP Dataset [4] The database was prepared by Biometric Research Center (UGC/CRC) at the Hong Kong Polytechnic University and freely available for academic, noncommercial use. The sample FKP image of different subjects are depicted in Fig. 28.32. It contains 7920 images in BMP image format with resolution 110×220. There were 165 (125:40) individuals participating in the enrollment process, including males and females. Among them, 143 subjects were 20–30 years old and the others were 30–50 years old. For each subject, six images per index/middle finger were acquired in two different sessions.

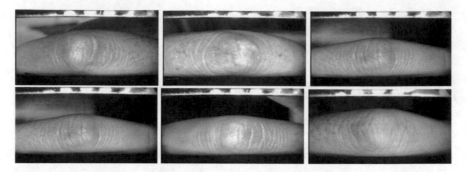

Fig. 28.32 Example images of PolyU FKP database

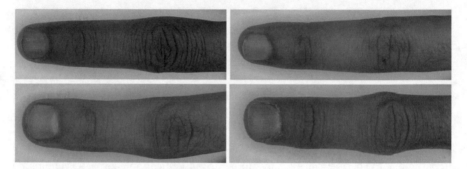

Fig. 28.33 Example images of PolyU contact-less FKI database

2. PolyU Contact-Less Finger Knuckle Images Database [2] The contact-less finger knuckle database includes 2515 middle-finger dorsal images collected from 503 volunteers from the Hong Kong Polytechnic University and IIT Delhi within two separate sessions with a gap of 7 years. The images are acquired by a contact-less ordinary camera and available in BMP image format for further research. Figure 28.33 shows the sample images of finger knuckle pattern collected from different individuals.

3. CASIA Multispectral Palm Print Dataset [1] The CASIA multispectral palm print database consist of full hand images, collected from 200 individuals. The left and right-hand samples from a subject are considered belonging to separate individuals, resulted in 2400 images. Figure 28.34 shows the sample images of multi spectral finger patterns collected from different individuals.

4. PolyU Finger Vein Dataset [3] The finger image database consists of 6264 images acquired from 156 volunteers over a period of 11 months using our imaging device. In this data set, about 93% of the individuals are younger than 30 years. The finger images were acquired in two separate sessions with a minimum interval

Fig. 28.34 Example images of CASIA MS palm print database

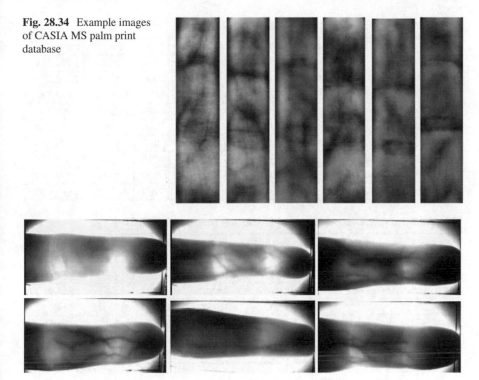

Fig. 28.35 Example images of PolyU contact-less finger vein database

of 1 month, a maximum interval of over 6 months. Figure 28.35 shows the sample images of finger vein patterns collected from different individuals.

28.4.2 Comparative Performance Analysis: Finger Knuckle Biometrics

The performance of above mentioned matching algorithms are computed on the most common performance evaluation parameters, like Correct Recognition Rate (CRR), Decidability Index (DI), Equal Error Rate(EER), Error under ROC Curve, and computation time. Likewise, there are several different testing protocols based on which any matching can be stated as true or false.

Testing Protocol 1 In this strategy, the different classes of PolyU FKP database like Right Middle (RM), Left Middle (LM), Right Index (RI), and Left Index (LI) are taken individually. Based on this, total of 5940 genuine and 974,160 impostor matches are reported [22, 43]. The complete detail about image selection is given in Table 28.2.

Table 28.2 Specifications of databases and testing strategies

Datasets	Subject	Pose	Images	Train	Test	Genuine	Impostor
PolyU FKI (Major)	503	5	2515	1509	1006	4527	2,272,554
PolyU FKI (Minor)	503	5	2515	1509	1006	4527	2,272,554
PolyU FKP (Major-Left)	330	12	3960	1980	1980	11,880	3,908,520
PolyU FKP (Major-Right)	330	12	3960	1980	1980	11,880	3,908,520
PolyU FKP (major-LI)	165	12	1980	990	990	5940	974,160
PolyU FKP (Major-LM)	165	12	1980	990	990	5940	974,160
PolyU FKP (Major-RI)	165	12	1980	990	990	5940	974,160
PolyU FKP (Major-RM)	165	12	1980	990	990	5940	974,160
PolyU FKP (Major-Full)	660	12	7920	3960	3960	23,760	15,657,840

Table 28.3 Comparative analysis over FKP database (results as reported in [22])

Algorithm	Full DB	LI	LM	RI	RM
Compcode [51]	1.38	1.88	1.88	1.44	1.17
BOCV [15]	1.83	2.20	2.29	1.89	1.64
ImCompcode+MagCode [54]	1.21	1.61	1.65	1.32	1.09
MoriCode [14]	1.20	1.54	1.69	1.60	1.24
MtexCode [14]	1.81	2.07	2.07	2.11	2.05
MoriCode and MtexCode [14]	1.04	1.32	1.45	1.24	1.06
Deep-Matching [22]	0.92	1.10	0.96	0.98	0.97

Testing Protocol 2 In this testing strategy, all subjects (660) and their corresponding poses (660∗12) are included for performance evaluation. A similar methodology is adopted for selection of training and test images per class. Thus, a total number of 15,657,840 impostor and 23,760 genuine matching scores are computed [22, 43].

The performance comparison of various state-of-the-art approaches on the basis of above discussed evaluation parameters is shown in Table 28.3. It gives the comparative analysis for Full PolyU finger-print database. As shown in Fig. 28.36a, a DET curve based comparative analysis is done in [14]. It clearly indicates that MoriCode method performs much better than the MtexCode method. Secondly, since MoriCode could keep more orientation information than CompCode, it could get better results than CompCode. Thirdly, the MoriCode-MtexCode scheme which integrates the multiple orientation and texture information performs overall better than using any of them individually. In addition, distance distributions of genuine matchings and imposter matchings of best performing MoriCode-MtexCode method is given in Fig. 28.36b.

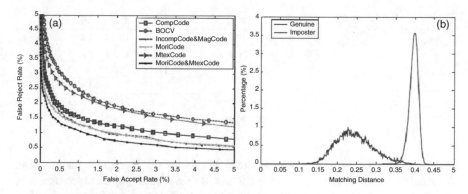

Fig. 28.36 (a) DET curve based comparative analysis, (b) genuine vs imposter score distribution [Image is taken from [14]]

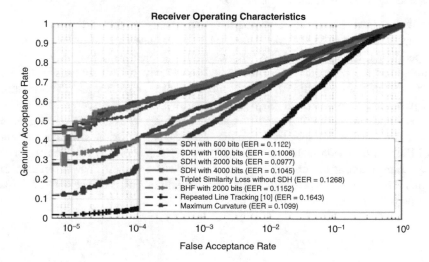

Fig. 28.37 Comparative ROC using triplet loss based LCNN with SDH and previous work [Image is taken from [48]]

28.4.3 Comparative Performance Analysis: Finger Vein Biometrics

In order to compare performance between various state-of-the-art studies, the same testing protocols and evaluation parameters are used, which we discussed in above section. Some of the well known studies are presented below:

1. Test 1 In this test, the comparative performance analysis between hand crafted and CNN approaches is discussed. As shown in Fig. 28.37, ROC curve based comparative analysis is done in [48], which used PolyU contact-less dataset for various experiments. The images collected during first session are only used for

Table 28.4 Comparative
analysis over FKP database
(results as reported in [8])

Algorithm	Index	Ring	Middle	Little
WLD [17]	14.08	12.98	13.99	19.14
MPC [10]	12.06	12.59	11.55	15.96
RLT [39]	17.17	28.79	28.92	30.87
NMRT [8]	19.17	17.72	19.33	20.68
Hessian Phase [8]	22.66	21.26	23.23	22.91
Deep-Matching [22]	6.24	7.23	6.23	10.97

training and then produced the binarized bit templates by which match score between corresponding templates are computed using Hamming distance measure. It is concluded that CNN based approaches like LCNN, supervised discrete hashing (SDH) can offer superior performance than hand crafted approaches like RLT, MCP etc and significantly reduce template size.

2. Test 2 In this test, we compared the performance of the various state-of-the-art approaches on CASIA MS dataset [1], as presented in. In order to perform experiments, left and right hand samples from a subject as belonging to separate individuals are considered, which resulted in effectively 200 subjects in CASIA MS dataset. For each subject, the first three samples as gallery and the remaining as probe are considered for finger vein matching. Matching scores between the gallery and probe samples were computed resulting in 1800 and 3330 genuine scores for CASIA datasets. Based on these scores, two error rates, false match rate (FMR) and false non match rate (FNMR) were computed. The decision threshold was determined at the operating point where FMR equalled FNMR. Finally, the equal error rates (EER) for four finger-vein modalities based on six state-of-the-art methods are reported in Table 28.4.

28.5   Conclusion

Remote health monitoring solutions are rapidly integrating medical health computations with biometric recognition of patients. On the same time technological advance of artificial intelligence and electronic hardware are making e-health devices more affordable and accessible. Finger based biometrics can be the most successful ways of identifying a patient in e-health system based on different physiological characteristics of finger like finger vein and finger knuckle based line texture. There have been some interesting efforts to develop finger based biometric solutions for e-health security and we have also presented an idea here in this direction.

Acknowledgements We acknowledge the Ph.D. Thesis "Multimodal Biometric Authentication using Palmer and Dorsal Hand Patterns" submitted to the Department of Electrical Engineering, National Institute of Technology Hamirpur, India as well as journal paper "Deepknuckle: revealing the human identity" published in Multimedia Tools and Applications and conference paper "FKQNet: a biometric sample quality estimation network using transfer learning" published in IEEE International Conference on Image Information Processing.

References

1. (2005–09) Casia multispectral palm print database (version 1.0). http://www.cbsr.ia.ac.cn/mspalmprint
2. (2009) Polyu contactless finger knuckle images database (version 1.0). http://www4.comp.polyu.edu.hk/~csajaykr/fn1.htm
3. (2009) Polyu finger image database (version 1.0). http://www4.comp.polyu.edu.hk/~csajaykr/fvdatabase.htm
4. (2009) Polyu finger-knuckle-print database. http://www.comp.polyu.edu.hk/biometrics
5. (2018) Digital information security in health care act.(disha). https://mohfw.gov.in/newshighlights/comments-draft-digital-information-security-health-care-actdisha
6. Badrinath G, Nigam A, Gupta P (2011) An efficient finger-knuckle-print based recognition system fusing sift and surf matching scores. In: International Conference on Information and Communications Security, Springer, pp 374–387
7. Bera A, Bhattacharjee D, Nasipuri M (2014) Hand biometrics in digital forensics. In: Computational Intelligence in Digital Forensics: Forensic Investigation and Applications, Springer, pp 145–163
8. Bhilare S, Jaswal G, Kanhangad V, Nigam A (2018) Single-sensor hand-vein multimodal biometric recognition using multiscale deep pyramidal approach. Machine Vision and Applications 29(8):1269–1286
9. Cappelli R, Ferrara M, Maltoni D (2010) Minutia cylinder-code: A new representation and matching technique for fingerprint recognition. IEEE Transactions on Pattern Analysis and Machine Intelligence 32(12):2128–2141
10. Choi JH, Song W, Kim T, Lee SR, Kim HC (2009) Finger vein extraction using gradient normalization and principal curvature. In: Image Processing: Machine Vision Applications II, International Society for Optics and Photonics, vol 7251, p 725111
11. Choi JH, Song W, Kim T, Lee SR, Kim HC (2009) Finger vein extraction using gradient normalization and principal curvature. In: Image Processing: Machine Vision Applications II, International Society for Optics and Photonics, vol 7251, p 725111
12. Delac K, Grgic M (2004) A survey of biometric recognition methods. In: Proceedings of the IEEE 46th International Symposium on Electronics in Marine, pp 184–193
13. Déniz O, Bueno G, Salido J, De la Torre F (2011) Face recognition using histograms of oriented gradients. Pattern Recognition Letters 32(12):1598–1603
14. Gao G, Yang J, Qian J, Zhang L (2014) Integration of multiple orientation and texture information for finger-knuckle-print verification. Neurocomputing 135:180–191
15. Guo Z, Zhang D, Zhang L, Zuo W (2009) Palmprint verification using binary orientation co-occurrence vector. Pattern Recognition Letters 30(13):1219–1227
16. Hillerstrom F, Kumar A, Veldhuis R (2014) Generating and analyzing synthetic finger vein images. In: Biometrics Special Interest Group (BIOSIG), 2014 International Conference of the, IEEE, pp 1–9
17. Huang B, Dai Y, Li R, Tang D, Li W (2010) Finger-vein authentication based on wide line detector and pattern normalization. In: Pattern Recognition (ICPR), 2010 20th International Conference on, IEEE, pp 1269–1272
18. Jain AK, Ross A, Prabhakar S (2004) An introduction to biometric recognition. IEEE Transactions on Circuits and Systems for Video Technology 14(1):4–20, https://doi.org/10.1109/TCSVT.2003.818349

19. Jaswal G, Kaul A, Nath R (2016) Knuckle print biometrics and fusion schemes–overview, challenges, and solutions. ACM Computing Surveys (CSUR) 49(2):34
20. Jaswal G, Nath R, Aggarwal D, Nigam A (2017) Fkqnet: A biometrie sample quality estimation network using transfer learning. In: Image Information Processing (ICIIP), 2017 Fourth International Conference on, IEEE, pp 1–6
21. Jaswal G, Nath R, Nigam A (2017) Deformable multi-scale scheme for biometric personal identification. In: Image Processing (ICIP), 2017 IEEE International Conference on, IEEE, pp 3555–3559
22. Jaswal G, Nigam A, Nath R (2017) Deepknuckle: revealing the human identity. Multimedia Tools and Applications 76(18):18955–18984
23. Jaswal G, Kaul A, Nath R (2018) Multiple feature fusion for unconstrained palm print authentication. Computers & Electrical Engineering 72:53–78
24. Jungbluth WO (1989) Knuckle print identification. Journal of forensic identification 39(6):375–380
25. Kang BJ, Park KR (2009) Multimodal biometric authentication based on the fusion of finger vein and finger geometry. Optical Engineering 48(9):090501
26. Kang BJ, Park KR, Yoo JH, Kim JN (2011) Multimodal biometric method that combines veins, prints, and shape of a finger. Optical Engineering 50(1):017201
27. Kong T, Yang G, Yang L (2014) A hierarchical classification method for finger knuckle print recognition. EURASIP Journal on Advances in Signal Processing 2014(1):44
28. Kralik M, Nejman L (2007) Fingerprints on artifacts and historical items: examples and comments. Journal of Ancient Fingerprints 1(1):4–13
29. Kumar A (2014) Importance of being unique from finger dorsal patterns: Exploring minor finger knuckle patterns in verifying human identities. IEEE Transactions on Information Forensics and Security 9(8):1288–1298
30. Kumar A, Ravikanth C (2009) Personal authentication using finger knuckle surface. IEEE Transactions on Information Forensics and Security 4(1):98–110
31. Kumar A, Wang B (2015) Recovering and matching minutiae patterns from finger knuckle images. Pattern Recognition Letters 68:361–367
32. Kumar A, Wu C (2012) Automated human identification using ear imaging. Pattern Recognition 45(3):956–968
33. Kumar A, Xu Z (2016) Personal identification using minor knuckle patterns from palm dorsal surface. IEEE Transactions on Information Forensics and Security 11(10):2338–2348
34. Kumar A, Zhou Y (2009) Human identification using knucklecodes. In: IEEE 3rd International Conference on Biometrics: Theory, Applications, and Systems, IEEE, pp 1–6
35. Kumar A, Zhou Y (2012) Human identification using finger images. IEEE Transactions on image processing 21(4):2228–2244
36. Lee EC, Park KR (2011) Image restoration of skin scattering and optical blurring for finger vein recognition. Optics and Lasers in Engineering 49(7):816–828
37. Li Z, Wang K, Zuo W (2012) Finger-knuckle-print recognition using local orientation feature based on steerable filter. In: International Conference on Intelligent Computing, Springer, pp 224–230
38. Maltoni D, Maio D, Jain AK, Prabhakar S (2009) Handbook of fingerprint recognition. Springer Science & Business Media
39. Miura N, Nagasaka A, Miyatake T (2004) Feature extraction of finger-vein patterns based on repeated line tracking and its application to personal identification. Machine vision and applications 15(4):194–203
40. Monro DM, Zhang Z (2005) An effective human iris code with low complexity. In: IEEE International Conference on Image Processing, IEEE, vol 3, pp III–277
41. Nigam A, Gupta P (2013) Quality assessment of knuckleprint biometric images. In: IEEE International Conference on Image Processing, IEEE, pp 4205–4209
42. Nigam A, Gupta P (2015) Designing an accurate hand biometric based authentication system fusing finger knuckleprint and palmprint. Neurocomputing 151:1120–1132

43. Nigam A, Tiwari K, Gupta P (2016) Multiple texture information fusion for finger-knuckle-print authentication system. Neurocomputing 188:190–205
44. Okoh E, Awad AI (2015) Biometrics applications in e-health security: A preliminary survey. In: International Conference on Health Information Science, Springer, pp 92–103
45. Qin H, El-Yacoubi MA (2017) Deep representation-based feature extraction and recovering for finger-vein verification. IEEE Transactions on Information Forensics and Security 12(8):1816–1829
46. Sanchez-Reillo R, Sanchez-Avila C, Gonzalez-Marcos A (2000) Biometric identification through hand geometry measurements. IEEE Transactions on pattern analysis and machine intelligence 22(10):1168–1171
47. Shariatmadar ZS, Faez K (2011) A novel approach for finger-knuckle-print recognition based on gabor feature fusion. In: Image and Signal Processing (CISP), 2011 4th International Congress on, IEEE, vol 3, pp 1480–1484
48. Xie C, Kumar A (2017) Finger vein identification using convolutional neural network and supervised discrete hashing. In: Deep Learning for Biometrics, Springer, pp 109–132
49. Yang J, Zhang X (2012) Feature-level fusion of fingerprint and finger-vein for personal identification. Pattern Recognition Letters 33(5):623–628
50. Yang W, Huang X, Zhou F, Liao Q (2014) Comparative competitive coding for personal identification by using finger vein and finger dorsal texture fusion. Information sciences 268:20–32
51. Zhang L, Zhang L, Zhang D (2009) Finger-knuckle-print: a new biometric identifier. In: 16th IEEE International Conference on Image Processing, IEEE, pp 1981–1984
52. Zhang L, Zhang L, Zhang D (2010) Monogeniccode: A novel fast feature coding algorithm with applications to finger-knuckle-print recognition. In: International Workshop on Emerging Techniques and Challenges for Hand-Based Biometrics, IEEE, pp 1–4
53. Zhang L, Zhang L, Zhang D, Zhu H (2010) Online finger-knuckle-print verification for personal authentication. Pattern recognition 43(7):2560–2571
54. Zhang L, Zhang L, Zhang D, Zhu H (2011) Ensemble of local and global information for finger-knuckle-print recognition. Pattern Recognition 44(9):1990–1998

Chapter 29
ECG Security Challenges: Case Study on Change of ECG According to Time for User Identification

Hoon Ko, Libor Mesicek, and Sung Bum Pan

29.1 Introduction

There are many ways to detect an identification by using a sensor, which is installed on touchable devices to evaluate a human's biometrics. It is easy to use them because all it has to do is to be worn on the body, then the device measures [1], processes and makes a decision. Usually, bio-information such as Electrocardiogram (ECG) has been used to check the human's health state and other bio-information such as a fingerprint, a face, a palm-print, hand geometry, a voice, a signature, and an iris, have been used in a security system, like as a form of authentication or identification. But now, with ECG, which has been used in the healthcare system, some of them are embarking on an authentication or an identification system [2]. However, the problem is that the measured bio-signal cannot be matched between a training set and a test set, according to the human's condition, what they are doing, and where they are. To know their identification, the measured value should be fixed, but the bio-information would be so dynamic. That's why it is necessary to measure the flow of the user's bio-information through periodic measuring: in the morning, afternoon, night, during exercise time, driving time, and other additional times. With the measurements of various situations, it can extract features. Once it analysis the periodic measure, it can find common patterns from the extracted patterns, then, it can connect between the two sides. By connect to connect, it can understand the bio-information's flow because it can be branched or linked from a root to a child node. In this chapter, it analysis the measured ECG, which had been measured in some

H. Ko (✉) · S. B. Pan
IT Research Institute, Chosun University, Gwangju, Republic of Korea
e-mail: skoh21@chosun.ac.kr; sbpan@chosun.ac.kr

L. Mesicek
Jan Evangelista Purkyne University in Usti nad Labem, Ústí nad Labem, Czech Republic

© Springer Nature Switzerland AG 2019
A. K. Singh, A. Mohan (eds.), *Handbook of Multimedia Information Security: Techniques and Applications*, https://doi.org/10.1007/978-3-030-15887-3_29

situations and describes the result. The rest of the sections consists of the following: Sect. 29.2 is concerned with the limitations of ECG, Sect. 29.3 deals with finding a pattern from a case study, Sect. 29.4 is a descriptive discussion, and finally, Sect. 29.5 presents the conclusion.

29.2   Limitations and Security Spec

29.2.1   Limitations

Each person has a unique and natural signal, such as ECG, which is from the heart [3]. It could be said that it is a bio-signal and that it can be processed into bio-information. Then the bio-information can be used to identify them by a computing system [4]. However, it is a sensory signal, so the feature from the signals can vary whenever they measure in different situations. It creates a big problem in security systems, which are supposed to be in use with this technique [5, 6]. Next, it shows the limitations of bio-information.

- According to the users' dynamic state, it finds the different measured value. Then the system doesn't accept the two values.
- As times goes by every day, the value can be changed.
- Depending on what you ate, the value will be changed.
- Depending on the time, such as in the morning, in the afternoon, or in the evening, the value also will be changed.
- If each person's state of health changes, the value can be different.

29.2.2   Security Spec

There are mechanisms of analyzing the bio-information like ECG in some situations, which is Security Association Database (SAD), used to define each parameter in Security Association (SA), which contains Security Policy Database (SPD) and Security Association (SA). SPD is the formalized table, which is used to describe how to connect to certain SA from IP Traffic and a SA is to share with security attributes to Security Parameter Index (SPI), Sequence Number Counter (SNC), Anti-Reply Window (ARW), Lifetime of this Security Association (LSA), SA Identification (SPI, destination address, AH/ESP), Encryption algorithms, Traffic Encryption Key, Network Parameter, Internet Security Association/Key Management Protocol (ISAKMP) and so on.

29.3 Case Study: Find a Pattern in a Scenario

This is a scenario about a women's life (Fig. 29.1).

> After her husband left to his company for work and her kids left for school, she drove from her home to her Fitness center, which normally takes 30 minutes. However in the morning, because she felt she had a slight illness from the weather, she decided to visit to the hospital. Then she went to a pharmacy to get her prescription filled. In the fitness center, she exercised for 60 minutes, and went to a Spa.

Case 1: While she drives to get the next place, she may need the security process with bio-information.

Case 2: While she exercise in the fitness center, she may need the security process with bio-information.

Also, the security process may be needed at any given time (blue dot in Fig. 29.1). The deliberation is if the measured value in blue dots would be matched, even if it is the little differences, as to when it measures the ECG at the same time but with the evaluated date. So, to fine-tune the connection of one day's evaluating value and the others' evaluating value is necessary.

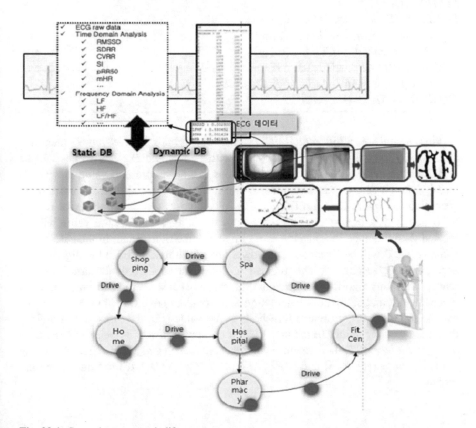

Fig. 29.1 Scenario: a woman's life

29.4   Pattern Finding Algorithm

The purpose of this study is to form a connection among all patterns, which is measured from one user and to identify it from some patterns. All ECGs contain P, Q, R, S, T, PR segments and a ST segment, and each parameter gets an individual value after evaluating the signals. In this study, to find the pattern, we use Q, R, S among them and to extract the pattern, it follows in the next algorithm.

Algorithm 1 Pattern Extract Algorithm

$Input_{[1,2,...,n]}$ <- $[ECG\ Signal_1, ECG\ Signal_2, ... ECG\ Signal_n]$
    P_1 <- $(Q,R,S)_1$;
    P_2 <- $(Q,R,S)_2$;
    :
    P_n <- $(Q,R,S)_n$;
$Find.common$ <- $[P_1, P_2, ..., P_n]$
$Threshhold$ <- $SD\ (Q, R, S)_{1, 2, ..., n}$;
$SET(Root(Q, R, S)$;
$DECISION(Equal.value || Child.value)$;
    $Overlap.Located$ <- $Equal.value$;
    $Branch.Linked$ <- $Child.value$;
$Evaluate\ (ARL, AFL, AFT, Cal\_STD)$;
$Process\ (Q, R, S || ARL, AFL, AFT, Cal\_STD)$
$OUTPUT$ <- $Result\ (Process)$;

First, it analyzes all incoming ECG signals and it finds Q, R, S values, then they arranged individually as an INPUT value with P_1, P_2 and P_n. The values will be a matrix type with Q, R, and S. Next, it tries to find a common value in $[P_1, P_2$ and $P_n]$, and it decides on root values. After making the decision, it separates them according to *Equal.value* and *Child.value*. With two values, it begins a tree named ECG tree with a hierarchical level. In the case of *Equal.value*, the value will be located with the node that has the same value. On the other hand, in the case of the *Child.value*, it will be located on the lower level by a linking from the higher node according to Q, R, and S. This process will be continuously done until the count reaches n. In this algorithm, it accepts a threshold because there is no exact matched value in Q, R, and S. So, after calculating each standard deviation of Q, R, and S, we use the standard deviation as a threshold. If the value is in the threshold, it defines that it is the same value. In the next step, it computes *average rise level (ARL), an average fall level (AFL), an average fall time (AFT)*, and Cal_STD. After combining the two groups *((Q, R, S)* and *(ARL, AFL, AFT, Cal_STD))*, it formulates the final output.

29.5   Discussion

As it has measured for 120 s, it then analyzed with five types of time for 5 s: from 0 to 5 s, from 1 to 5 s, from 2 to 5 s, from 3 to 5 s and from 4 to 5 s. Tables 29.1 and 29.2 show the measured value. Each group within the group has *ARL*, *AFL*, *AFT*, and *Cal_STD*.

We designed two graph groups with Tables 29.1 and 29.2 (Figs. 29.1 and 29.2). Each figure has each pattern which had been measured on the same day with a normal status. Next, we needed to compare to know what the differences are

Table 29.1 Measured value (*Q*, *R*, *S*)

Measured time	Q	R	S
0–1	−0.0325	0.4711	−0.4057
0–2	−0.0298	0.4840	−0.3926
0–3	−0.0324	0.5208	−0.3724
0–4	−0.0324	0.5327	−0.3718
0–5	−0.0312	0.5401	−0.3696
1–2	−0.0324	0.5267	−0.3721
1–3	−0.0288	0.5271	−0.3691
1–4	−0.0320	0.5414	−0.3680
1–5	−0.0301	0.5469	−0.3672
2–3	−0.0304	0.5342	−0.3685
2–4	−0.0329	0.5690	−0.3630
2–5	−0.0323	0.5658	−0.3639
3–4	−0.0316	0.5516	−0.3658
3–5	−0.0345	0.5668	−0.3607
4–5	−0.0447	0.5215	−0.4052

Table 29.2 Value analysis

Measured time	*ARL*	*AFL*	*AFT*	*Cal_STD*
0–1	0.5036	0.8769	45.0000	0.0889
0–2	0.5138	0.8766	44.6670	0.1012
0–3	0.5531	0.8932	45.0000	0.1069
0–4	0.5651	0.9044	45.1667	0.1043
0–5	0.5713	0.9097	45.3750	0.1082
1–2	0.5143	0.8801	45.4161	0.1119
1–3	0.5559	0.8962	45.0000	0.1147
1–4	0.5733	0.9093	45.2000	0.1089
1–5	0.5770	0.9141	45.4286	0.1124
2–3	0.5736	0.9136	45.5000	0.1174
2–4	0.6019	0.9320	45.6667	0.1074
2–5	0.5981	0.9297	45.8000	0.1126
3–4	0.5837	0.9580	46.0000	0.0963
3–5	0.6031	0.9379	46.0000	0.1101
4–5	0.5663	0.9268	46.0000	0.1224

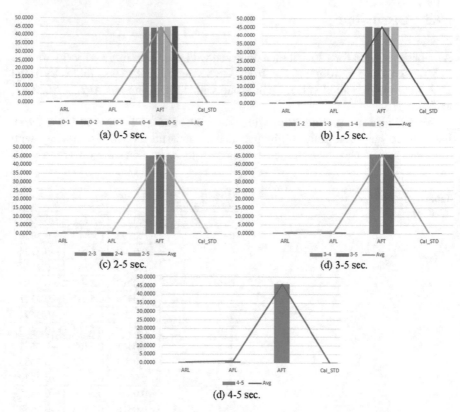

Fig. 29.2 Pattern graphs of (*ARL, AFL, AFT, Cal_STD*). (**a**) 0–5 s. (**b**) 1–5 s. (**c**) 2–5 s. (**d**) 3–5 s. (**e**) 4–5 s

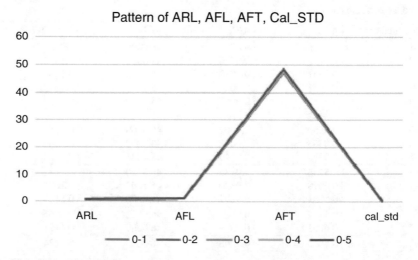

Fig. 29.3 Pattern graph of the previous day's ECG with a same user (1)

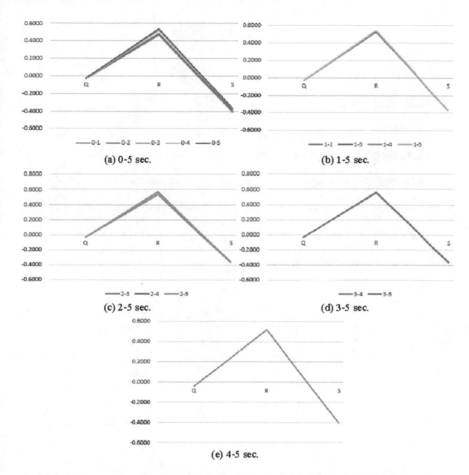

Fig. 29.4 Pattern graphs of (Q, R, S). (**a**) 0–5 s. (**b**) 1–5 s. (**c**) 2–5 s. (**d**) 3–5 s. (**e**) 4–5 s

between the normal status and other status of the user with other measured values from another day.

In Fig. 29.2, we could have the values of *ARL*, *ARF* and *Cal_STD* located between absolute-value (0 and 0.6) and the value of AFT is 45 through 46. Figure 29.3 is from the same user's pattern, which has a measured ECG from another day. By way of Figs. 29.2 and 29.3, we can define that the two figures are from same user (Fig. 29.4).

To compare them, we have measured the test user's ECG with the same method for the previous day and to speed up its identification, it only used 0–5 s value. We designed Fig. 29.5 with the same user's ECG, which has measured the previous day, then we found that the pattern value of *(Q, R, S)* is located almost within the same scope with Fig. 29.4.

We have measured five users, a user, b user, c user, d user and e user, then after extracting each *ARL*, *AFL*, *AFT, and Cal_STD*, we made Table 29.3 and Fig. 29.6.

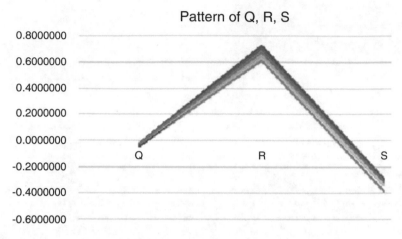

Fig. 29.5 Pattern graph of other day's ECG with a same user

Table 29.3 Analysis result of five users

Items	a user	b user	c user	d user	e user
ARL	0.4536	0.5087	0.7665	0.3314	0.4421
AFL	0.6183	0.6966	1.2844	0.5581	0.5638
AFT	453.3333	659.2000	52.8571	44.5000	570.4000
Cal_STD	0.0824	0.1007	0.1594	0.0593	0.0791

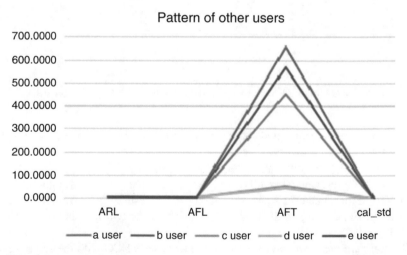

Fig. 29.6 Other users' pattern

The pattern's shape has the same type. However, the scope of value has a difference in *AFT*. The scope of the user of AFT is between 45 and 46, on the other hand, the scope of the rest of the three users are 453.333 (a user), 659.200 (b user), and

570.400 (e user). It means a, b, and e users are a different user. C user (52.8571) and d user (44.500) remain, however, with c user, there is also some difference with the test user. Finally, d user (44.5000) would be close to the test user.

29.6 Conclusion

A lots experts have been studying about security system such as an authentication and an identification which will use their bio-information like ECG. To authenticate or to identify, two values [Original value and test value] have to be exactly matched to go next process. So if two values are different, it would not accept to get next step. With another reason, for example, according to the users' health condition include a natural phenomenon, what food they eat, now what they are doing, the value also will be different. ECG has two sides, advantage and disadvantage. In the advantage side, each person has a unique signal. It means that if the system keeps the users' unique patterns, the system can be kept safe. A fingerprint is also a unique pattern for each person. The different point is that the fingerprint is not changed. If an attacker can hack into the system, the system will have serious risk. On the other hand, focusing on the disadvantage, it measures the ECG signal with the same users but it gets different value. Then, the computer may not be able to identify the users. To overcome the disadvantage, it has tried to know the users' signal trend, which means to know the patterns' similarities with the analyzed number. In this study, it analyzed the value from *ARL, AFL, ART, Cal_STD*. With these seven items (*ARL, AFL, ART, Cal_STD and Q, R, S*), it makes a pattern graph and threshold scope for a user. For the future, it needs to have a test for more users.

Acknowledgement This research was supported by Basic Science Research Program through the National Research Foundation of Korea (NRF) funded by the Ministry of Education (2018R1D1A1B07040679). This research was supported by Basic Science Research Program through the National Research Foundation of Korea (NRF), funded by the Ministry of Education (No. 2017R1A6A1A03015496).

References

1. C. Chan, S. Ginosar, T. Zhou, and A. A. Efros, "Everybody dance now,"arXiv preprint arXiv:1808.07371, 2018.
2. S. I. Safie, J. J. Soraghan, and L. Petropoulakis, "Ecg based biometric for doubly secure authentication," in Signal Processing Conference, 2011 19th European. IEEE, 2011, pp. 2274–2278.
3. P. Kumar, R. Saini, P. P. Roy, and D. P. Dogra, "A bio-signal based framework to secure mobile devices," Journal of Network and Computer Applications, vol. 89, pp. 62–71, 2017.
4. F. Gargiulo, A. Fratini, M. Sansone, and C. Sansone, "Subject identification via ecg fiducial-based systems: Influence of the type of qt interval correction," Computer methods and programs in biomedicine, vol. 121, no. 3, pp. 127–136, 2015.

5. T. N. Gia, M. Jiang, A.-M. Rahmani, T. Westerlund, P. Liljeberg, and H. Tenhunen, "Fog computing in healthcare internet of things: A case study on ecg feature extraction," in Computer and Information Technology; Ubiquitous Computing and Communications; Dependable, Autonomic and Secure Computing; Pervasive Intelligence and Computing (CIT/IUCC/DASC/PICOM), 2015 IEEE International Conference on. IEEE, 2015, pp. 356–363.
6. T. T. Khan, N. Sultana, R. B. Reza, and R. Mostafa, "Ecg feature extraction in temporal domain and detection of various heart conditions," in Electrical Engineering and Information Communication Technology (ICEEICT), 2015 International Conference on. IEEE, 2015, pp. 1–6.

Chapter 30
Analysis of Streaming Data Using Big Data and Hybrid Machine Learning Approach

Mamoon Rashid, Aamir Hamid, and Shabir A. Parah

30.1 Introduction

As of late, there has been a significant increase in growth of data. Data is produced from multiple sources like automobiles, banks, sensors, day-to-day human activities, social media etc. But the volume of data has grown beyond the computing power of traditional approaches of processing. There is the concept of Big Data [1]. Big Data has the main characteristics of volume, velocity and variety. It also encompasses variability, value, veracity and volatility which help in determining how important big data is. Big data can be either in structured or unstructured form. It can be either in a pre-stored form or can be generated in real-time. The attributes like value, volatility and veracity help in determining the importance of the data and usually data is important as it may give us useful insights regarding what decisions should a company make and what market strategy will be best. It can even allow political parties to target masses based on issues. It helps an organization in predicting the sales behavior. But older approaches of processing are unable to unravel the full potential of this data. They find just the portion of what actually is hidden inside the data. So, there has been an increase in approaches as to how Big Data can

M. Rashid
School of Computer Science and Engineering, Lovely Professional University, Jalandhar, Punjab, India

A. Hamid
Department of Computer Science and Engineering, Swami Vivekanand Institute of Engineering & Technology, Chandigarh, India

S. A. Parah (✉)
Department of Electronics and Instrumentation Technology, University of Kashmir, Srinagar, Jammu and Kashmir, India

© Springer Nature Switzerland AG 2019
A. K. Singh, A. Mohan (eds.), *Handbook of Multimedia Information Security: Techniques and Applications*, https://doi.org/10.1007/978-3-030-15887-3_30

be processed. One such approach is the Map Reduce [2]. Hadoop is one way to implement Map Reduce. Hadoop finds usage in industrial as well as academic research purposes.

Data is generated in large quantities on social media. Previously, information used to spread into little circles. Nowadays, people use social media to express their opinions about everything. They post about things and share images. Social network have received an upward surge and data generated from them is attaining higher values day by day. According to a survey, in one minute lakhs of tweets are sent, thousands of images are shared on Facebook and lakhs of videos are watched on YouTube [3].

Twitter is among the most used social networks. Users are able to tweet using a limited number of words so that it is read by everybody. There are tweets regarding many things including business establishments, movies, political parties, educational institutions, scientific projects etc. These tweets reflect sentiment of the people regarding various topics, products, movies. Every person has his own opinion regarding a topic or product. This sentiment gets reflected when the person tweets about that topic. The person may point out what were the positive things and what were negative ones. Companies will benefit immensely by getting this sentiment data as they can do target marketing and improve their market survey and research. There is a proposition that public opinion affects the stock price [4]. Market indicates the stock price, and what a person feels about anything will affect the market. So the sentiment of general public towards the company will impact the stock price of the company.

The existing tools are unable to handle such enormous quantities of data. The existing machines and algorithms are not able to provide the computing resources required. So, there is a need to design a model which will implement a method to capture the sentiment of people using social networks by utilizing social data in conjunction with Big Data.

One of the approaches is to do Sentiment Analysis. We get data from a social network and store it into Hadoop. Then we implement a classification algorithm using Map Reduce framework which will classify the data we have gathered based on what sentiments are hidden in it.

The number of users for social media is ever increasing and its role is evolving. Social media is a tool utilized by journalists, businessmen, educational institutes etc. to interact with the general public. They want to get what is the common perception regarding their interests [5]. So, there is a need to collect the data from social networks and analyze it to derive sentiments and opinions of people. Various machine learning algorithms can be used to perform sentiment analysis. Hadoop provides an efficient way of storing data collected from social networks. Map Reduce provides an efficient way of processing this data. So, data can be collected from Twitter and stored in HDFS. It can then be converted to a suitable form and then classification can be done using machine learning algorithms to derive sentiments. It will give interested parties an overview of public opinion regarding their interests.

Text can be classified according to what information is present in the text. Text classification can be done in two phases. In first phase, a model is built by training it with data we know what class it belongs to. First, we need to generate the dataset along with labels, then this data needs to be processed. Then model is trained after the data is vectored. In the second phase, we test the model by making it to classify previously unseen data. This data also needs to be processed and vectored before feeding it to the model. The various basic steps included are:

- First the data is collected and is assigned to classes. Class has its own label. Then this data is split into two halves, one for each phase.
- Then this data is changed like stop words, punctuation marks etc. are removed.
- After that, the data needs to be converted in a form understandable by the computer. This is called Vectorization. Actually, some features need to be selected from the data and then data is represented using those selected features.
- Then we need to select an algorithm which will classify our data and then we feed one half of data to the algorithm. The model learns from this data in this phase. This is the first phase.
- Then we feed the next half of data to the model and let the model classify it (Fig. 30.1).

In today's technological world, data is generated in enormous amounts. The sources of this data are diverse and almost every field generates some data. This data should be properly and efficiently stored and then processed so that we can analyze the underlying patterns. These patterns are of great importance in business decisions, elections, marketing strategy etc. One Big Data approach is for solving this problem is the use of Hadoop Cluster. Hadoop is a part of the apache project of the Apache Software Foundation. It is a framework based on java which is capable of processing very huge datasets. Hadoop runs in a distributed environment and it can process unstructured, heterogeneous data coming at high volume. A hadoop cluster is composed of racks. The number of nodes in one rack is not fixed and

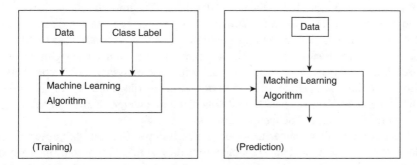

Fig. 30.1 Basic idea of data classification

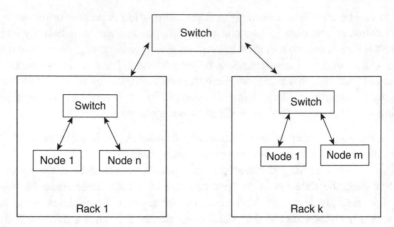

Fig. 30.2 Overview of a hadoop cluster

varies from 20 to 40. These racks are connected by a single network connecting device. There are master nodes and slave nodes in the hadoop cluster. Mater node is associated with managing the Hadoop Distributed File System. It also has the knowledge about which slave nodes contain the data of a particular file. The slave node is associated with carrying out the task. When a job is to be performed, the slave nodes are tasked with retrieval and processing of the data. Upon starting of a job, the slave node will find the location of data from the master node and retrieve the data and then process it (Fig. 30.2).

30.1.1 Significance of This Work for Multimedia Applications

Sentiment Analysis is one of the prime area where research is going on in terms of multimedia data mining and social network mining. The importance of this work lies in popularity of social networking domains like Twitter, Facebook and Flickr where a lot of multimedia stuff is getting generated by every second. This multimedia can be used effectively for research purposes to draw valuable insights in terms of sentiment analysis. Sentiment analysis with that of social multimedia help in analyzing opinions of people, various emotions and reading attitudes for data written in text languages. This work adds new dimension to undergo sentiment analysis and opinion mining for multimedia applications.

The outline of this chapter is structured as follows: Section 30.2 describes the related work on sentiment analysis of twitter data with different machine learning models. In Sect. 30.3, the problem is proposed and an approach for enhancing security on data storage is outlined. Section 30.4 discusses experimental setup and various results drawn. Conclusion and future scope of the approach is given in Sect. 30.5.

30.2 Literature Review

According to the authors in [6], big data processing is the main challenge today. Big data has many sources. So, size of data grows rapidly and storage and analysis becomes a problem. So, we need to find techniques to analyze this data as it finds its usage in diverse fields. Map Reduce is a technique of processing this data. Map Reduce consists of Map step and Reduce Step. Map Step in which the master node data is sliced into multiple sub-problems. A small piece of sub problems is given to worker node for processing and it is controlled by Job Tracker. Reduce Step which analyses and merges the data we get from Map. They discussed what tools Hadoop offers. It includes HDFS, Map Reduce, Flume, Zookeeper, HBase, Pig, Hive, Sqoop, Oozie and Flume. Hadoop can process large data sets in a distributed manner [7]. Map Reduce and HDFS are the main components of Hadoop. Hadoop makes use of these components to distribute data among many nodes and process them in parallel. It processes data which is large in quantity and can process structured as well as unstructured data. The main benefit of Hadoop is its ability to process unstructured data. HDFS cluster is formed by a number of datanodes. HDFS allows scale-out which provides fault tolerance and scalability. HDFS also provides cluster rebalancing which helps in fully utilizing the datanodes. MapReduce is the software framework that is associated with data processing. Map and Reduce are collectively referred to as MapReduce. Big data review in [8] has many obstacles to address. Data nowadays is mostly in unstructured form and is growing at a faster rate. So we need to divide data into many parts and process them in parallel. Also storing this huge amount of data will require lot of resources and money. Hadoop provides a solution for storage and processing. The storage portion of the Hadoop framework is provided by HDFS, while the processing functionality is provided by MapReduce. HDFS stores the data in a distributed manner. NameNode and DataNode comprise the HDFS. Name node is master and maintains the file system. It also keeps track of all the datanodes. The DataNodes store and retrieve data when requested by the clients or the NameNode. MapReduce is a framework in which large volume of unstructured data is processed across various clusters. The MapReduce framework works in two main phases i.e. Map phase and the Reduce phase. In Hadoop clusters are used to speed up data analysis, throughput and provide fault tolerance.

User opinions on social networks can be used to make predictions. A cluster of nodes in hadoop will process twitter data [9]. Analysis consists of many steps like Tokenization, Normalization, and Classification. Various types of dictionaries are used to determine polarity of user opinions expressed on twitter. A segment classifier will classify the tweets as positive, negative or neutral based upon the tokens in it. Twitter API is used to fetch data from twitter. Tweets are pre-processed like usernames, urls, special symbols, hashtags are removed and emoticons are converted into words [10]. Then Naïve-Bayes algorithm is applied for classification, which uses a wordnet dictionary. In Map phase, polarity of tokens is generated to check overall polarity of a tweet. In reduce phase, the authors are categorizing the polarity into specific class. Converting emoticons into equivalent words increases the efficiency of the system. A survey on multiple sentiment Analysis methods is presented in [11]. This proves to be of value to have an approximate understanding of sentiment evaluation techniques. At the end, the authors have drawn upon a contrast between various paper's method and issues along with the parameters used. A method for analyzing sentiments of twitter data is designed in [12]. It tried to establish a sentiment score to each entity by using a predefined dictionary. It also executed simple pronoun resolution by resolving pronouns to the closest entity in the tweet. SVM can be used to improve the classifier. Twitter data contains many sentiments which can be analyzed using Hadoop [13]. Twitter's API is used to get data from twitter. Then the data undergoes some processing. First removal of stop words is done. Then the tokens are changed into a structured form as they are mostly in unstructured form. Then emoticons are also translated for higher accuracy. Then Map-Reduce is used to find sentiment of each word and the sum gives the overall sentiment of the tweet.

Two map-reduces are discussed in [14]. In first map reduce, a sentence is detected and stop words, hashtags etc. are removed. Then we search for words which represent features and are then clustered. Then OpenNLP is used for POS Tagging. Phrase removal is done before stopword removal. In second mapreduce, a sentiwordnet dictionary is used, scores are given to words, which is averaged then to get overall value. Reviews given by customers on e-shopping websites have a lot of sentiment which need to be analyzed [15]. A dataset is collected and it undergoes some processing like Tokenization, Translating slang words, stemming etc. POS tagging is used in conjunction with Sentiword dictionary to calculate the sentiment. Sentiment analysis on news and blogs is performed in [16]. It splits prior work in the context of their specific task (sentiment analysis for news and blogs) into two categories. First category which—regards with techniques for automatically creating sentiment lexicon and the second one which relates to systems that analyze sentiment for entire documents. General sentiment analysis framework is discussed in [17]. It consists of steps like extracting relevant data from the source, pre-processing the data e.g. tokenization and stemming, training the classifier, then using it to determine polarity of new data e.g. tweets and at last checking the accuracy. SVM classifier in conjunction with clustering results for improvement in accuracy of classification than SVM alone provides is discussed in [18]. They used a set of rules to combine SVM with clustering. Here, additional information is obtained with help of clustering which improves classification of tweets. An open source tool for data mining Weka is used to perform sentiment analysis for movie reviews in [19]. Data was taken from twitter and other online review platforms like IMDB. Then data needs to be pre-processed. Then Naive Bayes classifier is used. Then the accuracy needs to be checked. The method of feature vectors to do sentiment analysis of twitter movie reviews is done in [20]. First a dataset needs to be created using tweets about movies. Then after pre-processing, feature vectors are created. Here first features of twitter are extracted, then the tweet is represented into keywords. Then a classification algorithm is used like Naive Bayes or support vector machine. Support Vector Machines have high accuracy than Naïve Bayes.

An algorithm is proposed in [21] which associates a sentiment with the data and tries to associate a strength value to the data also. The algorithm is lexicon-based and makes use of various lists of words. However, the performance of this algorithm was not well for positive sentiment when it was tested with data collected from MySpace. An approach of using twitter data for sentiment analysis is proposed using Hadoop in [22]. Flume is used to get data from twitter after creating a twitter application. This data gets stored in HDFS. Then Hive is used to analyze the various sentiments and inherent patterns of this data. An algorithm for sentiment analysis proposed in [23]. It is divided into four steps. First, the sentiment is recognized. It uses an algorithm based on WordNet dictionary to assign sentiment to a word. They proposed that synonyms of a word will have same sentiment as the word itself. This resulted in a corpus of data. For their presented approach, more the words in corpus, more will be the recall. Various classification algorithms can be used for sentiment analysis [24]. Decision trees have fast fitting speed and fast prediction speed, but have low accuracy. Naïve Bayes has high accuracy but has slow prediction speeds and consumes much time in training. An implementation of Naive Bayes on twitter data is shown in [25]. It makes use of SentiWordNet. SentiWordNet in combination Naïve Bayes can improve accuracy of tweet classification, by awarding sentiment score based on positivity or negativity of words in a tweet. For implementation of this system python with NLTK and python-twitter APIs are used. A comprehensive study on the challenge of detecting sentiment of words [26]. It considered words to be either positive or negative. Three languages were targeted by them; English, French and Hindi. But little work has been done in developing lexicons for languages other than English. The measures to bring security in data storage on public clouds is discussed in [27] by providing the extended model of Role Based Access Control where the authenticated users can only access the data in terms of roles with assigned permissions and restricts the unknown users from accessing data by adding variable constraints. The sentiment of youngsters is examined regarding the floods in Chennai in 2016 [28]. They used flume to get data from twitter and applying Naïve Bayes algorithm. They developed a dictionary to compare the tweets with and get a sentiment score.

Contrast between lexical based and model based techniques is given in [29]. Description of various algorithms is given like Support Vector Machine, Maximum Entropy, Multinomial Naive Bayes, and ok-Nearest Neighbour. They concluded that Model based methods have more accuracy than Lexicon based methods. Comparison of time taken by a file to process in Java without hadoop with the time taken in Hadoop is discussed in [30]. They compared files of different sizes, with results showing that Hadoop is the fastest approach. Due to growth in dataset, there is no decrease in accuracy of Naïve Bayes [31]. Naïve Bayes is able to scale up. Also, the number of cases which are classified correctly and the number of cases which are classified wrong decrease when the size of dataset grows. Also when the dataset increases, it benefits from parallelization of Hadoop, so processing time is reduced. Twitter data along with naive Bayes for evaluating the sentiments in twitter data is used in [32]. They combined it with a process which evaluates the results based on adjectives. This improves the accuracy of

Naïve Bayes. Firstly naive Bayes is implemented on collected tweets. It results in a set of true positive and false positive. The False Positive data is analyzed with the adjective evaluation technique then. Naïve Bayes with decision tables is combined in [33] for data mining. The results show that this combination resulted in improved statistics and various parameters were valued higher in combination than in Naïve Bayes. Also, it classified more correctly, resulting in more accurate information. Various methods and concepts of sentiment analysis on big data is shown in [34]. It has two approaches- one is based on Lexicons and another approach uses Machine Learning. Machine learning techniques are more popular and use various supervised and unsupervised learning algorithms. They perform better than Lexicon based techniques. The work on Big Data News Clusters is done in [35] and the authors managed Web News Big Data and categorizing it on the basis of text and content using different classifiers to provide the accurate news with less running time in clusters. Novel Approach for identifying lexicon set is presented in [36]. The authors in this research concluded that lexicon set specific to twitter is small and also transferable to domains. This research leads to a machine learning approach for the selection of features which are usually dependent on domains. Sentiment Analysis and Prediction System for Social Media is proposed in [37]. This prediction system helps in detection of real time events from large social media contents. Convolutional Neural Networks are used for classification for sentiments of various users. Sentiment Analysis for Chinese based Text is discussed in [38]. The authors have made use of sentiment dictionary to yield results. The sentiments are measured based on weight in this research and they conclude that this method is quite effective for performing sentiment analysis. Survey of multimodal sentiment analysis including images, video and human-human interaction is outlined in [39]. The emphasis has been given on text-based sentiment analysis with the use of machine learning models and construction of dictionaries. A hybrid approach has been implemented for sentiment analysis on twitter data in [40]. The approach used in this research is based on K-Means Cuckoo search method. This model provides effectiveness in reviews containing social issues.

30.3   Proposed Problem Approach

This section presents methodology of the proposed technique.

1. *Collection of Data:* Data can be collected from Twitter Data source using Twitter API. Twitter has millions of users who tweet billions of times in a week. One more imperative cause of using tweet data is that tweets are mostly in text, while on others, there are usually images, videos etc. Flume is used to get Twitter Data from twitter and store it in HDFS. Later, Hive is used to get this data in text form from HDFS. Then we manually edit the data to make it usable for our classifiers.
2. *Pre-Processing and Filtering:* The collected dataset from Twitter is in the form of raw data that needs to be filtered in order to do classification on the data.

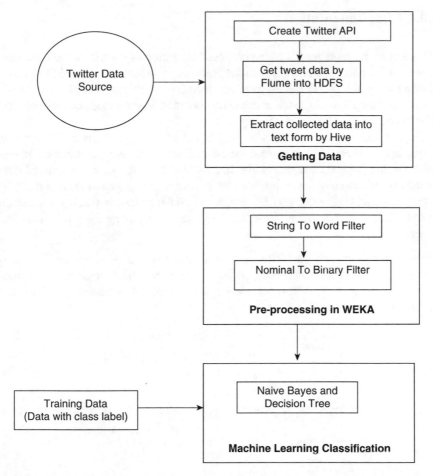

Fig. 30.3 Flowchart of proposed technique based on hybrid classifier

For the Filtration of the raw data, two filters from Weka are applied. They are StringToWord Filter and NominalToBinary Filter. It makes the data ready for use in classification algorithms.

3. *Classification using Map Reduce Platform:* A hybridised classification technique is then implemented. The algorithms used are Naïve Bayes and Decision Tree. Naïve (Fig. 30.3)

Bayes makes use of conditional probability and bayes theorem and it assumes that features are independent. The overall class probability is estimated by combining the estimated probability. Decision Tree makes use of decision rules. We will use the Weka implementations of these algorithms in hadoop library by using hadoop JARs.

30.4 Implementation

This section presents results of the proposed algorithm of Hybrid Naïve Bayes and Decision Tree and compares it with the Naïve Bayes Classifier. Figure 30.4 shows the summary of sentiment analysis results using Naïve Bayes Classifier. Out of 922 instances, Naïve Bayes Classifier correctly classified 748 instances and resulted into 174 in corrected instances previously.

Figure 30.5 shows the results of the proposed technique. It gives 797 correctly classified instances, 125 incorrectly classified instances. Kappa statistics of proposed technique is 0.7832, mean absolute error is 0.0967, root mean squared error is 0.2821, relative absolute error is 22.8956, root relative squared error is 61.3824, TP rate is 0.864, FP rate is 0.089, precision is 0.870, recall is 0.864, f-measure is 0.864. The comparison clearly marks an improvement by using the hybrid technique of classifiers.

Precision and Recall Precision and recall are the two measurements that are broadly utilized to evaluate execution in content mining, and in content investigation field like data recovery. These parameters are utilized for calculating precision and culmination separately.

$$\text{Precision} = \frac{\text{True Positive}}{\text{True Positive} + \text{False Positive}}$$

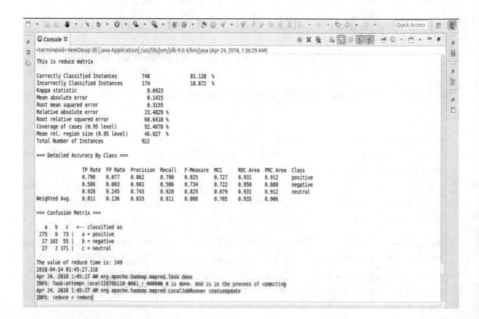

Fig. 30.4 Result extraction using Naïve Bayes classifier

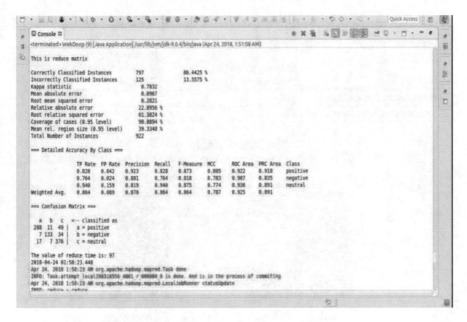

Fig. 30.5 Result extraction using proposed technique

$$Recall = \frac{True\ Positive}{True\ Positive + False\ Negative}$$

F-Measure The harmonic mean of precision and recall is called F-Measure. The esteem ascertained utilizing F-measure is a harmony amongst precision and recall.

$$F\ measure = \frac{2*recall*precision}{precision+recall}$$

Mean Absolute Error (MAE) The MAE calculates the standard size of the mistake in an display of gauges, lacking thinking about their bearing. It quantifies exactness for ceaseless factors.

$$MAE = \frac{1}{n} \sum_{j=1}^{n} \mid y_j - \hat{y}_j \mid$$

Root Mean Squared Error (RMSE) The RMSE is a quadratic scoring guideline that calculates the normal size of the mistake. The condition for the RMSE is provided in both of the references.

$$RMSE = \sqrt{\frac{1}{n} \sum_{j=1}^{n} \left(y_j - \hat{y}_j \right)^2}$$

Table 30.1 Comparison of proposed technique with existing technique based on classified instances

Parameters	Existing technique (Naïve Bayes classifier)	Proposed technique (hybrid classifier Naïve Bayes with Decision Tree)
Correctly classified instances	748	797
Incorrectly classified instances	174	125

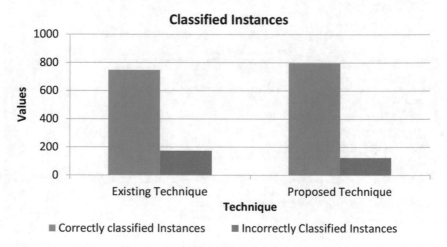

Fig. 30.6 Comparison of proposed technique with existing technique based on classified instances

Table 30.1 shows the comparison of proposed technique of Hybrid Classifier Naïve Bayes with Decision Tree with existing technique of Naïve Bayes Classifier based on classified instances as given in Figs. 30.4 and 30.5. Correctly classified instances of existing technique is 748 and that of proposed technique is 797. Incorrectly classified instances of existing technique is 174 and that of proposed technique is 125. As technique with more correctly classified instances and less incorrectly classified instances performs better, hence, proposed technique performs better as it has more number of correctly classified instances and less number of incorrectly classified instances.

Figure 30.6 shows comparison of proposed technique with existing technique based on classified instances as given in Figs. 30.4 and 30.5. It is clear from the figure that proposed technique give more number of correctly classified instances and less incorrectly classified instances and hence performs better.

30.5 Conclusion and Future Work

Previously, the work of Sentiment Analysis was implemented with Naïve Bayes which assumes that features selected are independent of each other and its accuracy of classifying entities is low and time taken is more. In this proposed and implemented work, the authors tried to implement a hybrid-classifier based on Naïve Bayes and Decision Tree. The hybrid-classifier has improved accuracy and takes less time to execute.

In future, data from other social sites can be used like Facebook with challenge of data in form of other than text. Moreover the implemented hybrid algorithm needs to be applied on HDFS with high performance clusters for in memory computation and efficient data processing on large datasets. This will largely result in the improvement of running time of jobs for processing.

References

1. Manyika, James, Michael Chui, Brad Brown, Richard Dobbs, Charles Roxburgh, Angela Hung Byers (2011). Big data: The next frontier for innovation, competition, and productivity. Report McKinsey Global Institute.
2. Dean, Jeffrey, Sanjay Ghemawat (2008). MapReduce: simplified data processing on large clusters. Communications of the ACM, 51(1): 107-113.
3. Temple, Krystal. (2012). What Happens in an Internet Minute? Inside Scoop.
4. Bollen, Johan, Huina Mao, Xiaojun Zeng (2011). Twitter mood predicts the stock market. Journal of Computational Science, 2(1):1-8.
5. Vargas, S., McCreadie, R., Macdonald, C., Ounis, I. (2016, March). Comparing Overall and Targeted Sentiments in Social Media during Crises. In ICWSM (pp. 695-698).
6. Sagiroglu, S., Sinanc, D. (2013, May). Big data: A review. In Collaboration Technologies and Systems (CTS), 2013 International Conference on (pp. 42-47). IEEE.
7. Sreedhar, C., Kavitha, D., Rani, K. A. Big Data and Hadoop. International Journal of Advanced Research in Computer Engineering & Technology (IJARCET) Volume, 3.
8. YashikaVerma, SumitHooda. (2015). A Review Paper on Big Data and Hadoop. International Journal of Scientific Research and Development, Volume 3, Issue 2, (pp. 682–684).
9. Ajinkiya Ingle, Anjali Kante, Shriya Samak, Anita Kumari. (2015). Sentiment Analysis of Twitter Data using Hadoop. International Journal of Engineering Research and General Science 3(6): 144-147.
10. Huma Pandey, Shikha Pandey (2016). Sentiment Analysis on Twitter Data-set using Naïve Bayes Algorithm. IEEE, 2nd International Conference on Applied and Theoretical Computing and Communication Technology: 416-419.
11. Abirami A M, Ms. V. Gayathri (2016). A Survey on Sentiment Analysis Methods and Approach. IEEE Eighth International Conference on Advanced Computing (ICoAC): 72-76.
12. Kumar, Sebastian. (2012). Sentiment Analysis on Twitter. IJCSI International Journal of Computer Science: 372–378.
13. Divya Sehgal, Ambuj Kumar Agarwal (2016). Sentiment Analysis of Big Data Applications using Twitter Data with the Help of HADOOP Framework. IEEE, 5th International Conference on System Modelling & Advancement in Research Trends: 251-255.
14. Jalpa Mehta, Jayesh Patil, Rutesh Patil, Mansi Somani, Sheel Varma. (2016). Sentiment Analysis on Product Reviews using Hadoop. International Journal of Computer Applications 142(11): 38-41.
15. Ravi Babu. (2017). Sentiment Analysis of reviews for E-Shopping Websites. International Journal of Engineering and Computer Science 6(1): 19965-19968.
16. Godbole, N., Srinivasaiah, M. & Skiena, S. (2007). Large-Scale Sentiment Analysis for News and Blogs. Proceedings of the International Conference on Weblogs and Social edia (ICWSM).

17. Luiz F. S. Coletta, Nadia F. F. da Silva, Eduardo R. Hruschka, Estevam R. Hruschka Jr. (2014). Combining Classification and Clustering for Tweet Sentiment Analysis. IEEE Brazilian Conference on Intelligent Systems, 210-215.
18. Vaishali Sarathy, Srinidhi S, Karthika S. (2015). Sentiment Analysis Using Big Data From Social Media:23rd IRF International Conference: 40-45.
19. Rajni Singh, Rajdeep Kaur. (2015). Sentiment Analysis on Social Media and Online Review, International Journal of Computer Applications 121(20): 44-48.
20. Akshay Amolik, Niketan Jivane, Mahavir Bhandari and Dr. M Venkatesan (2016). Twitter Sentiment Analysis of Movie Reviews using Machine Learning Techniques. International Journal of Engineering and Technology, 7(6):2038–2044.
21. Cui, Zhang, Liu, Ma. (2011). Emotion tokens: Bridging the gap among multilingual twitter sentiment analysis. Information Retrieval Technology: 238–249.
22. Abhinandan P Shirahatti, Neha Patil, Durgappa Kubasad and Arif Mujawar (2015). Sentiment Analysis on Twitter Data using Hadoop. International Journal of Emerging Technology in Computer Science and Electronics, 14(2): 831–837.
23. Kim, Hovy (2006). Identifying and analyzing judgment opinions. Proceedings of HLT/-NAACL: 200–207.
24. Thakor (2017). A Survey Paper on Classification Algorithms in Big Data. International Journal of Research Culture Society 1(3): 21-27.
25. Ankur Goel, Jyoti Gautam, Sitesh Kumar (2016). Real Time Sentiment Analysis of Tweets Using Naive Bayes. IEEE 2nd International Conference on Next Generation Computing Technologies (NGCT-2016) Dehradun: 257-261.
26. Rao, Ravichandran. (2009). Semi-supervised polarity lexicon induction, Conference of the European Chapter of the Association for Computational Linguistics: 675–682.
27. M Rashid, R Chawla (2013). Securing Data Storage by Extending Role Based Access Control. International Journal of Cloud Applications and Computing, 3(4), 28-37. DOI: https://doi.org/10.4018/ijcac.2013100103.
28. Priya. V, S Divya Vandana. (2016). Chennai Rains Sentiment-An Analysis Of Opinion About Youngsters Reflected In Tweets Using Hadoop. International Journal of Pharmacy & Technology, 8(3): 16172-16180.
29. Warih Maharani. (2013). Microblogging Sentiment Analysis with Lexical Based and Machine Learning Approaches. IEEE International Conference of Information and Communication Technology (ICoICT): 439-443.
30. Mrigank Mridul, Akashdeep Khajuria, Snehasish Dutta, Kumar N. (2014). Analysis of Big data using Apache Hadoop and Map Reduce. International Journal of Advanced Research in Computer Science and Software Engineering 4(5): 555-560.
31. Bingwei Liu, Erik Blasch, Yu Chen, Dan Shen and Genshe Chen (2013). Scalable Sentiment Classification for Big Data Analysis Using Naive Bayes Classifier. IEEE International Conference on Big Data: 99-104.
32. Mohit Mertiya, Ashima Singh. (2016). Combining Naive Bayes and Adjective Analysis for Sentiment Detection on Twitter. *International Conference on Inventive Computation Technologies (ICICT),* Coimbatore, pp. 1-6. DOI: https://doi.org/10.1109/INVENTIVE.2016.7824847.
33. Shivangi Sharma. (2017). Design and Implementation of Improved Naive Bayes Algorithm for Sentiment Analysis on Movies Review. International Journal of Innovative Research in Computer and Communication Engineering, 5 (1): 285-291
34. Edison M, A. Aloysius (2016). Concepts and Methods of Sentiment Analysis on Big Data. International Journal of Innovative Research in Science Engineering and Technology 5(9):16288-16296.
35. Sukhpal Kaur, Mamoon Rashid (2016). Web News Mining using Back Propagation Neural Network and Clustering using K-Means Algorithm in Big Data. Indian Journal of Science and Technology, Vol 9(41), DOI: https://doi.org/10.17485/ijst/2016/v9i41/95598.
36. Ghiassi, M., & Lee, S. (2018). A domain transferable lexicon set for Twitter sentiment analysis using a supervised machine learning approach. *Expert Systems with Applications*, *106*, 197-216.

37. Yoo, S., Song, J., & Jeong, O. (2018). Social media contents based sentiment analysis and prediction system. *Expert Systems with Applications*, *105*, 102-111.
38. Zhang, S., Wei, Z., Wang, Y., & Liao, T. (2018). Sentiment analysis of Chinese micro-blog text based on extended sentiment dictionary. *Future Generation Computer Systems*, *81*, 395-403.
39. Soleymani, M., Garcia, D., Jou, B., Schuller, B., Chang, S. F., & Pantic, M. (2017). A survey of multimodal sentiment analysis. *Image and Vision Computing*, *65*, 3-14.
40. Pandey, A. C., Rajpoot, D. S., & Saraswat, M. (2017). Twitter sentiment analysis using hybrid cuckoo search method. *Information Processing & Management*, *53*(4), 764-779.

Chapter 31
An Efficient Lung Image Classification Using GDA Based Feature Reduction and Tree Classifier

K. Vasanthi and N. Bala Kumar

31.1 Introduction

Around the global analysis, lung cancer affected patient's leads to death because of its delayed disease prediction and treatment [1]. So as to improve patients' survival rate, early prediction of lung cancer is prerequisite one [2]. Image mining is utilized to decide the information from the Image dataset by utilizing a few strategies like Image grouping, Image classification [3], and image representation [31, 32] based outline and association rule mining. In the examination, image classification assumes a noteworthy part to analyze the lung cancer image from the dataset images [4].

The preprocessing technique is likewise utilized in this work to acquire the correct outcome. In the stage of pre-processing, the morphological technique has been utilized to eject the undesirable information from the considered dataset image [5, 6]. To evacuate and filter the aggravating noisy data from lung cancer images, image pre-processing is applied to the input image [9]. The feature extraction method is utilized to limit the one of a kind dataset by manipulative some changed over highlights [7, 26]. To determine the feature extraction of lung image geometrical as well as statistical properties technique has been utilized to extricate images. Feature extraction is a movement of changing the input information into a coordinating arrangement for image mining assignment [8, 10]. Various features can be excluded from images by concerning statistical methods, image transform along with texture-based techniques [11]. When managing an expansive measure of image repository the greater part of the image information that progresses toward becoming an important, image next to the procedure of feature extraction [12]. It helps in increasing the execution of numerous classifiers, limiting the execution

K. Vasanthi · N. B. Kumar (✉)
Department of Computer Science, Pioneer College of Arts and Science, Coimbatore, India

© Springer Nature Switzerland AG 2019
A. K. Singh, A. Mohan (eds.), *Handbook of Multimedia Information Security: Techniques and Applications*, https://doi.org/10.1007/978-3-030-15887-3_31

time also makes the unassuming as well as laid-back to results [13, 28–30]. In the examination work, the real difficulties for lung cancer identification incorporate feature extraction, feature reduction and classification [14].

In feature extraction, the present study, for the most part, centers on planning latest features to enhance the depiction and separation of lung images [15]. In any case, these feature extraction techniques can't resolve the intra-class variety and between class vagueness issue [16, 27]. For classification, with the advancement of medicinal imaging innovation, various unlabeled information are produced [17]. Notwithstanding, the present significant classifiers require marks to train. A few methodologies have been connected to characterize the typical and unusual lung image [18]. This work has been essentially centered on recognizing and order of lung cancer medical images in light of the minimum distance computation of the nearest neighbor technique.

The structure of this chapter is depicted as follows: the existing research chapters related to medical imaging and its various approaches are detailed in Sect. 31.2, the purpose of the lung image classification system is discussed in Sect. 31.3, the proposed methodology is provided in Sect. 31.4, Sect. 31.5 explains the classification results of the proposed work and the conclusion part is explained in Sect. 31.6 along with its future work.

31.2 Survey of Existing Literatures

Désir et al. [19] exhibited an image classification system that can separate amongst ordinary and obsessive images. Distinctive feature spaces for segregation are explored and assessed utilizing a Support Vector Machine (SVM). The tests on expanded databases are required, these first outcomes demonstrate that effective PC based mechanized classification of typical versus obsessive images of the distal lung is attainable.

In 2018 Zia urRehman et al. [20] introduced a precise examination of the current nodules discovery strategies with the objective to summarize current patterns and future difficulties. The applicable chapters are chosen from IEEE Xplore, science direct, PubMed, and the web of science databases. Each chapter is fundamentally reviewed keeping in mind the end goal to outline its philosophy and results for further examination. The investigation uncovered that few strategies demonstrate potential advancement in the field yet at the same time require a change to defeat numerous difficulties like, the maximum sensitivity with low False Positive (FP) rate, and giving powerful procedures that are effective across over various databases.

In 2017 Abdillah et al. [21] executed and investigated the image processing strategy for the location of lung cancer. In this exploration, proposed a discovery technique for lung cancer in light of image segmentation. Marker control watershed and region developing methodology is utilized to a section of the CT scan image. Location stages are trailed by image improvement utilizing image filtering, segmentation along with feature extraction. By analyzing the exploratory outcomes, we found the efficiency of the presented approach. The outcomes demonstrate that the best approach for fundamental feature recognition is obtained with concealing strategy which has maximum precision and robust.

In 2014 Kuruvilla, J., and Gunavathi, K. [22] displayed a PC supported classification technique in CT images of lungs created utilizing Artificial Neural Network (ANN). The whole lung is divided from the CT images and the parameters were ascertained from the segmented image. Some factual parameters were utilized for ordering the medical dataset images. The classification procedure is finished by feed forward back propagation neural systems.

A gathering Classification Aided by Clustering (CAC) technique was proposed by Lee et al. in 2010 [23] to enhance the execution of computerized lung nodule recognition. The strategy exploits the Random Forest (RF) and designs a procedure for a hybrid RF based lung nodule separation which is done by clustering. A few tests were completed including the proposed strategy and in addition to two other existing strategies. The parameters of the classifiers are fluctuated to recognize the performance rate of the image classifiers. The analyses were directed utilizing lung scans of 32 patients including 5721 images inside which nodule areas were set apart by master radiologists.

In 2017 Bhatnagar et al. [24] clarified the classification of normal as well as abnormal images of lung cancer by the feature extraction (GLCM) and feature reduction (PCA) algorithm. With the assistance of consequence phase cancer will be assessed. With the assistance of dataset and result, the patient's survival rate must be evaluated. The algorithm performance is analyzed in terms of accuracy and error rate.

31.3 Purpose of Medical Image Classification

In the field of medical image processing, the monitoring and diagnosing the individual's diseases is very essential. Due to the late diagnosis of individual's diseases (lung cancer), the mortality rate is high [25]. The detection of abnormal lung images at an early stage is necessary to reduce the patient's death rate. Additionally, detailed information related to lung image classification gives maximum accuracy in the diagnosis process. The main goal of digital image processing is to enhance diagnosis accuracy by applying the development techniques in lung dataset images.

31.4 Methodology

The main motive of the methodology is to classify the normal and abnormal portion of the medical image i.e. lung. This study comprises an effective technique that can be utilized to classify the images. This process consists of pre-processing, feature extraction, feature reduction, and classification.

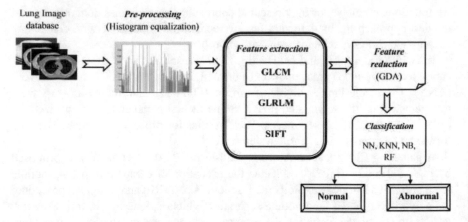

Fig. 31.1 The diagrammatic representation of the proposed work

- Preprocessing: The intention of image preprocessing is to attain high-quality lung images [33].
- Feature Extraction and Reduction: In both pattern recognition as well as image classification process, feature selection is an important data processing step.
- Classification: Based on the selected features, we can classify the lung images as normal and abnormal.

The methodology of the proposed lung cancer image classification work is depicted in Fig. 31.1. With the help of feature extraction and reduction algorithm (GDA), the optimal features are chosen and then the lung dataset images are classified as normal and abnormal, based on the selected features by using the four different classifiers such as NN, KNN, NB, and RF.

31.4.1 Image Pre-processing

In the pre-processing stage, Histogram Equalization (HE) is utilized to check the reasonableness of the extracted region. HE is typically accomplished by adjusting the histogram of the image pixel gray levels in the spatial area in order to re-distribute them consistently. It is generally done on too dark or too bright images in order to enhance upgrade image quality and to enhance acknowledgment execution. HE should be possible in three stages, in particular

- Evaluate the histogram of input lung image
- Evaluate the normalized sum of the histogram
- Change over the input image into an output image

The HE formula is given in the Eq. (31.1).

$$H(e) = round \left(\frac{cdf(e) - cdf_{min}}{(W \times H) - cdf_{min}} \times (G - 1) \right) \tag{31.1}$$

where, $H(e)$—the value of histogram, cdf—cumulative distribution function, cdf_{min}—minimum non zero value of cdf, W—width, H—height and G—the number of grey levels.

31.4.2 Feature Extraction

Feature extraction is a form of dimensionality reduction in the recognition of image patterns as well as image processing. At the point, when the data of an algorithm is too huge to be in any way prepared and it is suspected to be famously redundant then the input will be changed into a reduced set of image features. There are many feature-extraction systems that are accessible. In the proposed study, three strategies are utilized to extricate the desired features that are

- Gray Level Co-occurrence Matrix (GLCM)
- Gray Level Run Length Matrix (GLRLM)
- Scale Invariant Feature Transform (SIFT)

Gray Level Co-Occurrence Matrix (GLCM) A numerical method of investigating texture that assumes the spatial relationship of pixels is the GLCM, also called as the gray-level spatial dependence matrix. It is named as a second-order measure, the reason is: it measures the relationship between neighboring pixels. A GLCM is represented by a matrix where the pixel range of gray levels and number of rows and columns are equal, G, in the image.

The matrix element $p(i, j| d_1, d_2)$ indicates the equivalent value segregated by a pixel distance (d1 and d2). In the work, the features that are extracted using GLCM are depicted as in Table 31.1.

Gray Level Run Length Matrix (GLRLM) Next to that GLCM feature, the GLRLM is mainly for extracting higher order statistical texture information. The number of gray levels G, in the image is decreased by re-quantization prior to the accumulation of the matrix. The features that are extracted using this GLRLM are deliberated in Table 31.1. The GLRLM is developed as takes after:

$$K(\theta) = (r(u, v)/\theta), 0 \le u \le N_r, 0 \le v \le K_{max} \tag{31.2}$$

where N_r the maximum is gray level, K_{max} is the maximum length and u, v is a matrix size values.

Scale Invariant Feature Transform (SIFT) SIFT is a computer vision technique, extracts local features that can describe the cancer types which have the almost same characteristic. The features extorted by the SIFT are invariant to image scale,

Table 31.1 Features of GLCM and GLRLM

Features	Description
GLCM (10 features)	
Autocorrelation	It defines the correlation between image pixels separated by different time intervals
Contrast	This feature measures the local variations of lung image
Correlation	This feature measures the linear dependency of gray levels on the nearest pixel value of the image
Dissimilarity	It measures the dissimilarity of the features through the path based on Eigenvector
Cluster prominence	It is a measure of the asymmetry of an image
Cluster shade	The matrix skewness is measured by this feature (image pixels) based on the uniformity
Entropy	This feature measures the distribution change of the lung image in a specific region and it's supporting to represent the texture image
Energy	In a particular region, the lung image disorders are measured by energy feature, it helps to segment the image
Homogeneity	It evaluates the uniformity of non-zero entities
Maximum probability	Maximum probability defines the product of its distribution function and the probability density function of the image
GLRLM (3 features)	
Gray-level nonuniformity (GLN)	GLN evaluates the similarity of gray level values throughout the considered input lung image. If the values are not equal, GLN is small
Run length nonuniformity (RLN)	RLN evaluates the length's similitude of keeps running all through the image; The RLN is expected little if the run lengths are indistinguishable all through the image
Run percentage (RP)	RP is the biggest when the length of runs is 1 for every gray level in a specific direction

rotation, along with illumination condition. The steps involved in SIFT are explained as:

1. *Scale-space extrema detection*: The main stage of calculation searches over all scales as well as image areas. It is actualized efficiently by utilizing a distinction of-Gaussian capacity to recognize potential intrigue points that are invariant scale as well as orientation.
2. *Key point localization*: At every area, key focuses are chosen based on the similarity measures i.e. neighboring image pixels in a similar scale.
3. *Orientation assignment*: For each key point area, at least one orientation is doled out dependent on the image gradient. The tasks performed on lung image dataset that has been changed in respect to the allocated orientation, scale, and area for each feature set, in this manner giving invariance to these changes.
4. *Key point descriptor*: At this progression, SIFT includes vector is created and afterward neighborhood image values are estimated at the chosen scale in the locale around each key point. These are changed into a representation that takes

into consideration critical levels of neighborhood shape distortion also change in illumination.

Finally, the best outcomes were accomplished with a 4 × 4 cluster of histograms with 8 orientation receptacles in each. So the descriptor of SIFT that was utilized is 4 × 4 × 8 = 128 measurements. Accordingly, 128 SIFT vector is extricated for each key point.

31.4.3   Feature Reduction Using GDA

Feature reduction algorithms are utilized to separate just fundamental features from the feature vector database and after that store those as diminished feature vector database. Thus, it attains the reduced set of features as output which depicts the best features of lung image. The lung image similarity is analyzed by matching reduced feature vectors of input lung image with reduced feature vector database using the proposed GDA technique.

Generalized Discriminant Analysis (GDA) The GDA is used for multi-class classification issues i.e. it overcomes the overlap problem of classes in the feature space. GDA is generally designed for non linear classification based on the kernel function (φ). The step by step procedure in the GDA feature reduction is deliberated as follows:

Step 1: Assume the original space is S and then transform the original space to new high dimensional feature space.

$$T : \varphi : S \rightarrow T \tag{31.3}$$

Step 2: From the database, the non-linearly mapped data is calculated as in two ways: namely within the class data and between the class and scatter matrix using Eqs. (31.4) and (31.5),

$$\text{Within the class data } G^{\phi} = \sum_{k=1}^{k} N_k n_k^{\phi} \left(n_k^{\phi} \right)^{T} \tag{31.4}$$

$$\text{Between the class and scatter matrix } H^{\phi} = \sum_{k=1}^{k} \sum_{s \in S_k} \phi(s)\phi(s)^{T} \tag{31.5}$$

where, N_k represents the number of samples in the s_k in T and n_k^{φ} is the mean of s_k and k is a vector of weights.

Step 3: Projection Matrix Ratio: The main objective of GDA is to maximize the projection matrix ratio by finding

$$P_{opt}^{\phi} = \arg\max \frac{\left|(P^{\phi})^T G^{\phi} P^{\phi}\right|}{\left|(P^{\phi})^T H^{\phi} P^{\phi}\right|} = [p_1^{\varphi}, \ldots\ldots, p_n^{\varphi}] \tag{31.6}$$

For the generalized eigen values problem $G^{\phi} p_i^{\phi} = \lambda_i H^{\phi} p_i^{\phi}$, the vector p^{φ} can be evaluated as the solution and it lies in the span of all training samples in T, Where, α_{ki} are some real weights and s_{ki} is the ith sample of class k.

$$p^{\phi} = \sum_{k=1}^{K} \sum_{i=1}^{N_k} \alpha_{ki} \phi(s_{ki}), \alpha = \alpha_{ki}, i = 1, \ldots N_k \tag{31.7}$$

Step 4: Kernel Matrix and Diagonal Matrix: The solution is obtained by solving the Eq. (31.8).

$$\lambda = \frac{\alpha^T K_m D_m K_m \alpha}{\alpha^T K_m K_m \alpha} \tag{31.8}$$

The expansion of the kernel and the diagonal matrix is defined as, $K_m = (K_{ab})_{a=1, \ldots K, b=1, \ldots K}$, $D_m = (D_{m(k)})_{k=1, \ldots K}$. The k_{th} on the diagonal has the elements which are equal to $1/N_k$. By solving the eigen value problem yields the coefficient vector α it defines the projection vectors $p^{\phi} \in T$. A projection of a testing vector s_{test} is evaluated as

$$(p^{\phi})^T \phi(s_{test}) = \sum_{k=1}^{k} \sum_{i=1}^{N_k} \alpha_{ki} W(s_{ki}, s_{test}) \tag{31.9}$$

By using this feature reduction (GDA) algorithm, the best subset of features are selected from the GLCM, GLRLM, and SIFT.

31.4.3.1 Reduced Feature Set

The features are extracted from the Lung image dataset using GLCM, GLRLM, and SIFT. From that, the "best subset" of features is constructed based on the similarity with which each attribute is selected. The beneficial features of the images are extracted using the presented GDA dimensionality reduction technique and are provided as input for classification purposes.

31.4.4 Lung Image Classification

After the feature extraction and reduction of lung dataset images, the normal and abnormal lung image classification is done by various classifiers such as NN, KNN, NB, and RF. The procedure involved in each classifier is clearly explained in the below section.

(A) Neural Network NN is a type of artificial intelligence that impersonates some functions of the person mind. It has a tendency to store experiential knowledge. NN consists of a sequence of layers (input, hidden and output); each layer comprises a set of neurons as in the human brain. In this network, all neurons of every layer are linked by weighted functions to all neurons on the previous and succeeding layers. The structure of NN is shown in Fig. 31.2.

Input Layer In NN, the purpose of the input layer is for receiving the extracted features as input. These sources of input (tests or examples) are typically standardized within the values delivered by activation functions. This standardization results in better precision for the scientific tasks performed by the system.

Hidden Layer Activation function applies to a hidden layer if it is accessible and the weights in the hidden node need to test using training data and it is denoted by AF. An activation function performs a mathematical operation on the signal output. The operation of NN is to add the product of the input signal associated weight and output. The activation function is calculated by the following equation:

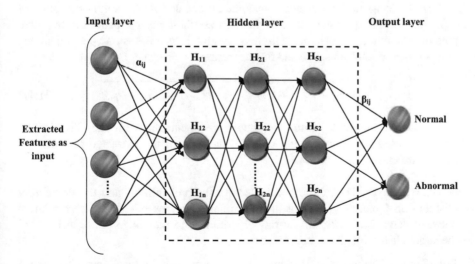

Fig. 31.2 Structure of NN

$$AF_i = \sum_{j=1}^{h} \alpha_j{}^* \left(\frac{1}{1 + \exp\left(-\sum_{i=1}^{N} I_i \beta_{ij} \right)} \right) \qquad (31.10)$$

where, $I_i \rightarrow$ image features which we are taken as input, $\alpha_j \rightarrow$ weight function between the input, as well as hidden layer, $\beta_{ij} \rightarrow$ weight function between the hidden and output layer, h, are the number of hidden neurons.

Output Layer The use of this output layer is for producing as well as presenting the final network outputs as normal and abnormal of lung images, it results from the task performed by the neurons in the previous layers.

(B) K-Nearest Neighbor For classification purpose, KNN classifier is used which is a non-parametric one. One advantage is that there is no need for any prior knowledge about the data structure in the training set. In the KNN algorithm, the classification of an object is fully based on distance from its neighbors. KNN process consists of three rules: (a) the set of stored records, (b) know the distance metric between stored and unknown record to classify and (b) recognize the KNN and use the corresponding class label in order to evaluate the class label of unknown record.

Step by Step Procedure
Step 1: Initially, the input data are stored in the training set and the unknown patterns are in the test set.
   Step 2: Using the Euclidean distance measure, calculate the similarity values of input images based on the extracted features i.e. the k nearest pattern to the input pattern. The minimum distance with least k value is taken. Assume p and q are the two points in Euclidean space and for measuring the distance, Eq. (31.11) is used.

$$E_d(p, q) = \sqrt{(p_1 - q_1)^2 + (p_2 - q_2)^2 + \cdots + (p_n - q_n)^2} \qquad (31.11)$$

   Step 3: Classes of k nearest neighbors are documented for the classification process. Based on the minimum distance measure of the extracted features, the images are classified.

(C) Naïve Bayes This algorithm deals with the probabilities and the Probability Distribution Function (PDF) of attained image features based on its correlation between them. The main aim of this algorithm is to maximize the probability of the target class with given image features.

Initialization Probability Distribution Function of given image features is depicted as $P_f(C_l | f_1, f_2, \ldots f_n)$

Conditional Probability In Bayes' theorem, the conditional probability that an image feature f belongs to a class l can be calculated from the Eq. (31.12).

$$P_f(C_l|f) = p_f(C_l) \frac{p_f(f|C_l)}{p_f(f)}, \qquad (31.12)$$

where

$$p_f(f|C_l) = \prod_{i=1}^{n} p(f_i|C_l) \quad i = 1, 2, \ldots, n \qquad (31.13)$$

From the Eq. (31.12), $P_f(C_l|f)$ defines a pattern classification problem since it finds the probability that the given feature f belongs to the class l and then select the optimum class by choosing the class with the highest probability among all possible classes C, which can minimize the classification error.

Highest Probability Class By combining Eqs. (31.12) and (31.13), the Naive Bayes classifier can be summarized as the following equation:

$$C = \arg\max c_l P_f(C_l) \prod_{i=1}^{n} p_f(f_i|C_l) \qquad (31.14)$$

where the denominator p_f is omitted since the value is the same for all class. Based on the high probability class the lung images are classified.

(D) Random Forest (RF) An RF multi-way classifier comprises various trees; by the randomization function we can develop the tree structure. The leaf nodes of each tree are named by appraisals of the posterior division over the lung image classes. An image is characterized by sending it down each tree, then aggregating the achieved leaf distributions. The diagrammatic representation of the RF classifier is portrayed in Fig. 31.3.

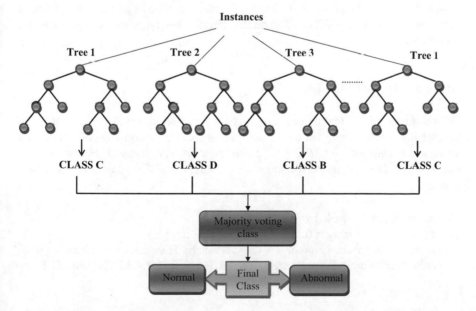

Fig. 31.3 Structure of RF classifier

Initialization Assume T_s indicates the set of all trees, C_s indicates class set, L_s indicates set of all leaves for a given tree.

Posterior Probabilities At the time of the training process, for each class, posterior probabilities are calculated by $P_p(L(I) = c)$ at each leaf node and are found for each tree. These probability functions are computed as the ratio of the number of images I of class c that reach l to the total number of images that reach l. L(I) is the class-label c for the image I.

Classification The test image is analyzed for every arbitrary tree until the point that it achieves a leaf node. All the posterior probabilities are then averaged and the maximum average is assigned as the classification of the input image. RF can manage high dimensional data, using an expansive number of trees in the troupe.

31.4.4.1   Error Rate Analysis

By evaluating the error rate of each classifier, the system performance level is analyzed. The Mean Square Error (MSE) rate is defined as the difference between the observed and target values for each trial with different iteration numbers, and the best structure was found by the minimum value of the MSE. MSE function is evaluated by.

$$MSE = \sqrt{\frac{1}{N} \sum_j \left(P_j - \hat{P}_j\right)^2} \tag{31.15}$$

where N is the total number of prediction, P_j and $\hat{P}_j$ are the target and observed time series respectively. In MSE calculation, the iterations are repeated until the optimal weight is achieved.

31.4.4.2   Attained Solution

With the help of the feature extraction, reduction, and image classifiers, the lung dataset images are classified as normal and abnormal (cancer images). Here, the images are classified by NN, KNN, Naïve Bayes and Random Forest classification algorithm and its performances are analyzed in the result and discussion section.

Pseudo code for Proposed work
Input: Lung dataset images (normal and abnormal images)
 Preprocessing: i) image preprocessing is done by Histogram Equalization (HE).
 Feature Extraction: Features are extracted using GLCM, GLRLM and SIFT.

Feature Reduction: Based on the similarity measures of extracted features, reduced set of features is attained by the applied GDA.

Image classification: Classification is done by four different classifiers such as NN, KNN, Naïve Bayes and RF

Output: Finally, the lung images are classified as normal and abnormal.

31.5 Result and Analysis

This section discusses the classification results of the lung image with proposed and existing method. This simulation process is implemented by MATLAB 2015 a with 4GB RAM and i5 processor. Validation of numerical results is done for the diagnosis of the normal and abnormal image and the analyzed measures are sensitivity, specificity, and accuracy etc. The results attained for the different classifiers is compared with the existing algorithm and are described in the below section. Figure 31.4 shows the sample lung images which we are taken for the classification analysis.

Table 31.2 shows the performance analysis of the proposed model. This table depicts the result of this study illustrated by performance measures such as accuracy, sensitivity, specificity, FPR, and FDR. Here 6 sample images are taken in the first column, then the next section shows the images processed under histogram equalization and then next column visualized that those images are normal or abnormal. In this study, the proposed model (RF) is compared to three existing models (KNN, NB, and NN). The comparison result shows that the maximum performance achieved in the RF classifier compared than other classifiers.

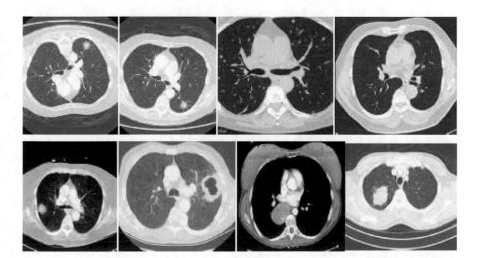

Fig. 31.4 Sample lung images

Table 31.2 Performance analysis of four classifiers

FDR	RF	58	56	59	56	57
	NN	48	49	49	51	53
	NB	46	46	45	48	45
	KNN	60	61	61	59	55
FPR	RF	70	64	64	68	66
	NN	65	62	64	60	65
	NB	58	57	60	63	62
	KNN	60	55	66	65	62
Sensitivity	RF	95	96	95	93	95
	NN	90	90	91	88	86
	NB	85	86	87	86	84
	KNN	87.45	88.96	85.36	89.74	82.03
Specificity	RF	94	94	94	92	94
	NN	90	86	87	85	84
	NB	81	80	78	78	82
	KNN	75.69	89.63	84.36	79.45	87.95
Accuracy	RF	92	93	96	95	94
	NN	80	83	84	86	87
	NB	78	80	81	81	82
	KNN	68	66	64	70	65

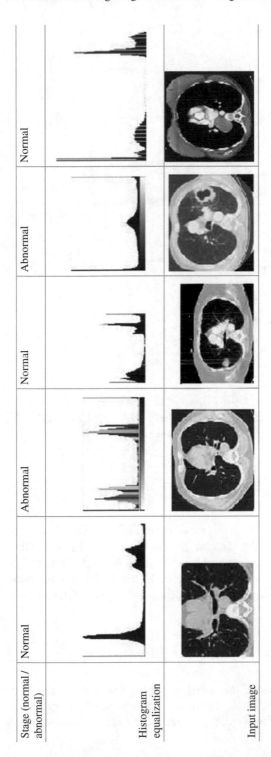

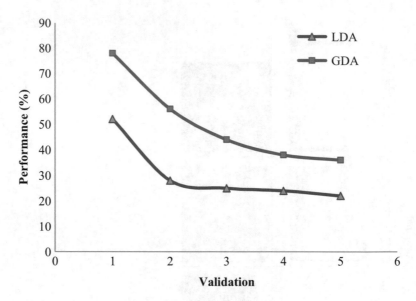

Fig. 31.5 Performance of feature reduction analysis

31.5.1   Feature Reduction Analysis

Figure 31.5 shows the performance of the feature reduction analysis. The features are reduced with the help of GDA in the proposed study. The graph scored that for every validation GDA performs high performance than LDA.

31.5.2   Comparative Analysis

Figure 31.6a–d shows the comparative analysis of performance such as accuracy, sensitivity, specificity, FDR, and FPR. The bar graphs depict that RF with GDA gives optimal values for all the images compared to KNN, NB, and NN. In Fig. 31.6a shows the accuracy reaches a maximum in RF-GDA as 97.99% and minimum in KNN, similarly, other Fig. 31.6b–d attains the optimal value in RF-GDA.

31.5.3   Error Rate Analysis

Figure 31.7 shows the analysis of MSE rate based on varying testing data. The MSE can be analyzed by finding the difference between predicted into the target value. Here, the low MSE rate is considered an optimal result. For the comparison of all the optimization techniques, RF with GDA optimizes the solution and get an optimal result that means minimum MSE value.

Table 31.3 shows the performance measures of RF-GDA by varying classifying conditions. After feature reduction, the images are classifying based on some conditions. Some conditions and their performance result are elaborated in the above table. In condition, 90% as training and 10% as testing in the classification technique gives high performance than others. That means if we trained the data as a high percentage the accuracy and the other performances result also improved.

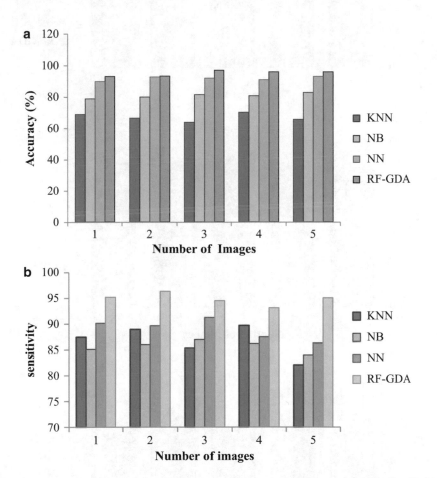

Fig. 31.6 Comparative Analysis of Performance measures (**a**) Accuracy, (**b**) Sensitivity, (**c**) Specificity, (**d**) FPR and (**e**) FDR

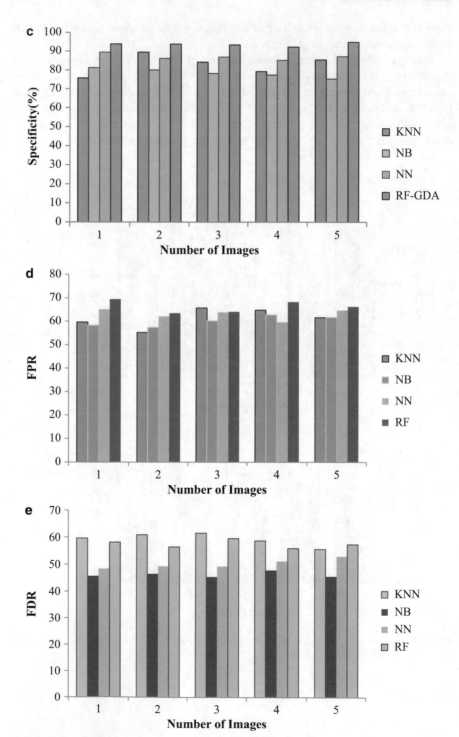

Fig. 31.6 (continued)

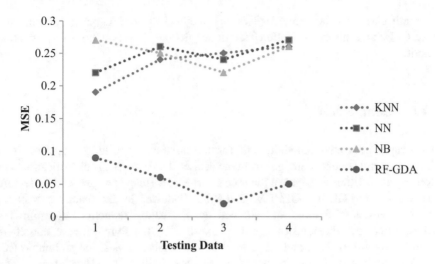

Fig. 31.7 MSE analysis

Table 31.3 Performance measures based on training and testing conditions

Input image	Training/testing	Performance measures of RF-GDA				
		Accuracy	Specificity	Sensitivity	FPR	FDR
1	90%/10%	97.99	95.03	96.34	83.25	75.12
2	80%/20%	90.32	90.68	93.47	80.15	74.56
3	70%/30%	87.45	85.64	90.11	79.63	71.34
4	60%/40%	85.45	83.47	85.44	74.12	70.98

Fig. 31.8 Comparative analysis of the four classifiers

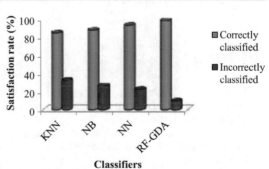

31.5.4 Comparison of Classifiers

Figure 31.8 shows the comparison of classification techniques based on their satisfaction rate. Here, KNN achieves the satisfaction rate in the range of 82%, the NB classifier classifies correctly as 83.15%, and wrongly as 32.14%, then for NN achieves the satisfaction rate as 90.22% in classified correctly and incorrectly as 25%, Coming to proposed model (RF-GDA) reaches 95.64% satisfaction rate in correctly classified and below 10% in incorrectly classified. As per the comparison result of above all classification techniques, RF-GDA gets a high classification result.

31.6   Conclusion

The chapter presented a methodology for the classification of lung images to attain the normal and abnormal images from the dataset. The lung image classification was done by three different stages of the process which are image pre-processing, feature extraction using GLCM, GLRLM, and SIFT. Followed by the feature extraction, the best subset of features are attained by the feature reduction algorithm i.e. GDA. After that, the lung images are classified by the four different classifiers such as KNN, NB, NN, and RF. Based on the result analysis, the technique RF-GDA is efficient for feature reduction as well as classification of lung images. The classification performance of RF-GDA method shows minimum error rate, better classification accuracy compared to other algorithms. This chapter can be further extended to test in a large number of medical lung images with reduced computation time. The selection of the best subset of features is finished because in this study we still need to do the iterative procedure in GDA to find the superior features and the authors expect that the existing technology can be developed based on speeding up the computation time. Also, the most optimal features will be attained for the exact nodule classification by introducing the combination of innovative neural networks with inspired metaheuristic optimization algorithms.

References

1. Li, J., Wang, Y., Song, X., & Xiao, H. (2018). Adaptive multinomial regression with overlapping groups for multi-class classification of lung cancer. Computers in Biology and Medicine, 100, 1–9.
2. Kashyap, A., Gunjan, V. K., Kumar, A., Shaik, F., & Rao, A. A. (2016). Computational and Clinical Approach in Lung Cancer Detection and Analysis. Procedia Computer Science, 89, 528–533.
3. Wei, G., Ma, H., Qian, W., Han, F., Jiang, H., Qi, S., & Qiu, M. (2018). Lung nodule classification using local kernel regression models with out-of-sample extension. Biomedical Signal Processing and Control, 40, 1–9.
4. Lu, Z., Liu, Y., Xu, J., Yin, H., Yuan, H., Gu, J., … Xie, B. (2018). Immunohistochemical quantification of expression of a tight junction protein, claudin-7, in human lung cancer samples using digital image analysis method. Computer Methods and Programs in Biomedicine, 155, 179–187.
5. Song, Y., Cai, W., Huang, H., Zhou, Y., Wang, Y., & Feng, D. D. (2015). Locality-constrained Subcluster Representation Ensemble for lung image classification. Medical Image Analysis, 22(1), 102–113.
6. Wang, Y., & Feng, L. (2018). Hybrid feature selection using component co-occurrence based feature relevance measurement. Expert Systems with Applications, 102, 83–99.

7. Bhuvaneswari, C., Aruna, P. and Loganathan, D., 2014. Classification of lung diseases by image processing techniques using computed tomography images. International Journal of Advanced Computer Research, 4(1), p. 87.
8. Song, Q., Zhao, L., Luo, X. and Dou, X., 2017. Using deep learning for classification of lung nodules on computed tomography images. Journal of healthcare engineering, 2017.
9. Dwivedi, S.A., Borse, R.P. and Yametkar, A.M., 2014. Lung Cancer detection and Classification by using Machine Learning & Multinomial Bayesian. IOSR Journal of Electronics and Communication Engineering (IOSR-JECE), 9(1), pp. 69-75.
10. Keerthana, P., Thamilselvan, P. and Sathiaseelan, J.G.R., Detection of Lung Cancer in MR Images by using Enhanced Decision Tree Algorithm.
11. Kaznowska, E., Depciuch, J., Łach, K., Kołodziej, M., Koziorowska, A., Vongsvivut, J., Cebulski, J. (2018). The classification of lung cancers and their degree of malignancy by FTIR, PCA-LDA analysis, and a physics-based computational model. Talanta, 186, 337–345.
12. Nagarajan, G., Minu, R. I., Muthukumar, B., Vedanarayanan, V., & Sundarsingh, S. D. (2016). Hybrid Genetic Algorithm for Medical Image Feature Extraction and Selection. Procedia Computer Science, 85, 455–462.
13. Ramos-González, J., López-Sánchez, D., Castellanos-Garzón, J. A., de Paz, J. F., & Corchado, J. M. (2017). A CBR framework with gradient boosting based feature selection for lung cancer subtype classification. Computers in Biology and Medicine, 86, 98–106.
14. Azhar, R., Tuwohingide, D., Kamudi, D., Sarimuddin, & Suciati, N. (2015). Batik Image Classification Using SIFT Feature Extraction, Bag of Features and Support Vector Machine. Procedia Computer Science, 72, 24–30.
15. Mohammed M., Al Samarraie, Md Jan Nordin, Ghassan Jasim Al-Anizy, 2015, Texture classification using random forests and support vector machines, Journal of Theoretical and Applied Information Technology, Vol. 73 No. 2, pp. 232-238.
16. P. Thamilselvan and J. G. R. Sathiaseelan, 2016, Detection and Classification of Lung Cancer MRI Images by using Enhanced K Nearest Neighbor Algorithm, Journal of Science and Technology, Vol 9(43), pp. 1-7.
17. Froz, B. R., de Carvalho Filho, A. O., Silva, A. C., de Paiva, A. C., Acatauassú Nunes, R., & Gattass, M. (2017). Lung nodule classification using artificial crawlers, directional texture and support vector machine. Expert Systems with Applications, 69, 176–188.
18. Katuwal, R., Suganthan, P. N., & Zhang, L. (2017). An ensemble of decision trees with random vector functional link networks for multi-class classification. Applied Soft Computing.
19. Désir, C., Petitjean, C., Heutte, L., Thiberville, L., & Salaün, M. (2012). An SVM-based distal lung image classification using texture descriptors. Computerized Medical Imaging and Graphics, 36(4), 264–270.
20. Zia ur Rehman, M., Javaid, M., Shah, S. I. A., Gilani, S. O., Jamil, M., & Butt, S. I. (2018). An appraisal of nodules detection techniques for lung cancer in CT images. Biomedical Signal Processing and Control, 41, 140–151.
21. Abdillah, B., Bustamam, A. and Sarwinda, D., 2017, October. Image processing based detection of lung cancer on CT scan images. In Journal of Physics: Conference Series (Vol. 893, No. 1, p. 012063). IOP Publishing.
22. Kuruvilla, J., & Gunavathi, K. (2014). Lung cancer classification using neural networks for CT images. Computer Methods and Programs in Biomedicine, 113(1), 202–209.
23. Lee, S. L. A., Kouzani, A. Z., & Hu, E. J. (2010). Random forest based lung nodule classification aided by clustering. Computerized Medical Imaging and Graphics, 34(7), 535–542.
24. Bhatnagar, D., Tiwari, A.K., Vijayarajan, V. and Krishnamoorthy, A., 2017, November. Classification of normal and abnormal images of lung cancer. In IOP Conference Series: Materials Science and Engineering (Vol. 263, No. 4, p. 042100). IOP Publishing.
25. Lakshmanaprabu S. K, Sachi Nandan Mohanty, K. Shankar, Arunkumar N, Gustavo Ramireze, Optimal deep learning model for classification of lung cancer on CT images, Future Generation Computer Systems, October 2018. https://doi.org/10.1016/j.future.2018.10.009

26. K. Shankar, Mohamed Elhoseny, Lakshmanaprabu S K, Ilayaraja M, Vidhyavathi RM, Majid Alkhambashi. Optimal feature level fusion based ANFIS classifier for brain MRI image classification. Concurrency Computat Pract Exper. 2018;e4887. https://doi.org/10.1002/cpe.4887
27. Lakshmanaprabu, S. K., Shankar, K., Khanna, A., Gupta, D., Rodrigues, J. J., Pinheiro, P. R., & De Albuquerque, V. H. C. (2018). Effective Features to Classify Big Data Using Social Internet of Things. IEEE Access, 6, 24196-24204.
28. Shankar, K., Lakshmanaprabu, S. K., Gupta, D., Maseleno, A., & de Albuquerque, V. H. C. (2018). Optimal feature-based multi-kernel SVM approach for thyroid disease classification. The Journal of Supercomputing, 2018. https://doi.org/10.1007/s11227-018-2469-4
29. Lakshmanaprabu SK, K. Shankar, Deepak Gupta, Ashish Khanna, Joel J. P. C. Rodrigues, Plácido R. Pinheiro, Victor Hugo C. de Albuquerque, "Ranking Analysis for Online Customer Reviews of Products Using Opinion Mining with Clustering," Complexity, vol. 2018, Article ID 3569351, 9 pages, 2018. https://doi.org/10.1155/2018/3569351.
30. T. Avudaiappan, R. Balasubramanian, S. Sundara Pandiyan, M. Saravanan, S. K. Lakshmanaprabu, K. Shankar, Medical Image Security Using Dual Encryption with Oppositional Based Optimization Algorithm, Journal of Medical Systems, Volume 42, Issue 11, pp. 1-11, November 2018. https://doi.org/10.1007/s10916-018-1053-z
31. Elhoseny, M., Ramírez-González, G., Abu-Elnasr, O. M., Shawkat, S. A., Arunkumar, N., & Farouk, A. (2018). Secure medical data transmission model for IoT-based healthcare systems. IEEE Access, 6, 20596–20608.
32. Shehab, A., Elhoseny, M., Muhammad, K., Sangaiah, A. K., Yang, P., Huang, H., & Hou, G. (2018). Secure and robust fragile watermarking scheme for medical images. IEEE Access, 6, 10269-10278.
33. Sonali, Sima Sahu, Amit Kumar Singh, S.P. Ghrera, Mohamed Elhoseny, An approach for denoising and contrast enhancement of retinal fundus image using CLAHE, Optics & Laser Technology, Available online 5 July 2018 (DOI: https://doi.org/10.1016/j.optlastec.2018.06.061)

Chapter 32
Deep Neural Networks for Human Behavior Understanding

Rajiv Singh and Swati Nigam

32.1 Introduction

Human behavior understanding is popular among researchers and attracted a lot of attention in last decade. It has potential applications in a person's daily life viz. security, surveillance, human-computer interaction, animation, sports, and several other significant applications [1, 2]. Majority of behavior understanding techniques are primarily based on facial expression and activity recognition. A successful behavior understanding technique must be capable of representing facial features and action unit features efficiently and effectively. These features reduce difference between same classes and enhance difference between different classes [3].

For behavior understanding, numerous handcrafted feature learning techniques for activity recognition and emotion recognition have been developed in literature [4]. Initial attempts to recognize emotions were mostly depended on geometric features such as angle, distance and position. Later on, an enormous work has been performed using other feature descriptors like scale invariant feature transform (SIFT) [5], histogram of oriented gradients (HOG) [6], Gabor features [7], local binary patterns (LBP) [8], etc. Several techniques on activity recognition have been presented using a variation of feature descriptors like spatio-temporal features [9], fusion of features [10], motion history images [11], etc. All these techniques deal with different behavior paradigms for real-time performance application.

Hence we see, features demonstrate a significant role in machine learning based human behavior understanding. However, selection of such features is a crucial

R. Singh (✉)
Department of Computer Science, Banasthali Vidyapith, Banasthali, Rajasthan, India

S. Nigam
Computer Science and Engineering Department, S. P. Memorial Institute of Technology, Kaushambi, Uttar Pradesh, India

© Springer Nature Switzerland AG 2019
A. K. Singh, A. Mohan (eds.), *Handbook of Multimedia Information Security: Techniques and Applications*, https://doi.org/10.1007/978-3-030-15887-3_32

task as those features are affected by occlusion, varying pose, alignment and illumination [12]. Hence, behavior understanding problem has become even more complicated. To deal with aforesaid challenges, in recent years, many intelligent techniques including deep learning models have been developed. In comparison to machine learning model, deep models have various advantages viz. (1) need less effort (2) need less domain knowledge (3) provide a general description of various modalities (4) automatic feature learning. Deep learning models can be applied on object segmentation [13], detection [14], natural language processing [15], image classification [16], person re-understanding [17], signature verification [18] tracking [19], expression recognition [20] and activity recognition [21].

Motivated by the above facts, in this chapter, we present a comparative analysis of deep learning models based emotion recognition and activity recognition approaches. Deep architectures and their usefulness have been discussed in this chapter. CK+ dataset for emotion recognition and Skoda dataset for activity recognition have been used for this purpose. Experimental results demonstrate that deep models outperform other existing methods in literature.

The rest of the chapter is organized as follows: In Sect. 32.2, preliminaries of deep learning technique based networks are discussed, Sect. 32.3 gives description of deep learning based emotion recognition techniques and Sect. 32.4 gives description of deep learning based activity recognition techniques. Finally, Sect. 32.5 concludes this study.

32.2 Deep Neural Networks

The process of learning involves retrieval and updation of existing knowledge or behavior with experience. Formally, a system learns from the experience ε with respect to the task τ and a performance metric μ, if its performance on τ as computed by μ increases with ε. Here, experience ε may be composed of elements such as Data, instances, feature, attribute, class, cluster, opinion; task τ may include prediction, classification, optimization, navigation, synthesis; and performance μ may include accuracy, precision, speed, storage, unambiguity, reliability. Precisely, a learning model should be capable of defining few parameters such as what to learn, how learning data is acquired and how to supply those data into the system [22].

A general architecture of human behavior understanding systems using machine learning approach is shown in Fig. 32.1 whereas using deep learning approach is shown in Fig. 32.2. The narrow discrimination can be understood from Figs. 32.1 and 32.2. As deep models deal with the problem of obtaining hierarchical representation, hence Fig. 32.2 shows a layered unsupervised learning hierarchy for initialization of all layers. It retrieves various levels of best possible features simultaneously using this hierarchical representation. These hierarchical features may be pixel, edge, shape, size, distance, etc.

Deep models can be implemented in three ways using Convolutional Neural Networks, Restricted Boltzmann Machine and Autoencoder [22].

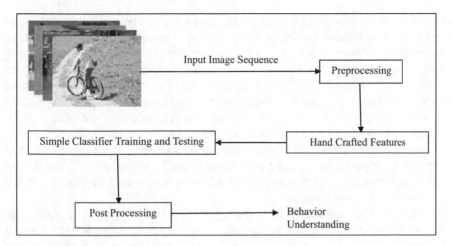

Fig. 32.1 Machine learning model for human behavior understanding

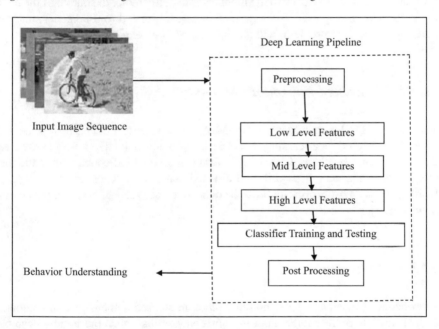

Fig. 32.2 Deep learning model for human behavior understanding

32.2.1 Convolutional Neural Networks

Deep networks consist of several neuron layers. As number of layers increases, networks get deeper and deeper. Basically, convolution neural network (CNN) is a feed forward neural network (FFNN). It has four type of layers that are part of every

CNN. These are convolution layer, pooling layer, ReLU layer, and fully-connected layer. Other than these four basic layers, the image input layer supplies the data to be analysed. Other layers that may be incorporated are batch-normalization layer and soft-max layer. Each and every layer is used for a specific purpose. These layers perform input of data, its analysis, extract relevant features and classify them. Input may be 2D binary, greyscale or color image or any kind of video streams. CNN is used for several tasks like segmentation, detection, classification, etc. [23].

Another version of CNN is called recurrent neural network (RNN). It is a self-feedback neural network (SFNN). It easily deals with time series related data and applied in the problems of future prediction. Based on the structure in which loop has been formed, the RNN may have four categories that are one-one, one-many, many-one and many-many.

Main difference between CNN and RNN is that we can supply only present input to the CNN whereas we can supply present as well as past input to the RNN. Internal memory of RNN is large so that it stores all the input. RNN stores output of present layer and send it for feedback to the input layer to help predict the output of the next layer. RNN is mostly used in the prediction of data related to time series, natural language processing problems and machine translation, etc. [24].

32.2.2   Restricted Boltzmann Machine

The Restricted Boltzmann Machine (RBM) provides a general stochastic type neural network. It is used as a learning model in Deep belief network (DBN) as well as deep Boltzmann Machine (DBM). DBN forms an undirected connection at the top two layers of the neural network and directed connections between lower layers. Unlike to DBN, DBM forms undirected connections between all layers of the neural network [25].

32.2.3   Autoencoder

Autoencoder is used as a basic building block in stacked autoencoder. An autoencoder is used to represent the input in such a way so that this representation can be used to reconstruct the input. It results into target output which is same as the input. Dimensions of these input and output are also same. The best possible autoencoder is that in which reconstruction error is minimum and representation delivers correct features as input [26].

32.3 Emotion Recognition

This section performs an analysis of various existing emotion recognition methods that have incorporated recent deep learning based techniques. For this purpose, numerous facial expression recognition datasets have been used. Few benchmark datasets are JAFFE dataset [27], Cohn-Kanade dataset [28], Extended Cohn-Kanade dataset [29], Yale dataset [30] and MMI dataset [31], etc. Here we present results for Extended Cohn-Kanade dataset (CK+) [29].

32.3.1 CK+ Dataset Results

Extended Cohn–Kanade (CK+) dataset [29] is used in most of the techniques developed for emotion recognition whether they are machine learning based or deep learning based. CK+ dataset contains facial expression images of 123 human subjects of age group 18 to 50. The dataset can be divided in different groups like groups divided based on gender (e.g. number of men and women) and groups based on race (number of Euro-American, Afro-American and others). Images are captured from different viewing angles out of which 593 images are captured in full frontal position. Figure 32.3 shows a few samples of CK+ dataset.

For a better analysis, we have compared few deep learning techniques. These techniques are 3DCNN [32], 3DCNN-DAP [32], DTDN [33], DTGN [33], DTAGN (WS) [33], DTAGN (Joint) [33], DNN [34], CNN [34], TOP-1 [35], TOP-2 [35], CNN [36], Exp-Net [36], IACNN [36], AUDN [37], BDBN [38], FP + SAE [39] and CNN [40]. Figure 32.4 shows comparative evaluation of recognition accuracy of these methods. In Fig. 32.4, we see that the method DTAGN (Joint) [33] performs better when compared to other methods with a recognition accuracy of 97.2% which is the highest for CK+ dataset.

32.3.2 SFEW Dataset Results

The Static Facial Expressions in the Wild (SFEW) [41] is generated from selected frames of the AFEW dataset. This selection is based on certain key frames and

Fig. 32.3 CK+ dataset samples

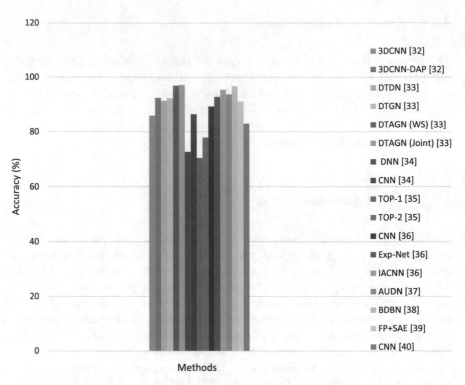

Fig. 32.4 Recognition accuracy of deep learning techniques for CK+ dataset

facial features. The most common version of the SFEW dataset is SFEW 2.0. The
dataset includes six fundamental emotions that are angry, happy, disgust, sad, fear,
surprised and one more emotion which is neutral. This dataset is divided in three
sets for training, testing and validation. Training set consists of 958 images, test set
consists of 372 images and validation set consists of 436 images.

For analysis purpose, we have compared a few deep learning techniques. These
are Levi [42], Ng [43], Li [44], Ding [45], Pons [46], Liu [47], Cai [48], Meng [36],
Kim [49] and Yu [50]. Figure 32.5 shows comparative evaluation of recognition
accuracy of various methods. In Fig. 32.5, one can observe that all these methods
have comparable accuracy, however method Yu [50] demonstrates the highest
accuracy of 55.96% for SFEW dataset.

32.4   Activity Recognition

In this section, we perform an analysis of various existing activity recognition
methods that have incorporated deep networks. For this purpose, several activity
recognition datasets have been used. Few benchmark activity datasets are Opportu-

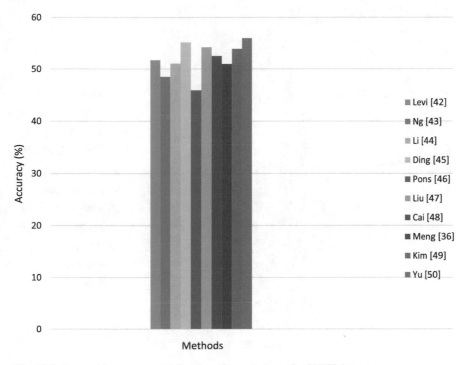

Fig. 32.5 Recognition accuracy of deep learning techniques for SFEW dataset

nity dataset [51], PAMAP dataset [52], Skoda dataset [53], mHealth dataset [54], and UCF 101 dataset [65], etc. Here, we present results for Skoda dataset [53].

32.4.1 Skoda Dataset Results

The Skoda Mini Checkpoint dataset [53] is an industrial dataset which consists of workers of an assembly-line in a vehicle production scenario. These actions are same as those actions which are performed at quality assurance checkpoint of any production environment. The dataset contains ten activities that are writing on a notepad, open the hood, close the hood, checking the gap between the door, open the door, close the door, closing of both the doors, checking the steering wheel of the car, open and close the box, and checking the box.

Figure 32.6 shows comparative evaluation of a few deep learning techniques for better analysis. These techniques are CNN [55], CNN [56], Baseline CNN [57], DeepConvLSTM [57], DCLSTM [58], DeActive [59], SMM [60], bLSTMs [61], AM [62], CNN [63] and DRNN [64]. From observing Fig. 32.6, we see that many methods show an accuracy above 90 but method SMM [60] shows a very high accuracy of 99.6%.

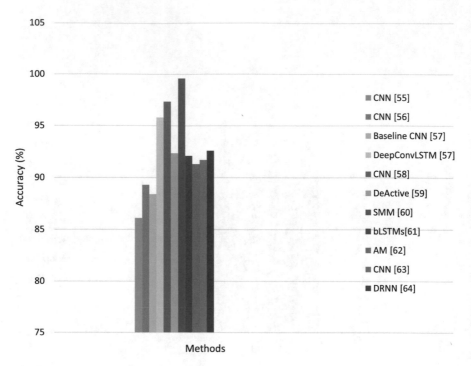

Fig. 32.6 Accuracy of different deep learning methods for Skoda dataset

32.4.2 UCF 101 Dataset Results

The UCF101 activity dataset [65] includes 13,320 real videos of 101 types from
YouTube. Action videos in this dataset have been captured with large camera
motion, changing appearance, pose, sale, view angle. Background conditions are
also different such as cluttered background and variation in illumination conditions.
These 101 videos are categorized in five different categories that are sports events,
body movement, human-object interaction, human-human interaction and play
music.

Compared methods are C3D [66], FSTCN [67], LTC [68], TDD [69], Fusion
[70], Conv Fusion [70], TSN [71], ResNet [72], ST-ResNet [72], Net [73], LSTM
[74] and RNN [75]. The results are shown in Fig. 32.7. In Fig. 32.7, one can see that
almost all the methods show comparable accuracy. However, method ST-ResNet
[72] shows a little higher accuracy of 94.6%.

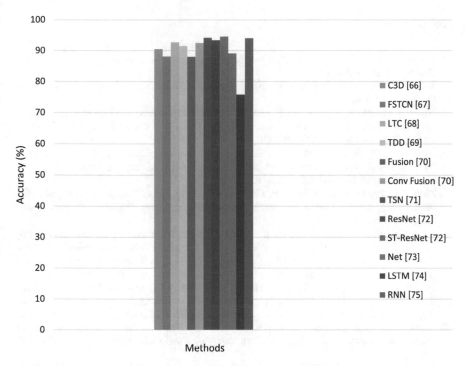

Fig. 32.7   Accuracy of different deep learning methods for UCF 101 dataset

32.5   Conclusions

This chapter presents an analysis of human behavior understanding techniques in terms of facial expression and activity recognition. The analysis depends on techniques based on deep learning models. Approaches that used deep learning for emotion and activity recognition are discussed. For extensive analysis, experimental results have been demonstrated for benchmark datasets. These datasets are CK+ [29] and SFEW [41] datasets for facial expression recognition, and Skoda [53] and UCF 101 [65] datasets for activity recognition. From the study, it is shown that method DTAGN (Joint) [33] performs better in comparison to other methods for CK+ dataset and method Yu [50] is better as compared to other methods for SFEW dataset. Similarly for activity analysis, method SMM [60] and method ST-ResNet [72] are better when compared to other methods for Skoda and UCF 101 datasets, respectively. The results show effectiveness of deep learning in human behavior understanding. In future, deep learning techniques can be explored for crowd scene analysis and micro-expression recognition which will improve human behavior understanding process.

Acknowledgments   This study is sponsored by Science and Engineering Research Board, Department of Science and Technology, Government of India via grant no. PDF/2016/003644.

References

1. Russell, S. J., & Norvig, P. (2016). Artificial intelligence: a modern approach. Malaysia; Pearson Education Limited.
2. Sonka, M., Hlavac, V., & Boyle, R. (2014). Image processing, analysis, and machine vision. Cengage Learning.
3. Nigam, S., Singh, R., & Misra, A. K. (2019). Towards intelligent human behavior detection for video surveillance. In Censorship, Surveillance, and Privacy: Concepts, Methodologies, Tools, and Applications (pp. 884-917). IGI Global.
4. Nigam, S., Singh, R., & Misra, A. K. (2018). A Review of Computational Approaches for Human Behavior Detection. Archives of Computational Methods in Engineering, 1-33. https://doi.org/10.1007/s11831-018-9270-7.
5. Zhao, K., Chu, W. S., De la Torre, F., Cohn, J. F., & Zhang, H. (2016). Joint patch and multi-label learning for facial action unit and holistic expression recognition. IEEE Transactions on Image Processing, 25(8), 3931-3946.
6. Nigam, S., Singh, R., & Misra, A. K. (2018). Efficient facial expression recognition using histogram of oriented gradients in wavelet domain. Multimedia Tools and Applications, 1-23.
7. Emambakhsh, M., & Evans, A. (2017). Nasal patches and curves for expression-robust 3D face recognition. IEEE transactions on pattern analysis and machine intelligence, 39(5), 995-1007.
8. Nigam, S., Singh, R., & Misra, A. K. (2018). Local Binary Patterns based Facial Expression Recognition for Efficient Smart Applications, Machine Learning Paradigms: Theory and Applications, Security in Smart Cities, Studies in Computational Intelligence Series, Springer.
9. Kerola, T., Inoue, N., & Shinoda, K. (2017). Cross-view human action recognition from depth maps using spectral graph sequences. Computer Vision and Image Understanding, 154, 108-126.
10. Nigam, S., & Khare, A. (2016). Integration of moment invariants and uniform local binary patterns for human activity recognition in video sequences. Multimedia Tools and Applications, 75(24), 17303-17332.
11. Sharma, C. M., Kushwaha, A. K. S., Nigam, S., & Khare, A. (2011, September). On human activity recognition in video sequences. In Computer and Communication Technology (ICCCT), 2011 2nd International Conference on (pp. 152-158). IEEE.
12. Salah, A. A., Gevers, T., Sebe, N., & Vinciarelli, A. (2010, August). Challenges of human behavior understanding. In International Workshop on Human Behavior Understanding (pp. 1-12). Springer, Berlin, Heidelberg.
13. Kamnitsas, K., Ledig, C., Newcombe, V. F., Simpson, J. P., Kane, A. D., Menon, D. K., ... & Glocker, B. (2017). Efficient multi-scale 3D CNN with fully connected CRF for accurate brain lesion segmentation. Medical image analysis, 36, 61-78.
14. Hoo-Chang, S., Roth, H. R., Gao, M., Lu, L., Xu, Z., Nogues, I., ... & Summers, R. M. (2016). Deep convolutional neural networks for computer-aided detection: CNN architectures, dataset characteristics and transfer learning. IEEE transactions on medical imaging, 35(5), 1285.
15. Young, T., Hazarika, D., Poria, S., & Cambria, E. (2018). Recent trends in deep learning based natural language processing. IEEE Computational Intelligence Magazine, 13(3), 55-75.
16. Wang, J., Yang, Y., Mao, J., Huang, Z., Huang, C., & Xu, W. (2016). Cnn-rnn: A unified framework for multi-label image classification. In Proceedings of the IEEE conference on computer vision and pattern recognition (pp. 2285-2294).
17. Zheng, Z., Zheng, L., & Yang, Y. (2017). A discriminatively learned cnn embedding for person reidentification. ACM Transactions on Multimedia Computing, Communications, and Applications (TOMM), 14(1), 13.
18. Hafemann, L. G., Sabourin, R., & Oliveira, L. S. (2016, July). Writer-independent feature learning for offline signature verification using deep convolutional neural networks. In Neural networks (IJCNN), 2016 international joint conference on (pp. 2576-2583). IEEE.
19. Leal-Taixé, L., Canton-Ferrer, C., & Schindler, K. (2016). Learning by tracking: Siamese cnn for robust target association. In Proceedings of the IEEE Conference on Computer Vision and Pattern Recognition Workshops (pp. 33-40).

20. Shima, Y., & Omori, Y. (2018, August). Image Augmentation for Classifying Facial Expression Images by Using Deep Neural Network Pre-trained with Object Image Database. In Proceedings of the 3rd International Conference on Robotics, Control and Automation (pp. 140-146). ACM.
21. Ronao, C. A., & Cho, S. B. (2016). Human activity recognition with smartphone sensors using deep learning neural networks. Expert Systems with Applications, 59, 235-244.
22. Goodfellow, I., Bengio, Y., Courville, A., & Bengio, Y. (2016). Deep learning (Vol. 1). Cambridge: MIT press.
23. Litjens, G., Kooi, T., Bejnordi, B. E., Setio, A. A. A., Ciompi, F., Ghafoorian, M., ... & Sánchez, C. I. (2017). A survey on deep learning in medical image analysis. Medical image analysis, 42, 60-88.
24. Zeng, Z., Li, Z., Cheng, D., Zhang, H., Zhan, K., & Yang, Y. (2018). Two-Stream Multirate Recurrent Neural Network for Video-Based Pedestrian Reidentification. IEEE Transactions on Industrial Informatics, 14(7), 3179-3186.
25. Aldwairi, T., Perera, D., & Novotny, M. A. (2018). An evaluation of the performance of Restricted Boltzmann Machines as a model for anomaly network intrusion detection. Computer Networks, 144, 111-119.
26. Sankaran, A., Vatsa, M., Singh, R., & Majumdar, A. (2017). Group sparse autoencoder. Image and Vision Computing, 60, 64-74.
27. Dailey, M. N., Joyce, C., Lyons, M. J., Kamachi, M., Ishi, H., Gyoba, J., & Cottrell, G. W. (2010). Evidence and a computational explanation of cultural differences in facial expression recognition. Emotion, 10(6), 874.
28. Kanade, T., Cohn, J. F., & Tian, Y. (2000). Comprehensive database for facial expression analysis. In Automatic Face and Gesture Recognition. Proceedings. Fourth IEEE International Conference on (pp. 46-53). IEEE.
29. Lucey, P., Cohn, J. F., Kanade, T., Saragih, J., Ambadar, Z., & Matthews, I. (2010, June). The extended cohn-kanade dataset (ck+): A complete dataset for action unit and emotion-specified expression. In Computer Vision and Pattern Recognition Workshops (CVPRW), 2010 IEEE Computer Society Conference on (pp. 94-101). IEEE.
30. Yale facial expression database, http://vision.ucsd.edu/content/yale-face-database.
31. Pantic, M., Valstar, M., Rademaker, R., & Maat, L. (2005, July). Web-based database for facial expression analysis. In 2005 IEEE international conference on multimedia and Expo (p. 5). IEEE.
32. Liu, M., Li, S., Shan, S., Wang, R., & Chen, X. (2014, November). Deeply learning deformable facial action parts model for dynamic expression analysis. In Asian conference on computer vision (pp. 143-157). Springer, Cham.
33. Jung, H., Lee, S., Yim, J., Park, S., & Kim, J. (2015). Joint fine-tuning in deep neural networks for facial expression recognition. In Proceedings of the IEEE International Conference on Computer Vision (pp. 2983-2991).
34. Jung, H., Lee, S., Park, S., Kim, B., Kim, J., Lee, I., & Ahn, C. (2015, January). Development of deep learning-based facial expression recognition system. In Frontiers of Computer Vision (FCV), 2015 21st Korea-Japan Joint Workshop on (pp. 1-4). IEEE.
35. Spiers, D. L. (2016). Facial emotion detection using deep learning. Doctoral Dissertation, UPPSALA Universitet.
36. Meng, Z., Liu, P., Cai, J., Han, S., & Tong, Y. (2017, May). Identity-aware convolutional neural network for facial expression recognition. In Automatic Face & Gesture Recognition (FG 2017), 2017 12th IEEE International Conference on (pp. 558-565). IEEE.
37. Liu, M., Li, S., Shan, S., & Chen, X. (2015). Au-inspired deep networks for facial expression feature learning. Neurocomputing, 159, 126-136.
38. Liu, P., Han, S., Meng, Z., & Tong, Y. (2014). Facial expression recognition via a boosted deep belief network. In Proceedings of the IEEE Conference on Computer Vision and Pattern Recognition (pp. 1805-1812).

39. Fathallah, A., Abdi, L., & Douik, A. (2017, October). Facial Expression Recognition via Deep Learning. In Computer Systems and Applications (AICCSA), 2017 IEEE/ACS 14th International Conference on (pp. 745-750). IEEE.
40. Li, W., Li, M., Su, Z., & Zhu, Z. (2015, May). A deep-learning approach to facial expression recognition with candid images. In Machine Vision Applications (MVA), 2015 14th IAPR International Conference on (pp. 279-282). IEEE.
41. Dhall, A., Goecke, R., Lucey, S., & Gedeon, T. (2011, November). Static facial expression analysis in tough conditions: Data, evaluation protocol and benchmark. In Computer Vision Workshops (ICCV Workshops), 2011 IEEE International Conference on (pp. 2106-2112). IEEE.
42. Levi, G., & Hassner, T. (2015, November). Emotion recognition in the wild via convolutional neural networks and mapped binary patterns. In Proceedings of the 2015 ACM on international conference on multimodal interaction (pp. 503-510). ACM.
43. Ng, H. W., Nguyen, V. D., Vonikakis, V., & Winkler, S. (2015, November). Deep learning for emotion recognition on small datasets using transfer learning. In Proceedings of the 2015 ACM on international conference on multimodal interaction (pp. 443-449). ACM.
44. Li, S., & Deng, W. (2018). Reliable Crowdsourcing and Deep Locality-Preserving Learning for Unconstrained Facial Expression Recognition. IEEE Transactions on Image Processing.
45. Ding, H., Zhou, S. K., & Chellappa, R. (2017, May). Facenet2expnet: Regularizing a deep face recognition net for expression recognition. In Automatic Face & Gesture Recognition (FG 2017), 2017 12th IEEE International Conference on (pp. 118-126). IEEE.
46. Pons, G., & Masip, D. (2018). Multi-task, multi-label and multi-domain learning with residual convolutional networks for emotion recognition. arXiv preprint arXiv:1802.06664.
47. Liu, X., Kumar, B. V., You, J., & Jia, P. (2017, July). Adaptive Deep Metric Learning for Identity-Aware Facial Expression Recognition. In CVPR Workshops (pp. 522-531).
48. Cai, J., Meng, Z., Khan, A. S., Li, Z., O'Reilly, J., & Tong, Y. (2018, May). Island Loss for Learning Discriminative Features in Facial Expression Recognition. In Automatic Face & Gesture Recognition (FG 2018), 2018 13th IEEE International Conference on (pp. 302-309). IEEE.
49. Kim, B. K., Lee, H., Roh, J., & Lee, S. Y. (2015, November). Hierarchical committee of deep cnns with exponentially-weighted decision fusion for static facial expression recognition. In Proceedings of the 2015 ACM on International Conference on Multimodal Interaction (pp. 427-434). ACM.
50. Yu, Z., & Zhang, C. (2015, November). Image based static facial expression recognition with multiple deep network learning. In Proceedings of the 2015 ACM on International Conference on Multimodal Interaction (pp. 435-442). ACM.
51. Roggen, D., Calatroni, A., Rossi, M., Holleczek, T., Förster, K., Tröster, G., ... & Doppler, J. (2010, June). Collecting complex activity datasets in highly rich networked sensor environments. In Networked Sensing Systems (INSS), 2010 Seventh International Conference on (pp. 233-240). IEEE.
52. Reiss, A., & Stricker, D. (2012, June). Introducing a new benchmarked dataset for activity monitoring. In Wearable Computers (ISWC), 2012 16th International Symposium on (pp. 108-109). IEEE.
53. Zappi, P., Lombriser, C., Stiefmeier, T., Farella, E., Roggen, D., Benini, L., & Tröster, G. (2008). Activity recognition from on-body sensors: accuracy-power trade-off by dynamic sensor selection. In Wireless sensor networks (pp. 17-33). Springer, Berlin, Heidelberg.
54. Banos, O., Garcia, R., Holgado-Terriza, J. A., Damas, M., Pomares, H., Rojas, I., ... & Villalonga, C. (2014, December). mHealthDroid: a novel framework for agile development of mobile health applications. In International Workshop on Ambient Assisted Living (pp. 91-98). Springer, Cham.
55. Zeng, M., Nguyen, L. T., Yu, B., Mengshoel, O. J., Zhu, J., Wu, P., & Zhang, J. (2014, November). Convolutional neural networks for human activity recognition using mobile sensors. In Mobile Computing, Applications and Services (MobiCASE), 2014 6th International Conference on (pp. 197-205). IEEE.

56. Alsheikh, M. A., Selim, A., Niyato, D., Doyle, L., Lin, S., & Tan, H. P. (2016, February). Deep Activity Recognition Models with Triaxial Accelerometers. In AAAI Workshop: Artificial Intelligence Applied to Assistive Technologies and Smart Environments.
57. Ordóñez, F. J., & Roggen, D. (2016). Deep convolutional and lstm recurrent neural networks for multimodal wearable activity recognition. Sensors, 16(1), 115.
58. Mohammad, Y., Matsumoto, K., & Hoashi, K. (2018). Primitive activity recognition from short sequences of sensory data. Applied Intelligence, 1-14.
59. Hossain, H. M., Al Haiz Khan, M. D., & Roy, N. (2018). DeActive: Scaling Activity Recognition with Active Deep Learning. Proceedings of the ACM on Interactive, Mobile, Wearable and Ubiquitous Technologies, 2(2), 66.
60. Qian, H., Pan, S. J., & Miao, C. (2018). Sensor-based Activity Recognition via Learning from Distributions. The Thirty-Second AAAI Conference on Artificial Intelligence (AAAI-18), 6262-6269.
61. Hammerla, N. Y., Halloran, S., & Ploetz, T. (2016). Deep, convolutional, and recurrent models for human activity recognition using wearables. arXiv preprint arXiv:1604.08880. In Proc. IJCAI.
62. Murahari, V. S., & Ploetz, T. (2018). On Attention Models for Human Activity Recognition. arXiv preprint arXiv:1805.07648. https://arxiv.org/abs/1805.07648.
63. Ravi, D., Wong, C., Lo, B., & Yang, G. Z. (2016, June). Deep learning for human activity recognition: A resource efficient implementation on low-power devices. In Wearable and Implantable Body Sensor Networks (BSN), 2016 IEEE 13th International Conference on (pp. 71-76). IEEE.
64. Murad, A., & Pyun, J. Y. (2017). Deep recurrent neural networks for human activity recognition. Sensors, 17(11), 2556, doi: https://doi.org/10.3390/s17112556.
65. Soomro, K., Zamir, A. R., & Shah, M. (2012). UCF101: A dataset of 101 human actions classes from videos in the wild. arXiv preprint arXiv:1212.0402, CRCV-TR-12-01.
66. Tran, D., Bourdev, L., Fergus, R., Torresani, L., & Paluri, M. (2015). Learning spatiotemporal features with 3d convolutional networks. In Proceedings of the IEEE international conference on computer vision (pp. 4489-4497).
67. Sun, L., Jia, K., Yeung, D. Y., & Shi, B. E. (2015). Human action recognition using factorized spatio-temporal convolutional networks. In Proceedings of the IEEE International Conference on Computer Vision (pp. 4597-4605).
68. Varol, G., Laptev, I., & Schmid, C. (2018). Long-term temporal convolutions for action recognition. IEEE transactions on pattern analysis and machine intelligence, 40(6), 1510-1517.
69. Wang, L., Qiao, Y., & Tang, X. (2015). Action recognition with trajectory-pooled deep-convolutional descriptors. In Proceedings of the IEEE conference on computer vision and pattern recognition (pp. 4305-4314).
70. Feichtenhofer, C., Pinz, A., & Zisserman, A. (2016). Convolutional two-stream network fusion for video action recognition. In Proceedings of the IEEE Conference on Computer Vision and Pattern Recognition (pp. 1933-1941).
71. Wang, L., Xiong, Y., Wang, Z., Qiao, Y., Lin, D., Tang, X., & Van Gool, L. (2016, October). Temporal segment networks: Towards good practices for deep action recognition. In European Conference on Computer Vision (pp. 20-36). Springer, Cham.
72. Feichtenhofer, C., Pinz, A., & Wildes, R. (2016). Spatiotemporal residual networks for video action recognition. In Advances in neural information processing systems (pp. 3468-3476).
73. Bilen, H., Fernando, B., Gavves, E., Vedaldi, A., & Gould, S. (2016). Dynamic image networks for action recognition. In Proceedings of the IEEE Conference on Computer Vision and Pattern Recognition (pp. 3034-3042).
74. Srivastava, N., Mansimov, E., & Salakhudinov, R. (2015, June). Unsupervised learning of video representations using lstms. In International conference on machine learning (pp. 843-852).
75. Lev, G., Sadeh, G., Klein, B., & Wolf, L. (2016, October). Rnn fisher vectors for action recognition and image annotation. In European Conference on Computer Vision (pp. 833-850). Springer, Cham.

Chapter 33
Digital Image Forensics-Gateway to Authenticity: Crafted with Observations, Trends and Forecasts

Neeru Jindal and Kulbir Singh

33.1 Introduction-Forensic Classification and Publication Trends

The authenticity of the information conveyed by digital images is becoming one of the key challenges for our society and strongly challenging the future digital media security applications [1]. Nowadays, affordable and sophisticated graphics editing software allows for the creation of fake photos, which easily puzzle our perception of reality.

Firstly, the word named as 'Forensics' was used in China (the year 1248) by Song Ci [2] in his book Washing Away of Wrongs written to solve criminal cases of suicide. Later on, in sixteenth-century, Europe and French medical practitioners began to study the causes and effects of death [3, 4]. Francois Immanuele Fodere, a French physician wrote a book named as 'A Treatise on Forensic Medicine and Public Health' in the eighteenth century on it [5].

Basically, forensics science is used to check and then decide the reality of criminal cases in courts [6–9]. Analog and digital forensics are the main classifications of forensics as shown in Fig. 33.1. Analog or classical forensics has main focused on traces of physical evidence whether wrong or not in reality [10]. However, Digital forensics is categorized into computer and multimedia forensics [11]. Computer forensics helps the investigators/detectives to extract the trustworthy evidence from computers in the real world applications [12].

Multimedia Forensics restores lost parts of digital media by creating instruments to manifest the changes [10, 13]. It is the challenging task and never-ending competition between forgery creators and detectors in the Multimedia science

N. Jindal (✉) · K. Singh
ECED Department, Thapar Institute of Engineering and Technology, Patiala, Punjab, India
e-mail: neeru.jindal@thapar.edu; ksingh@thapar.edu

© Springer Nature Switzerland AG 2019
A. K. Singh, A. Mohan (eds.), *Handbook of Multimedia Information Security: Techniques and Applications*, https://doi.org/10.1007/978-3-030-15887-3_33

Fig. 33.1 Forensics taxonomy

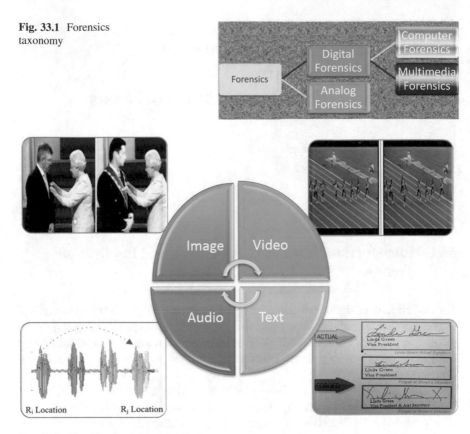

Fig. 33.2 Classification of multimedia forgery

forensics. To detect forged regions; broadly forensics can be classified as shown in Fig. 33.2.

To explore the literature of the science field, Web of Science (WOS) was the only accessible international multi-disciplinary database until 2004. Later on, many scientific databases like Scopus and Google Scholar were preferred by researchers. There was a high association between these all, so in 2008, Falagas et al. [14] presented a table of comparison between them on the basis of content coverage as a well practical utility. It was observed that WOS has more literature coverage from 1900 and its journals are written in English [15]. In the same context, Fig. 33.3 shows the publication trends in multimedia forgery detection using WOS database for the years 2005–2018.

In summary, it is observed that doctored image data is spreading at high frequency and highlights the situation that creates curiosity and sometimes needs among the users to verify the truthfulness of this data. To find the answer to this issue, the research community proposed several approaches [16–19], that was broadly classified into Active and Passive, discussed in next sections. Due to

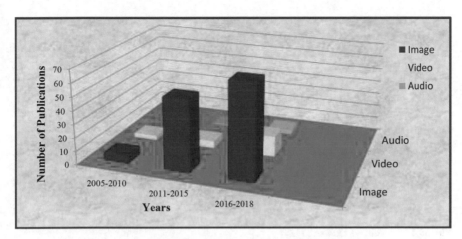

Fig. 33.3 Publication trends in the multimedia forgery detection field from 2005 to 2018 using WOS

technological advances over the last few years, passive approaches have come to be used in forensic studies [20, 21].

This chapter presents a framework for image forensics and in Sect. 33.2, we give types of the image forensic and its trends. In Sect. 33.3, several techniques for multimedia forgery detection and its common processing approach is presented. Finally, Sect. 33.4 concludes the chapter with open issues of forensics.

33.2 Image Forensics

The dire need to check the integrity of digital images and on the basis of facts and figures (Figs. 33.3, 33.6, and 33.7) authors felt the motivation to write this chapter. The adulteration of images dates back to the 1850s when photographs were modified by manual techniques of manipulation of their negatives, which provided quite satisfactory results [22]. The process of image scanning began and, consequently, the concept of two-dimensional digital image representation using binary numbers started so that it's processing can be done by using electronic means. In 2014, Albrecht's [23] research on Fraud took a form of 'Fraud Scale' given in Fig. 33.4. According to this Fraud Scale; high situational pressure, safe opportunity to commit fraud and low personal integrity of employees causes the victim to fraud.

Basically, photography dates back to eleventh century to the development of pinhole camera called obscura (dark room) and has seen continuous developments in the imaging technology. Till the previous decade, photos were captured on films which had been developed to get the negative and using them the photos (positives) were printed [24]. Shortly after the advent in 1814, photography was preferred for making portraits. Further, portrait photographers started retouching

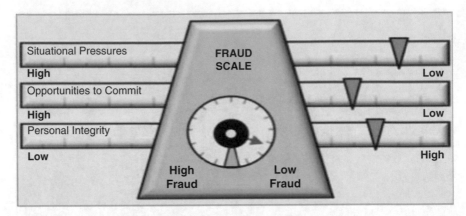

Fig. 33.4 Albrecht's Fraud scale [23]

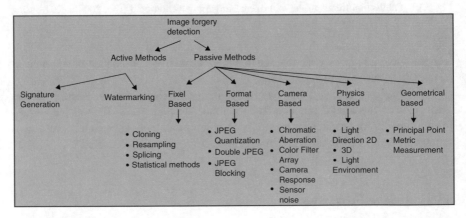

Fig. 33.5 Image Forgery Detection types

their photographs to please the customers. Later, attempts have been made to alter an image and modify its contents. Many such cases have been notorious that raise ethical questions. For the enhancement of image forensic work and helping the researchers, an amazing effort of Hany Farid [9, 46, 51, 132], Professor in Dartmouth College, the USA in this field is known across the globe. Figure 33.5 shows image forgery classification.

The two possible ways for image forgery recognition are (1) Active and (2) passive methods. The active approaches detect the modification because the information is embedded e.g. in watermarking and signature generation. The passive approaches do not need the original image. The passive approaches are generally classified into five types [25].

- *Pixel or object-dependent methods*: detects the statistical anomalies and correlations at the pixel level due to forgery.

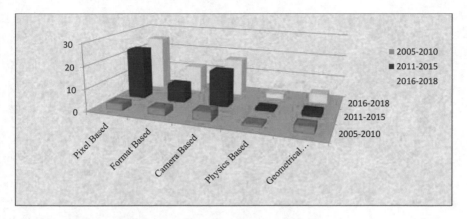

Fig. 33.6 Image forensic approaches trends indexed by Web of Sciences

- *Format-dependent methods*: identify the statistical correlations causes due to compression methods.
- *Camera dependent methods*: exploits artifacts arise due to the camera lens, sensors, or on-chip post-processing methods.
- *Physically dependent methods*: detects irregularities in the 3D interface between the physical objects, light, and cameras.
- *Geometry dependent methods*: take dimensions of objects and their relative positions in the cameras.

Pixel is the building block of an image. When an image tampers, anomalies are introduced into the pixel level correlations which can be analyzed and detected by statistical techniques. Copy move forgery detects the similarity between the copied and pasted segment of the same image. The CMFD techniques are generally classified into two categories viz.; Block matching and Key point matching schemes [26, 27]. Various researchers have made an effort to develop a robust algorithm based on block matching approach useful for the detection of CMF. It has been observed from Fig. 33.6 that pixel-based image forgery is growing research area in recent years. However, Fig. 33.7 shows that CMF is capturing the attention in Pixel based techniques from the last 13 years. A common approach to CMF detection is discussed in the next section.

33.3 Common Approach of Pixel Based Image Forensic

Several digital image tampering detection techniques are proposed by researchers nowadays. Figure 33.8 shows the general approach [28, 29] that is followed to detect the forgery.

Some pre-processing operations are performed on test input images like filtering, resizing, gray-scale to RGB conversion etc. for the performance enhancement

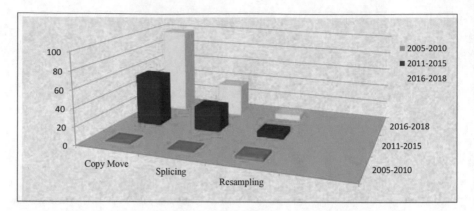

Fig. 33.7 Pixel based approaches trends indexed by Web of Sciences

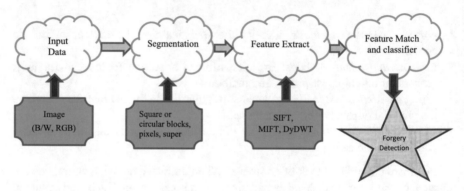

Fig. 33.8 A Common Approach for Image Forgery Detection

[30, 31]. This is often done to make the data more suitable for the succeeding stages. Segmentation is becoming popular among authors to get non-overlapping and semantically independent image patches (IP), especially in the case of hybrid detection techniques.

In Feature extraction, a number of Features are extracted for every IP of the image which helps to distinguish it from other IPs of the image [32–35]. The number of features to be extracted solely depends upon the authors. In particular, significant and informative features need to be extracted and features that are selected must be responsive to image manipulations. The desirable attribute of chosen features and formed feature vectors is that they should have low dimensions, as this will lower the computational complications of training as well as classifications.

Now, after feature extraction, an appropriate is selected from existing methods or is developed. An image database for the training of classifier is selected. According to algorithm requirement, relevant parameters are obtained and then exploited for the classification. Pre-processing of features is useful in reducing the features dimensionality excluding deterioration of the performance of classification based on machine-learning. For dimensionality diminution, generally Singular Value Decomposition and Principal Component Analysis are used [36, 37].

A classifier [38] categorizes the given database into two classes: genuine and forged digital images. Based on the extracted set of features, a suitable classifier is once more selected. Humongous priming set is more likely to give a better classifier in terms of performance. Phase correlation and lexicographical sort [39–41] are frequently used classifiers in case of block-based techniques.

Finally, morphological operations [42, 43] are performed to lower false positive rate. In case of multiple copy-move forgeries, similar patches having the same shift vectors are shown by the single color. Hence, image tampering may affect an individual person, society, our economy and so on. The main focus is: to study and observe pixel based forgery detection types; CMFD, Splicing and Resampling under one umbrella. Then, it will be followed by new challenges and future trends of image Forensics.

33.3.1 Copy Move Forgery Approach

Copy Move Forgery (CMF) techniques are passive approaches which work on the assumption that forgery possibly amends the fundamental statistics of the original image without leaving visual cues. The aim of CMF is to localize the similar patches in forged images. Figure 33.9 is an example of CMF.

The existing CMFD schemes are, generally, classified into the following categories:

- Block-based techniques [44–46]
- Keypoint-based techniques [47–49].

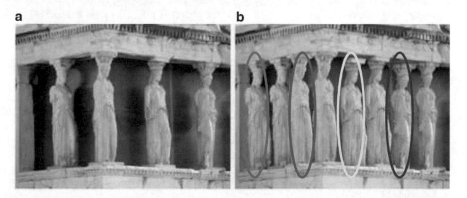

Fig. 33.9 (a) Genuine Image (b) Doctored Image, some statutes are added (circled) in between to make the image more attractive

The methodology of block-based CMFD techniques segments the test image into either overlapping or non-overlapping blocks followed by any transform on each block. Similar statics blocks are separated on the basis of the chosen comparison criterion. Though, the key point based methods involve the extraction of interest points in an image. They extract local features of distinguishing between genuine and duplicated regions.

33.3.1.1 Block Generation Schemes

Block generation schemes can be classified into the following groups (Tables 33.1 and 33.2):

1. Frequency transform based [31, 40, 50]
2. Texture and Intensity-based [55, 56]
3. Moments-invariant based [53, 54]
4. Transforms domain [57–59]
5. Dimensions reduction based [37, 51, 52]
6. Radix Sort and others [60]

Table 33.1 Feature extraction methods for block-based schemes

Methods	Authors
Frequency transforms [discrete cosine transforms, Fourier transforms, fractional Walsh Hadmard transforms, DWT, DyWT, Wiener filter]	Li et al. [61], Li et al. [62], Huang et al. [63], Cao et al. [64], Zhao and Guo [65], Shao et al. [66], Yang et al. [67], Zhang et al. [68], Muhammad et al. [69], Deng et al. [70], Ketenci and Ulutas [71], Kumar et al. [72], Shin [73]
Texture and intensity • Intensity [nine dimension feature average intensity using CPU and GPU] • Pattern [Gabor feature, multiresolution Local Binary pattern] • Color [color, spatial, grayscale]	Davarzani et al. [74], Gan and Zhong [75], Hsu and Wang [76], Vladimirovich and Valerievich [77], Lynch et al. [78], Singh and Raman [79]
Moments invariant [central moments, Krawtchouk's moments, Zernike moments, exponential moments, blur invariant moments]	Bilgehan and Uluta [80], Le and Xu [81], Mahdian and Saic [82], Ryu et al. [83], Hu [84]
Log polar transforms [Fourier Mellin transforms, log polar Fourier transforms, polar harmonic transforms, polar cosine transforms, polar sine transforms]	Bayram et al. [85], Li et al. [86], Li and Yu [87], Li [88] and Wu et al. [89]
Dimension reduction [SVD, locally linear embedding (LLE), PCA]	Ting and Rang-Ding [90], Ardizzone et al. [91]
Radix Sort and others [multi scale auto convolution]	Lin et al. [60], Wang et al. [92]

Table 33.2 Feature matching methods for block-based schemes

Methods	Authors
Sorting [Lexicographica, KD tree radix, others]	Bilgehan and Uluta [80], Shin [73], Cao et al. [64], Davarzani et al. [74], Gan and Zhong [75], Huang et al. [63], Kumar et al. [72], Le and Xu [81], Li et al. [62, 86], Ryu et al. [83], Wang et al. [92], Zhao and Guo [65], Mahdian and Saic [82], Ting and Rang-Ding [90], Christlein et al. [26], Singh and Raman [79], Lynch et al. [78]
Hash	Bayram et al. [85], Vladimirovich and Valerievich [77], Li and Yu [87], Ryu et al. [83]
Correlation	Myna et al. [93], Shao et al. [66], Zhang et al. [68]
Euclidean distance	Kashyap and Joshi [94] and Hussain et al. [38]
Others	Sekeh et al. [95], Hsu and Wang [76], Li et al. [62], Murali et al. [96], Shin [73], Wu et al. [89], Ardizzone et al. [91]

Observations of Block-Based Techniques

The existing block-based schemes, deal with a large number of blocks along with their feature vectors. Some common techniques use frequency transform for the feature extraction and lexicographical sorting for feature matching. Frequency transform methods are robust to the addition of noise, JPEG compression, and filtration, yet are vulnerable to geometrical attacks like translation, scaling, rotation etc. Due to the regular shape of blocks, these techniques yield very low recall rate.

Consequently, researchers have tried to find more efficient feature extraction as well as matching techniques in contrast to geometrical attacks. To handle transformation operations, researchers also studied the moment, log-polar transform precisely. Texture features mostly occur in natural scenes like a tree, grass, clouds along with smoothness, coarseness in the images. Mostly used identical feature are color, intensity and pattern information in the identical textures in the image. Further, to improve the computational time, dimensions of the images are reduced using PCA, DWT, and SVD. Meanwhile, Radix sorts, KDTree, and LSH have also familiarized matching techniques. Still, the improvement is around-the-clock developed; keypoint-based methods appear to attain improved performance.

33.3.1.2 Keypoint-Based CMFD Techniques

Keypoint-based CMFD approaches to detect the image forgery without block division in pre-processing. Features (corners, edge, and blobs) of the image are presented with descriptors. Basically, reliability is enhanced with the descriptors. Now, both descriptors and features are categorized and coordinated to detect copied regions (Tables 33.3 and 33.4).

Observations of Key Point-Based CMFD Techniques

Key point-based methods also become well-known and popular among researchers. SIFT techniques perform well in copy-move forgery detection and in geometrical

Table 33.3 Feature extraction schemes for Keypoint-based CMFD techniques

Methods	Authors
SIFT	Amerini et al. [97], Anand et al. [98], Farukh et al. [99], Huang et al. [100], Jaberi et al. [101], Shen et al. [102]
Harris corner Detector	Harris and Stephens [103], Chen et al. [104], Zhao and Zhao [105], Zheng and Chang [106]
SURF	Bo et al. [107], Mishra et al. [108]

Table 33.4 Feature matching techniques according to keypoint-based CMFD techniques

Methods	Authors
Nearest neighbour [best bin search, 2NN, g2NN,]	Chen et al. [104], Huang et al. [100], Jaberi et al. [101], Mishra et al. [108], Zhao and Zhao [105], Farukh et al. [99], Amerini et al. [97]
Others	Anand et al. [98], Shen et al. [102]

transformation operations. However, SIFT needs improvement to detect flat, smooth or highly identical forged area in texture. The features extracted by this method produce large false positives in texture applications. Overall, SIFT is the most widely used an algorithm for feature extraction in comparison of SURF and Harris corner Detector. CMF detection based on the g2NN procedure provides the maximum performance in case of multiple CMF detections. It also needs to concentrate on the issues of low recall rate and robustness. Selection of relevant features for accurate matching technique as well maintaining the computation time is open research field. However, very few keypoint features and descriptor techniques are applied to the nearest neighbor schemes and then evaluating their values in CMF detection.

33.3.2 Splicing

Image splicing is a technique for the amalgamation of two or more images, with altering the genuine image considerably to create a forged image, as shown in Fig. 33.10.

Splicing forgery detection methods can be categorized into six groups (Table 33.5):

1. Bi Coherence feature based
2. Camera Response function based
3. Pixel Correlation based
4. DWT and DCT based
5. Invariant image moments
6. Others

Fig. 33.10 Shows an example of image splicing or paste-up

Table 33.5 Splicing based forgery detection schemes

Methods	Authors
Bi-coherence features based	Ng and Chang [109], Ng et al. [110], Hsu and Chang [111]
Camera response function based	Hsu and Chang [111], Fang et al. [112], Lin et al. [113]
Pixel correlation based	Wang et al. [114], Hsu and Chang [115], Mushtaq and Ajaz [116]
DCT and DWT based	Lin and Wu [118], Li et al. [117]
Invariant image moments	Zhao et al. [119], Zhang et al. [120]
Others	Qu et al [121], Hussain et al. [122]

Observations from Splicing Forgery Detection

The nonlinear property is the main advantage of using bi-coherence features, as the image splicing forgery operation is too nonlinear. The spliced images are produced from dissimilar images thereby the inconsistencies of the image features and camera features are the main source in identifying the forged regions of the images. Camera response algorithms more depend on its intrinsic characteristics in comparison of inconsistencies and discontinue of spliced images. Pixel correlation-based algorithms were effectively applicable to uncompressed images to detect forgeries. These algorithms involve lesser feature vectors, but the challenges are associated to deal with post-processing operations, like blurring. Although the improvement in splicing forgery detection for geometrical transformations is also continually advancing using DWT and DCT methods, still to manage the strong post-processing operations is an open research area. For that reason, invariant image moment algorithms were found invariant to geometric transformations, but when spliced regions are minor in size their false positive rate is increased. Many existing techniques and tools are developed by researchers to detect splicing forgeries. Still, these methods may not be fit to solve many challenging applications.

Fig. 33.11 Example of resampling

Table 33.6 Resampling-based forgery detection schemes

Methods	Authors
Subsampling based, liner parametric model based	Birajdar and Mankar [123], Qiao et al. [124]
JPEG resampling, upscale crop based, spectral-based	Chen et al. [125], Singh and Aggarwal [126], Chen et al. [127]
Rescale detection, upsampling based	Birajdar and Mankar [129], Tu et al. [128], Kao et al. [130]
Non-intrusive approach	Cao et al. [131]
Detecting traces of resampling	Popescu and Farid [132]

33.3.3   Resampling

Resampling an image requires an interpolation method and linear or cubic interpolations are very popular and this fact was exploited by the authors of [3]. A new image with changed height and/or width is created in resampling. Upsampling is increasing the image size; whereas downsampling is reducing the size, an example is shown in Fig. 33.11.

Resampling of a 2D image can be broken down into two 1D resampling passes. Firstly, horizontal resampling is implemented by producing an image with a different width and the same height. Then, this middle image is resampled vertically to change its height with the same width (Table 33.6).

Observations for Resampling Forgery Detection
From a splicing forensic point of view, there are two main fronts: Resampling detection methods generally do not perform on JPEG compressed images, and downscaling is not accurately detectable in comparison of up-scaling. It has been observed from literature simulations that large spectral resolution enables the peak detector to distinguish between shifted and original JPEG peaks. Further, resampling detection also uses the concept of color filter array (CFA) interpolation

inside the camera. In the pixel domain, noise is added in the JPEG image as a pre-processing step before using a re-sampling detector. The re-sampling detector produces inferior results as compared with uniform noise addition. Finally, we also observed that scaling can be detected in the re-sampling operation also. A natural extension of this work would be an improvement in forgery detection rate (performed on a different database of unaltered and interpolated images) as each resampling detector is used according to the requirement of applications.

Although, mostly approaches guarantee good accuracy, but they fail on real-life forgeries. In real life, the forged area will never have a uniform boundary. Another issue that has to be investigated is more detection rate of downscaling. Since most of the resampling algorithms consider the case of scaling, still further focus on rotation and other geometrical transformations is required.

33.4 Future Directions and Conclusion

On the basis of the existing problems in current research status, several future directions for CMFD research are provided in this subsection based on the existing problems.

33.4.1 Future Directions

- *Benchmark and standard dataset*. Dataset for CMFD evaluation should include original images and corresponding forged images with different resolution, diverse forged images with regions (smooth or texture) which have different size in various geometric transformation (rotation, scaling, etc.), the forged region saved individually as images, the distorted images with post-processing methods (JPEG compression, AWGN, noise contamination, blurring, etc.). Besides, the corresponding ground truth maps and post-processing methods with open-source code (MATLAB, OpenCV) also should be included in the dataset.
- *Effectiveness and robustness*. CMFD methods should be effective to detect the forged regions in distorted doctored images as mentioned in *benchmark dataset*. It is worth exploring efficient local invariant feature and descriptors extraction, high-speed method of feature matching, and accurate localization method.
- *Deep learning*: It is comparatively few CMFD methods based on deep learning. CMFD methods based on deep learning are hard repeatable and used for comparison because of the difference of the training set and testing set. The researchers study deep Deep Boltzmann Machines, Deep Auto-Encoders, and Convolution Neural Networks [133–135]. These methods have shown remarkable performance in Artificial Intelligence (AI) applications (Fig. 33.12) such as object recognition, natural language processing, and several others.

Fig. 33.12 Machines can learn

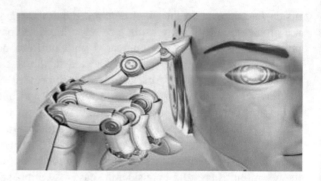

- *Performance evaluation:* There are limited numbers of performance parameters such as precision, recall, an F1 measure used for all forgery detection methods. There is a need to define further metrics for accurate assessment of algorithms such as lighting inconsistencies, color filter array etc..

33.4.2 Conclusion

This chapter, starting from the definition of forensics, general approach, classification, presented a concise survey on pixel-based image forgery detection between 2005 and 2018. Firstly, we discuss the origin of forensics and the common process involved in the image forensics workflow to further classify it. Specifically, in the Multimedia Forensics classification, we discussed the significance of pixel-based image forgery detection based on a passive approach. We categorized this technique in three types: Copy-move, splicing, resampling and listed the associated publications and observations. Furthermore, we categorized the copy-move regions in block-based and keypoint based methods which are implemented to detect CMF. Open challenges that can influence pixel-based techniques are also discussed. Overall, forensics is a flourishing and in trend research field able to detect forgery of doctored images. We can design more efficient algorithms in the future to overcome the weaknesses of existing methods using latest technologies like machine learning, deep learning etc.

References

1. Amerini I, Ballan L, Caldelli R, Del Bimbo A, Del Tongo L, Serra G (2013) Copy-move forgery detection and localization by means of robust clustering with j-linkage. Signal Process Image Commun 28(6):659–669
2. Forensics Timeline (2011) Cbsnews.com. Archived from the original on 2011-06-29

3. A Brief Background of Forensic Science (2009) Archived 2009-12-16 at the Wayback Machine

4. Ci S, Brian EM (1981) The washing away of wrongs: forensic medicine in thirteenth-century China. Ann Arbor: Center for Chinese Studies, Univ of Michigan,. Print. p. 3

5. Burkhard M. (2016) Handbook of Forensic Medicine. Sussex: Wiley Blackwell. p. 10. ISBN 9780470979990. Archived from the original on 2016-05-05

6. Battiato S, Farinella GM, Messina E, Puglisi G (2012) Robust image alignment for tampering detection. IEEE Trans Inf Forensics Secur 7(4):1105–1117

7. Tziakouris G (2018) Cryptocurrencies-A Forensic Challenge or Opportunity for Law Enforcement? An Interpol Perspective. IEEE Security & Privacy 16(4): 92-94

8. Pearson H (2005) Image manipulation: CSI: cell biology. Nature.434:952-953

9. Farid H (2006) Exposing digital forgeries in scientific images. In: Proceedings of the 8th workshop on multimedia and security, Geneva. pp 29-36

10. Bohme R, Freiling FC, Gloe T, Kirchner M (2009) Multimedia forensics is not computer forensics. In: Geradts ZJMH, Franke K, Veenman CJ (eds) Computational forensics. Springer, Berlin, pp 90-103

11. Reith M, Carr C, Gunsch G (2002) An examination of digital forensic models. Int J Digital Evid 1(3):1–12

12. Rogers M (2003) The role of criminal profiling in the computer forensics process. Comput Secur 22(4):292–298

13. Caldelli R, Amerini I, Picchioni F, De Rosa A, Uccheddu F (2009) Multimedia forensic techniques for acquisition device identification and digital image authentication. In: Handbook of research on computational forensics, digital crime and investigation: methods and solutions, pp 130-154

14. Falagas ME, Pitsouni EI, Malietzis GA, Pappas G (2008) Comparison of PubMed, Scopus, Web of Science, and Google Scholar: strengths and weaknesses. The FASEB Journal Life Sciences Forum 22:338-342

15. Chadegani AA, Salehi H, Yunus MM, Farhadi H, Fooladi M, Farhadi M, Ebrahim NA (2013) A Comparison between Two Main Academic Literature Collections: Web of Science and Scopus Databases. Asian Social Science 9(5):18-26

16. Pandey RC, Singh SK, Shukla KK (2016) Passive forensics in image and video using noise features. Journal Digital Investigation: The Int. J. of Digital Forensics & Incident Response.19(c):1-28

17. Mushtaq S, Mir HA (2014) Digital image forgeries and passive image authentication techniques: a survey. Int J Adv Sci Technol. 73:15-32

18. Ansari MD, Ghrera S, Tyagi V. (2014) Pixel-based image forgery detection: a review. IETE J Educ. 55: 40-46

19. Huynh T, Huynh K, Le T, Nguyen S (2015) A survey on image forgery detection techniques. In: Computing & communication technologies-research, innovation, and vision for the Future (RIVF) CanTho, Vietnam, pp 71-76

20. Vaishnavi D, Subashini TS (2015) A passive technique for image forgery detection using contrast context histogram features. International Journal of Electronic Security and Digital Forensics 7(3): 278-289

21. Panda S, Mishra M (2018) Passive Techniques of Digital Image Forgery Detection: Developments and Challenges" In book: Advances in Electronics, Communication and Computing, pp.281-290

22. Souza AdRF, Sousa SdLS, Franco DP (2017) Horus - A Computational Tool for Digital Image Forensics Through Artificial Intelligence and Pattern Comparison. In: chapter Multimedia Forensics Guidebook: Image, Audio, Video, 6(11)

23. Wayne DF, Bryant SP, Cook J, Kirschbaum D (2014) An Ounce of Prevention: A Guide for Combating Fraud in Construction. The Construction Lawyer 34(3):17-21

24. Masoner L A Brief History of Photography and the Camera. https://www.thesprucecrafts.com/brief-history-of-photography-2688527

25. Asghar K, Habib Z, Hussain M (2017) Copy-move and splicing image forgery detection and localization techniques: a review. Australian Journal of Forensic Sciences, 49(3):281-307
26. Christlein V, Riess C, Jordan J, Riess C, Angelopoulou E (2012) An Evaluation of Popular Copy-Move Forgery Detection Approaches. IEEE Trans. Inf. Forensics Secur. 7:1841–1854
27. Al-Qershi OM, Khoo BE (2013) Passive detection of copy-move forgery in digital images:state-of-the-art.ForensicSci.Int 231(1-3):284–295
28. Lin W, Khan SU, Yow KC, Qazi T, Madani SA, Xu CZ, Kołodziej J, Khan Ia, Li H, Hayat K (2013) Survey on blind image forgery detection. IET Image Process 7: 660–670
29. Birajdar GK, Mankar VH (2013) Digital image forgery detection using passive techniques: a survey. Digit. Investig 10:226-245
30. Peng F, Nie YY, Long M (2011) A complete passive blind image copy-move forensics scheme based on compound statistics features. Forensic Science International 212(1-3):e21-e25
31. Hashmi MF, Anand V, Keskar AG (2014) Copy-move image forgery detection using an efficient and robust method combining un-decimated wavelet transform and scale invariant feature transform. AASRI Procedia. 9: 84-91
32. Fridrich J, Soukal D, Lukas J (2003) Detection of copy-move forgery in digital images. In: Proceedings of the Digital Forensic Research Workshop, Cleveland, OH, USA, pp. 55-61
33. Li L, Li S, Zhu H, Chu SC, Roddick JF, Pan JS (2013) An efficient scheme for detecting copy-move forged images by local binary patterns. Journal of Information Hiding and Multimedia Signal Processing 4(1):46-56
34. Garfinkel SL (2006) Forensic feature extraction and cross-drive analysis. Digital investigation, 71-81
35. Lin X, Li JH,Wang SL, ChungLiew AW, Xiao FC, Huang S (2018) Recent Advances in Passive Digital Image Security Forensics: A Brief Review. Engineering.4(1):29-39
36. Pan X, Lyu S (2010) Region duplication detection using image feature matching. IEEE Transactions on Information Forensics and Security 5(4):857-867
37. Kang X, Wei S (2008) Identifying tampered regions using singular value decomposition in digital image forensics In: Proceedings of the International Conference on Computer Science and Software Engineering, Wuhan, China, pp 926-930
38. Hussain M, Muhammad G, Saleh SQ, Mirza AM, Bebis G (2012) Copy-move image forgery detection using multi-resolution weber descriptors. In: Proceedings of the 8th International Conference on Signal Image Technology and Internet Based Systems, Naples, Italy pp 395-401
39. Zhu Y, Shen XJ, Chen HP (2017) Covert copy-move forgery detection based on color LBP. Acta Automatica Sinica 43(3):390-397
40. Li G, Wu Q, Tu D, Sun S A (2007) sorted neighborhood approach for detecting duplicated regions in imageforgeries based on DWT and SVD. In: Proceedings of the IEEE International Conference on Multimedia and Expo, Beijing, China. pp 1750-1753
41. Lin HJ, Wang CW, Kao YT (2009) Fast copy-move forgery detection. WSEAS Transactions on Signal processing 5(5):188-197
42. Wang JW, Liu GJ, Zhang Z, Dai Y, Wang Z (2009) Fast and robust forensics for image region-duplication forgery. Acta Autom Sin 35(12):1488–1495
43. Zhang J, Feng Z, Su Y (2008) A new approach for detecting copy-move forgery in digital images. In: 11th IEEE Singapore international conference on communication systems, 2008. ICCS 2008. IEEE, Washington, pp 362–366
44. Li G, Wu Q, Tu D, Sun S (2007) A sorted neighborhood approach for detecting duplicated regions in image forgeries based on DWT and SVD. In: 2007 IEEE international conference on multimedia and expo, pp 1750–1753
45. Myrna A, Venkateshmurthy M, Patil C (2007) Detection of region duplication forgery in digital images using wavelets and log-polar mapping. In: International conference on conference on computational intelligence and multimedia applications, Washington, IEEE, pp 371-377
46. Popescu AC, Farid H (2004) Exposing digital forgeries by detecting duplicated image regions. Department of Computer Science, Dartmouth College, Tech. Rep. TR2004-515

47. Li S, Zhang A, Zheng Y, Zhu T, Jin B (2009) Detection of copymove image forgeries based on sift. J PLA Univ Sci Technol (NatSci Ed) 10(4):339-343
48. Avola D,Cinque L,Foresti GL, Massaroni C, Pannone D (2017) A keypoint-based method for background modeling and foreground detection using a PTZ camera. Pattern Recognition Letters,96: 96-105
49. Shivakumar B, Santhosh Baboo S (2011) Detection of region duplication forgery in digital images using surf. Int J Comput Sci Issues (IJCSI) 8(4):199-205
50. Fridrich AJ, Soukal BD, Lukáš AJ (2003) Detection of copymove forgery in digital images. In: Proceedings of digital forensic research workshop. Citeseer
51. Popescu A, Farid H. (2004) Exposing digital forgeries by detecting duplicated image regions. Dartmouth College; Technical Report TR2004-515; Hanover, New Hampshire
52. Zimba M, Xingming S (2011) Detection of image duplicated regions affected by rotation, scaling and translation using block characteristics of DWT coefficients. Int J Digit Content Technol Appl. 5:143-150
53. Hmimid A, Sayyouri M, Hassan (2014) Image Classification Using Novel Set of Charlier Moment Invariants. WSEAS Trans Signal Process, 10:156-167
54. Ryu SJ, Lee MJ, Lee HK (2010) Detection of copy-rotate-move forgery using Zernike moments. In: Böhme R, Fong PWL, Safavi-Naini R (eds) Information hiding. Springer, Berlin, pp 51-65
55. Ardizzone E, Bruno A, Mazzola G (2010) Copy-move forgery detection via texture description. In: Proceedings of the 2nd ACM workshop on multimedia in forensics, security and intelligence.ACM, New York, pp 59–64
56. Wang J, Liu G, Li H, Dai Y, Wang Z (2009) Detection of image region duplication forgery using model with circle block. In: International conference on multimedia information networking and security, MINES'09, vol 1. IEEE, Washington, pp 25-29
57. Mallat S, Zhong S (1992) Characterization of signals from multiscale edges. IEEE Transactions on Pattern Analysis and Machine Intelligence 14(7):710-732
58. Patil DP, Landge L (2016) Detection of Digital Image Forgery using Transformation Domain. Int J of Engineering Research & Technology.5 (6):599-602
59. Lai S; Bohme R (2013) Block convergence in repeated transform coding: JPEG-100 forensics, carbon dating, and tamper detection. In: Proceedings of the International Conference on Acoustics, Speech and Signal Processing, pp 3028-3032
60. Lin Z, He J, Tang X, Tang CK (2009) Fast, automatic and finegrained tampered jpeg image detection via DCT coefficient analysis. Pattern Recognit 42(11):2492–2501
61. Li W, Yu N, Yuan Y (2008) Doctored JPEG image detection. In: Proceedings of the Int. Conf. Multimed. Expo 2, IEEE, pp 253-256
62. Li X, Zhao Y, Liao M, Shih FY, Shi YQ (2012) Passive detection of copy-paste forgery between JPEG images. J. Cent. South Univ 19: 2839-2851
63. Huang Y, Lu W, Sun W, Long D (2011) Improved DCT-based detection of copy move forgery in images. Forensic Sci. Int. 206: 178-184
64. Cao Y, Gao T, Fan L, Yang Q (2012) A robust detection algorithm for copy-move forgery in digital images. Forensic Sci. Int. 214: 33-43
65. Zhao J, Guo J (2013) Passive forensics for copy-move image forgery using a method based on DCT and SVD. Forensic Sci. Int. 233: 158-166
66. Shao H, Yu T, Xu M, Cui W (2012) Image region duplication detection based on circular window expansion and phase correlation. Forensic Sci. Int. 222:71–82
67. Yang B, Sun X, Chen X, Zhang J, Li X (2013) An efficient forensic method for copy move forgery detection based on DWT-FWHT. Radio Eng. 22: 1098-1105
68. Zhang J, Feng Z, Su Y (2008) A new approach for detecting copy-move forgery in digital images, In: 11th IEEE Singapore International Conference on Communication Systems, ICCS 2008 pp 362-366
69. Muhammad G, Hussain M, Bebis G (2012) Passive Copy Move Image Forgery Detection Using Undecimated Dyadic Wavelet Transform. Digit. Investig. 9:49-5

70. Deng Y, Wu Y, Zhou L (2012) Detection of copy-rotate-move forgery using Dual Tree Complex Wavelet Transform. Adv. Sci. Lett. 16:32-38
71. Ketenci S, Ulutas G (2013) Copy-move forgery detection in images via 2D-Fourier Transform. In: Proceedings of the 36th Int. Conf. Telecommun. Signal Process. pp 813-816
72. Kumar S, Desai J, Mukherjee S (2013) A Fast DCT Based Method for Copy Move Forgery Detection, In: Proceedings of the Second International Conference on Image Information Processing (ICIIP-2013). IEEE pp 649-654
73. Shin Y (2013) Fast Detection of Copy-Move Forgery Image using DCT. J. Korea Multimed. Soc. 16: 411-417
74. Davarzani R, Yaghmaie K, Mozaffari S, Tapak M (2013) Copy-move forgery detection using multiresolution local binary patterns. Forensic Sci. Int. 231: 61-72
75. Gan Y, Zhong J (2014) Image copy-move tamper blind detection algorithm based on integrated feature vectors. J. Chem. Pharm. Res. 6:1584-1590
76. Hsu HC, Wang MS (2012) Detection of copy-move forgery image using Gabor descriptor. In: Proceedings of the International Conference Anti-Counterfeiting, Secur. Identification, ASID, pp 1-4
77. Vladimirovich KA, Valerievich MV (2014) A Fast Plain Copy-Move Detection Algorithm Based on Structural Pattern and 2D Rabin-Karp Rolling Hash. In: Proceedings of the 11th International Conference ICIAR, pp 461-468
78. Lynch G, Shih FY, Liao HYM (2013) An efficient expanding block algorithm for image copy-move forgery detection. Inf. Sci. (Ny.) 239:253-265
79. Singh J, Raman B (2012) A high performance copy-move image forgery detection scheme on GPU. Adv. Intell. Soft Comput. 131:239-246
80. Bilgehan M, Uluta M (2013) Detection of Copy-Move Forgery Using Krawtchouk Moment, In: Proceedings of the 8th International Conference on Electrical and Electronics Engineering (ELECO), pp 311-314
81. Le Z, Xu W (2013) A robust image copy-move forgery detection based on mixed moments. In: Proceedings of the International Conference Softw. Eng. Serv. Sci. ICSESS, IEEE pp 381-384
82. Mahdian B, Saic S (2007) Detection of copy-move forgery using a method based on blur moment invariants. Forensic Sci. Int. 171:180-189
83. Ryu SJ, Kirchner M, Lee MJ, Lee HK (2013) Rotation invariant localization of duplicated image regions based on zernike moments. IEEE Trans. Inf. Forensics Secur. 8:1355-1370
84. Hu MK (1962) Visual Pattern Recognition by. Moment Invariants. IRE Trans. Inf. Theory 2:179–187
85. Bayram S, Sencar HT, Memon N (2009). An Efficient And Robust Method for Detecting Copy-Move Forgery, In: Proceedings of the International Conference on Acoustics, Speech and Signal Processing (ICASSP). IEEE pp 1053-1056
86. Li J, Li X, Yang B, Sun X (2014) Segmentation-based Image Copy-move Forgery Detection Scheme. IEEE Trans. Inf. Forensics Secur. 60(13):1-12
87. Li W, Yu N (2010) Rotation robust detection of copy-move forgery. In: Proceedings of the International Conference on Image Processing, ICIP. pp 2113-2116
88. Li Y (2013) Image copy-move forgery detection based on polar cosine transform and approximate nearest neighbor searching. Forensic Sci. Int. 224:59-67
89. Wu Q, Wang S, Zhang X (2010) Detection of image region-duplication with rotation and scaling tolerance, In: Proceedings of the Second International Conference, ICCCI. pp 100-108
90. Ting Z, Rang-Ding W (2009) Copy-move forgery detection based on SVD in digital image. In: Proceedings of the 2nd International Congress on Image and Signal Processing, CISP'09 pp 0–4
91. Ardizzone E, Bruno A, Mazzola G (2015) Copy–Move Forgery Detection by Matching Triangles of Keypoints. IEEE Trans on Inf Forensics and Security. 2084 - 2094
92. Wang T, Tang J, Zhao W, Xu Q, Luo B (2012) Blind detection of copy-move forgery based on multi-scale autoconvolution invariants. Commun. Comput. Inf. Sci. 438-446

93. Myna AN, Venkateshmurthy MG, Patil CG (2008) Detection of region duplication forgery in digital images using wavelets and log-polar mapping, In: Proceedings of International Conference on Computational Intelligence and Multimedia Applications, ICCIMA 2007. pp 371-377

94. Kashyap A, Joshi SD (2013) Detection of Copy-Move Forgery Using Wavelet Decomposition. In: Proceedings of International Conference on Signal Processing and Communication (ICSC). pp 1–3

95. Sekeh AM, Maarof MA, Rohani MF, Mahdian B (2013) Efficient image duplicated region detection model using sequential block clustering. Digit. Investig.10: 73-84

96. Murali S, Anami BS, Chittapur GB (2012) Detection of Digital Photo Image Forgery. In: Proceedings of International Conference on Advanced Communication Control and Computing Technologies. IEEE pp 9166

97. Amerini I, Ballan L, Caldelli R, Bimbo A, Del SG (2011) A SIFT-based forensic method for copy - move attack detection and transformation recovery. IEEE Trans. Inf. Forensics Secur. 6:1099-1110

98. Anand V, Hashmi M, Farukh Keskar AG (2014) A Copy Move Forgery Detection to Overcome Sustained Attacks Using Dyadic Wavelet Transform and SIFT Methods, In: Proceedings of 6th Asian Conference on Intelligent Information and Database Systems (ACIIDS). pp 530-542

99. Farukh M, Anand V, Keskar AG (2014) Copy-move Image Forgery Detection Using an Efficient and Robust Method Combining Un-decimated Wavelet Transform and Scale Invariant Feature Transform. AASRI Procedia 9: 84-91

100. Huang H, Guo W, Zhang Y (2008) Detection Of Copy-Move Forgery in Digital Images Using SIFT Algorithm, In: Proceedings of Pacific-Asia Workshop on Computational Intelligence and Industrial Application. IEEE pp 272-276

101. Jaberi M, Bebis G, Hussain M, Muhammad G (2013b) Accurate and robust localization of duplicated region in copy–move image forgery. Mach. Vis. Appl 25:451-475

102. Shen X, Zhu Y, Lv Y, Chen H (2013) Image Copy-Move Forgery Detection Based on SIFT and Gray Level, In: Proceedings of International Conference on Information Technology and Management Innovation (ICITMI2012) pp 3021-3024

103. Harris C, Stephens M (1988) A Combined Corner and Edge Detector. In: Proceedings of Alvey Vision Conference. Alvey Vision Club, pp 23.1–23.6

104. Chen L, Lu W, Ni J, Sun W, Huang J (2013) Region duplication detection based on harris corner points and step sector statistics. J. Vis. Commun. Image Represent.24:244-254

105. Zhao J, Zhao W (2013) Passive forensics for region duplication image forgery based on harris feature points and local binary patterns. Math. Probl. Eng.1-12

106. Zheng J, Chang L (2014) Detection Technology of Tampering Image Based on Harris Corner Points. J. Comput. Inf. Syst. 10:1481-1488

107. Bo X, Junwen W, Guangjie L, Yuewei D (2010) Image Copy-Move Forgery Detection Based On SURF, In: Proceedings of International Conference on Multimedia Information Networking and Security. IEEE. pp 889–892

108. Mishra P, Mishra N, Sharma S, Patel R (2013) Region duplication forgery detection technique based on SURF and HAC. Sci. World J.1-8

109. Ng T, Chang S (2004) A model for image splicing. In International conference on image processing ICIP'04 Singapore. pp1169-1172

110. Ng T, Chang SF, Sun Q (2004) Blind detection of photomontage using higher order statistics. In: International Symposium on Circuits and Systems (ISCAS'04) Vancouver, Canada. pp V-688-V-691

111. Hsu YF, Chang S (2010) Camera response functions for image forensics: An automatic algorithm for splicing detection. IEEE Trans Inform Forensics Secur 5:816-825

112. Fang Z, Wang S, Zhang X (2009) Image splicing detection using camera characteristic inconsistency. In: Proceedings of International Conference on Multimedia Information Networking and Security (MINES'09) Hubei, China. pp 20-24

113. Lin Z, Wang R, Tang X, Shum H-Y (2005) Detecting doctored images using camera response normality and consistency. In: Proceedings of conference on computer vision and pattern recognition (CVPR) San Diego, CA, USA. IEEE pp 1087-1092

114. Wang W, Dong J, Tan T (2009) Effective image splicing detection based on image chroma. In: Proceedings of 16th IEEE International Conference on Image Processing (ICIP) Cairo, Egypt. pp 1257-1260

115. Hsu F, Chang S (2006) Detecting image splicing using geometry invariants and camera characteristics consistency. In: Proceedings of IEEE International Conference on Multimedia and Expo. Seattle, USA. Pp 549-552

116. Mushtaq S, Ajaz H (2014) Novel method for image splicing detection. In: Proceedings of International conference on advances in computing, communications and informatics (ICACCI), Delhi, India. pp 2398-2403

117. Li X, Jing T, Li X (2010) Image splicing detection based on moment features and Hilbert-Huang Transform. In: Proceedings of IEEE international conference on information theory and information security (ICITIS), Beijing, China. pp 1127–1130

118. Lin S, Wu T (2011) An integrated technique for splicing and copy-move forgery image detection. In: Proceedings of International congress on image and signal processing (CISP) Shenyang, China. pp 1086-1090

119. Zhao X, Li S, Wang S, Li J, Yang K (2012) Optimal chroma-like channel design for passive color image splicing detection. EURASIP J Adv Signal Process.2012:1-11

120. Zhang Z, Zhou Y, Kang J, Ren Y (2008) Study of image splicing detection. In: Proceedings of Advanced Intelligent Computing Theories and Applications. With Aspects of Theoretical and Methodological Issues. Springer, Shanghai, China. pp 1103-1110

121. Qu Z, Qiu G, Huang J (2009) Detect digital image splicing with visual cues. In: Proceedings of Information Hiding, Berlin, Springer. pp 247-261

122. Hussain M, Saleh SQ, Aboalsamh H, Muhammad G, Bebis G (2014) Comparison between WLD and LBP descriptors for non-intrusive image forgery detection. In: Proceedings of IEEE international symposium on innovations in intelligent systems and applications (INISTA), Alberobello, Italy. pp 197-204

123. Birajdar GK, Mankar VH (2018) Subsampling-Based Blind Image Forgery Detection Using Support Vector Machine and Artificial Neural Network Classifiers. Arab J Sci Eng 43:555-568

124. Qiao T, Zhu A, Retraint F (2018) Exposing image resampling forgery by using linear parametric model. Multimed Tools Appl 77:1501-1523

125. Chen Z, Zhao Y, Ni R (2017) Detection of operation chain: JPEG-Resampling-JPEG. Signal Processing: Image Communication 57: 8-20

126. Singh RD, Aggarwal N (2017) Detection of upscale-crop and splicing for digital video authentication. Digital Investigation 21: 31-52

127. Chen C, Ni J, Shen Z, Shi YQ (2017) Blind Forensics of Successive Geometric Transformations in Digital Images Using Spectral Method: Theory and Applications: 2811-2824

128. Tu CT, Lin HJ, Yang FW, Chang HW (2014) Approximate Detection Method for Image Up-Sampling. KSII Transactions on Internet & Information Systems 8(2):462-482

129. Birajdara GK, Mankar (2014) VH Blind method for rescaling detection and rescale factor estimation in digital images using periodic properties of interpolation. Int. J. Electron. Commun. (AEÜ) 68: 644-652

130. Kao YT, Lin HJ, Wang CW, Pai YC (2012) Effective Detection for Linear Up-Sampling by a Factor of Fraction. IEEE Transactions on Image Processing 21(8): 3443 - 3453

131. Cao G, Zhao Y, Ni R (2012) Forensic identification of resampling operators: A semi non-intrusive approach. Forensic Science International 216: 29-36

132. Popescu AC, Farid H (2005) Exposing digital forgeries by detecting traces of resampling. IEEE Transactions on Signal Processing 53(2): 758-767

133. Ciresan DC, Meier U, Masci J, Maria Gambardella L, Schmidhuber J (2011) Flexible, high performance convolutional neural networks for image classification. In: Proceedings of International Joint Conference on Artificial Intelligence, Barcelona, Spain. pp 1237-1242

134. Krizhevsky A, Sutskever I, Hinton GE (2012) Image net classification with deep convolutional neural networks. In Advances in neural information processing systems 2:1097-1105
135. Ji S, Xu W, Yang M, Yu K (2013) 3D convolutional neural networks for human action recognition. IEEE Trans Pattern Anal Mach Intell 35:221–231

Chapter 34
Resource Allocation in Co-Operative Relay Networks for IOT Driven Broadband Multimedia Services

Javaid A. Sheikh, Mehboob-ul- Amin, Shabir A. Parah, and G. Mohiuddin Bhat

34.1 Introduction

The Internet of Things (IoT) is considered to future revolutionary step in the cellular technology. IoT services are predicted as a key parameter for further push in the growth in cellular technology. It has been estimated that about 30 billion cellular IOT based connected devices will be deployed by 2025 and also 7 billion Low-Power Wide-Area (LPWA) modules are predicted to account in 2025. Cellular based IOT is likely to offer services like service meters, machines for retailing, automotive marine management, smart traffic system, traffic information in real time to the vehicle in automotive sector, security reporting and critical and other medical services.

To enable these services the cellular IOT requires the following parameters:

- Battery life should be large
- Cost of the devices should be low
- Deployment cost should be as minimum as possible
- Extended network coverage
- Handling capability for support of large number of devices

This chapter presents a cellular LTE based IoT solution that meets above mentioned requirements and enhances the core and radio and networks. The prime necessity of any radio network needs to work with simple and low cost devices. The future networks need to work in cohesion with the transmission and higher layer

J. A. Sheikh · M.-u. Amin · S. A. Parah (✉)
Department of Electronics and Instrumentation Technology, University of Kashmir, Srinagar, Jammu and Kashmir, India

G. M. Bhat
Institute of Technology, Zakura Campus, University of Kashmir, Srinagar, Jammu and Kashmir, India

© Springer Nature Switzerland AG 2019
A. K. Singh, A. Mohan (eds.), *Handbook of Multimedia Information Security: Techniques and Applications*, https://doi.org/10.1007/978-3-030-15887-3_34

protocols such that the devices consume less power, which will eventually extend the battery life over the years. For deep indoor and rural areas extended coverage is required therefore the network elements need to handle subscription, charging, and MIMO support for small packages. The Long Term Evolution (LTE) integration with Cat.1 devices has a capability to support IoT, while LTE-A enhances the battery life up-to 10 years without power saving mode. Introduction of two emerging technologies: emTC (enhanced machine type communication) and NB-IOT (Narrow Band Internet of things) further optimizes the coverage and can support large number of devices in downlink communication.

The use of multiple antenna at every node (BS/RN) is necessary requirement for designing next generation communication system to meet growing demands of high information rate for both uplink as well as downlink. The performance of the cellular system is then dependent on allocation of resource blocks in the wireless environment. For achieving optimal resource allocation tradeoff exists between the maximization of aggregate system throughput and user fairness. A major hurdle in resource allocation is the inter-user-interference arising due to multiple users operating in parallel. In contrast to the earlier resource allocation using single antenna mode MIMO techniques enable resource allocation with precise degrees of freedom and spatial separation of users. Multi-antenna system allows the steering of the signals towards intended users, thus increase the received power and at the same time limit the interference caused to non–intended users. The deployment of RNs in the cellular systems proves to be a promising technology for optimal power allocation in a cooperative environment. The cell edge users suffering from worst signal-to-interference-noise (SINR) are served well by RNS deployed at various positions in the cell. Various techniques and schemes have been proposed and found in the literature to improve the performance of cooperative cellular networks. The modest scheme of single relay selection was proposed in [1]. The best possible relay selection coupled with resource allocation with single user was investigated in [2, 3]. The relay site planning and its impact has been discussed in [4]. Optimal relay placement was proposed in [5].

In this chapter relay based cooperative resource allocation problem has been investigated for downlink cellular networks. The RNs are placed at various positions of cell ($k = 1, 2, 3$). MIMO channel modeling and Power allocation is formulated as an optimization problem to maximize the link rate, capacity (Information rate) and mean SINR on both relay and access links.KKT condition is used to derive optimal values for power allocation coefficients on both relay and access links.

34.2   Optimization Techniques

Optimization has been the traditional method of searching the optimum mathematical solution to a problem which encompasses maximization or minimization of an objective or effectiveness function, for both unconstrained and vulnerable to certain constraints on the parameters of the function. For different multimedia applications the nature of the utility function dictates the type of optimization problem. Traditionally, the solutions of resource management consider video as an isolated application in the network thus solving a convex optimization problem. For example, the better the quality is required for higher the data rate at which the video can be transmitted, guarantees perceived by the user and hence the higher the efficacy for the user [6, 7].

For multimedia applications based real time network, (e.g. IPTV, Voice over IP (VoIP) etc.) they must be delivered along with video. For such applications utility non-convex functions are considered the optimum functions for solutions. Since the allocated transmission rate and the inelasticity of real time applications which do not improve or degrade gracefully produces non-convexity. Further significant QOS drop out results in reduction in data rate below certain limit [8, 9].

Resolving the non-convex optimization problem (due to multiple applications) within the restrictions of the mm-Wave network is therefore the challenge for 5G which includes the practical consideration of the execution time of the algorithm [10, 11]. The most popular optimization techniques

1. Lagrangian Dual Decomposition Sub-gradient Algorithm
2. Rate Allocation Game
3. Nash Bargaining Solution

34.2.1 Lagrangian Dual Decomposition Sub-Gradient Algorithm

Lagrangian dual decomposition sub gradient has been the most widely and earliest optimization algorithm for optimization process.In convex optimization gradient search method has been widely used. Gradient of the function is recommended for gradient search, and the search direction is defined to be optimized at the current point as the first derivative of the function is the gradient. The gradient projection controlled by the Lagrange multiplier finds the optimum solution to the convex problems [12]. However, gradient search methods are inappropriate to convex optimization which is non-differentiable. A sub-gradient approach to the Lagrangian algorithm which enables solution of non-differentiable convex problems. The alternate solution will be iterative algorithm is generated replacing the gradient based method [13]. In this method the updating of Lagrange multiplier at each iteration is carried out. The implementation of the algorithm requires message-passing in order to communicate the Lagrange multiplier from each network device to a central calculation point at each iteration [14]. However the network over-headiness is the main disadvantage of message passing which may reduce the application based data transmission rate.

34.2.2   Rate Allocation Game

Game theory uses set of mathematical tools for analyzing the interactive decision process. In rate allocation game each player is selfish therefore it is considered as non-cooperative resource allocation process therefore distributed implementation is aided. The connecting objectives of the wireless devices in the network uses the principle of handling mechanism. The number of players, in a game is dependent on strategies chosen by network to describe the game. In this method, the consequences of player ranges and other player priorities are taken into consideration in such a way, so as to maximize the utility. The rational player in principle will chose those priorities that have good response to the opinions, he should possess about the approach of his counterparts.

Price will be low if few players will be competing for available resources. The price for requesting more resource is higher for higher competition. The satisfaction will decrease if price increases, so an optimum is reached where no user desires to depart because their satisfaction will be reduced if the price goes up, which is the importance of excess demand. Following illustration explains how game will be implemented in mm-wave network (Fig. 34.1).

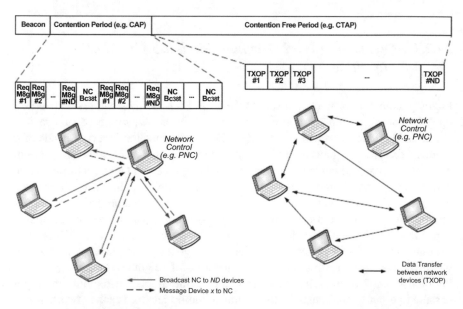

Fig. 34.1 Hybrid MAC framework based implementation of the rate allocation game

34.2.3 Nash Bargaining Solution

The game-theoretic method is the Nash Bargaining Solution (NBS). The fair allocation of resources is possible in this case of game-theoretic approach. The disagreement point is acceptable to each known play in this scheme. The Nash product NBS is used to allocate resources optimally by maximizing, which is the product of utilities in the channel time allocation problem corresponds to the set of lower CTA limits. The NBS does not require iterative bargaining among users is an axiomatic bargaining solution, which means that it accordingly message passing is avoided. However, for non-convex functions neither NBS nor Rate Allocation Game are applicable.

34.3 Cognitive Radio Technology for Efficient Resource Allocation in 5G Networks

With the increase in number of mobile users, there is a thirst for bandwidth that needs to be allocated for all the users without traffic among them. In the fast changing environment having own demands of fast and reliable communication and connectivity. Better understanding of communication theory and electromagnetic is required for the continuous demands and need for wireless communication systems. Increasing demand for spectrum in fourth and Fifth Generation (5G) mobile networks results in the rapid development of reliable wireless devices. Therefore the scarcity of wireless resources is the crucial challenge to the already burdened scarce wireless systems and many determinations are taken to come out of this problem. The FCC (Federal Communication Commission) observed that the current licensed spectrum is significantly underutilized [15]. Hence, Cognitive radio (CR) approach is having much interest in the use of resource allocation in mobile networks. A cognitive radio (CR) is classified as a radio that can be configured and programmed dynamically to explore the best wireless channels in its neighborhood to mitigate user interference and to overcome congestion [16, 17]. The available channels in the wireless spectrum are automatically detected by the cognitive radio and then accordingly modifies its transmission or reception parameters to allow more simultaneous wireless communications in a given spectrum band at a given location. This process is known as dynamic spectrum management. The communication between secondary users can be categorized into two parts in -band either in underlay mode (shared spectrum) or overlay mode (dedicated spectrum) and secondly out-of-band where the Unlicensed spectrum is adopted by other wireless technologies such as Blue-tooth or Wi-Fi direct [18]. The primary user is known as the licensed user since they have allocated bandwidth and the secondary user is the unlicensed user as they do not have any allocated bandwidth. Here, we propose an algorithm where the unused bandwidth of primary users is allocated to secondary users using cognitive radio technology [19, 20].

34.4   Proposed System Model

Consider a discrete time channel with Ergodic time varying gain g(t) and noise power n(t). Assuming power gain p(t) follows Gaussian Distribution Statistics p(g) and the power gain p(t) is independent of channel input. The channel gain g(t) varies with each instant of time 't', having some correlation overtime. In a fading environment g(t) is constant over some block of time T, after which g(t) changes to a new value based on Gaussian distribution p(g). Let P be the average transmit signal power. $N_0/2$ denote the noise power spectral density of n(t). B be the bandwidth of LTE channel. The received SINR is then given as:

$$\gamma(t) = P \, g(t) / N_0.B \qquad (34.1)$$

The distribution of $\gamma(t)$ depends upon distribution of g(t).

We are considering the system with n_t transmit antennas and n_r receive antennas. The transmitted signal in each symbol period is denoted by $n_t \times 1$ complex vector X where x_i ($x_i \in X$) refers to transmitted signal from ith antenna. We assume that the total power of the complex transmitted signal X is constrained to P, irrespective of number of transmit antennas (n_t). The Expectation value is written as

$$E\left[x^*x\right] = P \qquad (34.2)$$

The received signal Y is given by

$$Y = Hx + n \qquad (34.3)$$

H is the $n_r \times 1$ complex channel gain matrix, h_{ij} represents the channel fading coefficient from the ith transmit antenna to the jth receive antenna, 'n' is Additive White Gaussian noise (AWGN). The output of each receive is given as P_r. The average SINR at each receive antenna is defined as

$$SINR = P_r/\sigma^2 \qquad (34.4)$$

where, σ^2 is the identical noise power at each of receive antenna.

The following assumptions are taken into account

1. No power losses ($P_t = P_r$)
2. Channel State Information known at receiver but not always at transmitter.

The proposed model is incorporated in co-operative LTE-A networks, where we are having a Base station (BS), Relay Node (RN), Mobile Station (MS/UE). The MS or UE is connected to both BS as well as RN. We assume that the backhaul link between BS and RN is positioned in such a way that no wastage of resource occurs and proper interference coordination occurs. Since UE is connected to both BS as well as RN, so in order to avoid interference at the UE, BS transmits to the

UE and RN simultaneously during timeslot 't' and during time slot ('1 − t') RN transmits to the UE. The direct link is modeled by Rayleigh fading channel and the access link is modeled by Rician fading channel. We model the backhaul relay link simply by AWGN, since it may impose limit to the capacity of access link. Our main focus is laid to evaluate the expression for the capacity of this fading access link and to compare it with fading direct link capacity. The modified capacity in a MIMO environment of the system model can be written as:

$$C = \min \left\{ \log_2 \det \left[\left(I + \frac{g}{n_t} \right) H H' \right] \right\} \tag{34.5}$$

I is the diagonal matrix of receive antennas 'n_r', g is the gain at transmitter antenna. H is the channel matrix. In order to achieve maximum capacity, the optimum distribution of the transmitted signal x_i for the ith antenna from BS to the UE with MIMO channel gain g(t) is assumed to be Gaussian distribution for large number of random variables according to Central limit theorem. The overall channel capacity is the sum of all sub-channel capacities from the ith transmit antenna of BS to the jth receive antenna of the user equipment and is formulated as:

$$C_d = \sum_{i=1}^{r_o} \log_e \left(I + \frac{P_{ri}}{\sigma^2} \right) \tag{34.6}$$

$r_0 = \min(n_t, n_r)$. P_{ri} is the received power at the ith sub channel. C_d is the direct link capacity.

Case 1. When CSI is not known at transmitter, then we apply Equal transmit power allocation algorithm.

Case 2. When CSI is known at transmitter we apply Adaptive transmit power allocation.

Case 1. Equal Transmit Power Allocation
In this case, the power allocated to sub-channel i is given by

$$P_i = \frac{P}{n_t}, i = 1, 2, \ldots \ldots n_t \tag{34.7}$$

and

$$P_{ri} = \frac{\lambda_i P}{n_t} \tag{34.8}$$

$$C_d = \sum_{i=1}^{r_o} \log_e \left(I + \frac{\lambda_i P}{n_t \sigma^2} \right) \tag{34.9}$$

$$= \log_e \prod_{i=1}^{r_o} \left(I + \frac{\lambda_i P}{n_t \sigma^2} \right) \tag{34.10}$$

Case 2. Adaptive Transmit Power Allocation
In this case transmitter knows the channel state information, the transmit power is allocated to the ith transmit antenna of BS as

$$P_i = \left(\mu - \frac{\sigma^2}{\lambda_i} \right) \text{ for i} = 1, 2 \ldots .. n_t \tag{34.11}$$

μ is the mean power confined to

$$\sum_{i=1}^{r_o} P_i = P \tag{34.12}$$

The power received at the UE is given as

$$P_{ri} = \left(\lambda_i \mu - \sigma^2 \right) \tag{34.13}$$

Substituting value in equation

$$C_d = \sum_{i=1}^{r_o} \log_e \left[I + \frac{\lambda_i \mu - \sigma^2}{\sigma^2} \right] \tag{34.14}$$

$$C_d = \sum_{i=1}^{r_o} \log_e \left[I + \left(\frac{\lambda_i \mu}{\sigma^2} - 1 \right) \right] \tag{34.15}$$

Replacing 1 by I (diagonal matrix)

$$C_d = \sum_{i=1}^{r_o} \log_e \left[1 + \frac{\lambda_i \mu}{\sigma^2} - 1 \right] \tag{34.16}$$

$$C_d = \sum_{i=1}^{r_o} \log_e \left(\frac{\lambda_i \mu}{\sigma^2} \right) \tag{34.17}$$

For transmitted signal x the Expectation value for power constraint is given as,

$$E \left(xx^* \right) = P \tag{34.18}$$

The capacity C of channel for transmitting mutual information from x to y I(x,y) is given by

$$C_d = {}_{p(x):E(xx^*)=P} \ E_H \ \left\{ max I \ (x; y) \right\} \tag{34.19}$$

p(x) represents the distribution of transmitted signal x for direct link.

When the channel state Information is not known at transmitter and assumed to be known at receiver only, the channel output pair at the user equipment will be given as (Y,H)

$$C_d = \max_{p(x):tr\left(E\left(xx^*\right)\right)<P} I\left(x:Y,H\right) \qquad (34.20)$$

As per the information theory, the mutual information of the event is inversely proportional to the happing of the event $I(x,y) \alpha 1/P(x_i)$, so in order to maximize the mutual information rate from the transmitted signal x to the received signal y at the user equipment (UE), we have to decrease the probability. In order to decrease the probability we have to increase randomness or simply Entropy.

34.5 Optimal Resource Allocation

The resource allocation problem considers the Maximization of Entropy in order to maximize the information rate I(x,y). We consider following cases:

1. When provided with testable information
2. When no testable information is provided

Consider the information I about a data x that is to be transmitted from one node (BS/RN) to another node (UE). We assume this information takes values in subsets $\{X_1, X_2, X_3, \ldots \ldots \ldots \ldots \ldots X_n\}$. Considering this information has no constraints on the expectations of the functions f_k.

$$X \in \left(\sum_{i=1}^{n} X_i\right) \qquad (34.21)$$

The Expectation value of X_i is $f_k(x_1)$.
The PDF F_k can be written as

$$\sum_{i=1}^{n} P_r\left(x_i\right) f_k\left(x_i\right) = F_k \qquad (34.22)$$

Since the probabilities must sum to unity

$$\sum_{i=1}^{n} P_r\left(x_i\right) = 1 \qquad (34.23)$$

For the maximum information rate the probability distribution function can be written as:

$$P_r\left(x_i\right) = \frac{1}{Z\left(\lambda_i \ldots \ldots \ldots \ldots, \lambda_m\right)} e^{[\lambda_i f_i(x_i) + - - - - - - - - + \lambda_m f_m(x_i)]} \qquad (34.24)$$

where $Z(\lambda_i \ldots \ldots \ldots \ldots, \lambda_m)$ is the normalization constant.

If $\sum_{i=1}^{n} P_r(x_i) = 1$,

$$Z(\lambda_i \ldots \ldots \ldots, \lambda_m) = \sum_{i=1}^{n} e^{[\lambda_i f_i(x_i) + - - - - - - - + \lambda_m f_m(x_i)]} \qquad (34.25)$$

λ_m Parameters are Lagrange's multipliers whose value are determined by constraints according to following equation:

$$F_m = \frac{\partial}{\partial \lambda_m} \log Z(\lambda_i \ldots \ldots \ldots, \lambda_m) \qquad (34.26)$$

This equation does not have any closed loop solution and can be solved only by numerical methods.

When there are 'm' mutually exclusive happing events, and for no reason we favor any one of the event over the others. This condition will lead to the maximum possible value of information or entropy. Since we are having 'm' exclusive happing events, we distribute N quanta of probability among the 'm' possibilities. Let

$$p_i = \frac{n_i}{N} \qquad (34.27)$$

p_i is the probability of the ith event, while n_i is the number of quanta that were assigned to ith event.

Using multinomial distribution,

$$P_r(P) = W m^{-N} \qquad (34.28)$$

W is the weighted matrix and is known as multiplicity of the outcome and is given as

$$W = \frac{N!}{n_1! n_2! \ldots \ldots \ldots n_m!} \qquad (34.29)$$

The most probable result is the one which maximizes W. In order to maximize W, we maximize any of the monotonic increasing function W

$$\frac{1}{N} \log W = \frac{1}{N} \log \frac{N!}{n_1! n_2! \ldots \ldots n_m!} \qquad (34.30)$$

$$= \frac{1}{N} \log \frac{N!}{(N p_1)! (N p_2)! \ldots \ldots \ldots (N p_m)!} \qquad (34.31)$$

$$\frac{1}{N} \left(\log N! - \sum_{i=1}^{m} \log (N p_i)! \right) \qquad (34.32)$$

Taking limit N→infinity (Striling approximation)

$$\lim_{N \to infinity} \left(\frac{1}{N} \log W \right) = \lim_{N \to infinity} \frac{1}{N} \left(N \log N - \sum_{i=1}^{m} N p_i \log (N p_i) \right)$$
(34.33)

$$= \lim_{N \to infinity} \log N - \sum_{i=1}^{m} p_i \log (N p_i)$$
(34.34)

$$\lim_{N \to infinity} \log N - \log N \sum_{i=1}^{m} p_i - \sum_{i=1}^{m} p_i \log p_i$$
(34.35)

$$= \lim_{N \to infinity} \left(1 - \sum_{i=1}^{m} p_i \right) \log N - \sum_{i=1}^{m} p_i \log p_i$$
(34.36)

$$= -\sum_{i=1}^{m} p_i \log p_i$$
(34.37)

$$= \sum_{i=1}^{m} p_i \frac{1}{\log p_i}$$
(34.38)

$$= H(P)$$
(34.39)

This is the maximum achievable entropy Shannon Entropy. Resource allocation on direct link is formulated as

$$R_d = \frac{1}{2} I [X_d]$$
(34.40)

$$= \frac{1}{2} \left[W_d C_d (P_{xi}) \right.$$
(34.41)

$$R_d = \frac{1}{2} \left[\frac{1}{N} \log W_d C_d (P_{xi}) \right]$$
(34.42)

$$\frac{1}{2} \left[\frac{1}{N} \log \frac{N!}{N (p_1)! + N (p_2)! - - - - N (p_m)!} \right] . C_d (P_{xi})$$
(34.43)

$$= \frac{1}{2} [C_d (P_{xi})] . \frac{1}{N} \log \left(N! - \sum_{i=1}^{m} \log (N p_i)! \right)$$
(34.44)

Taking N→infinity (Sterling approximation)

$$\frac{1}{2}C_d\,(P_{xi})\,\text{limit}\,(N \rightarrow \text{infinity})\left(1 - \sum_{i=1}^{m} p_i\right)logN - \sum_{i=1}^{m} p_i logp_i$$

$$(34.45)$$

$$\frac{1}{2}C\,(P_{xi})\sum_{i=1}^{m} p_i \frac{1}{logp_i} \qquad (34.46)$$

$$\frac{1}{2}C_d\,(P_{xi})\,H(p) \qquad (34.47)$$

This is the expression for direct link capacity in absence of relay nodes. After the deployment of RNs in system model, we consider two links; relay and access link. Resource allocation on these links is formulated as the following optimization problem and needs to be searched for non-convex solutions in order to maximize the capacity of the whole contour via the kth RN:

$$R_m = \min\{C_{RL}, C_{AL,}\} \qquad (34.48)$$

where R_m is the total channel efficiency, C_{RL} and $C_{AL,}$ are the channel capacity of relay and access link respectively. Thus the overall end-to end rate can be established using following equation:

$$\max_{\chi} \sum_{i=1}^{m} R_m \qquad (34.49)$$

The variable set χ will lead ads to the exponential growth of the problem size leading to system complexity. The solution lies in maximizing the variable set χ using Lagrange's dual problem as,

$$\max_{\chi} f\,(\lambda)$$

subject to $\lambda \geq 0$, where $\lambda = [\lambda_{1,k}, \lambda_{2,k}, \ldots \quad \ldots \quad \ldots \quad \ldots \, . \, \lambda_{m,k}]$ denotes the Lagrange multiplier vector subject to following constraints:

$$t_1 + t_2 = t,\, p_{RL} \leq P_b,\, p_{AL} \leq P_r,\, p_{RL} \geq 0 \, and \, p_{AL} \geq 0$$

where p_{RL}, p_{AL} are the power allocation coefficients on relay and access link respectively, P_b and P_r are power at BS and RN respectively.

Substituting, Eq. (34.48) in Eq. (34.49)

$$\max_{\chi} \sum_{i=1}^{m} \{C_{RL} = C_{AL,}\} \qquad (34.50)$$

To optimize the capacity, the arguments in min (.) of Eq. (34.48) must be equal

$$C_{RL} = C_{AL},$$

Thus Eq. (34.50) can be written as

$$\max_{\chi} \sum_{i=1}^{m} \sum_{k=1}^{3} \frac{1}{2} \left\{ C_{RL,k\left(\frac{1}{v_m}\right)} + C_{AL,k\left(\frac{1}{v_m}\right)} \right\} \tag{34.51}$$

The Lagrangian cost function L for the given optimization problem can be formulated as under

$$L = T_1 \sum_{i=1}^{m} \log_2 \left(1 + \frac{P_i \, p_{RL} \sigma_i^2}{\sigma_n^2} \right) + \mu' \left(P_b - \sum_{i=1}^{m} p_i \, p_{RL} \right)$$

$$+ T_2 \sum_{i=1}^{m} \log_2 \left(1 + \frac{P_i \, p_{AL} \sigma_i^2}{\sigma_n^2} \right) + \rho \left(P_r - \sum_{i=1}^{m} p_i \, p_{AL} \right) \tag{34.52}$$

where μ'' *and* ρ are the Lagrangian multipliers associated with relay and access link respectively.

Strong duality of Eq. (34.52) implies the following condition and is solved using KKT condition:

$$\sum_{i=1}^{m} T_1 \log_2 \left(1 + \frac{P_i \, p_{RL} \sigma_i^2}{\sigma_n^2} \right) + T_2 \sum_{i=1}^{m} \log_2 \left(1 + \frac{P_i \, p_{AL} \sigma_i^2}{\sigma_n^2} \right)$$

$$= \sum_{i=1}^{m} \sum_{k=1}^{3} [(\mu' P_i \, (p_{RL} - P_b) \, (\rho P_i \, (p_{AL} - P_r)] \tag{34.53}$$

After solving Eq. (34.53) using KKT we get following value for power allocation coefficients on both relay and access link,

$$p_{RL} = \frac{\sum_{i=1}^{m} \sum_{k=1}^{3} \left[\left(P_i \mu' - \frac{\sigma_n^2}{\sigma_i^2} \right) \right]}{\sum_{i=1}^{m} \sum_{k=1}^{3} (P_b)} \tag{34.54}$$

$$p_{AL} = \frac{\sum_{i=1}^{m} \sum_{k=1}^{3} \left[\left(P_i \rho - \frac{\sigma_n^2}{\sigma_i^2} \right) \right]}{\sum_{i=1}^{m} \sum_{k=1}^{3} (P_r)} \tag{34.55}$$

The power allocated to the ith user is directly dependent on user defined function σ_i^2. Increasing the σ_i will increase the power allocated to the ith user. Thus the resulting power allocation will result in the water filling phenomenon subject to the constraint $p_{RL} \leq P_b, p_{AL} \leq P_r$.

34.6 Results and Discussions

In this section the performance of MIMO relay networks is evaluated in terms of
channel capacity and SINR using analytical framework discussed in Sect. 34.3.
Three possible positions for RN deployment in cell is considered ($k = 1, 2, 3$). Direct
link is assumed to be in absence of RNs. The relay and access links at predefined
positions of k are modeled using both MIMO and SISO channels and comparisons
are drawn out.

Figure 34.2 shows the variation of ergodic capacity in Mbps of relay link in
accordance with SINR (dB) values. Figure reveals that there is no significant
increase in capacity. Capacity starts increasing at higher SINRs at all positions of k.
MIMO channel capacity at all k positions is greater than SISO capacity and results
in water filling phenomenon. For $k = 3$ (MIMO) there is 700% increase in capacity
as compared to direct link.

Figure 34.3 shows the variation of ergodic capacity in Mbps of access link
in accordance with SINR (dB) values. Access link capacity shows significant
improvement as the SINR increases from 2 dB to 20 dB. The access link quality
does not get detreated at lower SINR values. This enables the access link to serve
the cell edge users, which experience low SINR. There is an overall 450% increase
in capacity as SINR increases from 2 dB to 20 dB.

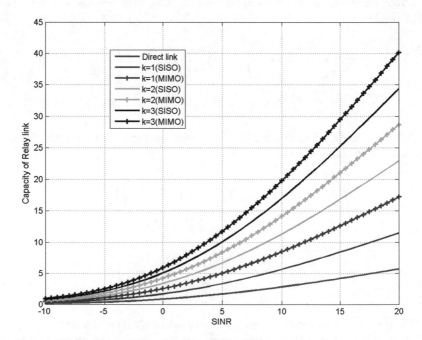

Fig. 34.2 Ergodic capacity in Mbps of relay vs. SINR (dB)

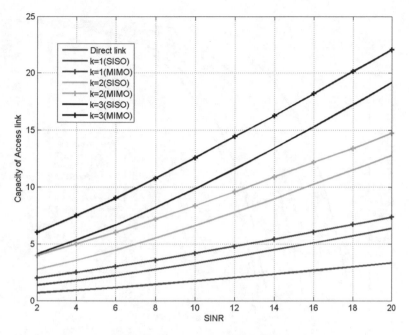

Fig. 34.3 Ergodic capacity in Mbps of access link vs. SINR (dB)

Figure 34.4 shows variation of mean relay link SINR vs. CDF. At fifth percentile CDF level for k = 3 (MIMO) the SINR is almost 5 dB as compared to 1 dB for direct link. Thus overall 400% increase in SINR is achieved.

Figure 34.5 shows the variation of mean access link SINR vs. CDF of end-to-end rate. Again at fifth percentile CDF level the direct link SINR is almost 1 dB. With relay deployment at predefined positions of k, the SINR of the access link increases significantly. At k = 3 (MIMO) for the fifth percentile CDF level the SINR increases to 7 dB. Thus there is almost 600% increase in SINR for the cell edge users.

Figure 34.6 shows the link rate of relay and access link vs. CDF. At fifth percentile CDF level, the link rate due to direct link is negligible. Thus there is no connectivity for cell edge users due to power limiting capacity of base stations. When RN is deployed at the predefined positions of k, link rate shows improvement at lower percentile level of CDF. The figure reveals that at higher percentile CDF levels (>90%), the MIMO relay capacity falls as compared to SISO relay capacity. Thus MIMO introduces a significant improvement in link rate for cell edge users where non line of sight communication prevails.

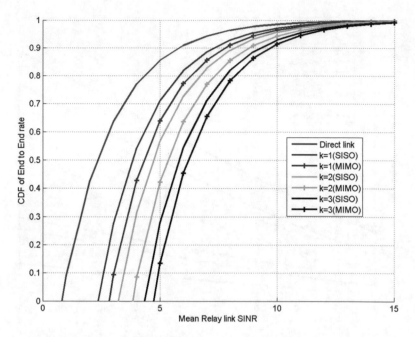

Fig. 34.4 Mean relay link SINR vs. CDF of End-to-End rate

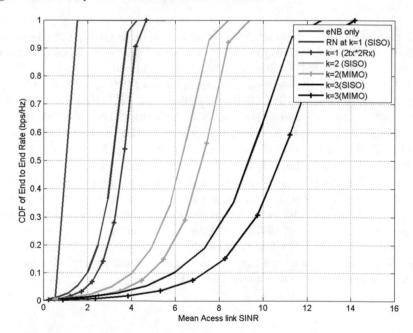

Fig. 34.5 Mean access link SINR vs. CDF of End-to-End rate

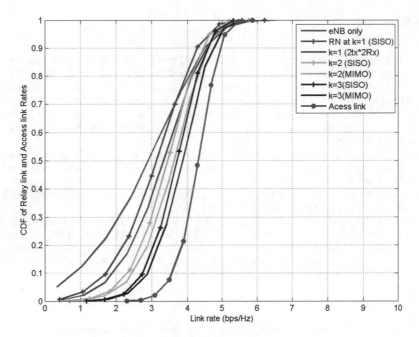

Fig. 34.6 Link rate vs. CDF of relay and access link

34.7   Conclusion

In this chapter resource allocation problem of MIMO based cooperative relay networks for multimedia delivery content has been described. The resource allocation for millimeter meter wave based 5G based multimedia communication with specific applications to IOT has also been considered. The proposed model provides a convenient and accurate approach to model, generate and transmit video traffic over the 5G driven IOT networks. The proposed scheme can be considered for practical solutions to solve the dynamic resource allocation challenge for multimedia delivery contents in future networks due to its ability to provide accurate results for the most common video codecs. This can be beneficial especially for networks with limited resources like WiMAX and LTE besides 5G networks. The proposed method also provides quality solution for sum rate maximization in MIMO relay networks. fifth percentile CDF level was chosen for cell edge users to reflect the performance of these users from coverage and connectivity prospective. The analytical framework for optimal solution was verified using simulation results performed on Matlab software. The results confirmed the effectiveness of proposed method in terms of capacity, SINR and link rate with much higher computational gains.

References

1. J. Cai, X. Shen, J. Mark, A. Alfa, Semi-distributed user relaying algorithm for amplify-and-forward wireless relay networks, IEEETrans. Wireless Commun. 7 (4) (2008) 1348–1357.
2. B. Saleh, O. Bulakci, J. Hamalainen, S. Redana, B. Raaf, Analysis of the impact of site planning on the performance of relay deployments, IEEE Trans. Veh. Technol. 61 (7) (2012) 3139–3150.
3. Mattia Minelli, Maode Ma, Marceau Coupechoux, Jean-Marc Kelif, Marc Sigelle, Philippe Godlewski, Optimal relay placement in cellular networks, IEEE Trans.WirelessCommun. 13 (2) (2014) 998-1008.
4. M. H. Islam, Z. Dziong, K. Sohraby, M. F. Daneshmand, R. Jana, Capacity-optimal relay and base station placement in wireless networks, in: Proceedings of 2012 IEEE Int. Conf. Inf. Netw. 1-3 February 2012.
5. W. Guo and T.O Farrell, Relay deployment in cellular networks: planning and optimization, IEEE J. Sel.AreasCommun. 31 (8) (2013) 1597-1606.
6. Qian Li, Rose Qingyang Hu, Yi Qian, Geng Wu, Intracell Cooperation and resource allocation in a heterogeneous network with relays, IEEE Trans. Veh. Technol. 62 (4) (2013) 1770-1784.
7. Paul Arnold, Veselin Rakocevic, Oscar Ramos, Joachim Habermann, Algorithms for adaptive radio resource management in relay-assisted LTE-A networks, in: Proceedings of 77th IEEE Vehicular Technology Conference, 2-5 June 2013, pp. 1-5.
8. Xiaoxia Zhang, Xuemin Sherman Shen, Liang-Liang Xie, Joint subcarrier and power allocation for cooperative communications in LTE-A networks, IEEE Trans.WirelessCommun. 13 (2) (2014) 658-668.
9. S. H. Song, Ali F. Almutairi, K. B. Letaief, Outage-capacity based adaptive relaying in LTE-A networks, IEEE Trans.WirelessCommun. 12 (9) (2013) 4778-4787.
10. HonghaoJu, Ben Liang, Jiandong Li, Xiaoniu Yang, Dynamic joint resource optimization for LTE-A relay networks, IEEE Trans.WirelessCommun. 12 (11) (2013) 5668-5678.
11. Liu, Y. Liu, H. Xiang, W. Luo, Polite water-filling for weighted sum-rate maximization in MIMO B-MAC networks under multiple linear constraints, IEEE Trans. Signal Process. 60 (2) (2012) 834–847.
12. Monowar Hasan, Ekram Hossain, Dong In Kim, Resource allocation under channel uncertainties for relay-aided device-to-device communication underlaying LTE-A cellular networks, IEEE Trans. Wireless Commun. 13 (4) (2014) 2322-2338.
13. Javaid A Sheikh, Mehboobul Amin, SA Parah, G.M Bhat, "Towards Green Capacity in Massive MIMO based 4G LTE-A cell using Beam-forming Vector based Sectored Relay Planning" Wireless Personal Communication, Springer DOI: 10.1007/s11277-017-4809-8.
14. Javaid A Sheikh, Mehboobul Amin, SA Parah, G.M Bhat, "Impact of Antenna and Beam selection based Sectored Relay Planning on the performance evaluation of 4G LTE-A tri-sectored cell" Digital Communication Networks, Elsevier, https://doi.org/10.1016/j.dcan.2017.08.006.
15. K.Naidu, R. B.Battula Swift Resource Allocation in Wireless Networks, IEEE Transactions on Vehicular Technology Volume: 67, Issue: 7, July 2018.
16. Alia Asheralieva; Tony Q. S. Quek; Dusit Niyato An Asymmetric Evolutionary Bayesian Coalition Formation Game for Distributed Resource Sharing in a Multi-Cell Device tp Device Enabled Cellular Network, IEEE Transactions on Wireless Communications 2, Volume: 17, Issue: 6, 208
17. Hongliang Zhang; Lingyang Song; Ying Jun Zhang "Load Balancing for 5G Ultra-Dense Networks Using Device- to- Device Communications IEEE Transactions on Wireless Communications Year: 2018, Volume: 17, Issue: 6 Page s: 4039 – 4050
18. Jiaheng Wang; Yongming Huang; Shi Jin; Robert Schober; Xiaohu You; Chunming Zhao "Resource Management for Device-to-Device Communication: A Physical Layer Security Perspective" IEEE Journal on Selected Areas in Communications Year: 2018, Volume: 36, Issue: 4 Page s: 946 – 960

19. Resource allocation for Device-to-Device Communications Underlaying Heterogeneous Cellular Networks Using Coalitional Games Yali Chen; Bo Ai; Yong Niu; Ke Guan; Zhu Han IEEE Transactions on Wireless Communications Year: 2018, Volume: 17, Issue: Page s: 4163 – 4176
20. Bushra Ismaiel; Mehran Abolhasan; Wei Ni; David Smith; Daniel Franklin; Abbas Jamalipour, "Analysis of Effective Capacity and Throughput of Polling-Based Device –to-Device Networks", IEEE Transactions on Vehicular Technology Year: 2018, Volume: 67, Issue: 9

Chapter 35
Supercomputing with an Efficient Task Scheduler as an Infrastructure for Big Multimedia Processing

Hamid Reza Boveiri

35.1 Introduction

Task-scheduling optimization plays an essential role for different computational environments such as multiprocessor systems in which a number of processing elements are coupled, and perform as a whole high-performance supercomputer [1]. In such systems, each application program is decomposed into smaller and maybe dependent subprograms named tasks. Some tasks need the data generated by other tasks so that there will be precedence constraints among them. On this basis, each application program can be formulated as a Directed Acyclic Graph (DAG) so-called task graph. Considering a task graph, nodes indicate tasks, and edges are precedence constraints among them. There are two kinds of scheduling based on the nature of the problem at hand; in static scheduling, all the parameters needed such as required-execution-times of tasks, communication-costs, and precedence-constraints are available beforehand since they would be produced during the program's compiling step. The main objective is to derive an appropriate topological order of tasks from the given task-graph, and assign them to a number of computational elements (here the processors) respecting the tasks' precedence constraints in such a way that some criteria such as overall finish-time of the given application program, or total energy consumption by processors is minimized [2, 3]. This is an NP-hard problem from the time complexity perspective so that the exact methods may not be able to respond in a predefined and restricted time budget, especially for large scale inputted samples [4].

One real-world state-of-the-art example of the demanding areas is indeed big data processing that needs a huge amount of computational capacity, and multimedia is

H. R. Boveiri (✉)
Sama Technical and Vocational Training College, Islamic Azad University, Shoushtar Branch, Shoushtar, Iran
e-mail: boveiri@samashoushtar.ac.ir; boveiri@ieee.org

© Springer Nature Switzerland AG 2019
A. K. Singh, A. Mohan (eds.), *Handbook of Multimedia Information Security: Techniques and Applications*, https://doi.org/10.1007/978-3-030-15887-3_35

responsible for more than 80% of the big data all over the world. Another state-of-the-art computational-hungry application is related to the development of deep learning or deep neural networks, on the other words, which is the predominant technology to process and analyze multimedia content, where hundreds to thousands staked neural layers consume billions of operations, and cannot be operational unless providing efficient high-performance supercomputing environments. Some other real-world applications requiring such a high-performance supercomputer infrastructure can be enumerated as biomedicine and bioinformatics [5, 6], space and urbane surveillance and smart city [7–9], to mention a few.

Most of conventional task scheduling methods which are applicable for such kinds of architectures are based on the list-scheduling technique [10] in which a list of ready tasks so-called ready-list is created. Then, at each step, a task with the most priority in the ready-list is selected and assigned to the processor that allows the Earliest Start Time (EST), until all the tasks in the task-graph are scheduled and assigned. On this basis, the achieved makespan or finish-time is dominated by which order of tasks to be selected. Although, there are a number of priority measurements used as heuristics to navigate search process in the problem's space, all of them are biased to some sorts of inputted samples [11]. On the other hand, although there are a large number of heuristic approaches proposed for this problem (that most are bios to some kinds of samples, as mentioned), the application of metaheuristics to this problem has not been attended a lot. The Author was the first who proposed an Ant Colony Optimization (ACO) [12–15], and Cellular Learning Automata (CLA)-based [16, 17] approaches to tackle this problem; nevertheless, we believe the application of metaheuristics to this problem should be further investigated according to the no free lunch theorem [18]. In other words, based on this renown and accepted theorem in the community, there may be other metaheuristics, though week in other applications, demonstrating significant results and performance in this specific problem, and this deserves much consideration.

Cuckoo Optimization Algorithm (COA) is a novel swarm-intelligence-based metaheuristic first introduced by Rajabioun in 2011 [19]. It is inspired from the exotic parasite-brooding behavior of a bird family called cuckoo, and shows an outstanding potential to solve some sorts of theoretical and practical optimization problems [20]. In this paper, an enhanced version of COA with two novelties and improvements in the egg-laying phase is proposed to cope with the static task-graph scheduling problem in multiprocessor supercomputing environments. This Enhanced COA (named E-COA) is equipped with an adaptive coefficient tuning strategy, and an efficient non-stochastic egg-laying mechanism, which significantly improve the local and global search potentiality of the basic COA. we believe that the most important contributions of this study are as follows: (1) Static task-scheduling problem in homogeneous multiprocessor supercomputing environments is formulated in a comprehensive way using an easy-to-understand taxonomy, notations and definitions. (2) For the first time, an efficient and novel high-performance approach based on an enhanced version of COA has been proposed to tackle the problem, which has a significant potentiality in terms of performance. (3) A novel non-stochastic egg-laying mechanism along with an adaptive coefficient tuning strategy is applied to the COA which can be exploited as an efficient local search for a large number of other metaheuristic algorithms.

The rest of the paper is organized as follows. The following Section is devoted to the literature review and related works. Problem formulation of task scheduling problem in multiprocessor supercomputing environment is explained in Sect. 35.3. Section 35.4 introduces the proposed approach and details and philosophies behind it. Sections 35.5 and 35.6 are devoted to the implementation details and experimental results, respectively. Finally, the paper is concluded in the last Section.

35.1.1 Highlights and Contributions

Task-scheduling optimization plays an essential role for different computational environments such as multiprocessor system in which a number of processing elements are coupled, and perform as a whole high-performance supercomputer. One real-world state-of-the-art example of the demanding areas is indeed big data processing that needs a huge amount of computational capacity, and multimedia is responsible for 80% of the big data all over the world [21]. Worse mentioning that the proliferation of the Internet and user-generated content, and the growing prevalence of cameras, mobile phones, and social media all are contributing factors to worsen the situation, and to increasingly elevate the necessity of high-performance supercomputing environments as the underlying infrastructure to elicit hidden knowledge from row multimedia data [22]. Another state-of-the-art computational-hungry application is related to the development of deep learning or deep neural networks, on the other words, which is the predominant technology to process analyze multimedia content, where hundreds to thousands staked neural layers consume billions of operations, and cannot be operational unless providing efficient high-performance supercomputing environments [23].

In this paper, an enhanced version of COA with two novelties and improvements in the egg-laying phase is proposed to cope with the static task-graph scheduling problem in multiprocessor environments. This Enhanced COA (named E-COA) is equipped with an adaptive coefficient tuning strategy, and an efficient non-stochastic egg-laying mechanism, which significantly improve the local and global search potentiality of the basic COA. We believe that the most important contributions of this study are as followings: (1) Static task-scheduling problem in homogeneous multiprocessor supercomputing environments is formulated in a comprehensive way using an easy-to-understand taxonomy, notations and definitions. (2) For the first time, an efficient and novel high-performance approach based on an enhanced version of COA has been proposed to tackle the problem, which has a significant potentiality in terms of performance. (3) A novel non-stochastic egg-laying mechanism along with an adaptive coefficient tuning strategy is applied to the COA which can be exploited as an efficient local search for a large number of other metaheuristic algorithms.

35.2 Related Works

Optimized task scheduling is a fundamental factor to achieve high-performance in different computational environments. Based on the different natures of different architectures given for task scheduling, different objectives, definitions, notations and formulations can be considered.

One of the widest spread, and most important groups of high-performance environments is homogeneous multiprocessor systems. In such architectures, all the processing elements have an identical processing power, and are connected together using a very fast data bus with huge bandwidth also referred to as tightly coupled systems. All the processing nodes in the system work coordinately as a whole, and seem to be one system with high processing capability and throughput. Most the conventional approaches reported in the literature to cope with the task scheduling problem in such environments, e.g. HLFET[1] [24], ISH[2] [25], CLANS[3] [26], LAST[4] [27], ETF[5] [28], DLS[6] [29], and MCP[7] [30], are working based on the list-scheduling method in which a set of ready tasks is created as a ready-list in each iteration. The ready tasks are either those without any parents or without any unscheduled ones. In each iteration, the task with the most priority in the ready-list is chosen to be allocated to that computational unit (processor) allowing the Earliest Start Time (EST), until all the tasks in the task-graph are scheduled. References [1, 2, 4, 10] are of the most complete reviews on these systems and the corresponding task scheduling problem.

It should be emphasized that in the realm of scheduling, each category has its own review, taxonomy, definition, datasets and literature varying based on the different natures of the structure and architecture in-use, and the objectives to be satisfied. That is, a certain heuristic or meta-heuristic approach proposed for one specific kind of scheduling problem cannot be applied for the others but with some/huge number of modifications in the encoding/decoding mechanism, input datasets and the utilized algorithm. In addition, an approach efficient for one certain scheduling problem is not necessarily as so for the others based on the no free lunch theorem [18], and we need a comprehensive study and various sets of experiments to proof that. On this basis, each comparison study can be made on its own category; for example, we are not able to compare an COA-based approach introduced for job-shop scheduling, or for task scheduling in smart grid environment with our approach proposed for homogeneous multiprocessor supercomputing system.

---

[1] Highest Level First with Estimated Time.

[2] Insertion Scheduling Heuristic.

[3] Which uses the cluster-like CLANs to partition the task graph.

[4] Localized Allocation of Static Tasks.

[5] Earliest Time First.

[6] Dynamic Level Scheduling.

[7] Modified Critical Path.

35.3   Problem Formulation

In this section, problem formulation for task scheduling problem in multiprocessor environment will be explained. A directed acyclic graph $G = \{N, E, W, C\}$ called task-graph is considered as a model to formulate a parallel application program executed on a multiprocessor supercomputing environment, where

$$N = \{n_1, n_2, \ldots, n_n\},$$
$$E = \left\{(n_i, n_j) \mid n_i, n_j \in N\right\},$$
$$W = \{w_1, w_2, \ldots, w_n\},$$
$$C = \left\{c(n_i, n_j) \mid (n_i, n_j) \in E\right\},$$

in which N is a set of nodes, E is a set of edges, W is the set of the weights of the nodes, C is the set of the weights of the edges, and n is the number of the nodes in the task-graph.

Figure 35.1 shows a sample task-graph for a real application program comprised of nine different tasks. In such a graph, nodes are indicating tasks to be executed on the processors of system, and edges specify precedence constraints among tasks. Actually, existence of each edge such as $(n_i, n_j) \in \mathbf{E}$ demonstrates that the task n_i must be finished before the task n_j can be started. Accordingly, n_i is called a parent, and n_j is called a child. Nodes without any parents and nodes without any children are called "entry nodes" and "exit nodes", respectively. Also there are nodes' weights such as w_i indicating the necessary execution-time for the task n_i, and edges' weights such as $c(n_i, n_j)$ specifying the required time for data transmission from task n_i to the task n_j so-called communication costs. If a pair of tasks e.g. n_i and n_j are executed on a same processor e.g. on the processor p_m, the communication cost can be neglected, and considered as zero between them because the data generated by n_i, and needed by n_j, is available in the local memory of p_m; hence, the necessity of data transfer between the processors is obviated.

Execution times of the tasks, communication costs, and precedence constraints among them are generated during the program compiling-stage. Tasks is distributed over the predefined m available processors considering their precedence so that the overall finish-time (or makespan) of the tasks could be minimized.

Most of the related approaches to static scheduling problem use list-scheduling as the undelaying technique to find optimum task-order to assign to the processors. The philosophy behind list-scheduling techniques is to make a ready-list by gathering the ready tasks in the current iteration. Ready tasks are the ones without any parent or without any unscheduled parent. In continuum, a priority measure is considered to specify the priority of each ready task where the most priority task in the ready list should be chosen, removed, and assigned to the processor providing the earliest-start-time (EST). The ready-list should be updated repeatedly, until all the tasks in the task-graph are scheduled.

It should be noted if all the predecessors (parents) of a task e.g. n_i were executed on the same processor e.g. p_j, $EST(n_i, p_j)$, i.e. the earliest-start-time, would be

Fig. 35.1 The task graph of a
program with nine tasks
inside [31]

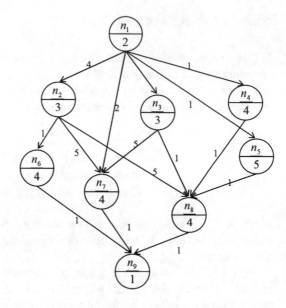

$Avail(p_j)$, that is, the earliest time at which p_j is available to execute the next task; in other respects, the earliest-start-time of the task n_i on the processor p_j should be computed using

$$EST\left(n_i, p_j\right) = \begin{cases} 0, & if\ n_i = entery - node \\ \max_{n_k \in Parent(n_i)} \begin{cases} (AFT\left(n_k\right)), & if\ processor\left(n_k\right) = p_j \\ \left(AFT\left(n_k\right) + c\left(n_k, n_i\right)\right), & else \end{cases} \end{cases}$$
(35.1)

where $AFT(n_k) = AST(n_k) + w_k$ is the actual finish-time of the task n_k, and $Parents(n_i)$ is the set of all the parents of n_i, $AST(n_k)$ is the actual start-time of the task n_k computed using (35.2).

$$AST\ (n_k) = \min_{j=1}^{m}\left(\max\left(Avail\left(p_j\right), EST\left(n_k, p_j\right)\right)\right)$$
(35.2)

At last, the total finish-time of the given application program, we want to execute in parallel, can be computed using (35.3).

$$makespan = \max_{i=1}^{n}\left(FT\left(n_i\right)\right)$$
(35.3)

Let's suppose a given task-graph with n nodes represented via its adjacency matrix, an efficient implementation of the EST method to map all the n tasks over a given m identical processors is a member of O(mn^2), from the time-complexity prespective [32]. A comprehensive list of the aforementioned notations applied to

Table 35.1 A comprehensive list of the notations applied to formulate the task-graph scheduling in multiprocessor supercomputing environments

Symbol	Description
$G = (N, E, W, C)$	A given task graph
$N = \{n_1, n_2, \ldots, n_n\}$	Set of tasks in the task graph
$E = \{(n_i, n_j) \mid n_i, n_j \in N\}$	Set of edges (precedence constraints) among tasks in the task graph
$W = \{w_1, w_2, \ldots, w_n\}$	Set of the required execution times of the tasks
$C = \{c(n_i, n_j) \mid (n_i, n_j) \in E)$	Set of the communication costs (delays) among tasks in the task graph
n	The number of tasks in the task graph
entry-node	A node without any parents
exit-node	A node without any children
$P = \{p_1, p_2, \ldots, p_m\}$	The set of the processors in the system
m	The number of processors in the system
Ready-List[ ]	Current set of the tasks ready to be scheduled considering precedence constraints among tasks
Avail (p_m)	The earliest time when the processor p_m is ready to execute the next task
AFT (n_k)	The actual finish-time of task n_k
AST (n_k)	The actual start-time of task n_k
EST $(n_i, C_{a,b})$	The earliest start-time of task n_i on the processor p_m
Parents(n_i)	Set of all the parents of n_i
Children(n_i)	Set of all the children of n_i
Processor (n_k)	A function that returns the processor no. on which task n_k is executed
makespan	The total finish time of a parallel program, or scheduling length

formulate and model the task-graph scheduling on multiprocessor supercomputing environment is summarized in Table 35.1.

35.4 The Proposed Approach

35.4.1 Cuckoo Optimization Algorithm (COA)

Cuckoo Optimization Algorithm (COA) is a swarm-intelligence-based metaheuristic first introduced by Rajabioun [19] which is inspired from the exotic lifestyle of a bird family called the cuckoo. Specific egg-laying and breeding characteristics of cuckoos called parasite-brooding is the basis of constituting this novel optimization algorithm. Each solution vector in the COA is represented by a "habitat" which is the current location of either a mature cuckoo in the society or an individual egg. Mature cuckoos lay their eggs in some other birds' nests by mimicking their eggs' color, pattern and size. If these eggs cannot be recognized and killed by the host birds, they grow and become a mature cuckoo, too. The aforementioned parasite-brooding behavior along with the migration of societies (groups) of cuckoos hopefully lead them to converge and find the best location for breeding and reproduction. Actually, these the most profitable locations supposed to be the global optima of the given objective function of the problem under the investigation. Although the COA has revealed substantial potentiality in some sorts of applications which leads gaining an increasing popularity in the past few years, it has not been studied and applied a lot yet.

The most important reason, in our mind, is that the description of the basic COA algorithm and its associated flowchart and pseudo-code in the proposing manuscript (i.e. Ref. [19]) are very obscure and confusing so that even we could not implement it without the help of the corresponding Author, Mr. Ramin Rajabioun. Anyway, some applications can be numerated as multi-objective task scheduling in heterogeneous systems [33], load balancing in transshipment terminal [34], cancer classification [35], and prediction of blast-induced ground vibration [36].

Figure 35.2 shows the flowchart of the basic cuckoo optimization algorithm (COA). At the first step, the COA generates a randomly distributed initial population of N_{pop} solutions, where N_{pop} denotes the size of population. In COA, each solution of the given problem is represented by a "habitat vector" e.g. $H_i = [x_{i,1}, x_{i,2}, \ldots, x_{i,Nvar}]^T$, which indicates the location of either a mature cuckoo or an individual egg, where each $x_{i,j}$ is an optimization parameter (decision variable) for the solution H_i, N_{var} is the total number of optimization parameters (i.e. the dimension of each solution vector), and T denotes as vector transposition. In this way, the algorithm starts with a candidate habitat matrix with the size of $N_{pop} \times N_{var}$. Then, the desirability of each randomly generated habitat is calculated using a corresponding fitness function. The fitness function can be shown by f so that $f_i = f(H_i) = f(x_{i,1}, x_{i,2}, \ldots, x_{i,Nvar})$ is the desirability (fitness value) of the i-th habitat. If the minimization is to be under the consideration, the lower fitness value is achieved, the better solution is obtained.

After initialization, the population of the habitats (solutions) is subjected to some repeated cycles, $iter = 1, 2, \ldots, iter_{max}$, of the search process. In each iteration, firstly, a randomly-produced number of eggs ($Negg_i, i = 1, 2, \ldots, N_{pop}$) is supposed for each initial cuckoo's habitat. In the nature, each cuckoo lays from 5 to 20 eggs, which are suitable as the upper and lower bounds of egg-dedication to each cuckoo for most of the problems. Another habit of real cuckoos is that they lay eggs within a limited distance from their habitats called Egg Laying Radius (ELR). In an optimization problem with upper and lower bound as x_{max} and x_{min} for all the decision variables, respectively, each cuckoo has an ELR which is proportional to the total number of eggs laid by all the cuckoos, the number of current cuckoo's eggs, and also the difference between x_{max} and x_{min}. On this basis, the ELR for each cuckoo to lay her eggs is defined as

$$ELR_i = \alpha \times \frac{Negg_i}{Total\ number\ of\ eggs} \times (x_{max} - x_{min}), \tag{35.4}$$

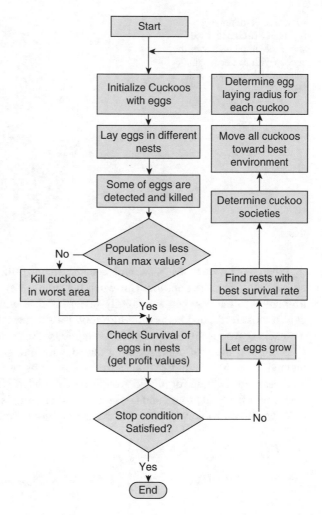

Fig. 35.2 The flowchart of the basic COA [19]

where $Negg_i$ is the number of eggs laid by the i-th cuckoo, and α is the egg-laying coefficient, a real value constant supposed to tune the maximum value of ELR.

In this way, each cuckoo starts laying eggs randomly in some other host bird's nests within her ELR. Figure 35.3 gives a clear view of this concept. After all the cuckoos' eggs are laid, some of them that are less similar to host birds' eggs are detected by the hosts, and are thrown out of the nest; therefore, $p\%$ of all the eggs (usually 10%) with less profit values will be killed after egg-laying process. Obviously, these eggs had no chance to grow and contribute to the society. Rest of the eggs grow, and are considered as mature cuckoos i.e. their habitats are included in the habitats' set to be selected for the next iterations. In addition, another interesting point about laying eggs by cuckoos is that only one egg in a nest has the chance to grow. On this basis, we check all the eggs' locations, and those eggs in the same locations (with an epsilon tolerance) will be killed except one on them.

Fig. 35.3 Random egg
laying in ELR, central red
star is the initial habitat of the
cuckoo with five eggs; pink
stars are the eggs in new nests
[19]

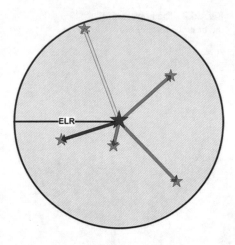

When young cuckoos grow and become mature, they live in their own area
and society for some duration. But when the time for egg-laying approaches, they
immigrate to the new and supposedly better habitats with more similarity of their
eggs to host birds, and also with more food for the new chicks. On this basis, after
the cuckoo groups are formed in different areas, the society with best profit value
is selected as the goal point for other cuckoos to immigrate. A k-means clustering
method is used (a k ranging from 3 to 5 seems to be sufficient in the simulations),
and mean profit value for all the groups are calculated. The maximum mean profit
determines the goal group, and consequently that group's best habitat (H_{best}) is the
new destination habitat for all the cuckoos to migrate using (35.5).

$$H_{i.j}^{new} = H_{i.j}^{old} + F \times \text{rand}(0.1)$$

$$\times \left(H_{best.j} - H_{i.j}^{old} \right) \mid i = 1, 2, \ldots, N_{pop} \; and \; j = 1, 2, \ldots, N_{var}$$

$$(35.5)$$

where F is the migration coefficient, and *rand* $(0, 1)$ generates random number in
the range of $[0, 1]$. As it is shown in Fig. 35.4, it is worth mentioning that cuckoos
do not fly all the way to the destination habitat when they move toward the goal
point, but they only fly a part of the way (λ) and also with some deviation (φ). A λ
randomly selected in range of $(0, 1)$, and φ generated randomly in range of $(-\pi/6, +\pi/6)$ are introduced suitable for good convergence in the basic COA [19]; therefore,
the migration coefficient (F) should be tuned up accordingly.

Fig. 35.4 The immigration of cuckoos in groups toward the globally best habitat [19]

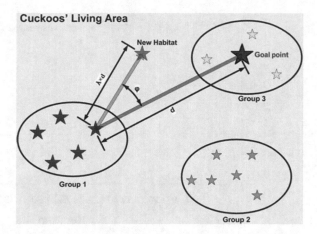

Fig. 35.5 ELR coefficient reduction used in the proposed approach, and its effect on searching of the problem space

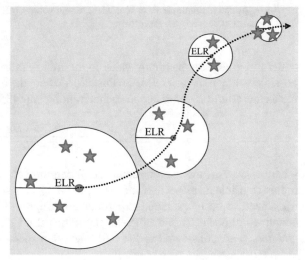

35.4.2 Improvement 1: Adaptive Egg-Laying Coefficient Tuning

The egg-laying radius (ELR) coefficient (α) used in Eq. (35.4) is a parameter to control the length of ELR which is the maximum distance among which a cuckoo can lay her eggs. Higher α lets cuckoos to lay eggs in farer distance which is suitable for the exploration of search space (as global search) while lower α bonds this distance in favor of the exploitation and local search. To make a balance between exploration and exploitation, a logical idea, as shown in Fig. 35.5, is that this parameter should be high in the first iterations to help with the exploration (as global search), and be decreased with iterations to help with the exploitation (as local search). We argue that this reduction should not be in a linear form, i.e. α is

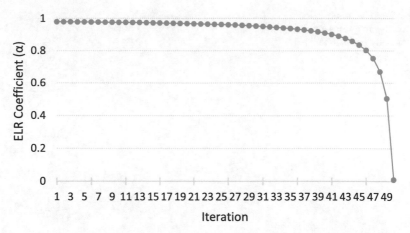

Fig. 35.6 Adaptive nonlinear ELR coefficient tuning based on Eq. (35.6), where α_{max}, α_{min}, and $iter_{max}$ are 1.0, 0.01, and 50, respectively

better to be near its maximum value in the first iterations while near its minimum possible value in the last ones. On this basis, α_t i.e. the egg-laying radius coefficient for the iteration t is computed in each iteration using (35.6).

$$\alpha_t = \alpha_{max} - \frac{\alpha_{max} - \alpha_{min}}{iter_{max} - iter + 1} \qquad (35.6)$$

where α_{min}, α_{max} are the minimum and maximum values considered for egg-laying radius coefficient, respectively. Simply, the α_{min} can be assumed as zero, and just α_{max} need to be investigated experimentally. Figure 35.6 shows a sample of this adaptive nonlinear ELR coefficient tuning based on the (35.6), where α_{max}, α_{min}, and $iter_{max}$ are considered as 1.0, 0.01, and 50, respectively.

35.4.3 Improvement 2: Effective Non-stochastic Egg-Laying

In the proposed egg-laying mechanism, the ELR for each cuckoo is divided to some identical tracks and sectors based on the number of the eggs to be laid. The cuckoos with odd and even numbers alternately lay their eggs in clockwise and counterclockwise fashions, respectively. That is, the first cuckoo is clockwise, the second is counterclockwise, and so on. Then, each cuckoo lay her eggs one-by-one in the next track and sector in a spiral manner like the ones demonstrated in Fig. 35.7. We argue that random egg-laying in ELR formerly showed in Fig. 35.3 is not efficient. Using random egg-laying, in an un neglectable number of cases, most of the eggs are laid in the same region so that other regions in ELR remain uninvestigated. Instead, using the proposed non-stochastic egg-laying strategy, all the regions in ELR have a quota, and this improves diversification of solutions, and avoids stagnation.

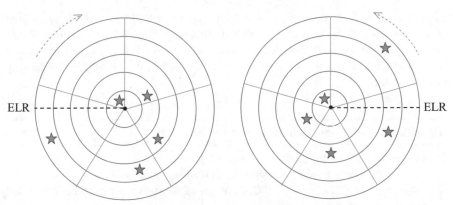

Fig. 35.7 The proposed non-stochastic egg-laying approach. Left: clockwise egg-laying for an odd cuckoo with five eggs. Right: counterclockwise egg-laying for an even cuckoo with five eggs

	$H[n_1]$	$H[n_2]$	$H[n_3]$	$H[n_4]$	$H[n_5]$	$H[n_6]$	$H[n_7]$	$H[n_8]$	$H[n_9]$
A typical Habitat, briefly as H	1.0	0.71	0.65	0.85	0.9	0.5	0.41	0.3	0.1

Corresponding task-order extracted from the upper Habitat	n_1	n_5	n_4	n_2	n_3	n_6	n_7	n_8	n_9

$C_{1,2}$ n_4 n_3 n_8 n_9
$C_{1,1}$ n_1 n_5 n_2 n_6 n_7

0 1 2 3 4 5 6 7 8 9 10 11 12 13 14 15 16 17 18 19 20 21 22 23 24 25 26 27 28 29 30

Fig. 35.8 A typical habitat and its corresponding task-order as well as the final EST task-mapping on two processors demonstrated by a Gantt chart

35.4.4 The Proposed Approach

In the proposed approach, each solution called a "scheduling" which is equivalent to a "habitat" in COA. Actually, a habitat or scheduling is just a list with the length of n, where n is the number of tasks in the given task-graph. Accordingly, each element/cell of this list is associated with one individual task of the inputted task-graph e.g. $H[1]$ is associated with Task n_1, $H[2]$ is associated with the task n_2, and so on. The value of each cell is the priority of selecting that task which is a real number in the range of [0, 1]; the higher priority, the sooner selected for scheduling. Figure 35.8 shows a typical habitat and its corresponding task-order as well as the final task-mapping on two processors demonstrated by a Gantt chart, where the inputted task-graph is the one showed in Fig. 35.1. On this basis, the COA's duty is to properly adjusting the values of cells (priorities) so that the optimum scheduling can be eventuated. To do this, first of all, a set of habitats is created as the cuckoos' population (Algorithm 1), and each cell's value is initiated randomly in the range of [0, 1] using Algorithm 2. In the following, each habitat e.g. *habitat* [i] is evaluated, and final makespan achieved is computed as the habitat's fitness value using Algorithm 3. To do this, first of all, the corresponding task-order based on the tasks' priorities in the habitat is extracted. Secondly, this task-order is distributed over the processors using the EST method, and the overall finish-time (makespan) is calculated which is also considered as the fitness/objective value or the desirability of this habitat.

Algorithm 1 Parameter Definition and Initialization

01: int $n \leftarrow the\_number\_of\_tasks\_in\_the\_task\_graph$;

02: int $m \leftarrow the\_number\_of\_processors\_in\_computing\_environment$;

03: int $Ready\text{-}List$ $[1..n]$ $\leftarrow$ 0; {"Current set of the tasks ready to be scheduled considering precedence constraints"}

04: int $rear \leftarrow$ 0; {"The number of ready-tasks in the $Ready\text{-}List$ [ ] at each iteration"}

05: int $Parents$ $[1..n]$ $\leftarrow$ 0; {"The number of yet unscheduled parents for all the tasks"}

06: int w $[1..n]$ $\leftarrow$ Required execution times of the tasks

07: int AFT $[1..n]$ $\leftarrow$ 0; {"The actual finish-time for each task"}

08: int $Task\text{-}order$ $[1..n]$; {"The task order extracted from a habitat vector"}

09: int $N_{pop} \leftarrow the\_number\_of\_cuckoos\_in\_the\_population$;

10: int $N_{var} \leftarrow n$; {"the_number_of_optimization_parameters"}

11: int $Negg_{min}$, $Negg_{max} \leftarrow the\_minimum\_and\_maximum\_numbers\_of\_eggs\_for\_each\ cuckoo$;

12: int $N_{max} \leftarrow N_{pop}$ + $Negg_{max}$ * N_{pop}; {"The maximum number of habitats (cuckoos and eggs) may exist at the same time"}

13: float $habitats$ $[1..N_{max}, 1..N_{var}]$ $\leftarrow$ 0; {"To retain the location of cuckoos as well as eggs"}

14: float $x_{min} \leftarrow$ 0; {"the_minimum_bounds_for_optimization_parameters"}

15: float $x_{max} \leftarrow$ 1; {"the_maximum_bounds_for_optimization_parameters"}

16: int N_{egg} $[1..N_{pop}]$; {"The number of eggs for each cuckoo"}

17: float ELR $[1..N_{pop}]$; {"The egg-laying radius for each cuckoo"}

18: float α_{min}, $\alpha_{max} \leftarrow the\_minimum\_and\_maximum\_for\_egg\_laying\_coefficients$;

19: float α; {"The egg-laying coefficient for each iteration"}

20: float ε; {"The epsilon coefficient for each iteration"}

21: flaot F; {"The migration coefficient for each iteration"}

22: int $iter$; {"The main counter"}

23: int $C_{max} \leftarrow the\_maximum\_number\_of\_iterations$;

24: int GB_Index; {"The index of global best habitat"}

Algorithm 2 Habitat Initialization Function

01: **for** i = 1 **to** N_{pop}

02:     **for** d = 1 **to** N_{var}

03:         $habitat$ $[i, d]$ = x_{min} + $rand$ (0, 1) * (x_{max} - x_{min});

04:   **next**d
    05:   *habitats* $[i]$.*fitness* $\leftarrow$ *evaluate_scheduling_function* (*habitats* $[i]$);
    06: **next**i

Algorithm 3 Evaluate_Scheduling_Function

01:   *Parents* $[1..n]$ $\leftarrow$ The total number of parents for each task;
02:   *rear*$\leftarrow$ 0;   {"Initializing the number of ready-tasks in the *Ready-List* [ ]"}
03:   **for**$t = 1$ **to**n {"For all the tasks in the task-graph"}
04:     **for**$j = 1$ **to**n {"Regeneration of the *Ready-list* [ ]"}
05:       **if**$Parents$ $[j] = 0$ **then**
06:         AddQueue $(n_j, Ready\text{-}List[\ ])$;   {"Insert n_j in to the rear of *Ready-List* [ ]"}
07:           *rear*$\leftarrow$*rear*+ 1;
08:       **endif**
09:     **next**j
10:     **for**$j = 1$ **to***rear*   {"For all the ready-tasks in the *Ready-List* [ ]"}
11: **if**$habitat$ $[i, Ready\text{-}List$ $[j]] >max$**then**
12:         *max_index*$\leftarrow$$j$;
13:         *max*$\leftarrow$*habitat* $[i, Ready\text{-}List$ $[j]]$
14:       **endif**
15:     **next**j
16:     *Task-order* $[t]$ $\leftarrow$*Ready-List* $[max\_index]$;
17:     DeleteQueue $(Ready\text{-}List$ [ ], *Task-order* $[t]$); {"Delete the selected task from the *Ready-List* [ ]"}
18:     **for**$j = 1$ **to**n {"For each child of the selected task i.e. *Task-order* $[t]$"}
19:       **if**$Task\text{-}order$ $[t]$$\in$$Parents$ (n_j) **then**$Parents$ $[j] = Parents$ $[j]$ - 1;
20:     **next**j
21:   **next**t
    22:   {"The start of assigning extracted *Task-order* $[1..n]$ to the m processors using EST method"}
23:   **for**$t = 1$ **to**n {"For the task-order generated by *habitat* $[i]$"}
24:     AFT $[t] = AST$ $(n_t) + w$ $[t]$;   {"Calculating actual finish-time for each task using Eqs. (35.1) and (35.2)"}
25:   **next**t
26: *makespan*$\leftarrow$ MAX $(AFT$ $[1..n])$; {"The maximum finish-time among all the tasks using Eq. (35.3)"}

Then, the main loop starts (Algorithm 4); in which iteration, all of the habitats are selected one-by-one, and subjected to the following operations:

1. The number of eggs can be laid by this cuckoo (associated to this habitat) is selected randomly in the range of $[Negg_{min}, Negg_{max}]$; this range should be selected experimentally which is trade-off between time-budget and perfor-

mance. Indeed, the more eggs, consume the more Fitness Function Evaluations (FFEs) i.e. the more time, but the better overall performance.

2. The egg-laying coefficient (α) for this iteration is computed based on the selected α_{min} and α_{max} using Eq. (35.6).
3. The egg laying radius (ELR) is calculated for each cuckoo based on her number of eggs using Eq. (35.4).
4. Each cuckoo lays her eggs inside her calculated ELR using the non-stochastic mechanism explained in Sect. 35.4.3 (Algorithm 5).

Algorithm 4 The Main Iteration

01: **for**$iter = 1$ **to**C_{max}
02:    update N_{egg} [$1..N_{pop}$];   {"Update the number of eggs for each cuckoo randomly in the range of [$Negg_{min}$, $Negg_{max}$]"}
03:    update α;{"Update the egg-laying coefficient for this iteration using (6)"}
04:    update ELR [$1..N_{pop}$];   {"Update the egg-laying radius (ELR) for each cuckoo using (4)"}
05:    call *egg_laying_function*;
06:    call *egg_killing_function*;
07:    **for**$i = 1$ **to**N_{pop}
08:        *habitats* [i].*fitness* ← *evaluate_scheduling_function* (*habitats* [i]);
09:    **next**i
10:    sort *habitat* [$1..N_{max}$, $1..N_{var}$] based on their fitness values, and pick the first N_{pop}habitats;
11:    GB_Index ← 1;   {"The global best cuckoo will be the first one after sorting"}
12:    call *migration_function*;
13: **next**$iter$
14: print *habitat* [GB_Index].*fitness*;

Algorithm 5 Egg_Laying_Function

01:    N_{max} ← N_{pop};
02:    **for**$i = 1$ **to**N_{pop} {"Egg-laying for each cuckoo"}
03:        **for**$j = 1$ **to**N_{egg} [i]
04:            N_{max} ← $N_{max} + 1$;   {"Assign a new habitat for the newly generated egg"}
05:            *habitat* [N_{max}, $1..N_{var}$] = *habitat* [i, $1..N_{var}$] + *rand* (-1, 1) * *ELR* [i]; {"Egg-laying in ELR"}
06:    **next**j, i

In continuum of the current iteration, all the eggs in the same locations (using an ε tolerance) are recognized and killed without any evaluation (just like the description in the basic COA) using Algorithm 6. The value of ε tolerance should be investigated experimentally, or one in the basic COA paper should be considered [19]. Then, the survived eggs are evaluated like the randomly-generated habitats described above.

These eggs along with the previous habitats are sorted in ascending order of their produced makespans (fitness values), and the first N_{pop} number of better habitats are selected as the next population. This population is decomposed to the several clusters, and the best cluster then the best habitat in this cluster is selected for the migration phase. In the migration phase (Algorithm 7), all the cuckoos (habitats) move from their locations toward the best global cuckoo using Eq. (35.5), and this changes the priority of tasks in each habitat which leads different scheduling orders and makespans.

Algorithm 6 Egg_Killing_Function

01: **for** $i = 1$ **to** N_{pop} - 1   {"Kill the eggs in the same locations"}
02:     **for** $j = i$ **to** N_{pop}
03:        find all the habitats within the epsilon distance of habitat [i] and kill them;
04: **next** j, i

Algorithm 7 Migration_Function

01: **for** $i = 1$ **to** N_{pop}
02:     **for** $j = 1$ **to** N_{var}
03:        $habitat [i, j] = habitat [i, j] + F * rand (0, 1) * (habitat [GB\_Index, j] - habitat [i, j])$;   {"The migration phase using (5)"}
04: **next** j, i

By means of this operations, whole the population will be move toward the best solution, and finally converge to an optimal/suboptimal solution. This solution is the best one has been found so far, and is the final selected solution of the proposed approach in the current run. A flowchart of these operations is also illustrated in the Fig. 35.9.

35.5   Competitor Approaches

35.5.1   The HLFET Algorithm

The Highest Level First with Estimated Times (HLFET) [24] is a list-scheduling approach using static level (simply *SLevel*) of nodes as priority measurement. *SLevel* of a node n_i is the length of the longest path from n_i to an *exit-node* exclude all the communication delays (edges' weights). To compute the *SLevel* of each task, the task graph should be traversed in the reversed topological order using (35.7).

$$SLevel (n_i) = \max_{j \in Children(n_i)} \left(SLevel (n_j) \right) + w_i, \tag{35.7}$$

Fig. 35.9 The flowchart of
the proposed E-COA
approach

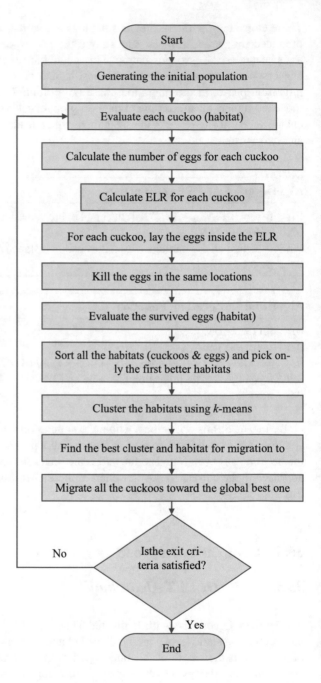

where **Children**(n_i) is the set of all the children of n_i. In each iteration, a ready-list in the descending order of *Slevel* is created, and the first node in the list is selected to be mapped to the processors using non-insertion EST. The non-insertion EST refers to as the processor that provides the earliest start time is selected for assigning, and if the assigning produced a gap (idle time-slot) in the processor, the algorithm simply neglect the gap, while insertion-based EST try to fill the produced gab by the next existing tasks at the expense of an extra computational cost. The ready-list is updated at the end of each iteration by inserting the new nodes ready-to-be-executed-now, and these operations continue until all the nodes are scheduled.

35.5.2 The MCP Algorithm

The Modified Critical Path (MCP) algorithm [30] is another list-scheduling approach exploiting as late as possible (*ALAP*) of the nodes as the priority measurement. *ALAP* start-time of a node e.g. n_i is a priority measurement to indicate how far the start-time of n_i can be postponed without increase the overall finish-time. The *ALAP* of each node e.g. n_i can be computed by traversing the task graph in its topological order using the followings,

$$ALAP\,(n_i) = \min_{j \in Children(n_i)} \left(CPL, ALAP\,(n_j) - c\left(n_i, n_j\right) \right) - w_i, \qquad (35.8)$$

where the Critical Path Length (*CPL*) is the length of the longest path exists in the given task graph. In each iteration after the computation of *ALAP* for all the nodes in the ready-list (ties are broken by considering the *ALAP* of the children of the nodes), the node with the most *ALAP* is selected and mapped to the processor using the EST with insertion-based approach described above.

35.5.3 The DLS Algorithm

The Dynamic Level Scheduling (DLS) algorithm [29] is working on the base of a synthetic heuristic measure named Dynamic Level (*DL*), where *DL* is calculated using $DL = SLevel - EST$ i.e. the difference between the *SLevel* of a node and its earliest-start-time on all the processors. In each iteration after the computation of the *DL* for each node in the ready-list on all over the processors, the DLS selects the node-processor pair producing the largest *DL* is selected to schedule, and these operations continue until all the nodes are scheduled.

35.5.4 The ETF Algorithm

The Earliest Time First (ETF) algorithm [28] exploits the dynamic earliest-start-times for each node in the ready-list over all the existing processors using Eqs. (35.1) and (35.2). In each iteration, ETF elects the node-processor that provide the smallest EST (ties are broken by selecting the node with the higher *SLevel* priority). The ready-list is updated at the end of each iteration by inserting the new nodes ready-to-be-executed-now, and these operations continue until all the nodes are scheduled.

35.5.5 The ISH Algorithm

The Insertion Scheduling Heuristic (ISH) algorithm [25] exploit the aforementioned *SLevel* as the priority measurement to assign priority to the nodes and sort them it each iteration. The substantial novelty associated to this algorithm is its exploitation of the idle time slots (the schedule holes) in the partial schedules i.e. it tries to fill the holes created during the scheduling by inserting other unscheduled nodes into them. This is a kind of insertion-based EST method, although with a lower computation costs than the others like MCP.

35.6 Implementation Details and Configurations

The proposed approach was implemented on a Pentium IV (8-thread 3.9 GHz i7–3770K processor) desktop computer with Microsoft Windows 7 (X64) platform using Microsoft Visual Basic 6.0 programming language. The initial population of the proposed E-COA approach was 20 cuckoos ("habitats" or solutions), where each cuckoo is able to lay from 2 to 5 eggs. The egg-laying was based on the non-stochastic mechanism introduced in Sect. 35.4.3, with adaptive egg-laying radius tuning using Eq. (35.6), where α_{max} and α_{min} were set to 1.0 and 0.01, respectively. The total number of iterations was set to 1000; however, the algorithm was terminated after $n \times 100$ Fitness Function Evaluations (FFEs) (since the number of iteration is not a fair metric for termination of algorithms under the comparison). Also, if all the population reach to a same point, the algorithm is considered as converged, and hence is terminated though it has unused iterations or EFFs. Other details about the configuration of the proposed E-COA approach are summarized in Table 35.2.

Table 35.2 The configuration of the proposed E-COA approach

Algorithm	Parameter	Symbol	Value
E-COA (The Proposed Approach)	ELR coefficient	α_{max}	1.0
		α_{min}	0.01
	Migration coefficient	F	$\pi/6 \times rand(0, 1)$
	The No. of clusters	c	1
	The minimum No. of eggs for each Cuckoo	$Negg_{min}$	2
	The maximum No. of eggs for each Cuckoo	$Negg_{max}$	5
	Epsilon tolerance to kill the eggs in the same locations	ε	1.00E-08
	The population size		20
	Total No. of iterations	C_{max}	1000
	Total No. of fitness function evaluation	FFE	$n \times 100$
	Other termination criteria	–	Identical population

35.6.1   The Utilized Dataset

To do a rational judgment, a set of 125 random task graphs are exploited for comparison study and the evaluations [37]. These random task graphs are with the different shapes based on the three following parameters:

- *Size* (n): The number of nodes in the given task graph. Five different values as size are considered {32, 64, 128, 256, and 512}.
- *Communication-to-Computation Ratio* (CCR): To show how much a graph is intensive from computational or communicational perspective. The execution time of the nodes in the task-graph were randomly chosen from the uniform distribution with mean equal to the specified average computation cost that was 50 time-instance. The weight of each edge was also randomly selected from the uniform distribution with mean equal to average-computation-cost $\times CCR$. Five different values of *CCR* were considered {0.1, 0.5, 1.0, 5.0, and 10.0}, so that selecting 0.1 makes the generated task-graphs computation intensive, while selecting 10.0 makes them communication intensive.
- *Parallelism:* The average number of children for each node in the task graph. Increasing this parameter makes the generated graphs fully connected, while lower parallelism makes the generated task graphs dispersed. Five different values of parallelism were selected {3, 5, 10, 15, and 20}.

35.6.2   Comparison Metrics

It should be noted that because of the various structural parameters, the archived makespans for the aforementioned random graphs are in a wide range; therefore, the Normalized Schedule Length (*NSL*), which is a normalized metric, is used. It can be computed for every inputted graph by dividing the *makespan* (schedule length) to a lower bound. Although different lower bounds can be assumed, we chose the sum of weights of the nodes on the computational critical path of the graph as in (35.9).

$$NSL = \frac{Schedule\ Length}{\sum_{n_i \in CP} w_i},\tag{35.9}$$

where *CP* is the set of nodes on the longest computational path inside the given task graph (a computational path is a regular path excluding the communication costs along the path). Worth mentioning that such lower bounds are theoretical and may not always be possible to achieve, i.e. the optimal schedule length is often some larger than this bound.

Another extensively used metric for empirical study in the realm of task scheduling is "*speedup*" which is the ratio of assigning all the tasks to a single processor (i.e. the aggregation of all the task's execution times) to the obtained schedule length (*makespan*) using many processors. In other words,

$$Speedup = \frac{\sum_{i=1}^{n} w_i}{Schedule\ Length}.\tag{35.10}$$

Obviously, the lower *NSL* means the better performance, whilst the higher *speedup* is a consequence of the better performance.

35.7   The Experimental Results

35.7.1   The Convergence of the Proposed Approach

As said in the Sect. 35.6, one of the algorithm's termination criteria is that all the population reach in an identical point. Obviously, no further investigation can be achieved by the population halted in such this situation, and this is regarded as the convergence of the algorithm. On the other hand, reaching the maximum number of iterations or Fitness Function Evaluations (FFEs) is regarded as the algorithm divergence. Figure 35.10 shows a sample of algorithm execution for the task-graph showed in Fig. 35.1. We can say that the proposed approach is converged in this

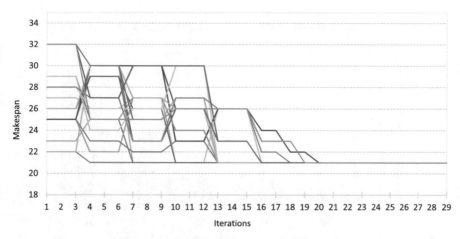

Fig. 35.10 A sample of the execution of the proposed approach for the task-graph in Fig. 35.1. The algorithm was terminated after 29 iterations and the minimum makespan achieved was 21 time-slots

diagram based on the population's convergence. Since there are 125 random task-graphs and each of which is subjected to 10 independent runs, there will be 1250 independent runs in overall, among them 160 runs i.e. 12.8% of all the runs end up without convergence; however, most of diverged runs belong to those task-graphs with maximum number of nodes in the dataset (i.e. 512-node task-graphs). When we double the maximum number of iterations and FFEs, only 20 runs i.e. 1.6% of all the runs end up without convergence, which shows the capability of the proposed approach to achieve better solutions and results provided enough time budget.

35.7.2   The Experimental Study and Results

All the final experiments are conducted using all the aforementioned 125 random task graphs as inputted samples. Each task-graph is subjected to 10 independent runs, and the average of these runs is considered for each graph in all the subsequent diagrams. The first set of experiments are conducted regarding different graphs' sizes to investigate the impact of this primarily shape parameter. Figures 35.11 and 35.12 illustrate the achieved results in *NSL* and *speedup* for the proposed E-COA approach besides other aforementioned traditional counterparts, respectively. Of course, The lesser *NSL*, the better performance, while the higher *speedup*, the higher efficiency. The entire 125 random task graphs are used in this set of experiments, and the results are favored the proposed E-COA approach. Generally speaking, the achieved *NSL*s and *speedup*s grows and descends, respectively, proportionate to the increase in the inputted graph sizes (tough the relation in not linear). In the

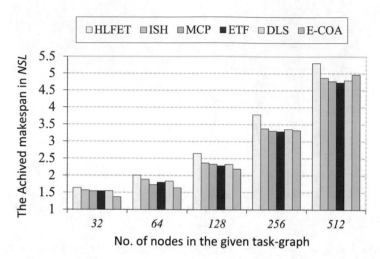

Fig. 35.11 The achieved results (in *NSL*) of the proposed approach besides its traditional counterparts on the entire 125 random task-graphs with respect to the different graph sizes (*m*, i.e. the no. of processors is set to 2)

average *NSL* and *speedup*, the performance ranking of the approaches is {E-COA, ETF, MCP≈DLS, ISH, HLFET}. It should be noted that each ranking in this paper starts with the best approach, and ends with the worst one with respect to the given comparison metric; that is, the E-COA was the best (especially with the small-scale inputs), ETF was a little bit worse, MCP and DLS were moderate and about identical (MCP was slightly better than DLS), and the ISH and HLFET were the worst methods. Worth mentioning that the number of processors was set to two in these experiments for each approach to produce the most possible compact scheduling. Restricting the number of processors is a key experiment revealing how efficient an approach is in terms of lacking sufficient resources; however, all the presented experiments were done again using very large number of processors (i.e. 32 ones), and the achieved ranking were exactly identical with the above, which certified the conclusions. In addition, the effect of increase in the number of processors, and detailed results using higher number of processors are presented and evaluated in the following.

For investigating the effect of the number of processors used, another set of experiments are conducted. Figures 35.13 and 35.14 show the diagrams of the achieved *NSL*s and *speedup*s of the entire 125 random task-graphs regarding utilization of different numbers of processors ranging from 2 processors to the 32 ones, respectively. Again, the performance ranking of the approaches is {E-COA, ETF, MCP≈DLS, ISH, HLFET}, and the proposed E-COA approach is the winner of the race versus to other methods in most of the cases. It can be seen that the difference among the performance of the proposed E-COA approach and their

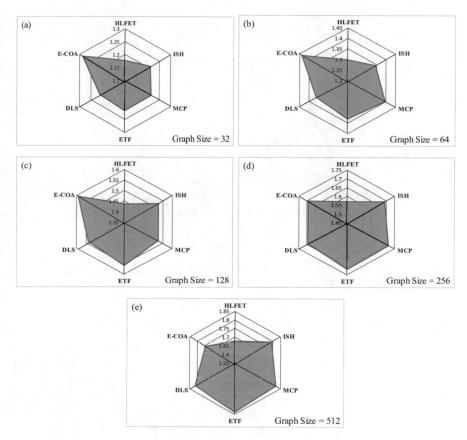

Fig. 35.12 The achieved *speedup* kiviat graphs for the proposed E-COA approach besides its counterparts on the entire 125 random task-graphs with respect to the different graph sizes (*m*, i.e. the no. of processors is set to 2). (**a**) Graph-Size = 32, (**b**) Graph-Size = 64, (**c**) Graph-Size = 128, (**d**) Graph-Size − 256, (**e**) Graph-Size = 512

counterparts is decreased regarding the increase in the number of processors used, and this can be interpreted that the strength of the E-COA approach is where the number of processors in restricted, and we are subjected to the lack of computational resources.

Finally, Figs. 35.15 and 35.16 show the average *NSL*s and *speedup*s achieved by all the experiments conducted on entire 125 random task-graphs, respectively. As a rule, we can say that the final performance ranking is {E-COA, ETF, MCP≈DLS, ISH, HLFET}; that is, the E-COA is the best (especially with the small-scale inputs), ETF is a little bit worse, MCP and DLS are moderate and almost identical (their rankings change alternately in the different experiments), and the ISH and HLFET are the worst methods from the performance point of view.

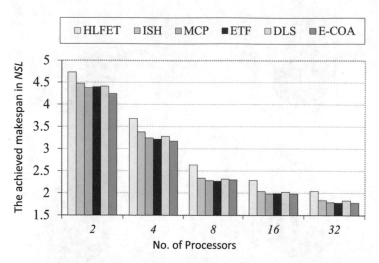

Fig. 35.13 The diagram of the achieved *NSL*s of the entire 125 random task graphs regarding the different number of utilized processors

35.8   Conclusion

In this paper, an enhanced version of Cuckoo Optimization Algorithm (COA) named E-COA was introduced to tackle with the static task-graph scheduling problem in homogeneous multiprocessor supercomputing environments. The proposed E-COA approach was equipped with an adaptive coefficient tuning strategy, and an efficient non-stochastic egg-laying mechanism, which significantly improve the local and global search potentiality of the basic COA. The main duty of the E-COA was to find the best possible sequence of tasks for the given task-graph by manipulating the priority variables associated to each task, and then, the Earliest Start Time (EST) first strategy was used to assign the sequence obtained by E-COA to the existing processors in the system. For a comprehensive unbiased experimental study, a set of 125 random task graphs were used to evaluate the proposed approach. These random task graphs had different shape parameters in size, *CCR* and the parallelism. Different sets of experiments were conducted, and finally, the proposed E-COA approach was the winner of the race on most the cases in comparison with different traditional methods such as HLFET, ISH, ETF, MCP and DLS. As a rule, the final performance ranking was {E-COA, ETF, MCP, DLS, ISH, and HLFET}; that is, E-COA was the best approach, ETF was slightly worse, DLS and MCP were moderate and their rankings were fluctuated based on the different shape parameters, and finally the ISH and HLFET were the worst from the performance point of view. All of these were of strong evidences to demonstrate the capability and superiority of the proposed E-COA approach for static task-graph scheduling in the high-performance multiprocessor supercomputing environments.

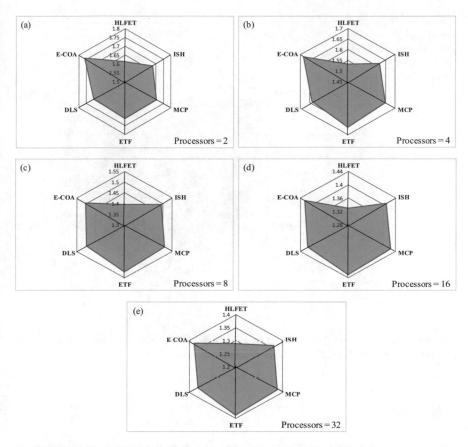

Fig. 35.14 Kiviat diagrams for achieved *speedup* of the entire 125 random task graphs regarding the different number of utilized processors. (**a**) Processors = 2, (**b**) Processors = 4, (**c**) Processors = 8, (**d**) Processors = 16, (**e**) Processors = 32

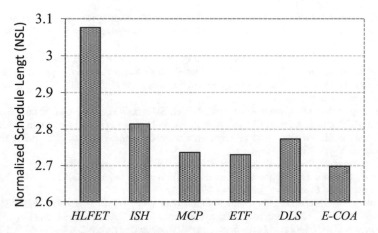

Fig. 35.15 The average *NSL* of all the experiments conducted on entire 125 random task-graphs.

Fig. 35.16 The average
speedup of all the
experiments conducted on
entire 125 random
task-graphs

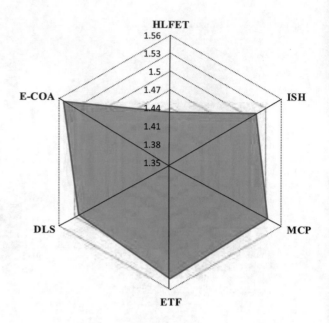

Acknowledgements This work was supported by Sama Technical and Vocational Training College, Islamic Azad University, Shoushtar Branch, Shoushtar, Iran.

References

1. Buyya, R., High Performance Cluster Computing: Architecture and Systems, Volume I, Prentice Hall, Upper SaddleRiver, NJ, USA, 1999.
2. Cao, Jiannong, Alvin TS Chan, Yudong Sun, Sajal K. Das, and MinyiGuo. "A taxonomy of application scheduling tools for high performance cluster computing," *Cluster Computing* 9, no. 3 (2006): 355-371.
3. M Elhoseny, X Yuan, HK ElMinir, and AM Riad, "An energy efficient encryption method for secure dynamic WSN", *Security and Communication Networks*, Wiley, 9(13): 2024-2031, 2016.
4. Kwok, Y. K. and Ahmad, I., "Benchmarking and comparison of the task graph scheduling algorithms," *Journal of Parallel and Distributed Computing*, vol. 59, no. 3, pp. 381-422, 1999.
5. Nandi, Asoke K., Basel Abu-Jamous, and Rui Fa. Integrative cluster analysis in bioinformatics. John Wiley & Sons, 2015.
6. Mohamed Elhoseny, Ahmed Abdelaziz, Ahmed Salama, AM Riad, Arun Kumar Sangaiah, Khan Muhammad, A Hybrid Model of Internet of Things and Cloud Computing to Manage Big Data in Health Services Applications, *Future Generation Computer Systems*, Elsevier, Accepted March 2018, In Press.
7. Xiong, Yonghua, Shaoyun Wan, Jinhua She, Min Wu, Yong He, and Keyuan Jiang. "An energy-optimization-based method of task scheduling for a cloud video surveillance center." *Journal of Network and Computer Applications* 59 (2016): 63-73.
8. Xiaohui Yuan, Mohamed Abouelenien, and Mohamed Elhoseny, A Boosting-based Decision Fusion Method for Learning from Large, Imbalanced Face Data Set, *Quantum Computing: An Environment for Intelligent Large Scale Real Application*, Springer, 2017

9. Elhoseny H., Elhoseny M., Riad A.M., Hassanien A.E. (2018) A Framework for Big Data Analysis in Smart Cities. In: Hassanien A., Tolba M., Elhoseny M., Mostafa M. (eds) *The International Conference on Advanced Machine Learning Technologies and Applications (AMLTA2018)*. AMLTA 2018. Advances in Intelligent Systems and Computing, vol 723. Springer, Cham.

10. Boveiri, H. R., "List-Scheduling Techniques in Homogeneous Multiprocessor Environments: A Survey," *International Journal of Software Engineering and Its Applications*, vol. 9, no. 4, pp. 123-132, 2015.

11. Boveiri, H. R., "An Efficient Task Priority Measurement for List-Scheduling in Multiprocessor Environments," *International Journal of Software Engineering and Its Applications (IJSEIA)*, vol. 9, no. 5, pp. 233-246, May 2015.

12. Boveiri, H. R., "ACO-MTS: A new approach for multiprocessor task scheduling based on ant colony optimization." In: *Intelligent and Advanced Systems (ICIAS), 2010 International Conference on*, pp. 1-5. Kuala Lumpur, 2010.

13. Boveiri H. R., "A Novel ACO-Based Static Task Scheduling Approach for Multiprocessor Environments," *International Journal of Computational Intelligence Systems*, vol. 9, no. 5, pp. 800-811, 2016.

14. Boveiri, Hamid Reza, and Raouf Khayami. "Static Homogeneous Multiprocessor Task Graph Scheduling Using Ant Colony Optimization." *KSII Transactions on Internet & Information Systems* 11, no. 6 (2017).

15. Boveiri, Hamid Reza, Raouf Khayami, Mohamed Elhoseny, and M. Gunasekaran. "An efficient Swarm-Intelligence approach for task scheduling in cloud-based internet of things applications." *Journal of Ambient Intelligence and Humanized Computing* (2018): 1-11. https://doi.org/10.1007/s12652-018-1071-1

16. Boveiri, H. R., "Assigning Tasks to the Processors for Task-Graph Scheduling in Parallel Systems Using Learning and Cellular Learning Automata," In: *Proceeding of the 1st National Conf. on Comp. Eng. and Info. Tech*, pp. 1-8, Shoushtar, Iran, Feb. 2014 (in Farsi).

17. Boveiri, H. R., "Multiprocessor Task Graph Scheduling Using a Novel Graph-Like Learning Automata," *International Journal of Grid and Distributed Computing*, vol. 8, no. 1, pp. 41-54, Feb. 2015.

18. Wolpert, David H., and William G. Macready. "No free lunch theorems for optimization." *IEEE transactions on evolutionary computation* 1, no. 1 (1997): 67-82.

19. Rajabioun, Ramin. "Cuckoo optimization algorithm." Applied soft computing 11, no. 8 (2011): 5508-5518.

20. Boveiri, H. R. and Elhoseny, M., "A-COA: an adaptive cuckoo optimization algorithm for continuous and combinatorial optimization," Neural Comput & Applic, pp. 1-25, 2018. https://doi.org/10.1007/s00521-018-3928-9

21. Zhu, Wenwu, Peng Cui, Zhi Wang, and Gang Hua. "Multimedia big data computing." *IEEE multimedia* 3 (2015): 96-105.

22. Ota, Kaoru, Minh Son Dao, Vasileios Mezaris, and Francesco GB De Natale. "Deep learning for mobile multimedia: A survey." *ACM Transactions on Multimedia Computing, Communications, and Applications (TOMM)* 13, no. 3s (2017): 34.

23. Hatcher, William Grant, and Wei Yu. "A Survey of Deep Learning: Platforms, Applications and Emerging Research Trends." *IEEE Access* 6 (2018): 24411-24432.

24. Thomas L. Adam, K. Mani Chandy and J. R. Dickson, "A comparison of list schedules for parallel processing systems," *Communications of the ACM*, vol. 17, no. 12, pp. 685-690, 1974.

25. Kruatrachue, B. and Lewis, TG., "Duplication Scheduling Heuristics (DSH): A New Precedence Task Scheduler for Parallel Processor Systems," Technical report, Oregon State University, Report No.: OR 97331, Corvallis, 1987.

26. Carolyn, M. C., and Gill, H., "Automatic determination of grain size for efficient parallel processing," *Communications of the ACM*, vol. 32, no. 9, pp. 1073-1078, 1989.

27. Baxter, J. and Patel, JH., "The LAST Algorithm: A Heuristic-Based Static Task Allocation Algorithm," In: *Proceeding of the 1989 Int'l Conf. Parallel Processing*, pp. 217-222, Aug. 1989.

28. Hwang, JJ., Chow, YC., Anger, FD. and Lee, CY., "Scheduling Precedence Graphs in Systems with Interprocessor Communication Times," *SIAM J. Computing*, vol. 18, no. 2, pp. 244-257, Apr. 1989.
29. Sih, GC. and Lee, EA., "A Compile-Time Scheduling Heuristic for Interconnection-Constrained Heterogeneous Processor Architectures," *IEEE Trans. Parallel and Distributed Systems*, vol. 4, no. 2, pp. 75-87, Feb. 1993.
30. Wu, MY. and Gajski, DD., "Hypertool: A Programming Aid for Message-Passing Systems," *IEEE Trans. Parallel and Distributed Systems*, vol. 1, no. 3, pp. 330-343, Jul. 1990.
31. Hwang, R., Gen, M. and Katayama, H., "A comparison of multiprocessor task scheduling algorithms with communication costs," *Computer & Operations Research*, vol. 35, no. 3, pp. 976-993, 2008.
32. Boveiri, H. R. "Task Assigning Techniques for List-Scheduling in Homogeneous Multiprocessor Environments: A Survey." *International Journal of Software Engineering and Its Applications* 9, no. 12 (2015): 303-312.
33. Akbari, Mehdi, and Hassan Rashidi. "A multi-objectives scheduling algorithm based on cuckoo optimization for task allocation problem at compile time in heterogeneous systems," *Expert Systems with Applications* 60 (2016): 234-248.
34. Bazgosha, Atiyeh, Mohammad Ranjbar, and NeginJamili. "Scheduling of loading and unloading operations in a multi stations transshipment terminal with release date and inventory constraints," *Computers & Industrial Engineering* 106 (2017): 20-31.
35. Elyasigomari, V., D. A. Lee, H. R. C. Screen, and M. H. Shaheed. "Development of a two-stage gene selection method that incorporates a novel hybrid approach using the cuckoo optimization algorithm and harmony search for cancer classification." *Journal of Biomedical Informatics* 67 (2017): 11-20.
36. Faradonbeh, RoohollahShirani, and MasoudMonjezi. "Prediction and minimization of blast-induced ground vibration using two robust meta-heuristic algorithms." *Engineering with Computers* (2017): 1-17.
37. Boveiri, H. R. (2018), "125 random task-graphs for multiprocessor task scheduling", *Mendeley Data*, v2. https://doi.org/10.17632/4fycv9td56.2

Chapter 36
IoT for Healthcare: System Architectures, Predictive Analytics and Future Challenges

Ghanshyam Singh

36.1 Introduction

Internet-of-Things (IoT) is the notion so called "things" being interconnected via the Internet, which enabling them to exchange information. Recently, it has emerged as one of the most trending topics of technology. The function of IoT reduces the gap between real world objects and their virtual representations in information and communication systems [1]. The term "things" can be any type of object able to generate or consume information [1]. In the IoT, the devices gather and share information directly with each other and the cloud that making it possible to collect, record and analyse new data streams faster and more accurately. Due to its multidisciplinary approach, the IoT has been remarkable in revolutionizing several aspects of traditional healthcare paradigms and not just being limited to the health informatics. Before the IoT idea being widely accepted, several challenging issues still need to be addressed and both technological as well as social knots must be untied. The challenging issues are making a full interoperability of interconnected devices with higher degree of smartness by enabling their adaptation and autonomous behaviour, while guaranteeing trust, privacy, and security. Moreover, the IoT idea poses several new problems with the networking aspects. In fact, the things composing the IoT will be characterized by low resources in terms of both computation and energy capacity. Therefore, the proposed solutions need to pay special attention to resource efficiency besides the obvious scalability problems [2]. Further, the advancement in areas like data science, multimedia, cloud computing, machine learning and artificial intelligence as well as rapid proliferation of wearable devices, the IoT leads in providing efficient healthcare solutions.

G. Singh (✉)
Department of Electrical and Electronics Engineering Sciences, Auckland Park Kingsway
Campus, University of Johannesburg, Johannesburg, South Africa
e-mail: ghanshyams@uj.ac.za

© Springer Nature Switzerland AG 2019
A. K. Singh, A. Mohan (eds.), *Handbook of Multimedia Information Security:
Techniques and Applications*, https://doi.org/10.1007/978-3-030-15887-3_36

Several industrial, standardization and research fraternity are currently involved in the activity of development of solutions to fulfil the technological requirements such as:

- provides different visions of IoT paradigm coming from different scientific communities with explanations;
- reviews the enabling technologies and illustrates which are the major benefits of spread of this paradigm in daily-life, and
- offers an analysis of the major research issues the scientific community still has to face.

The IOT itself syntactically composed of two terms: (1) pushes towards a network oriented vision of IoT, and (2) focus on generic objects to be integrated into a common framework. It shall not be forgotten, anyway, that the words "Internet" and "Things", when put together, assume a meaning which introduces a disruptive level of innovation into present information and communication technology (ICT) world. In fact, IoT semantically means a world-wide network of interconnected objects uniquely addressable, based on standard communication protocols.

Recent advancements in IoT and e-Health are aimed to provide simple and efficient solutions in order to make available personalized, preventive and collaborative form of healthcare. This goal of IoT for e-Healthcare bring together researchers and practitioners from both academia and industry into a common platform, to showcase the state-of-the-art research and development in this field, addressing the key necessities and challenges while applying IoT in medical sciences and healthcare. With the pervasive advancement of IoT in healthcare, it also faces critical challenges across the globe such as shortage of cost-effective and accurate smart medical sensors, lack of uniform standards and interoperability across the e-Healthcare devices, heterogeneity and multi-dimensionality of the data from healthcare sector, and the trust issues pertaining to privacy and security of data pose significant obstacles before the extensiveness of IoT for healthcare.

The IoT is a global network infrastructure as shown in Fig. 36.1, linking physical and virtual objects through the exploitation of data capture and communication capabilities. This infrastructure includes existing and involving Internet and network developments. It will offer specific object-identification, sensor and connection capability as the basis for the development of independent cooperative services and applications. These will be characterized by a high degree of autonomous data capture, event transfer, network connectivity and interoperability [2]. Presently IoT links the Internet with sensors and a multitude of devices, mostly using IP-based communications. In the healthcare industry, IoT provides options to remote monitoring, early prevention, and medical treatment for institutionalized patients. For IoT, people or objects can be equipped with sensors, actuators, Radio-Frequency Identification (RFID) tags, etc as shown in Fig. 36.1 which facilitates access by patients' caregivers. For example, RFIDs tags of patients or patients' personal devices are decipherable, identifiable, locatable, and controllable via IoT applications [3].

Fig. 36.1 IoT and its
constituents

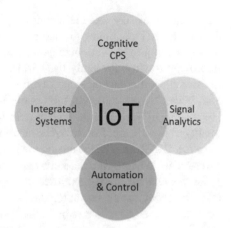

In general, IoT is a loosely coupled, decentralized, dynamic system in which trillions of everyday smart objects are endowed with smartness to increase their own capacities, seamlessly communicate and cooperate despite their physical/functional heterogeneity. To face such an increasing complexity of IoT scenario, its composing devices emphasizes the need of autonomic and cognitive approaches for the system design, especially for the management aspects. The Cyber-Physical System (CPS), a new generation of digital system, mainly focuses on complex inter-dependencies and integration between cyberspace and physical world. It consists of highly integrated computation, communication, control, and physical elements. Two main functional components are: (1) the advanced connectivity that ensures real-time data acquisition from the physical world and information feedback from the cyber space and (2) intelligent data management, analytics and computational capability that constructs the cyber space. The use of CPS aims to increase the implementation of large-scale systems by improving the adaptability, autonomy, efficiency, functionality, reliability, safety, and usability of such systems. IoT enables a broad-range of smart applications and services to manage with challenges which has been faced by individuals as well as healthcare sector [4]. The IoT has dynamic capabilities to connect D2M (Device-to-Machine), O2O (Object-to-Object), P2D (Patient-to-Doctor), P2M (Patient-to-Machine), D2M (Doctor-to-Machine), S2M (Sensor-to-Mobile), M2H (Mobile-to-Human), T2R (Tag-to-Reader). Thus, the IoT intelligently connects humans, machines, smart devices, and dynamic systems in order to assure an effective healthcare system [5]. Although, the demographic change required to develop novel functionalities as well as integrating new technologies into home automated environments. In the healthcare dominion, the IoT devices are expected to change the overall functioning of healthcare by decentralising. The chronic disease patients are expected to be remotely monitored by small sensor devices, making it possible to detect bad conditions before they get really bad and thereby avoid hospitalisation in several cases. Furthermore, the doctors' consultations are also anticipated to partly occur remotely in the future, consequently it is expected to lower the costs of healthcare with more than 20%. As the technology for collecting, analysing and transmitting data in the IoT continues to mature but there is no shortage of predictions about how it is going to revolutionize healthcare by dramatically minimizing the costs and improving quality. Presently the wireless sensor-based systems are in the demand to assemble patient medical data even which was never before available for analysis and delivering healthcare to the people for whom it was not previously available. Hence, the IoT-driven systems are able to radically reduce the costs and improve quality of healthcare. Recently, the customer intelligence market of IoT is expected to have a CAGR of 43.01% during the period 2018–2024, mainly driven by growing investments in healthcare market by governments and various other stakeholders [6].

In this chapter, I have explored in depth the role of IoT in healthcare delivery, take a close look at the technological aspects which make it a reality and examine the opportunities and challenges of the IoT poses for healthcare currently. I start with an introduction to the IoT which is still a relatively new concept with a growing number of practical applications across industries. The key technologies that will drive the future IoT will be related to smart sensor technologies like advanced MEMS (micro-electro-mechanical-systems) sensors, bio-electronics, the nanotechnology and miniaturization of the sensing devices. Further, the role of cyber-physical system (CPS), signal processing, automation and control with integrated circuit, particularly at millimetre and terahertz frequency as shown in Fig. 36.1 will be very challenging for fourth industrial evolutions. In Fig. 36.1, the main concepts, technologies and standards are highlighted and classified with reference to the IoT visions. The technologies for use throughout IoT-driven healthcare systems are as follows.

- Sensors—collect patient data/information
- Microcontrollers—process, analyse and wirelessly communicate the data/information
- Microprocessors—enable rich graphical user interfaces, and
- Healthcare-specific gateways—sensor data is further analysed and sent to the cloud.

36.1.1 Sympathetic IoT

IoT-associated with healthcare systems are based on the fundamental definition of IoT as a network of devices that connect directly with each other to capture and share essential data through a secure service layer (SSL) which connects to a central control server in the cloud. The concept of devices connected directly with each other is authorized devices to gather information on their own without human intervention. The emergence of IoT, in which devices are connected directly to data as well as to each other, is imperative due to following two reasons:

1. Advances in sensor and connectivity technology are allowing devices to collect, record and analyse data, which means devices being able to collect patient data over the time that can be used to help enable preventive

healthcare as well as allow prompt diagnosis of sensitive complications and promote understanding a therapy to help in the improvement of a patient's health parameters.

2. The ability of devices to gather data on their own and removes the limitations of human-entered data—automatically obtaining the data that is required by doctors. Thus the automation reduces the risk of error, which increases efficiency, lower the costs and improvements in quality of care is the demand of future healthcare industry.

36.1.1.1   IoT Architecture

The architecture of IoT comprise several layers, starting from the edge technology layer at the bottom to the application layer at the top, as shown in Fig. 36.2 [7]. The two lower layers contribute to data capturing, while the two higher layers are responsible for data utilization in concern applications. The working functionality of the layers is as follows:

1. Edge technology layer—this is a hardware layer that includes data collection components which provide identification and information storage, information collection, information processing, communications, control and actuation. The potential component of this layer technology is as follows.

   (a) RFID systems: are the most important components of IoT which enable data transmission by a highly portable device such as RFID tag. The RFID reader reads the tag and processes the achieved data according to the demand of a specific application. This system can be used to monitor healthcare objects in real-time, without the need of being in the line-of-sight. Further the data transmitted by the tag may provide device identification or location information [8].

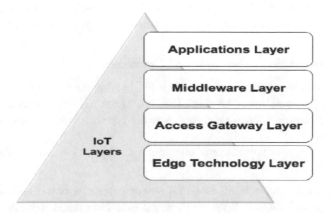

Fig. 36.2 The layered architecture of IoT [7]

    (b) Wireless sensor networks (WSNs): is consist of a large numbers of sensing nodes, which report the sensing results to special nodes called sinks [9].

2. Access gateway layer—is responsible for data handling, including data transmission, message routing, and publishing and subscribing messages. It sends to the middleware layer information received from the edge layer, using communications technologies [9].

3. Middleware layer—is a software platform that provides abstraction to applications from things. Further, it offers several services such as device discovery and management, data filtering, data aggregation, semantic data analysis, access control, and information discovery.

4. Applications layer—is the top layer which is responsible for delivery of various applications to different IoT users. It consists of two sub-layers [10]:

    (a) Data management sub-layer: It provides directory service, quality-of-service, cloud-computing technologies, data processing, machine-to-machine (M2M) services, etc.

    (b) Application service sub-layer: It is responsible for interfacing to end users and enterprise applications running on top of the IoT applications layer.

36.1.1.2   IoT Components

As the IoT consist of different components which work together to realize the IoT concept. Mainly these components are as follows.

1. Physical Objects IoT Component

This component of IoT collect, identify, and monitor information about patients in their environments. The physical devices are connected to the Internet, and transform patients related information obtained in the physical world into data for the digital world.

2. Communication Technologies IoT Component

The most common types of networks for IoT healthcare applications for the patients are Personal Area Networks (PANs), Local Area Networks (LANs), and Wide Area Networks (WANs) and each network type involves a number of wireless technologies.

The most frequently used communication technologies in IoT healthcare applications are as follows:

    (a) ZigBee: It is the IEEE 802.15.4 standard for low-power and short-range, based on Low Rate Wireless Personal Area Network (LR-WPAN). It is less expensive than Bluetooth and operates in the 2.4 GHz ISM band.

(b) Bluetooth: It is the IEEE 802.15.1 standard for low-power short distance radio frequency which facilitates point-to-point and point-multipoint configurations, based on Wireless Personal Area Network (WPAN) and operates at 2.4 GHz. However, these devices are cheap significantly reduces power consumption, and is aimed among others novel healthcare applications.

(c) Light Fidelity (Li-Fi): It is optical, visible light communication (VLC) system using light instead of radio waves in a manner similar to Wi-Fi [11], which uses rapid pulses of visible light between 400 and 800 THz for data transmission. The transceiver-fitted LED lamps is used by Li-Fi for transmitting and receiving information. However, it has security issues such as reliability and network coverage. In the reliability, the path of transmission will cause disruption in the communication due to the interface from external light sources such as sunlight/normal bulbs as well as it cannot provide data in an area where are obstacles. However, this communication technique has several advantages such as low-cost, no room for eavesdropping and avoids the problem of overlapping frequencies.

(d) Wi-Fi: This communication system operates on three different non-interoperable technologies, which are Direct Sequence Spread Spectrum, Frequency Hopping Spread Spectrum (FHSS), and Infrared (IR). However, there are several Wi-Fi versions, such as IEEE 802.11x (Wireless LAN or WLAN). It provides both point-to-point and point-multipoint configurations. Moreover, IEEE 802.11n provides a good performance with the maximum data rate 600 Mbps, and uses 2.4 GHz or 5 GHz RF bands. Wi-Fi security can be provided by the following protocols:

- Wired Equivalent Privacy is the first security protocol used for Wi-Fi,
- Wi-Fi Protected Access is a much stronger security protocol for Wi-Fi, and
- Wi-Fi Protected Access II is the improvement of Wi-Fi Protected Access, which includes the strong Advanced Encryption Standard.

(e) Long Term Evolution (LTE): It is a 4G wireless broadband standard which provides Uplink data rate up to 75 Mbps, and DownLink data rate up to 300 Mbps. It is cost effective solution for M2M services for IoT for healthcare applications, including monitoring, and tracking patients and devices.

(f) Long Term Evolution-Advanced (LTE-A): It is advanced 4G mobile communication standard, which is a significant enhancement of the LTE and provides up to three times higher data rates than LTE with lower latency [12]. LTE-A should be backward compatible with LTE equipment, so upgraded M2M services can take advantage of existing LTE networks.

The traditional IoT concept comprises of low-power edge devices that collect data which is transmitted to centralized high-performance head nodes and then analyzed and visualized the data on the head nodes to generate results as well as actionable information. However, this concept poses potential challenges and overheads, arising from the transmission of data between the edge and head devices.

Further, due to the limited bandwidth resources, this concept also results significant delays in retrieving the required results. These bandwidth bottlenecks could be unaffordable in some applications such as healthcare monitoring, where the latency of data analysis and visualization must satisfy stringent realtime constraints in order to prevent medical emergencies. Furthermore, the data transmission between the edge and head nodes can also result significant energy overheads [13, 14].

(g) Millimeter/Terahertz Communication: It will be employed in 5G communication which enhances the data rate up to 1000 times than that of 4G.

36.1.1.3 Applications of IoT Component

The use of IoT component is responsible for data formatting and arranging its flow for specific applications [15]. It provides healthcare and assistance to users through smart technologies. By replacing wireless sensors inside the home, on clothes and personal items, it becomes possible to monitor, in a way that preserves the privacy, the macroscopic behaviour of the person as well as to compile statistics, to identify precursors of dangerous behavioural abnormalities, and finally to activate alarms or prompt for remote actions by appropriate assistance procedures. Moreover, it enables users to read/view their health information through smart applications, such as ECG monitoring applications, diabetes therapy management applications, etc. Information processing is handled in applications layer. The information processing technologies for IoT healthcare applications include cloud and fog computing. The healthcare applications that depend on utilizing input from the physical world. These data can be sent to a cloud integrated with an IoT system for convenient and efficient storage, processing, and management [16]. For example, proposes three-component system for AAL (Ambient Assisted Living) healthcare applications, which consist of a sensor gateway at the sensor network level, network communication at the level of Internet-connected devices and applications, and a cloud platform at the topmost level for collecting data from the communication network [17]. The cloud-based approach enhances healthcare solutions by improving accessibility and quality of healthcare, and reducing costs [18]. The cloud computing can deliver three types of services [19]:

(a) Infrastructure as a Service: Infrastructure includes hardware and software, such as storage devices, networks, data, applications, and operating systems. Users can request for a certain infrastructure configuration, and then the cloud takes the administration and management duties off their shoulders.
(b) Platform as a Service: The cloud can provide a set of services and tools that facilitate convenient creating and efficient running of users' applications. Users can fully control their applications in the cloud but they are limited by not being able to use the operating system, hardware, and network infrastructure of the cloud.
(c) Software as a Service: This provides applications available to the users over the web.

Fog computing extends cloud computing. It is a distributed computing infrastructure that provides the same application services to end-users as cloud computing such as data processing, storage, and execution of applications. However, the application services are handled at the network edge in a smart device instead of a remote data centre in the cloud. The goal of fog computing is to improve the efficiency and reduce the amount of transported data to the cloud [20].

36.1.2   IoT Action in Healthcare

The IoT plays a significant role in a broad range of healthcare applications, from managing chronic diseases at one end of the spectrum to preventing disease at the other. Several healthcare applications are presented in Fig. 36.3 and here some examples are summarized as follows.

Clinical Care: The hospitalized patients whose physiological status requires close attention can be constantly monitored using IoT-driven, non-invasive monitoring technique. This type of solution employs sensors to collect comprehensive physiological information and uses gateways and the cloud to analyse and store the information and then send the analysed data wirelessly to caregivers for further analysis and review. It replaces the process of having a health professional come by at regular intervals to check the patient's vital signs, instead providing a continuous automated flow of information. In this way, it simultaneously improves the quality

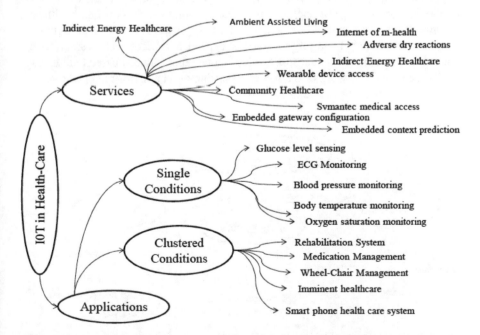

Fig. 36.3 Role of IoT in healthcare applications

of care through constant attention and lowers the cost of care by eliminating the need for a caregiver to actively engage in data collection and analysis.

Remote Monitoring: There are people all over the world whose health may suffer because they don't have ready access to effective health monitoring. However small, powerful wireless solutions connected through the IoT are now making it possible for monitoring to come to these patients instead of vice-versa. These solutions can be used to securely capture patient health data from a variety of sensors, apply complex algorithms to analyse the data and then share it through wireless connectivity with medical professionals who can make appropriate health recommendations.

As a result, patients with chronic diseases may be less likely to develop complications, and acute complications may be diagnosed earlier than they would be otherwise. For example, patients suffering from cardiovascular diseases who are being treated with digitalis could be monitored around the clock to prevent drug intoxication.

Early Intervention/Prevention: The healthy and active people can also benefit from IoT-driven monitoring of their daily activities and well-being. A senior living alone, for example, may want to have a monitoring device that can detect a fall or other interruption in everyday activity and report it to emergency responders or family members.

These are just a few examples of IoT-based healthcare solutions, and many more are emerging. IoT in healthcare are mainly classified in two major classes: (1) applications and (2) services as illustrated in Fig. 36.3. In present times, IoT is being applied in a wide range of applications including domestic monitoring, healthcare, environment sensing, agriculture and more. The application of IoT in configuration of a smart environment and self-conscious independent devices such as smart living, smart items, smart health, and smart cities among others are discussed here briefly.

The healthcare network of the IoT is consisting of: (1) platform, (2) architecture and (3) topology as discussed in Fig. 36.4.

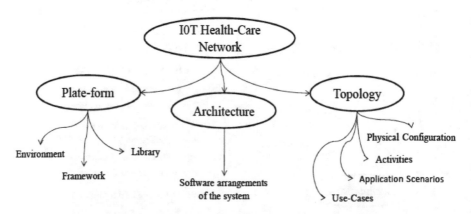

Fig. 36.4 The constituent of IoT healthcare networks

36.2 Enabling Technologies: IoT in Healthcare

The successful use of the IoT discussed in the preceding healthcare network relies on several enabling technologies. Without these, it would be difficult to achieve the usability, connectivity and capabilities required for applications in areas such as health monitoring.

Smart Sensors: The smart sensors which combine a sensor and a microcontroller, make it possible to harness the power of the IoT for healthcare by accurately measuring, monitoring and analyzing a variety of health status indicators. These can include basic vital signs such as heart rate and blood pressure, as well as levels of glucose or oxygen saturation in the blood. Smart sensors can even be incorporated into pill bottles and connected to the network to indicate whether a patient has taken a scheduled dose of medication. For smart sensors to work effectively, the microcontroller components must incorporate several essential capabilities.

Low-Power Operation: Low-power operation is essential to keeping device footprint small and extending battery life, characteristics that help to make IoT devices as usable as possible. Freescale, which has long offered low-power processing, is working now to enable completely battery-free devices that utilize energy harvesting techniques through the use of ultra-low-power DC-DC converters [21].

Integrated Precision-Analog Capabilities: Integrated precision-analog capabilities make it possible for sensors to achieve high accuracy at a low cost. Freescale offers this enabling technology within microcontrollers which contain analog components, such as high-resolution analog-to-digital converters (ADCs) and low-power op-amps [22].

Graphical User Interfaces (GUIs): The emergence of IoT is reshaping the relationship with computing technology, including the interface paradigms that we use to interact with digital technology. A graphical user interface (GUI) is an interface through which a user interacts with electronic devices and other appliances. Its design requirements vary dramatically in embedded applications. However, this variation has increased to unprecedented levels with the proliferation of smart devices and IoT. Some implementations are best served by simple GUIs that support minimal system resources, such as a small-footprint system-on-chip, using software rendering to a framebuffer. At the other end of the spectrum, some applications require feature-rich GUIs with advanced 3D graphics, shading, animation, and image transforms; these typically use hardware acceleration on dedicated graphics processors. The GUIs improve usability by enabling display devices to deliver a great deal of information in vivid detail and by making it easy to access that information. Freescale's i.MX applications processors with high graphics-processing performance support advanced GUI development.

Gateways: Gateways are the information hubs that collect sensor data, analyze it and then communicate it to the cloud via wide area network (WAN) technologies. Gateways can be designed for clinical or home settings; in the latter, they may be part of larger connectivity resource that also manages energy, entertainment and other systems in the home. The Freescale Home Health Hub reference platform includes a gateway component. Medical device designers can also use the platform to create remote-access devices for remote monitoring [23].

Wireless Networking: Wireless networking removes the physical limitations on networking imposed by traditional wired solutions like Ethernet and USB. Freescale offers microcontrollers that support wireless connectivity for devices based on popular wireless standards such as Bluetooth and Bluetooth Low Energy (BLE) for personal area networks (PAN) used with personal devices and Wi-Fi and Bluetooth for local area networks (LAN) in clinics or hospitals, which leads us to a key challenge for the IoT in healthcare standards [24, 25].

36.2.1 Connectivity Standards: IoT Devices to Work Together

The connectivity standards represent an inherent challenge for any environment in which a large number of complex devices need to communicate with each other—which is exactly the case for the IoT in healthcare.

Fortunately, the standards organizations are working now to create guidelines for wireless communications between monitoring devices and with healthcare providers. In wireless technology, IEEE standards for LANs define Wi-Fi (IEEE 802.11) and ZigBee (IEEE 802.15.4) networks. Standards for PANs include Bluetooth and BLE, as well as IEEE 802.15.4j and IEEE 802.15.6, which are the IEEE standards associated with the body area network (BAN). Standards for cellular networks include GSM/UMTS and CDMA. Proprietary wireless networks still play something of a role in healthcare environments in general and IoT applications in particular, but that role seems to be shrinking as the industry continues to move toward standards-based architectures.

36.2.2 Issues in Healthcare

The potential challenges in healthcare is presented in this section particularly, emphasized on interoperability challenges which limit data sharing and obstruct patient-centred care fostered by healthcare interoperability which would otherwise allow patients to access and control their own health information as discussed in Fig. 36.5.

Interoperability: The healthcare interoperability depicts the ability for heterogeneous information technology systems and software applications like Electronic Health Record (EHR) system, to communicate, exchange data, and use the exchanged data [26]. The secure and scalable data sharing is essential to provide effective collaborative treatment and care decisions for patients. The data sharing

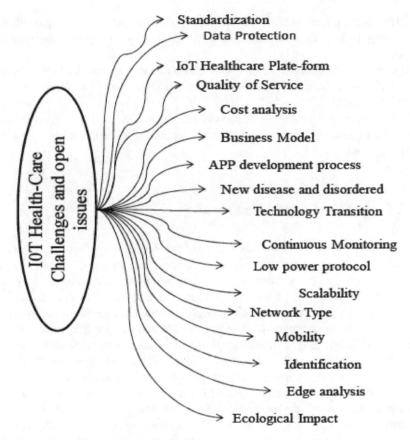

- Standardization
- Data Protection
- IoT Healthcare Plate-form
- Quality of Service
- Cost analysis
- Business Model
- APP development process
- New disease and disordered
- Technology Transition
- Continuous Monitoring
- Low power protocol
- Scalability
- Network Type
- Mobility
- Identification
- Edge analysis
- Ecological Impact

Fig. 36.5 IoT healthcare challenges and open issues

helps improve investigative accuracy [27] by gathering confirmations/recommendations from a group of medical experts, as well as preventing inadequacies [28] and errors in treatment plan and medication [29, 30]. Also, the aggregated intelligence and insights [31–33] helps medical practicenor to understand patient needs and apply more effective treatments. Even with the importance of medical data sharing, presently the healthcare systems frequently require patients to obtain and share their own medical records with other service providers either via physical paper copies or electronic hard disk copies. This process of obtaining and sharing medical records is ineffective for the following reasons:

- It is slow since copies of medical data must be prepared, delivered, and picked up by patients.
- It is insecure because data copies may be lost or stolen during their physical transmission by patients from one location to another.
- It is incomplete since as patient health history may be fragmented because their data is stored in disparate and siloed systems. There is no single source that stores

all the medical records of an individual, therefore patients must be responsible for keeping track ofhealth services record in order to request copies of their medical history.

- It lacks context because current healthcare systems are provider-centric instead of patient-centric, thereby preventing patients from taking control of their own health records.
- The ineffective data sharing process in healthcare results lack of trust between providers and the lack of interoperability between health IT systems and applications.

36.2.3 Patient-Centred Healthcare

The healthcare industry is shifting from volume-based care—in which providers are incentivized to provide more treatments because payment is proportional to the quantity of care, to the value-based care that promotes patient-centred care with higher quality, in which patients are informed and involved in clinical decision making [30]. In patient-centred care model, patients are capable of incorporating Patient Reported Experience Measures (PREM) and Patient Recorded Outcome Measures (PROM) [31], such as symptoms or health status, collected from their wearable and mobile devices into their medical history. The patients should also be given easy access to their medical records with a comprehensive view of their entire health history, which could potentially reduce information fragmentation and inaccuracy caused by communication delays or coordination errors and in turn improve the care continuity and quality [32]. Ideally, all the health systems would provide automatic notifications for patients to access their clinical data in real-time records are entered into the system or when lab results are available. Further, in the patient-centric care it is necessary for patients to control when and to whom their health data is shared and to choose what pieces of information they would be willing to share. The healthcare systems currently, do not provide the means for patients to modify or revoke a provider's access to their data. As a result, once a provider has cared for a patient or has obtained access to patient data that data is permanently in possession of the provider. When a patient visits different providers many times throughout their lifetime, their health and other sensitive personal data is available at several sites. This diffusion increases the risk of data theft because it only takes one provider lacking sufficient and up-to-date security practices to put patient information vulnerable to attack. Alternately, a patient may wish to release their medical records to a new provider, which is not easily accomplished. The interoperability is also a fundamental concept to support a patient-centric model that improves quality of care for individual patients. In practice, barriers exist in the healthcare technical infrastructure that impedes interoperability and thus patient-centred care, including:

- *Information security and privacy concerns*: Even though the need for data sharing, it increases the risk of sensitive data breaches without a highly secure infrastructure [7]. The service providers could face severe financial and legal consequences [6] when data is compromised. The lack of trust between providers because of security regulations, care providers must be able to identify other providers and also trust their identities before any patient health-related communication occurs [33]. The trust relationships often exist between in-network providers and/or health organizations but they are particularly difficult to establish when the data receiving care office does not use the same health system with a shared provider directory, such as in a private practice or a hospital network.
- *Scalability concerns*. The medical data may contain large volumes of data like medical images, especially in cancer patients or patients with chronic conditions. These large-scale datasets are difficult to share electronically due to limitations in bandwidth or restrictive firewall settings, such as in rural areas [21].

36.3 Privacy and Security Issues

I have addressed the most common privacy issues in IoT applications healthcare users along with IoT-based solutions that are known in the literature.

(1) Risks of Patients' Privacy Exposure

A Personal Health Record (PHR) is an individual electronic record of health-related information that conforms to the nationally recognized interoperability standards. PHR can be drawn from multiple sources while being managed, shared and controlled by the individual [22]. The PHRs are reported to the e-health centre directly, and the primary privacy and security issue is to keep the patients' PHRs confidential. Li et al. [23] proposed a method to encrypt each PHR with one-to-many encryption methods. Encryption algorithms with efficient key management have been used to encrypt each PHR file [24]. A healthcare system can be divided into two security domains, namely, public domains (PUDs) and personal domains (PSDs), according to the different users' data access requirements. PUDs consist of users who need access based on their professional roles, such as doctors, nurses and medical researchers. In practice, a PUD can be mapped to an independent economic sector, such as healthcare, government or insurance sectors. For each PSD, its users are personally associated with a data owner (such as family members or close friends), and they make accesses to PHRs based on access rights assigned by the owner [25]. Ukil et al. [34] presents a privacy measurement scheme that detects and analyzes sensitive content of time-series sensor data. It measures the amount of privacy, to make a decision whether to release private data or not.

(2) Threats of Cyber-Attacks on Privacy

Cyber attacks can inject false data into a system, causing critical damage in IoT applications. It is fundamental to provide the adequate level of protection against cyber-attacks in in smart home applications for the disabled. However, the resource-constrained nature of many of IoT devices present in a smart home environment do not allow to implement the standard security solutions. Tajer et al. [35] proposed a framework that guarantees detection of the cyber attacks and recovering from them. Different controlling agents, distributed across the network, constitute the attack detection subsystem. System recovery involves iterative local processing and message passing. Nguyen et al. [36] proposed a new distributed cyber attack detection algorithm, based on the decision cost minimization strategy. It is shown that is a suitable solution for detection of both known and unknown cyber attacks.

(3) Data Eavesdropping and Data Confidentiality

Generally, the health data of patients, including the disabled, are held under the legal obligations of confidentiality, and made available only to the authorized caregivers. It is important to prevent stealing data from storage or eavesdropping on them while they flow over the wireless links. For example, a popular IoT-based disabled glucose monitoring and insulin delivery system utilizes wireless communication links, which are frequently used to launch privacy attacks. Data eavesdropping may cause damage to the disabled by breaching the disabled's privacy. Li et al. [37] propose rolling-code cryptographic protocols and body-coupled communication to mitigate the eavesdropping on disabled's health data. Miaou et al. [38] propose a bi-polar multiple-base data hiding technique for images, where a pixel value difference between an original image and its default JPEG lossy decompressed image is taken as the number conversion base. The algorithm allows to hide, e.g., doctors' digital seals and PHR within a still image. The still image could be a logo of a hospital identifying where the PHR comes from. A diagnostic report and a biomedical signal, such as an electrocardiogram (ECG), can also be hidden in an image. The proposed approach allows hiding multiple data types in the same image. All these data can be separated and restored perfectly by the intended users [38]. Data confidentiality can be improved by using Public Key Encryption (PKI). PKI creates an effective approach to data encryption as it can provide high level of confidence for exchanging information in an insecure environment. Atzori et al. [39] presents a conceptual design and a prototype implementation of a system based on IoT gateways that aggregate health sensor data and resolve privacy issues through digital certificates and PKI data encryption.

(4) Identity Threats and Privacy of Stored Data

The identity threat, information security, privacy and stored data protection should systematically be addressed at the design stage. In numerous cases, it added on later once the intended functionality, which is not only limits the effectiveness of the added-on identity threat, information security and privacy measures, but also is less efficient in terms of the cost of implementation. Moreover, the IoT objects do not always have enough computing power to implement all the relevant security layers / functionalities therefore the heterogeneity of objects becomes very challenging in this context. Similarly, the heterogeneity of privacy policies needs to be taken into account.

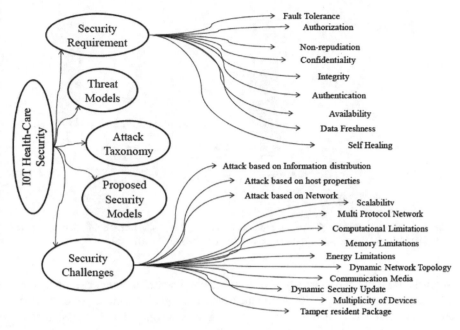

Fig. 36.6 IoT healthcare security challenges

36.3.1   Capacity of IoT Market

There are numerous customers who are interested in services of IoT. The capacity of market of the IoT defines a PWC [40], the number of connected devices to IoT, according to their forecast, will grow to 30 billion in 2020. IoT is a network of everyday objects embedded with sensors, actuators, and connectivity which enables them to send and receive data, and this technology has gained importance with wide scope of applications in various fields such as utilities, education, etc. Adoption of this advanced technology in healthcare sector is one of the fastest among other end-use industries (Fig. 36.6).

From the Fig. 36.7 it is clearly shown that the IoT market is growing with high speed. IoT connects multiple devices in an organization via the wireless sensor networks and cloud services which provides access to operational technology networks and information technology. Further, IoT solutions and services need to provide secure access to authorized users as well as protect confidential and personal data. The major factors driving the growth of the global IoT security market is increasing adoption of cloud-based services and solutions in various sectors, which has led to storage of vast volumes of data on the cloud that could be vulnerable to cyber-attack and data theft. Another factor driving the growth of the global IoT security market is increasing the number of connected devices in organizations worldwide, and increasing concerns related to security of devices and data privacy. The global IoT security market is segmented on the basis of network security components, end user, and region. On the basis of navigation security components

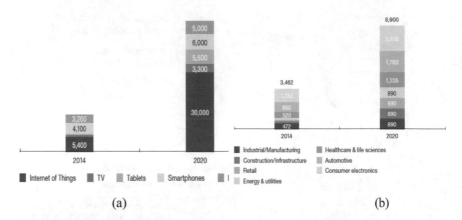

Fig. 36.7 The capacity of IoT market forecasts from IDC, PwC analysis (**a**) connected devices (in millions) [40] and (**b**) potential applications (in billion US $) up to 2020 [6]

segmentation, the hardware segment is expected to contribute major revenue share and expected to maintain its dominance over the forecast period. Among all the end user segments, the industrial sector segment accounted for highest revenue contribution to the global IoT market, owing to factors such as increasing adoption of IoT solutions in manufacturing industry to boost production, improve quality, and cost efficiency of products [6]. Further, the adoption of cloud is increasing due to the flexibility and scalability offered by it to small and medium scale enterprise/companies. To securing confidential data on cloud, the security systems are in demand which is major factor to drive the global IoT security market. The increasing need for data-centric security solutions for various security controls for the information itself stored and processed in database systems, primary computing and network infrastructures, as well as applications accessing the data is driving the market. The cost of IoT security solutions may impact the growth of the market initially. However, as consumers are increasingly drawn to the conveniences and benefits of IoT devices the IoT market is expected to witness the growth globally. However, errors in real-time responses being generated by the security systems, over reliance on technology, and complexes in the systems could lead to damage. These are the major factors for the restraining the growth of the global IoT security market.

The growth of IoT transform the healthcare industry and enable the emergence ofthe Internet of Medical Things (IoMT). One of the applicationdomains that will be most impacted by the IoT is the healthcare industry [41], which will give rise to the Internet of Medical Things (IoMT). The IoT is expected to have aprofound $1.1–$2.5 trillion annual economic impact in the healthcare domain by 2025 [42]. Recent interest in future IoT systems arises from a variety of challenging characteristics, such as capability, adaptability, resiliency, safety, security, and usability. As the biggest computer network, IoT produces massive information from a network of physical devices, which enables the communication and exchange of data. The computer networks are considered as the major contributor to handle 50 petabytes of data available on the Internet. Therefore, traditional technology cannot handle such data size. Although cutting-edge tools are proposed to analyze and extract useful knowledge from vast and diverse data streams, to attain the benefits of IoT, the identification of things, the integration and management of heterogeneous data and knowledge-based decision systems are required. Innovative solutions on technologies of identification, information, and knowledge systems are sought to attain throughput goals within efficiency constraints for orders of magnitude improvements.

36.4   Conclusion

The recent developments in the area of IoT show a great promise for providing solutions for healthcare. However, there are many privacy and security challenges in IoT healthcare applications for the users. This chapter presents IoT, its layered architecture, and its role in the healthcare industry. It describes privacy and security services and proposes viewing confidentiality as the intersection of privacy and security. It describes the range of IoT healthcare applications along with their classification. It investigates privacy and security issues in IoT healthcare applications for users, and reviews IoT-based solutions known in the literature. The long-predicted IoT revolution in healthcare is already underway as new use cases continue to emerge to address the urgent need for affordable, accessible care. For the meantime, we are seeing the IoT building blocks of automation and machine-to-machine communication continue to be established, with the addition of the service layer completing the infrastructure. This revolution by providing end-to-end processing and connectivity solutions for IoT-driven healthcare solutions, working toward establishing standards for these solutions and accelerating innovation for organizations eager to realize the benefits of the IoT in healthcare. The exponential growth of the Internet of Things connections, and the invested funds convince companies to have a high financial interest in this direction. Growing markets provide a high profit margin of the projects. The goal of this feature topic is to present state-of-the-art original research, and latest advances and innovations in key theories, techniques, schemes, applications, and solutions for Blockchain, as well as to identify emerging research topics and examine the future.

References

1. Rolf H. Weber and Romana Weber, "Internet of Things: Legal Perspective," Heidelberg: Springer, 2010.
2. A. J. Jara, M. A. Zamora, and A. F. G. Skarmeta, "HWSN6: Hospital Wireless Sensor Networks based on 6LoWPAN technology: Mobility and fault tolerance management," Proc. 7th IEEE Int. Conf. on Computational Science and Engineering, Vancouver, Canada, Aug. 2009, vol. 2, pp. 879-848.

3. R. Tesoriero, J. A. Guled, M. D. Lozano, and V. M. R. Penichet, "Tracking autonomous entities using RFID technology," IEEE Trans. on Consumer Electronics, vol. 55(2), pp. 650-655, May 2009.
4. C. M. Medaglia and A. Serbanati, "An Overview of Privacy and Security Issues in the Internet of Things," In: D. Giusto, A. Iera, G. Morabito, and L. Atzori (eds) "The Internet of Things", Springer: New York, 2010.
5. P. Yang, W. Wu, M. Moniri, and C. C. Chibelushi, "Efficient object localization using sparsely distributed passive RFID tags," IEEE Transactions on Industrial Electronics, 60(12), pp. 5914-5924, 2013.
6. https://www.marketresearchengine.com/reportdetails/iot-healthcare-market
7. F. Firouzi, B. Farahani, M. Ibrahim, and K. Chakrabarty, "Keynote paper: From EDA to IoT eHealth: promises, challenges, and solutions," IEEE Transactions on Computer-Aided Design of Integrated Circuits and Systems, 37(12), 2965-2978, 2018.
8. S. Amendola, R. Lodato, S. Manzari, C. Occhiuzzi, and G. Marrocco, "RFID technology for IoT-based personal healthcare in smart spaces," IEEE Internet of Things Journal, 1(2), 144-152, 2014.
9. L. Atzori, A. Lera, and G. Morabito, "The internet of things: A survey," Computer Networks, vol. 54(15), pp. 2787-2805, Oct. 2010.
10. X. Jia, Q. Feng, T. Fan, Q. Lei, "RFID technology and its applications in internet of things (IoT)" Proc. 2nd IEEE Int. Conf. on Consumer Electronics, Communications and Networks (CECNet), Yichang, Apr. 2012, pp. 1282-1285.
11. L. Grobe, A. Paraskevopoulos, J. Hilt, D. Schulz, F. Lassak, F. Hartlieb, C. Kottke, V. Jungnickel, and K. D. Langer, "High-speed visible light communication systems," IEEE Communications Magazine, vol. 51(12), pp. 60-66, 2013
12. P.K. Wali and D. Das, "A novel access scheme for IoT communications in LTE-Advanced network," Proceeding of the IEEE Int. Conf. on Advanced Networks and Telecommunications Systems, New Delhi, India, Dec. 2014, pp. 1-6.
13. V. Raghunathan, C. Schurgers, S. Park, andM. B. Srivastava, "Energy aware wireless microsensor networks," IEEE Signal Processing Magazine, vol. 19(2), pp. 40–50, Mar 2002.
14. T. T.-O. Kwok and Y.-K. Kwok, "Computation and energy efficient image processing in wireless sensor networks based on reconfigurable computing," Proc. Int. Conf. Parallel Processing Workshops, 2006, pp. 50-58.
15. D. Chen, G. Chang, L. Jin, X. Ren, J. Li, and F. Li, "A novel secure architecture for the internet of things," Proc. 5th IEEE Int. Conf. on Genetic and Evolutionary Computing, Xiamen, China, Aug. 2011, pp. 311-314.
16. C. Doukas, and I. Maglogiannis, "Bringing IoT and cloud computing towards pervasive healthcare," Proc. 6th IEEE Int. Conf. on Innovative Mobil and Internet Services in Ubiquitous Computing (IMIS), Palermo, July 2012, pp. 922-926.
17. J. Cubo, A. Nieto, and E. Pimentel, "A Cloud-Based Internet of Things Platform for Ambient Assisted Living," Sensors J., vol. 14 (8), pp. 14070-14105, Aug. 2014.
18. G. Garkoti, S.K. Peddoju, and R. Balasubramanian, "Detection of insider attacks in cloud based e-healthcare environment," Proceeding of the IEEE Int. Conf. on Information Technology, Bhubaneswar, Dec. 2014, pp. 195-200.
19. C.H. Liu et al., "Secure PHR access control scheme for healthcare application clouds," Proceeding of the IEEE 42nd Int. Conf. on Parallel Processing, Lyon, Oct. 2013, pp. 1067-1076.
20. F. Bonomi, R. Militi, J. Zhu, and S. Addepalli, "Fog Computing and Its Role in The Internet of Things," Processing of the 1st Edition of the ACM MCC Workshop on Mobil Cloud Computing, Helsinki, Finland, Aug. 2012, pp. 13-16.
21. A. Sawand, S. Djahel, Z. Zhang, and F. Nait-Abdesselam, "Toward energy-efficient and trustworthy eHealth monitoring system," China Communications, vol. 12(1), pp. 46– 65, 2015.
22. J.S. Khan, V. Aulakh, and A. Bosworth, "What it takes: Characteristics of the ideal personal health record," Health Aff (Millwood), vol. 28(2), pp. 369-376.

23. M. Li, S. Yu, Y. Zhen, K. Ren, and W. Lou, "Scalable and secure sharing of personal health records in cloud computing using attribute-based encryption," IEEE Trans. on Parallel and Distributed System, vol. 24(1), pp. 131-143, Mar. 2012
24. Y. Ren, R.W.N. Pazzi, and A. Boukerche, "Monitoring patients via a secure and mobile healthcare system," IEEE Wireless Communications, vol. 17(1), pp. 59-65, Feb. 2010.
25. M. Li, S. Yu, Y. Zhen, K. Ren, and W. Lou, "Scalable and secure sharing of personal health records in cloud computing using attribute-based encryption," IEEE Trans. on Parallel and Distributed Systems, vol. 24(1), pp. 131-143 March 2012.
26. Fadele Ayotunde Alaba, Mazliza Othman, Ibrahim Abaker Targio Hashem and Faiz Alotaibi, "Internet of Things security: A survey" Journal of Network and Computer Applications, vol. 88(15), pp. 10-28, June 2017.
27. S R Islam, D. Kwak, M. H. Kabir, M. Hossain, and K. S. Kwak, "The internet of things for health care: a comprehensive survey", IEEE Access, 3, pp. 678-708, 2015.
28. I. Lee and Kyoochun Lee, "The internet of things (IoT): Applications, investments, and challenges for enterprises," Business Horizons, vol. 58(4), pp. 431-440, 2015.
29. D. Miorandi, Sabrina Sicari, Francesco De Pellegrini, and Imrich Chlamtac, "Internet of things: Vision, applications and research challenges," Ad Hoc Networks, vol. 10(7), pp. 1497- 1516, 2012.
30. J. Gubbi, Rajkumar Buyya, Slaven Marusic, and M. Palaniswami. "Internet of Things (IoT): A vision, architectural elements, and future directions," Future Generation Computer Systems, vol. 29(7), pp. 1645-1660, 2013.
31. Partha Pratim Ray, "A survey on internet of things architectures," Journal of King Saud University-Computer and Information Sciences, vol. 30(3), pp. 291-319, 2018.
32. S. Sicari, Alessandra Rizzardi, Luigi Alfredo Grieco, and Alberto Coen-Porisini, "Security, privacy and trust in internet of things: The road ahead," Computer Networks, vol. 76, pp. 146-164, 2015.
33. R. Roman, J. Zhou, and Javier Lopez, "On the features and challenges of security and privacy in distributed internet of things," Computer Networks, vol. 57(10) pp. 2266- 2279, 2013.
34. A. Ukil, S. Bandyopadhyay, and A. Pal, "IoT-privacy: To be private or not to be private," Proceeding of the IEEE Conference on Computer Communications Workshops (INFOCOM WKSHPS), Toronto ON, Apr. 2014, pp. 123-124.
35. A. Tajer, S. Kar, H.V. Poor, and S. Cui, "Distributed joint cyber attack detection and state recovery in smart grids," Proceeding of the IEEE Int. Conf. on Smart Grid Communications, Brussels, Belgium, Oct. 2011, pp. 202-207.
36. H.D. Nguyen, S. Gutta, and Q. Cheng, "An active distributed approach for cyber attack detection," Proceeding of 44th IEEE Asilomar Conf. on Signals, Systems and Computers, Pacific Grove, CA, Nov. 2010, pp. 1540-1544.
37. C. Li, A. Raghunathan, and N. K. Jha, "Hijacking an insulin pump: Security attacks and defenses for a diabetes therapy system," Proceeding of 13th IEEE Int. Conf. on e-health Networking, Applications and Services, Columbia, MO, June 2011, pp. 150-156.
38. S.G. Miaou, C.M. Hsu, Y.S. Tsai, and H. M. Chao, "A secure data hiding technique with heterogeneous data-combining capability for electronic patient records," Proc. of the 22nd Annual International Conference of the IEEE Engineering in Medicine and Biology Society, vol. 1, Chicago IL, July 2000, pp. 280-283.
39. L. Atzori, A. Lera, and G. Morabito, "The internet of things: A survey," Computer Networks, 54(15), pp. 2787-2805, Oct. 2010.
40. www.pwc.com
41. Y. Yuehong, Y. Zeng, X. Chen, and Y. Fan, "The internet of things in healthcare: An overview," Journal of Industrial Information Integration,vol. 1, pp. 3–13, 2016.
42. J. Manyika, M. Chui, J. Bughin, R. Dobbs, P. Bisson, and A. Marrs, "Disruptive technologies: Advances that will transform life, businessand the global economy," Tech. Rep., May 2013.

Chapter 37
Internet-of-Things with Blockchain Technology: State-of-the Art and Potential Challenges

Ghanshyam Singh

37.1 Introduction

Internet-of-Things (IoT) is the class of cyber–physical systems (CPSs) that influence internet technology for interactions between the physical and cyber-world. It represents a broader move to the vision of pervasive or ubiquitous computing [1]. The IoT has emerged as most important new technology since the arrival of Internet and the global researcher's fraternity are now turning to signal processing to support and augment new IoT services and make existing applications less expensive and more practical. It is expanding with a fast pace and researcher in [2] predict that IoT devices will grow to 26 billions by 2020, which are 30 times the estimated number of devices deployed in 2009. Moreover, some forecasts [3, 4] anticipate a fourfold growth in Machine-to-Machine (M2M) connections by 2021, which may be related to a broad spectrum of applications. Presently, most IoT solutions rely on the centralized server-client paradigm, connecting to cloud servers through the Internet. Although this solution may work properly nowadays, the expected growth suggests that new paradigms will have to be proposed. Among such proposals, decentralized architectures have been suggested in the past to create large Peer-to-Peer (P2P) Wireless Sensor Networks (WSNs) [5–7], but some pieces were missing in relation to privacy and security until the arrival of blockchain technology. Therefore, as it is illustrated in Fig. 37.1, in the last years pre-IoT closed and centralized mainframe architectures evolved towards IoT open-access cloud-centred alternatives, being the next step the distribution of the cloud functionality among multiple peers which is supported by blockchain technology. This technology is able to track, coordinate, carry out transactions and store information from a large

G. Singh (✉)
Department of Electrical and Electronics Engineering Sciences, Auckland Park Kingsway Campus, University of Johannesburg, Johannesburg, South Africa
e-mail: ghanshyams@uj.ac.za

© Springer Nature Switzerland AG 2019
A. K. Singh, A. Mohan (eds.), *Handbook of Multimedia Information Security: Techniques and Applications*, https://doi.org/10.1007/978-3-030-15887-3_37

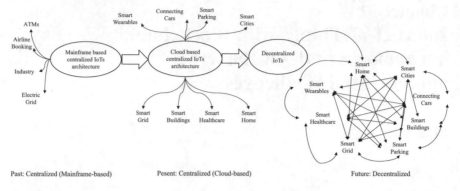

Fig. 37.1 Evolution of the IoT architectures [8]

number of devices, enabling the creation of applications that require no centralized cloud. The blockchain as a technology is used for democratizing the future IoT [9], since it addresses the current critical challenges for its massive adoption:

- Various IoT solutions are still expensive because of costs related to the deployment and maintenance of centralized systems.
- Maintenance is a challenging issue to distribute regular software updates to millions of smart devices,
- The privacy and secrecy are a challenging issue of future IoT solutions, and
- To enhance the trust and security, transparency is essential, consequently opensource approaches should be considered when developing the next generation of IoT solutions.

Therefore, this chapter studies such similarities and analyses the advantages that blockchain can bring to IoT despite its current practical limitations. Moreover, the main Blockchain-integrated IoT (BIoT) architectures and improvements that have already proposed are reviewed. Furthermore, the most relevant future challenges for the application of blockchain to IoT are detailed. Several authors have previously presented surveys on the application of blockchain on different application areas. For instance, in [10] it is provided an extensive description on the basics of blockchain and smart contracts, and it is given a good overview on the application and deployment of BIoT solutions. However, the characteristics of the ideal BIoT architecture and possible optimizations which need to performed for creating BIoT applications are missing in the reported literatures. It is worth to mentioned that the systematic reviews presented in [11], which analyse the sort of topics that deal blockchain integrated IoT when proposing the use of blockchain.

This chapter presents a holistic approach of blockchain integrated IoT scenarios including its basics with applications as well as most relevant aspects involved on their development, deployment and optimization. Also, review the potential contribution of blockchain for revolutionizing the IoT industry and confront today challenges. The remainder of this chapter is organized as follows. Section 37.2 describes the basics of blockchain technologies. Section 37.3 presents the most relevant BIoT applications. Section 37.4 reviews critical aspects to be optimized in a blockchain in order to adapt it to an IoT application. Section 37.5 describes the main limitations of current BIoT applications. Section 37.6 identifies further medium-term challenges and proposes recommendations for IoT developers. Finally, Sect. 37.7 is devoted to conclusions.

37.2 Blockchain Technology

The blockchain is most popular type of distributed lager technology (DLT), which is a distributed and decentralized ledger of transactions used to manage a constantly increasing set of records. Further, to store a transaction in the ledger, the majority of participating nodes in the blockchain network should agree and record their consent. Also, a set of transactions are grouped together and allocate a block in the ledger, which is chained of blocks and each block encompasses a times-tamp and hash function with the previous block to link the blocks together. The hash function validates the integrity and non-repudiation of the data inside the block. Furthermore, to keep all participating nodes of the blockchain network updated, each user holds a copy of the original ledger and all nodes are synchronized and updated with newly change. Blockchain delivers a high level of transparency by sharing transaction details between all participants nodes involved in the transactions and in this environment, no need for a third party which improve business friendliness, guarantees a trusted work-flow and blockchain eliminates the single point of failure which affects the entire system. Moreover, blockchain provides better security since it uses public key infrastructure that protects against malicious actions. The participating nodes of the blockchain network place their trust in the integrity and security features of the consensus mechanism. Although the concept of blockchain was originated as a tool for a cryptocurrency, it is not necessary to develop a cryptocurrency to use a blockchain and build decentralized applications [8]. A blockchain, as its name implies, is a chain of timestamped blocks that are linked by cryptographic hashes. To introduce the reader into the inner workings of a blockchain, the next subsections describe its basic characteristics and functioning.

37.2.1 Function of Blockchain Technology

In order to use a blockchain, first create a peer-to-peer (P2P) network with all the nodes interested in use of a blockchain. Every node of the network receives two keys: (1) a public key, which is used by the other users for encrypting the messages sent to a node, and (2) a private key, which allows a node to read (decrypting) such messages. In practice, the private key is used for signing blockchain transactions to approve such transactions, while the public key works like a unique address. Only the user with the proper private key is able to decrypt the messages encrypted with the corresponding public key that is symmetric cryptography. A detailed explanation of its workings is presented in [10]. When a node carries out a transaction, it signs and then broadcasts to its one-hop peers. The fact of signing the transaction in a unique way enables authenticating it and guarantees integrity. As the peers of node that broadcasts the transaction receive the signed transaction, they verify that it is valid before retransmitting it to other peers, thus, contributing to its spread through the network. The transactions disseminated in this way and that are considered valid by the network are ordered and packed into a timestamped block by special nodes called miners. The election of the miners and the data included into the block depend on a consensus algorithm. The blocks packed by a miner are then broadcast back into the network. Then the blockchain nodes verify that the broadcast block contains valid transactions and that it references the previous block of the chain by using the corresponding hash. If such conditions are not fulfilled, the block is discarded. However, if both conditions are verified successfully, the nodes add the block to their chain and updating the transactions.

37.2.2 Types of Blockchains

There are different types of blockchains depending on the managed data, availability of such data, and actions performed by a user. Thus, it can be distinguished between public and private, and permissioned and permission-less blockchains. It is important to indicate that some authors use the terms public/permission-less and private/permissioned as synonyms, what may be coherent when talking about cryptocurrencies, but that is not the case for IoT applications, where it is important to distinguish between authentication and authorization. However, such distinctions are still in debate. In public blockchains anyone can join the blockchain without the approval of third-parties, being able to act as a simple node or as miner/validator. In the case of private blockchains, the owner restricts network access. Many private blockchains are also permissioned in order to control which users can perform transactions, carry out smart contracts or act as miners in the network, but not all private blockchains are necessarily permissioned. It can also be distinguished between blockchains aimed exclusively at tracking digital assets and blockchains that enable running certain logic. Moreover, there are systems that make use of tokens while others do not and such tokens are not necessarily related to the existence of a cryptocurrency, but they may be used as internal receipts that prove that certain events happened at certain time instants.

37.2.3 Prerequisite for Using a Blockchain

Before investigating into the details to employ a blockchain technology or IoT applications, initially, we emphasized that a blockchain is not always the best solution for every IoT scenario. Precisely, in order to determine if the use of a blockchain is appropriate, a developer should decide if the following features are necessary for an IoT application:

- *Decentralization*: IoT applications demand decentralization when there is not a trusted centralized system.
- *P2P exchanges*: In IoT most communications drive from nodes to gateways that route data to a remote server or cloud. Communications among peers at a node level are not very common, except for specific applications, like in intelligent swarms or in fog computing systems [12]. There are also other paradigms that foster communications among nodes at the same level, as it happens in fog computing with local gateways [13, 14].
- *Payment system*: Some IoT applications require to perform economic transactions with third parties, but not many. Moreover, economic transactions can still be carried out through traditional payment systems, although they usually imply to pay transaction fees and it is necessary to trust banks or middlemen.
- *Public sequential transaction logging*: Various IoT networks collect data that need to be timestamped and stored sequentially. However, such needs may be easily fulfilled with traditional databases, especially in cases where security is guaranteed or where attacks are rare.
- *Robust distributed system*: Distributed systems can also be built on top of clouds, server farms or any form of traditional distributed computing systems. The need of this feature is not enough to justify the use of a blockchain:

  (1) There also has to be at least a lack of trust in the entity that manages the distributed computing system.
  (2) Some IoT applications may need to keep a record of every transaction to maintain traceability that is known as micro-transaction collection, for auditing purposes or because Big Data techniques will be applied later [15, 16].

In these situations, a sidechain may be useful, however other applications do not need to store every collected value. Figure 37.2 shows a generic flow diagram that allows for determining the type of blockchain that is necessary depending on the characteristics of an IoT system.

37.3   Blockchain Integrated IoT Applications

Blockchain technology has been applied in various fields. Smart contracts can be applied in many practical cases, including international transfers, mortgages or crowd funding. Ethereum is arguably the most popular blockchain-based platform for running smart contracts, although it can actually run other distributed applications and interact with more than one blockchain. In fact, Ethereum is characterized by being Turing-complete, which is a mathematical concept that indicates that Ethereum's programming language can be used to simulate any other

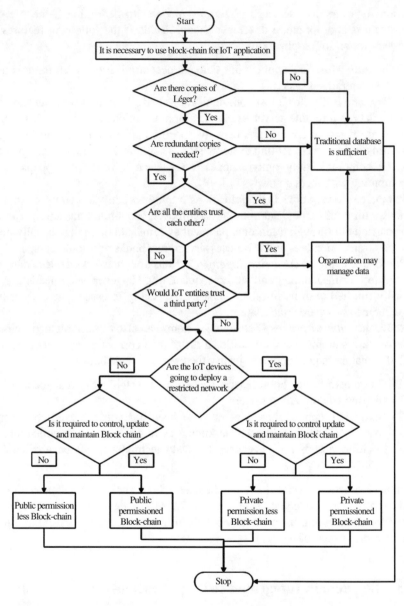

Fig. 37.2 Flow diagram for deciding when to use blockchain in an IoT application [8]

language. Beyond cryptocurrencies and smart contracts, blockchain technologies can be applied in different areas (the most relevant are shown in Fig. 37.3) where IoT applications are involved [17], like sensing, data storage, identity management, timestamping services, smart living applications, intelligent transportation systems [18], wearables, supply chain management [19], mobile crowd sensing, cyber law

Fig. 37.3 Potential applications IoT integrated blockchain

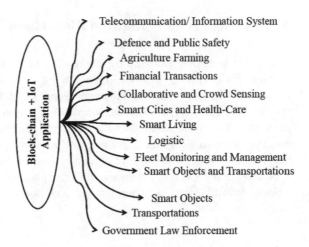

Telecommunication/ Information System

Defence and Public Safety

Agriculture Farming

Financial Transactions

Collaborative and Crowd Sensing

Smart Cities and Health-Care

Smart Living

Logistic

Fleet Monitoring and Management

Smart Objects and Transportations

Smart Objects

Transportations

Government Law Enforcement

Block-chain + IoT Application

and security in mission-critical scenarios [20]. Blockchain can also be used in IoT agricultural applications. The system is based on the use of Radio Frequency Identification (RFID) and a blockchain, being its aim to enhance food safety and quality, and to reduce losses in logistics. Several researchers focused on managing IoT devices through a blockchain, which proposed a system able to control and configure IoT devices remotely. The system stores public keys in Ethereum while private keys are saved on each IoT device. The authors indicate that the use of Ethereum is essential, since it allows them to write their own code to run on top of the network. Moreover, updating the code on Ethereum modifies the behaviour of the IoT devices, what simplifies maintenance and bug corrections. The energy sector can also be benefited from the application of a blockchain to IoT or to the Internet of Energy (IoE) [21]. The healthcare BIoT applications are found in the literature as well. For instance, in [8] it is presented a traceability application that makes use of IoT sensors and blockchain technology to verify data integrity and public accessibility to temperature records in the pharmaceutical supply chain. This verification is critical for the transport of medical products in order to ensure their quality and environmental conditions. The work described in [22], which presents a generic smart healthcare system that makes use of IoT devices, cloud and fog computing [15], and a blockchain. IoT low-level security can also be enhanced by integrating blockchain technology. Specifically, it can be improved remote attestation, which is the process that verifies whether the underlying Trusted Computer Base (TCB) of a device is trustworthy. Finally, it should be mentioned that Big Data can be leveraged by blockchain technology, therefore, several researchers [15] reviewed the main blockchain-based solutions to gather and control massive amounts of data that may be collected from IoT networks.

37.4   Design of an Optimized Blockchain for IoT Applications

Blockchain technologies is full of several benefits to IoT, however it has not been planned explicitly for IoT environments. In order to optimize them, several authors studied BIoT performance in different scenarios and analysed various potential aspects, but mainly focus on the performance of consensus algorithms. Further, it is stated that the implementation of the consensus protocols in hardware is probably the most promising way for improving the performance of any consensus method. Besides the consensus algorithm, other elements of the blockchain can be adapted to be used in IoT networks. Further, different parts of a blockchain are analysed in order to determine possible optimizations as follows.

37.4.1   Architecture

The architecture that supports a blockchain used for IoT applications should have to be adapted to the amount of traffic that such applications usually generate. This is a concern for traditional cloud-based architectures, which, as it is illustrated in Fig. 37.4, evolved towards more complex edge and fog computing-based architectures. From Fig. 37.4, it can be observed that three architectures depend on a cloud, although, in practice, the dependency degree varies a great deal. In the case

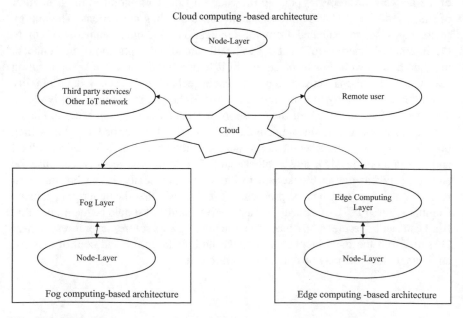

Fig. 37.4 IoT architecture evolution scenarios

of a cloud-based architecture, the data collected by the Node Layer are forwarded directly to the cloud through IoT gateways without further processing that the one needed for protocol conversion. There are also gateways that perform more sophisticated tasks, but in most cloud-centered applications, most processing is carried out in the cloud. However, note that traditional cloud-centered IoT architectures have certain inherent vulnerabilities [19], being the most relevant the fact that the cloud is a point of failure: if the cloud is down due to cyberattacks, maintenance or software problems, the whole system stops working. In addition, it is important to emphasize that if a single IoT device is compromised, it may disrupt the whole network by performing Denial of Service (DoS) attacks, eavesdropping private data [23], altering the collected data or misleading other systems [24]. Therefore, once an IoT device connected to the cloud or to a central server is breached, the rest of the nodes may be compromised. In contrast, the blockchain-based systems do not rely on a unique central server/cloud. Moreover, the transactions are verified cryptographically, consequently when malicious activities from a compromised device are detected, the system can reject its blockchain updates. However, other two architectures depicted in Fig. 37.4 are more recent and offload part of the processing from the cloud- to the edge-computing of the network. Thus, Edge- and fog computing can be used to support physically distributed, low-latency and quality-of-service (QoS)-aware applications that decrease the network traffic and the computational load of traditional cloud computing systems. Fog computing is based on a set of local gateways able to respond fast to IoT node requests through specific services and such nodes can also interact with each other and, when required, with the cloud. The researchers conclude that a BIoT architecture should be as close as possible to the Fully Distributed approach, but in some scenarios where computational power or cost are limiting factors, other approaches may be more appropriate. It is also proposed a novel blockchain-based architecture that makes use of software defined networks (SDN) to control the fog nodes of an IoT network. The system makes use of a cloud to perform compute-intensive tasks, while providing low-latency data access through fog computing. The fog nodes are the ones that are distributed, providing services and interaction with the blockchain. However, the achieved results indicate that the architecture reduces delays, increases throughput and it is able to detect real-time attacks on the IoT network.

37.4.2   Cryptographic Algorithms

The public-key cryptography algorithms are essential for providing security and privacy in a blockchain however, resource-constraint IoT devices struggle with the computing requirements of modern secure cryptographic schemes [25]. Specifically, asymmetric cryptography based on Rivest–Shamir–Adleman (RSA) is slow and power consuming when implemented on IoT devices. Therefore, when choosing the right cryptographic scheme, it should be taken into account not only the computational load and the memory requirements, but also the consumed energy.

37.4.3   Message Timestamping

In order to track modifications on the blockchain, transactions have to be both signed and timestamped and later task should be performed in a synchronized way such that the timestamping servers are commonly used. Traditional schemes rely on having trustworthiness on the server, which signs and timestamps transactions with its own private key. Nonetheless, no one deters the server from signing past transactions. For such a reason, diverse authors have proposed secure mechanisms.

37.4.4   Consensus Mechanisms, Mining and Message Validation

For proper functioning of the blockchain, the consensus is the key technique which is basically consists in a mechanism that determines the conditions to be reached in order to conclude that an agreement has been reached regarding the validations of the blocks to be added to the blockchain. The most egalitarian (and idealistic) consensus mechanism consists in giving to all the miners the same weight when voting and then deciding according to the majority of the votes. The work performed usually involves doing some calculations until a solution is found, a process that is commonly known as mining. In the case of the Bitcoin blockchain, mining consists in finding a random number (called nonce) that will make the SHA-256 hash of the block header to have at the beginning certain number of zeroes. Therefore, miners have to demonstrate that they have performed certain amount of work to solve the problem. Once the problem is solved, it is really easy for other nodes to verify that the obtained answer is correct. However, this mining process makes the blockchain inefficient in throughput, scalability, and in terms of energy consumption, what is not desirable in an IoT network. Due to the problems previously mentioned, several alternative consensus methods have been proposed. The following are the most relevant:

- Proof of stake (PoS) is a consensus mechanism that requires less computational power than Proof of Work (PoW), so it consumes less energy. In a PoS-based blockchain, it is assumed that the entities with more participation on the network are the ones less interested in attacking it. Thus, the miners have to prove periodically that they own certain amount of participation on the network. Since this scheme seems unfair, because the wealthiest participants are the ones ruling the blockchain, other variants have been proposed.
- Delegated Proof-of-Stake (DPoS) is a consensus algorithm maintaining irrefutable agreement on the truth across the network, validating transactions and acting as a form of digital democracy, and is similar to PoS, but stakeholders instead of being the ones generating and validating blocks, they select certain delegates to do it. Since less nodes are involved in block validation, transactions

are performed faster than with other schemes. In addition, delegates can adjust block size and intervals, and, if they behave dishonestly, they can be substituted easily.

- Transactions as Proof-of-Stake (TaPoS) is a PoS variant. While in PoS systems only some nodes contribute to the consensus, in TaPoS all nodes that generate transactions contribute to the security of the network.
- Proof-of-Activity (PoA) consensus algorithms were proposed due to the main limitation of PoS systems based on stake age: it is accumulated even when the node is not connected to the network. Thus, PoA schemes have been proposed to encourage both ownership and activity on the blockchain, rewarding stakeholders who participate instead of punishing passive stakeholders. A similar approach is proposed by Proof of-Stake-Velocity (PoSV). It is implemented by Reddcoin, which is based on the concept of velocity of money. Such a concept indicates how many times a unit of currency flows through an economy and is used by the members of a society during a certain time period. Usually, the higher the velocity of money, the more transactions in which it is used and the healthier the economy.
- PBFT (Practical Byzantine Fault Tolerance) is a consensus algorithm that solves the Byzantine Generals Problem for asynchronous environments and it assumes that less than a third of the nodes are malicious. For every block to be added to the chain, a leader is selected to be in charge of ordering the transaction and such a selection has to be supported by at least 2/3 of the all nodes, which have to be known by the network.
- Delegated BFT (DBFT) is a variant of BFT where, in a similar way to Delegated Proof-of-Stake (DPoS) consensus algorithms which is fast, efficient, decentralized, and highly flexible blockchain design, some specific nodes are voted to be the ones generating and validating blocks.
- The Ripple consensus algorithm was proposed to reduce the high latencies found in many blockchains, which are in part due to the use of synchronous communications among the nodes.
- Stellar Consensus Protocol (SCP) is a implementation of a consensus method called Federated Byzantine Agreement (FBA). It is similar to PBFT but, whilst in PBFT every node queries all the other nodes and waits for the majority to agree, in SCP the nodes only wait for a subset of the participants that they consider important.
- BFTRaft is a BFT consensus scheme based on the Raft algorithm, which is aimed at being simple and easy to understand for students. Such an aim makes Raft assume simplifications that rarely hold in practice, like the fact that nodes only fail by stopping. Thus, BFTRaft enhances the Raft algorithm by making it Byzantine fault tolerant and by increasing its security against diverse threats.
- Sieve is a consensus algorithm proposed by IBM Research that has already been implemented for Hyperledger-Fabric. Its objective is to run nondeterministic smart contracts on a permissioned blockchain that makes use of BFT replication. In such a scenario, Sieve replicates the processes related to nondeterministic smart contracts and then compares the results. If a divergence is detected among

the results obtained by a small number of processes, they are sieved out. However, if the number of divergent processes is excessive, the whole operation is sieved out.

- Tendermintis a consensus algorithm that can host arbitrary application states and can only tolerate up to a 1/3 of failures. In Tendermint, blockchain participants are called validators and they propose blocks of transactions and vote on them. A block is validated in two stages (pre-vote and pre-commit) and it can only be committed when more than 2/3 of the validators pre-commit it in a round.
- Bitcoin-NG implements a variant of the Bitcoin consensus algorithm aimed at improving scalability, throughput and latency. The developers performed experiments with 1000 nodes and concluded that Bitcoin-NG scales optimally, only limited by the bandwidth of the nodes and the latency related to the propagation time of the network.
- Proof-of-Burn (PoB) is a consensus method that requires miners to show proof of their commitment to mining by burning some cryptocurrency through an unspendable address. The idea behind PoB is that, instead of burning resources (e.g., energy in the case of many PoW implementations), cryptocurrency is burnt as it is considered as expensive as such resources.
- Proof-of-Personhood (PoP) is a consensus mechanism that makes use of ring signatures and collective signing to bind physical to virtual identities in a way that anonymity is preserved. A very similar concept is Proof-of-Individuality (PoI), which is currently being developed on Ethereum by the PoI Project. Finally, it is worth noting that private blockchains, which control user access, reduce the probability of Sybil attacks, so they do not require costly mining algorithms and economic incentives are removed.

37.4.5 Blockchain Updating/Maintenance and Protocol Stack

The construction of an IoT network requires deploying a huge number of devices which embed certain firmware that is usually updated to correct bugs, prevent attacks or just to improve some functionality. In general, IoT devices had to be updated manually or with Over-The-Air (OTA) updates. With context to the protocol stack, some authors suggested changes on the traditional OSI stack to adapt it to blockchain technologies. The most relevant is the so-called "Internet of Money" (IoM), which proposes a set of five layers that operate on TCP/IP which are as follows:

- A Ledger Layer that creates ledgers and issues assets.
- A Payment and Exchange Layer.
- A Pathfinding Layer that calculates the optimal set of atomic operations to be executed for the desired value transfer or exchange.
- A Contract Layer that controls balances through certain running code.

- An Application Layer that allows for developing applications and user interfaces. More research is still needed in order to study the need for specific stacks and to analyze their performance in comparison to other traditional OSI-based stacks.

37.5   Current Challenges for BIoT Applications

Currently, the emerging technologies in IoT ecosystem like Cyber-Physical Systems (CPS) [26], telemetry [27] or 4G/5G broadband communications are facing several challenges particularly, the case of mission-critical scenarios escalates additional concerns. By employing blockchain technology with IoT is complex process to fulfil the operational and technical requirements. The main factors are described as follows discussed in Fig. 37.5.

37.5.1   Privacy

All the users of a blockchain are identified by their public key or its hash which means that the anonymity is not guaranteed. Since all the transactions are shared, therefore it is possible for third-parties to analyse such transactions and infer the actual identities of the participants [28]. Privacy is even more complex in IoT environments because IoT devices can reveal private user data that could be stored in a blockchain whose privacy requirements differ from one country to another. Some proposed solution also enhances security by using a certificate system for authentication and by enabling the hash function substitution if it is compromised. It is also worth reveal that the system can be pinched to limit the amount of temporal data stored, which is useful for IoT devices with less storage space. Alternative approach focused on solving the privacy and robustness problems

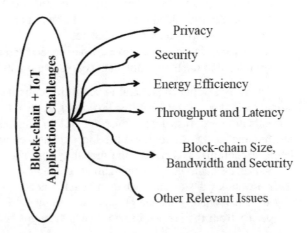

Fig. 37.5 Potential application challenges of Blockchain with IoT

derived from using centralized identity management systems is described in which the authors emphasize the need for providing automatic authentication systems for IoT applications where scalability is needed and where device heterogeneity and mobility are common. To deal with such challenges, the researchers present a blockchain-based system for IoT smart homes that extracts appliance signatures automatically in order to identify both the appliances and their users. However, the access management to IoT networks is challenging. In many IoT applications, secrecy is not necessary, but the privacy of the transactions is required in certain scenarios when the collected data may allow for monitoring and predicting people behaviour. This has already been an issue in fields like RFID-based transportation card systems, where the stored information is supposedly anonymous, but in practice it may be collected by third parties [29]. The issue is even more problematic when adding a blockchain, since transactions are shared among peers, what in certain fields like industry or financial systems, allows for monitoring the activity of competitors. Therefore, solutions have to be proposed to mitigate these privacy issues. Another possible solution for preserving privacy is the use of homomorphic encryption and such type of encryption allows third-party IoT services to process a transaction without revealing the unencrypted data to those services. Finally, the mechanisms previously mentioned require a relevant number of computational resources, consequently its applicability to resource-constrained IoT devices is currently limited.

37.5.2 Security

Conventionally, in order to guarantee its security following three requirements have to be fulfilled by an information system:

- *Confidentiality*: The most sensitive information should be protected from unauthorized accesses.
- *Integrity*: It guarantees that data are not altered or deleted by unauthorized parties. It is also usually added that, if an authorized party damages the information, it should be possible to undo the changes.
- *Availability*: Data can be accessed when needed and regarding confidentiality, the part related to the transaction data is associated with their privacy.

Current IoT applications tend to centralize communications which supports the stored data, such an approach is valid as long as the administrators of the centralized infrastructure are trusted and while the system remains robust against attacks [30] and internal leaks. In contrast, the blockchain technologies are characterized by being decentralized, therefore the global system should keep on working. For an individual user, the key for maintaining confidentiality is a good management of their private keys, since it is what an attacker needs in conjunction with the public key to impersonate someone or steal something from them. In order to avoid key tampering from the service provider (which might become compromised), before sending any message, two verifications are performed: it is checked that the public key of the receiver is the one used by other clients when communicating with the same user, and that such a key has not changed unexpectedly over time.

37.5.3   Energy Efficiency

IoT end-nodes usually make use of resource-constrained hardware that is powered by batteries. Therefore, energy efficiency is key to enable a long-lasting node deployment. However, many blockchains are characterized by being power-hungry. In such cases most of the consumption is due to two factors:

- Mining: Blockchains like Bitcoin make use of massive amounts of electricity due to the mining process, which involves a consensus algorithm (PoW) that consists in a sort of brute force search for a hash.
- P2P communications: P2P communications require edge devices that have to be powered on continuously, which could lead to waste energy. Some researchers proposed energy efficient protocols for P2P networks [31], but the issue still has to be studied further for the specific case of IoT networks. In relation to P2P communications, they are essential for a blockchain to communicate peers and distribute blocks, so the more updates a blockchain receives, the more energy consumption is dedicated to communications. To reduce the number of updates, mini-blokchains may allow IoT nodes to interact directly with a blockchain, since they only keep the latest transactions and lower the computational requirements of a full node.

37.5.4   Throughput and Latency

IoT deployments may require a blockchain network able to manage large amounts of transactions per time unit which is a limitation in certain networks. For instance, Bitcoin's blockchain has a theoretical maximum of seven transactions per second, although it can be increased by processing larger blocks or by modifying certain aspects of the node behavior when accepting transactions. In comparison, other networks are remarkably faster. With context to latency, it is important to note that blockchain transactions take some time to be processed. In relation to the consensus latency, it can be stated that the complexity of the consensus process is more important in terms of latency than individual hashing.

37.5.5 Blockchain Size, Bandwidth and Infrastructure

Blockchains grow periodically as users store their transactions, what derives into larger initial download times and in having to make use of more powerful miners with larger persistent memories. Blockchain compression techniques should be further studied, but the truth is that most IoT nodes would not be able to handle even a small fraction of a traditional blockchain. Moreover, note that many nodes have to store large amounts of data that are of no interest for them, what can be regarded as a waste of computational resources. This issue could be avoided by using lightweight nodes, which are able to perform transactions on the blockchain, but who do not have to store it. However, this approach requires the existence in the IoT hierarchy of certain powerful nodes that would maintain the blockchain for the resource constrained nodes, which implies a certain degree of data centralization.

Another alternative would consist in the use of a mini-blockchain. Such a kind of blockchain introduces the use of an account tree, which stores the current state of every user of the blockchain. Thus, only the most recent transaction has to be stored on the blockchain together with the account tree. Therefore, the blockchain only grows when new users are added to the blockchain. In addition, note that transaction and block size have to be scaled according to the bandwidth limitations of IoT networks: many small transactions would increase the energy consumption associated with communications, while a few large ones may involve big payloads that cannot be handled by some IoT devices. Regarding the infrastructure, certain elements are required to make the blockchain work properly, including decentralized storage, communication protocols, mining hardware, address management or network administration. Part of these needs are being fulfilled by the industry progressively, creating specific equipment for blockchain applications. For instance, miners have evolved from simple CPU-based systems, to more sophisticated equipment that harnesses the power of Graphics Processing Units (GPUs), Field-Programmable Gate Arrays (FPGAs) or Application Specific Integrated Circuits (ASICs).

37.5.6 Other Relevant Issues

37.5.6.1 Adoption Rate

One of the factors that may prevent a wide adoption of a BIoT application is the fact that a blockchain enables pseudo-anonymity. Governments may demand a strong link between real-world and online identity. Moreover, since IoT transactions can be carried out internationally, it may not be clear who should perform the identification. Further, the value and security of a blockchain increases with the number of users, also being more difficult to perform the feared 51% attacks. Moreover, the miner adoption rate also influences the capacity of a network to process transactions, therefore, the computational power brought by miners should be high enough to handle the transactions received from the IoT devices in a blockchain integrated IoT deployment.

37.5.6.2   Usability

In order to ease the work of developers, blockchain access Application Programming Interface (APIs) should be as user friendly as possible. The same should be applied to the APIs to manage user accounts.

37.5.6.3   Multi-chain Management

In some cases, the proliferation of blockchains has derived into the necessity of having to deal with several of them at the same time. This can also happen in an IoT scenario, where, for instance, sensor values may be stored in a private blockchain.

37.5.6.4   Versioning and Forks

Blockchains can be forked for administrative or versioning purposes. Once a blockchain is forked, it is not easy to carry out transactions between both chains.

37.5.6.5   Mining Boycott

Miners end up deciding which transactions are or are not stored in the blockchain, so they are able to censor certain transactions for economic or ideological reasons. This issue can happen when the number of conspiring miners are above 51% of the total, so small chains and blockchains that delegate their decisions on a subset of miners are susceptible to this kind of boycotts. Therefore, miners have to be chosen wisely and, when smart contracts have been signed, mis-behaviours should be sanctioned.

37.5.6.6   Smart Contract Enforcement and Autonomy

Legal rules have still to be developed to enforce smart contracts and resolve disputes properly. Some work is being performed for binding real-world contracts with smart contracts, but this is still an issue to be further studied.

37.6   Further Challenges and Recommendations

Even with the promising benefits and excellent foreseen future of BIoT, there are potential challenges in the development and deployment of existing and planned systems which will need further investigation as discussed in Fig. 37.6:

- *Complex technical challenges*: Potential issues regarding the scalability, security, cryptographic development and stability requirements of novel BIoT applications is still need to address. Further, this technology face design limitations in transaction capacity, in validation protocols or in the implementation of smart contracts. Moreover, the potential methods to solve the tendency to centralized approaches should be introduced.
- *Interoperability and standardization*: The adoption of BIoT requires the compromise of all stakeholders in order to achieve full interoperability and integration with legacy systems. The adoption of collaborative implementations and the use of international standards for collaborative trust and information protection will be needed. For example, the authentication across multiple authorities or organizations requires Federated Identity Management (FIM) [32]. At an international scale, such a FIM currently exists only at a low Level of Assurance (LoA), thus, higher LoAs will be needed.
- *Blockchain infrastructure*: It is required to create a comprehensive trust framework or infrastructure which fulfil all the requirements for the use of blockchain in IoT systems. Several state-of-the-art approaches that address issues such as trust depend on inter-domain policies and control. For example, the governments should set up a blockchain infrastructure to support use cases of public interest.
- *Organizational, governance, regulatory and legal aspects*: In addition to the technological challenges, shaping the regulatory environment is one the biggest issues to unlock the potential value of BIoT. It is possible that some developers fake their blockchain performance in order to attract investors driven by the expected profits.

Fig. 37.6 The open research challenges of blockchain technology and IoT

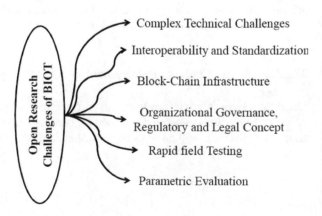

- *Instant field testing*: Presently, different types of blockchains for diverse applications is needing to be optimized and when users interested to combine blockchain with IoT systems, the first step is to figure out which blockchain is fulfil their requirements. Therefore, it is necessary to establish a mechanism to test different blockchains. This approach should be split into two main phases: (1) standardization and (2) testing. In the standardization phase, after a wide understanding of the supply chains, markets, products, and services, all the requirements have to be analysed and agreed. When a blockchain is created, it should be tested with the agreed criteria to validate if the blockchain works as needed. In the case of the testing phase, different criteria should be evaluated in terms of privacy, security, energy efficiency, throughput, latency, blockchain capacity or usability, among others [33].

37.7 Conclusions

Recently the blockchain offer to IoT a platform for distributing trusted information which defy non-collaborative organizational structures. This chapter presented the state-of-the art of blockchain technologies and proposed significant scenarios for blockchain integrated IoT applications in fields like healthcare, logistics, smart-cities or energy management. Moreover, it presented a holistic approach to blockchain integrated IoT scenarios with a thorough study of the most relevant aspects involved in its design. Nevertheless, the adoption of the paradigm opens a wide area of short- and medium-term potential applications that could disrupt the industry and probably, the economy. The global reality is a complex mix of different stakeholders in the IoT ecosystem, therefore it is necessary to reassess the different activities and actors involved in the near-future economy. We can conclude that blockchain integrated IoT is still in its nascent stage, and beyond the its earliest developments and deployments, broader applications will require additional technological research advances to address the specific demands, together with the collaboration of organizations and governments.

References

1. M. Weiser, "Hot topics-ubiquitous computing", *Computer*, 26(10), 71–72, 1993.
2. Forecast: The Internet of Things, Worldwide, 2013, Gartner, Stamford, CA, USA, Nov. 2013.
3. White Paper: Cisco Visual Networking Index: Global Mobile Data Traffic Forecast Update, 2016–2021. San Jose, CA, USA, Mar. 2017.
4. M. Suárez-Albela, P. Fraga-Lamas, T. M. Fernández-Caramés, A. Dapena, and M. González-López, "Home automation system based on intelligent transducer enablers," Sensors, vol. 16, no. 10, no. 1595, pp. 1–26, Sep. 2016.
5. P. Triantafillou, N. Ntarmos, S. Nikoletseas, and P. Spirakis, "NanoPeer networks and P2P worlds," in Proc. 3rd Int. Conf. Peer-Peer Comput., Linkoping, Sweden, Sep. 2003, pp. 40–46.

6. M. Ali and Z. A. Uzmi, "CSN: A network protocol for serving dynamic queries in large-scale wireless sensor networks," in Proc. 2nd Annu. Conf. Commun. Netw. Services Res., Fredericton, NB, Canada, May 2004, pp. 165–174.

7. S. Krco, D. Cleary, and D. Parker, "P2P mobile sensor networks," in Proc. 38th Annu. Hawaii Int. Conf. Syst. Sci., Big Island, HI, USA, Jan. 2005, p. 324c.

8. Tiago M. Fernández-Caramés, and Paula Fraga-Lamas, "A **Review** on the **Use** of **Blockchain** for the **Internet** of **Things**," IEEE Access, vol. 6, pp. 32979–33001, 2018.

9. Device Democracy: Saving the Future of the Internet of Things, IBM, New York, NY, USA, 2015.

10. K. Christidis and M. Devetsikiotis, "Blockchains and smart contracts for the Internet of Things," IEEE Access, vol. 4, pp. 2292–2303, 2016.

11. J. Yli-Huumo, D. Ko, S. Choi, S. Park, and K. Smolander, "Where is current research on blockchain technology?—A systematic review,"PLoS ONE, vol. 11, no. 10, p. e0163477, 2016.

12. J. S. Preden, K. Tammemäe, A. Jantsch, M. Leier, A. Riid, and E. Calis, "The benefits of self-awareness and attention in fog and mist computing," Computer, vol. 48, no. 7, pp. 37–45, Jul. 2015.

13. M. Suárez-Albela, T. M. Fernández-Caramés, P. Fraga-Lamas, and L. Castedo, "A practical evaluation of a high-security energy-efficient gateway for IoT fog computing applications," Sensors, vol. 17, no. 9, p. 1978, Aug. 2017.

14. D. Datla et al., "Wireless distributed computing: A survey of research challenges," IEEE Commun. Mag., vol. 50, no. 1, pp. 144–152, Jan. 2012.

15. H. Cai, B. Xu, L. Jiang, and A. V. Vasilakos, "Iot-based big data storage systems in cloud computing: Perspectives and challenges," IEEE Internet Things J., vol. 4, no. 1, pp. 75–87, Jan. 2017.

16. M. Marjani et al., "Big IoT data analytics: Architecture, opportunities, and open research challenges," IEEE Access, vol. 5, pp. 5247–5261, 2017.

17. Panarello, A., Tapas, N., Merlino, G., Longo, F., & Puliafito, A. (2018). Blockchain and IoT Integration: A Systematic Survey. Sensors, 18(8), 2575.

18. A. Lei, H. Cruickshank, Y. Cao, P. Asuquo, C. P. A. Ogah, and Z. Sun, "Blockchain-based dynamic key management for heterogeneous intelligent transportation systems," IEEE Internet Things J., vol. 4, no. 6, pp. 1832–1843, Dec. 2017.

19. N. Kshetri, "Can blockchain strengthen the Internet of Things?" IT Professional, vol. 19, no. 4, pp. 68–72, 2017.

20. N. Kshetri, "Blockchain's roles in strengthening cybersecurity and protecting privacy," Telecommun. Policy, vol. 41, no. 10, pp. 1027–1038, 2017.

21. O. Blanco-Novoa, T. M. Fernández-Caramés, P. Fraga-Lamas, and L. Castedo, "An electricity-price aware open-source smart socket for the internet of energy," Sensors, vol. 17, no. 3, p. 643, Mar. 2017.

22. M. A. Salahuddin, A. Al-Fuqaha, M. Guizani, K. Shuaib, and F. Sallabi, "Softwarization of Internet of Things infrastructure for secure and smart healthcare," Computer, vol. 50, no. 7, pp. 74–79, Jul. 2017.

23. Q. Xu, P. Ren, H. Song, and Q. Du, "Security enhancement for IoT communications exposed to eavesdroppers with uncertain locations," IEEE Access, vol. 4, pp. 2840–2853, 2016.

24. T. Yu, X. Wang, and A. Shami, "Recursive principal component analysisbased data outlier detection and sensor data aggregation in IoT systems," IEEE Internet Things J., vol. 4, no. 6, pp. 2207–2216, Dec. 2017.

25. N. Li, D. Liu, and S. Nepal, "Lightweight mutual authentication for IoT and its applications," IEEE Trans. Sustain. Comput., vol. 2, no. 4, pp. 359–370, Oct./Dec. 2017.

26. P. Fraga-Lamas, D. Noceda-Davila, T. M. Fernández-Caramés, M. Díaz-Bouza, and M. Vilar-Montesinos, "Smart pipe system for a shipyard 4.0" Sensors, vol. 16, no. 12, p. 2186, Dec. 2016.

27. D. L. Hernández-Rojas, T. M. Fernández-Caramés, P. Fraga-Lamas, and C. J. Escudero, "Design and practical evaluation of a family of lightweight protocols for heterogeneous sensing through BLE beacons in IoT telemetry applications," Sensors, vol. 18, no. 1, p. 57, Dec. 2017.
28. S. Meiklejohn et al., "A fistful of bitcoins: Characterizing payments among men with no names," Commun. ACM, vol. 59, no. 4, pp. 86–93, Apr. 2016.
29. T. M. Fernández-Caramés, P. Fraga-Lamas, M. Suárez-Albela, and L. Castedo, "Reverse engineering and security evaluation of commercial tags for RFID-based IoT applications," Sensors, vol. 17, no. 1, p. 28, Dec. 2016.
30. R. M. Jabir, S. I. R. Khanji, L. A. Ahmad, O. Alfandi, and H. Said, "Analysis of cloud computing attacks and countermeasures," in Proc. 18th Int. Conf. Adv. Commun. Technol. (ICACT), Pyeongchang, South Korea, Jan./Feb. 2016.
31. S. Miyake and M. Bandai, "Energy-efficient mobile P2P communications based on context awareness," in Proc. IEEE 27th Int. Conf. Adv. Inf. Netw. Appl. (AINA), Barcelona, Spain, Mar. 2013, pp. 918–923.
32. E. Birrell and F. B. Schneider, "Federated identity management systems: A privacy-based characterization," IEEE Security Privacy, vol. 11, no. 5, pp. 36–48, Sep./Oct. 2013.
33. P. K. Sharma, M.-Y. Chen, and J.-H. Park, "A software defined fog node based distributed blockchain cloud architecture for IoT," IEEE Access, vol. 6, pp. 115–124, Sep. 2017.

Index

© Springer Nature Switzerland AG 2019
A. K. Singh, A. Mohan (eds.), *Handbook of Multimedia Information Security:*
Techniques and Applications, https://doi.org/10.1007/978-3-030-15887-3